# Lecture Notes in Computer Science 14798

The series Lecture Notes in Computer Science (LNCS), including its subseries Lecture Notes in Artificial Intelligence (LNAI) and Lecture Notes in Bioinformatics (LNBI), has established itself as a medium for the publication of new developments in computer science and information technology research, teaching, and education.

LNCS enjoys close cooperation with the computer science R & D community, the series counts many renowned academics among its volume editors and paper authors, and collaborates with prestigious societies. Its mission is to serve this international community by providing an invaluable service, mainly focused on the publication of conference and workshop proceedings and postproceedings. LNCS commenced publication in 1973.

Angelo Sifaleras · Fuhua Lin
Editors

# Generative Intelligence and Intelligent Tutoring Systems

## 20th International Conference, ITS 2024 Thessaloniki, Greece, June 10–13, 2024 Proceedings, Part I

Springer

*Editors*
Angelo Sifaleras
University of Macedonia
Thessaloniki, Greece

Fuhua Lin
Athabasca University
Athabasca, AB, Canada

ISSN 0302-9743 ISSN 1611-3349 (electronic)
Lecture Notes in Computer Science
ISBN 978-3-031-63027-9 ISBN 978-3-031-63028-6 (eBook)
https://doi.org/10.1007/978-3-031-63028-6



This Springer imprint is published by the registered company Springer Nature Switzerland AG
The registered company address is: Gewerbestrasse 11, 6330 Cham, Switzerland

# Preface

The 20th International Conference on Intelligent Tutoring Systems (ITS 2024) was held in Thessaloniki, Greece, from June 10 to June 13, 2024.

ITS 2024 is evolving to a new concept of Artificial Intelligence which can be found in various disciplines and can serve human education and well-being. This new concept is named: Generative Intelligence. Generative Intelligence concerns various AI systems, techniques, architectures, methods, or tools based on machine learning in particular deep learning which can be used to generate texts, images, solutions, and environments, able to enhance Human Intelligence, cognitive capacities, memory, and learning. Instead of trying to reproduce human behavior or recognize human traits using artificial intelligence techniques or learning analytics, Generative Intelligence provides means to increase human cognitive potential.

The conference featured eight distinct tracks in which the concepts mentioned above contribute to the increase of Generative Intelligence. Each track included (but was not limited to) a list of topics of interest which can be found below. Submitted papers refer to one of the tracks here below.

Conference tracks

T1: Generative Intelligence in Tutoring Systems

The goal of this track was to show how new techniques inspired by artificial intelligence and new methods in education can improve learning and teaching and generate the capacity for knowledge acquisition. The topics of this track include generative learning strategies, distance education, learning analytics for tutoring systems, deep learning and machine learning for tutoring systems, online and distance learning, generative learner models, emotion recognition, human-machine interaction, case-based reasoning, cognitive modeling, open learning, authoring systems, cultural learning, and adaptive learning.

T2: Generative Intelligence in Healthcare Informatics

The goal of this track was to show the progress of AI tools for increasing the propagation of healthcare techniques and their efficiency. Informatics provides means to improve the prediction, analysis, and treatment of disease and patients' control over their own care. The topics of this track were AI and telemedicine, medical image processing, virtual systems for healthcare, learning analytics in medicine, progress of AI for non-pharmacological Alzheimer's treatments, predictive modeling of healthcare, intelligent tutoring systems in medicine, machine learning and deep learning in healthcare, AI in medical education, AI in public health, home management of healthcare, neurofeedback techniques, games for healthcare, virtual reality (VR), and augmented reality (AR).

T3: Human Interaction, Games, and Virtual Reality

The goal of this track was to show the progress of interactive games using generative intelligence techniques. Intelligent games can adapt to the characteristics of the player and can be used to enhance learning, skills, memory, cognitive capacities, brain-computer interaction, and strategic decisions. They can be used in various applications (education, healthcare, group management, decision support systems, industry control). Multimedia allows an increase in the receptivity of sensors and reactions. The topics of this track included Brain-Computer Interaction (BCI), game design, intelligent immersive games, multi-agent systems, educational games, social games, generative simulations, theory of games, reinforcement learning in games, virtual and generative reality, simulation training, emotions recognition, neurofeedback games, generative scenario design, human interaction with games, multimedia technologies in games, fuzzy systems in games, artificial intelligence in games, and games content generation.

T4: Neural Networks and Data Mining

This track was a crucible for innovation, where the latest techniques in machine learning intersect with the rich, untapped data of educational environments, aiming to revolutionize the pedagogical landscape and pave the way for a future where intelligent tutoring systems are as nuanced and insightful as the educators they seek to augment. The topics of this track include supervised machine learning, genetic algorithms, Markovian regulation, smart sensor networks, determinate regulation, games and strategies, fuzzy systems, web information processing, applications of data mining in social sciences, data-driven reasoning, deep learning and statistical methods for data mining, big data mining, algorithms for data mining, ethical data analytics, and data mining for recommendation.

T5: Generative Intelligence and Metaverse

This track was dedicated to exploring the innovative synthesis of generative algorithms and the boundless educational landscapes within virtual environments. We delved into how generative AI is revolutionizing personalized learning experiences, creating dynamic content, and fostering engaging educational models that are as limitless as the Metaverse itself. Participants gained insights into the latest advancements, discussed the integration of AI-driven pedagogies in virtual spaces, and engaged with groundbreaking research that shapes the future of learning. Here, educators, technologists, and researchers came together to craft the nexus of next-generation learning platforms–where intelligence generation meets the expanse of the Metaverse, setting a new paradigm in digital education. The topics of this tracks included technology and creativity around Metaverse, gaming and interactivity, mixed reality and virtual world, social and digital identity, extended reality, digital art, social communication, applications of Metaverse in health, and global Metaverse.

T6: Security, Privacy, and Ethics in Generative Intelligence

As we step into an era where AI's capabilities to generate content are nearly indistinguishable from human output, we must also navigate the complex web of security challenges, privacy concerns, and ethical dilemmas that accompany these advancements. This track offered a multidisciplinary forum for examining the safeguarding of digital identities, the protection of intellectual property, and the moral imperatives guiding AI interactions in educational settings. Experts, scholars, and practitioners from around the globe converged to share their wisdom, debate best practices, and forge strategies to ensure that generative intelligence develops in a manner that is secure, respects privacy, and adheres to the highest ethical standards. Together, we will chart the course for responsible stewardship of AI technologies that enhance learning while honoring the trust placed in them by educators and learners alike. The topics of this track included commercial security, data privacy and security, web security, applied cryptography, authentication, identity management and biometrics, electronic payments, culture of ethics, business and human rights, diversity and inclusion in teaching and learning, environmental ethics, machine learning and security, cloud computing and data outsourcing security, mobile payments, security in games, security of peer-to-peer networks, security metrics, sustainability, language-based security, security and privacy for the Internet of Things, and socio-technical security.

T7: Generative Intelligence for Applied Natural Language Processing

This track was dedicated to unearthing and showcasing the transformative power of generative models that are reshaping the way we interact with language in computational settings. It served as a beacon for those who are leveraging these advancements to build sophisticated tutoring systems capable of understanding, generating, and personalizing language-based interactions. The topics of this track included language modeling, domain ontologies, computational linguistics, cognitive semantics, text mining, translation, question answering, dialogue systems, information retrieval, speech recognition and synthesis, discourse, machine translation, and lexical semantics.

T8: Generative Intelligence for Autonomous Robots and Learning

Generative intelligence with robots includes a variety of new criteria that provide more human characteristics to robots. Such elements concern emotions, mood, and facial expressions which give a more realistic interaction with humans. They transform robots into useful human-like companions. The topics of this track included but were not limited to emotional robots, voice recognition, intelligent agents, autonomous robots, planning and Goal reasoning, entertainments robotics, intelligent systems and robotics, applications of autonomous intelligent robots, sensors and vision systems for robots, generative exploration in hazardous situations, extraction of environment maps, robots in medicine, and teaching robots.

The call for scientific papers solicited works presenting substantive new research results in using generative artificial intelligence (GenAI), advanced computer technologies and interdisciplinary research for enabling, supporting, and enhancing human learning.

The international Program Committee consisted of 78 leading members (32 senior and 46 regular) of the Intelligent Tutoring Systems and AI communities, assisted by additional external reviewers.

Research papers came from 25 countries and were each reviewed by three reviewers through a double-blind process. ITS 2024 retained the strict and high standards in the review process that were established during the previous years, and which have rendered it a top-flight, rather selective, and high-quality conference. This year, 35 papers were accepted as full, whereas 28 papers were accepted as short. We believe that the selected full papers describe some very significant research and the short papers some very interesting new ideas.

The management of the review process and the preparation of the proceedings was handled through the EasyChair platform.

ITS 2024 had two outstanding Invited Speakers in the plenary sessions: Eftychios Protopapadakis (University of Macedonia, Greece), a renowned figure in Machine Learning, Optimization, and Computer Vision, and Gianna Martinengo, CEO of Didael Knowledge Technologies Services and President of Women &Tech ETS, specializing in Learning and AI (Milano, Italy). Both are leaders in different specialized areas of the ITS field. In addition, ITS 2024 had an excellent Tutorial Speaker: Panagiotis Fotaris (University of Brighton, UK), specializing in Digital Games and User Experience Design.

Moreover, ITS 2024 hosted two workshops, one under the title: Breaking Barriers with Generative Intelligence (BBGI'24) and another one under the title: Digital Transformation in Higher Education. Empowering Teachers and Students for Tomorrow's Challenges (Back2Basics). The program of ITS 2024 also included a panel on Potential Ways of Creative Use of Gen AI (e.g., ChatGPT) in Computer Science Departments.

In addition to the contributors mentioned above, we would like to thank all the authors, the members of the Program Committees of all tracks, the external reviewers, and the Steering Committee members as well as the Hosting Institution of the Conference, the University of Macedonia, in Thessaloniki, Greece.

We finally would like to acknowledge that ITS 2024 was held under the auspices of the Institute of Intelligent Systems (IIS) and was organized by Neoanalysis Ltd, under the guidance of Kitty Panourgia, the Organization Chair, and her team.

April 2024

Fuhua Lin
Angelo Sifaleras

# Organization

## Conference Committee

## Program Committee Chairs

| | |
|---|---|
| Oscar Lin | Athabasca University, Canada |
| Angelo Sifaleras | University of Macedonia, Greece |

## Program Advising Chairs

| | |
|---|---|
| Maiga Chang | Athabasca University, Canada |
| Yugo Hayashi | Ritsumeikan University, Japan |
| Christos Troussas | University of West Attica, Greece |
| Seiji Isotani | Harvard University, USA |

## Organization Committee

### Organization Chair

| | |
|---|---|
| Kitty Panourgia | Neoanalysis Ltd., Greece |

### Organization Members

Maria Lafazani
Iias Petrodaskalakis
Kostantina Traka
Paula Dona
Isaak Tselepis

## Program Committees

### Senior Program Committee

| | |
|---|---|
| Roger Azevedo | University of Central Florida, USA |
| Emmanuel Blanchard | Le Mans University, France |

| | |
|---|---|
| Benedict Du Boulay | University of Sussex, UK |
| Bert Bredeweg | University of Amsterdam, The Netherlands |
| Stefano A. Cerri | LIRMM, University of Montpellier, France |
| Maiga Chang | Athabasca University, Canada |
| Michel Desmarais | École Polytechnique de Montréal, Canada |
| Cyrille Desmoulins | Université Grenoble Alpes, France |
| Claude Frasson | University of Montreal, Canada |
| Sabine Graf | Athabasca University, Canada |
| Yugo Hayashi | Ritsumeikan University, Japan |
| Wu-Yuin Hwang | National Dong-Hwa University, Taiwan |
| Seiji Isotani | Harvard University, USA |
| Lewis Johnson | Alelo Inc., USA |
| Charalampos Karagiannidis | Aristotle University of Thessaloniki, Greece |
| Kinshuk | University of North Texas, USA |
| Vivekanandan Kumar | Athabasca University, Canada |
| Amruth Kumar | Ramapo College of New Jersey, USA |
| Susanne Lajoie | McGill University, Canada |
| Nian-Shing Chen | National Taiwan University, Taiwan |
| Alessandro Micarelli | Roma Tre University, Italy |
| Phivos Mylonas | Ionian University, Greece |
| Riichiro Mizoguchi | Japan Advanced Institute of Science and Technology, Japan |
| Roger Nkambou | Université du Québec à Montréal, Canada |
| Elvira Popescu | University of Craiova, Romania |
| Demetrios Sampson | University of Piraeus, Greece |
| Filippo Sciarrone | Roma Tre University, Italy |
| Marco Temperini | Sapienza University of Rome, Italy |
| Stefan Trausan-Matu | Politehnica University of Bucharest, Romania |
| Christos Troussas | University of West Attica, Greece |
| Julita Vassileva | University of Saskatchewan, Canada |
| Panagiotis Vlamos | Ionian University, Greece |

## Program Committee

| | |
|---|---|
| Mohammed Abdel Razek | Al-Azhar University, Egypt |
| Galia Angelova | Bulgarian Academy of Sciences, Bulgaria |
| Renu Balyan | SUNY Old Westbury, USA |
| Maria Lucia Barron-Estrada | Instituto Tecnológico de Culiacán, Mexico |
| Azza Basiouni | Liwa College, UAE |
| Hamdi Ben Abdessalem | University of Chicoutimi, Canada |
| Jesus G. Boticario | UNED, Spain |
| Tharrenos Bratitsis | University of Western Macedonia, Greece |

| | |
|---|---|
| Ting-Wen Chang | Beijing Normal University, China |
| Chih-Yueh Chou | Yuan Ze University, Taiwan |
| Evandro Costa | Federal University of Alagoas, Brazil |
| Ali Akber Dewan | Athabasca University, Canada |
| Georgios Evangelidis | University of Macedonia, Greece |
| Nikolaos Fachantidis | University of Macedonia, Greece |
| Reva Freedman | Northern Illinois University, USA |
| Ashok Goel | Georgia Tech, USA |
| Xiaoqing Gu | East China Normal University, China |
| Ella Haig | University of Portsmouth, UK |
| Yusuke Hayashi | Hiroshima University, Japan |
| Dimitrios Hristu-Varsakelis | University of Macedonia, Greece |
| Qun Jin | Waseda University, Japan |
| Srecko Joksimovic | University of South Australia, Australia |
| Mizue Kayama | Shinshu University, Japan |
| Georgia Koloniari | University of Macedonia, Greece |
| Blair Lehman | Educational Testing Service, USA |
| Chao-Lin Liu | National Central University, Taiwan |
| Carla Limongelli | Roma Tre University, Italy |
| Pin-Chuan Lin | Mount Saint Vincent University, Canada |
| Frederick Li | University of Durham, UK |
| Mirko Marras | University of Cagliari, Italy |
| Wolfgang Müller | University of Education Weingarten, Germany |
| Silvia Margarita Baldiris Navarro | University of Cartagene, Colombia |
| Kuo-Liang Ou | National Hsin-Chu University of Education, Taiwan |
| Sasha Poquet | University of South Australia, Australia |
| Eftychios Protopapadakis | University of Macedonia, Greece |
| Valéry Psyché | TÉLUQ University, Canada |
| Ricardo Queiros | Agostinho Neto University, Portugal |
| Ioannis Refanidis | University of Macedonia, Greece |
| Flippo Sciarrone | Universitas Mercatorum, Italy |
| Riina Vuorikari | ALL DIGITAL, Belgium |
| Dunwei Wen | Athabasca University, Canada |
| Stylianos Xinogalos | University of Macedonia, Greece |
| Milos Kravcik | DFKI GmbH, Germany |
| Shaozi Li | Xiamen University, China |
| Theodore Kaskalis | University of Macedonia, Greece |

## Steering Committee

### Chair

| | |
|---|---|
| Claude Frasson | University of Montreal, Canada |

### Members

| | |
|---|---|
| Stefano A. Cerri | LIRMM, University of Montpellier and CNRS, France |
| Maiga Chang | Athabasca University, Canada |
| Amruth Kumar | Ramapo College of New Jersey, USA |
| Yugo Hayashi | Ritsumeikan University, Japan |
| Isabel Fernandez-Castro | University of the Basque Country, Spain |
| Guy Gouardères | University of Pau and Pays de l'Adour, France |
| Alan Lesgold | University of Pittsburgh, USA |
| James Lester | North Carolina State University, USA |
| Alessandro Micarelli | Roma Tre University, Italy |
| Roger Nkambou | Université du Québec à Montréal, Canada |
| Giorgos Papadourakis | Hellenic Mediterranean University, Greece |
| Elliot Soloway | University of Michigan, USA |
| John Stamper | Carnegie Mellon University, USA |
| Daniel Suthers | University of Hawaii, USA |
| Stefan Trausan-Matu | University Politehnica of Bucharest, Romania |
| Christos Troussas | University of West Attica, Greece |

## Advisory Committee

### Members

| | |
|---|---|
| Luigia Carlucci Aiello | Sapienza University of Rome, Italy |
| Kinshuk | University of North Texas, USA |
| Demetrios Sampson | University of Piraeus, Greece |

## Workshop 1: Breaking Barriers with Generative Intelligence (BBGI)

### Chair

| | |
|---|---|
| Azza Basiouni | Liwa College Abu Dhabi, UAE |

### Senior Program Committee

| | |
|---|---|
| Claude Frasson | University of Montreal, Canada |
| Oscar Lin | Athabasca University Canada |
| Kinshuk | University of North Texas, USA |

### Program Committee

| | |
|---|---|
| Michael Lin | Mount Saint Vincent University, Canada |
| Xiaokun Zhang | Athabasca University, Canada |
| Khaled Shaalan | British University in Dubai, UAE |
| Ahmed Al-Gindy | Canadian University Dubai, UAE |
| Ray Al-Barazie | Liwa College Al Ain, UAE |
| Beenu Mago | Skyline University College, UAE |
| Rasha Hasan | Liwa College Abu Dhabi, UAE |
| Said Salloum | University of Salford, UK |

## Workshop 2: Back2Basics

### Chairs

| | |
|---|---|
| Anastasios Economides | University of Macedonia, Greece |
| Maria Perifanou | University of Macedonia, Greece |

### Program Committee

| | |
|---|---|
| Alexandros Mikroyanidis | Open University, UK |
| Carlos Santos | University of Aveiro, Portugal |
| Tobias Ley | Danube University Krems, Austria |
| Maka Eradze | University of Aquila, Italy |
| Stavros Nikou | University of Strathclyde, UK |
| Rita Santos | University of Aveiro, Portugal |
| Luis Pedro | University of Aveiro, Portugal |
| Panagiotis Kosmas | University of Limassol, Cyprus |

# Invited Talks

# Unleashing Potential: Harnessing the Power of Generative AI in Intelligent Tutoring Systems

Eftychios Protopapadakis

Department of Applied Informatics, University of Macedonia,
156 Egnatia Street, GR-546 36 Thessaloniki, Greece
eftprot@uom.edu.gr

**Abstract.** Intelligent Tutoring Systems (ITS) fueled by Generative AI (genAI) provide an exceptional opportunity to revolutionize education. Offering personalized learning experiences, tailored to individual needs and preferences, is not an easy task, yet it becomes easier by the year. In this keynote, we explore how genAI-powered ITS can transcend the limitations of traditional education models, paving the way for a new era of cognitive empowerment and skill development.

Through advanced algorithms and adaptive learning techniques, genAI-powered ITS can deliver targeted instruction, personalized practice problems, and immersive simulations that foster critical thinking and problem-solving skills. By leveraging the unique capabilities of generative AI, educators can further boost the human cognitive potential, moving beyond rote memorization to cultivate deep understanding and mastery.

However, alongside the promise of genAI-powered ITS come inherent challenges that must be addressed. Biases embedded within AI algorithms and concerns regarding data privacy and security demand careful consideration. Yet, by proactively addressing these challenges and fostering collaboration between AI developers, educators, and policymakers, we can ensure the responsible and ethical application of genAI in education.

The importance of collaboration and partnership between AI and human educators is a topic worthy of investigation. By combining the expertise of AI algorithms with the guidance and mentorship of teachers, we can create a symbiotic relationship that enhances the learning experience and maximizes student outcomes. Together, we can envision a future where genAI-powered ITS play a central role in democratizing education, empowering learners of all backgrounds to reach their full potential and contribute meaningfully to society.

**Keywords:** Intelligent Tutoring Systems · Generative AI · Personalized Learning · Cognitive Potential · Educational

# Sharing from Experience: Competencies for "Intelligent Dialogues" with Emerging Technologies

Gianna Martinengo

CEO and Founder of Didael KTS and President of Women&Tech® ETS, DKTS: Digital Knowledge Technologies Services, Via Ampère 61/A, 20131 Milan, Italy
gianna.martinengo@didaelkts.it

**Abstract.** We have witnessed the various phases of technologies supporting human learning and at the same time of artificial intelligence since 1982, mainly by means of business initiatives, within hundreds of projects of private and public interest including many EU pre-competitive ones. Lessons learned and tips for the future are at the core of our talk. The main issues we privilege are knowledge, competencies, and ethics for the future of modern, interactive AI including human learning as a first priority. As a side effect, we will shortly describe our efforts for women, by demonstrating the interest of a true complementarity between genders, as a source of innovation in society: future business as well as academic initiatives. Last, we briefly quote our contribution to the EU Parliament for the AI act recently approved. We are proud to see the initial implementation of an AI office, dedicated to the certification of AI products and services, as we proposed, motivated and documented in our written reports in 2021.

**Keywords:** digital transformation · AI · ethics · change management · evolving society · women's empowerment

# Contents – Part I

# Contents – Part II

**Neural Networks and Data Mining**



**Generative Intelligence and Metaverse**

# Generative Intelligence and Tutoring Systems

# Using Large Language Models to Support Teaching and Learning of Word Problem Solving in Tutoring Systems

Jaime Arnau-Blasco(✉), Miguel Arevalillo-Herráez, Sergi Solera-Monforte, and Yuyan Wu

Departament d'Informàtica, Universitat de València, 46100 Burjassot, Valencia, Spain
{jaime.arnau,miguel.arevalillo,sergi.solera,yuyan.wu}@uv.es

**Abstract.** The latest developments in Large Language Models (LLMs) open the door to significantly improving scaffolding and support when supervising word problem-solving. In this paper, we examine the potential of a large variety of open models for solving different types of arithmetical problems and discuss the potential implications for the development of Intelligent Tutoring Systems (ITSs). The results reported show that relatively small LLMs are able to correctly solve around two-thirds of single-stage word problems, obtaining a similar performance as children. Nevertheless, their behavior varies in terms of their ability to provide the correct solution for specific conceptual schemes. Beyond their potential as a problem-solving tool, the research presented opens the door to using LLMs for the implementation of virtual agent-based students.

**Keywords:** Large Language Models · Word problem solving · Intelligent Tutoring Systems

## 1 Introduction

Proficiency in problem-solving is closely linked to academic success in educational contexts, while difficulty in this skill is associated with academic challenges and potential failure in school [11,17]. In the development of problem-solving skills, word problems have become a crucial component of the mathematics curriculum, aiding in the development of students' mental abilities, logical analysis, and creative thinking skills.

Intelligent Tutoring Systems (ITSs) have emerged as a valuable tool for enhancing students' problem-solving skills, particularly in the domain of word problems. These systems leverage artificial intelligence and interactive interfaces to provide personalized learning experiences tailored to individual students' needs. By offering step-by-step guidance, feedback, and hints, ITSs help learners develop critical thinking and mathematical reasoning abilities essential for tackling complex word problems effectively. Some examples of ITSs designed specifically for word problem-solving include AnimalWatch [5], MathCAL [7], Ms. Lindquist [15], PAT (Pump Algebra Tutor) [16] and HINTS [2,13].


A. Sifaleras and F. Lin (Eds.): ITS 2024, LNCS 14798, pp. 3–13, 2024.
https://doi.org/10.1007/978-3-031-63028-6_1

Recent advances in Natural Language Processing (NLP) and strong evidence that narratives and chatbot-mediated help can enhance learning experiences for children [25] have encouraged the integration of chatbots to provide student support [8]. Some initiatives in this direction include Mathbot [14], the adapted version of HINTS presented in [1,3] or the integration of a chatbot to support scaffolding in an existing platform described in [8]. However, most existing math-focused chatbots use traditional rule-based algorithms and neglect the transformative capabilities of generative Artificial Intelligence (AI) [8].

Indeed, new Large Language Models (LLMs) such as ChatGPT [34] or other freely available alternative models like LLaMA 2 [29] present numerous new opportunities in education. The largest models, with several tens of billions of parameters, exhibit surprising capabilities or behaviors that were not specifically programmed [36]. These skills are known in the literature as emergent abilities [33], ranging from performing specific tasks to understanding linguistic nuances, making logical inferences, and even generating creative content unexpectedly. Such skills, especially those related to task decomposition into simpler steps, can be leveraged to generate AI-based agents that support scaffolding in math-related tasks. Nevertheless, we need to take into account that these agents are prone to errors, and hence rigorous testing is essential to ensure their reliability and effectiveness in assisting learners.

In this paper, we examine the reliability of a wide range of open LLMs in the context of word problem-solving. As the majority of scaffolding methods primarily focus on guiding learners through individual steps of problem-solving processes rather than providing comprehensive support across the entire problem-solving task, we have focused on single-step problems and analyzed the performance according to the skills required to solve the step. The research presented serves as an initial exploration into assessing the capabilities of LLMs to support scaffolding strategies in learning word problem-solving. This includes their potential application either as a feedback mechanism or integrated within collaborative learning settings to deploy virtual students who interact with children to jointly discover solutions to word problems.

## 2 Skill-Based Categorization

A word problem presents a scenario where quantities are connected, and at least one of them needs to be determined through calculation. Solving these problems requires performing arithmetic operations such as addition, subtraction, multiplication, and division. Although word problems can describe a large variety of different situations, solving them involves applying a limited set of conceptual schemes. These conceptual schemes are linked to the semantics of word problems and have proven effective in predicting problem difficulty accurately [24], outperforming the predictive power of the number of arithmetic operations that are necessary to solve the problem. When solving word problems involving non-negative numbers, three additive schemes and three multiplicative schemes have been typically identified in the literature. The three additive schemes, described in [24] for situations involving natural numbers are change, combine, and additive comparison. Additionally, another scheme called equalize is mentioned in other studies but can be considered a combination of other problem schemas [30] and we do not use it in our study. Regarding multiplicative schemes, we can differentiate between isomorphism of measures, multiplicative comparison, and product of measures [32]. Furthermore, each conceptual scheme is subdivided into specific subtypes, offering a detailed understanding of the required problem-solving skills. These subtypes include 2 types of combine (C1, C2), 6 types of change (CH1–CH6), 6 types of additive comparison (AC1–AC6), 3 types of isomorphism of measures (IM1–IM3), 6 types of multiplicative comparison (MC1–MC6), and 3 types of product of measures (PM1–PM3).

## 3 Methodology

### 3.1 Dataset

To evaluate the performance of the different LLMs considered in this work at solving each type of conceptual scheme, we used the SVAMP (Simple Variations on Arithmetic Math word Problems) dataset [23]. SVAMP contains 1,000 math word classified entries, each featuring a problem statement and a question. An example is shown in Fig. 1. The label refers to the operations involved in the calculation of the solution: subtraction, multiplication, common division, or addition. As this labeling is insufficient for accurately capturing the intrinsic difficulty associated with each problem, we re-labeled the entire dataset by assigning each problem another label that matched the conceptual scheme involved in calculating the solution, according to the conceptual scheme taxonomy previously described in Sect. 2. In addition, to concentrate on evaluating each model's ability to offer assistance for individual steps in problem-solving processes, we eliminated problems that cannot be solved in a single step. These tasks were performed by an expert in mathematics education. To minimize errors, the process was repeated twice with a two-week interval between the two classifications. There was only one disagreement in one label, which was carefully examined to determine the correct designation. The resulting dataset contained a total of 741 single-step problems. This collection included representative labeled instances of all three subtypes of isomorphism of measures, four out of the six subtypes of additive comparison, both subtypes of combination, and all six types of change. The number of samples in each conceptual scheme is shown in Table 1.

### 3.2 LLMs Considered

We have examined the performance of several LLMs at solving the problems in the re-labeled version of the SVAMP dataset. We prioritize affordable models that can be seamlessly integrated into existing or new systems at minimal expense. Hence, the tested models were chosen considering their open-source nature, ease of deployment, computational cost, and compatibility with the constraints imposed by our available hardware. All models considered belong to the

```
{
 "ID": "chal-2",
 "Body": "Dan had $3 left with him after he bought a candy bar.
         If he had $4 at the start",
 "Question": "How much did the candy bar cost?",
 "Equation": "( 4.0 - 3.0 )",
 "Answer": 1.0,
 "Type": "Subtraction",
},
```

**Fig. 1.** SVAMP problem example.

**Table 1.** Number of samples in each class. Classes include conceptual schemes subtypes that appear in the dataset, namely 2 types of combine (C1, C2), 6 types of change (CH1–CH6), 4 types of additive comparison (AC1, AC3–AC5) and 3 types of isomorphism of measures (IM1–IM3).

| Classes | IM1 | IM2 | IM3 | C1 | C2 | CH1 | CH2 | CH3 | CH4 | CH5 | CH6 | AC1 | AC3 | AC4 | AC5 |
|---|---|---|---|---|---|---|---|---|---|---|---|---|---|---|---|
| Samples | 76 | 72 | 66 | 79 | 65 | 22 | 40 | 17 | 39 | 10 | 24 | 188 | 19 | 8 | 16 |
| Total | 741 | | | | | | | | | | | | | | |

LLaMA 2 [29] family, and can easily be obtained from Ollama[1] or HuggingFace[2], facilitating the replication of the experiments. We used the foundation model from Meta [29], but also other re-trained and/or fine-tuned models for specific tasks. They have all been evaluated in their 7 and 13 billion parameter versions, to assess the effect of larger models on the results. The different models involved in our comparison are summarized in Table 2.

**Table 2.** Summary of models considered

| Family | Training | Model name |
|---|---|---|
| LLaMA 2 | General purpose | Foundation [29] |
| | | Beluga [18] |
| | | Vicuna [9] |
| | Reasoning/maths problems | MetaMath [35] |

The Foundation [29], Beluga [18] and Vicuna models [9] have all been trained with data not related to mathematical problems, and problem-solving capabilities are an emergent ability [33]. The MetaMath model [35] was trained with the MetaMathQA dataset, which is specialized in mathematical reasoning. Its inclusion in the comparison aims to assess the effect of training with specific data.

[1] https://ollama.ai.

[2] https://huggingface.co.

### 3.3 Experimental Setting

Our experiments were run on a system equipped with a single NVIDIA RTX 4090 GPU, with 24 GB of memory. The prompt used was shared among the different LLMs. It started with "Solve the following exercise: " and was followed with the problem body and question. For example, the prompt for the problem example shown in Fig. 1 was *"Solve the following exercise: Dan had $3 left with him after he bought a candy bar. If he had $4 at the start. How much did the candy bar cost?"*

The format of the system response varied across different LLMs and depended on the exercise. In some cases, the result was given at the beginning of the response and was followed by an explanation. In other cases, the answer was provided at the end of the response. To cope with all the different variations, a parser was used to filter the system response. To this end, all numbers in the response were extracted and compared to the answers provided in the dataset. A solution was considered correct if any of these numbers matched the correct answer. While this method inherently identifies incorrect solutions, there is a possibility of evaluating an incorrect solution as correct if the correct answer to the problem is embedded within an explanation. This scenario is more likely to happen when the problem involves intermediate quantities with the same numeric value as the problem solution, a situation that is highly improbable in single-step problems. In this case, the problem would be considered as correctly solved once the value of the intermediate quantity is found. For each LLM, we manually tested this potential situation on a collection of 10 random problems extracted from SVAMP that were evaluated as correct, and it never happened. Although this sample of 10 problems represents only around 2% of all problems correctly solved, we considered that the effect of this potential situation is limited and would not significantly alter the results reported.

## 4 Results

The performance achieved with each model is expressed in Table 3 as the percentage of correctly solved problems for each conceptual scheme type and subtype. The last row in the table summarizes the performance under a single number, which represents the percentage of problems correctly solved by each LLM.

The positive effect of fine-tuning the model with a dataset in a close domain reflects on the results obtained by MetaMath [35], which is especially relevant for the smaller models. A higher performance is clear and consistent across all types for the 7 billion parameter models. For the largest models, MetaMath also shows a substantially better performance for the change (CH) and additive comparison (AC) conceptual schemes, but the Foundation model behaves better for the combine (C) type, and similar performance is observed for isomorphism of measure (IM).

In addition, the improvement achieved by the 13 billion parameter models as compared to the 7 billion one is quite noticeable along all models and most

**Table 3.** Detailed results for each conceptual scheme type and subtype, expressed as the percentage of correctly solved problems. Values in bold represent the highest for a particular conceptual scheme when the number of parameters is fixed to the same value.

| | 7 billion parameters | | | | 13 billion parameters | | | |
|---|---|---|---|---|---|---|---|---|
| C Scheme | Foundation | Beluga | Vicuna | MetaMath | Foundation | Beluga | Vicuna | MetaMath |
| IM1 | 63.16 | 43.42 | 47.37 | **69.74** | **78.95** | 50.00 | 67.11 | 73.68 |
| IM2 | 31.94 | 19.44 | 19.44 | **34.72** | **52.78** | 29.17 | 37.50 | 43.06 |
| IM3 | **63.64** | 30.30 | 45.45 | **63.64** | 71.21 | 53.03 | 46.97 | **80.30** |
| IM | 52.80 | 31.31 | 37.38 | **56.07** | **67.76** | 43.93 | 50.93 | 65.42 |
| C1 | 41.77 | 29.11 | 39.24 | **46.84** | **56.96** | 43.04 | 46.84 | 51.90 |
| C2 | **67.69** | 48.46 | 41.54 | 66.15 | **76.92** | 53.84 | 46.15 | 69.23 |
| C | 53.47 | 33.33 | 40.28 | **55.56** | **65.97** | 47.92 | 46.53 | 59.72 |
| CH1 | **81.82** | 36.36 | 45.45 | 54.55 | 68.18 | 36.36 | 63.64 | **72.73** |
| CH2 | 57.5 | 45.00 | 37.50 | **87.50** | 70.00 | 57.50 | 60.00 | **75.00** |
| CH3 | 70.59 | 23.53 | 47.06 | **82.35** | 76.47 | 41.18 | 47.06 | **88.24** |
| CH4 | **69.23** | 33.33 | 46.15 | **69.23** | 41.03 | 35.90 | 53.85 | **79.49** |
| CH5 | **60.00** | 30.00 | 50.00 | 50.00 | **70.00** | 60.00 | 30.00 | 50.00 |
| CH6 | 16.67 | 8.33 | 45.83 | **83.33** | 62.50 | 54.17 | 50.00 | **91.67** |
| CH | 59.21 | 31.58 | 44.08 | **74.34** | 61.84 | 46.71 | 53.95 | **78.29** |
| AC1 | 54.79 | 38.83 | 38.83 | **68.09** | 61.17 | 51.60 | 52.66 | **62.23** |
| AC3 | 52.63 | 10.53 | 15.79 | **57.89** | 10.53 | 31.58 | 57.89 | **84.21** |
| AC4 | 37.50 | 12.50 | 12.50 | **75.00** | 37.50 | 25.00 | 50.00 | **87.50** |
| AC5 | 18.75 | 6.25 | 25.00 | **68.75** | 31.25 | 25.00 | 56.25 | **81.25** |
| AC | 53.95 | 35.35 | 35.81 | **67.44** | 55.81 | 48.84 | 53.02 | **65.12** |
| Overall | 53.85 | 32.39 | 38.60 | **63.29** | 61.94 | 46.29 | 51.42 | **67.21** |

conceptual schemes. This is aligned with the arguments provided in [36] that link emergent abilities to larger models with a higher number of parameters.

It is also interesting to compare the solving ability of the LLMs to that of children, based on well-established previous studies by other researchers. The results in Table 4 are taken from [21], and indicate the percentage of correct solutions in several studies, for each conceptual scheme. Although researchers used a distinct set of word problems, resulting in potential fluctuations in absolute success rates, the values presented can be used as a scale of relative difficulty levels for children. Surprisingly, although values in Tables 3 and 4 are on a similar scale, it can be observed that they do not correlate in terms of the relative difficulty associated with each scheme. For example, while data in Table 4 show that students have fewer problems facing the C1 than the C2 conceptual scheme, LLMs show a higher performance with the C2 scheme. Similarly, LLMs show relatively higher performance for CH3, while children seem to face more difficulty in dealing with this conceptual scheme when compared to others within the same type. Another interesting effect can be observed when comparing AC vs C types. Children seem to find the AC type more challenging, the same as models that have been trained with general-purpose datasets. However, the performance of

MetaMath is just the opposite and seems to perform generally better on the AC conceptual scheme. These differences suggest that the LLMs fail to replicate the mathematical aptitude observed in children, showing significantly different behaviour. These differences could be exploited when using LLMs to support students with learning difficulties or special needs [10], using a language model specifically adept at their learning weaknesses.

**Table 4.** Results obtained in several studies for each conceptual scheme, expressed as a percentage of correctly solved problems [21]. For ease of comparison, the results for the generally best-performing tested model (MetaMath with 13 billion-parameter) are replicated as a reference in the rightmost column of both tables.

| | Carpenter et al. [6] | Fischer [12] | Nesher & Teubel [22] | Nesher & Katriel [20] | Nesher [19] | MetaMath [35] (13 billion) |
|---|---|---|---|---|---|---|
| Year | 1981 | 1979 | 1975 | 1978 | 1981 | 2024 |
| Level | 1st | 2nd | 5th | 2nd-6th | 2nd-6th | – |
| C1 | 86 | – | – | 79 | 79 | 51.90 |
| C2 | 46 | 14 | – | 46 | 52 | 69.23 |
| CH1 | 79 | – | – | 87 | 82 | 72.73 |
| CH2 | 72 | 30 | – | 70 | 75 | 75.00 |
| CH3 | 51 | – | – | 62 | 72 | 88.24 |
| CH4 | – | – | – | 75 | 77 | 79.49 |
| CH5 | – | 5.5 | – | – | 48 | 50.00 |
| CH6 | – | – | – | – | 49 | 91.67 |
| AC1 | 67 | – | – | – | 76 | 62.23 |
| AC3 | 23 | – | 87 | – | 65 | 84.21 |
| AC4 | – | – | 81 | – | 66 | 87.50 |
| AC5 | – | – | 43 | – | 60 | 81.25 |
| | Steffe & Johnson [27] | Riley et al. [24] | | Tamburino [28] | Vergnaud [31] | MetaMath [35] (13 billion) |
| Year | 1971 | 1981 | | 1980 | 1976 | 2024 |
| Level | 1st | 1st | 2nd | K | 2nd–6th | – |
| C1 | 67 | 100 | 100 | 83 | – | 51.90 |
| C2 | 35 | 39 | 70 | 18 | – | 69.23 |
| CH1 | 67 | 100 | 100 | 89 | – | 72.73 |
| CH2 | 43 | 100 | 100 | 91 | 85 | 75.00 |
| CH3 | 41 | 56 | 100 | 8 | – | 88.24 |
| CH4 | 41 | 78 | 100 | 64 | 70 | 79.49 |
| CH5 | 67 | 28 | 80 | 32 | – | 50.00 |
| CH6 | 35 | 39 | 70 | – | 69 | 91.67 |
| AC1 | – | 28 | 85 | – | – | 62.23 |
| AC3 | – | 17 | 80 | – | – | 84.21 |
| AC4 | – | 28 | 90 | – | – | 87.50 |
| AC5 | – | 11 | 65 | – | – | 81.25 |

## 5 Conclusions

In this paper, we have examined the performance of several LLMs at solving word problems. Results show that relatively simple models with 13 billion parameters can reach similar performance as children, opening new opportunities for technology-supported learning. Potential uses include the design of scaffolding strategies based on conversational agents that advise the student while solving the problems, or the implementation of collaborative learning settings that use these agents to simulate human behavior and play the role of classmates.

In between our findings, the observed capabilities of LLMs seem to differ from those of children, exhibiting notably distinct proficiency levels in tackling various conceptual schemes. This aspect is particularly interesting and useful when considering the integration of virtual agent-based students into collaborative environments. In this case, the observed differences in skill levels compared to those of children are a desirable feature that can contribute to enriching the learning experience by providing diverse perspectives on problem-solving. Further research is also needed to identify potential reasons for these differences, that could stem from the training data utilized to construct the model, potentially skewed towards adult-centric content.

However, despite the positive results, the solving abilities exhibited by the LLMs tested still do not reach sufficient accuracy to allow them to replace other advanced ad-hoc feedback mechanisms specifically designed to offer adaptive support, e.g. [13]. Some recent works have examined the possibility of using LLMs to generate an intermediate representation that allows monitoring of the student's solution [4], and this is another research line that deserves further exploration.

We should also note several limitations of the present study, which has only considered 8 different models with a maximum size of 13 billion parameters. Enhanced emergent capabilities are noted to be more prominent in larger-scale models, as highlighted in [36]. Some recent models are considerably larger, reaching 530 billion parameters in the transformer-based Megatron-Turing Natural Language Generation (MT-NLG) model [26]. Although using such models on educational systems may prove unfeasible in the majority of cases, it is imperative to investigate the impact of quantization for downsizing larger models, aiming to reach the optimal balance between cost and performance.

Another aspect that deserves attention is the design of the prompt. While the one used seems a natural choice, an investigation of other alternatives may yield higher performance. Other designed prompts may be better suited to offer direct assistance to students or create agents intended to seamlessly integrate as virtual classmates in collaborative environments. In addition, the results have underscored the high influence of the training dataset on performance, observing a notable benefit when a domain-adapted dataset is used for training. The substantially different behaviour offered by each model can be leveraged to implement different profiles and endow agents with specific performance-related traits. Lastly, we shall also mention as a limitation of the study that the dataset was labeled by a single expert. Although it is a fairly straightforward labeling task for an expert and was performed twice with a two-week gap, the participation of multiple experts in the process would have enhanced the labeling's reliability.

Despite the limitations mentioned above, the research presented in this paper represents an initial exploration that underscores the potential of LLMs as problem-solving tools. However, further research is necessary for the development of agents capable of seamlessly integrating into computerized systems dedicated to teaching mathematical problem-solving skills.

**Acknowledgements.** This research has been supported by project TED2021-129485B-C42, funded by MCIN/AEI/10.13039/501100011033 and the European Union "NextGenerationEU"/PRTR; and pre-doctoral grant ACIF/2021/439, funded by the Valencian Regional Government.

## References

1. Albornoz-De Luise, R.S., Arevalillo-Herráez, M., Arnau, D.: On using conversational frameworks to support natural language interaction in intelligent tutoring systems. IEEE Trans. Learn. Technol. **16**(5), 722–735 (2023)
2. Arevalillo-Herráez, M., Arnau, D., Marco-Giménez, L.: Domain-specific knowledge representation and inference engine for an intelligent tutoring system. Knowl.-Based Syst. **49**, 97–105 (2013)
3. Arnau-González, P., Arevalillo-Herráez, M., Albornoz De Luise, R., Arnau, D.: A methodological approach to enable natural language interaction in an intelligent tutoring system. Comput. Speech Lang. **81**, 101516 (2023). https://doi.org/10.1016/j.csl.2023.101516
4. Arnau-González, P., Mamolar, A.S., Katsigiannis, S., Althobaiti, T., Arevalillo-Herráez, M.: Toward automatic tutoring of math word problems in intelligent tutoring systems. IEEE Access **11**, 67030–67039 (2023). https://doi.org/10.1109/ACCESS.2023.3290478
5. Beal, C.R.: AnimalWatch: an intelligent tutoring system for algebra readiness. In: Azevedo, R., Aleven, V. (eds.) International Handbook of Metacognition and Learning Technologies. SIHE, vol. 28, pp. 337–348. Springer, New York (2013). https://doi.org/10.1007/978-1-4419-5546-3_22
6. Carpenter, T.P., Moser, J.M., Hiebert, J.: Problem structure and first-grade children's initial solution processes for simple addition and subtraction problems. J. Res. Math. Educ. **12**(1), 27–39 (1981)
7. Chang, K.E., Sung, Y.T., Lin, S.F.: Computer-assisted learning for mathematical problem solving. Comput. Educ. **46**(2), 140–151 (2006)
8. Cheng, L., Croteau, E., Baral, S., Heffernan, C., Heffernan, N.: Facilitating student learning with a chatbot in an online math learning platform. J. Educ. Comput. Res., 07356331241226592 (2024)
9. Chiang, W.L., et al.: Vicuna: An open-source chatbot impressing GPT-4 with 90%* ChatGPT quality, March 2023. https://lmsys.org/blog/2023-03-30-vicuna/
10. Cunha-Pérez, C., Arevalillo-Herráez, M., Arnau, D.: Design and evaluation of a set of methodological strategies for learning a second language in students with down syndrome using computer-based instruction. IEEE Trans. Learn. Technol. **17**, 172–180 (2024). https://doi.org/10.1109/TLT.2023.3242170
11. Duckworth, A.L., Yeager, D.S.: Measurement matters: assessing personal qualities other than cognitive ability for educational purposes. Educ. Res. **44**(4), 237–251 (2015)
12. Fischer, J.P.: L'enfant et le comptage. IREM, Strasbourg, a paraitre (1979)
13. González-Calero, J.A., Arnau, D., Puig, L., Arevalillo-Herráez, M.: Intensive scaffolding in an intelligent tutoring system for the learning of algebraic word problem solving. Br. J. Educ. Technol. **46**(6), 1189–1200 (2015). https://doi.org/10.1111/bjet.12183

14. Grossman, J., Lin, Z., Sheng, H., Wei, J.T.Z., Williams, J.J., Goel, S.: MathBot: transforming online resources for learning math into conversational interactions. In: AAAI 2019 Story-Enabled Intelligence (2019)
15. Heffernan, N.T., Koedinger, K.R.: An intelligent tutoring system incorporating a model of an experienced human tutor. In: Cerri, S.A., Gouardères, G., Paraguaçu, F. (eds.) ITS 2002. LNCS, vol. 2363, pp. 596–608. Springer, Heidelberg (2002). https://doi.org/10.1007/3-540-47987-2_61
16. Koedinger, K.R., Anderson, J.R.: Illustrating principled design: the early evolution of a cognitive tutor for algebra symbolization. Interact. Learn. Environ. **5**(1), 161–179 (1998)
17. Ma, L.: Knowing and Teaching Elementary Mathematics: Teachers' Understanding of Fundamental Mathematics in China and the United States. Routledge, New Jersey (2020)
18. Mahan, D., Carlow, R., Castricato, L., Cooper, N., Laforte, C.: Stable beluga models. https://huggingface.co/stabilityai/StableBeluga2
19. Nesher, P.: Levels of description in the analysis of addition and subtraction word problems. In: Carpenter, T.P., Moser, J.M., Romberg, T. (eds.) Addition and Subtraction: Developmental Perspective. Lawrence Erlbaum Associates, Hiilsdale (1981)
20. Nesher, P., Katriel, T.: Two cognitive modes in arithmetic word problem solving. In: Second Annual Meeting of the International Group for the Psychology of Mathematics Education, Osnabruck, West Germany (1978)
21. Nesher, P., Greeno, J.G., Riley, M.S.: The development of semantic categories for addition and subtraction. Educ. Stud. Math. **13**(4), 373–394 (1982)
22. Nesher, P., Teubal, E.: Verbal cues as an interfering factor in verbal problem solving. Educ. Stud. Math., 41–51 (1975)
23. Patel, A., Bhattamishra, S., Goyal, N.: Are NLP models really able to solve simple math word problems? In: Proceedings of the 2021 Conference of the North American Chapter of the Association for Computational Linguistics: Human Language Technologies, pp. 2080–2094. Association for Computational Linguistics, Online, June 2021
24. Riley, M.S., Greeno, J.G., Heller, J.L.: Development of children's problem-solving ability in arithmetic. In: Ginsburg, H.P. (ed.) The Development of Mathematical Thinking, pp. 153–196. Academic Press, New York (1984)
25. Ruan, S., et al.: Supporting children's math learning with feedback-augmented narrative technology. In: Proceedings of the Interaction Design and Children Conference, pp. 567–580 (2020)
26. Smith, S., et al.: Using DeepSpeed and Megatron to train Megatron-turing NLG 530b, a large-scale generative language model (2022)
27. Steffe, L.P., Johnson, D.C.: Problem-solving performances of first-grade children. J. Res. Math. Educ. **2**(1), 50–64 (1971)
28. Tamburino, J.L.: An analysis of the modelling processes used by kindergarten children in solving simple addition and subtraction story problems. Ph.D. thesis, University of Pittsburgh (1981)
29. Touvron, H., et al.: Llama 2: Open foundation and fine-tuned chat models. arXiv preprint arXiv:2302.13971 (2023)
30. Vergnaud, G.: A classification of cognitive tasks and operations of thought involved in addition and subtraction problems. In: Carpenter, T.P., Moser, J.M., Romberg, T.A. (eds.) Addition and Substraction: A Cognitive Perspective, pp. 39–59. Erlbaum, Hillsdale (1982)

31. Vergnaud, G., Durand, C.: Structures additives et complexité psychogénétique. Revue française de pédagogie, pp. 28–43 (1976)
32. Vergnaud, G.: Multiplicative structures. In: Lesh, R., Landau, M. (eds.) Acquisition of Mathematics Concepts and Processes, pp. 127–174. Academic Press, New York (1983)
33. Wei, J., et al.: Emergent abilities of large language models. Trans. Mach. Learn. Res. **2022** (2022). https://openreview.net/forum?id=yzkSU5zdwD
34. Wu, T., et al.: A brief overview of ChatGPT: the history, status quo and potential future development. IEEE/CAA J. Automatica Sinica **10**(5), 1122–1136 (2023)
35. Yu, L., et al.: MetaMath: Bootstrap your own mathematical questions for large language models. arXiv preprint arXiv:2309.12284 (2023)
36. Zhao, W.X., et al.: A survey of large language models. arXiv preprint arXiv:2303.18223 (2023)

# A Generative Approach for Proactive Assistance Forecasting in Intelligent Tutoring Environments

Yuyan Wu(✉), Miguel Arevalillo-Herráez, and Sergi Solera-Monforte

Departament d'Informàtica, Universitat de València, 46100 Burjassot, Valencia, Spain
{yuyan.wu,miguel.arevalillo,sergi.solera}@uv.es

**Abstract.** Adaptive user feedback facilitates the delivery of personalized assistance to students struggling with self-learning and enhances their overall learning effectiveness. However, numerous studies on student behavior have revealed that they may not consistently utilize help-seeking functions. Deciding when a system should assist students during the dynamic learning process poses a challenge. We propose a new approach called Transformer4HELP, which enables the system to proactively assist students in their learning process interactions in a generative way. We employ an auto-regressive masking strategy to train a decoder-based transformer for prediction, assessing the necessity of providing help at each time step based on the likelihood that intervention may benefit the user's actions. To evaluate this approach, we used real behavioral data from students engaged in solving arithmetic mathematical problems. The experimental results demonstrate the effectiveness of the proposed method, reaching an AUC of 0.84 when predicting whether the student needs help.

**Keywords:** Intelligent Tutoring Systems · assistance dilemma · proactive hints · problem solving · transformer

## 1 Introduction

Intelligent Tutoring Systems (ITSs) provide customized guidance to students, offering adaptive feedback and hints tailored to each individual's learning progress, enriching their learning experiences. Providing targeted assistance to students can optimally mitigate their frustration produced by the learning process, fostering motivation and improving learning outcomes. However, researchers have found that students do not always display appropriate help-seeking behaviors. Some fail to utilize hints when they are genuinely needed (help avoidance), while others overuse hints to solve problems they could tackle independently (help abuse) [3,17]. This has garnered attention within the research community at ITSs, addressing the challenge of deciding when and whether to assist students, named the assistance dilemma.


A. Sifaleras and F. Lin (Eds.): ITS 2024, LNCS 14798, pp. 14–26, 2024.
https://doi.org/10.1007/978-3-031-63028-6_2

The assistance dilemma can be defined as a trade-off problem, attempting to balance information giving and withholding to achieve optimal learning outcomes [14]. A fundamental aspect of the assistance dilemma is discovering instances when students are unproductive and subsequently deciding how and what hints the virtual tutor should offer. To tackle this challenge, early studies primarily focused on on-demand graded hints [19,20], in which students asked the system for help. In common cases, students indicated their need for help by pressing the Help button option. Nevertheless, these approaches sometimes led to undesirable student behaviors, ranging from help avoidance to help abuse [3,7]. One possible solution to avoid these suboptimal behaviors is to implement unsolicited hints, where the system proactively offers assistance to students without them having to request it.

In this work, we focus on autonomously identifying situations that warrant assistance and introduce an approach proficient in automatically detecting instances where aid is needed. In typical e-learning contexts, students iteratively interact with the system performing a series of actions. We capture and organize these interactions throughout the session in a chronological sequence. Then, we predict the need for assistance by leveraging the historical behaviors of previous students to determine if the current student's progress is becoming unproductive and whether intervention is warranted. The method has been validated in a dataset that includes records of student behavior during arithmetic maths problem-solving tasks. The results demonstrate the potential of the method for the task at hand.

## 2 Related Work

### 2.1 Assistance Dilemma and Proactive Hints

Building on the work of Aleven et al. [14], unsolicited hints or feedback have emerged as solutions to prevent help avoidance and help abuse. However, literature on mechanisms to provide this type of hints is surprisingly scarce, despite the potential benefits associated with their implementations. In between relevant works, a recent proposal introduced a framework aimed at understanding students' help-seeking behavior through the analysis of action sequences that ended in help requests [12]. With regard to particular implementations, Fossati et al. [10] presented the linked list Tutor, which generates proactive feedback using a procedurally constructed knowledge model derived from prior student interactions. The results demonstrated the tutor's effectiveness in facilitating student learning, including proactive feedback brings its performance closer to that of a human tutor. Maniktala et al. [16] introduced the HelpNeed model to predict when students require assistance and determine the appropriate hints to provide in logic problems. This approach built upon and extends the Hint Factory [20], which employed a Markov Decision Process to predict the necessary hints. Additionally, it incorporated related features into various machine learning techniques to classify whether students are currently in a productive or unproductive state. The results demonstrated that using proactive hints effectively promotes the appropriate utilization of help, reducing instances of help avoidance and help abuse. More recently, Maniktala et al. [15] incorporated students' hint usage into the HelpNeed model and demonstrated its effectiveness in significantly reducing false positive cases, thereby improving the system's performance in assisting student behavior. Additionally, Alam et al. [1] introduced a deep reinforcement learning policy that leverages autoencoder-based feature learning to offer proactive assistance. The results underscored the effectiveness of this approach.

### 2.2 Sequence Modelling

Proactive hints can be formulated as a sequence modelling problem. The system needs to model a sequence of user actions, learn the probability of previous actions, and then predict the most likely next action based on contextual information. Finally, the system decides whether to provide help or not based on the predicted action.

Recurrent Neural Networks (RNNs) and their variants, such as Gated Recurrent Units (GRU) and Long Short-Term Memory (LSTM), have gained popularity for modeling sequences of user behaviors. For instance, GRU4Rec [11] incorporates RNN into session-based GRU with ranking loss, yielding effective results. Other prevalent research is based on attention-based neural networks. As the transformer's structural model has achieved great success in numerous domains such as Natural Language Processing and Computer Vision, the structure has also been applied to recommender systems. Some representative examples are Kand and McAuley [13] and BERTRec [21]. The former introduced a two-layer transformer decoder known as SASRec, designed to capture users' sequential behaviors. This model was unidirectional and employed a causal attention mask. The latter used a deep bidirectional self-attention to model sequences of user behavior.

We hypothesize that the approach used in sequence recommendation can be applied in the context of proactive assistance. The key difference lies in our emphasis on help actions rather than a general sequential recommendation, where all actions have equal importance. Additionally, transformer-based approaches have shown effectiveness in capturing dependencies between sequence elements.

## 3 Proposed Method

Motivated by the success of next-action prediction in sequence recommendation systems, existing methods have excelled in modeling the correlations between actions by considering an item as an action. Since we also work with sequences, we propose that next-step help prediction can be transformed into a form of next-action prediction. However, instead of considering all possible actions, we particularly focus on help actions. In the context of problem-solving, we hypothesize that the number of actions is finite and propose a decoder-based model to learn the inner relationships among these actions. Subsequently, we utilize the probability of help actions at each time step to determine whether assistance is needed in the current moment or not.

The general architecture we have applied has been imported from the Natural Language Processing field. In particular, similar to SASRec [13], we have used a scaled-down version of GPT-2 [18] as the model's structure. For simplicity, we refer to the proposed model as Transformer4HELP. Transformer4HELP comprises the integration of an embedding layer, stacked decoder blocks, and a prediction layer, as described below.

**Data Input**. Students' attempts to solve a problem in an ITS were recorded as a sequence of actions $S^u = (S_1^u, S_2^u, ..., S_{|S^u|}^u)$. For training, we converted the input sequence into a fixed-length input $S = (s_1, s_2, ..., s_N)$, where $N$ is the maximum length of the model's input. Padding was applied when the sequence length was less than the model input length, filling the right-hand side of the sequence up to $N$. When the sequence length was longer, the sequence was truncated by eliminating the last actions.

**Embedding Layer**. We use embedding matrix $AE \in \mathbb{R}^{|A| \times d}$ to encode student actions into matrices, where $|A|$ is all possible actions could have in the system, and $d$ represents the latent dimensionality. As the order of actions is essential, positional embedding $PE \in \mathbb{R}^{N \times d}$ is added to represent position information. The information transferred into the next layer is defined as:

$$E = AE + PE \tag{1}$$

Furthermore, we include the duration of each action as part of the embedding representation.

**Stacked Decoder Block**. A stacked decoder block combines a masked self-attention layer and a point-wise feed-forward network. Self-attention is computed through Scaled Dot-Product Attention [22]:

$$Attention(Q, K, V) = softmax(\frac{QK^T}{\sqrt{d_k}})V \tag{2}$$

where query $Q$, key $K$, and value $V$ are projected from the same matrix with different learned projection matrices. The scale factor $\sqrt{d_k}$ is used to avoid overly large values of the inner product. Self-attention allows capturing the dependencies between representation pairs without regard to their distance in the sequences. Masked self-attention is applied to mask actions that occur in future time steps, to prevent information leakage during prediction. Following attention sub-layer, a fully connected feed-forward network is applied to endow non-linearity. This involves two linear transformations with a GELU action in between. Moreover, to improve data representation, we applied multiple masked self-attention operations (multi-head attention) in parallel and concatenated the outputs, instead of using a single masked self-attention.

$$FFN(x) = GELU(xW_1 + b_1)W_2 + b_2 \tag{3}$$

where $x$ is the output of previous attention sub-layer, $W_1$ and $W_2$ are $d \times d$ matrices and $b_1$, $b_2$ are d-dimensional vectors.

**Prediction Layer.** After several stacked decoder blocks that adaptively and hierarchically extract information about previous actions, a linear layer is used to map information into an output matrix $O \in \mathbb{R}^{N \times |A|}$, and the softmax function is used to convert the output to the predicted next action probabilities.

## 4 Experimental Setting

To evaluate the proposed method, we have used a large amount of data captured by using an Intelligent Tutoring System called HINTS (Hypergraph-based Intelligent Tutoring System) [2,6], which was specifically designed to teach arithmetic and algebraic word problem-solving. This ITS follows a typical workflow, which unfolds as follows: a student initiates the problem-solving process, communicates their problem-solving steps to the system, receives feedback from the system, and engages in alternating interactions until the problem is successfully solved as depicted in Fig. 1.

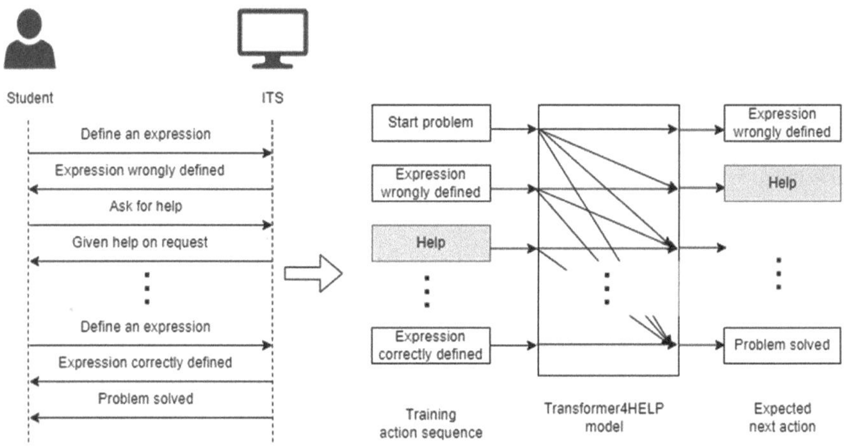


**Fig. 1.** A simplified diagram illustrating user interaction in HINTS and training of Transformer4HELP. At each time step, the model considers all prior system actions and predicts the next action, with a particular focus on identifying actions related to providing assistance.

The system classifies user action intentions and provides relevant feedback. While there are two types of actions in this context (user actions and system actions), the system actions are the ones that furnish crucial information about user actions. Consequently, we exclusively employ system actions as training sequences. These sequences are fed into Transformer4HELP, which calculates the probabilities of actions in the next time step. It is essential to underscore that our ultimate evaluation criterion is not the specific next-step action, but rather whether the next-step action provides assistance.

### 4.1 Dataset

The dataset was recorded as 222 students aged 10–13 in primary school solved a variable number of arithmetic math problems in a HINTS version that supported on-demand help by pressing a button. The dataset recorded both user actions and system feedback in session logs. Actions that students could perform while solving a problem were defining a letter, defining a quantity by using other quantities, writing an equation, interacting with the user interface, or requesting help. The response to the first three actions was whether the action was correct, while a help request triggered a dialogue box suggesting a next step. This allowed us to combine the user action and the system response under 14 different actions, namely: clean equation box, clean expression box, correct equation, incorrect equation, correct expression, incorrect expression, expression already defined, expression operands error, wrong letter definition, correct letter definition, correct quantity, wrong quantity, help request and new problem. Using this encoding, we produced a total of 2144 sequences with a total of 14939 actions, after discarding sequences with less than 3 actions. 1602 of these actions were help requests, which is around 10.7% of total actions.

### 4.2 Model Training

To train the model, we designed a custom loss function that combines two cross-entropy terms: one to compute the overall loss among all actions and another to specifically calculate the loss when determining whether the action is a help request or not. The cross-entropy loss function is defined as follows:

$$L = -\sum_{s \in S} \sum_{t \in [2,\ldots,N]} O_{st} \cdot log(O'_{st}) \tag{4}$$

where $O'_{st}$ represent the predicted probability of action $s$ in time step $t$ and $O_{st}$ is the true probability distribution. Note that we ignore the term where the action output is the action used for padding. In addition, we apply a factor $\lambda$ to decide the relative importance of the two losses. Thereby, the final loss is defined as:

$$L_{final} = L_{all} + \lambda L_{help} \tag{5}$$

The AdamW optimizer with $\beta_1 = 0.9$, $\beta_2 = 0.999$ and weight decay of 0.01 were used for training. We set the initial learning rate to 0.0005 and the batch size to 32, using a linear decay learning rate scheduler. We also implemented an early stopping mechanism to mitigate the risk of overfitting and enhance the model's generalization capability. Specifically, we configured the stopping condition to halt training after 50 epochs if the validation loss does not improve.

We set the maximum sequence length $N = 50$, head number $h = 1$, transformer blocks $L = 1$, and embedding dimension $d = 50$. For hyperparameter $\lambda$ in Eq. 5, we set it to 10.0. We split the dataset into train, validation, and test sets with a ratio of 6:2:2. All our experiments were conducted on a computer equipped with a 13th generation i7 processor with 128 RAM and a single NVIDIA RTX 3090 GPU with 24 GB of memory, running Ubuntu 20.04.4 LTS. The required model implementations used Python 3.9 with version 2.0 of the open-source Pytorch.

### 4.3 Evaluation Metric

Despite the model being trained to predict the next-step action, our evaluation exclusively focuses on help prediction. We assume the action help has label 1 and the remainder with label 0. Since the model computes the probability of all actions, we extract the probability of the action help in each time step. To better judge the model's ability to predict the need for help using a score, we used the Area Under the Curve (AUC) as an evaluation metric of classification performance. This metric AUC is calculated by aggregating the area under the Receiver Operating Characteristic (ROC) curve. The bigger the area, the more accurate the predictor. Formally, the formula for calculating AUC is defined as follows:

$$\int_0^1 f(x)dx \tag{6}$$

where $f(x)$ is the function of the ROC curve.

The ROC curve is a two-dimensional graphical representation utilized in binary classification. On the vertical axis, the True Positive Rate (TPR), also known as sensitivity, expresses the ratio of correctly classified positive samples to the total number of positive. The horizontal axis represents the False Positive Rate (FPR), referred to as 1-specificity, which signifies the proportion of correctly classified negative samples out of the total negative samples. At each point along the curve, its coordinates (fpr, tpr) are computed based on the actual class labels of the samples and their predicted probabilities of being positive. A well-performing classification model's ROC curve exhibits a distinctive feature: as the False Positive Rate decreases, the True Positive Rate simultaneously increases. That is, the curve resides near the upper-left corner, signifying that the model possesses a strong discriminative capability.

The ROC curve provides a way to visualize the trade-off between the true positive rate and the true negative rate and is insensitive to the threshold used for classification. This is particularly relevant in our concrete scenario, as setting a low threshold would lead to an excessive level of assistance while a high threshold would result in minimal support. This leaves the threshold decision as an opportunity to fine-tune Transformer4HELP, adapting the level of assistance provided to each user based on their preferences.

# 5 Results and Discussion

## 5.1 Comparison to Other Methods

As there are limited existing methods in the current state of the art, we are unable to conduct direct comparisons between Transformer4HELP and other models. In order to assess the effectiveness of our proposed model, we have formulated a straightforward help prediction policy. This baseline policy allows us to establish a basis for comparison between the outcomes of the two approaches.

**Mistake-Based Help Prediction Policy.** Intuitively, students are more inclined to seek help in their subsequent actions when they make mistakes while solving a problem. Mistaken actions from the past can influence future behaviors, with a more pronounced effect when the time interval between the erroneous behavior and the subsequent moment is shorter, gradually diminishing as the interval lengthens. Based on this idea, we developed a weighted function for past actions and used it to determine the probability that the next-step action would be a help request. The specific details are outlined as follows:

$$\begin{aligned} M(t) &= e^{-a \cdot t} \\ MT(t) &= flip(M(t)) \\ output &= \sum_{t=1}^{t} MT(t), \text{where } s_t = \text{ mistake action} \end{aligned} \tag{7}$$

We calculate the weight for each time step action using the function $M(t)$, where the variable $a$ represents an increasing factor concerning time, and $t$ denotes the number of the current time step since the problem was initiated. Recognizing the impact of actions over time is influenced by the proximity of time intervals, we employ a "flip" function to order the weights from smallest to largest. The ultimate output value is determined by aggregating all the weights associated with actions taken at time steps related to mistakes. In this case, we set $a = 0.5$ and take into account this approach as a baseline to compare with.

**Transformer4HELP.** The proposed model uses single-head attention and a causal attention mask for left-to-right unidirectional modeling. The goal is to predict the next action for each position in a sequence. We take the probability of help in each time step to compute the value of AUC.

**Table 1.** HELP prediction performance on our dataset across the training, validation, and test sets. The best results are highlighted in bold.

| Method | train set AUC | validation set AUC | test set AUC |
|---|---|---|---|
| Baseline | 0.61 | 0.42 | 0.52 |
| Transformer4HELP | **0.87** | **0.90** | **0.84** |

ROC curves for training, validation, and test sets are illustrated in Fig. 2. These curves provide insights into the model's performance in predicting help requirements. Corresponding AUC values are presented in Table 1 to assess the overall model performance. These results clearly demonstrate the superior performance of our proposed model, Transformer4HELP, compared to the baseline. It is important to note that while students may be more inclined to seek help following frequent mistakes, this is not the sole determinant of performance; other contributing factors can also influence the baseline's performance.

In contrast, Transformer4HELP uses past actions to predict the next-step action with remarkable results. The AUC scores of the model were 0.87, 0.90, and 0.84 for the training, validation, and test sets, respectively. Compared to the baseline, the performance of each group improved by 0.26, 0.48, and 0.32, respectively.

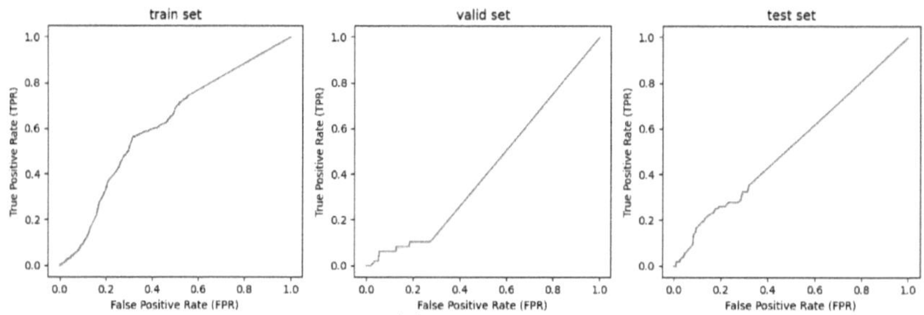


(a) Baseline

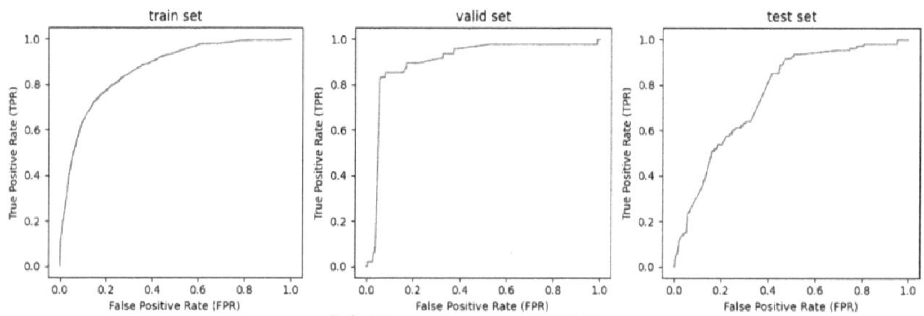


(b) Transformer4HELP

**Fig. 2.** ROC curves in both approaches

## 5.2 Ablation Study

In this section, we describe three ablation experiments, addressed to assess the contribution of the loss function, the addition of temporal information to the model, and the model complexity.

With regard to the loss function, we have studied the model's performance when using cross entropy for all actions, binary cross entropy for help actions, and a mixture of both. Table 2 represents the model's performance based on different loss functions. In the evaluation of the model's generalization performance on the test set, the best performance was achieved by combining the two loss functions, resulting in an improvement close to 0.1 in the AUC value.

**Table 2.** HELP prediction performance on our dataset across the training, validation, and test sets with different loss functions using Transformer4HELP. The best results are highlighted in bold.

| Method | train set AUC | validation set AUC | test set AUC |
|---|---|---|---|
| cross-entropy | 0.83 | 0.88 | 0.73 |
| binary cross entropy | 0.79 | 0.85 | 0.75 |
| combine two losses | **0.87** | **0.90** | **0.84** |

The second experiment attempted to quantify the impact of including timing information in the model. In Table 3, the method "Transformer4HELP-time feature" indicates that no timing information was incorporated into the sequence embedding representation. These results support the addition of timing information to enhance the model's performance.

**Table 3.** HELP prediction performance on our dataset across the training, validation, and test sets using Transformer4HELP with or without time interval information. The best results are highlighted in bold.

| Method | train set AUC | validation set AUC | test set AUC |
|---|---|---|---|
| Transformer4HELP | **0.87** | **0.90** | **0.84** |
| Transformer4HELP-time feature | 0.84 | 0.88 | 0.77 |

In our exploration of model complexity, we conducted experiments with varying numbers of heads and transformer blocks. Table 4 indicates that increasing the number of heads or deepening the model does not yield improvements in model performance.

**Table 4.** HELP prediction performance on our dataset across the training, validation, and test sets using Transformer4HELP with different heads and transformer blocks. The best results are highlighted in bold.

| head | transformer block | train set AUC | validation set AUC | test set AUC |
|---|---|---|---|---|
| 1 | 1 | **0.87** | **0.90** | **0.84** |
| 1 | 2 | 0.84 | 0.90 | 0.78 |
| 2 | 1 | 0.85 | 0.89 | 0.77 |
| 2 | 2 | 0.85 | 0.90 | 0.76 |

## 6 Conclusion

In this work, we have presented a novel approach to capture student action relationships for proactive help prediction, addressing the assistance dilemma problem in intelligent tutoring systems. The proposed model, Transformer4HELP, was built upon a transformer decoder-based architecture. It was designed to model student actions and predict whether the next-step action would be a help request, within the context of a concrete problem-solving scenario. We validated the proposed model and the experimental results indicated the effectiveness, achieving an AUC of 0.84 on the test set.

However, it is important to acknowledge the limitations of this study. One key limitation is the relatively small dataset size we used for our analysis, particularly regarding the scarcity of help action occurrences. When employing deep learning techniques, having a larger dataset is often advantageous for model performance. In addition, the dataset is constrained by its reliance on short-term session logs, which prevents us from creating a user model for each student due to the lack of user information. In real-world problem-solving scenarios, students's personality traits and knowledge acquisition patterns play a significant role in seeking help behavior. Furthermore, due to the lack of publicly available datasets, the proposed method has only been evaluated on one specific dataset. Therefore, we are unable to conduct experiments to demonstrate the generalizability of the method to other ITSs.

In future work, we plan to augment the dataset scale to enhance the model's fitting performance. To further improve the next-step help prediction, we would like to develop user models to align more effectively with individual learning processes. Furthermore, we plan to validate the effectiveness of this approach in real-world scenarios, investigating the impact of a proactive help approach on the student's learning experience. In addition, we consider of special interest the integration of the presented method with some of our recent research, aiming at improving the results presented in this paper. In this direction, we shall consider the possibility of combining the predictions offered by the proposed transformer architecture with others coming from different modalities. These modalities include affective information extracted by using physiological signals [24], cameras [9,23] or text-based classification methods [4]; as well as student success predictions computed using different techniques such as Item Response Theory (IRT) [5]. We are especially interested in the potential impact of accurate predictions of the need for assistance in educational settings, including students with special needs [8].

**Acknowledgements.** This research has been supported by pre-doctoral grant ACIF/2021/439, funded by the Valencian Regional Government; and project TED2021-129485B-C42, funded by MCIN/AEI/10.13039/501100011033 and the European Union "NextGenerationEU"/PRTR.

## References


1. Alam, N., Mostafavi, B., Chi, M., Barnes, T.: Exploring the effect of autoencoder based feature learning for a deep reinforcement learning policy for providing proactive help. In: Wang, N., Rebolledo-Mendez, G., Dimitrova, V., Matsuda, N., Santos, O.C. (eds.) Artificial Intelligence in Education. CCIS, vol. 1831, pp. 278–283. Springer, Cham (2023). https://doi.org/10.1007/978-3-031-36336-8_43
2. Albornoz-De Luise, R.S., Arevalillo-Herráez, M., Arnau, D.: On using conversational frameworks to support natural language interaction in intelligent tutoring systems. IEEE Trans. Learn. Technol. **16**(5), 722–735 (2023)
3. Aleven, V., Mclaren, B., Roll, I., Koedinger, K.: Toward meta-cognitive tutoring: a model of help seeking with a cognitive tutor **16**(2), 101–128 (2006)
4. Arevalillo-Herráez, M., Arnau-González, P., Ramzan, N.: On adapting the DIET architecture and the rasa conversational toolkit for the sentiment analysis task. IEEE Access **10**, 107477–107487 (2022). https://doi.org/10.1109/ACCESS.2022.3213061
5. Arevalillo-Herráez, M., Katsigiannis, S., Alqahtani, F., Arnau-González, P.: Fusing ECG signals and IRT models for task difficulty prediction in computerised educational systems. Knowl. Based Syst. **280**, 111052 (2023). https://doi.org/10.1016/j.knosys.2023.111052
6. Arevalillo-Herráez, M., Arnau, D., Marco-Giménez, L.: Domain-specific knowledge representation and inference engine for an intelligent tutoring system. Knowl.-Based Syst. **49**, 97–105 (2013)
7. Baker, R.S., Corbett, A.T., Koedinger, K.R., Wagner, A.Z.: Off-task behavior in the cognitive tutor classroom: When students "game the system". In: Proceedings of the SIGCHI Conference on Human Factors in Computing Systems, pp. 383–390 (2004)
8. Cunha-Pérez, C., Arevalillo-Herráez, M., Arnau, D.: Design and evaluation of a set of methodological strategies for learning a second language in students with down syndrome using computer-based instruction. IEEE Trans. Learn. Technol. **17**, 172–180 (2024). https://doi.org/10.1109/TLT.2023.3242170
9. Deramgozin, M.M., Jovanovic, S., Arevalillo-Herráez, M., Ramzan, N., Rabah, H.: Attention-enabled lightweight neural network architecture for detection of action unit activation. IEEE Access **11**, 117954–117970 (2023). https://doi.org/10.1109/ACCESS.2023.3325034
10. Fossati, D., Di Eugenio, B., Ohlsson, S., Brown, C., Chen, L.: Generating proactive feedback to help students stay on track. In: Aleven, V., Kay, J., Mostow, J. (eds.) ITS 2010. LNCS, vol. 6095, pp. 315–317. Springer, Heidelberg (2010). https://doi.org/10.1007/978-3-642-13437-1_56
11. Hidasi, B., Karatzoglou, A., Baltrunas, L., Tikk, D.: Session-based recommendations with recurrent neural networks. In: Bengio, Y., LeCun, Y. (eds.) 4th International Conference on Learning Representations, ICLR 2016, San Juan, Puerto Rico, 2–4 May 2016, Conference Track Proceedings (2016)
12. Horta-Bartomeu, R., Santos, O.C.: A time-aware approach to detect patterns and predict help-seeking behaviour in adaptive educational systems. In: Hsiao, S.I., Sahebi, S.S., Bouchet, F., Vie, J. (eds.) Proceedings of the 14th International Conference on Educational Data Mining, EDM 2021, virtual, June 29 - July 2, 2021. International Educational Data Mining Society (2021)
13. Kang, W., McAuley, J.: Self-attentive sequential recommendation. In: 2018 IEEE International Conference on Data Mining (ICDM), pp. 197–206. IEEE Computer Society, Los Alamitos (2018)

14. Koedinger, K.R., Aleven, V.: Exploring the assistance dilemma in experiments with cognitive tutors. Educ. Psychol. Rev. **19**, 239–264 (2007)
15. Maniktala, M., Chi, M., Barnes, T.: Enhancing a student productivity model for adaptive problem-solving assistance. User Model. User-Adap. Inter. **33**(1), 159–188 (2023)
16. Maniktala, M., Cody, C., Isvik, A., Lytle, N., Chi, M., Barnes, T.: Extending the hint factory for the assistance dilemma: a novel, data-driven help need predictor for proactive problem-solving help. J. Educ. Data Mining **12**(4), 24–65 (2020)
17. Price, T.W., Zhi, R., Barnes, T.: Hint generation under uncertainty: the effect of hint quality on help-seeking behavior. In: André, E., Baker, R., Hu, X., Rodrigo, M.M.T., du Boulay, B. (eds.) AIED 2017. LNCS (LNAI), vol. 10331, pp. 311–322. Springer, Cham (2017). https://doi.org/10.1007/978-3-319-61425-0_26
18. Radford, A., et al.: Language models are unsupervised multitask learners. OpenAI Blog **1**(8), 9 (2019)
19. Razzaq, L., Heffernan, N.T.: Hints: is it better to give or wait to be asked? In: Aleven, V., Kay, J., Mostow, J. (eds.) ITS 2010, Part I. LNCS, vol. 6094, pp. 349–358. Springer, Heidelberg (2010). https://doi.org/10.1007/978-3-642-13388-6_39
20. Stamper, J., Barnes, T., Lehmann, L., Croy, M.: The hint factory: automatic generation of contextualized help for existing computer aided instruction. In: Proceedings of the 9th International Conference on Intelligent Tutoring Systems Young Researchers Track, pp. 71–78 (2008)
21. Sun, F., et al.: BERT4Rec: sequential recommendation with bidirectional encoder representations from transformer. In: Proceedings of the 28th ACM International Conference on Information and Knowledge Management, CIKM 2019, pp. 1441–1450. Association for Computing Machinery, New York (2019)
22. Vaswani, A., et al.: Attention is all you need. Adv. Neural Inf. Process. Syst. **30** (2017)
23. Wu, Y., Arevalillo-Herráez, M., Arnau-González, P.: Improved action unit detection based on a hybrid model. IEEE Access **11**, 77585–77595 (2023). https://doi.org/10.1109/ACCESS.2023.3297266
24. Wu, Y., Arevalillo-Herráez, M., Katsigiannis, S., Ramzan, N.: On the benefits of using hidden Markov models to predict emotions. In: Bellogín, A., Boratto, L., Santos, O.C., Ardissono, L., Knijnenburg, B.P. (eds.) UMAP 2022: 30th ACM Conference on User Modeling, Adaptation and Personalization, Barcelona, Spain, 4–7 July 2022, pp. 164–169. ACM (2022). https://doi.org/10.1145/3503252.3531323

# Combined Maps as a Tool of Concentration and Visualization of Knowledge in the Logic of Operation of the Intelligent Tutoring Systems

Viktor Uglev(✉) and Georgy Smirnov

Siberian Federal University, Zheleznogorsk, Russia
vauglev@sfu-kras.ru

**Abstract.** The issue of generalizing and concentrating learning situation data in human learner interaction with ITS is described. The resolution of this issue is important for making reasoned decisions that are considered credible by a human learner. Various approaches to data concentration and visualization are considered, among which mapping has a special place. Using the example of the Cognitive Maps of Knowledge Diagnosis (CMKD) method, it is shown how data can be generalized by concentrating them into parametric maps and then forming and visualizing a combined map. The algorithm of synthesizing the combined map and the principle of its interpretation are given. An experiment with master's students who interpreted and evaluated ITS recommendations accompanied by different types of maps in CMKD notation is described. The data example of one of the master's students studying the "Intelligent Data Analysis" course shows the process of visualization of data about the learning situation. The analysis of the experimental results showed an increased effectiveness of ITS decision perception when using the data from the combined map and visualizing its simplified fragment.

**Keywords:** Intelligent Tutoring Systems · cognitive visualization · decision making · Cognitive Maps of Knowledge Diagnosis · Combined Map

## 1 Introduction

The decision-making mechanism in Intelligent Tutoring Systems (ITS) plays a central role in the development of an intelligent solver (planner). Since the control object is a human learner, the complexity of the task of developing effective decisions directly depends on the flexibility of describing and evaluating the learning situation. Due to the variety of input parameters taken into account by the planner, a simple sorting of their combinations in the form of rules is inefficient and leads to the need to propose other ways of organizing the processing of knowledge bases in ITS. One of the approaches is a step-by-step concentration of knowledge about the learning situation.


A. Sifaleras and F. Lin (Eds.): ITS 2024, LNCS 14798, pp. 27–39, 2024.
https://doi.org/10.1007/978-3-031-63028-6_3

The methods of the bottom-up approach, to which generative intelligence based on artificial neural networks belongs, are very good for generalization, but they do not allow obtaining explainable (reasoned) decisions. The use of XAI methods [1] does not yet allow to reconstruct an acceptable quality of causal relationships. In this regard, the main mechanism for realizing the logic of an intelligent planner are mainly methods of the top-down artificial intelligence (ontologies and recommendation/expert system [18,21]). But they also rely on the mechanism of knowledge concentration when making decisions. One of the trends in the development of modern ITS is the use of cognitive visualization methods [10]. Our paper is devoted to describing the process of transition from input data to explainable decisions, relying on the mechanism of mapping and cognitive visualization.

## 2 Existing Solutions

The standard tools of data concentration in LMS (e.g., Moodle, Canvas, Blackboard, D2L Brightspace, etc.) or in developed AI-oriented tutoring systems [3,12], start generalization by extracting data from the digital educational footprint, grouping them and generalizing them statistically (concentration). In doing so, a number of problems arise related to *evaluation* of the learning situation as a complex object of consideration. These problems are mainly related to the necessity of:

1. considering the heterogeneous nature of the data (overcoming the difficulty of simultaneously describing structural, functional, target and operational data about the object of visualization);
2. considering the dynamics of indicators (overcoming the temporal variability and generalization of frequency properties);
3. considering different points of view (overcoming differences in subjective emphasis and personal targets in the evaluation of the learning situation);
4. considering different aspects of analysis (overcoming the heterogeneity of the interpretation of the situation with respect to multiple key properties);
5. considering various decisions (overcoming the difficulty of choosing one of the alternatives or synthesizing a compromise decision);
6. considering the specifics of the subjective perception of the recipient of the answer (overcoming the difficulty of setting accents in the argumentation when presenting the ITS decision to a person).

Most ITS decisions are oriented to the solution of the task of control, i.e. to the development of pedagogical action adequate to the situation. It is important to get an answer to the following question: how to motivate a human learner to choose a proper action in the educational environment, which will lead to "the best" results (achievement of educational goals) as predicted by the system? At the same time, any decision should be explained to the person in natural language or other form, if he/she doubts the adequacy of the work of intelligent algorithms.

ITS developers implement the following items as methods of summarizing information from the learner model and digital footprint to assess the learning situation:

- averaging based on statistical and probabilistic approaches (e.g., [2]);
- classification based on a typical behavioral model (pre-identified patterns and clusters [17]);
- recognition of the situation by neural network models [13];
- calculation of the model of the subject area in the form of an ontology [7];
- calculation of rule collections from knowledge bases of recommender systems [18];
- integrated visualization of the learning environment and learner model [25].

As was shown in [10,19], graphic tools are a powerful trend for explaining decisions. The methods of cognitive visualization are of the greatest interest as they have the greatest potential for data concentration. Let us compare the possibilities of knowledge concentration (convolution) in relation to the six problematic aspects of analyzing a learning situation given above (see Table 1).

**Table 1.** Possibilities for interpreting different aspects of analyzing a learning situation with ITS graphic tools

| Basic technologies | Example | 1 | 2 | 3 | 4 | 5 | 6 |
|---|---|---|---|---|---|---|---|
| Kohonen Self-Organizing Maps (SOM) | [16] | – | – | – | – | – | – |
| Clustering methods | [9] | – | – | – | – | – | – |
| Ontologies and semantic networks | [8] | V | ~V | V | V | ~V | ~V |
| OLAP | [5] | ~V | – | – | V | – | – |
| Chernoff faces | [4] | ~V | – | – | ~V | – | – |
| UGVA method | [24] | V | V | – | ~V | – | – |
| Pictograph boards (dashboards) | [6] | ~V | ~V | – | – | – | – |
| Cognitive maps | [14,25] | ~V | ~V | ~V | – | – | ~V |

As can be seen from Table 1, it is problematic to take advantage of all generalization possibilities using a single data processing mechanism in ITS without forming a detailed ontology of the subject area. This approach is extremely time-consuming and complex [8]. In addition, there are also the following peculiarities of generalization: clear steps, combination of different types of uncertainty, the need for interpretability of the image and its interactivity. Therefore, let us consider the development of the method of cognitive maps. Let us use the method of cognitive maps of knowledge diagnosis (CMKD) to solve this task. The purpose of this paper is to demonstrate how parametric maps and the CMKD method (via combined maps) can increase the level of student confidence in ITS assessment of the learning situation. For this purpose, in Sect. 3 we will describe the principle of synthesizing a parametric map and converting it into a combined map, as well as the rules for interpreting it during operation of the ITS planner. In Sect. 4 we will describe the experiment with the master's students and in Sect. 5 we will give the results of the experiment and summarize the experience gained.

# 3 Method

## 3.1 Methodological Approach to Data Generalization

The mechanism of concentration of the data collected in the digital educational footprint by ITS mechanisms involves a step-by-step generalization from a common substrate of parameters and sets of their values to the formation of a complete decision of the tutoring system and informing about it the human learner. For this purpose, the input data are transformed according to the following *sequence of steps*:

1. extraction of digital educational footprint data from ITS logs and their statistical generalization for each parameter (averaging and determining the direction of change - operating with single values);
2. translation of each generalized parameter to its qualitative assessment (fuzzification operation based on the fuzzy logic method [26]);
3. independent expert evaluation of various aspects of the object/process under consideration, represented by vectors of qualitative assessments, concerning key aspects of analysis and models, the logic of which is simulated by ITS (e.g. particular models of student, teacher and subject tutor);
4. formation of a compromise alternative at the intersection of particular decisions and preparation of a set of arguments justifying this decision (corresponds to the stage of logical concentration according to [21]);
5. identification of 1–2 key arguments from the set of justifying arguments, their display in the logic of internal targets of the student in order to accelerate the perception of the recommendations of the tutoring system (increasing the effectiveness of the pedagogical impact and increasing the credibility of ITS decisions).

These steps are schematically shown in Fig. 1 and conditionally correspond to overcoming six problems related to analyzing complex objects/situations, which were listed in Sect. 2. It is problematic to operate with a set of data in steps 3–5, without involvement of special structures. Therefore, we will use the mapping mechanism to solve this problem.

## 3.2 CMKD Method

Mapping, as a data concentration method, is widely used when there is a need for complex representation of complex objects. The term "cognitive map" was introduced to describe cognitive functions of the brain in the works on neurophysiology by E. Tolman [20]. Let us consider one of the mapping methods called Cognitive Map of Knowledge Diagnosis (CMKD).

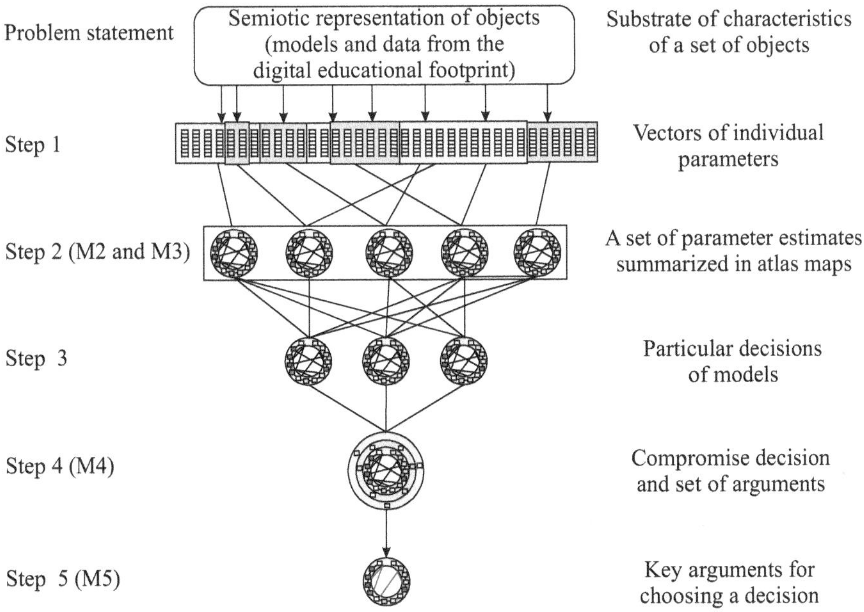


**Fig. 1.** Scheme of step-by-step generalization of data in the implementation of the ITS decision-making process

CMKD is a mapping method that provides a compact representation (visualization) of semiotic structures (syntactic, semantic, and pragmatic data) applied to the diagnosis of an instance of an object/process in order to improve the quality of making decisions and their reasoning. This method reflects the concept of applied semiotics [15] and can be adapted to different subject areas. For example, in [25] it is used to visualize the learning situation when working with ITS. Developing this idea, it should be noted that CMKD map can be displayed in different modes:

1. basic map ($M1$) reflecting invariant basic structures (excluding pragmatic and denotation data);
2. personalized map ($M2$) reflecting the object in relation to a specific pragmatic approach (excluding only denotation data);
3. particular map ($M3$) reflecting the object in relation to a particular aspect of analysis and point of view;
4. combined map ($M4$) reflecting the combination of particular maps (an atlas) and emphasizing the most significant elements from different maps (e.g., reflecting only problematic points in different aspects and points of view);
5. simplified particular map ($M5$) reflecting the central tendency/accent and excluding everything else (as a rule, on the basis of one particular map which is the most suitable for argumentation of decisions).

In analytical systems, where the CMKD notation is implemented for the purpose of demonstration to the user, it is provided by mechanisms of interactive interaction: it is possible to move between maps at the initiative of a person, as well as to refer to the objects associated with its elements.

For ITS, the role of each map is indicated by corresponding designation in Fig. 1. Examples of each of these maps are shown in Fig. 2. The letter $u$ on the maps denotes didactic units of the course and the letter $t$ denotes topics of the course. While the use of maps 1, 2, 3 and 5 in implementing ITS logic is well enough described in [25], the combined map should be considered in more detail.

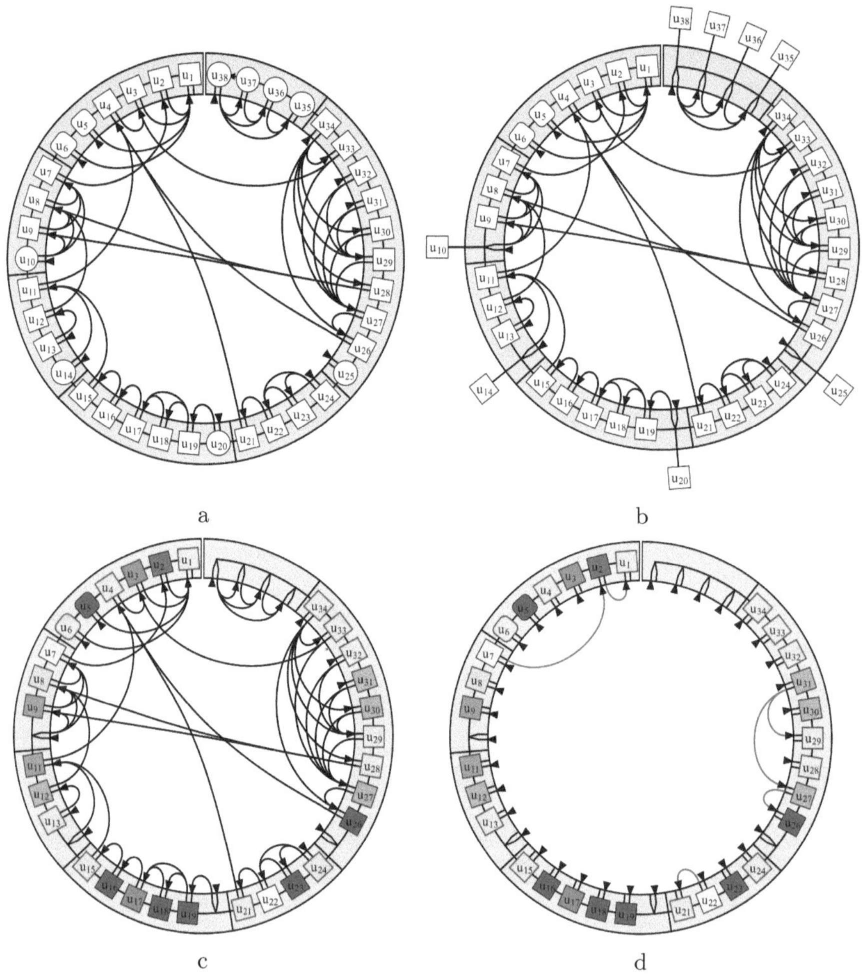


**Fig. 2.** Examples of basic ($M1$, a), personalized ($M2$, b), particular ($M3$, c) and simplified particular ($M5$, d) CMKD maps describing different states of learning situation analysis on the example of the learning process in the "Intelligent Data Analysis" (IDA) course based on ITS

### 3.3 Combined Map as an Element of ITS Operation Logic

As mentioned above, the combined map of knowledge diagnosis ($M4$) in ITS is intended to perform a metric concentration of data on problems identified as a result of the diagnosis of the current learning situation. To synthesize it, it will be necessary to have particular maps from the atlas generated for all models and aspects of analysis ($M3$) simulated by the system. Each of these particular maps has not only structural elements (syntactics) in the combined map, but also a set of semantic links among themselves (semantics) and with other entities (e.g., targets, competencies, and tasks corresponding to pragmatics). The process of synthesizing a combined map can be conditionally represented as the following algorithm in pseudocode (see Algorithm 1).

**Algorithm 1.** Enlarged steps for synthesizing a combined map

Form a common pool of objects $W$ of the structure (didactic units $u$), tasks, targets and competencies with a through index $i$
Load particular maps $M3$ with through index $j$ from the atlas
**for** j **do**
    **if** (the element $i$ is present in the map $M3_j$) and (an estimate of the negative contribution $\theta_i$ (*) > of the threshold value $\alpha_i$) **then**
        Include the object $w_i$ as $m4_k$ in $M4$, as well as those entities from $W$ that had semantic links with the problematic element
        **if** $w_i$ was previously included in $M4$ **then**
            Increase the significance level $\beta_k$ of the object $m4_k$ and corresponding problematic links
        **end if**
    **end if**
**end for**
Group the elements $M4$ by object type
Estimate the average value $\beta_k$ (denote the result by $\beta_W$) with respect to the whole $M4$ taking into account the weights of semantic links (*)
**for** k **do**
    **if** $\beta_k < (\beta_W/2)$ **then**
        Exclude $m4_k$ from $M4$ as having little influence on decision making in the context of the entire learning situation
    **end if**
**end for**
**if** the map to be visualized for user **then**
    **for** k **do**
        Modify each block (shape, lettering, line style, etc.) to display the most important parameters (e.g., value trends)
        Color coding of each block according to the selected color scale reflecting the degree of "problem"
    **end for**
**end if**

Symbol (*) in the algorithm denotes operations that are performed using an additional mechanism of expert systems. The result of this algorithm is that a set of significant entities and the links between them are built in the form of a single structure, reflecting the reconstruction of the student's state (in the opinion of ITS) at the current moment in time and in relation to a particular decision-making task. An example visualization of a combined map in CMKD notation is shown in Fig. 3. Here in block $S$ competencies from the curriculum are grouped and block $\Psi$ includes target preferences.

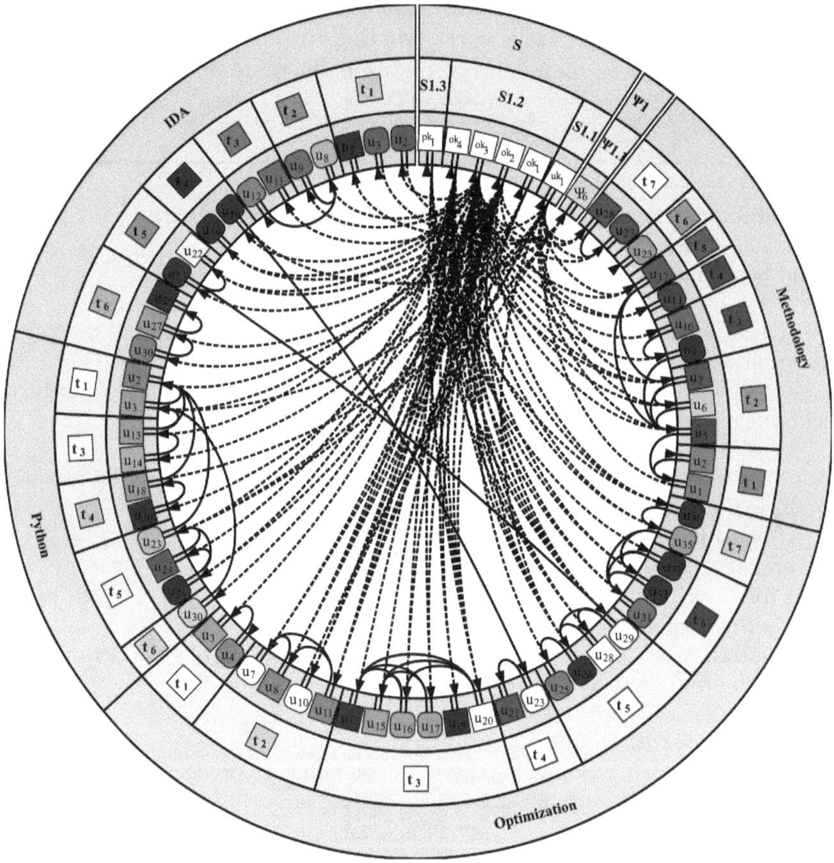


**Fig. 3.** Example of the combined map in CMKD notation

Interpretation of the combined map is that an intelligent solver (in case the map is processed by ITS) or a decision maker (in case the map is demonstrated to a person) has a possibility to simultaneously cover the most significant structural elements of the analyzed object/process, their links between each other, values of indicators characterizing them and target settings.

In the process of implementing the ITS operation logic, the combined map becomes the basis for the majority of decisions, because it concentrates the most significant indicators and displays semantics of links between objects. If we rely on the idea that different models simulated by the tutoring system have their own fragments of the knowledge base, their interaction through the analysis of the combined map allows us to implement the strategy of working out compromise decisions by the blackboard mechanism [11].

## 4 Experiment

The experiment on the use of CMKD in organizing the work of the experimental ITS AESU was conducted by us at the end of 2023 on a group of master's students (9 people) of the specialty "Informatics and Computer Science" at Siberian Federal University. The following research hypothesis was put forward: graphic support of ITS recommendations about problems in the current learning situation will be faster to be understood and accepted for execution by a student if the arguments are concentrated on the cognitive maps of knowledge diagnosis with the possibility of interactive interaction.

For all courses of the first academic term, data on their structure, semantics, and priorities of the teacher model were formalized. Students took entrance and intermediate tests in each course, as well as indicated their priorities by answering questionnaires. In particular, through the questionnaires each student noted the priority didactic units of the course, the most important goals of the course, and the priority competencies to be developed. All answers were recorded in the learner model and taken into account when forming the individual course composition and educational trajectory.

The results of individual work with the learning material were used to record the digital educational footprint, assess the level of mastery of didactic material (knowledge aspect) and the level of development of each of the 8 competencies measured by ITS. The approach we used to assess the competencies is described in detail in [23].

Within a particular course, the intelligent planner formed a recommendation to work with the learning material in a natural language form, which could be supplemented by one of the types of maps. The maps were implemented as an interactive graphic block, allowing to get extended data about each depicted element, when the student hovered over or highlighted it.

For a particular learning situation, the student was given a textual recommendation to repeat the learning material (repetition) and the reasons for the system to include it in the recommendation. It was synthesized on the basis of a combined map. The first stage of the experiment included only the text recommendation. In the second stage, the student was presented with a recommendation for a different learning situation, but accompanied with a particular map (the reasons and the main emphasis on repetition were also indicated) without the possibility of changing the aspect of consideration (the most meaningful aspect was automatically selected). In the third stage, the map was shown with the possibility of switching aspects by the student. In the final (fourth) stage, a simplified map was presented. At each stage, the degree of usefulness, comprehensibility and credibility of the recommendation text was clarified. In addition, the time of studying the text part of the answer, the map and answers to accompanying questions was recorded.

Let us describe an example of a learning situation for one of the students for the course "Intelligent Data Analysis" (IDA, its basic and personalized CMKD are shown in Fig. 2a-b). At a certain moment of its study an atlas of particular maps was formed (an example of such a map is shown in Fig. 2c, reflecting the competency aspect for the competency $uk1$ "Can critically analyze problem situations on the basis of a systematic approach"). The analysis of the map allows us to identify "problematic" didactic units $u2$ and $u27$, which should be repeated first of all. But the presence of semantic links within the course shows that this competency depends significantly on the knowledge of $u1$.

After the formation of the combined map, which was shown in Fig. 3, the following peculiarities of the learning situation can be noted:

- the didactic unit $u1$ creates "problems" not only for $u11$, but also for $u2$, but also for $u7$ in the knowledge aspect and in relation to competency $uk1$;
- there is a dependency in the neighboring course "Software implementation of mathematical models" in Python ($u27$), which creates additional difficulties in the overall learning process;
- the influence of $u2$ and $u5$ on the mastery of the learner's priority course objective $\psi6$ is recorded.

This not only shifts the focus of the recommendation from $u7$ and $u31$ to $u2$ and $u27$, but also gives a "personal" coloring to the arguments presented to explain the recommendation.

Obviously, the display of a combined map in the process of the dialog explaining the recommendations would be unnecessary. Therefore, the competency aspect $uk1$ was emphasized during the simplification process, and the map was simplified to the form shown in Fig. 2d. More details about the process of synthesizing a dialog accompanied by maps can be found in [22].

## 5 Results and their Analysis

In the course of the experiment, 480 evidences were recorded from 25 questionnaires and tests of the learning process. In the process of analyzing the learning situation according to the experiment described above, an additional 218 evidences were obtained from each student. A summary of the data for the group of master's students is presented in (see Table 2).

In 86% of cases, the key reason for trusting a recommendation supported by a simplified map was the personalized reference to personal learning goals. This indicates that combined maps are effective in identifying emphases in the data, but it is unnecessary to demonstrate them to students. This indicates that combined maps are effective at identifying emphases in the data, but they are too complicated to be demonstrated to students. We were surprised to see that the particular map with the option to select an aspect of the analysis $M3$ received the best response from students: it was preferred to the simplified map in 89%

**Table 2.** Experiment results

| Stage number and map type | Average number of clicks on the map | Average number of aspect changes, times | Average time to assess the situation, min. | Average level of trust (a Likert scale) |
|---|---|---|---|---|
| 1. No map | – | – | 2:13 | It's difficult |
| 2. $M3$ with a major aspect | – | 8 | 2:16 | I'm more likely to trust |
| 3. $M3$ when changing aspect | 14.3 | 7.3 | 2:18 | I'm more likely to trust |
| 4. $M5$ | 8.3 | 5.1 | 1:53 | I'm more likely to trust |

of cases and to the recommendation text alone in 100% of cases. When evaluating 100% of learning situations, it was noted that it is desirable to allow the student to learn the algorithms, rules and guidelines for obtaining quantitative and qualitative grades from the text of the recommendation demonstrated by the ITS. In general, it can be stated that the hypothesis of the study was confirmed: students not only tend to trust (accept) recommendations with maps more often, but also consciously record a personal need in the expected result of the educational work.

The difficulties we had to face in conducting the experiment were the following: first, the need to formalize the data for all courses in a standard form (not all teachers appreciated the detailed description of their course models); second, the interpretation of the map in the second stage of the experiment took a long time because the students had to become familiar with the CMKD notation (when the experiment is repeated, the speed of interpretation will be higher); third, the experimental group was not large. For these reasons, we consider the results to be preliminary and in need of a larger-scale experiment. Perhaps demonstration of the combined map to the students is unnecessary.

The use of the mapping method, and in particular of combined maps in CMKD notation, allows not only to automate the decision-making process, but also to form a system of arguments by the method from [22]. This is in line with the general approach to using explainable artificial intelligence in ITS [12]. A more flexible approach can only be implemented by using an ontological description of the subject area. But this will specify the work of the whole ITS for a particular course and will be incommensurably more labor-intensive than the use of CMKD.

## 6 Conclusion

The combined maps play an important role in ITS operation, i.e. the concentration of knowledge about the problems of the learning situation. But this is only a part of the cross-cutting analysis [25], which is aimed at improving the quality of personalization of the learning process and increasing the student's confidence in ITS decisions. Although the experimental data we have obtained are only preliminary, we can evaluate them as positive and will continue our work in this direction.

The scalability of the proposed approach to analyzing the learning situation using the mapping mechanism was verified by us on several groups of students of different technical degrees. If the course description in ITS and the formation of evaluation and test materials are correct, as well as data on the student's personal preferences are sufficient, the algorithm of knowledge concentration in the form of a combined map and its automatic analysis provide a meaningful argumentative dialog guided by a student.

Our current research directions in the field of ITS operation logic implementation are combination of CMKD method with other methods of cognitive visualization (in particular, with UGVA method [24]); exploring the possibility of multi-agent implementation of interaction between teacher, student and subject tutor models on the basis of combined maps; as well as organization and carrying out of complex experiment in the educational process in Siberian Federal University.

## References

1. Baker, R.S.: Stupid tutoring systems, intelligent humans. Int. J. Artif. Intell. Educ. **26**, 600–614 (2016)
2. Birnbaum, A.: Some latent trait models and their use in inferring an examinee's ability. Statistical theories of mental test scores (1968)
3. Brusilovsky, P.: AI in education, learner control, and human-AI collaboration. Int. J. Artif. Intell. Educ. **33**(1560–4306), 15 (2023). https://doi.org/10.1007/s40593-023-00356-z
4. Chernoff, H.: The use of faces to represent points in K-dimensional space graphically. J. Am. Stat. Assoc. **68**(342), 361–368 (1973)
5. Djedaini, M., Drushku, K., Labroche, N., Marcel, P., Peralta, V., Verdeaux, W.: Automatic assessment of interactive OLAP explorations. Inf. Syst. **82**, 148–163 (2019)
6. Few, S.: Information Dashboard Design: The Effective Visual Communication of Data. O'Reilly Media, Inc., Sebastopol (2006)
7. Gavrilova, T.A., Kokoulina, L.: Using ontology engineering to design an artificial intelligence course. In: Uskov, V.L., Howlett, R.J., Jain, L.C. (eds.) Smart Education and e-Learning 2019. SIST, vol. 144, pp. 201–207. Springer, Singapore (2019). https://doi.org/10.1007/978-981-13-8260-4_19
8. Gavrilova, T., Kuznetsova, A., Lesheva, I.: On the issue of the development of ontologies of scientific and academic work. In: XXI National Conference of Artificial Intelligence, vol. 1, pp. 60—67. Print-Express, Smolensk, Russia (2023). (in Russian)
9. Gorban, A.N., Zinovyev, A.: Fast and user-friendly non-linear principal manifold learning by method of elastic maps. In: 2015 IEEE International Conference on Data Science and Advanced Analytics (DSAA), pp. 1–9. IEEE (2015)
10. Ilves, K., Leinonen, J., Hellas, A.: Supporting self-regulated learning with visualizations in online learning environments. In: Proceedings of the 49th ACM Technical Symposium on Computer Science Education, pp. 257—262. Association for Computing Machinery, New York (2018)

11. Jackson, P.: Introduction to Expert Systems. Addison-Wesley Pub. Co., Reading (1999)
12. Khosravi, H., et al.: Explainable artificial intelligence in education. Comput. Educ. Artif. Intell. **3**, 100074 (2022). https://doi.org/10.1016/j.caeai.2022.100074
13. Pan, T., Feng, G., Liu, X., Wu, W.: Using feature interaction for mining learners' hidden information in MOOC dropout prediction. In: Frasson, C., Mylonas, P., Troussas, C. (eds.) ITS 2023. LNCS, vol. 13891, pp. 507–517. Springer, Cham (2023). https://doi.org/10.1007/978-3-031-32883-1_45
14. Peer, M., Brunec, I.K., Newcombe, N.S., Epstein, R.A.: Structuring knowledge with cognitive maps and cognitive graphs. Trends Cogn. Sci. **25**(1), 37–54 (2021)
15. Pospelov, D., Osipov, G.: Applied semiotics. News Artif. Intell. **1**, 9–35 (1999). (in Russian)
16. Qian, J., et al.: Introducing self-organized maps (SOM) as a visualization tool for materials research and education. Results Mater. **4**, 100020 (2019)
17. Roux, L., Nodenot, T., Etcheverry, P., Dagorret, P., Marquesuzaa, C., Lopistéguy, P.: A classification approach to recognize on-task student's behavior for context aware recommendations. In: Crossley, S., Popescu, E. (eds.) ITS 2022. LNCS, vol. 13284, pp. 161–170. Springer, Cham (2022). https://doi.org/10.1007/978-3-031-09680-8_15
18. Rybina, G., Slinkov, A.: The implementation of the ontological approach to control of the processes of designing integrated expert systems based on the problem-oriented methodology. In: Kovalev, S.M., Kuznetsov, S.O., Panov, A.I. (eds.) RCAI 2021. LNCS (LNAI), vol. 12948, pp. 354–364. Springer, Cham (2021). https://doi.org/10.1007/978-3-030-86855-0_25
19. Sinatra, A., Graesser, A.C., Hu, X., Goldberg, B., Hampton, A.J.: Design Recommendations for Intelligent Tutoring Systems: Volume 8-Data Visualization. A Book in the Adaptive Tutoring Series, US Army Combat Capabilities Development Command–Soldier Center (2020)
20. Tolman, E.: Cognitive Maps in rats and men. Psychol. Rev. **55**(4), 189–208 (1948)
21. Uglev, V.: Implementation of decision-making methods in Intelligent Automated Educational System focused on complete individualization in learning. AASRI Procedia **6**, 66–72 (2014). https://doi.org/10.1016/j.aasri.2014.05.010
22. Uglev, V.: Explanatory didactic dialogue in the Intelligent Tutoring Systems based on the Cross-Cutting approach. In: Frasson, C., Mylonas, P., Troussas, C. (eds.) ITS 2023. LNCS, vol. 13891. pp. 371–380. Springer, Cham (2023). https://doi.org/10.1007/978-3-031-32883-1_34
23. Uglev, V., Shangina, E.: Assessment and visualization of course-level and curriculum-level competency profiles. In: Gervasi, O., et al. (eds.) ICCSA 2023. LNCS, vol. 14104, pp. 478–493. Springer, Cham (2023). https://doi.org/10.1007/978-3-031-37105-9_32
24. Uglev, V., Sychev, O.: Evaluation, comparison and monitoring of multiparameter systems by Unified Graphic Visualization of Activity method on the example of learning process. Algorithms **15**(21) (2022). https://doi.org/10.3390/a15120468
25. Uglev, V., Sychev, O., Gavrilova, T.: Cross-cutting support of making and explaining decisions in intelligent tutoring systems using cognitive maps of knowledge diagnosis. In: Crossley, S., Popescu, E. (eds) ITS 2022. LNCS, vol. 13284, pp. 51–64. Springer, Cham (2022). https://doi.org/10.1007/978-3-031-09680-8_5
26. Zadeh, L.A., Aliev, R.A.: Fuzzy Logic Theory and Applications: Part I and Part II. World Scientific Publishing, New Jersey (2018)

# Fast Weakness Identification for Adaptive Feedback

Raymond Morland[1(✉)], Lawrence Wang[2], and Fuhua Lin[1]

[1] Athabasca University, Athabasca, AB T9S 3A3, Canada
rmorland1@learn.athabascau.ca, oscarl@athabascau.ca
[2] University of Alberta, Edmonton, AB T6G 2R3, Canada
lxwang@ualberta.ca

**Abstract.** Identifying and addressing areas of weakness of online learning students early on is critically important to prevent minor issues from becoming major obstacles to their success. It is desirable to have a tool that allows learners to conduct personalized formative assessment on demand anytime during their course study. To minimize the cognitive load of a learner and facilitate the iterative learning process, a pedagogical strategy is to identify a singular weak skill each formative assessment and to provide adaptive feedback for remediation for the learner to close the gap between his/her current performance and the expected mastery criteria. As one gap closes, another gap may be identified afterward, renewing the formative assessment and feedback loop. For such singular weakness identification, minimizing the time spent or the number of questions on each assessment is crucial for maintaining learner engagement. On the other hand, it is also critical to ensure that the result of the assessment is reliable to provide effective feedback. To balance the accuracy and efficiency of the assessment, we propose three algorithms for fast and adaptive weakness identification based on the good arm identification (GAI) problem in multi-armed bandit-based machine learning. We evaluate the sensitivity and performance of the proposed algorithms through simulation.

**Keywords:** Adaptive Learning · Formative Assessment · Multi-armed Bandits · Simulated Learners · Knowledge Tracing · Knowledge Components

## 1 Introduction

Formative assessments are essential in the educational process, as they provide timely opportunities for students to close the gap between their current performance and the expected criteria. By identifying and addressing areas of weakness early on, students can prevent minor issues from becoming major obstacles to their success. However, most existing research for conducting formative assessment is for classroom-based educational environments, in which the most efficient way of gathering evidence about student weaknesses and taking actions for improvement is face-to-face interaction between teachers and students [1]. In online education, especially asynchronous online learning (AOL) or Self-directed learning (SDL), such face-to-face discussions are infeasible. In AOL, feedback on curriculum-embedded assignments, quizzes, and projects may not


A. Sifaleras and F. Lin (Eds.): ITS 2024, LNCS 14798, pp. 40–54, 2024.
https://doi.org/10.1007/978-3-031-63028-6_4

be as immediate as in traditional classroom settings. The delay in receiving feedback can hinder the learning process, as students may move on to new topics without fully understanding or correcting mistakes from previous lessons. Also, providing personalized feedback to each student can be challenging for instructors, especially in courses with many participants. In SDL, self-assessment is common, and external feedback is limited unless the learner seeks it out from peers, mentors, or through other means. In adaptive learning systems (ALS), it is pivotal to generate immediate feedback and formative assessments that are integrated into the learning path, using these inputs to adjust the learning experience in real time.

Thus, automated formative assessment and feedback mechanisms are desirable for online learning. However, to be helpful, they should address specific student needs or misunderstandings as effectively as personalized, instructor-led feedback. Gareis (2007) specifies two criteria to ensure formative assessment is beneficial for the student [2]. First, it must convey the student's progress in learning the material. Second, it must specify steps to continue learning. Therefore, by identifying a student's learning weaknesses and strengths, formative assessments can help identify the next steps the student should take in their learning path. Furthermore, to be maximally beneficial, formative assessments should be made available anytime and on-demand during a course. To make this possible, formative assessments can be administered using intelligent tutoring systems.

Intelligent tutoring systems can generate automated feedback that reduces discrepancies between current and desired performance. To generate effective feedback, it is crucial to focus on how well the task is being performed [3]. Given a set of knowledge components (KCs) (or learning objectives or skills), formative assessment is performed by asking a set of questions to the learners and analyzing the responses of the learner. Depending on the pedagogical strategy the teacher prefers, a formative assessment can terminate once one or several "weak" or "un-mastered" KCs or the weakest KCs are detected, and the remediation feedback can be generated by further investigating about the foremost weak KCs using the chain of weakness [4].

In formative assessment, minimizing the time spent or the number of questions on each formative assessment is crucial for maintaining engagement [5], reducing cognitive load, providing timely and frequent feedback, encouraging reflection, supporting personalized learning, enhancing motivation, and ensuring efficient use of time. These elements collectively contribute to a more effective and engaging learning experience. On the other hand, it is also critical to ensure that formative assessment is reliable to generate feedback. Therefore, there is a need for balancing the accuracy and efficiency of the assessment. To meet this need, in this paper, we model a formative assessment process as a *good arm identification* (GAI) problem in machine learning [6] and propose three fast and adaptive weakness identification algorithms. The sensitivity and performance of the proposed algorithms is verified by simulation.

The rest of the paper is organized as follows. Related work is reviewed in Sect. 2. Section 3 formulates the weakness identification problem and the proposed algorithms to solve the problem. Next, our simulation setup, experimental results and discussions are presented in Sect. 4. Finally, we conclude the paper and point out future research directions in Sect. 5.

## 2 Related Work

Our approach for adaptive feedback generation is involved with knowledge tracing in intelligent tutoring systems, and bandit algorithms in machine learning. Efficiently identifying the exact learning items that would prove most useful to a student's study can be classified as a Knowledge Tracing (KT) problem. KT research has been studied in similar intelligent tutoring systems under a broad range of methods to effectively track the learning progress of a student [7]. These models rely on dynamically updating student knowledge states based on their responses to provide personalized feedback and adaptivity, which may not be as relevant in scenarios in formative assessment where student mastery does not evolve.

Several innovative approaches to adaptive testing have been developed to quickly identify students' weaknesses. Kingsbury and Houser (2008) introduced ICAT: An Adaptive Testing Procedure, which is designed to efficiently identify students' areas of strength and weakness compared to traditional adaptive testing methods [8]. Yigit, Sorrel, and de la Torre (2018) discuss using the Jensen–Shannon divergence index in CD-CAT to improve attribute classification accuracy with very short test lengths, allowing for quick identification of students' weaknesses [9]. These approaches represent a significant advancement in adaptive testing, offering more personalized, efficient, and accurate methods for identifying and addressing students' weaknesses. However, their algorithms can be enhanced to better handle uncertainty in student responses. In this research, we use techniques from machine learning to deal with ambiguities in student data and make more nuanced inferences about their knowledge states.

Multi-armed bandits are a reinforcement learning mechanism that traditionally aims to maximize the attained reward from a set of items with varying, unknown reward distributions [10]. The rewards of these items, referred to as arms, can be probability distributions. The arms, in our context, refer to the KCs in a domain and the rewards of the arms mean the proficiencies or knowledge states of a learner. One heuristic for choosing arms that addresses the exploration-exploitation dilemma in the multi-armed bandit problem is Thompson Sampling [10], which may use beta distributions to characterize the state of each arm. The beta distribution is handy for representing knowledge about probabilities [11]. Our model adopts Beta distributions to maintain empirical observations.

Kano et al. consider a novel stochastic multi-armed bandit problem called *good arm identification* (GAI) [6], where a good arm is defined as an arm with expected reward greater than or equal to a given threshold. They proposed an algorithm to solve the *exploration-exploitation dilemma of confidence* that GAI faces. In the context of weakness identification through adaptive assessment, the standard bandit model of exploration-exploitation does not accurately apply as we are only concerned with the identification of a weak arm rather than best arm identification as best arm identification is much more time-consuming [4, 6]. Therefore, in this paper we model our problem as *good-arm identification* modified to identify *weak* arms. This approach is purely explorative in nature and aims to quickly identify any such arm(s) less than a specified threshold.

Another multi-armed bandit framework relevant to our case is *multi-armed bandits with correlated arms* proposed by Gupta et al. [12]. We use it to model dependency among knowledge components or learning objectives. As such, our algorithm borrows ideas developed for correlated arms such as the concept of *pseudo-rewards*: sampling arm $k$ may generate reward $r_1$ for itself, but similar, correlated rewards $r_2$ may be associated with correlated arm $l$ [12].

# 3 Problem Formulation

The goal of formative assessment is to identify and close the gap between the status of student learning and the desired learning objective. Placing appropriate demands on learners with the ZPD assists them to close the gap. As one gap closes, new learning goals are identified or another gap is identified, renewing the formative assessment feedback loop [1]. Figure 1 shows the process of iteratively generating feedback about remediation action, in which a singular weak skill each formative assessment is identified.

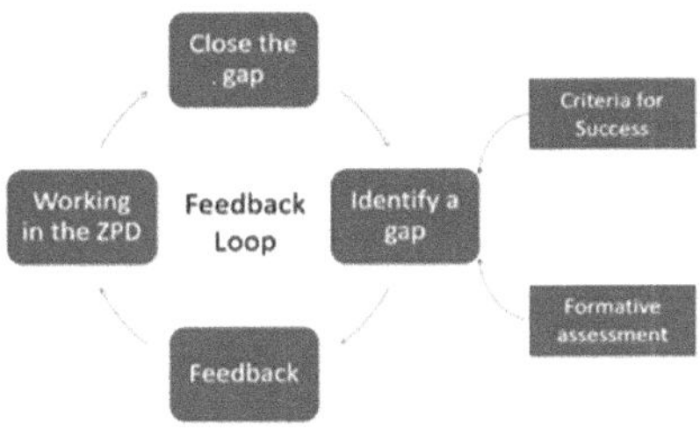


**Fig. 1.** The process of iteratively generating feedback about remediation action, in which a singular weak skill each formative assessment is identified.

## 3.1 Domain Model

The goal of our research is to allow educators and students to efficiently identify their critical weaknesses in a particular subject. The set of all topics that the subject consists of and their relationships to each other can be described by a domain model. The domain model consists of a set of knowledge components or learning objectives, hereafter referred to as KCs, modelled as a graph-like structure where the nodes represent the KC, and the edges represent the dependencies between them. We can use the dependencies of the KCs to our advantage; i.e., if a KC is dependent on another, we can extract information from both simply by sampling either one. Using this KC structure, we can approach the problem of identifying weak KCs as a multi-armed bandit "good arm identification" problem.

### 3.2 Student Model

To provide appropriate question sequencing, a student model of the learners' abilities is needed. For a student $s$ learning within a domain consisting of $K$ knowledge components: each knowledge component $i \in \{1, 2, \ldots, K\}$ is associated with their mastery in $i$. This mastery level represents the skill level of student $s$ in KC $i$. In our Beta-Bernoulli MAB, a student's abilities, and history in KC $i$ are modelled as a beta distribution with shape parameters $(\alpha_i, \beta_i)$ and values $(\mu_i, \sigma_i^2)$. The student's mastery of KC $i$ is represented by the mean, $\mu_i$, of this distribution. Therefore, the mean represents the probability that the student will respond correctly to a question from KC $i$. The shape parameters represent the number of questions the student has answered correctly, $\alpha_i$, and incorrectly, $\beta_i$, for KC $i$.

### 3.3 Transition Model

The transition model in an adaptive learning system maps an individual learner and their current knowledge state to their next logical knowledge state. In adaptive formative assessment, an instructor can specify the following parameters: mastery threshold and confidence level, or error rate. To define what makes an arm weak, we instate a mastery threshold $\xi$ as a hyperparameter. More generally, the instructor can specify a mastery threshold denoted as $\xi_i$ for each KC or arm $i$. If our empirical mean reward $\mu_i$ for arm $i$ is below $\xi_i$, that is, $\mu_i < \xi_i$, we can define it as weak.

### 3.4 Bandit Model

The standard MAB model cannot be directly used to model the weakness identification problem in formative assessment since we are simply interested in the identification of a weak arm, not the exploitation of rewards. Also, even though identifying the weakest skill or KC would be ideal, identifying the best arm requires drawing many arms. In our problem, the arms of the MAB are represented by KCs. A bad arm is also called a weak arm or a weak KC. The system sequentially chooses KCs, selects questions from those KCs, and observes independent noisy responses to the questions by the student. If the student answers a question correctly, the corresponding arm, or KC, gets a reward. This means updating the student model's beta distribution parameters for that KC based on the correctness of the answer. The goal for the MAB is to select questions so that a weak KC for the student can be identified confidently with as few questions as possible.

**Sampling Policies.** We call the procedure of choosing the next arm to pull the sampling policy of the MAB. The sampling policy is responsible for determining the next arm to pull to minimize the number of questions to ask a student. To do this we want the sampling policy to find the current estimated weak KC so that we can find an actual weak KC quicker. This is central to the bad, or weak, arm identification problem. In this paper we explore three alternative sampling policies: High Degree of Confidence (HDoC), Thompson, and Random. The HDoC policy is modified from the HDoC algorithm introduced by Kano et al. [6]. The following function determines the score,

$\tilde{\mu}_i(t)$, of KC $i$ for round $t$:

$$\tilde{\mu}_i(t) = \hat{\mu}_i(t) + \sqrt{\frac{\log t}{2N_i(t)}} \tag{1}$$

Where $N_i(t)$ is the number of times KC $i$ has been sampled as of round $t$ and $\hat{\mu}_i(t)$ is the empirical mean of the KC at round $t$. The arm with the lowest score is sampled so that if it is weak, it can be identified quickly.

The Thompson sampling policy we implement follows the traditional Thompson sampling algorithm for MABs [10]. During each sampling round, the beta distributions of each arm are sampled and the arm with the lowest sampled value is pulled. This arm is likely to have the highest probability of being weak, i.e. the lowest mean value. The random sampling policy naïvely selects a random arm and pulls it. It gives no preference based on the beta distributions of the arms.

**Updating Empirical Means.** After a question from a KC is presented to the student and after the student provides a response, the student model is updated based on the reward provided. This means updating the student model's beta distribution for the KC. Following our usage of beta distributions, the most practical way to update the empirical mean of each distribution to their respective posterior distribution is to update the $\alpha$ and $\beta$ values. A correct answer yields updated parameters $(\alpha + 1, \beta)$, whereas an incorrect answer yield $(\alpha, \beta + 1)$ [11].

**Stopping Criterion.** For the MAB to terminate the question asking process, one of the stopping criteria must be met. All three algorithms will stop when there are no arms available to pull or when a weak arm is found. Arms are removed when they are determined to be strong. However, each algorithm implements a different procedure for determining whether an arm is weak or strong after a reward has been received. For the HDoC sampling policy we use the idea of score, like that used in the sampling policy and described by Kano et al. [6]. For any arm with distribution $Beta(\alpha, \beta)$ we have the following confidence bound scores $\overline{\mu}_i(t)$ and $\underline{\mu}_i(t)$:

$$\overline{\mu}_i(t) = \hat{\mu}_i(t) + \sqrt{\frac{\log(\frac{4KN_i^2(t)}{\delta})}{2N_i^2(t)}} \tag{2}$$

$$\underline{\mu}_i(t) = \hat{\mu}_i(t) - \sqrt{\frac{\log(\frac{4KN_i^2(t)}{\delta})}{2N_i^2(t)}} \tag{3}$$

Where $\hat{\mu}_i(t)$ is the empirical mean of the beta distribution for arm $i$ at round $t$, $N_i(t)$ is the number of times arm $i$ is sampled at round $t$, and δ is our accepted error rate, adjusted as a hyperparameter. This scoring function will be used to determine if we have collected sufficient samples from a particular arm $i$ to justify outputting $i$ as weak.

For the Thompson algorithm, we employ the standard cumulative distribution function (CDF) and error rate δ to determine whether the mean of an arm $i$ is greater than ξ within a degree of confidence. For the random algorithm we naively classify an arm as weak if the mean of its beta distribution is less than ξ. Otherwise, we classify it as strong. The random algorithm does not have a well-defined measure of confidence about whether an arm is weak or strong. This makes it a good candidate to compare to for algorithms that do.

**Pseudo-Rewards.** To take advantage of the KC mapping and dependencies we implement the idea of pseudo-rewards. Correlated bandit problems have already implemented variations of this concept [12]. In these problems, arms that are highly correlated or dependent on one another allow information from both arms to be attained by sampling merely one. For example, given dependent KC $i_1$ and $i_2$, a correct answer of arm $i_1$ allows us to update $(\alpha_{i_1} \leftarrow \alpha_{i_1} + 1, \beta_{i_1} \leftarrow \beta_{i_1})$ and $(\alpha_{i_2} \leftarrow \alpha_{i_2} + \frac{1}{c}, \beta_{i_2} \leftarrow \beta_{i_2})$, where $c$ is the pseudo-reward factor. In our experiments, we set $c = 2$ to emulate a soft dependency between these arms.

### 3.5 Weak KC Identification Algorithms

The algorithms for weak KC identification are described as follows. The graph $\boldsymbol{G} = (\boldsymbol{KC}, \boldsymbol{E})$ represents the domain model. Where $\boldsymbol{E}$ represents the dependency relations between two KCs in the domain. The set of available arms is represented by $\boldsymbol{A}$. The mastery threshold ξ, error rate δ, and pre-sample count $\pi$, are input parameters. The number of rounds the algorithm needs to find a weak KC is represented by $t$. The output of the algorithms is the first KC detected as weak, if any, and the number of rounds to find the weak KC $t$. The pseudocode for the algorithms is shown in Figs. 2, 3, and 4.

**Algorithm 1. Weak KC Identification with HDoC Sampling ($\boldsymbol{G}, \boldsymbol{A}, \xi, \delta, \pi$)**

Sample each KC in $\boldsymbol{A}$ $\pi$ times.
Initialize $t \leftarrow \pi$
**repeat**
Select KC $i^*$ satisfying $i^* = argmin_{i \in \boldsymbol{A}}(X_i(t)),\ X_i(t) = \hat{\mu}_i(t) + \sqrt{\frac{\log t}{2N_i(t)}}$
Set $t \leftarrow t + 1$
Select random question from KC $i^*$and get response from student
**if** response is correct, then update $\alpha_{i^*}(t) \leftarrow \alpha_{i^*}(t) + 1$
**else** update $\beta_{i^*}(t) \leftarrow \beta_{i^*}(t) + 1$
Update dependent KCs of $i^*$ from $\boldsymbol{G}$ with pseudo-rewards
**if** $\underline{\mu}_{i^*}(t) \geq \xi$ **then** delete $i^*$ from $\boldsymbol{A}$
**else if** $\bar{\mu}_{i^*}(t) < \xi$ **then** output $i^*$as weak KC; **break**;
**until** $\boldsymbol{A}$=∅

**Fig. 2.** Weak KC Identification Algorithm using HDoC sampling

**Algorithm 2. Weak KC Identification with Thompson Sampling ($G, A, \xi, \delta, \pi$)**

Sample each KC in $A$ $\pi$ times.
Initialize $t \leftarrow \pi$
**repeat**
Select KC $i^*$ satisfying $i^* = argmin_{i \in A}(X_i(t))$, $X_i(t) = Beta(\alpha_i, \beta_i)$
Set $t \leftarrow t + 1$
Select random question from KC $i^*$and get response from student
**if** response is correct, then update $\alpha_{i^*}(t) \leftarrow \alpha_{i^*}(t) + 1$
**else** update $\beta_{i^*}(t) \leftarrow \beta_{i^*}(t) + 1$
Update dependent KCs of $i^*$ from $G$ with pseudo-rewards
**if** $1 - CDF(\xi, \alpha_{i^*}, \beta_{i^*}) \geq 1 - \delta$ **then** delete $i^*$ from $A$
**else if** $1 - CDF(\xi, \alpha_{i^*}, \beta_{i^*}) < \delta$ **then** output $i^*$as weak KC; **break**;
**until** $A = \emptyset$

**Fig. 3.** Weak KC Identification Algorithm using Thompson sampling

**Algorithm 3. Weak KC Identification with Random Sampling ($G, A, \xi, \delta, \pi$)**

Sample each KC in $A$ $\pi$ times.
Initialize $t \leftarrow \pi$
**repeat**
Select random KC $i^*$ from $A$
Set $t \leftarrow t + 1$
Select random question from KC $i^*$and get response from student
**if** response is correct, then update $\alpha_{i^*}(t) \leftarrow \alpha_{i^*}(t) + 1$
**else** update $\beta_{i^*}(t) \leftarrow \beta_{i^*}(t) + 1$
Update dependent KCs of $i^*$ from $G$ with pseudo-rewards
**if** $mean(\alpha_{i^*}, \beta_{i^*}) \geq \xi$ **then** delete $i^*$ from $A$
**else if** $mean(\alpha_{i^*}, \beta_{i^*}) < \xi$ **then** output $i^*$as weak KC; **break**;
**until** $A = \emptyset$

**Fig. 4.** Weak KC Identification Algorithm using Random sampling

## 4 Simulations

We verify our proposed MAB methods through simulations using two methods. First, we run simulations based on data from experiments on real students using a traditional student model. Secondly, we generate random domain graphs and simulate students based on a simple student mastery model.

### 4.1 Simulations with Real-Student Dataset Using IRT

We use the DBE-KT22 dataset [13] to simulate a domain model and initialize the parameters of the student model. It is a knowledge-tracing dataset based off an undergraduate databases course. The dataset includes a KC-KC mapping which provides the graph structure of the domain and which we utilize to test the efficacy of our algorithms. In addition to this graph structure, the dataset includes over 1000 transaction records of various students who have taken an online practice assessment, containing information regarding the correctness of every student's answer to each question they encountered. To model our simulated learners, we assume every separate transaction instance is representative of an individual student and use their answers to model a sample student in this population. Another piece of information this dataset includes is the ground-truth difficulty of each question, which we use to calibrate the mastery levels of our simulated learners.

We firstly preprocessed the dataset and performed a statistical analysis upon our findings. Upon doing so we analyzed the relative difficulty of mastering each KC $i$ by simply computing the probability of any unique student answering a question involving $i$ correctly, and maintaining a probability distribution for $i$ for every student $S$. For questions involving multiple KC's $i_1, i_2, \ldots i_n$, answers contribute to each probability distribution equally. Questions are also further subdivided based off the dataset's ground-truth difficulty level. From this we extract, for each KC-difficulty pair, the mean probability of any student from our sample population answering correctly. These distributions are first sampled, then inserted into Eq. (4) to randomly initialize the α values for each of our simulated learner's—such a strategy ensures that our simulation accurately reflects a real-world scenario with realistic student's and mastery levels that are not arbitrarily determined. In addition, we also analyze the correlations between KC correctness, and have found that certain KC's have statistically significant correlations, which also adhere to the KC-KC domain mapping the dataset provides. These correlations were also used in our initialization of simulated learner masteries to represent how students who have mastered one KC may be more likely to master a similar or pre-requisite KC.

Simulations using the DBE-KT22 dataset operated under Item Response Theory (IRT) fundamentals. In IRT, certain models exist to map a student's latent ability in a particular KC to the probability that that student will answer it correctly, such as the 1-parameter logistic model (1PLM). Consider a student $s$ learning within a domain consisting of $K$ knowledge components: each KC $i \in \{1, 2, \ldots, K\}$ is associated with a latent ability $\theta_i$, also referred to as their mastery in $i$. We utilize an IRT model taken from the Stanford paper "Deep Knowledge Tracing" [14]:

$$P(correct|\alpha, \beta) = c + \frac{1 - c}{1 + e^{\beta - \alpha}} \tag{4}$$

Where $\alpha = \theta_i$ represents the student mastery, $\beta$ represents the difficulty to the question given, and $c$ is the probability of guessing a correct answer—in a four-option multiple choice question, this would be 0.25.

The above equation is used to model the behavior of our artificial learners—that is, the student AI used in our simulation. Each simulated learner possesses a particular mastery level $\alpha_i$ for every $i$, which paired with the above equation allows us to simulate the correctness of this student's response given any question. These values are ground-truths, initialized upon the creation of the learner, and our model must identify any such $\alpha_i$ that is underneath a given mastery threshold—that is, it is considered weak.

### 4.2 Simulations with Random Domain Graphs and Simulated Students

In addition to simulating learners using the DBE-KT22 dataset and IRT, we developed a second set of simulations to test the generalizability of our MAB model. In this second set of simulations, we generate random domain graphs for our artificial learners. These random graphs are generated as DAGs using the NetworkX Python library[1]. We confirm that each is acyclic and directed before using them in the simulation. The number of nodes, $n_N$, in a graph is set to the number of KCs that we would like in our simulated domain model. The number of edges, $n_E$, is randomly set to a number in the range [2, $n_N \times (n_N - 1)$]. Each student for each simulation is generated with a different random graph. Once the graph is built for a simulated student, the nodes, i.e. the KCs for the student model, must be initialized.

To model the simulated student's ground truth mastery levels, we use the following equation, from [4], to determine their proficiency $\mu_{KC}(s)$:

$$\mu_{KC}(s) = w1 \times apt(s) + w2 \times pre(KC) \tag{5}$$

Where $apt(s)$ is the aptitude of the student and $pre(KC)$ is the ratio of the number of $KC$'s prerequisites the student has mastered to the number of prerequisites $KC$ has. The values $w1$ and $w2$ are tunable parameters. The value for $apt(s)$ is set to a random value in the range [0.1, 1] for all simulations except those testing the differences in aptitudes. For those simulations three categories of aptitude are defined: weak, with values in the range [0.1, 0.3]; medium, with values in the range [0.4, 0.6]; and strong, with values in the range [0.7, 1].

The filling in of the student model for a graph is performed in a breadth-first fashion starting with the first layer nodes, i.e. those without any prerequisites. For these nodes $\mu_{KC}(s)$ is set to $apt(s)$, the aptitudes at this layer correspond directly to the student's mastery of the KC. For the second layers and above, the above equation is used to calculate $\mu_{KC}(s)$ taking into consideration the student's mastery of the KC's prerequisites. Because we need to determine both the $\alpha$ and $\beta$ parameters for each KC, for each node in every layer we generate a random integer value for $\alpha$ in the range [200, 500] and use it along with $\mu_{KC}(s)$ to calculate the $\beta$ parameter for the KC. In this way we can generate random domain DAGs and translate them into ground-truth student models for testing artificial learners.

When these artificial students provide answers to questions their beta distributions are sampled. This represents answering a question based on the student model we have defined for the artificial learners. If a random value between 0 and 1 is less than the sample, we consider the student to have answered the question correctly. Because we would like to simulate the answering of multiple-choice questions, we have adjusted the sample by adding a guess factor. The guess factor takes into consideration the number of

[1] https://networkx.org/.

choices in a multiple-choice question and represents the probability of a student correctly guessing the answer. The adjusted probability of getting a question correct is defined as:

$$P(correct|\alpha, \beta) = Beta(\alpha, \beta) + \frac{1 - Beta(\alpha, \beta)}{N} \tag{6}$$

Where $N$ is the number of choices in the multiple-choice question. Compare this to the IRT formulation in the previous section. This is a simpler function for the probability that the student will answer a question correctly. It aligns well to our definition of mastery threshold and our Beta-Bernoulli MAB model.

### 4.3 Experiments and Results

The evaluation of our MAB algorithms is based on the correctness of each algorithm's output weak arm in comparison to the artificial learner's ground-truth weak arms. That is, the algorithm is correct if the output arm $a \in A_W$ where $A_W$ is the set of all ground-truth weak arms as defined by $\xi$ and the artificial learner's KC proficiencies. If $A_W = \varnothing$ then the model is only correct if it has not output an arm. We are also concerned with the number of questions the MAB asks before the algorithm terminates, i.e., the efficiency of the algorithm. Four experiments were conducted for each simulation method using each MAB algorithm.

**Experiment 1: KC Count.** The number of KCs varies from 2 to 16. The other parameters, error rate, threshold, and aptitude, are kept constant at $\delta = 0.15$, $\xi = 0.7$, student aptitude = medium for DBE-KT22, and $apt(s)$ to a random value between 0.1 and 1 for random graphs, respectively. Results are shown in Figs. 5a and 5b.

**Experiment 2: Mastery Threshold.** The mastery threshold varies from 0.2 to 0.9 while keeping the other parameters, KC count, error rate, and aptitude, constant. These other parameters are set to KC count = 16, $\delta = 0.15$, student aptitude = medium for DBE-KT22, and $apt(s)$ to a random value between 0.1 and 1 for random graphs, respectively. These results are shown in Figs. 5c and 5d.

**Experiment 3: Aptitude.** We test three levels of aptitude: weak, medium, and strong. These aptitudes for the random graph experiment are described in Sect. 4.2. For experiments using the IRT model, weak students suffer a flat 0.5 mastery penalty to all KC's, medium students' mastery is not changed, and strong students benefit from a 0.5 increase. The other parameters are set to KC count = 16, $\delta = 0.15$, and $\xi = 0.7$. Results are shown in Figs. 5e and 5f.

**Experiment 4: Error Rate.** The error rate varies from 0.05 to 0.35 with a step size of 0.05. The other parameters are set to KC count = 16, $\xi = 0.7$, student aptitude = medium for DBE-KT22, and $apt(s)$ to a random value between 0.1 and 1 for random graphs. Results are shown in Figs. 5g and 5h.

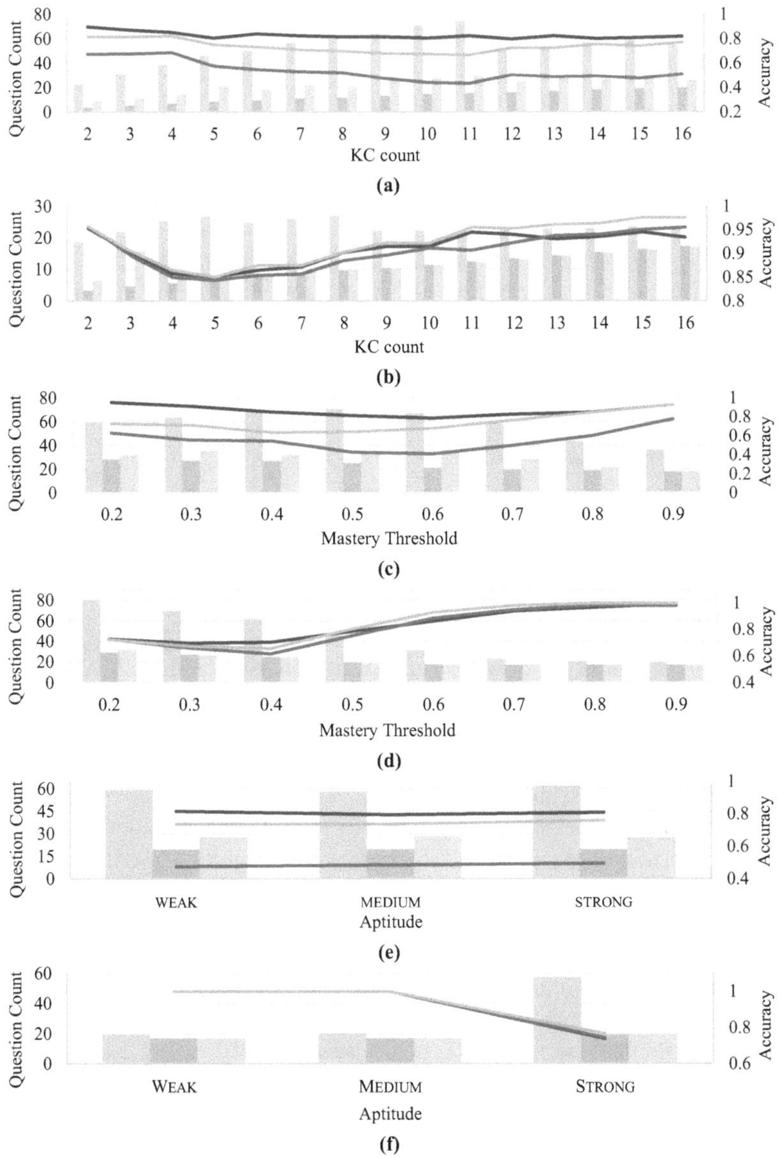


**Fig. 5.** (**a**) KC count experiments with DBE-KT22 dataset. (**b**) KC count experiments with random graphs. (**c**) Mastery threshold experiments with the DBE-KT22 dataset. (**d**) Mastery threshold experiments with random graphs. (**e**) Aptitude experiments with the DBE-KT22 dataset. (**f**) Aptitude experiments with random graphs. (**g**) Error rate experiments with the DBE-KT22 dataset. (**h**) Error rate experiments with random graphs.

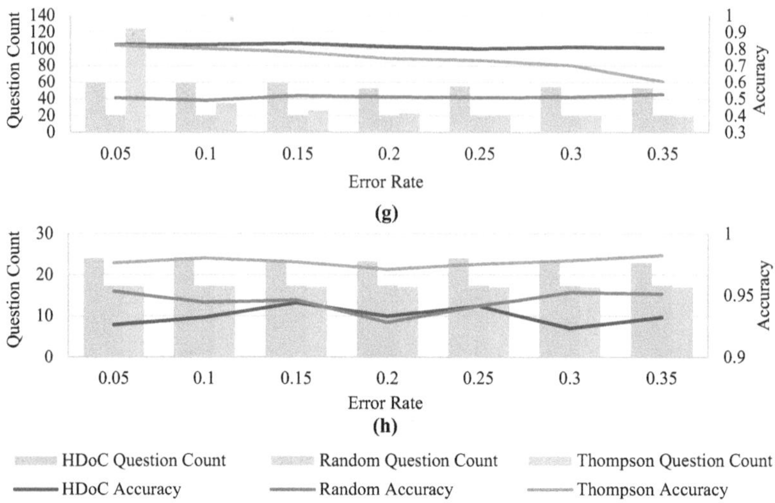


**Fig. 5.** (*continued*)

### 4.4 Discussion

Our simulations demonstrate the various tradeoffs between the three MAB algorithms we have developed. In simulations using the DBE-KT22 dataset, we see that Thompson algorithm uses far fewer questions than the HDoC algorithm, whereas HDoC is more accurate. While the random algorithm is the least accurate of the three algorithms in these simulations, it uses the least number of questions. The differences between the algorithm accuracies are less apparent in the second set of simulations using random graphs. In these experiments the Thompson and HDoC algorithms only slightly outperform the random algorithm in each of the experiments. In these experiments, a similar number of questions were asked to the DBE-KT22 experiments. With the HDoC algorithm again asking more questions on average than both Thompson and random algorithms. In general, the data from the two methods of simulation show similar trends. However, in the simulations using random graphs, we see much higher accuracies for each algorithm without as pronounced a difference between each that is seen the DBE-KT22 experiments. The trends that were seen in both simulations show how effective our algorithms are for efficiently finding weak KCs.

From Figs. 5c and 5d, we see how adjusting the mastery threshold $\xi$ changes the accuracy and required questions of the algorithms. Increasing the threshold results in much higher algorithmic accuracy and a lower number of questions required. From Figs. 5e and 5f, we see that our model operates well even with students of varying aptitudes. However, in the random graph simulations, Fig. 5f, we see a sharp drop in accuracy for strong students. This may be due to the differing definitions of mastery and must be examined further. From Figs. 5g and 5h, this experiment provides the most unexpected results. We would expect that with an increased error rate, the number of questions required for our algorithm to return would decrease significantly, but this is not the case. We see that generally, as we increase the allowed error rate for our algorithm a corresponding decrease in accuracy and sample complexity follows. Note that because here error rate is dependent on the variance of the beta distributions, it is undefined for the naive random selection algorithm. Overall, from the results of our simulations, we believe that the Thompson and HDoC algorithms are good candidates for use in an MAB system for formative assessment. However, there are some limitations and room for improvement. First, we do not consider "partial credit" answers (e.g., based on the usage of hints or on the response time). Also, we did not model the soft or probabilistic pre-requisites among learning objectives in the proficiency model. Second, the proposed algorithm can be easily extended to generate multiple weak skills. Third, by defining the opposite arm selection rule in the algorithm, we can generate the strong learning objectives as adaptive feedback to the student as encouragement.

## 5 Conclusion and Future Work

We have presented the results of simulations using three different algorithms that can be used in an MAB for identifying weakness or strengths of students from our results we are confident that the Thompson sampling algorithm and, to a lesser extent, the HDoC algorithm would be effective when used in an online adaptive formative assessment system. The main advantage of these algorithms is that they allow the instructor to specify the accuracy and efficiency criteria and that they effectively balance them with a bandit algorithm. From our experiments, we find that the overall performance of the proposed algorithms is quite consistent even after accounting for different variables. The complexity is relatively small and particularly serviceable in a practical setting where questions may be limited in nature and scope. In our future work, we will work to develop methods for automated feedback generation that adapt to varied feedback strategies or students' needs. We will also refine and develop further the random graph model for use in future simulation studies. The differences we discovered between the simulations using the random graph strategy and the simulations using the student dataset will be investigated. Furthermore, we will consider "partial credit" answers (e.g., based on the usage of hints or on the response time) and the soft or probabilistic pre-requisites among learning objectives in the proficiency model. Finally, we will evaluate the proposed approach to measure its actual effectiveness in real-world learning settings.

**Acknowledgments.** We acknowledge the support of the Natural Sciences and Engineering Research Council of Canada (NSERC), Alberta Innovates, and Athabasca University, Canada.

**Disclosure of Interests.** The authors have no competing interests to declare that are relevant to the content of this article.

## References

1. Heritage, M.: Formative Assessment: Making it Happen in the Classroom. Corwin, Thousand Oaks (2010)
2. Gareis, C.R.: Reclaiming an important teacher competency: the lost art of formative assessment. J. Pers. Eval. Educ. **20**, 17–20 (2007). https://doi.org/10.1007/s11092-007-9044-5

3. Hattie, J., Timperley, H.: The power of feedback. Rev. Educ. Res. **77**(1), 81–112 (2007). https://doi.org/10.3102/003465430298487
4. Lin, F., De Silva, S.: An approach to generating adaptive feedback for online formative assessment. In: Frasson, C., Mylonas, P., Troussas, C. (eds.) ITS 2023. LNCS, vol. 13891, pp. 88–99. Springer, Cham (2023). https://doi.org/10.1007/978-3-031-32883-1_8
5. Vie, J.J., Popineau, F., Bruillard, É., Bourda, Y.: A Review of recent advances in adaptive assessment. In: Peña-Ayala, A. (eds.) Learning Analytics: Fundaments, Applications, and Trends. Studies in Systems, Decision and Control, vol. 94, pp. 113–142. Springer, Cham (2017). https://doi.org/10.1007/978-3-319-52977-6_4
6. Kano, H., Honda, J., Sakamaki, K., Matsuura, K., Nakamura, A., Sugiyama, M.: Good arm identification via bandit feedback. Mach. Learn. **108**, 721–745 (2019). https://doi.org/10.1007/s10994-019-05784-4
7. Corbett, A.T., Anderson, J.R.: Knowledge tracing: Modeling the acquisition of procedural knowledge. User Model. User-Adap. Inter. **4**, 253–278 (1994). https://doi.org/10.1007/BF01099821
8. Kingsbury, G.G., Houser, R.L.: ICAT: An adaptive testing procedure for the identification of idiosyncratic knowledge patterns. Zeitschrift für Psychologie/J. Psychol. **216**(1), 40–48 (2008). https://doi.org/10.1027/0044-3409.216.1.40
9. Yigit, H.D., Sorrel, M.A., de la Torre, J.: Computerized adaptive testing for cognitively based multiple-choice data. Appl. Psychol. Meas. **43**(5), 388–401 (2019). https://doi.org/10.1177/0146621618798665
10. Lattimore, T., Szepesvári, C.: Bandit Algorithms. Cambridge University Press, Cambridge (2020)
11. Almond, R.G., Mislevy, R.J., Steinberg, L.S., Yan, D., Williamson, D.M.: Bayesian Networks in Educational Assessment. Springer, New York (2015). https://doi.org/10.1007/978-1-4939-2125-6
12. Gupta, S., Chaudhari, S., Joshi, G., Yagan, O.: Multi-armed bandits with correlated arms. IEEE Trans. Inf. Theory **67**(10), 6711–6732 (2021). https://doi.org/10.1109/TIT.2021.3081508
13. Abdelrahman, G., Abdelfattah, S., Wang, Q., Lin, Y.: DBE-KT22: a knowledge tracing dataset based on online student evaluation (2022). https://doi.org/10.21203/rs.3.rs-2192747/v1
14. Piech, C., et al.: Deep knowledge tracing. In: Advances in Neural Information Processing Systems (2015). https://doi.org/10.48550/arXiv.1506.05908

# QuizMaster: An Adaptive Formative Assessment System

Fuhua Lin[1], Raymond Morland[1](✉), and Hongxin Yan[2]

[1] Athabasca University, Athabasca, AB T9S 3A3, Canada
oscarl@athabascau.ca, rmorland1@learn.athabascau.ca
[2] School of Computing, University of Eastern Finland, Joensuu, Finland
hongya@student.uef.fi

**Abstract.** In this paper, we introduce QuizMaster, an innovative web-based adaptive learning system designed for conducting formative assessment on-demand anytime during students' course study. QuizMaster reduces learner time spent on assessment and accelerates formative feedback delivery. Leveraging a Multi-Armed Bandit algorithm for question sequencing and feedback, it ensures intelligent assessment processes. Additionally, we employ Large Language Models to auto-generate questions, enhancing instructor productivity. When deployed, QuizMaster will serve to assess adaptive algorithms for formative assessment in real-world learning scenarios. Through our detailed analysis of the QuizMaster architecture, we demonstrate how to leverage reinforcement learning and generative intelligence in the development of systems for formative assessment.

**Keywords:** Adaptive Learning Systems · Intelligent Tutoring Systems · Multi-armed Bandits · Reinforcement Learning · Personalized Learning · Formative Assessment · Generative Intelligence

## 1 Introduction

Formative assessment can be an integral part of the learning process in formal educational settings [1]. It differs from summative assessment in that it is meant to be an assessment *for* learning and not an assessment *of* learning through grading [2]. The goal of formative assessment is to provide individualized feedback to enhance learners' understanding of the subject materials and guide their studies. Therefore, formative assessment aids the student by helping them bridge the gap between their knowledge state and their learning goal, i.e., mastery of the learning objectives (LOs). While formative assessment can be fundamental to a student's learning process, current self-quizzes for formative assessment face two significant limitations. First, feedback provided in the self-quizzes may be generic and lack the depth needed for students to gain a nuanced understanding of their mistakes, hindering targeted improvement. Second, developing high-quality self-quizzes requires extensive resources, time, and expertise. Institutions with limited resources may face challenges creating effective, diverse, and engaging quiz content. Thus, we aim to provide a solution to both problems by employing course modelling, reinforcement learning techniques, and large language models in a web-based adaptive formative assessment system – QuizMaster, introduced in this paper.


A. Sifaleras and F. Lin (Eds.): ITS 2024, LNCS 14798, pp. 55–67, 2024.
https://doi.org/10.1007/978-3-031-63028-6_5

QuizMaster is a fully-fledged client-server application comprised of web-based interfaces, an application server, and a database. The goal of QuizMaster is to shorten the assessment-feedback cycle of formative assessment. It accomplishes this goal in three ways: a) reducing the time that learners spend on assessments, b) providing instantaneous automated feedback to the learner, and c) decreasing the time instructors spend developing content for assessments. In these ways, QuizMaster can increase efficiency for both students and instructors. To increase the learning efficiency for students, QuizMaster employs a Multi-armed Bandit algorithm to provide adaptive feedback and question sequencing. To increase the question creation efficiency for instructors, QuizMaster leverages large language models to create questions for assessments. These approaches together allow QuizMaster to provide a learning environment for students to undergo efficient formative assessment and receive individualized feedback.

The remainder of this paper is organized as follows. Related work and background information are reviewed in Sect. 2. The QuizMaster implementation is discussed in Sect. 3. In Sect. 4, evaluations of the various components and our proposed testing, both simulation and in-person, are discussed. Finally, in Sect. 5, we conclude the paper with a discussion about the system and future work.

## 2 Background and Related Work

Reviews of systems designed to provide automated feedback have been performed previously [3], including for specific domains such as programming instruction [4]. McLaughlin and Yan (2017) reviewed various delivery methods for formative assessment [5]. While the research into tools for formative assessment is extensive, most of these systems are limited in scope and are specialized in their domain. We seek to develop a generalized system that can be used for different knowledge domains. To this end, we need a simple and general algorithm to provide adaptive formative feedback.

Traditional adaptive learning systems (ALS) focus on forming a robust student model to estimate a learner's knowledge state. This estimated knowledge state, or mastery of knowledge components, is used for question sequencing. Traditional ALS algorithms include Bayesian and Logistic Knowledge Tracing [6], Item Response Theory [7], and Partial-Observable Markov decision processes [8]. While research into these algorithms is extensive, they do have limitations. These algorithms typically require a set of parameters that are difficult to tune [9, 10]. They may also require making assumptions about a learner's mastery of a subject beforehand. This may require pretesting or relying on self-assessment by the learner, potentially leading to inaccurate initial data being used to calibrate parameters. To address these limitations, we have chosen to utilize Multi-armed Bandit (MAB) algorithms.

MABs are a class of reinforcement learning algorithm that seeks to provide a solution to the exploitation-exploration problem. MABs are a recent addition to the field of adaptive learning. A recent survey by Mui et al. (2021) explores the various use cases of MABs in ALSs [11]. MAB algorithms have been shown to be simpler to implement while remaining as effective as traditional algorithms when used for formative assessment [9, 13]. Lattimore and Szepesvári (2020) provide a comprehensive introduction to the topic of MABs [12]. The goal of an original MAB is to maximize the total reward they receive while minimizing the regret of making choices. The decisions surrounding managing this trade-off and the choice of sampling policies they use differentiate MAB algorithms. By using an MAB algorithm, we show how the number of questions asked during assessment to detect mastery can be reduced, thus increasing student efficiency.

One of the most challenging and time-consuming aspects of formative assessment is the generation of appropriate questions. The questions asked in an assessment must be relevant to the LOs of the course. Therefore, subject matter experts with sufficient domain knowledge usually create the questions for the course. However, due to the substantial cost of time and resources that question generation requires, developing systems that automatically generate questions is an active area of research [14]. We aim to provide efficient ways for instructors to generate effective questions for use with QuizMaster by turning to large language models (LLMs) for assistance.

With the recent developments in LLMs, there has been a growing interest in their use for building and integrating with ALSs. One application of LLMs in ALS that may prove fruitful is in the generation of questions for assessments [15]. The use of generative AI systems such as OpenAI's ChatGPT may lead to an increase in instructor productivity by reducing the time they spend on manually crafting course content. One example of this increase in productivity is using these models to generate programming questions by integrating an LLM with a web-based user interface [16]. However, LLMs are not yet in a state of development where it is safe to use them without humans in the loop. Therefore, while an increase in efficiency may be realized by instructors when creating content, an expert's evaluation of the questions is still required before they are presented to students [14].

## 3 System Overview

One of the primary goals of QuizMaster is to contribute to the research and development of functioning formative assessment systems. Therefore, we provide the following thorough explanation of the system architecture and each of the various modules that QuizMaster is composed of.

### 3.1 System Architecture

QuizMaster is implemented using a client-server architecture (see Fig. 1). This architecture allows for flexibility in separating the concerns of the client applications and the server application. Two client applications accessing a single server application, one for students and another for instructors, have been designed and developed in the architecture. Both the student and instructor applications utilize the open-source ReactJS framework[1].

**Student Interface.** The student interface consists of an assessment component and a student profile. Through the assessment component, students can take quizzes and receive formative feedback. It provides the presentation for the quizzes while the server executes the logic of the adaptive algorithms. From the assessments home screen, the

[1] https://react.dev/.

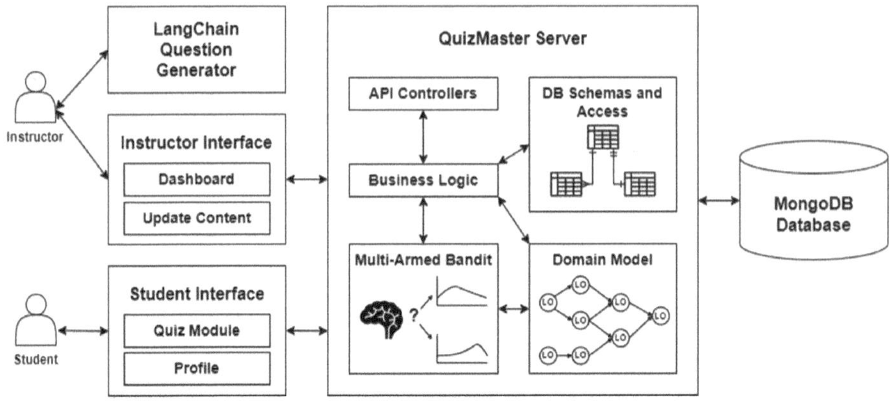


**Fig. 1.** The System Architecture of QuizMaster

student selects a course and a unit from that course to begin a quiz. The student can only choose from courses for which they are registered. After they have chosen the course, they will be able to select the unit they want to be tested in. Presently QuizMaster supports multiple-choice and interactive questions. The interactive data structures and algorithm questions are sourced from OpenDSA[2] (see Figs. 2 and 3). Future work will involve integrating other assessment types.

During a quiz the student is presented with a single question at a time. They select their answers and press the submit button. While a timer indicating the amount of time a user has been on a question is shown below the questions, a timer indicating the total time spent on the quiz appears in the upper right-hand corner. The number of questions that a student will be presented with is determined by the MAB algorithm. However, the number of questions will not be more than the budget of the quiz. The budget is displayed beneath the question beside the timer. After the student completes a quiz, they are shown the results view (see Fig. 7). This page provides summative feedback as well as the formative feedback including the weak LO and the recommended remedial learning materials. Along with the formative feedback, the students' chain of weak learning objectives is displayed as a graph. This serves to recommend the sequence of LOs that the student should study to improve their proficiency in their weak LO. How this chain of weak LOs is generated is discussed in Sect. 3.5. The student interface also has a profile page where students can view the results of their completed quiz sessions and update their profile information.

**Instructor Interface.** The instructor interface allows instructors to create and maintain course models. When an instructor signs in, they are presented with the courses assigned to them. Instructors can view and update the information associated with each course, including the individual units, learning objectives, quiz parameters, and questions. There are two types of multiple-choice questions present in QuizMaster: expert-generated and LLM-generated. The LLM-generated questions will be further discussed in the Content Library section. The expert-generated questions are developed by the instructor and then

[2] https://opendsa-server.cs.vt.edu/.

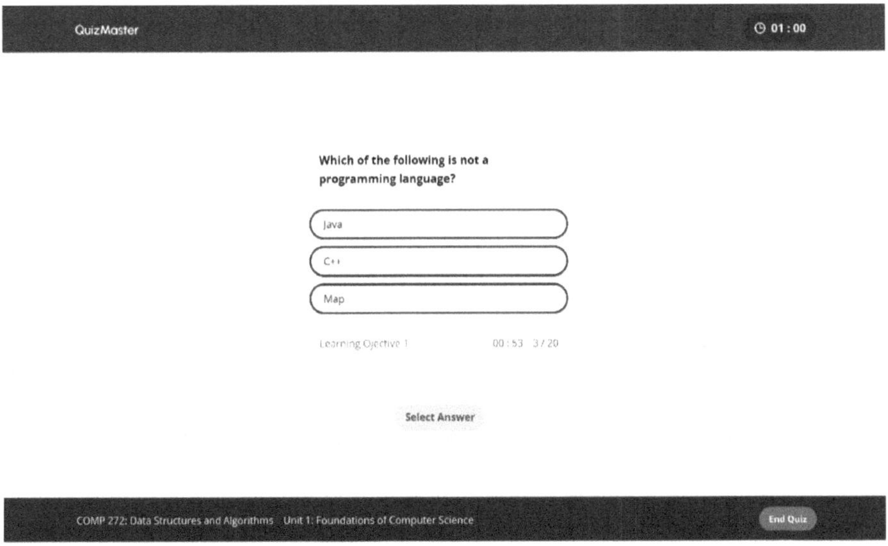


**Fig. 2.** Example of a multiple-choice question. The student selects what they think the best option is and submits it. Another question is presented if a stopping criterion is not met.

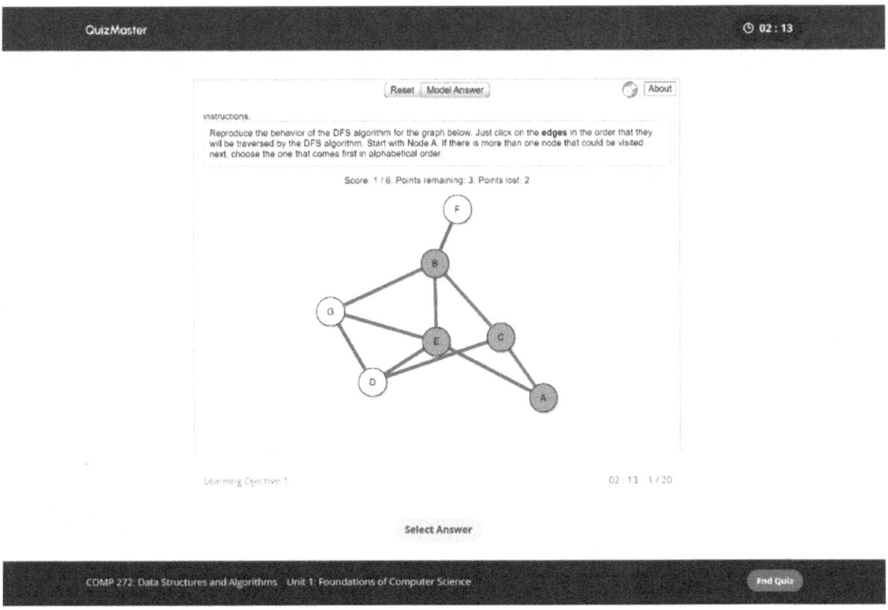


**Fig. 3.** Example of an interactive-type question. This figure shows that a student is performing an auto assessed graph question. We can observe that the student has scored one out of six points, there are three points remaining, and the student has lost two points. We use the open-source material provided by OpenDSA for these interactive questions.

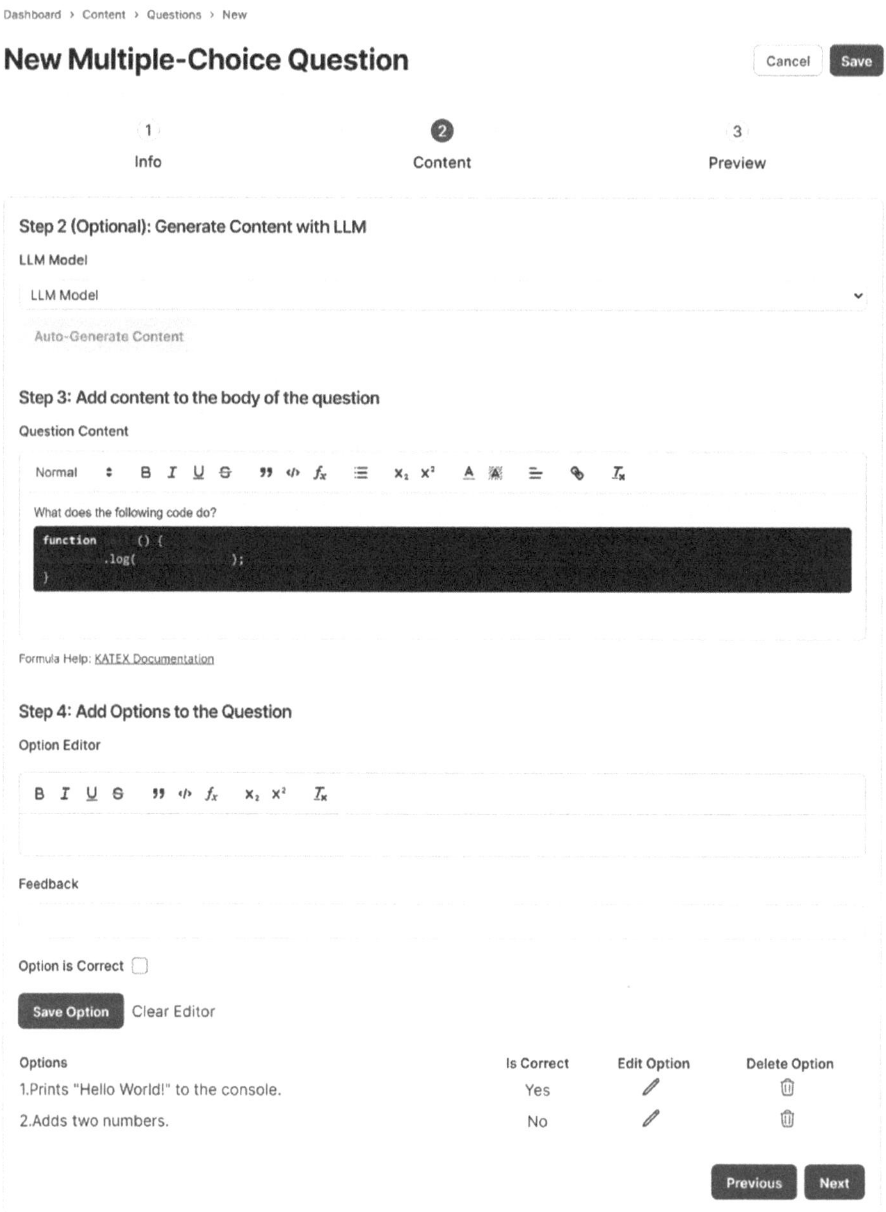


**Fig. 4.** The Instructor interface for creating multiple-choice questions. This screenshot shows the question content step in the question generation form. At this step the instructor adds the content to the body of the question as well as the options.

input into the system manually (see Fig. 4). The LLM-generated questions produced using separate scripts are entered manually into the form after the instructor validates them.

Rich text format is used for question creation, allowing different formatting and variability in content so that the questions can be more than only plain text. For instance, code can be displayed using code blocks with formatting that depends on the programming language. Images can also be included in the content of the question.

When entering questions, the instructor must select the appropriate learning objective to associate with them. This association will automatically include them as potential candidate questions when the MAB algorithm selects their LO during a quiz. This mechanism is another time-saving benefit QuizMaster offers, along with having the LLM generate questions. Here, instructors only need to enter the questions without manually sequencing the questions for each assessment. This method can save instructors precious time that can be spent on more important teaching tasks.

**Server Application.** The server, implemented as a NodeJS[3] application, consists of modules for the API controller, business logic, MAB, domain model, and database access and schemas, as shown in Fig. 1. The modularity of the server architecture gives the application flexibility when components need to be added, updated, and removed. This flexibility will be especially important for QuizMaster to be developed into a robust and versatile ALS platform.

**Database.** All the application data entities and content are stored as documents in a MongoDB[4] database. The NoSQL document-based MongoDB gives us the flexibility and ease of use we need for QuizMaster.

### 3.2 Content Library

The QuizMaster content library consists of the questions available for quizzes. QuizMaster currently focuses on multiple-choice and interactive-type questions. These questions can be auto-graded in formative assessment for immediate feedback because they have definite answers. The interactive questions, obtained from the open-source materials provided by OpenDSA, integrate directly into the student application. We chose to integrate OpenDSA questions because initial testing will focus on the content from a course in data structures and algorithms. Including interactive exercises will allow us to evaluate the effectiveness of having incorporated different question types.

To improve instructor efficiency, LLM-generated multiple-choice questions are included in the content library after experts verify their validity. The LLM-generated questions QuizMaster uses are generated with LangChain[5] using OpenAI's GPT3.5 and GPT4 models as described by Jhajj et al. in [15]. Instructors must manually verify each question before they submit them to the database. They can edit them to their liking from within the instructor interface. An example of a question generated using the LangChain question generator module is shown in Fig. 5.

[3] https://nodejs.org/.
[4] https://www.mongodb.com/.
[5] https://www.langchain.com/.

Sure! Here are ten multiple choice questions on the concept of data structures, each with four options and an explanation for the correct answer.

Question 1: Which of the following is a type of data structure?
A) Java
B) Binary Tree
C) HTML
D) JavaScript

Correct Answer: B) Binary Tree
Explanation: A binary tree is a data structure in which each node has at most two children, which are referred to as the left child and the right child.
...

**Fig. 5.** An example response from the LangChain question generator when prompted to return ten multiple choice questions on the concept of data structures.

### 3.3 Course Model

One essential component of QuizMaster is the course model. The course model specifies the relationships among the set of knowledge components in a course. Students must progress through the course model by exposure to each of the knowledge components in an appropriate way for learning. In QuizMaster, the course model represents the prerequisite relationships among LOs of a section and/or unit in a course. These relationships are represented as an AND/OR graph described in [17]. The graph structure of the course model is considered when updates are made to the student model for LOs and when the system searches for weak LOs. Figure 6 illustrates an example of course models, the course model for COMP272 Data Structure used in QuizMaster.

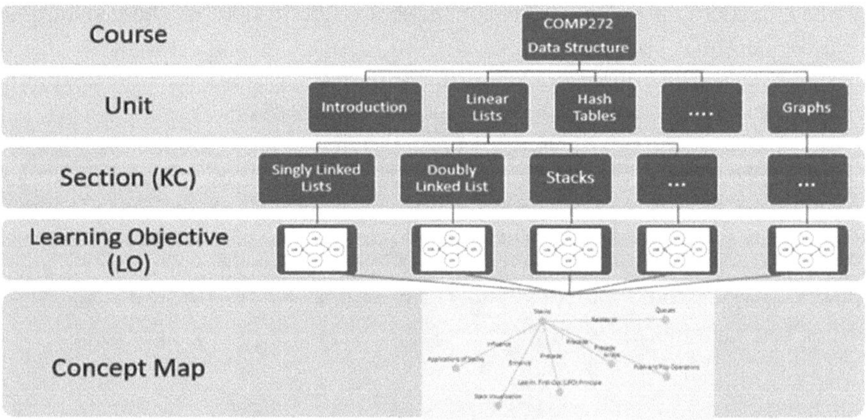


**Fig. 6.** An example of course models used in QuizMaster for a data structures and algorithms course.

### 3.4 Question Sequencing and Student Model

QuizMaster utilizes an MAB algorithm for question sequencing and mastery detection. The MAB technique that QuizMaster utilizes is the hybrid algorithm for the Dilemma of Confidence HDoC algorithm described by Kano et al. [18], which is modified to find the weak arms as described in [19]. The HDoC algorithm is a form of upper confidence bound (UCB) sampling policy that estimates whether an arm is strong within a degree of confidence above a threshold. In QuizMaster, the arms of the bandit correspond to the LOs, so pulling an arm means asking the student a question. A student's answers to a question are binary, either right or wrong. Thus, the student's proficiency for a given LO can be modelled as a Beta distribution with the alpha and beta parameters corresponding to the correct and incorrect answers, respectively. This model of student progress defines the student model of the system. It represents an estimate of the student's knowledge state during the quiz. The task of the MAB algorithm is to determine the next LO to draw a question from so that sufficient evidence can be collected to determine whether the LO is a strong or weak one for the student. The QuizMaster MAB seeks to find weak LOs for a student to invest more learning efforts in.

The QuizMaster question sequencing and mastery detection work as follows. Initially, the system has no information on the student's knowledge state for the LOs in a unit; therefore, a pre-sample is conducted. In the pre-sample, each LO is sampled an equal number of times, with questions drawn randomly from the LOs. The number of pre-sampling rounds is a parameter set by the instructor. Responses, in the form of answers, are sent to the server, and the parameters for the beta distributions of each sampled LO are updated accordingly. This update may have cascading effects, known as pseudo-rewards, as the LOs with which the sampled LO has prerequisite relationships may also be updated. Once the pre-sample is completed, the main loop of the MAB algorithm is entered. After the LO update is complete with the final pre-sample question being answered, the stopping criterion is checked. The quiz will stop when one of the following conditions is met:

- The budget is reached, i.e., the maximum number of questions allowed is asked.
- The algorithm determines that there are no weak LOs, i.e., all LOs are strong.
- The algorithm is confident that it has found one or more weak LO.

If no stopping criterion applies, the MAB samples another LO. The MAB determines which LO to draw a question from based on the HDoC sampling policy. The system presents the student with an available question from that LO, chosen at random. The system will continue to ask questions in this sample-update-check loop until one of the stopping criteria is met.

### 3.5 Formative Feedback Generation and Presentation

At the end of a quiz session when a stopping criterion is met, the results of the quiz and the formative feedback are presented to the student (see Fig. 7). To produce the formative feedback, the chain of weakness in the LO-graph is calculated. A graph search is conducted to calculate the foremost weak LO, as described by Lin and De Silva in [17]. This search finds the weak LOs that have the most significant learning potential.

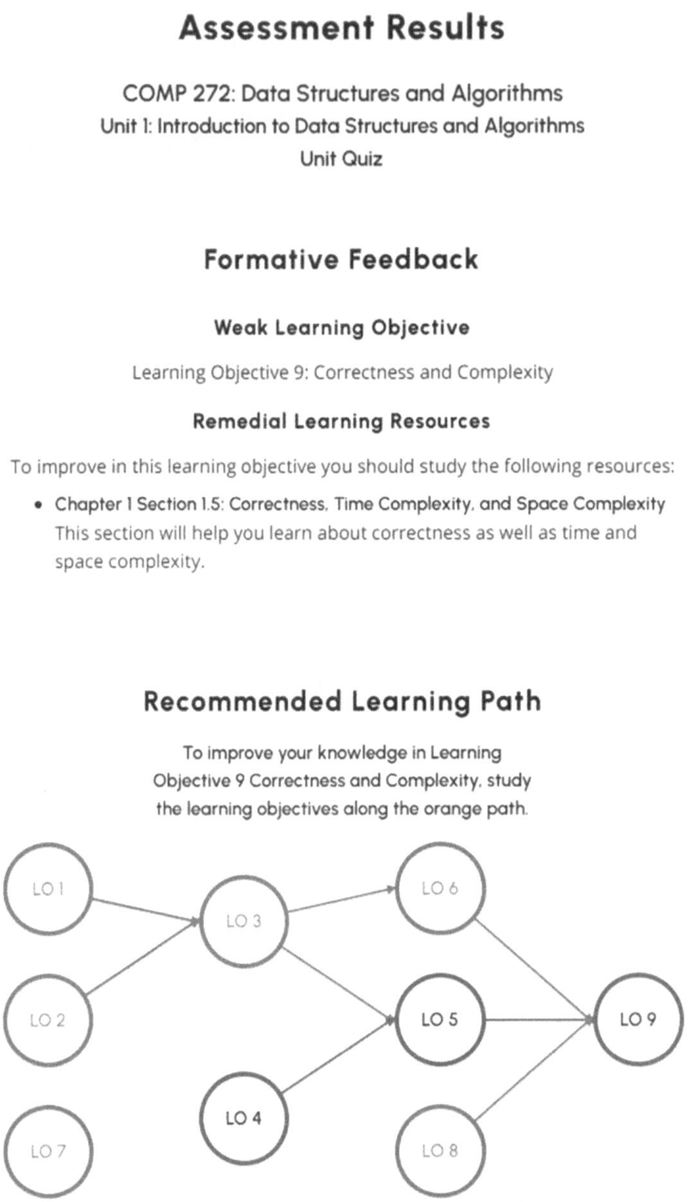


**Fig. 7.** Assessment results screen shown to the student after they have completed an assessment. The screen shows the formative feedback provided to the student and a recommended learning path. Students can access this screen from their profile by clicking on the corresponding completed quiz session.

That is, they are the LOs that may be the optimal ones for the student to spend time improving upon. This is an active line of research in our group, hoping to generate even more personalized feedback corresponding to individuals' weaknesses.

## 4 Evaluation of Methods and Future Testing

QuizMaster is the culmination of several research studies into algorithms and techniques for formative assessment in adaptive learning within the Intelligent Educational Systems research group at Athabasca University, Canada. Preliminary simulation tests have been conducted on the HDoC sampling policy used in QuizMaster's MAB algorithm [19]. Using AI students, these simulations have shown promising results for reducing the number of questions asked before a weak LO could be found. Evaluations of the LLM question generation technique have shown it is effective at creating domain-specific multiple-choice questions [15]. We will use the questions generated for this study in our student and simulation testing. Other work in our group has also shown how LLMs can be used in adaptive practicing systems [20]. The technique for finding the chain of weak LOs within the graph-based domain model is based on the results of simulation testing to generate adaptive feedback for formative assessment [17]. The simulations in this study showed that MABs combined with a graph-based domain model can be effective at finding weak LOs in formative assessment. Now that QuizMaster has integrated these techniques, they can be evaluated with real students.

Testing with real students will focus on assessing a set of LOs for an intermediate-level data structures and algorithms course. We will quiz students with a version of expert-generated questions and a version of LLM-generated questions to compare the effectiveness of different question-generating techniques. We will also compare the HDoC and other MAB sampling algorithms by evaluating the student's mastery and question sequencing effectiveness. Our testing will also include an opportunity for students and instructors to provide us with feedback about using the system so that we can further enhance the user experience and interaction.

## 5 Conclusions and Future Work

We introduced QuizMaster, a fully-fledged web-based formative assessment system. It can save students time on assessment, providing immediate feedback to learners on weak learning objectives, and increasing instructor efficiency in creating quiz questions. Through our discussion of the QuizMaster architecture, we demonstrate its effectiveness for providing formative assessment by integrating reinforcement learning and generative intelligence. This makes QuizMaster a valuable addition to the general formative feedback applications discussed in the literature. It is important to present fully engineered systems in academic literature to benefit others who need them.

As discussed above, the next step for developing the QuizMaster system will be testing with students in real-world learning scenarios. After this testing, we will continue to develop the QuizMaster system so that it can manage more general learning use-cases. Future enhancements to QuizMaster will include the auto-generation of questions in the instructor interface as well as more personalized feedback generation. The potential for

LLM and other generative technologies to enhance systems such as ours is significant, and we will continue to research ways to leverage these technologies.

Finally, the end goal of our testing and development is for QuizMaster to become a fully general formative assessment tool. We intend for QuizMaster to be capable of integrating with popular learning management systems using the learning tools interoperability (LTI) standard. This will allow QuizMaster to be used alongside a vast number of applications, helping both students and instructors reach their goals more efficiently.

**Acknowledgments.** We acknowledge the support of the Natural Sciences and Engineering Research Council of Canada (NSERC), Alberta Innovates, and Athabasca University, Canada. Additionally, we thank Michael Dupuis, Supun De Silva, and Diptanshu Mandal for their efforts in implementing the prototype of QuizMaster.

**Disclosure of Interests.** The authors have no competing interests to declare that are relevant to the content of this article.

## References

1. Black, P., Wiliam, D.: Assessment and classroom learning. Assess. Educ. Princ. Policy Pract. **5**(1), 7–74 (1998). https://doi.org/10.1080/0969595980050102
2. Bennett, R.E.: Formative assessment: a critical review. Assess. Educ. Princ. Policy Pract. **18**(1), 5–25 (2011). https://doi.org/10.1080/0969594X.2010.513678
3. Deeva, G., Bogdanova, D., Serral, E., et al.: A review of automated feedback systems for learners: classification framework, challenges and opportunities. Comput. Educ. **162**, 104094 (2021). https://doi.org/10.1016/j.compedu.2020.104094
4. Keuning, H., Jeuring, J., Heeren, B.: A systematic literature review of automated feedback generation for programming exercises. ACM Trans. Comput. Educ. **19**(1), 3:1–3:43 (2018). https://doi.org/10.1145/3231711
5. McLaughlin, T., Yan, Z.: Diverse delivery methods and strong psychological benefits: a review of online formative assessment. J. Comput. Assist. Learn. **33**, 562–574 (2017). https://doi.org/10.1111/jcal.12200
6. Pelánek, R.: Bayesian knowledge tracing, logistic models, and beyond: an overview of learner modeling techniques. User Model. User-Adap. Inter. **27**, 313–350 (2017). https://doi.org/10.1007/s11257-017-9193-2
7. Jia, J., Le, H.: The design and implementation of a computerized adaptive testing system for school mathematics based on item response theory. In: Lee, LK., Hou U, L., Wang, F.L., Cheung, S.K.S., Au, O., Li, K.C. (eds.) ICTE 2020. CCIS, vol. 1302, pp. 100–111. Springer, Singapore (2020). https://doi.org/10.1007/978-981-33-4594-2_9
8. Rafferty, A.N., Brunskill, E., Griffiths, T.L., Shafto, P.: Faster teaching by POMDP planning. In: Biswas, G., Bull, S., Kay, J., Mitrovic, A. (eds.) AIED 2011. LNCS, vol. 6738, pp. 280–287. Springer, Heidelberg (2011). https://doi.org/10.1007/978-3-642-21869-9_37
9. Melesko, J., Ramanauskaite, S.: Time saving students' formative assessment: algorithm to balance number of tasks and result reliability. Appl. Sci. **11**, 6048 (2021). https://doi.org/10.3390/app11136048
10. Clement, B., Roy, D., Oudeyer, P.-Y., Lopes, M.: Multi-armed bandits for intelligent tutoring systems. J. Educ. Data Min. **7**(2), 20–48 (2015). https://doi.org/10.5281/zenodo.3554667

11. Mui, J., Lin, F., Dewan, M.A.A.: Multi-armed bandit algorithms for adaptive learning: a survey. In: Roll, I., McNamara, D., Sosnovsky, S., Luckin, R., Dimitrova, V. (eds.) AIED 2021. LNCS, vol. 12749, pp. 273–278. Springer, Cham (2021). https://doi.org/10.1007/978-3-030-78270-2_49
12. Lattimore, T., Szepesvári, C.: Bandit Algorithms. Cambridge University Press, Cambridge (2020)
13. Melesko, J., Novickij, V.: Computer adaptive testing using upper-confidence bound algorithm for formative assessment. Appl. Sci. **9**, 4303 (2019). https://doi.org/10.3390/app9204303
14. Bachiri, Y. A., Mouncif, H.: Artificial intelligence system in aid of pedagogical engineering for knowledge assessment on MOOC platforms: Open EdX and Moodle. Int. J. Emerg. Technol. Learn. **18**(5), 144–160 (2023). https://doi.org/10.3991/ijet.v18i05.36589
15. Jhajj, G., Lin, F., Dewan, M.A.A., Yan, H.: LLM-powered question generation using domain models for formative assessment. Manuscript submitted for publication (2024)
16. Hassany, M., Brusilovsky, P., Ke, J., et al.: Authoring worked examples for Java programming with human-AI collaboration. arXiv preprint (2023). https://doi.org/10.48550/arXiv.2312.02105
17. Lin, F., De Silva, S.: An approach to generating adaptive feedback for online formative assessment. In: Frasson, C., Mylonas, P., Troussas, C. (eds.) ITS 2023. LNCS, vol. 13891, pp. 88–99. Springer, Cham (2023). https://doi.org/10.1007/978-3-031-32883-1_8
18. Kano, H., Honda, J., Sakamaki, K., et al. Good arm identification via bandit feedback. Mach. Learn. **108**, 721–745 (2019). https://doi.org/10.1007/s10994-019-05784-4
19. Morland, R., Wang, L., Lin, F.: Fast Weakness identification for adaptive feedback. In: Lin, O., Sifaleras, A. (eds.) ITS 2024, LNCS, vol. 14798, pp. 40–54 (2024)
20. Kabir, M.R., Lin, F.: An LLM-powered adaptive practicing system. In: Proceedings of the Workshop on Empowering Education with LLMs - the Next-Gen Interface and Content Generation 2023, co-located with 24th International Conference on Artificial Intelligence in Education (AIED 2023), Tokyo, Japan (2023)

# Preliminary Systematic Review of Open-Source Large Language Models in Education

Michael Pin-Chuan Lin[1(✉)], Daniel Chang[2], Sarah Hall[1], and Gaganpreet Jhajj[3]

[1] Mount Saint Vincent University, Halifax, NS, Canada
{michael.lin,sarah.hall1}@msvu.ca
[2] Simon Fraser University, Burnaby, BC, Canada
dth7@sfu.ca
[3] Athabasca University, Athabasca, AB, Canada
gjhajj1@learn.athabascau.ca

**Abstract.** This work-in-progress study aims to explore and analyze the growing impact of large language models (LLMs) in the fields of education and industry. We preliminarily review how LLMs can be integrated into educational contexts with their technical features, open-source nature, and applicability. Through a systematic search, we have identified a selection of open-source LLMs that have been released or significantly updated post-2021. This initial search indicates a thriving field with immense potential for both academic and industry applications. While LLMs hold promise for education, some challenges need to be addressed. These include limited application of open-source LLMs, concerns regarding data privacy, content accuracy, and potential biases. It is critical to carefully consider these factors before deploying LLMs in educational settings. However, our preliminary research highlights the versatility of LLMs in generating educational content and supporting diverse instructional strategies. This suggests a shift towards more adaptive and personalized learning environments. By assessing the suitability of these models for educational purposes, our study lays the foundation for future research aimed at fully maximizing the potential of open-source LLMs to transform teaching and learning practices. As our work progresses, we plan to expand our investigation to explore the broader implications of LLMs on educational outcomes and pedagogical contexts. Ultimately, our goal is to facilitate dynamic, inclusive, and effective learning experiences across various educational environments.

**Keywords:** Large Language Models · Open-Source · AI in Education · Educational Technology · Pedagogical Innovation

## 1 Introduction and Literature

The large language models (LLMs), such as GPT-3 and its variants, have greatly impacted education [7, 8]. Computational tools at such high levels can generate human-like text and engage in nuanced conversations, promising to enhance educational methodologies and outcomes [3, 14]. This capability allows for personalized feedback and supports


A. Sifaleras and F. Lin (Eds.): ITS 2024, LNCS 14798, pp. 68–77, 2024.
https://doi.org/10.1007/978-3-031-63028-6_6

various instructional strategies, such as virtual tutoring and interactive learning environments [4]. They have been demonstrated to provide quick and correct responses to student inquiries across different research studies [3, 11, 13]. Additionally, LLMs could assist instructors in course development, lesson planning, assessment, and educational evaluation, representing a paradigm shift in pedagogy and assessments to incorporate these tools [13]. These functionalities show the potential of LLMs in delivering personalized learning experiences, a shift in the paradigm of teaching and assessment methods. In this preliminary research, we are going to explore the expanding influence of LLMs on education, focusing on how they can be useful in creating and facilitating learning, with a particular interest in the challenges and benefits associated with their use, mainly regarding open-source models.

However, despite the advantages that come from the use of LLMs within educational contexts, there are some substantive barriers to such wide implementation. One major gap is the limited exploration and application of open-source LLMs, where proprietary models, such as OpenAI's ChatGPT, have been extensively used in various sectors, with little investigation of open-source alternatives offering similar benefits (Merrick et al., 2022). The nature of models such as OpenAI's ChatGPT is that they are black boxes, and there is little knowledge of their training methods or materials [16]. Open-source models promise a step towards providing explainability in AI systems [16]. The existing literature generally supports the use of open-source software in education, for being affordable, adaptable, and encouraging collaboration and innovation [1, 15, 20] but lacks a systematic understanding of how open-source LLMs have been used. Open-source LLMs give educators the opportunity to adapt and personalize these technologies according to their particular instructional requirements. With that, cutting-edge AI tools should be accessible to all and bring down barriers to equitable and inclusive learning environments [11, 18, 21]. Explainable AI systems are crucial in education as they ensure that AI tools are transparent and understandable to learners and educators [9]. This transparency builds trust between all stakeholders and AI systems by providing insight into their decision-making process [9].

This research will address the existing research gap by exploring the range of LLMs available, focusing on open-source models, and evaluating their suitability for educational purposes. By investigating the technical features, open-source nature, and potential educational applications of LLMs, we will deepen our understanding of how these technologies can be effectively integrated into educational settings to enhance and create dynamic, inclusive, and effective learning experiences.

## 2 Methods

### 2.1 Research Questions

The study is guided by two primary research questions:

1. What are the current available LLMs in the market, across both educational and industry sectors, and which of these are open-source? How have these available LLMs been used?

2. How do LLMs' technical features and open-source nature influence their suitability for educational applications in English-speaking contexts?

These questions aim to explore the landscape of LLMs, focusing on open-source models, and to identify the challenges and potential solutions for their adoption in education.

## 2.2 Search Strategy

Our study follows Snyder's recommendation for the review procedure, including the design, conduct, analysis, and structuring of the review [19]. These phases ensure that our study can offer new insights or propositions related to the use of open-source LLMs in education.

### 2.2.1 Eligibility Criteria

During the Conduct phase, as Synder (2019) mentioned, we searched these open-source LLMs by partially following the established PRISMA guidelines for the systematic review procedure [17]. Consequently, the eligibility criteria for selecting LLMs for this review were defined as follows:

- Open Source: Only LLMs that are openly available and free to use were considered.
- Language: The LLMs must primarily support English, given the focus on applicability in English-speaking educational contexts.
- Release Date: The LLMs included in the study must have been released or significantly updated after 2021. This criterion ensures that the review focuses on the most recent advancements in the field.
- Predecessor: If the LLM has its predecessor, the predecessor is excluded. For instance, LLaMA was excluded since Meta released LLaMA 2 in July of 2023.

Table 1 below has been populated with the full compendium of inclusion and exclusion criteria employed:

**Table 1.** LLM Inclusion and Exclusion Criteria

| Inclusion Criteria | Exclusion Criteria |
|---|---|
| Open-source | Not open-source |
| Language in English | LLM is not supported in English |
| Released after 2021 | Released before 2021 |
| Include the latest model | Predecessor is found, such as LLaMA |

### 2.2.2 Consulted Sources

The search for relevant literature and resources on open-source LLMs involved consulting several key databases and popular search platforms to ensure comprehensive subject area coverage. The search sources included Google Scholar, Google, GitHub, and Hugging Face. These sources were chosen for their wide reach and diverse collection of academic literature, technical documentation, open-source projects, and community discussions relevant to LLMs and their application in education and industry.

## 2.3 Screening and Selection

Our research carefully gathered a vast collection of LLMs, aiming to offer a comprehensive overview of the LLMs currently used in educational settings. To achieve this goal, we implemented a thoughtful selection process to identify the most relevant and innovative LLM applications. Through this method, we were able to extract valuable insights regarding the trends and patterns that are crucial in the field of educational technology.

### 2.3.1 Data Collection

The search for relevant information was guided by a set of established terms aimed at capturing the breadth and depth of LLMs and their applications between December 2023 to the end of January 2024. The terms included "Large Language Models", "Top Large Language Models", "Large Language Models in Education", "Top Large Language Models in Industry", "Open Source Large Language Models", and "Transformer Models". From these terms, two main search strings were formulated:

(("Large Language Models" OR "Large Language Model" OR "Top Large Language Models" OR "Top LLM" OR "LLM" OR "LLMs" OR "Transformer Models") AND ("Education" OR "Industry"))

(("Open Source Large Language Models" OR "Open Source Large Language Model" OR "Open Source LLM" OR "Open Source Transformer Models") AND ("Education" OR "Industry"))

These search strings were strategically designed to capture the most relevant and recent contributions to the field of Educational Technology and the use of AI in Education. We then organized the data into various columns in a spreadsheet, such as the name of LLM, owner, open-source (Yes/No), release date, user interface (Yes/No), used in education or research (Yes/No), Used case in industry (Yes/No/note), intended users, limitations, website, and notes.

### 2.3.2 Data Analysis

The collected data underwent a rigorous evaluation by the first and second authors, chosen for their expertise in Educational Technology and AI applications in education. This qualitative synthesis aimed to identify and categorize the LLMs based on the established criteria. Discrepancies between reviewers were resolved during several sessions of research meetings. Finalized results for these discrepancies were settled during the meetings. Our review methodological framework supports the objective of mapping the landscape of open-source LLMs and their readiness for educational adoption, highlighting technical barriers and proposing pathways to mitigate these challenges.

## 3 Results

Our investigation offers new insights into the evolving domain of open-source LLMs and their applications within educational and industry sectors. By analyzing the findings in a systematic manner, we shed light on the current state and future possibilities of LLMs in improving educational experiences and industrial processes. This section provides a comprehensive understanding of the capabilities and practical applications of LLMs, laying the foundation for the in-depth analysis that will follow.

### 3.1 Analysis of Current Open-Source LLMs in Educational and Industry Sectors

The exploration of open-source LLMs in today's market reveals a growing field of technology that holds potential for both educational and industry applications. To address research question 1, a systematic search initially identified a total of 41 LLMs. However, after applying our inclusion criteria, we narrowed it down to 13 open-source LLMs that were released or significantly updated post-2021, (see Table 2). This highlights a crucial moment in the accessibility and utilization of these advanced computational tools. Table 3 provides a chronological assessment of these models, starting from the most recent release and going back to the earliest.

Upon analysis, it was found that only one LLM, called Cohere Sandbox, explicitly recognized for its application in educational settings. Most of the LLMs, do not directly mention their potential for educational usage. However, Llemma is noted for its ability to solve math problems. This finding indicates that the field is still in its early stages of development, with the potential for educational use starting to emerge, but not yet extensively explored.

In various industry applications, LLMs demonstrate their utility in different ways. They can be used for tasks such as text generation, conversational AI, and specialized research support. For example, GPT-J and Bloom exhibit a wide range of capabilities, showcasing their versatility. MPT from the MosaicML Foundation Series and LLaMA2 by Meta have gained broad adoption due to their robust performance and scalability, which are essential for large-scale applications. Additionally, Cohere Sandbox's partnerships with major tech entities like Oracle and Google Cloud indicate direct applications for improving business operations through language models.

**Table 2.** Overview of Open-Source LLMs Released Post-2021: Accessibility, Application in Education, and User Interface Availability

| Metrics | Count | Details |
|---|---|---|
| Total Open-Source LLMs | 13 | All identified LLMs are open-source |
| LLMs with User Interface | 1 | Only 1 LLM offers user interface |
| LLMs Used in Education | 2 | 2 LLMs have mentioned uses in education or potential educational applications |
| Earliest Release Date | 2021-06-01 | Earliest release date of included LLMs |
| Latest Release Date | 2023-11-01 | Latest release date of included LLMs |

These technologies have a broad range of users, including the general public, researchers, and various industries. This highlights their widespread appeal and potential impact. This analysis not only examines the current state of open-source LLMs but also emphasizes their potential to make significant contributions to both educational outcomes and advancements in various industries.

**Table 3.** Comparative Overview of Open-Source LLMs

| LLM | Owner | Release Date | User Interface | Education Usage |
|---|---|---|---|---|
| GPT-J | Stella Biderman | 2021/06 | No | No |
| Bloom | BigScience | 2022/07 | No | No |
| GODEL | Microsoft | 2022/10 | No | No |
| Cohere Sandbox | Cohere | 2022/11 | Yes | Yes |
| Alpaca | Stanford University | 2023/03 | No | No |
| Guanaco | CausalLM | 2023/04 | No | No |
| OpenLLaMA | Openlm-research | 2023/04 | No | No |
| MPT | MosaicML Foundation Series | 2023/05 | No | No |
| Falcon | Technology Innovation Institute | 2023/06 | No | No |
| LLaMA2 | Meta | 2023/07 | No | No |
| Vicuna-13b | LMSYS | 2023/08 | No | No |
| Llemma | EleutherAI | 2023/10 | No | Yes |
| Orca 2 | Microsoft | 2023/11 | No | No |

## 3.2 Suitability and Open-Source LLMs for Educational Integration

To address research question 2, we further analyzed whether LLMs' technical features and open-source nature can influence their suitability for educational purposes. LLMs like GPT-J, Bloom, GODEL, Cohere Sandbox, and Alpaca are open-source, which means that they are readily available to developers and researchers. This accessibility allows for customization and integration of these models into educational platforms, enabling the creation of innovative teaching and learning tools that can be freely adapted to fulfill diverse educational requirements.

Our classification also reveals various industry applications for these LLMs, ranging from text generation to partnerships with major technology companies (such as Cohere Sandbox). These applications demonstrate the versatility and potential of LLMs in educational settings. For example, text generation can create dynamic educational content for both instructors and students, while conversational AI features can support interactive learning and personalized tutoring systems. Cohere Sandbox, in particular, explicitly mentions its educational use and provides a user-friendly interface, highlighting its direct applicability to educators and learners. Our preliminary finding may suggest that the technical strengths utilized in industry contexts hold great promise for enhancing educational experiences.

While the analyzed open-source LLMs possess extensive capabilities, it is essential to consider their limitations when assessing their suitability for educational purposes. The data provides insights into these models' limitations, such as technical constraints and the absence of user interfaces (excluding Cohere Sandbox). These limitations indicate areas that require further development in order to fully unlock the educational potential of LLMs.

The technical features and open-source nature of LLMs provide a strong foundation for their adoption and adaptation in educational contexts. The results indicate that while current applications may lean towards industry, the underlying capabilities of these models are highly relevant and adaptable for educational purposes.

## 4 Discussion and Implications

The preliminary review of the currently available and popular LLMs of this study provides insight into both education and industry. We discuss the implications of LLMs' technical features, specifically focusing on their emerging usefulness and applicability in educational contexts.

Our findings indicate that several open-source LLMs, such as GPT-J, Bloom, GODEL, and Cohere Sandbox, share foundational technological strengths, as they exhibit diversity in adaptability and educational integration. Table 4 offers recommendations for how these LLMs can be integrated to support pedagogy. This open-source feature not only democratizes the use of advanced AI technologies but also promotes innovation by allowing developers and technologists to apply these models in various educational settings [1, 15]. Additionally, the inherent flexibility of open-source models can greatly expedite the creation of personalized learning experiences, interactive content, and automated assessments, aligning with the shift toward adaptive, active, and student-centred learning environments [10, 11]. For example, GPT-J's text generation capabilities could be used to support creative writing modules, while Bloom's multilingual support makes it useful in linguistically diverse educational settings. Cohere Sandbox, on the other hand, stands out for its explicit educational orientation and user-friendly interface that facilitates practical application by educators and learners.

Moreover, the comparison highlights the distinct advantages of each LLM's approach to common educational requirements, such as personalized learning pathways and automated assessment tools. For instance, the flexibility of open-source models like GPT-J and Bloom allows for extensive customization, which aligns well with pedagogical models that emphasize adaptive learning and student engagement.

However, the value of LLMs in education goes beyond their technical capabilities [7, 8]. The societal and ethical implications of deploying such advanced AI tools in educational settings require careful consideration. Concerns regarding data privacy, the accuracy of LLM-generated content (e.g., misinformation and hallucinations), and the potential reinforcement of biases present significant challenges [2, 5, 8, 13]. While Cohere Sandbox may excel in providing transparency and ease of use, other models like GPT-J and Bloom may need additional support to ensure ethical application, given

**Table 4.** Applying LLMs into education

| LLM | Possible Educational Applications |
|---|---|
| GPT-J | Suitable for supporting writing and generative purposes |
| Bloom | Multilingual support and use in linguistically diverse settings |
| Cohere Sandbox | General educational data processing |
| Alpaca | Providing feedback to students; educational administration |
| Guanaco | Multilingual translation |
| MPT | Suitable for business education and training for social media |
| Falcon | General educational inquiries |
| Vicuna-13b | General educational inquiries but limited in its accuracy of factual knowledge and math capabilities |
| Llemma | Suitable for math education |
| Orca 2 | Suitable for creating step-by-step instructions or reasoning tasks |

their broader generative nature. Therefore, integrating LLMs into educational platforms necessitates a robust framework for ethical use, emphasizing transparency, accountability, and the inclusion of diverse perspectives in model training and application [6, 12, 13].

The findings of this study highlight some overlaps between the industrial applications of LLMs and their potential educational uses. The versatility demonstrated by LLMs in tasks such as text generation, conversational AI, and data analysis suggests numerous opportunities for educational applications [4, 13]. For instance, the ability of LLMs to generate diverse and complex textual content can reform the creation of educational materials and provide customized resources for diverse students [8]. Furthermore, the capabilities of conversational AI can facilitate the development of virtual tutors and interactive learning environments, offering personalized feedback and support to students [4, 13].

Cohere Sandbox serves as a model for directly applying LLMs to enhance teaching and learning, as it explicitly mentions its educational applications and offers a user-friendly interface. By providing a user interface, barriers for educators and students are significantly reduced, making it easier to explore and harness the capabilities of LLMs in educational settings. This highlights the importance of developing user-friendly platforms and tools that can leverage the power of LLMs to support educational objectives.

## 5 Conclusion and Future Directions

In this work-in-progress research, we continue the systematic and empirical evaluation of open-source LLM systems. We intend to find out their relevance and suitability for educational purposes. These first findings provide a simple understanding of the current state and the possible potential of LLMs in this field. Acknowledging the preliminary nature of our work, we are ready to broaden our view by tapping into more academic databases. This strategic expansion aims to better understand how open-source LLMs could be seamlessly woven into educational methodologies, examining adaptability, practical implementation, and overall efficacy in enriching teaching and learning environments [12, 13]. Some open-source LLMs suffer partially from the same black box criticisms as their proprietary counterparts [16]. However, future work into open-source LM development will inherently increase the explainability of such systems. Future studies must pay attention to the implications of LLMs on educational outcomes, that is, learning outcomes, student engagement, and the cultivation of analytical and critical thinking skills. Similarly, we need further research on customizing LLMs under various pedagogical contexts, such as language learning and STEM disciplines.

In conclusion, incorporating open-source LLMs into educational spheres does indicate a transformational turn in pedagogical methodologies. Taking it upon ourselves to hone down on these technological advancements, mitigating their inherent constraints, and making our collective alliance with educators, technologists, and policymakers, hopefully, will unleash the full spectrum of possibilities provided by LLMs. This collaborative effort would provide dynamic, inclusive, and productive learning experiences across varied environments [12–14].

**Acknowledgments.** This research was funded by ML's institutional conference funding from Mount Saint Vincent University.

**Disclosure of Interests.** The authors have no competing interests to declare that are relevant to the content of this article.

## References

1. Carmichael, P., Honour, L.: Open source as appropriate technology for global education. Int. J. Educ. Dev. **22**(1), 47–53 (2002). https://doi.org/10.1016/S0738-0593(00)00077-8
2. Chan, C.K.Y.: A comprehensive AI policy education framework for university teaching and learning. Int. J. Educ. Technol. High. Educ. **20**(1), 38 (2023). https://doi.org/10.1186/s41239-023-00408-3
3. Chang, D.H., Lin, M.P.-C., Hajian, S., Wang, Q.Q.: Educational design principles of using AI Chatbot that supports self-regulated learning in education: goal setting, feedback, and personalization. Sustainability **15**(17), 12921 (2023). https://doi.org/10.3390/su151712921
4. Fui-Hoon Nah, F., Zheng, R., Cai, J., Siau, K., Chen, L.: Generative AI and ChatGPT: applications, challenges, and AI-human collaboration. J. Inf. Technol. Case Appl. Res. **25**(3), 277–304 (2023). https://doi.org/10.1080/15228053.2023.2233814
5. Gill, S.S., et al.: Transformative effects of ChatGPT on modern education: emerging era of AI Chatbots. Internet Things Cyber Phys. Syst. **4**, 19–23 (2024). https://doi.org/10.1016/j.iotcps.2023.06.002
6. Grassini, S.: Shaping the future of education: exploring the potential and consequences of AI and ChatGPT in educational settings. Educ. Sci. **13**(7) (2023). https://doi.org/10.3390/educsci13070692
7. Jeon, J., Lee, S.: Large language models in education: a focus on the complementary relationship between human teachers and ChatGPT. Educ. Inf. Technol. **28**(12), 15873–15892 (2023). https://doi.org/10.1007/s10639-023-11834-1

8. Kasneci, E., et al.: ChatGPT for good? On opportunities and challenges of large language models for education. Learn. Individ. Differ. **103**, 102274 (2023). https://doi.org/10.1016/j.lindif.2023.102274
9. Khosravi, H., et al.: Explainable artificial intelligence in education. Comput. Educ. Artif. Intell. **3**, 100074 (2022). https://doi.org/10.1016/j.caeai.2022.100074
10. Lin, M.P.C.: A proposed methodology for investigating chatbot effects in peer review. (Unpublished doctoral dissertation). Faculty of Education, Simon Fraser University, Canada (2020)
11. Lin, M.P.C., Chang, D.: CHAT-ACTS: a pedagogical framework for personalized chatbot to enhance active learning and self-regulated learning. Comput. Educ. Artif. Intell. **5**, 100167 (2023). https://doi.org/10.1016/j.caeai.2023.100167
12. Memarian, B., Doleck, T.: Fairness, accountability, transparency, and ethics (FATE) in artificial intelligence (AI) and higher education: a systematic review. Comput. Educ. Artif. Intell. **5**, 100152 (2023). https://doi.org/10.1016/j.caeai.2023.100152
13. Meyer, J.G., et al.: ChatGPT and large language models in academia: opportunities and challenges. BioData Min. **16**(1), 20 (2023). https://doi.org/10.1186/s13040-023-00339-9
14. Milano, S., McGrane, J.A., Leonelli, S.: Large language models challenge the future of higher education. Nat. Mach. Intell. **5**(4), 333–334 (2023). https://doi.org/10.1038/s42256-023-00644-2
15. Müller, M., Schindler, C., Slany, W.: Engaging students in open source: establishing FOSS development at a university. In: Proceedings of the 52nd Hawaii International Conference on System Sciences, pp. 7721–7730 (2019)
16. Ollion, É., Shen, R., Macanovic, A., Chatelain, A.: The dangers of using proprietary LLMs for research. Nat. Mach. Intell. **6**(1), 4–5 (2024). https://doi.org/10.1038/s42256-023-00783-6
17. Rethlefsen, M.L., et al.: PRISMA-S: an extension to the PRISMA statement for reporting literature searches in systematic reviews. Syst. Rev. **10**, 1–19 (2021). https://doi.org/10.1186/s13643-020-01542-z
18. Salas-Pilco, S., Xiao, K., Oshima, J.: Artificial intelligence and new technologies in inclusive education for minority students: a systematic review. Sustainability **14**(20), 13572 (2022). https://doi.org/10.3390/su142013572
19. Snyder, H.: Literature review as a research methodology: an overview and guidelines. J. Bus. Res. **104**, 333–339 (2019). https://doi.org/10.1016/j.jbusres.2019.07.039
20. Williams Van Rooij, S.: Adopting open-source software applications in U.S. higher education: a cross-disciplinary review of the literature. Rev. Educ. Res. **79**(2), 682–701 (2009). https://doi.org/10.3102/0034654308325691
21. Yang, H., Kyun, S.: The current research trend of artificial intelligence in language learning: a systematic empirical literature review from an activity theory perspective. Australas. J. Educ. Technol. **38**(5), 180–210 (2022). https://doi.org/10.14742/ajet.7492

# Jill Watson: Scaling and Deploying an AI Conversational Agent in Online Classrooms

Sandeep Kakar(✉), Pratyusha Maiti, Karan Taneja, Alekhya Nandula, Gina Nguyen, Aiden Zhao, Vrinda Nandan, and Ashok Goel

Georgia Institute of Technology, Atlanta, GA, USA
{skakar6,pmaiti6,ktaneja6,anandula3,gnguyen37,yzhao750,vrinda, ag25}@gatech.edu

**Abstract.** We present a highly performant and scalable conversational virtual teaching assistant, Jill Watson, to enhance teaching presence in online classrooms. Jill Watson leverages the generative AI capabilities of ChatGPT and the underlying OpenAI's GPT large language models, along with dense passage retrieval and retrieval-augmented text generation to answer student questions about instructor-approved courseware anytime and anywhere. This courseware may include natural language text from textbooks, user guides, video lesson transcripts, course websites, and class syllabi. This version of Jill Watson has been deployed in several classes with close to 1300 students at the Georgia Institute of Technology as well as in two community colleges in the Technical College System of Georgia. We have found that Jill Watson enhances the positives of conversational courseware (such as answering questions and engaging in conversations anytime and anyplace) and suppresses the negatives of large language models (such as biases and hallucinations).

**Keywords:** Virtual Teaching Assistants · Intelligent Tutors · Conversational AI Agents · Conversational Courseware · Intelligent Textbooks

## 1 Introduction

The growing popularity of online programs in higher and continuing education [1] has lent much urgency to reducing the gap between the learning experience of online and in-person learners. Online classes may have hundreds, if not thousands, of students, and they typically deliver educational content asynchronously. While this dramatically expands the reach of education delivery, it also makes it challenging for instructors to adequately attend to the learning needs of their students. Many student questions in an online classroom may go unanswered or not be answered in a timely fashion. This gap between the online and in-person

This research has been supported by NSF Grants #2112532 and #2247790 to the National AI Institute for Adult Learning and Online Education. We thank members of the Design Intelligence Laboratory for their contributions to this work.


A. Sifaleras and F. Lin (Eds.): ITS 2024, LNCS 14798, pp. 78–90, 2024.
https://doi.org/10.1007/978-3-031-63028-6_7

modes of instruction can impede effective learning by online learners [2,3]; lead to low student engagement [4]; and adversely impact retention in the program [5]. Unfortunately, there are no cost-effective means of having enough human teachers who can answer all questions posed by online students anytime and from anywhere to alleviate this gap.

Artificial intelligence-based virtual teaching agents (VTAs) can help alleviate the lack of student-teacher interactions in online classrooms if they are easily scalable and cost-effective [6]. To this end, we have developed a new version of Jill Watson, a virtual teaching assistant (VTA) that leverages generative AI. With OpenAI's ChatGPT at its core, Jill Watson can answer student questions and engage in extended conversations anytime and anywhere. By itself, ChatGPT is a conversational agent based on the GPT family of large language models (LLMs). While ChatGPT has an uncanny ability to answer questions and converse with users with a human-like text, it suffers from two major drawbacks. First, LLMs underlying ChatGPT are trained on a massive corpus of text data on the internet, and they implicitly store their knowledge in model parameters. ChatGPT relies on this knowledge to answer user queries. As such, if used in a classroom, ChatGPT's answers may not reflect the instructor's expectations based on the class materials, thus failing to support the desired learning outcomes. Second, LLMs are statistical models that answer a simple probability question - given a training data set and a string of words, what is the most probable next word? As a result, LLMs, and hence, ChatGPT, are prone to hallucinations, i.e., they can generate factually incorrect answers devoid of reality (hallucinations) [7], or even undesirable speech [8]. This in part is where Jill Watson comes in. Though having ChatGPT at its core, Jill Watson mitigates hallucinations by using retrieval-augmented text generation (RAG) [9] with dense passage retrieval (DPR) [10] to constrain ChatGPT to answer student questions using only the class materials provided by the instructor. Further, Jill Watson also employs moderation to block irrelevant questions from being processed and to block answers containing harmful speech.

Our work makes several contributions. First, Jill Watson is highly scalable and optimal for learning at scale. It has been deployed across several classes with up to several hundred students at multiple institutions. It can answer questions based on natural language text from instructor-approved documents of any length, including textbooks, user guides, transcripts from video lessons, text from presentation slides, course websites, and class syllabi, schedules, and policies. In theory, given enough computing infrastructure, there is no limit to the number of classes, students, or institutions that can benefit from Jill Watson deployments.

Second, Jill Watson is conversational. It allows students to use a private chat window enabled as a Learning Tools Interoperability (LTI) [11] tool in class Learning Management Systems (LMSs) to ask follow-up questions and converse about course material within the confines of its knowledge base. This interactivity can motivate students to explore content-related questions; answer questions related to course-related activities; and prompt reflection on course content. Thus, Jill Watson may enhance student's cognitive engagement with the courseware.

Third, Jill Watson is appropriate for a classroom setting due to grounding in the approved instructional material, thereby increasing the trust of the VTA by both students and instructors. The provenance of its answers is not only checked for grounding, but they are also filtered through built-in guard rails against undesirable speech and irrelevant questions.

Fourth, Jill Watson is cost-effective as it relies on pre-trained models along with RAG to provide relevant answers to student questions while minimizing hallucinations. The alternative to this is computationally intensive and expensive fine-tuning of underlying LLMs using hard-to-obtain training datasets with fidelity to courseware. This eliminates the cost of creating proprietary models while making it easy to incorporate ongoing technological enhancements in the fast-paced space of LLMs and AI agents.

## 2 Related Work

The Community of Inquiry model [2,3] points to the centrality of teaching presence, i.e., the presence of teacher-student interactions in the classroom, to achieve effective learning outcomes through individual reflection (cognitive presence) and collaborative construction of knowledge (social presence). Given that provisioning adequate teaching presence in online classrooms is often challenging, their work admits technical intervention through VTAs. VTAs can answer questions about course logistics and content anytime and anywhere, thereby amplifying interaction between human instructors and students and hence, increasing teaching presence.

In a first for VTAs, Goel and Polepeddi introduced the original version of Jill Watson built on top of IBM's Watson platform in 2018 [12]; hence the name. This version of Jill Watson answered students' questions on class discussion forums of online classes based on a digital library of previously asked questions and human answers to those questions. However, this version of Jill Watson showed demographic bias because the data of the previously asked questions skewed toward majority groups [13]. As a result, the next version of Jill Watson was constrained to answer questions related only to course syllabi, schedules, and policies [6]. This Jill Watson not only helped the students by providing them with a 24/7 question-answering service, but it also supported teachers by offloading routine question-answering and thereby saving precious time. However, the construction of a Jill Watson agent for a new class was prohibitively expensive because the need for training it anew on data for the new class required several tens of hours of manual effort. Further, Jill Watson could only answer a limited type of questions, and that too standalone questions; it could not engage in extended conversation. Goel et al. extended this work with a question-answering AI agent embedded in a natural language user guide to answer questions about another AI agent [14].

In contrast to versions of Jill Watson grounded in a well-defined corpus of relevant but limited knowledge discussed above, open-ended question-answering models such as ChatGPT based on LLMs derive their knowledge from large non-specific textual training datasets sourced from across the internet and other natural language sources. As noted in the previous section, such models may give answers that are either irrelevant or factually incorrect. These issues are mitigated by using retrieval augmented generation (RAG) with LLM-based models [9]. Very recently, Wang et al. report an implementation of a retrieval-based chatbot for use in education [15]. While they validate this approach with a set of 20 questions, they do not report having deployed their VTA in live classes. In the same vein, Taneja et al. present a conceptual design of the Jill Watson version presented here and evaluate its performance using standard datasets while comparing it to a chatbot constructed using the OpenAI Assistant API [16].

## 3 Overview of Jill Watson's Architecture

Unlike previous versions, the new version of Jill Watson is deployed as an LTI tool in the class LMS and students interact with it through a private chat window. This affords a private channel of communication between a learner and Jill Watson. In addition, LTI-based deployments offer easy scalability across several alternative LMSs such as Canvas and Blackboard.

A Jill Watson agent for a class has a modular architecture with functionality enabled by three modules - the agent knowledge base, the agent memory, and the question-answer pipeline.

### 3.1 Knowledge Base

The first step in generating a Jill Watson agent for a new class is to create its knowledge base by preprocessing natural language courseware provided by the instructor as PDF documents or text parsed from the course website. Figure 1 illustrates the document preprocessing step, which is performed before agent runtime and hence, it does not affect runtime latency. We use the Adobe PDF Extract API to extract text from the PDF documents. All text is sectioned into pages which are further divided into paragraphs. The paragraphs are then grouped into passages of at least 500 characters (about 100 words). There is a 50% overlap between consecutive passages for redundancy and continuity of context across passages. The raw text in these passages often has special characters, unwanted spaces, and formatting anomalies. We prompt ChatGPT with these passages to generate passages with clean text along with a 2-3-word long header. ChatGPT is also used to generate a summary of the clean text to make implicit information in passages more explicit. The clean passages along with their headers and summaries are then served to a text encoder to generate two sets of embeddings that are stored in the agent knowledge base for later use in dense passage retrieval.

### 3.2 Agent Memory

A MongoDB database stores information about agent-student interactions to serve as a source of student-specific question history for conversation. This eliminates reliance on LMS to provide this information. This is important as LMS often do not store the question history.

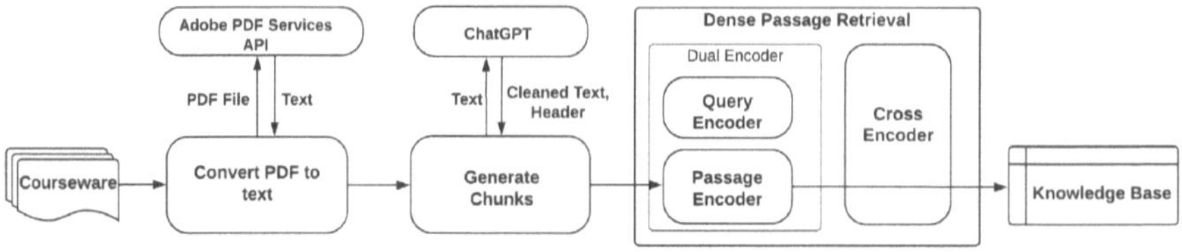


**Fig. 1.** Jill Watson document preprocessing

### 3.3 Question Answering

Figure 2 shows Jill Watson's runtime architecture. The runtime performs the following functions - Jill-Watson-LMS interaction; co-reference resolution; skill classification for relevant document selection; question-answering; and moderation. A REST server enables Jill-Watson-LMS interaction by exposing Jill Watson as an API. This allows for integration with any LTI-compatible LMS.

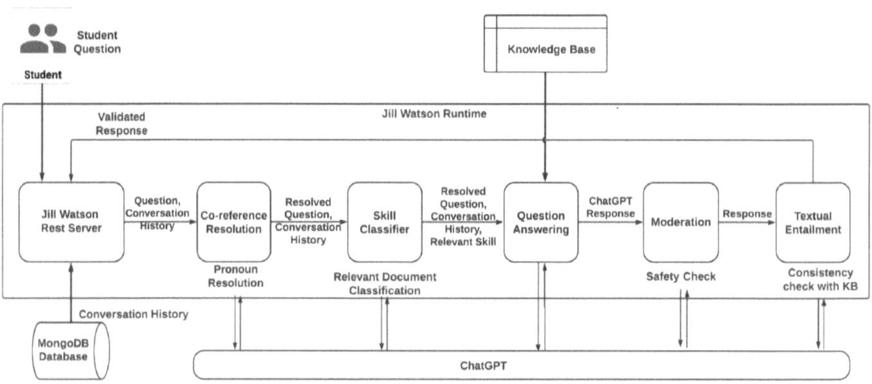


**Fig. 2.** Jill Watson runtime architecture

Co-reference resolution replaces indirectly referenced entities (pronouns) in a query with explicit nouns or noun phrases based on the conversation history [17]. This ensures the continuity of dialog. The resolved query is then input into a skill classifier to determine the skill required to answer it. Queries that require content retrieval are forwarded to the Contextual Answering Skill; irrelevant queries and greetings are trivially answered, respectively, by the Irrelevant Skill and Greeting Skill.

Figure 3 illustrates the implementation of Jill Watson's contextual answering pipeline. Contextual answering involves answering questions based on relevant information retrieved from the knowledge base. Jill Watson uses dense passage retrieval for this task [10]. First, based on the required skill, we retrieve relevant passages with clean text and their summaries along with their embeddings from the knowledge base. Second, we compute query embeddings of the co-reference-resolved queries. Third, we compute the similarity of the query embedding with context embeddings for each passage as well as its summary text. The similarity score of a passage is the maximum of the two numbers. Fourth, we sort the passages in decreasing order of similarity and select k passages with similarity above a threshold. To improve retrieval accuracy, we introduce a cross-encoder in our design to re-rank the selected k passages, which are then grouped into batches of five for prompt construction.

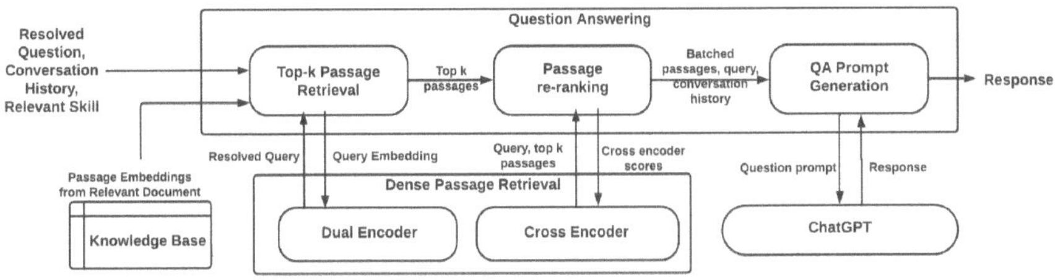


**Fig. 3.** Contextual answering pipeline

Prompt construction for the question-answering constrains ChatGPT to only answer student queries if the context has the requisite information, or else, refuse to answer. Further, it should be able to respond to follow-up questions to converse. For the latter, we use the conversation history for the current user extracted from the agent memory. We construct a prompt with the first batch of passages as context, conversation history, and resolved user query. If ChatGPT fails to answer the question using the first batch of passages, we use the second batch of passages, and so on, until ChatGPT generates a valid answer. The validity of the answer is checked by prompting ChatGPT. If a valid answer is not found from any of the batches, Jill Watson lets the student know that it cannot answer that question based on the provided context.

A textual entailment module checks the response for consistency against the context retrieved from the knowledge base. The task assesses the logical relationship between a context (C) and a hypothesis (H), where C entails H, contradicts H, or is neutral to H. We incorporate these checks to validate whether context C fully supports the generated answer A. If not, the answer is either rejected or flagged with a low-confidence warning, prompting users to verify the answer independently. Our method utilizes ChatGPT for textual entailment, with instruction-based prompts yielding the highest recall for identifying non-entailed answers.

Finally, to ensure safe and relevant responses, Jill Watson checks input queries and responses for harmful text using the OpenAI Moderation API. The API allows Jill Watson to detect different categories of harmful text and discard such text with an appropriate message to the user.

# 4 Results and Discussion

The current version of Jill Watson has been deployed since Summer 2023 in several classes at the Georgia Institute of Technology (Gatech) as well as classes at two community colleges - Wiregrass College and Columbus College - in the Technical College System of Georgia. Table 1 lists some salient information for these deployments along with natural language documents that Jill Watson uses in each class to converse with students. These include instructor handouts, textbooks, lecture transcripts, and text parsed from course websites. Figure 4 shows the accuracy of Jill Watson's responses to a large number of synthetically created questions for a wide variety of documents used in deployment in alternative courses. These responses were graded by humans. The accuracy ranges from 75% to 97%. Lower accuracy is mostly traced to parsing challenges posed by tables commonly found in syllabi.

Tables 2, 3, and 4 show demographic data for the Fall 2023 Knowledge-based AI class at the Georgia Institute of Technology and the English class at Wiregrass College, and they illustrate that the two student bodies have starkly different gender, age, and ethnicity distributions.

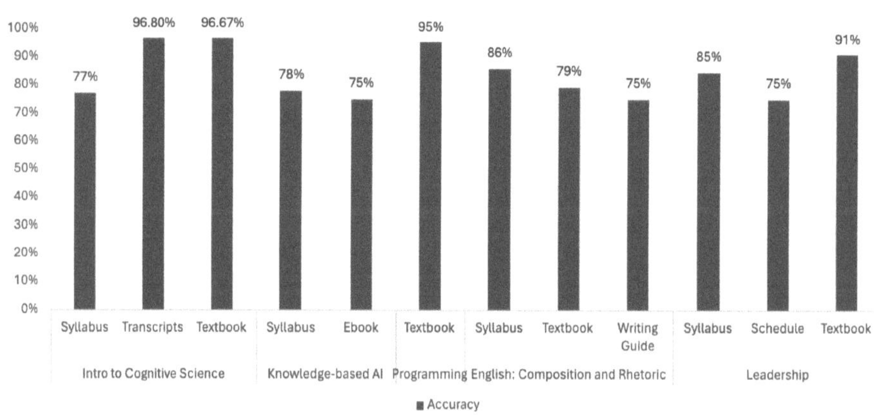


**Fig. 4.** Accuracy of Jill Watson responses to synthetically created questions for various documents.

**Table 1.** Jill Watson deployments. In addition to the knowledge base components listed, Jill Watson also answers questions about class syllabus, schedule, and policies.

| Semester | Institution | Course | Knowledgebase components | # Students |
|---|---|---|---|---|
| Summer 2023 | Gatech | Human-Computer Interaction | Course website | 385 |
| Summer 2023 | Gatech | Knowledge-based AI | E-textbook | 216 |
| Summer 2023 | Gatech | Intro to Cognitive Science | –Textbook<br>–Video transcripts | 115 |
| Fall 2023 | Gatech | Knowledge-based AI | E-textbook | 198 |
| Fall 2023 | Wiregrass College | English: Composition and Rhetoric | –MLA Writing Guide<br>–E-textbook<br>–Instructor handouts | 100 |
| Spring 2024 | Gatech | Knowledge-based AI | –E-textbook<br>–Course website | 223 |
| Spring 2024 | Gatech | Intro to Cognitive Science | –Textbook<br>–Video lecture transcripts | 58 |
| Spring 2024 | Wiregrass College | English: Composition and Rhetoric | –MLA writing guide<br>–E-textbook<br>–Instructor handouts | 60 |
| Spring 2024 | Columbus College | Leadership | Course readings | 15 |

**Table 2.** Student Gender Distribution

| Course (Fall 2023) | Female | Male |
|---|---|---|
| Knowledge-based AI | 28.54% | 71.46% |
| English: Composition and Rhetoric | 78.00% | 22.00% |

**Table 3.** Student Age Distribution

| Course (Fall 2023) | 17–24 | 25–34 | 35–44 | 45–54 | 55–64 |
|---|---|---|---|---|---|
| Knowledge-based AI | 12.50% | 64.79% | 17.08% | 4.16% | 1.45% |
| English: Composition and Rhetoric | 67.50% | 23.50% | 6.00% | 2.00% | 1.00% |

**Table 4.** Student Race/Ethnicity Distribution

| Course (Fall 2023) | American Indian/Alaskan Native | Asian | Black/ African American | Hispanic/Latino | Two or more | Unk | White |
|---|---|---|---|---|---|---|---|
| Knowledge-based AI | 0 | 51.25% | 3.54% | 6.45% | 2.71% | 2.50% | 33.54% |
| English: Composition and Rhetoric | 1.00% | 1.00% | 40.00% | 11.50% | 4.5% | 0 | 42.00% |

**Table 5.** Example of a real student conversation with Jill Watson from the Knowledge-based AI class in Spring 2024 (conversation has been truncated for brevity). Note the depth of the conversation between the student and Jill Watson

| Turn | Student Question | Jill Watson's response |
|---|---|---|
| 1 | Do you have sample questions to quiz about means end analysis? | Certainly! Here are some sample questions to quiz your understanding of means-end analysis:<br>1. What is means-end analysis in problem-solving?<br>2. How does means-end analysis differ from generate and test?<br>3. What is the role of a heuristic in means end analysis?<br>4. Explain the concept of state spaces [...]<br>10. Can means-end analysis guarantee computational efficiency or optimality of the solution? Explain.<br>If you have any specific questions or need further explanation on any topic related to means-end analysis, feel free to ask! |
| 2 | Means ends analysis is a universal problem solving technique. It is not guaranteed to provide a solution. It attempts to solve a problem by traversing through a potential state space [...] Is this correct for the first one? | Yes, your understanding of means-end analysis is correct for the first question. Means-end analysis is a universal problem- solving technique that aims to solve a problem by reducing the differences or distance between the current state and the goal state. It involves traversing through a potential state space and applying operators or moves to bring the current state closer to the goal state. [...] |
| 3 | Are the operators the potential moves being generated from a given state? | Yes, that's correct. In means-end analysis, the operators refer to the potential moves or actions that can be applied to a given state in order to progress towards the goal state. These operators represent the available actions or transformations that can be performed on the current state to generate new states. [...] |
| 4 | For question number 2, Means-End-analysis differs from generate and test because it is reducing the distance between the current state and the goal state. To get the states for means end analysis, the agent will generate [...] | Yes, you are correct in stating that means-end analysis differs from generate and test in terms of reducing the distance between the current state and the goal state. However, there are a few additional differences between the two problem-solving approaches: [...] |

Table 5 shows a real conversation between Jill Watson and a student in the Knowledge-based AI class. The student is using Jill Watson to test her skills and receive Jill Watson's feedback. This is an example of a student's deep engagement with the courseware. What is interesting is that though the student asks specifically about questions related to means-end analysis, Jill Watson generates questions for related topics taught in the class. ChatGPT also generates a good quality quiz to the same question, but it focuses solely on means-end analysis. This means that Jill Watson, by having access to course content, generates questions that encourage students to think more deeply about related concepts in the course. The ability of Jill Watson to support deeper understanding and critical thinking however requires more investigation.

Table 6 illustrates Jill Watson's ability to mitigate the hallucinatory behavior of ChatGPT. When asked about the concept of 'free will' in the context of the recommended textbook in the Intro to Cognitive Science class, Jill Watson

**Table 6.** Example where ChatGPT hallucinates an entire response but Jill Watson does not. The entirety of the ChatGPT response is a hallucination.

| |
|---|
| Question: How does Thagard explain the concept of 'free will' within the frameworks he discusses in his book "MIND: Introduction to Cognitive Science"? |
| **Jill Watson:** Thagard does not explicitly discuss the concept of "free will" within the frameworks he discusses in his book "MIND: Introduction to Cognitive Science." The book primarily focuses on explaining various aspects of intelligent behavior and the different approaches to modeling the mind. Thagard's emphasis is on understanding the nature of the mind and the cognitive processes that underlie intelligent behavior, rather than delving into philosophical concepts such as free will. |
| **ChatGPT 3.5:** In his book "MIND: Introduction to Cognitive Science," Thagard addresses the concept of free will within the context of cognitive science, exploring how cognitive processes give rise to our sense of agency and decision-making. Thagard's approach to free will in "MIND" is consistent with his broader views on consciousness and cognition, emphasizing the role of neural mechanisms and computational processes in shaping human behavior. While "MIND" covers a wide range of topics in cognitive science, including perception, language, and reasoning, Thagard's discussion of free will typically focuses on the following key points: [...] |

maintains fidelity to the source material, responding that there is no explicit mention of 'free will' while ChatGPT's elaborate response consists entirely of a hallucination and is not grounded in the actual content of the textbook.

Table 7 presents sample student comments gathered from the class discussion forums and surveys to gauge student perceptions regarding Jill Watson. The comments are reproduced without any editing, and they illustrate a positive student experience on the whole.

We close this section with two preliminary observations from the Knowledge-based AI class in 2023 indicating that access to Jill Watson may positively impact student performance. All students in this class were asked to consent to participate in an A/B experiment to measure the impact of Jill Watson on teaching presence using the Community of Inquiry instrument [18]. Those who consented to participate were randomly assigned to treatment and control groups. The treatment group was given access to Jill Watson, while the control group was not. The impact on teaching presence will be published elsewhere; we report here other important results. Figure 5 shows the proportion of students receiving final grades of A and C in the two groups. The proportion of students with an A in the treatment group is 3.9% higher than that in the control group; the proportion with a C in the treatment group is 4.4% lower than that in the control group.

**Table 7.** Student comments on Jill Watson from class discussion forums and surveys.

| |
|---|
| Student A: Does Jill provide any course content related answers? Student B: Yes, it does. It can answer questions like "What's common sense reasoning?" |
| Student A: Can you ask Jill how to do assignments and projects then? Student B: Yes, it will give you step by step general instructions on how to approach the assignment. It won't provide any extra information that's not already present in the assignment description. |
| Student C: The Jill Watson upgrade is a leap forward. With persistent prompting I managed to coax it from explicit knowledge to tacit knowledge. That's a different league right there, moving beyond merely gossip (saying what it has been told) to giving a thought-through answer after analysis. I didn't take it through a comprehensive battery of tests to probe the limits of its capability, but it's definitely promising. Kudos to the team. |
| Student D: +1 really like the upgrade - I am using it to actually learn the lecture material. One feature request would be to persist the conversation, I had closed the tab and lost my prompts. Again, kudos! |
| Student E: Jill helped me find out where I needed to go when I was lost on blackboard. |
| Student F: I often times need assistance with finding certain assignments and Jill Watson is very helpful with directing me towards the right place. |

Note that while this is a promising result, the statistical significance of this one data point and Jill Watson's causal relationship with it is undetermined.

We also compare the mean final raw score for those students in the treatment group who interacted with Jill Watson at least three times with that for students in the same group who did not. The mean scores are 91.4% and 86.6%, respectively, for the two populations. The probability that the null hypothesis that the two populations have identical mean values is true is $p = 0.007$, which is a statistically significant difference at the $p < 0.05$ level.

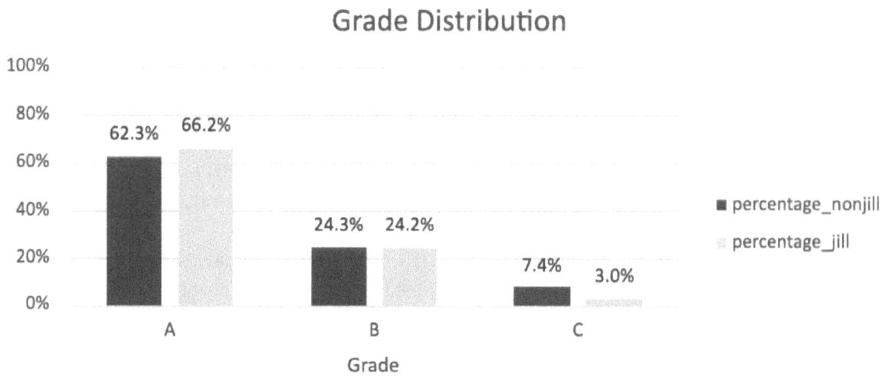


**Fig. 5.** Grade distribution in Knowledge-based AI in Fall 2023 class

## 5 Conclusion

We presented a highly performant and scalable conversational virtual teaching assistant, Jill Watson, based on the GPT family of LLMs. Jill Watson is resistant to hallucinations. It answers student questions and engages in extended conversations based on instructor-approved courseware anytime and anywhere using safe language, thus supporting both students and instructors. It has been deployed in several classes at the Georgia Institute of Technology and in two community colleges with about 1300 students. Qualitative feedback by students shows an encouraging level of engagement with the AI agent. We see preliminary evidence that Jill Watson may support deeper understanding of the subject matter but this needs to be investigated further. We also see preliminary indication that Jill Watson positively impacts student performance but this too needs to be explored further.

## References

1. Shah, D.: By The Numbers: MOOCs in 2021. https://www.classcentral.com/report/mooc-stats-2021. Accessed 14 Feb 2024
2. Garrison, D., Anderson, T., Archer, W.: Critical inquiry in a text-based environment: computer conferencing in higher education. Internet High. Educ. **2**, 87–105 (1999). https://doi.org/10.1016/S1096-7516(00)00016-6
3. Anderson, T., Rouke, L., Garrison, D.R., Archer, W.: Assessing teaching presence in a computer conferencing context. J. Asynchronous Learn. Netw. **5**(2), 1–17 (2001)
4. Estrada-Molina, O., Fuentes-Cancell, D.-R.: Engagement and desertion in MOOCs: systematic review. Comunicar **30**(70), 111–124 (2022)
5. Badali, M., Hatami, J., Banihashem, S.K., Rahimi, E., Noroozi, O., Eslami, Z.: The role of motivation in MOOCs' retention rates: a systematic literature review. Res. Pract. Technol. Enhanc. Learn. **17**(5) (2022). https://doi.org/10.1186/s41039-022-00181-3

6. Goel, A.: AI-powered learning: making education accessible, affordable, and achievable. arXiv:2006.01908v1 [cs.CY]. https://doi.org/10.48550/arXiv.2006.01908
7. Ji, Z., et al.: Survey of hallucination in natural language generation. ACM Comput. Surv. **55**(12), 1–38 (2023). https://doi.org/10.1145/3571730
8. Zhang, B., et al.: Comprehensive assessment of toxicity in ChatGPT, arXiv:2311.14685 [cs.CY]. https://doi.org/10.48550/arXiv.2311.14685
9. Li, H., et al.: A survey on retrieval-augmented text generation, arXiv:2202.01110 [cs.CL]. https://doi.org/10.48550/arXiv.2202.01110
10. Karpukhin, V., Oğuz, B., Min, S., et al.: Dense passage retrieval for open-domain question answering, arXiv:2004.04906v3 [cs.CL]. https://doi.org/10.48550/arXiv.2004.04906
11. 1Edtech's LTI Standards. https://www.1edtech.org/standards/lti. Accessed 22 Apr 2024
12. Goel, A.K., Polepeddi, L.: Jill Watson: a virtual teaching assistant for online education. In: Learning Engineering for Online Education: Theoretical Contexts and Design-Based Examples, 1st edn. Routledge, New York (2018)
13. Eicher, B., Polepeddi, L., Goel, A.K.: Jill Watson doesn't care if you're pregnant: grounding AI ethics in empirical studies. In: Proceedings of the 2018 AAAI/ACM Conference on AI, Ethics, and Society, New Orleans, LA, USA, pp. 88–94. ACM (2018)
14. Goel, A., Nandan, V., Gregori, E., An, S., Rugaber, S.: Explanation as question answering based on user guides. In: Explainable Agency in AI: Research and Practice. CRC Press, Boca Raton (2024). http://dx.doi.org/10.1201/9781003355281-4
15. Wang, K., Ramos, J., Lawrence, R.: ChatEd: a chatbot leveraging ChatGPT for an enhanced learning experience in higher education. arXiv:2401.00052 [cs.CY]. https://doi.org/10.48550/arXiv.2401.00052
16. Taneja, K., Maiti, P., Kakar, S., Guruprasad, P., Rao, S., Goel A.: A virtual teaching assistant powered by ChatGPT. In: Proceedings of Artificial Intelligence in Education: 25th International Conference, Recife, Brazil, AIED 2024. Springer (2024, Accepted for publication.)
17. Sukthanker, R., Poria, S., Cambria, E., Thirunavukarasu, R.: Anaphora and coreference resolution: a review. arXiv:1805.11824 [cs.CL]. https://doi.org/10.48550/arXiv.1805.11824
18. Arbaugh, J.B., Clevelan-Innes, M., Diaz, S.R., et al.: Developing a community of inquiry instrument: testing a measure of the Community of Inquiry framework using a multi-institutional sample. Internet High. Educ. **11**(3), 133–136 (2008). https://doi.org/10.1016/j.iheduc.2008.06.003

# Improving LLM Classification of Logical Errors by Integrating Error Relationship into Prompts

Yanggyu Lee[1], Suchae Jeong[2], and Jihie Kim[2](✉)

[1] Department of Computer Science and AI, Dongguk University, Seoul, Republic of Korea
yglee730@dgu.ac.kr

[2] College of AI Convergence, Dongguk University, Seoul, Republic of Korea
jihie.kim@dgu.edu

**Abstract.** LLMs trained in the understanding of programming syntax are now providing effective assistance to developers and are being used in programming education such as in generation of coding problem examples or providing code explanations. A key aspect of programming education is understanding and dealing with error message. However, 'logical errors' in which the program operates against the programmer's intentions do not receive error messages from the compiler. In this study, building on existing research on programming errors, we first define the types of logical errors that can occur in programming in general. Based on the definition, we propose an effective approach for detecting logical errors with LLMs that makes use of relations among error types in the Chain-of-Thought and Tree-of-Thought prompts. The experimental results indicate that when such logical error descriptions in the prompt are used, the average classification performance is about 21% higher than the ones without them. We also conducted an experiment for exploiting the relations among errors in generating a new logical error dataset using LLMs. As there is very limited dataset for logical errors such benchmark dataset can be very useful for various programming related applications. We expect that our work can assist novice programmers in identifying the causes of code errors and correct them more effectively.

**Keywords:** Logical Error · Programming Education · LLMs

## 1 Introduction

In recent developments in Natural Language Processing (NLP), Large Language Models (LLMs) have evolved to understand and infer the meaning of sentences or documents, allowing them to grasp context and understand the relationships between words more accurately. Such approach has significantly boosted the performance of LLMs in various NLP tasks, leading to technical advancements in each NLP domain [1]. In programming, LLMs focus on understanding the workings of source code and performing tasks such as code analysis and autocompletion. Recently, various LLMs, such as codex and codellama [2, 3], have emerged, enhancing the understanding of programming syntax to assist developers in their tasks more efficiently.


A. Sifaleras and F. Lin (Eds.): ITS 2024, LNCS 14798, pp. 91–103, 2024.
https://doi.org/10.1007/978-3-031-63028-6_8

While these LLMs serve developers' convenience, there is also the potential for their use in coding education for beginners. For example, students can use LLMs to generate solutions for practice problems not provided by instructors, facilitating more opportunities for code learning [4]. Currently, LLMs are primarily used for code generation [6] and explanation [7]. However, a crucial aspect of programming education is understanding and addressing programming error messages [5]. Understanding the process of interpreting and resolving error messages is necessary to facilitate efficient code learning.

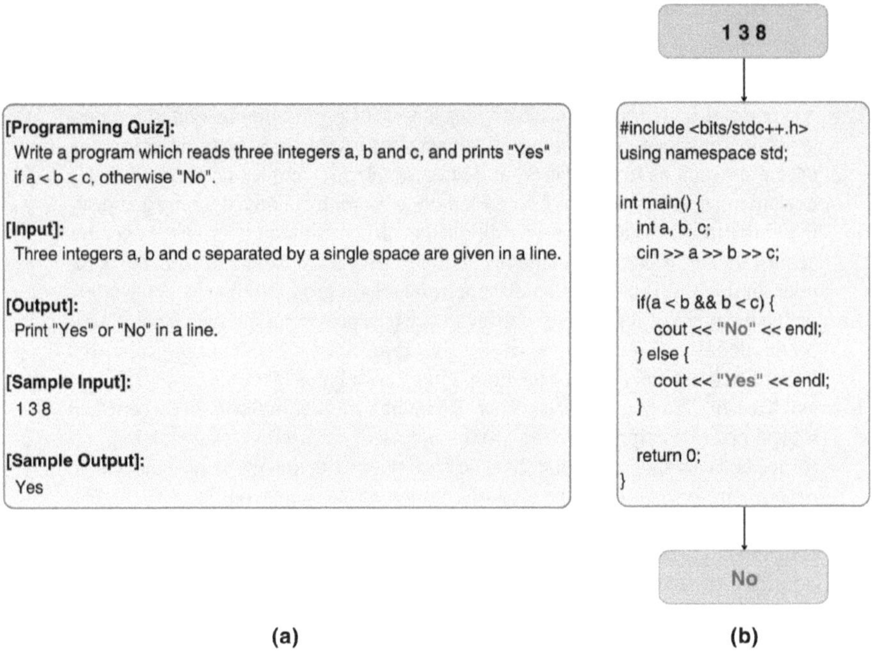


**Fig. 1.** The answer is incorrect, but no syntax error occurs when running; (a) is a programming problem that the user must solve; (b) is the incorrect answer code with a Condition Error.

When writing programming code, one particular type of error that requires special attention is logical error. Logic error refers to an error in which a program operates differently from the intention of the program writer and outputs an incorrect result. The significance of logical errors stems from the fact that, unlike compile errors, it is difficult for the novice programmer to self-correct. In the case of syntax errors, the compiler provides error messages, making it feasible to produce corrections. Simply following the code and making fixes enhances the ability to self-debug. However, for logical errors, often times there is no clear error message provided. Therefore, the debugging process involves understanding what the code does, identifying its functionality, and comparing it to the intended process. Novice programmers find this process challenging. Figure. 1 illustrates such a scenario where the C++ code written in **(b)** behaves differently from the intended purpose in **(a)**. It is a problem that a program that outputs "Yes" when a specific condition is satisfied by comparing the sizes of the input three integers must be implemented. In (b), the output was wrong by setting the condition differently from the part referred to in (a). That is, the error that occurred in Fig. 1 is due to a Condition Error. However, as it is syntactically correct, no error messages are received from the compiler, and the debugging process mentioned above becomes necessary. Detecting such errors and developing an approach for assisting the user holds educational potential [8].

In this paper, building on existing work on program analysis, we first divide the types of errors into ten categories and establish their respective concepts for the purpose of classifying logical errors more clearly. We then identify potential areas of confusion by understanding the relationships between errors and set an ordering in resolving them. Based on the defined concepts and relationships of errors, we propose a new approach for detecting logical errors with LLMs that makes use of relations among error types in the Chain-of-Thought (CoT) [12] and Tree-of-Thought (ToT) [13] prompts. We also undertake the task of generating specific logical error data from the correct code. The contributions of this paper include 1) defining the type of logical error and described the relationship between the types; 2) analyzing relationships between logical error types and reflecting them in LLM prompts, allowing the LLM to clearly distinguish between error types; 3) demonstrating effectiveness of the approach through an experiment where the classification accuracy increases by 21%.

## 2 Related Works

### 2.1 Automated Program Repair

Existing research on errors in source code has predominantly followed the Automated Program Repair (APR) paradigm [9, 16]. One notable example is [9], which introduces a method for fixing a broken program based on compiler-provided error messages. The model generates the corrected lines when given a program with errors along with the corresponding error messages. The work represents the errors and the error messages from the compiler in a graph format, enabling the model to modify multiple lines of code. Moreover, to address the data scarcity issue, the researchers intentionally broke programs for which labels did not exist, obtained error messages from the compiler. However, the approach cannot handle logical errors that do not come with specific error messages, and its focus on code recovery prevents users from understanding the root cause of errors. This paper aims to classify types of logical errors occurring in the code to enable users to understand the reasons behind the errors.

### 2.2 Teaching Programming to Beginners: An Instructor's Perspective on Educational Environment

When teaching coding to beginners, instructors often face the challenge of repeatedly explaining the same errors [14]. During practical sessions, students may spend considerable time fixing simple errors and inadvertently introduce repetitive mistakes. However, due to the large number of students compared to instructors in labs, individual students may need more frequent assistance from instructors. Students are often left to resolve errors independently, relying on error messages for guidance. While compile-time or runtime errors can be addressed to some extent by interpreting compiler-provided error messages, logical errors, which deviate from the intended behavior, often lack explicit error messages, making debugging a particularly upsetting experience. To alleviate these challenges, [17] introduces a prospective solution to enhance the performance of intelligent programming education systems by providing personalized feedback to learners. This study suggests a prospective resolution to mitigate the aforementioned issues. LLMs takes the programming problems as input attempted by students and the submitted code. It then identifies the types of logical errors present and provides this information as output, enabling students to understand the root causes of their errors independently. Understanding error messages is crucial for effective programming learning [5], and use of LLM based approaches could benefit programming novices.

## 3 Definition of Logical Error Types

In the past, there has been research on a classification system for common logical errors made by novice programmers [10]. The 11 error classifications explained in [10] list examples for each error type. However, a clear definition of the error type is not fully provided. In our research, we first present a definition of individual errors Table 1 for classification of logical errors. In order to cover logical errors in diverse programming languages, components of specific grammar such as class programming were excluded. The classification system we reconstructed can be applied to languages such as C, Java, and Python.

The '(11) Miscellaneous' category of errors defined in [10] encompasses issues arising from incorrectly placed semicolons or minor typos. These errors resemble compilation errors, but they can also be logical errors. When semicolons are misused, the compiler can interpret it as a long sentence. Also, typos in variable names can mislead the compiler. In such cases, it is difficult to set clear criteria and can be easily confused with other types of errors, so the category has been excluded from consideration.

Next, we created a view Fig. 2 to intuitively present the occurrence positions in the code and the relationships among the ten logical errors. Here, each type of logical error is represented as a node with the Type ID defined in Table 1 written on it.

We classified the structure of programs into 'Input', 'Process', and 'Output', according to the IPO pattern that many simple programs follow [15]. Subsequently, we distinguished the part used for declaration and initialization in Process and classified logical error types into four major groups: (1) Input, (2) Process: Declaration & Initialization, (3) Process: Remaining, and (4) Output. And we separated the relationships between errors into casual and coincidence relationships.

Casual relationships are represented by the sequence of the structure of programs 'Input', 'Process', and 'Output'. If an error occurs in one step, it may lead to subsequent errors in the following steps. For instance, if a program receives incorrect input in (1) Input, it can trigger errors in (2) Process: Declaration & Initialization, (3) Process: Remaining, and (4) Output. These casual relationships can obscure the logical error that needs to be classified, as one error can lead to another.

'Coincidence' relationships refer to when the criteria for classifying an error occurrence into a certain error type are ambiguous because the conceptual meaning of two

**Table 1.** Group types commonly occur while writing a code; Column 1 and 2 are list error types and names; Column 3 provides a description and examples of the error type

| Type | Category | Description and occurrence examples |
|---|---|---|
| (A) | Input | Errors arising from the inability to properly store input values properly<br>1. When not all given input values are received<br>2. When the data type of the variable the input value is incorrect |
| (B) | Output | Errors arising from non-compliance with the required output format<br>1. When the output format of the value in the variable is incorrect<br>2. When an incorrect string literal is output |
| (C) | Variable | Errors arising from incorrect use of variables<br>1. When the value stored in the variable is incorrect<br>2. When the data type of the variable is incorrectly specified |
| (D) | Computation | Errors caused by incorrect calculations<br>1. When calculating using incorrect values<br>2. When calculating using incorrect operations |
| (E) | Condition | Errors caused by incorrect use of conditional statements<br>1. When the conditional operation in the declaration part of the conditional statement is incorrect<br>2. When the condition in the declaration part of the conditional statement is insufficient |
| (F) | Branching | Errors caused by incorrect branching of the program<br>1. When the break in the loop is written incorrectly<br>2. When a conditional statement that should be written as if-else is written as if-if |
| (G) | Loop | Errors caused by incorrect use of loops<br>1. When the condition in the declaration part of the loop is incorrect<br>2. When the variable used in the declaration part of the loop is incorrect |
| (H) | Array/String | Errors caused by incorrect arrays or strings<br>1. When arrays or strings are initialized incorrectly<br>2. When referencing an incorrect index when using an array or string |
| (I) | Function | Errors caused by incorrect user-defined functions<br>1. When the parameters or return values of user-defined functions are incorrectly defined<br>2. When the arguments are incorrect when calling user-defined functions |
| (J) | Conceptual | Errors caused by incorrect concepts for problem-solving<br>1. When solving a different problem than the one presented<br>2. When the necessary loops or conditional statements are not written to solve the presented problem |

errors overlap. For example, an incorrect operation written in the declaration part of a conditional statement falls under both the Computation error and Condition error categories. If the existence of the conditional statement itself is incorrect, it also falls under

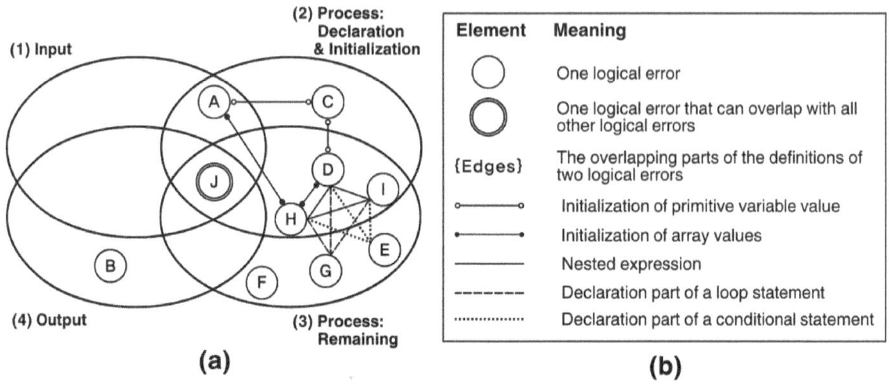


**Fig. 2.** Relationship diagram for types of logical errors; (a) divides error types into four areas and displays the relationships between the types in a graph form; (b) refers to the element in the graph of (a).

the Conceptual error category. These coincidence relationships can make the criteria for error classification unclear.

In Fig. 2, you can check the casual relationships according to the (1), (2), (3), and (4) groups where the nodes are located and the coincidence relationships through the edges between each node. You can also see the typical cases where coincidence relationships occur through the meanings of each edge. In this case, (J) Conceptual error can occur, overlapping with all other errors conceptually, so we depicted it as a node with two external lines.

Distinguishing and defining error types based on these casual and coincidence relationships enables us to identify potential confusion when multiple errors could be blended. This confusion can create ambiguity, making it difficult to pinpoint a single logical error in the code or leading to incorrect error classification. Providing clear criteria for such ambiguities enhances error classification performance using LLMs. Particularly, as seen in Fig. 2, there are complex coincidence relationships between nodes (D), (E), (G), (H), and (I). Therefore, it‘s essential to distinguish the criteria for this area clearly.

While we can specify which error will occur in each relationship to define the relationships between errors, setting and remembering this for all relationships is challenging. Therefore, we assign occurrence priorities to each error to be more applicable in general cases. To ensure convenience, we initially set the highest ordering for (J), which can overlap with all errors and concepts. Then, based on the casual relationships of the errors, we establish the order of arrangement as (J) > (A), (C) > (D), (E), (F), (G), (H), (I) > (B). Subsequently, we adjust the ordering of errors with clearly defined occurrence points among those having coincidence relationships, resulting in the order of arrangement (J) > (A) > (C) > (H) > (I) > (E) = (G) > (D) > (F) > (B). This approach allows us to identify the highest-ranked error when classifying a single logical error to which multiple concepts apply, thus helping to avoid ambiguous situations. Therefore, LLMs can classify logical errors on a more precise basis. Through this, we can inform novice programmers of the incorrect logic in the code more accurately.

# 4 Classification and Augmentation Using LLMs

The structure of the data used for classification is as follows. The labeling format is binary, with a value of 1 indicating the presence of the corresponding error type in the code and 0 indicating its absence. The distribution of the collected data is presented in Table 2. The data can be access on GitHub.[1]

**Table 2.** Distribution of logical error types collected for classification. The first row is the logical error type, and the second row is the number of data per logical error type.

| (A) | (B) | (C) | (D) | (E) | (F) | (G) | (H) | (I) | (J) |
|---|---|---|---|---|---|---|---|---|---|
| 10 | 10 | 5 | 9 | 12 | 8 | 10 | 8 | 8 | 6 |

Additionally, the data used for augmentation was only the code data that had been 'Accepted' as the correct answer for problems in the Introduction to Programming 1 (ITP 1) course.

## 4.1 Logical Error Classification Prompt

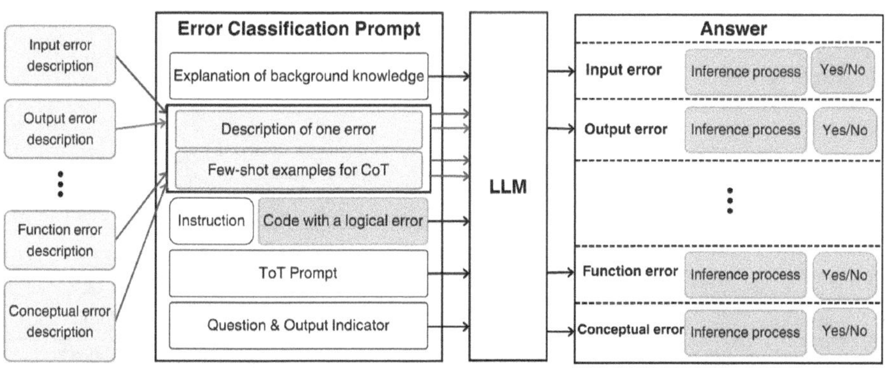


**Fig. 3.** This is the overall structure and process for classifying logical error types from incorrect answer codes.

We constructed a pipeline to observe the logical error classification performance of LLMs. Figure. 3 illustrates the process of the LLM classifying logical errors based on the provided information.

The Error Classification Prompt is composed of 'Explanation of background knowledge', 'Description of one error', 'Few-shot examples for CoT', 'Instruction', 'Code with a logical error', 'ToT Prompt' and 'Question & Output Indicator'.

[1] https://github.com/SChaeck/llm-logical-error-detection.

The 'Explanation of Background Knowledge' section explains the model of what a logical error is and lists the names of ten errors that will be used as classification criteria. This gives the LLM preliminary information on what task it needs to perform. 'Description of one error' uses ten descriptions written based on the concept of errors defined in Table 1 to describe each type of logical error. As only one error content exists in a single description, it's impossible to inform the LLM of the concept of all errors. Therefore, by writing about the restrictions on the occurrence of the described error, we have expressed its relationship with other errors. Through this, we provided cases where the concept of the error applies but should not occur. 'Few-shot examples for CoT [12]' provides instances for each error type. Each example consists of three average shots for each type of error. This helps the LLM distinguish the ten error types and understand where to focus. In 'Instruction', it asks the LLM if the previously explained error types exist in the code. 'Code with a logical error' is formatted as in Fig. 1, consisting of the problem the programmer wants to solve and the incorrect code for that problem. Finally, ToT prompts [13] are written to facilitate three experts sharing their thoughts step by step and providing feedback on each other's ideas, followed by 'Question & Output Indicator'. This enhances the accuracy of answers for complex errors that require inference.

Therefore, when one incorrect code is input, it generates ten prompts that verify different errors for this code, prompting the LLM with questions. Only the description changes during this process, while the rest remains unchanged. The LLM explains the inference process for each of the ten prompts and responds with Yes/No, indicating whether the specific error is present. This allows for identifying which logical errors exist in a given code.

## 4.2 Logical Error Augmentation Prompt

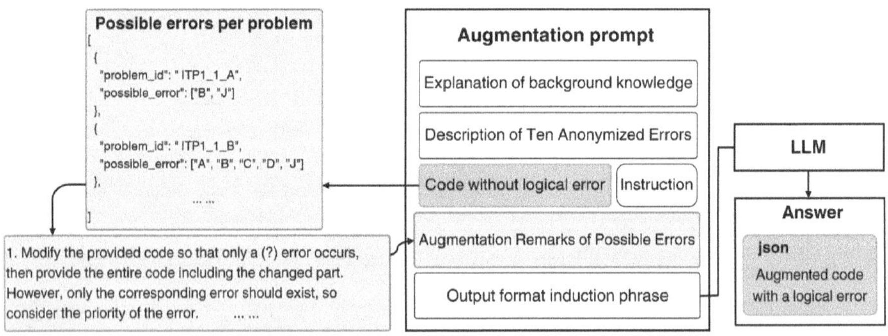


**Fig. 4.** Process and configuration of generating a code in which a logical error occurred from code with an 'Accepted' judgment.

We proposed a methodology for constructing a logical error dataset by creating augmentation prompts to induce specific logical errors from correct answer data. The overall process is illustrated in Fig. 4.

The augmentation prompt consists of an 'Explanation of background knowledge', 'Description of Ten Anonymized Errors', 'Code without logical error', 'Instruction',

'Augmentation Remarks of Possible Errors', and 'Output' format induction phrase'. In the 'Explanation of background knowledge' of the augmentation prompt, unlike the classification prompt, we explained what logical errors are. This was done as each error's enumeration is described with explanations in the subsequent 'Description of Ten Anonymized Errors'. The 'Description of Ten Anonymized Errors' provides detailed descriptions and scenarios for each error, using alphabet anonymization instead of direct names for all ten errors. This prevents augmentation based on the content of each error stored in the parametric memory, enabling a focus on the error classification concepts defined in the research. For instance, to avoid focusing solely on the term 'Input error' rather than the 'explanation for the Input error', the error type is provided to the LLM in the form of (A). Also, by providing the ordering of anonymized errors and explanations about the order, we ensured that the LLM considers the relationship between errors, preventing augmentation with incorrect errors. 'Code without logical error' comprises problem descriptions and correct code, similar to Fig. 1 (a). The instruction assigns the task of augmenting while including common mistakes novice programmers make. 'Augmentation Remarks of Possible Errors' only requests errors that can be augmented. Given the varying difficulty levels and unused syntax in the collected dataset problems, potential errors are compiled, and 'Augmentation Remarks of Possible Errors' are created based on the 'Code without logical error' problems. In 'Output format induction phrase,' the LLM is instructed to provide a JSON-formatted response. Subsequently, the LLM returns the code containing logical errors in JSON format based on the input prompts. This approach allows the construction of a dataset containing logically erroneous code examples. Augmentation results can be checked in Fig. 5.

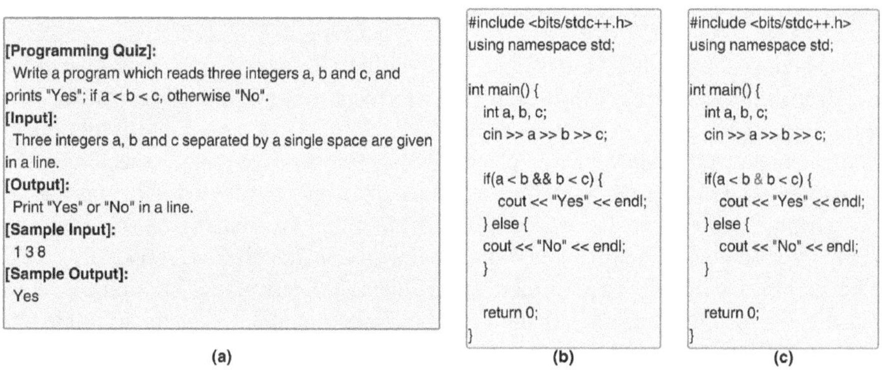


**Fig. 5.** Generation of code in which a specific logical error occurred from code with an 'Accepted' judgment; (a) is the problem we want to solve; (b) is code for 'Accepted' judgement; (c) is code where a logical error was generated.

## 4.3 Experimental Results

**Method of Collecting Experimental Data.** The labeled logical error dataset was relatively limited, requiring us to collect and label additional data manually. Then, from the data collected, we only utilized those labeled with the agreement of two annotators. The labeled data was used to evaluate the accuracy of Large Language Models (LLMs) in classifying logical error types and for augmentation tasks. The raw data was collected from the programming problem-solving platform AOJ (Aizu Online Judge) [11]. Specifically, we focused on problems from the ITP 1 course, which is part of AOJ's introductory programming courses. When users submit their solutions to programming problems and the system evaluates them, the submission information, including submission ID, submitter, submission status, and submission code, is stored on the server. This data is publicly accessible in API format.

**Results.** Looking at Table 3, we can see that the classification accuracy improves when a description is provided for errors, compared to when the description is not provided. When utilizing GPT-3.5-turbo, the classification accuracy for the prompts labeled 'Description not provided' was 35%. However, for the prompts categorized under 'Description provided,' the accuracy improved to 56%, indicating a 21% increase in classification performance. Additionally, we observe that the classification accuracy improves as the model's parameter increases. The performance improvement of GPT-4 compared to GPT-3.5-turbo is attributed to the difference in inferential capabilities based on the model's size. It is presumed that GPT-4 better understands the criteria for errors and can deeply contemplate changes caused by code execution. The False Positive Rate (FPR) is the ratio of instances where 'Yes' is output for incorrect errors when classifying the ten prompts generated from a single code. As errors are more effectively distinguished and classified, the FPR decreases. Therefore, the clearer the limitation of the error written in the description, the more distinguishable the relationship between errors will be, and the FPR will decrease. Additionally, this reduction can be seen in association with the improved inferential capabilities of the model.

Analyzing the results of GPT-4, we find that despite having relatively high inferential capabilities, it struggles to easily detect errors in areas that conceptually need more clarity, such as 'Computation error,' 'Branching error,' and 'Conception error.' 'Computation error' often occurs in places with incorrect operations, 'Branching error' in locations with incorrect branching, and 'Conception error' where the logic is flawed. Such abstract descriptions can confuse the LLM, making it challenging to understand which part of the code requires attention. On the other hand, errors clearly classified as 'Input error,' 'Output error,' >Variable error,' 'Condition error,' and 'Loop error' have well-defined locations, namely in the input statement, output statement, variable creation, condition statement declaration, and loop declaration, respectively. This indicates that the model can easily classify errors occurring only in specific parts of the code but struggles with errors present in ambiguous areas.

In Table 4, the augmented results are shown in Sect. 4.2. A total of 111 code samples were augmented using gpt-3.5-turbo. 'Right Augmentation" refers to cases where augmentation for a specific type of logical error was done correctly. The rest fall under 'Wrong Augmentation,' which is further divided into 'Other type of logical errors' and 'Not a logical error.' 'Other type of logical errors' pertains to cases where the code was generated with logical errors not requested. In contrast 'Not a logical error' denotes cases where a compilation error occurred, or the code provided the correct answer.

**Table 3.** Logical error classification results

| Error Type | GPT-3.5-Turbo | | | GPT-4 | |
|---|---|---|---|---|---|
| | Description not provided | Description provided | | Description provided | |
| | Acc | Acc | FPR | Acc | FPR |
| Input | 20% (2/10)) | 50% (5/10) | 0.06 | 100% (10/10) | 0.1 |
| Output | 20% (2/10) | 80% (8/10) | 0.1 | 100% (10/10) | 0.08 |
| Variable | 40% (2/5) | 60% (3/5) | 0.22 | 100% (5/5) | 0.12 |
| Computation | 67% (6/9) | 44% (4/9) | 0.12 | 55% (5/9) | 0.12 |
| Condition | 50% (6/12) | 67% (8/12) | 0.25 | 92% (11/12) | 0.125 |
| Branching | 38% (3/8) | 50% (4/8) | 0.188 | 63% (5/8) | 0.188 |
| Loop | 50% (5/10) | 50% (5/10) | 0.18 | 100% (10/10) | 0.1 |
| Array/String | 25% (2/8) | 50% (4/8) | 0.138 | 88% (7/8) | 0.275 |
| Function | 25% (2/8) | 63% (5/8) | 0.038 | 88% (7/8) | 0.075 |
| Conceptual | 0% (0/6) | 33% (2/6) | 0.167 | 67% (4/6) | 0.15 |
| **AVG** | **35% (30/86)** | **56% (48/86)** | **0.145** | **86% (74/86)** | **0.13** |

Overall, a higher augmentation success rate was observed for errors that are relatively easier to transform, such as (A) Input, (B) Output, and (J) Conceptual error. In contrast, for errors with lower ordering, like (D) Computation and (F) Branching error, more codes augmented into different errors were observed than the number of correctly generated codes. Interestingly, (E) Condition error showed a very low success rate, with 5 out of 8 'Not a logical error' cases resulting in compilation errors and 2 cases producing the same code as the original. This suggests that appropriate prompt engineering could improve the success rate.

**Table 4.** The result of augmentation with a specific type of logical error

| Error Type | Number of Augmented Codes | Right Augmentation | Wrong Augmentation | |
|---|---|---|---|---|
| | | | Other type of logical errors | Not a logical error |
| Input | 10 | 9 | 1 | 0 |
| Output | 13 | 11 | 1 | 1 |
| Variable | 10 | 4 | 2 | 4 |
| Computation | 10 | 1 | 6 | 3 |
| Condition | 10 | 1 | 1 | 8 |

*(continued)*

**Table 4.** (*continued*)

| Error Type | Number of Augmented Codes | Right Augmentation | Wrong Augmentation | |
|---|---|---|---|---|
| | | | Other type of logical errors | Not a logical error |
| Branching | 12 | 3 | 4 | 5 |
| Loop | 12 | 5 | 2 | 5 |
| Array/String | 11 | 4 | 2 | 5 |
| Function | 10 | 4 | 2 | 4 |
| Conceptual | 13 | 7 | 3 | 3 |
| **Total** | **111** | **49** | **24** | **38** |

An additional 73 code sets consisting of 49 "Right Augmentation" and 24 "other types of logical errors" can be utilized to evaluate the performance of the error classification model.

## 5 Conclusion

In this paper, we defined ten concepts of logical error types based on prior research and set an order to eliminate potential confusion from understanding the relationship between errors. Then, based on these clearly defined errors, we instructed GPT to classify these errors using CoT and ToT techniques, and evaluated its performance using a manually created dataset. Additionally, we proposed a methodology for creating a benchmark dataset by augmenting the correct code to generate logical errors using each error's definition. We also observed that as the model parameters increased, the inference performance improved, and a clearer redefinition of error types led to a higher classification performance.

**Limitations.** The limitation of this research lies in the insufficient consideration given to the unique characteristics of each programming language, as the newly defined category of logical errors has been applied across various programming languages. This makes it challenging to detect logical errors resulting from the misuse of language-specific syntax, such as class-based programming or pointers. Therefore, a more specialized approach that considers these language-specific characteristics is needed.

**Acknowledgments.** This research was supported by the MSIT (Ministry of Science and ICT), Korea, under the ITRC (Information Technology Research Center) support program (IITP-2024-2020-0-01789), and the Artificial Intelligence Convergence Innovation Human Resources Development (IITP-2024-RS-2023-00254592) supervised by the IITP (Institute for Information & Communications Technology Planning & Evaluation). Also, we would like to express our gratitude to HyeonJeong Jun for her assistance in dataset creation.

## References


1. Minaee, S., Mikolov, T., Nikzad, N., Chenaghlu, M., Socher, R., et al.: Large language models: a survey. arXiv preprint arXiv:2402.06196
2. Chen, M., Tworek, J., Jun, H., Yuan, Q., Pinto, H.P.O., et al.: Evaluating large language models trained on code. arXiv preprint arXiv:2107.03374
3. Rozière, B., Gehring, J., Gloeckle, F., Sootla, S., Gat, I., et al.: Code Llama: open foundation models for code. arXiv preprint arXiv:2308.12950
4. Finnie-Ansley, J., Denny, P., Becker, B.: The robots are coming: exploring the implications of OpenAI codex on introductory programming. In: ACE 2022: Proceedings of the 24th Australasian Computing Education Conference, pp. 10–19. ACM, New York (2022)
5. Leinonen, J., Hellas, A., Denny, P., et al.: Using large language models to enhance programming error messages. In: SIGCSE TS 2023. arXiv preprint arXiv:2210.11630 (2022)
6. Sarsa, S., Denny, P., Hellas, A., Leinonen, J.: Automatic generation of programming exercises and code explanations using large language models. In: ICER. arXiv preprint arXiv:2206.118 61v2 (2022)
7. MacNeil, S., Tran, A., Mogil, D., Bernstein, S., Ross, E., et al.: Generating diverse code explanations using the GPT-3 large language model. In: ICER 2022: Proceedings of the 2022 ACM Conference on International Computing Education Research, vol. 2, pp. 37–39. ACM, New York (2022)
8. MacNeil, S., Denny, P., Tran, A., Leinonen, J., Bernstein, S., et al.: Decoding logic errors: a comparative study on bug detection by students and large language models. arXiv preprint arXiv:2311.16017 (2023)
9. Yasunaga, M., Liang, P.: Graph-based, self-supervised program repair from diagnostic feedback. arXiv preprint (2020)
10. Alzahrani, N., Vahi, F.: common logic errors for programming learners: a three-decade literature survey (2021). https://doi.org/10.18260/1-2--36814
11. AOJ. https://judge.u-aizu.ac.jp/onlinejudge/
12. Wei, J., Wang, X., Schuurmans, D., Bosma, M., Ichter, B., et al.: Chain-of-thought prompting elicits reasoning in large language models. arXiv preprint (2022)
13. Yao, S., Yu, D., Zhao, J., Shafran, I., Griffiths, T.L., et al.: Tree of thoughts: deliberate problem solving with large language models. arXiv preprint (2023)
14. Bey, A., Champagnat, R.: Toward a smart tool for supporting programming lab work. In: Frasson, C., Mylonas, P., Troussas, C. (eds.) ITS 2023. LNCS, vol. 13891, pp. 290–297. Springer, Cham (2023). https://doi.org/10.1007/978-3-031-32883-1_25
15. Zelle, J.M.: Python Programming: An Introduction to Computer Science, p. 45. Franklin, Beedle & Associates, Inc. (2004)
16. Xia, C.S., Zhang, L.: Less training, more repairing please: revisiting automated program repair via zero-shot learning. In: Proceedings of the 30th ACM Joint European Software Engineering Conference and Symposium on the Foundations of Software Engineering, pp. 959–971 (2022)
17. Troussas, C., Papakostas, C., Krouska, A., Mylonas, P., Sgouropoulou, C.: Personalized feedback enhanced by natural language processing in intelligent tutoring systems. In: Frasson, C., Mylonas, P., Troussas, C. (eds.) ITS 2023. LNCS, vol. 13891, pp. 667–677. Springer, Cham (2023). https://doi.org/10.1007/978-3-031-32883-1_58

# Enhancement of Knowledge Concept Maps Using Deductive Reasoning with Educational Data

Hyunhee Choi[1], Hayun Lee[2], and Minjeong Lee[1,3,4](✉)

[1] LAIVDATA, Seoul, Republic of Korea
choihh00@gmail.com
[2] School of Computer Science and Engineering, Chung-Ang University, Seoul, Republic of Korea
hayun0406@cau.ac.kr
[3] Department of Computer Science and Engineering, Korea University, Seoul, Republic of Korea
[4] College of General Education, Chung-Ang University, Seoul, Republic of Korea
minjeonglee@cau.ac.kr

**Abstract.** Teacher-led lessons can successfully convey concepts depending on the teacher's preparation. However, it is challenging to convey a specific concept in an online environment without a well-designed learning path to guide students. Learning paths allow students to backtrack the prerequisite content from a specific lesson in which they are weak or skip to related content in which they have a strong understanding, resulting in efficient learning. Knowledge maps, as the basis of personalized learning paths, can be generated from educational data by deriving prerequisite relationships between two knowledge concepts. We have aimed to enhance knowledge maps by adding the prerequisite relationships obtained by applying deductive reasoning to previous maps. Using test data from Company D, we first generated prerequisite relationships using the least absolute shrinkage and selection operator, random forest, and hidden Markov model for three datasets of the company. Next, we derived additional prerequisite relationships by applying deductive reasoning. The results showed that the knowledge maps of the three datasets had accuracies of 59%, 55%, and 84%, respectively, which were 3%, 10%, and 4% higher than those of the prior maps. As a result, "at risk" students can perform better using the enhanced knowledge maps by applying deductive reasoning.

**Keyword:** Deductive Reasoning · Knowledge Map · Knowledge Concepts · Learning Path

## 1 Introduction

The World Education Forum (2020), a framework for "Education 4.0," introduced a novel learning technique that suggests a new educational paradigm involving advanced technology and automation connected to Industry 4.0. As artificial intelligence (AI) and


A. Sifaleras and F. Lin (Eds.): ITS 2024, LNCS 14798, pp. 104–116, 2024.
https://doi.org/10.1007/978-3-031-63028-6_9

big data are being applied to education, online education has played a crucial role in society, implying that the educational environment is evolving into a fully or partially online format [1].

In this era, the power of machine learning (ML), including deep learning, to predict future scores based on learning histories has been frequently touted in the field of education [2]. However, the application of AI or ML in the online learning environment can become ineffective if the learning path created for leading students lacks the appropriate design. This is because teacher-centered lessons focus on curriculum-prepared content delivery, whereas student-centered e-learning lessons focus on delivering the relevant knowledge that the students need at the time [3].

This paper demonstrates that already existing AI-generated learning paths can be enhanced using logic development methods. Our contributions are twofold. First, we have implemented deductive reasoning techniques in an educational setting to refine learning pathways for academic techniques. Second, we introduce a backtracking method aimed at supporting at-risk students. This approach has potential to provide tailored educational strategies that better meet the needs of individual students.

The remainder of this paper is organized as follows. Section 2 reviews the existing research results on determining prerequisite relations, deductions, and the extension of causality. In this study, the deductions were usually related to the syllogism. Section 3 discusses the methodology based on these concepts, and Sect. 4 presents the results of applying the methodology to experimental data. Finally, Sect. 5 concludes the study and offers directions for further research.

## 2 Related Work

Establishing a well-organized learning sequence as an educational content bundle is essential for efficient non-face-to-face learning. After sharing the research on creating a relationship based on the causal concept relationships between the methods of generating learning paths, we introduce syllogism to extend the existing relationships identified in the learning path.

### 2.1 Bregman Iterative Approach

**Decision from a Range of Conditional Probability Values.** Chen et al. [4] presented the KnowEdu system, which introduces a method for extracting KCs from educational materials and determining the prerequisite relationships for concepts that satisfy a predefined probability formula. The method for determining the prerequisite relationship follows the procedure described below:

a. Textbooks, educational materials, and other materials were converted into digital data using conditional random field model [5], and the main concepts were extracted.
b. The mastery statuses of the extracted concepts were expressed as 1 or 0 to obtain conditional probability values. For example, if concepts A and B are derived in the concept extraction step, the conditional probability values of Eq. 1 and Eq. 2 are obtained from the learning evaluation dataset.

$$p(A = 1|B = 1) \geq \alpha \tag{1}$$

$$p(B = 0|A = 0) \geq \alpha \tag{2}$$

c. If these conditional probability values satisfy a predetermined threshold (i.e., the probability of knowing concept A if concept B is known exceeds $\alpha$, and the probability of not knowing concept B if concept A is unknown exceeds $\alpha$), then a prerequisite relationship A → B exists. This relationship can help students focus on essentials. Moreover, Hwang et al. [6] introduced this feature to help students focus on essentials.

**Reference Distance (RefD).** Wang et al. [7] presented a link-based RefD method that measures antecedent and consequent relationships in learning. We consider two concepts, A and B. If A refers to B in many cases and B refers to A in a few cases, then the probability of B → A is high. Therefore, RefD is defined as follows:

$$RefD(A, B) = \frac{\sum_{i=1}^{k} r(c_i, B) \cdot w(c_i, A)}{\sum_{i=1}^{k} w(c_i, A)} - \frac{\sum_{i=1}^{k} r(c_i, A) \cdot w(c_i, B)}{\sum_{i=1}^{k} w(c_i, B)} \tag{3}$$

where

C = $\{c_1, \cdots, c_k\}$: concept space
$w(c_i, A)$: importance to $A$ of the concept $c_i$
$r(c_i, A)$: an indicator whether $c_i$ refers to $A$
$A$: books, papers, and other materials

Liang et al. [8] explained that hyperlinks, citations, and notes that are often used daily are examples of references.

**Using Latent Dirichlet Allocation (LDA).** Roy et al. [9] developed a supervised learning approach called PREREQ to identify the concept prerequisites. Each concept consists of a combination of topics; therefore, a pairwise-link LDA model [10] identifies the prerequisite of individual concepts. After creating a model using a dataset, a neural network classifier determines the prerequisites for concepts with unknown prerequisites.

## 2.2 Deduction and Syllogism

The simplest example of deductive reasoning is syllogism [11]. In deductive reasoning, only a specific conclusion is drawn from a general premise, whereas syllogism includes drawing a logical conclusion as well from the general premises. Syllogisms rely on two premises to draw conclusions. In this process, the true premise guarantees that the conclusion is also true. Recall a common historical syllogism:

*Premise 1: Socrates is a man (P → Q)*
*Premise 2: All men are mortal (Q → R)*
*Conclusion: Socrates is mortal (P → R)*

In other case, if a patient presents with fever, then a doctor considers that he has an infection; and if a doctor knows that the infection requires antibiotics, then the same conclusion can be drawn using this reasoning to prescribe antibiotics when the patient has fever [12]. This example can be expressed using the propositional formula as:

*Premise 1: Fever implies infection* $(P \rightarrow Q)$
*Premise 2: If there is an infected patient, a doctor prescribes antibiotics* $(Q \rightarrow R)$
*Conclusion: If a patient has fever, the patient needs antibiotics* $(P \rightarrow R)$

## 2.3 Expansion of Causality

Giannotti et al. [13] illustrated the use of supermarket sales data to expand or strengthen association rules using inductive and deductive methods. Associations (e.g., beer and diapers are likely to appear in the same basket [14]) are useful for explaining different buying habits, but are often too rare for practical use. Therefore, it is efficient to consider the combined results of ARM and deductive reasoning. By extending this work to the upper level, the rules of the lower level can be inferred from the updated rules. By expanding the relationships between products from the results of market basket analysis, the KC relationships leverage the rules of "a → b and b → c, then a → c" based on deductive reasoning, and the function of automatically calculating and displaying the probability of the prerequisite relationships defines the relationships more clearly.

## 2.4 Learning Path and Knowledge Concept Maps

Muhammad et al. [15] proposed that recommending a learning path suitable for students practically applies to improving the quality of online learning. Quality enhancement is possible by utilizing the benefits of learning paths. The main advantage of learning paths is that successive relationships between knowledge concepts (KCs) is defined according to the order of knowledge acquisition. This supports the study of learning content for a specific lack of content through backtracking. Moreover, if a specific learning content is sufficiently understood, then skipping related content enables efficient learning [16].

Chen [17] proposed a personalized e-learning system that extracts incorrect response patterns from learners' test results and constructs optimal learning paths. Gasparetti et al. [18] introduced a method that selects the learning object (LO) with the least difficulty associated with incorrectly answered test items as the start of the learning path and then uses a genetic algorithm to generate a learning path for an individual learner. Cai et al. [19] proposed a knowledge-tracing method that modeled learners' knowledge levels over time to accurately predict their learning situation. They also proposed a learning path recommendation algorithm based on a knowledge-tracing model and reinforcement learning. Siren and Tzerpos [20] used an ML classifier algorithm to extract keywords and automatically classified them to extract LOs; they then employed concept map data to generate learning paths containing two types of information—prerequisites and similarity. Alternatively, Choi and Lee [21] used the least absolute shrinkage and selection operator (LASSO) [22] as well as random forest (RF) [23]—which are variable selection techniques and supervised ML algorithms [24]—to obtain the relationship between knowledge components (KCs). Subsequently, a precursor between two KCs was determined by applying the hidden Markov model (HMM) [25]—a time-series model that concerns hidden and observed states—to generate a knowledge map based on learning paths generated from the prerequisite relationships between two LOs [26].

The research direction on learning paths or knowledge maps identified in the above cases implies that studies do not rely on a given curriculum, but they attempt to model it based on input data by considering the concept of causal relationships and probability. However, these studies present a disadvantage—they found a relationship between KCs [27, 28] only based on data as units of knowledge. Thus, creating a learning path or knowledge map that includes all the necessary KCs becomes impossible because real patterns cannot be observed owing to the structural problems of the training data. For example, experts may present the notable relationship between KCs in a curriculum, but this relationship may not be measured by a student's learning data. Moreover, suppose a pair of KCs exist, such as a "before" and an "after" KCs, it should yield a significant correlation but the level of difficulty of a particular KC may be mismanaged. If the "after" KC is observed to be simple, and all the students answer it correctly, the "before" KC would not be found to have any effect on the "after" KC. Therefore, no association between the two KCs would be found. To account for this, we used deductive reasoning to extend the causal relationship based on relationships not found in the data obtained.

## 3 Proposed Method

The purpose of this study is to create a learning path based on LASSO, RF, and HMM [21], and then add prerequisite relationships using deduction to the previous learning path to improve the accuracy of the generated knowledge map and learners' efficiency. Specifically, a hypothetical syllogism was employed as one of the deductive reasoning methods.

### 3.1 Data

To present the application results of the deduction in different cases, we used data from Company D in the Republic of Korea. Company D provides math learning services to K12 students in the Republic of Korea. In this experiment, we used the test results of three units—"Fractions and decimals," "Factors and multiples," and "Advanced fractions,"— which are studied by elementary school students in the sixth and seventh grades. For each dataset, we randomly sampled 2000 students. Because all three datasets have the same format, only the "Factors and multiples" dataset is introduced (see Table 1). The curriculum generated from the list of KCs shown in Table 1 represents single learning path. However, it does not provide information that allows skipping or backtracking as mentioned in the overview.

For each of the 2000 students, the data from KC36 through KC58 were coded with a value of 1 if they had mastered the corresponding KC and 0 otherwise as shown in Table 2.

According to the basic statistical results for KC48 to KC51 and KC53 to KC54, more than 90% students correctly answered the questions corresponding to each KC. For instances in which the average accuracy value was exceedingly high, signifying that the question was notably easy for most students, discerning the precedence or influence

**Table 1.** Title of KC36 through KC58 for the "Factors and multiples" unit

| KC ID | KC Title |
|---|---|
| KC36 | Finding factors |
| KC37 | Finding multiples |
| KC43 | Finding the greatest common divisor of two numbers |
| KC45 | Finding the least common multiple of two numbers |
| KC47 | Using multiplication to create equal-sized fractions |
| KC48 | Creating equal fractions using division |
| KC49 | Divide by 2 and 3 |
| KC51 | Divide by 2 to 9 |
| KC52 | Divide by 10 to 19 |
| KC53 | Divide by 20 to 39 |
| KC54 | Divide by multiple numbers |
| KC56 | Dividing the least common multiple of the denominators as the common denominator |
| KC57 | Size comparison of two fractions |
| KC58 | Size comparison of three fractions |

**Table 2.** Analysis data set for the "Factors and multiples" unit

| Student ID | KC36 | KC37 | KC43 | KC45 | ... | KC57 | KC58 |
|---|---|---|---|---|---|---|---|
| 1 | 1 | 1 | 1 | 0 | ... | 0 | 0 |
| 2 | 1 | 1 | 1 | 0 | ... | 1 | 0 |
| 3 | 1 | 1 | 1 | 0 | ... | 0 | 1 |
| ... | | | | | | | |
| 1999 | 1 | 1 | 1 | 1 | ... | 1 | 1 |
| 2000 | 1 | 1 | 0 | 0 | ... | 1 | 1 |

relationship between KCs solely through data analysis became challenging. In other words, it may be difficult to determine whether KC51 influenced the correct answer to KC53, which had a high average score only with ML results.

To conduct LASSO, RF, and HMM analyses (hereafter referred to as the LASSO/RF/HMM analysis) for generating a learning path or knowledge map, target KC relationships must be available to validate the predictive model's performance. This means that in addition to the test data used for analysis, the curriculum data utilized by teachers to assess its effectiveness must also be prepared. Table 3 displays specific information on KC51–54, which represents a subset of the complete target data available for the "Factors and multiples" unit.

**Table 3.** Target prerequisite relations on KC51–54 in the "Factors and multiples" unit

| No | Before KC | After KC | KC Title (Before KC) | KC Title (After KC) |
|---|---|---|---|---|
| 1 | KC51 | KC53 | Divide by 2–9 | Divide by 20–39 |
| 2 | KC52 | KC53 | Divide by 10–19 | Divide by 20–39 |
| 3 | KC51 | KC54 | Divide by 2–9 | Divide by multiple numbers |
| 4 | KC52 | KC54 | Divide by 10–19 | Divide by multiple numbers |
| 5 | KC53 | KC54 | Divide by 20–39 | Divide by multiple numbers |

### 3.2 Research Procedure

The procedure used in this study is shown in Fig. 1; it illustrates the sequence of data selection for analyses, data cleaning, creating prerequisite relationships, and expanding the causal relationships.

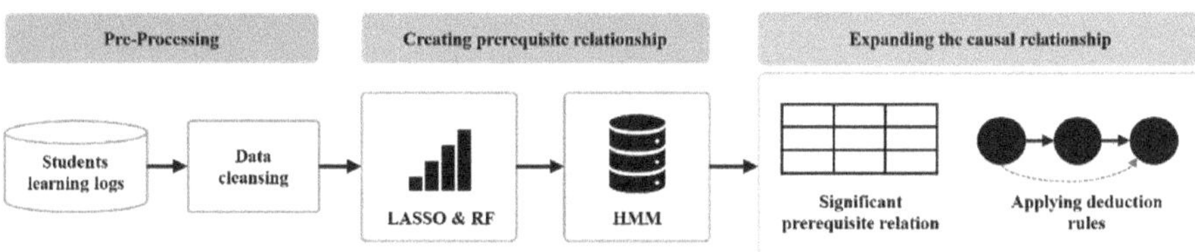


**Fig. 1.** System operating flow diagram of the research model

After selecting the data to be analyzed and removing extreme values that interfered with the generation of learning paths [29], we employed a linear LASSO model [22] and a nonlinear RF model [23] to select pairs of meaningful relationships. Among the various ML methods, LASSO and RF were used for relationship selection based on Wojtas and Chen [30]. To select significant relationships, we applied supervised learning instead of correlation analysis [31, 32]. This is based on the relationship between the regression and correlation coefficients [32].

Thereafter, the HMM [25] was applied to establish the prerequisite relationships between the related *KCs* as described by Choi and Lee [21]. The prerequisite relationships were determined based on the transition probabilities between the related *KC*s calculated using the HMM.

The final step was to expand the learning path created using LASSO, RF, and HMM. In this study, we expanded the number of relationships through a hypothetical syllogism, namely deduction, which derives a new hypothetical proposition from two previous ones. The defined rules are listed in Table 4.

For example, if there is a prerequisite relationship from KC01 to KC02 and a prerequisite relationship from KC02 to KC03, an additional relationship from KC01 to KC03 is created by applying the rule in Table 4. By expanding the learning path using deductive reasoning, we obtained a knowledge map that implies enhanced choices rather than a deterministic learning path.

**Table 4.** Hypothetical syllogism and propositions

| Rule of inference | Linear rule of inference |
|---|---|
| $P \rightarrow Q$<br>$Q \rightarrow R$<br>$\therefore P \rightarrow R$ | $(P \rightarrow Q) \land (Q \rightarrow R) \vdash P \rightarrow R$ |

The next step involved calculating and comparing the accuracy of the generated learning path with that of the knowledge map. The comparison before and after the expansion was based on the recall formula [33].

## 4 Results and Analysis

The prerequisite relationships for KC51–54 of the "Factors and multiples" unit generated by the LASSO/RF/HMM are displayed in Table 5, as the probability value that limits the prerequisite relationship when we compare it with the target relationships in Table 3. One reason that models do not efficiently represent target relationships is, as any data scientist would agree, owing to data problems. To circumvent this problem, a deduction was applied to the obtained relationship.

**Table 5.** Prerequisite relations derived from the LASSO/RF/HMM on KC51–54 in the "Factors and multiples" unit

| No | Before KC | After KC | KC Title (Before KC) | KC Title (After KC) |
|---|---|---|---|---|
| 1 | KC51 | KC52 | Divide by 2–9 | Divide by 10–19 |
| 2 | KC52 | KC53 | Divide by 10–19 | Divide by 20–39 |
| 3 | KC52 | KC54 | Divide by 10–19 | Divide by multiple numbers |
| 4 | KC53 | KC54 | Divide by 20–39 | Divide by multiple numbers |

Table 6 shows the results of applying the deduction to the prerequisite relationships in Table 5. The results are similar to the precedence relationships in the curriculum shown in Table 3.

The graphs in Tables 5 and 6 are shown in Fig. 2. Judging from the color of the edges connecting KC51 to KC53 and KC51 to KC54, the curriculum predicts that the acquisition of KC51 will affect the acquisition of KC53 or KC54; however, the LASSO/RF/HMM analysis shown in Fig. 2 (a) alone does not lead to this relationship. In contrast, when the deduction is applied to the relationships found in the LASSO/RF/HMM analysis shown on Fig. 2 (a), the antecedent relationships $KC51 \rightarrow KC53$, $KC51 \rightarrow KC54$, shown in red, are added. These results can be seen in the knowledge map on the right side of Fig. 2 (b).

**Table 6.** Prerequisite relations from the LASSO/RF/HMM+ deduction on KC51–54 in the "Factors and multiples" unit

| No | Before KC | After KC | KC Title (Before KC) | KC Title (After KC) |
|---|---|---|---|---|
| 1 | KC51 | KC52 | Divide by 2–9 | Divide by 10–19 |
| 2 | **KC51** | **KC53** | **Divide by 2–9** | **Divide by 20–39** |
| 3 | **KC51** | **KC54** | **Divide by 2–9** | **Divide by multiple numbers** |
| 4 | KC52 | KC53 | Divide by 10–19 | Divide by 20–39 |
| 5 | KC52 | KC54 | Divide by 10–19 | Divide by multiple numbers |
| 6 | KC53 | KC54 | Divide by 20–39 | Divide by multiple numbers |

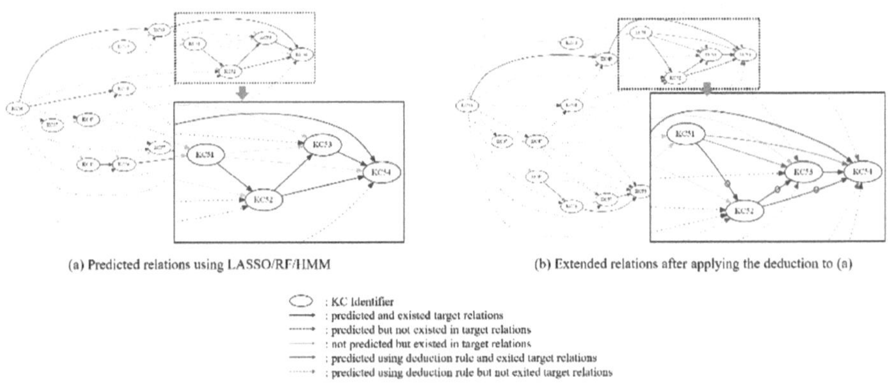


**Fig. 2.** Relationship obtained by the LASSO/RF/HMM and that obtained by adding the deduction on KC51–54 in the "Factors and multiples" unit.

The details are presented in Table 7. We confirmed that the accuracy of the model could be improved by applying the deduction to the LASSO/RF/HMM analysis results in all three datasets: "Fractions and decimals," "Factors and multiples," and "Advanced fractions".

We confirmed that the accuracy of the causal relationship analysis could be further increased by applying logic to the field of AI or machine learning. Moreover, it allowed to emphasize more focus on important KCs during learning by helping the KC that was affected or received in the preceding relationship to appear more clearly. Although the observed performance improvement was not significantly high, it is valuable that the approach identifies specific areas where students requiring performance enhancement should revisit.

Figure 3 presents the frequencies of inbound/outbound relations for each KC in the "Factors and multiples" unit. Figure 3 consists of three heatmaps illustrating the frequencies of appearance of KCs in the actual or estimated prerequisite relations within the "Factors and multiples" unit. In Fig. 3 (a), the values within the heatmap represent

**Table 7.** Recall before and after applying the deduction to the LASSO/RF/HMM analysis

| Data Set | *Recall* LASSO/RF/HMM | *Recall* LASSO/RF/HMM+ deduction | Change in accuracy |
|---|---|---|---|
| Fractions and decimals | 0.5625 | 0.5938 | 3% rise |
| Factors and multiples | 0.4545 | 0.5455 | 10% rise |
| Advanced fractions | 0.8070 | 0.8421 | 3% rise |

the total number of relations associated with each KC. Figure 3 (b) displays the number of affected or inbound relations for each KC, while Fig. 3 (c) shows the number of influencing or outbound relations for each KC. The first row of each heatmap indicates the number of occurrences of the corresponding KC in the target relationship initially defined by educational experts based on the curriculum. The second row displays the number of occurrences of each KC in the combined relationship, including the relations estimated using the LASSO/RF/HMM. The third row shows those of each KC in the integrated relationship extended through the deduction.

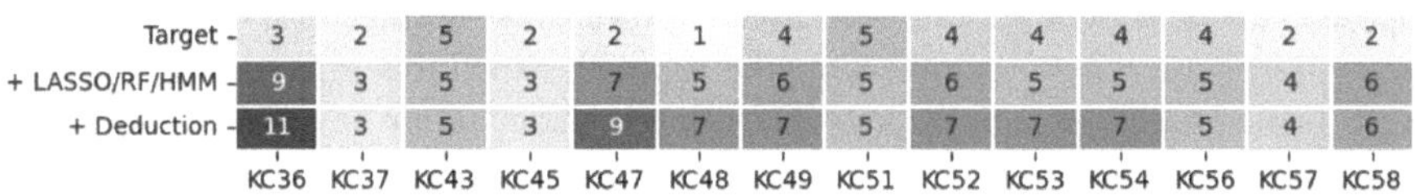


(a) Frequencies of inbound and outbound relations for each KC in the "Factors and multiples"

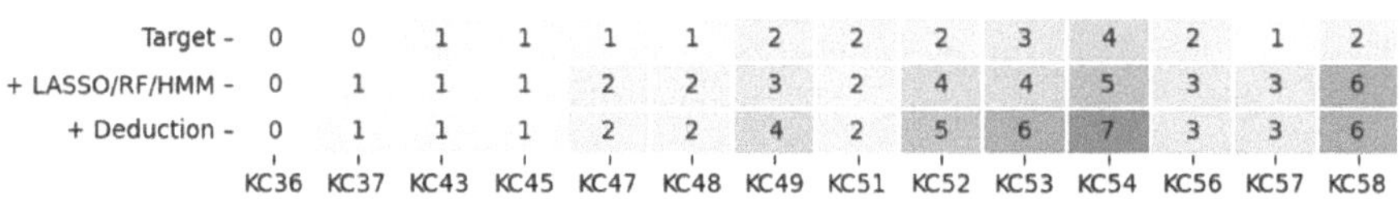


(b) Frequencies of inbound relations for each KC in the "Factors and multiples"

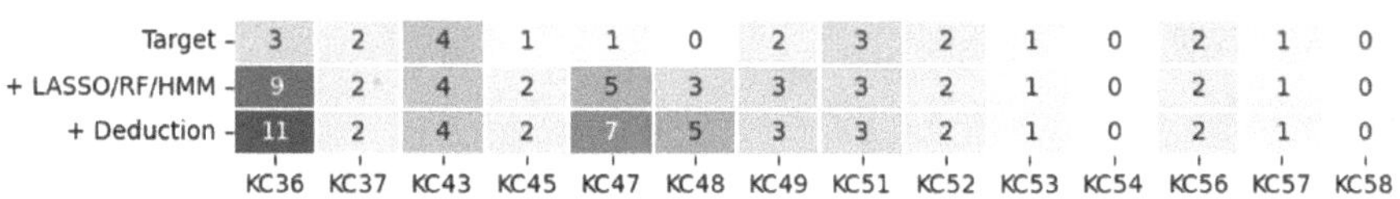


(c) Frequencies of outbound relations for each KC in the "Factors and multiples"

**Fig. 3.** Inbound and outbound frequencies of relations for KC36–KC58 in the "Factors and multiples" unit

In the first row of Fig. 3 (c), the values for KC47 and KC48, which indicates the number of times the corresponding KCs appeared to influence other KCs in the curriculum, are one and zero respectively. Subsequently, in the prerequisite relationships estimated by the LASSO/RF/HMM analysis, these figures increased to five and three, respectively, as presented in the second row of Fig. 3 (c). Finally, with the application of deduction, these numbers further increase to seven and five, respectively. This progression reveals that despite educational experts not originally categorizing KC47 and KC48 as major KCs in the "before KC" category, these KCs have the potential to serve as significant prerequisite elements in the learning process.

Thus, the application of deduction to the relations derived solely through LASSO/RF/HMM analysis has the potential to enhance the knowledge component map. This enhancement takes two forms: firstly, by uncovering additional meaningful relationships, and secondly, by highlighting the influential KCs that demand heightened attention during the learning process.

## 5 Conclusion and Further Study

This study presents a method for creating a learning path or knowledge map and expanding it through the deduction. The learning path that served as the basis before expansion was created using the data of Company D with ML algorithms, LASSO and RF, and then connecting them using HMM to obtain prerequisite relationships. In the case of $\alpha = 0.4$ in Eq. 1 and Eq. 2, the original accuracy was 56%, 45%, and 81%, respectively, for the three datasets, "Fraction and decimals," "Factors and multiples," and "Advanced fractions", which increased to 59%, 55%, and 84%, respectively, after adding the deduction. Suppose that if a student presents a KC with a lower-than-average or the lowest score, the recommendation involves reviewing the KC with which the original KC possesses a prerequisite relationship on the knowledge map. This may not be possible before the deduction for some KCs; however, utilizing a deduction technique allows the selection of one KC among the expanded feasible KCs. This results in an efficient learning recommendation for the "at risk" student with improved accuracies after the deduction [34]. However, using the deduction presents a problem—although it improves recall compared to the default learning path, the number of relationships that comprise the knowledge map increases to an infinite number. The future challenge is to create a rule that can filter out noise such as unnecessary relationships.

**Disclosure of Interests.** The authors have no competing interests to declare that are relevant to the content of this article.

## References

1. Bashir, A., Bashir, S., Rana, K., Lambert, P., Vernallis, A.: Post-COVID-19 adaptations; the shifts towards online learning, hybrid course delivery and the implications for biosciences courses in the higher education setting. Front. Educ. (FIE), 310 (2021). https://doi.org/10.3389/feduc.2021.711619
2. Abdelrahman, G., Wang, Q., Nunes, B.: Knowledge tracing: a survey. ACM Comput. Surv. **55**(11), 1–37 (2023). https://doi.org/10.1145/3569576
3. Bessadok, A.: Analyzing student aspirations factors affecting e-learning system success using a structural equation model. Educ. Inf. Technol. **27**(7), 9205–9230 (2022). https://doi.org/10.1007/s10639-022-11015-6

4. Chen, P., Lu, Y., Zheng, V.W., Chen, X., Yang, B.: KnowEdu: a system to construct knowledge graph for education. IEEE Access **6**, 31553–31563 (2018)
5. Lafferty, J., McCallum, A., Pereira, F.C.: Conditional random fields: probabilistic models for segmenting and labeling sequence data. In: Proceedings of the Eighteenth International Conference on Machine Learning (ICML 2001), San Francisco, CA, USA, pp. 282–289 (2001)
6. Hwang, G.J., Xie, H., Wah, B.W., Gašević, D.: Vision, challenges, roles and research issues of Artificial Intelligence in education. Comput. Educ. Artif. Intell. **1**, 100001 (2020). https://doi.org/10.1016/j.caeai.2020.100001
7. Wang, S., et al.: Using prerequisites to extract concept maps from textbooks. In: Proceedings of the 25th ACM International on Conference on Information and Knowledge Management, Indianapolis, Indiana, USA, pp. 317–326 (2016). https://doi.org/10.1145/2983323.2983725
8. Liang, C., Wu, Z., Huang, W., Giles, C.L.: Measuring prerequisite relations among concepts. In: Proceedings of the 2015 Conference on Empirical Methods in Natural Language Processing, Lisbon, Portugal, pp. 1668–1674 (2015). https://doi.org/10.18653/v1/D15-1193
9. Roy, S., Madhyastha, M., Lawrence, S., Rajan, V.: Inferring concept prerequisite relations from online educational resources. In: Proceedings of the AAAI Conference on Artificial Intelligence, Honolulu, Hawaii, USA, vol. 33, no. 01, pp. 9589–9594 (2019)
10. Nallapati, R., Cohen, W.: Link-PLSA-LDA: a new unsupervised model for topics and influence of blogs. In: Proceedings of the International AAAI Conference on Web and Social Media, Seattle, Washington, USA, vol. 2, no. 1, pp. 84–92 (2008)
11. Stylianides, G.J., Stylianides, A.J.: Proof in school mathematics: insights from psychological research into students' ability for deductive reasoning. Math. Think. Learn. **10**(2), 103–133 (2008). https://doi.org/10.1080/10986060701854425
12. Spooner, S.A.: Mathematical foundations of decision support systems. In: Berner, E.S. (ed.) Clinical Decision Support Systems. Health Informatics, pp. 23–43. Springer, New York (2007). https://doi.org/10.1007/978-0-387-38319-4_2
13. Giannotti, F., Manco, G., Pedreschi, D., Turini, F.: Experiences with a logic-based knowledge discovery support environment. In: Lamma, E., Mello, P. (eds.) AI*IA 1999. LNCS, vol. 1792, pp. 202–213. Springer, Heidelberg (2000). https://doi.org/10.1007/3-540-46238-4_18
14. Tsur, D., et al.: Query flocks: a generalization of association-rule mining. ACM SIGMOD Rec. **27**(2), 1–12 (1998). https://doi.org/10.1145/276305.276306
15. Muhammad, A., Zhou, Q., Beydoun, G., Xu, D., Shen, J.: Learning path adaptation in online learning systems. In: Proceedings of the 2016 IEEE 20th International Conference on Computer Supported Cooperative Work in Design (CSCWD), Nanchang, China, pp. 421–426. IEEE (2016). https://doi.org/10.1109/cscwd.2016.7566026
16. Murata, A., Fuson, K.: Teaching as assisting individual constructive paths within an interdependent class learning zone: Japanese first graders learning to add using 10. J. Res. Math. Educ. **37**(5), 421–456 (2006)
17. Chen, C.M.: Intelligent web-based learning system with personalized learning path guidance. Comput. Educ. **51**(2), 787–814 (2008)
18. Gasparetti, F., De Medio, C., Limongelli, C., Sciarrone, F., Temperini, M.: Prerequisites between learning objects: automatic extraction based on a machine learning approach. Telemat. Inform. **35**(3), 595–610 (2018)
19. Cai, D., Zhang, Y., Dai, B.: Learning path recommendation based on knowledge tracing model and reinforcement learning. In: Proceedings of the 2019 IEEE 5th International Conference on Computer and Communications (ICCC), Chengdu, China, pp. 1881–1885 (2019)
20. Siren, A., Tzerpos, V.: Automatic learning path creation using OER: a systematic literature mapping. IEEE Trans. Learn. Technol. **15**(4), 493–507 (2022)

21. Choi, H., Lee, M.: Analysis of prerequisite relation in knowledge graph using ElasticNet (LASSO)+ RF+ HMM: focusing on K-12 math. J. Digit. Contents Soc. **23**(10), 1981–1990 (2022). https://doi.org/10.9728/dcs.2022.23.10.1981
22. Tibshirani, R.: Regression shrinkage and selection via the lasso. J. R. Stat. Soc. Ser. B Stat Methodol. **58**(1), 267–288 (1996)
23. Breiman, L.: Random forests. Mach. Learn. **45**, 5–32 (2001)
24. Hastie, T., Tibshirani, R., Friedman, J.: Overview of supervised learning. In: Hastie, T., Tibshirani, R., Friedman, J. (eds.) The Elements of Statistical Learning. SSS, pp. 9–41. Springer, New York (2009). https://doi.org/10.1007/978-0-387-84858-7_2
25. Zucchini, W., MacDonald, I.L., Langrock, R.: Hidden Markov Models for Time Series: An Introduction Using R, 2nd edn. Chapman and Hall/CRC, London (2016)
26. Zhou, X., Li, Y., Yuan, L., Ma, G., Tan, X., Zhang, K., et al.: Learning path recommendation method based on knowledge map. In: Handbook of Research on Managerial Practices and Disruptive Innovation in Asia, pp. 171–184. IGI Global, Pennsylvania (2020)
27. Ritter, S., Anderson, J.R., Koedinger, K.R., Corbett, A.: Cognitive tutor: applied research in mathematics education. Psychon. Bull. Rev. **14**, 249–255 (2007)
28. Koedinger, K.R., Corbett, A.T., Perfetti, C.: The Knowledge-Learning-Instruction framework: bridging the science-practice chasm to enhance robust student learning. Cogn. Sci. **36**(5), 757–798 (2012). https://doi.org/10.1111/j.1551-6709.2012.01245.x
29. Osborne J., Overbay, A.: The power of outliers (and why researchers should ALWAYS check for them). Pract. Assess. Res. Eval. **9**, Article no. 6 (2019)
30. Wojtas, M., Chen, K.: Feature importance ranking for deep learning. Adv. Neural. Inf. Process. Syst. **33**, 5105–5114 (2020)
31. Cohen, I., Huang, Y., Chen, J., Benesty, J., et al.: Pearson correlation coefficient. Noise Red. Speech Process., 1–4 (2009). https://doi.org/10.1007/978-3-642-00296-0_5
32. Schmid Jr., J.: The relationship between the coefficient of correlation and the angle included between regression lines. J. Educ. Res. **41**(4), 311–313 (1947)
33. Goutte, C., Gaussier, E.: A probabilistic interpretation of precision, recall and *F*-score, with implication for evaluation. In: Losada, D.E., Fernández-Luna, J.M. (eds.) ECIR 2005. LNCS, vol. 3408, pp. 345–359. Springer, Heidelberg (2005). https://doi.org/10.1007/978-3-540-31865-1_25
34. Jang, Y., Choi, S., Jung, H., et al.: Practical early prediction of students' performance using machine learning and eXplainable AI. Educ. Inf. Technol. **27**, 12855–12889 (2022)

# Individualised Mathematical Task Recommendations Through Intended Learning Outcomes and Reinforcement Learning


Alexander Pögelt[1](✉), Katja Ihsberner[1], Norbert Pengel[2], Milos Kravcik[3], Martin Grüttmüller[1], and Wolfram Hardt[4]

[1] Leipzig University of Applied Sciences, Karl-Liebknecht-Straße 132, 04277 Leipzig, Germany
{alexander.poegelt,katja.ihsberner,martin.gruettmueller}@htwk-leipzig.de

[2] Leipzig University, Marschnerstraße 29a, 04109 Leipzig, Germany
norbert.pengel@uni-leipzig.de

[3] Educational Technology Lab, German Research Center for Artificial Intelligence (DFKI), Alt-Moabit 91C, 10559 Berlin, Germany
milos.kravcik@dfki.de

[4] Department of Computer Engineering, Chemnitz University of Technology, Straße der Nationen 62, 09111 Chemnitz, Germany
wolfram.hardt@informatik.tu-chemnitz.de



**Abstract.** Guiding students towards achieving the Intended Learning Outcomes (ILOs) of an academic module as part of a mentoring process presents a significant challenge, as it is important not only to emphasize the necessary skills, but also to consider the ongoing personal progress towards achieving a learning outcome. In addition, most educational content is presented in a 'one-size-fits-all' way, without taking into account the individual needs of students. In this paper we present a recommendation system based on Reinforcement Learning (RL) that derives its suggestions from the students' progress towards achieving the ILOs and the current relevance of the ILOs, according to the specific didactic design of the module. The taxonomy model proposed by Anderson and Krathwohl, serves as the groundwork for abstracting ILO progress, temporal relevance, and the affiliation of recommendation items. In the process of creating a recommendation pool, experts identified the mathematical concept and the taxonomy level addressed by existing e-assessments in order to identify their possible association with ILOs. The RL agent utilizes this dynamic measurement of the student's ILO progress - measured by the Bayesian knowledge tracing algorithm - to improve its recommendations, contributing to the ongoing personalisation of learning paths. In our evaluation, which utilized a test set of 129 mathematical tasks, the tested RL algorithms significantly outperformed a random baseline, underscoring the potential of this approach to enhance personalized learning within the realm of higher education mathematics.



**Keywords:** Recommender System · Reinforcement Learning · Intended Learning Outcomes · Mathematical Tasks




A. Sifaleras and F. Lin (Eds.): ITS 2024, LNCS 14798, pp. 117–130, 2024.
https://doi.org/10.1007/978-3-031-63028-6_10

# 1 Introduction

In the evolving landscape of higher education, the demand for delivering personalized learning paths tailored to the distinct needs and capabilities of each student is paramount, as it has been shown to significantly enhance learning outcomes, student satisfaction, motivation, and engagement [6]. However, the development of these personalized learning paths demands significant effort and continuous adaptation from educators, who must meticulously specify the Intended Learning Outcomes (ILOs), which define the knowledge and skills students should have acquired on successful completion of the module, and select and arrange the learning content accordingly to ensure that the learning objects contribute effectively to the achievement of the learning objectives [4]. Moreover, educators must continually monitor and adjust students' learning trajectories to optimize educational impact. To support this complex process, a variety of strategies and methods from the field of Intelligent Tutoring Systems (ITS) offer promising ways to create personalized learning experiences.

This paper presents a novel approach to the design of personalised learning in higher education mathematics by designing a system that focuses on the students' progress towards achieving ILOs, the current relevance and cognitive demand level of topics (based on the didactic model of the module), and the desired challenge level of the students. The aim of this process is to recommend relevant and suitable mathematical tasks, contributing to the effective and efficient achievement of the ILOs.

This work introduces a recommender system leveraging Reinforcement Learning (RL), with a focus on applying and comparing the Proximal Policy Optimization (PPO) [13] and the Deep Q Network (DQN) [11] algorithms. By evaluating their performance in recommending from a collection of 129 mathematical tasks across 312 topics, we aim to establish a benchmark against a random selection method. This comparison provides insights into the potential of combining ILO and RL to personalize learning by aligning task recommendations with students' progress and the challenge level they seek, directly contributing to the achievement of ILOs set by educators.

In the following sections, we first provide a reference to related work. Subsequently, we thoroughly introduce the design and implementation of our approach. Finally, we describe the experiments conducted and discuss them, before concluding the paper.

# 2 Related Work

A large part of the education technology research has focused on the implementation of the increasingly data-driven systems. However, people tend to trust humans more than algorithms, especially if the task is considered subjective or it requires consideration of individual uniqueness [8]. Therefore, it is crucial to give a close attention to specific learner characteristics in this process. A comprehensive meta-analysis [7] showed that digital tool use had a positive effect on student learning outcomes and can enhance learning in secondary school mathematics and science.

In recent research on adaptive learning recommendation systems, RL has been utilized to personalize educational processes effectively. An example of individualized educational support is a task recommender for the domain of mathematics based on RL and Item Response Theory (IRT) [12]. The recommendation used the estimated total score and item difficulty estimates derived from IRT. The results suggested that this method allowed for personalized and adaptive recommendations of items within the user-selected threshold while avoiding those with an already achieved target score.

Another approach is a knowledge graph-based, context-aware, recommender system algorithm, which was influenced by agent exploration in RL, for creating sequential learning-path recommendations [1]. The evaluation showed an enriched recommendation based on the learners' context, as well as a better discovery of relevant educational content.

[9] aimed at goal-oriented learning path recommendation and pointed out that previous methods still failed to recommend effective goal-oriented paths due to the under-utilizing of goals. Therefore they presented a Graph Enhanced Hierarchical Reinforcement Learning (GEHRL) framework for goal-oriented learning path recommendation. The framework divides learning path recommendation into two parts: sub-goal selection (planning) and sub-goal achieving (learning item recommendation). They employed a high-level agent as a sub-goal selector to select sub-goals for the low-level agent to achieve. Experiments demonstrated state-of-the-art performance of the framework.

Various RL-based strategies in educational recommendation systems typically utilize a Markov decision framework combined with specific RL algorithms to solve it. For example, [2] integrates the Markov framework with Deep Deterministic Policy Gradients to tailor online course recommendations to individual learner profiles. Similarly, [15] also employs a Markov framework alongside DQN to optimize learning paths by analyzing behavioral data. Additionally, [16] uses a Markov decision process enhanced with DQN to dynamically adapt content recommendations.

## 3 Design and Implementation

In the context of education, the principle of "Constructive Alignment" emphasizes the importance of aligning the ILOs (which reflect the goals and expectations of the educator for the students), learning activities (objects) and assessment of a module, to ensure that the designed learning experiences are effectively contributing to achieving the desired educational objectives [4]. To operationalize the mapping of ILOs, various models exist, with one of the most well-known being the revised Bloom's taxonomy by Anderson and Krathwohl [3]. This, comprising 6 cognitive process dimensions (remember, understand, apply, analyze, evaluate, create) and 4 knowledge dimensions (factual knowledge, conceptual knowledge, procedural knowledge, metacognitive knowledge), serves as the foundation for this work, as it provides a structured framework for classifying learning objectives and associated learning activities (objects). In the context of this research, ILOs are technically defined by a mathematical concept and a certain taxonomy level. It is essential to note that this model is hierarchical, meaning that addressing a specific level implies addressing all levels below it.

Within the domain of higher education mathematics described here, a vast, university-wide pool of tasks exists, utilized, maintained, and further developed by universities in Saxony, which comprises over 5000 mathematics tasks in the area of higher education mathematics that, once classified according to these taxonomies, can be effectively aligned with ILOs to achieve targeted educational objectives. The logical and structured progression of mathematical concepts allows for the strategic reuse of tasks across different learning objectives. This not only demonstrates the interconnectedness of mathematical topics, but also significantly improves the efficiency of resource utilization. By repurposing tasks, educators can enhance the use of existing educational materials, reducing the necessity to develop new tasks for each distinct learning objective and promoting a more sustainable approach to curriculum development. Additionally, within the existing task pool, a significant portion lacks student outcome data, limiting the applicability of conventional recommendation techniques. However, the approach proposed in this paper, focusing on the taxonomy-classification of tasks, enables dynamic and cross-module application even in the absence of outcome data.

For our technical implementation, we utilized two principal reinforcement learning algorithms: Proximal Policy Optimization (PPO) [13] and Deep Q Network (DQN) [11]. The PPO, an On-Policy method, i.e. it directly optimizes the policy currently making decisions, is known for its balance between performance and interpretability. It uses a trust region approach to ensure minimal deviation from the previous policy while seeking improvements [13]. Conversely, DQN is an Off-Policy method, optimizing a policy that is separate from the one generating the current data, that learns from a broader collection of past interactions through experience replay and fixed Q-targets [11]. This approach not only allows DQN to leverage historical data for learning but also enhances stability and efficiency in the learning process. Both PPO and DQN are model-free methods, meaning they learn optimal policies directly from interaction with the environment without constructing a model of the environment, which is particularly advantageous in complex or unknown environments where modeling the dynamics can be challenging. Both methods were implemented through the Ray RLlib library [10], providing a comprehensive framework for managing reinforcement learning experiments, and the Gymnasium package [17], offering a standardized interface for simulating a wide array of environments, thereby enabling the effective training and evaluation of our models.

### 3.1 Reinforcement Learning Environment

The presented recommendation problem of assigning optimal tasks for the efficient and targeted achievement of ILOs was modelled as a Markov Decision

Process (MDP), a common strategy in recommender systems known for its effectiveness in sequential decision-making and long-term outcome optimization [14]. With MDP, an agent aims to select an action $a$ from the set of all possible actions $A$ in a state $s$ from a set of states $S$ in order to reach a new state $s'$. This modelling approach is based on the assumption that the transition to the subsequent state $s'$ depends exclusively on the current state $s$ and not on previous states. This assumption is known as the Markov assumption and forms the basis of the MDP. For the state transitions, the agent considers the transition probabilities $P$ and the set of reward functions $R$ associated with these transitions. These reward functions are used to reward or penalise the agent for state changes. The objective of this method is to identify a policy that maximises the expected total reward. Encapsulating the state space, action space, reward functions and transition probabilities in the tuple $(S, A, R, T)$ provides a comprehensive definition of the MDP [18].

**State Space $S$.** The state space, also known as the agent's observation space, defines all possible states that can be assumed by the agent's environment. In our modelling, each state $s$ can be defined by a tuple $(ut, pl, st)$, where:

1. $ut$: Is a list of tasks that the student has already solved.
2. $pl$: Is a prioritization list representing the current relevance of each concept, influenced by the progress in the course and its didactic design. This is implemented as a dictionary, where each element includes:
   (a) The position in the prioritization list.
   (b) A taxonomy mapping determining the desired cognitive level at which the concept should be addressed in relation to the current state of the course.
3. $st$: Is the representation of a student, also represented as a dictionary. Each student contains:
   (a) A challenge level indicating how much the student desires to be challenged.
   (b) Progress on each concept. This is expressed by a taxonomy mapping describing the extent of the student's mastery of the concept at each cognitive level.

**Action Space $A$.** The action space describes all actions that the agent can choose in a given state. In our model, this encompasses all tasks that can be recommended.

**Reward Function $R$.** The reward function evaluates an action in a given state by a numerical value. In our model, we have integrated four different rewards that reflect the adaptation of a task to the required relevance, the contribution to the student's progress, the selection of new tasks for the student and the correspondence between the difficulty of a task and the desired challenge level of the student. The assignment of the Relevance Reward ranges from 0 to 100, and the Difficulty Reward and Reward for New Tasks functions range from 0 to 10. The Progress Reward typically ranges from 0 to 100 but can exceed 100 upon the achievement of ILOs, reflecting significant learning milestones.

1. Reward based on the relevance of the selected task is determined by the correspondence between the concepts and the addressed cognitive level recommended by the task and the prioritization list. The reward is computed for each concept, and subsequently, the average across all concepts is considered as the final relevance reward. For each concept $i$ in a recommended task, the reward is calculated as follows:
   (a) Calculation of the *Concept Relevance Factor (CRF)*:

$$CRF_i = \frac{|\text{prioritization list}| - \text{index of concept}_i}{|\text{prioritization list}|}$$

   (b) Calculation of the *Taxonomy Relevance Factor (TRF)*: For each concept $i$ that is both in the task and the prioritization list, the $TRF$ is calculated to reflect the alignment between the cognitive levels of the tasks and the requirements from the prioritization list. For cognitive levels $j$ that match exactly ($j \in$ matching levels), a factor of 1 is used. If a task addresses a concept at a lower cognitive level ($j \in$ lower levels) than specified in the prioritization list, a factor of 0.5 is used. Conversely, addressing a concept at a higher cognitive level ($j \in$ higher levels) than specified results in a factor of $-1$, penalizing the misalignment.

$$TRF_i = \frac{\sum_{j \in \text{matching levels}} 1 + \sum_{j \in \text{lower levels}} 0.5 + \sum_{j \in \text{higher levels}} -1}{|\text{J}|}$$

   (c) Calculation of the General *Relevance Reward (RR)*:

$$RR_i = (TRF_i \cdot CRF_i \cdot \text{weight}_i) \cdot 100$$

2. The reward for contributing to the student's learning progress, whose calculation is described in Subsect. 3.2, is calculated specifically for concepts that appear in the prioritization list and at cognitive levels that are addressed by these prioritized concepts. The calculation is performed for each relevant concept $i$, with a greater impact on improvements in more relevant concepts.
   (a) Calculate progress: Utilizing the Bayesian Knowledge Tracing (BKT) algorithm, which accounts for the possibility of regression as well as advancement in learning progress, we calculate the difference in student's mastery level before and after completing a recommended task. However, to ensure the reward is positive, negative values are set to 0. The difference is calculated on average over each cognitive level $j$:

$$diff_i = \frac{\sum_j \max(0, \text{value after}_{i,j} - \text{value before}_{i,j})}{|\text{J}|}$$

   (b) Calculation of General *Progress Reward (PR)*:

$$PR_i = diff_i \cdot 100$$

(c) Calculation of *Achieved Bonus*: This bonus is applied for each cognitive level $j$ where progress exceeds 90% ($j \in achieved$), denoting mastery. If mastery at any cognitive level regresses below this threshold, the bonus is retracted.

$$PR_i = PR_i + \sum_{j \in achieved} CRF_i \cdot 100$$

3. The *Difficulty Reward (DR)* is calculated based on the task difficulty for fulfilling the student's challenge level.

$$DR = \begin{cases} 10 & \text{if challenge level} >= \text{difficulty} \\ 0 & \text{else} \end{cases}$$

4. The *New Task Reward (NTR)* is awarded for each task recommended to the student that they haven't completed yet.

$$NTR = \begin{cases} 10 & \text{if tasks have not yet been completed by the student} \\ 0 & \text{else} \end{cases}$$

**Transition Probability *T*.** The transition probability quantifies the chance of moving from one state to another when an action is performed in a particular state. In our context, this represents the probability that the progress of a particular student will change as a result of the recommendation of a task.

### 3.2 Assessing Student Progress

In intelligent tutoring systems, the Bayesian Knowledge Tracing (BKT) algorithm was initially designed to track how students acquire skills over time. Its purpose is to estimate the likelihood of a student mastering a given skill based on their performance in tasks or tests requiring that skill [5].

Extending BKT's application beyond its original scope, we utilize it to monitor students' progression towards achieving ILOs within academic modules. This adaptation allows us to assess each student's advancement for specific concepts covered by recommended tasks and at every cognitive level associated with these concepts (encompassing all levels below), thereby offering a tailored approach to enhancing educational content recommendations.

The BKT relies on four primary parameters, which can be adapted to our context as follows:

- $P_{init}$: Initial probability of a student having achieved an ILO before attempting the recommended task
- $P_{transit}$: Probability of transitioning from not achieving to achieving an ILO upon attempting the recommended task
- $P_{slip}$: Chance of a student making an error despite having achieved the ILO
- $P_{guess}$: Likelihood of a correct answer without achieving mastery of the ILO

In our implementation, we assume that a student has not previously made progress in any ILO of the module, starting with $P_{init} = 0$. In each recommendation iteration, the test's success is used to estimate the new level of progress, becoming the new $P_{init}$ in the subsequent iteration. To determine $P_{transit}$ the concept weight, the cognitive level addressed in the recommended task and the task difficulty are multiplied together. $P_{slip}$ and $P_{guess}$ were assessed by mathematical experts on the basis of the task structure. The complete calculation is performed as follows:

For a correct solution to the recommended task, we determine $P_{obs=correct}$ using the formula:

$$P_{obs=correct} = \frac{P_{init} \cdot (1 - P_{slip})}{P_{init} \cdot (1 - P_{slip}) + (1 - P_{init}) \cdot P_{guess}}$$

If the solution is incorrect, $P_{obs=wrong}$ is calculated using the following formula:

$$P_{obs=wrong} = \frac{P_{init} \cdot P_{slip}}{P_{init} \cdot P_{slip} + (1 - P_{init}) \cdot (1 - P_{guess})}$$

Subsequently, these calculated probabilities are employed to assess the student's progress within the specific concept $i$ and cognitive level $j$:

$$Progress_{i,j} = P_{obs} + (1 - P_{obs}) \cdot P_{transit}$$

# 4 Experiments

## 4.1 Recommendation Pool

In order to create a recommendation pool to train the RL agent and measure students' progress in the ILOs, an experienced maths expert evaluated 129 existing online maths exercises taken from the learning management system OPAL and the integrated examination software ONYX. This selected set of tasks represents all the exercises available to students in a first-semester Bachelor's course at HTWK Leipzig. The 129 exercises reflect the breadth of the module and cover a total of 312 different concepts. Various criteria were taken into account when selecting the exercises:

**id** Reference of the task
**name** Name of the task
**link** Direct link to the task for the presentation of the recommendation
**difficulty** Overall difficulty of the task
**vector of weights** Refers to the differentiated assignment of significance or prominence to different concepts within a task
**vector of concepts** List of all concepts addressed in the task
**vector of process dimensions** Mapping of the addressed cognitive process dimension per concept

**vector of knowledge dimensions** Mapping of the addresed knowledge dimension per concept
**slip probability** Probability that a student who already has the skills required in the task can fail the task
**guess probability** Probability that a student who does not have the skills required in the task can solve the task by guessing

To obtain a detailed insight into the classification and assignment of tasks, refer to the following representative example:

**Task:** Replace the question mark with one of the following quantifier to make the following statement true:

$$\forall p \in \mathbb{N} : ?q \in \mathbb{Z} : \frac{p}{q} \in \mathbb{Q}$$

A. $\forall$... for all
B. $\exists$... there exists (at least one)
C. $\nexists$... there exists none
D. None of the above

The task engages students with concepts such as quantifiers, specifically the existential and universal quantifiers, and sets, including natural, real and rational numbers. It is classified under the cognitive process dimension of "understand" and the knowledge domain of "conceptual knowledge" for all its concepts, requiring the identification of the correct quantifier to make the statement true. The probability to slip is 0.1 due to the simplicity of the task and the absence of input fields other than the single choice boxes. The guess probability is 0.25, reflecting a chance of guessing the correct answer among the provided options. Overall, the task is classified as having low difficulty, with a rating of 0.1 (10% difficult), making it accessible for those with a foundational understanding of the involved mathematical concepts.

## 4.2 Experimental Setup

In our study, we train the RL models and observe their performance in simulated environments with virtual students. For this purpose, the environments were created wherein the RL-agent recommends a task to a randomly generated student, for which an outcome is estimated. As described in Subsect. 3.1, each environment consists of a student and a prioritization list for relevant concepts. In our experimental setup, both are generated with random parameters at each initialisation. For the prioritization list, a selection is made by choosing a random number of concepts with a random selection of taxonomy levels at which these concepts should be addressed. In order to simulate the processes of real students, simulated students are generated by assigning them a random ability level that represents their overall capability in handling tasks and a random progress, which is created by a random selection of concepts for which a random value of progress per cognitive level was determined. Additionally, a function was developed to determine whether a simulated student successfully completes a given task. This determination is based on calculating a success rate, which integrates the student's ability level, the difficulty of the task, and the discrepancy between the student's progress and the task's requirements. The success rate is computed as follows:

$$\text{success\_rate} = 0.5 + (a - 0.5) - (d - 0.5) - (\overline{g} - 0.3)$$

where $a$ represents the student's ability level, which varies from 0 to 1, $d$ indicates the difficulty level of the task, also ranging from 0 to 1. $\overline{g}$ denotes the average gap between the cognitive levels concepts are addressed in the task and the highest level in which the student has achieved any progress in these concepts, with values ranging from $-1$ to 1. Here, negative values indicate that the student's mean progress exceeds the cognitive levels adressed in the task. If this success rate exceeds 0.5, the task completion is considered successful, and the student's learning progress is updated as detailed in Subsect. 3.2.

### 4.3 Results

To evaluate the effectiveness of the trained models a comparative analysis was conducted against a random baseline across 1000 unique, randomly generated environments, as described in Subsect. 4.2. These settings were created to simulate diverse student progress levels and the relevance of ILOs, incorporating all 129 tasks as potential recommendations. Each model was required to issue a single recommendation per environment.

The outcomes, depicted in Fig. 1, are illustrated through two bar graphs, showcasing the average rewards received from the recommendations. The first graph offers a detailed breakdown by individual reward functions, revealing that PPO outperforms in 'Relevance Reward' and 'Progress Reward' categories, surpassing both DQN and the random baseline. The noticeable outperformance of both PPO and DQN in the 'Progress Reward' (PR) category compared to the random baseline may be attributed to their more effective selection of tasks that contribute to a student's progression. All three approaches show similar performance in the 'New Task Reward' category. This can be attributed to the test environment setup, where each model was required to issue only a single recommendation per environment, ensuring that the recommended task is inherently new and thus all models invariably score the full 10 points in this category. However, for 'Difficulty Reward' (DR), DQN's recommendations stand out, outperforming those of PPO and the random baseline, which suggests that DQN may have a better strategy for gauging or responding to task difficulty levels.

The second graph compares the total rewards obtained by the algorithms, highlighting that PPO achieves the highest improvement, outperforming the random baseline by an average of 36.61%. Meanwhile, DQN also demonstrates a notable advancement, being 30.49% better than the random selection. These findings underscore the efficacy of both RL algorithms and highlight the potential of RL to enhance personalized learning pathways in higher education mathematics.

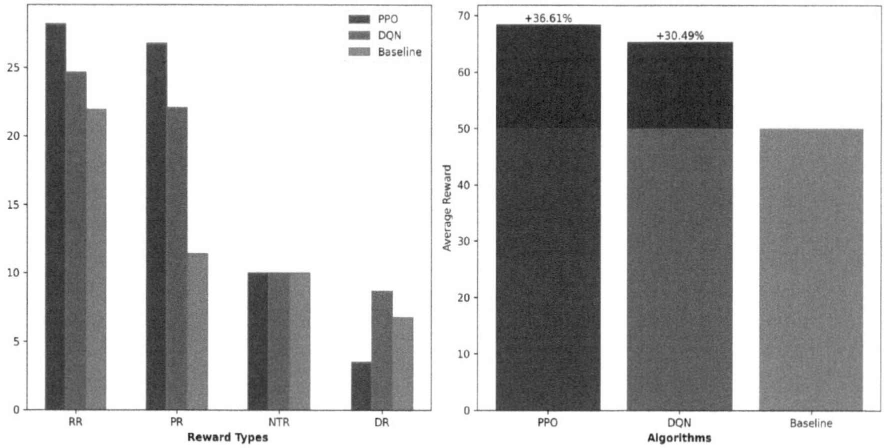


**Fig. 1.** Comparison of algorithms PPO and DQN, along with a random baseline, across four different reward functions (RR - Relevance Reward, PR - Progress Reward, NTR - New Task Reward, DR - Difficulty Reward) in the left bar charts. The right bar chart illustrates the cumulative reward comparison for PPO, DQN, and the baseline

## 5 Discussion

In this study, we introduced a RL-based recommendation system designed to support students in achieving ILOs. Our results showcase the system's efficacy, with the PPO algorithm outperforming a random baseline by 36.61%, and the DQN algorithm also showing a commendable performance improvement of 30.49% over the baseline. These findings highlight the practical utility of our approach in personalizing learning experiences.

Despite the promising outcomes, the reliance on expert-classified data introduces a potential for errors or subjective biases, suggesting a need for future studies to involve multiple independent raters to enhance the classification's reliability. A further limitation noted is the selection bias introduced by utilizing all tasks from a specific module as the recommendation pool. This approach does not account for the entire spectrum of possible tasks, potentially skewing the algorithms' performance when faced with a completely different set of tasks. Acknowledging this, future work should investigate the system's robustness and performance across a broader range of tasks, ensuring its effectiveness in universally enhancing learning outcomes. The results of this study, derived from a simulated environment, underscore the need for real-world testing to validate the RL-based system's effectiveness in actual educational settings. Conducting practical tests will be crucial for future work to identify potential challenges and confirm the system's impact on learning outcomes. Unlike related studies, such as [12], which base recommendations on statistical analyses, our approach provides the capability to recommend tasks for which no outcome data is available. Furthermore, the adaptability of the proposed methods, such as BKT and taxonomy classification, suggests broader applicability to diverse domains, opening avenues for future research. It is conceivable to extend this approach to create a generalized mathematics recommendation system suitable for various academic modules with distinct ILOs. Although our approach requires the classification of learning materials based on concepts and taxonomy levels, which poses a scalability challenge, it uniquely allows for module-transcendent use of these materials. In contrast to systems that recommend learning materials tailored to specific skills, our method enables a more individual selection of materials aligned with course-specific learning objectives. This facilitates contributions from multiple stakeholders, such as instructors, who can add to a shared pool of resources that others may use effectively.

## 6 Conclusion

This paper introduces an effective recommendation system designed for academic settings, assisting students attaining the predefined learning objectives of a module while considering the learner's individual progress and specific preferences for challenging tasks. By comparing the PPO and DQN algorithms against a random baseline, we have shown that both algorithms are more efficient in selecting appropriate tasks, indicating the potential of RL for enhancing the relevance of educational content recommendations.

While the outcomes are encouraging, we acknowledge the study's initial reliance on simulated environments. Future work will focus on real-world applications to better understand the system's practical benefits and limitations. This step is crucial for assessing the system's real impact on student learning and for making necessary adjustments to enhance its effectiveness.

By moving towards implementing and testing in actual educational settings, we aim to validate the system's potential to personalize learning at a broader scale. This research contributes to the ongoing discussion on integrating AI in education, highlighting the importance of further exploration to fully realize its benefits.

**Acknowledgments.** The authors would like to thank the German Federal Ministry of Education and Research (BMBF) for their kind support within the project *Personalisierte Kompetenzentwicklung und hybrides KI-Mentoring* (tech4compKI) under the project id 16DHB2211.

## References


1. Abu-Rasheed, H., Weber, C., Dornhöfer, M., Fathi, M.: Pedagogically-informed implementation of reinforcement learning on knowledge graphs for context-aware learning recommendations. In: Viberg, O., Jivet, I., Muñoz-Merino, P., Perifanou, M., Papathoma, T. (eds.) EC-TEL 2023. LNCS, vol. 14200, pp. 518–523. Springer, Cham (2023). https://doi.org/10.1007/978-3-031-42682-7_35
2. Agrebi, M., Sendi, M., Abed, M.: Deep reinforcement learning for personalized recommendation of distance learning. In: Rocha, Á., Adeli, H., Reis, L.P., Costanzo, S. (eds.) WorldCIST 2019. AISC, vol. 931, pp. 597–606. Springer, Cham (2019). https://doi.org/10.1007/978-3-030-16184-2_57
3. Anderson, L.W., Krathwohl, D.R.: A Taxonomy for Learning, Teaching, and Assessing: A Revision of Bloom's Taxonomy of Educational Objectives, complete Addison Wesley Longman Inc., New York (2001)
4. Biggs, J.: Enhancing teaching through constructive alignment. Higher Educ. **32**(3), 347–364 (1996). https://doi.org/10.1007/BF00138871
5. Corbett, A.T., Anderson, J.R.: Knowledge tracing: modeling the acquisition of procedural knowledge. User Model. User-Adap. Interact. **4**(4), 253–278 (1994). https://doi.org/10.1007/BF01099821
6. Fariani, R.I., Junus, K., Santoso, H.B.: A systematic literature review on personalised learning in the higher education context. Technol. Knowl. Learn. **28**(2), 449–476 (2023). https://doi.org/10.1007/s10758-022-09628-4
7. Hillmayr, D., Ziernwald, L., Reinhold, F., Hofer, S.I., Reiss, K.M.: The potential of digital tools to enhance mathematics and science learning in secondary schools: a context-specific meta-analysis. Comput. Educ. **153**, 103897 (2020)
8. Kizilcec, R.F.: To advance AI use in education, focus on understanding educators. Int. J. Artif. Intell. Educ. **34**, 1–8 (2023)
9. Li, Q., et al.: Graph enhanced hierarchical reinforcement learning for goal-oriented learning path recommendation. In: Proceedings of the 32nd ACM International Conference on Information and Knowledge Management, pp. 1318–1327 (2023)
10. Liang, E., et al.: RLlib: abstractions for distributed reinforcement learning. https://doi.org/10.48550/arXiv.1712.09381. http://arxiv.org/abs/1712.09381
11. Mnih, V., et al.: Playing Atari with deep reinforcement learning (2013). https://doi.org/10.48550/arXiv.1312.5602. http://arxiv.org/abs/1312.5602
12. Orsoni, M., Pögelt, A., Duong-Trung, N., Benassi, M., Kravcik, M., Grüttmüller, M.: Recommending mathematical tasks based on reinforcement learning and item response theory. In: Frasson, C., Mylonas, P., Troussas, C. (eds.) ITS 2023. LNCS, vol. 13891, pp. 16–28. Springer, Cham (2023). https://doi.org/10.1007/978-3-031-32883-1_2
13. Schulman, J., Wolski, F., Dhariwal, P., Radford, A., Klimov, O.: Proximal policy optimization algorithms. https://doi.org/10.48550/arXiv.1707.06347
14. Shani, G., Brafman, R.I., Heckerman, D.: An MDP-based recommender system. J. Mach. Learn. Res. **6**, 1265–1295 (2005)
15. Tan, C., Han, R., Ye, R., Chen, K.: Adaptive learning recommendation strategy based on deep q-learning. Appl. Psychol. Meas. **44**, 251–266 (2020). https://doi.org/10.1177/0146621619858674
16. Tang, X., Chen, Y., Li, X., Liu, J., Ying, Z.: A reinforcement learning approach to personalized learning recommendation systems. Br. J. Math. Stat. Psychol. **72**, 108–135 (2019). https://doi.org/10.1111/bmsp.12144. https://onlinelibrary.wiley.com/doi/abs/10.1111/bmsp.12144

17. Towers, M., et al.: Gymnasium, March 2023. https://doi.org/10.5281/zenodo.8127026. https://zenodo.org/record/8127025
18. Uther, W.: Markov decision processes. In: Sammut, C., Webb, G.I. (eds.) Encyclopedia of Machine Learning, pp. 642–646. Springer, New York (2010). https://doi.org/10.1007/978-0-387-30164-8_512

# Developing Conversational Intelligent Tutoring for Speaking Skills in Second Language Learning

Jeongmin Lee[1,2], Jin-Xia Huang[1,2](✉), Minsoo Cho[3], Yoon-Hyung Roh[1], Oh-Woog Kwon[1], and Yunkeun Lee[1]

[1] Electronics and Telecommunications Research Institute (ETRI), Daejeon, Korea
{faraway,hgh,yhroh,ohwoog,yklee}@etri.re.kr
[2] University of Science and Technology (UST), Daejeon, Korea
[3] Hyundai Motor Group, Seoul, Korea
minsoocho@hyundai.com

**Abstract.** In this study, we introduce a Conversational Intelligent Tutoring System designed to create an interactive and immersive learning experience aimed at improving the speaking abilities of second language learners. This system mimics a human tutor by engaging in role-play dialogues with the learner, based on predefined scenarios, and offers corrective feedback on the learners' utterance, while also engaging in chat to encourage student participation. The tutoring system includes a deep-learning classifier to assess students' utterances, a dialogue generator customized for responding to students' free-form chats, and a straightforward dialogue manager to determine the sequence of conversational turns. To tackle the challenge posed by the scarcity of tutoring dialogue resources, a significant hurdle for deep learning methods, we present a cost-effective approach that efficiently extends existing Korean dialogue datasets for the purpose of intelligent language tutoring. We carried out a series of experiments to compare various fine-tuned models based on language models of different sizes, and included a comparative analysis with ChatGPT. We discovered that smaller, specialized, fine-tuned models can either surpass or match the performance of GPT-4 in specific tutoring applications. Given the educational sector's demand for cost-effective solutions, our contributions, spanning system design, dataset development, and comparative analysis, serve as valuable references to address these needs.

**Keywords:** Conversational Intelligent Tutoring Systems · Second language learning · Generative AI for tutoring · Cost-effective Language Tutoring

---

J. Lee and J.-X. Huang—These authors equally contributed to this work.
M. Cho—This study was conducted while the author was affiliated with ETRI.


A. Sifaleras and F. Lin (Eds.): ITS 2024, LNCS 14798, pp. 131–148, 2024.
https://doi.org/10.1007/978-3-031-63028-6_11

## 1 Introduction

Conversational Intelligent Tutoring Systems (CITS) strive to replicate the experience of human tutors by conducting personalized one-on-one tutorial conversations tailored to an individual's needs. They provide immediate, human-like feedback on errors, misunderstandings, or misconceptions. CITS mostly adopt a goal-oriented dialogue architecture, facilitating error detection and correction for learners [1–3]. However, their specificity in objectives leads to inflexibility, risking the learning experience when users diverge from set scenarios [3, 4]. Additionally, the structured design of goal-oriented dialogue systems, which involves natural language understanding through detecting user intents, managing dialogue by predicting dialogue acts and states tracking, and generating responses, complicates educational content updates, potentially elevating maintenance costs [5]. As an alternative, although still in their infancy, open-domain dialogue systems, commonly referred to as chatbots, are also utilized in speaking education for second language learners [6, 7]. However, CITS aim to achieve specific learning goals through designated scenarios, and chatbot systems cannot achieve this purpose. In addition, they show limitations in assessing student errors and providing feedback.

In recent years, the development of large-scale language models (LLM) with billions to hundreds of billions of parameters has empowered these models to exhibit excellent performance across various tasks, marking significant progress in the field of natural language processing. ChatGPT [8] and similar AI-driven technologies have made significant strides in the field of education, offering personalized learning experiences, instant feedback, and interactive learning opportunities.

In this paper, using the latest LLM development, we aim to build a CITS through a simple system architecture, and offer learners flexible dialogue tutoring to improve second language learners' speaking skills. The system conducts dialogues with users through role-play according to given scenarios, assessing learners' responses, offering corrective feedback, while providing opportunities for spontaneous and free-flowing conversations.

Our contributions are as follows:

1) We present a streamlined system architecture for CITS designed for rapid implementation: a classifier to assess students' utterances, a dialogue generator specifically developed to produce responses to students' free-form chats, and a straightforward dialogue management module responsible for selecting the system's subsequent utterance types and navigating the dialogue in alignment with predefined scenarios.
2) We introduce an approach to leverage existing dialogue datasets for the swift and cost-effective creation of tutoring dialogue datasets. This approach addresses the notable scarcity of tutoring dialogue data necessary for training deep learning models, a significant barrier to the rapid adoption of state-of-the-art NLP technologies in the educational sector.
3) We conducted comprehensive experiments to evaluate a spectrum of fine-tuned models derived from language models with varying sizes, spanning from about half a billion to 13 billion parameters, incorporating a comparative analysis with ChatGPT (both GPT-3.5 and GPT-4). This series of experiments has shown that our efficient model stacks up against ChatGPT.

## 2 Related Work

### 2.1 Conversational Intelligent Tutoring Systems

Research into Intelligent Tutoring Systems (ITS) has continuously evolved. The language tutor plays a role similar to a language parent [9], promoting natural dialogue, creating situations sometimes resembling conversations with friends, and making efforts to understand learners' speech beyond their language proficiency level. At times, they are designed to mimic human tutors in encouraging learning motivation through free conversation [10].

AI and deep learning-powered ITS have drastically transformed tailored learning experiences across various educational domains, including programming education [11, 12], clinical or medical training [13, 14] and mental therapy [15, 16] like cognitive-behavioral therapy (CBT), influencing student achievements significantly [17]. By harnessing the power of AI and language models, these systems have significantly improved personalized learning across various fields. They foster better student performance in interactive and efficient learning environments, especially in case of CITS [6, 18, 19].

In the domain of CITS, existing research has predominantly utilized rule-based or goal-oriented dialogue systems, which are augmented with domain knowledge meticulously crafted by humans [2, 20, 21]. Goal oriented dialogue systems are designed to accomplish one or several specific tasks [22], including making restaurant, hotel, or taxi reservations [23], or providing movie recommendations [24, 25]. Open-domain dialogue systems, also known as chit-chat models, can be utilized for language learning. Their objective is to engage users in conversation and maintain interest through dynamic and captivating chats [4, 22].

In the realm of speaking tutoring, achieving educational objectives is crucial, a domain where goal-oriented dialogue systems shine. These systems are complemented by chit-chat systems, known for facilitating natural interactions with students. Numerous studies have underscored the importance of increased interactivity for students learning languages through free-form conversations, thus supporting the adoption of hybrid systems [4].

Moreover, CITS must accurately assess the correctness of human responses in order to provide relevant hints or feedback [1, 26]. AI dialogue systems are currently unable to meet these critical requirements, essential for acting as complete substitutes for real-life language instructors [27].

### 2.2 LLM-Integrated Second Language Learning

The era of language model advancements significantly contributes to language learning by providing access to abundant language data, personalized learning experiences [28, 29] improved language proficiency [30, 31], 24/7 accessibility [32, 33] supplementary learning tools, natural language generation [34] and effective feedback mechanisms [35].

In the domain of Large Language Models (LLM), ChatGPT has garnered significant attention for its accessibility. It is widely used for personal writing assistance and has quickly become integrated into Duolingo and other conversational educational systems [3, 36], owing to its proficiency in dialogue and feedback generation. Numerous researchers have undertaken comparative experiments involving ChatGPT to assess its capabilities in the educational sector [37, 38].

### 2.3 Dialogue Datasets for Deep Learning-Based Second Language Tutoring

Developing an CITS for language tutoring requires a specific dataset for training dialogue models. While traditional educational materials offer quality, their quantity may fall short for adequately training deep learning-based dialogue models.

DREAM [39] and CoQA [40], conversation-based Question-Answering datasets featuring multi-choice options and structured correct answers, respectively, have been employed for educational purposes owing to their organized format.

Tutoring conversations differ from general conversations in that students may provide answers that are not always correct. The tutoring system must evaluate these responses and offer appropriate feedback [22, 26]. However, achieving this requires additional annotations and educational feedback in tutoring dialogue datasets, incurring high costs.

DIRECT [26] and CIMA [22] are tutoring dialogue datasets enriched with additional annotations for both student and tutor utterances. They cater to reading comprehension for English learners and vocabulary acquisition in Italian for English speakers, respectively.

## 3 KORLINGS Dataset Construction

We aimed to create a tutoring dialogue dataset KORLINGS (Korean Language Speaking) specifically tailored for Korean as a Foreign Language (KFL) education with a focus on speaking skills. Our goal was to quickly and efficiently construct tutoring dialogue datasets in an economical manner. The method was to expand the existing dialogue dataset suitable for KFL learners.

### 3.1 Tutoring Dialogues with Annotations

We utilized an existing sentence-aligned multilingual dataset covering English, Korean, Japanese, and Chinese, initially created for machine translation purposes. This dataset was chosen due to its coverage of conversations in various scenarios such as travel, shopping, transportation, accommodation, restaurants, emergencies, etc., making it well-suited for foreign language teaching. Our dataset construction solely incorporated the Korean portion.

Following a real-world teaching approach, we envision the tutoring scenario as follows: students first learn a predefined dialogue scenario and then engage in role-play with an AI tutor. During this interaction, students may make common mistakes typical of second language learners. The tutor provides corrections to guide the student in rephrasing the utterance, allowing the conversation to progress. To simulate an educational environment resembling interactions between a human tutor and a student, we assumed that participants might occasionally engage in free-form chats outside the predefined scenario. Each dialogue encompasses three types of turns:

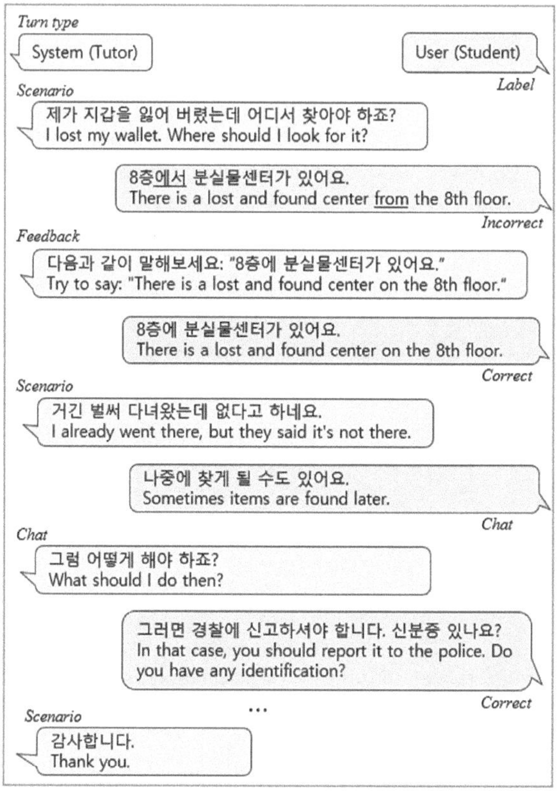


**Fig. 1.** Illustration of a multi-turn interaction between a student and a tutor.

*Scenario* Type: In this type, the tutor or student follows a given scenario. For tutor utterances, a *scenario* type would be added as an annotation. For student utterances, an annotation with a *correct* or *incorrect* label will be added, indicating whether students articulate a given scenario appropriately.
*Feedback* Type: This type pertains to a tutor utterance aimed at eliciting correct expressions when students fail to articulate the scenario type accurately.
*Chat* Type: This type is for the utterances outside of the predefined scenarios during the conversation.

Turn types are incorporated into tutor utterances, and labels are assigned to student utterances. An illustration of the dialogue scenario between the tutor and a student is depicted in Fig. 1. The utterances labeled with *Scenario* and *Correct* annotations are derived from existing scenarios. While those labeled with *Feedback*, *Chat*, and *Incorrect* annotations are newly constructed.

### 3.2 Dataset Statistics

The statistics for the multi-turn dialogues in the KORLINGS dataset are presented in Table 1. The "Dialogue" and "Scenario Turn" data are sourced from an existing bilingual dataset. The "Tutoring Turn" comprises the extended dataset, augmented with student incorrect utterances, tutor feedback, and chats, and is specifically employed in our study. A single turn encompasses a maximum of two utterances exchanged between the tutor and the student.

**Table 1.** Statistics of the KORLINGS dataset.

| | Train | Valid | Test | Total |
|---|---|---|---|---|
| Dialogue # | 3,483 | 398 | 398 | 4,279 |
| Scenario Turn # | 17,415 | 1,990 | 1,990 | 21,395 |
| Avg. turns | 5 | 5 | 5 | 5 |
| Tutoring Turn # | 26,645 | 3,105 | 3,107 | 32,857 |
| Avg. turns | 7.65 | 7.80 | 7.81 | 7.68 |

We adopted user utterances in tutoring turns labeled as *correct*, *incorrect*, and *chat* from the dataset above for user utterance assessment, using the existing scenario turns as the golden standard (Table 2).

**Table 2.** Distribution statistics of labels for student utterances assessment

| Labels | Train | Valid | Test | Total |
|---|---|---|---|---|
| Correct | 12,973 | 1,360 | 1,372 | 15,705 |
| Incorrect | 7,013 | 737 | 743 | 8,493 |
| Chat | 4,119 | 830 | 805 | 5,754 |
| Total | 24,105 | 2,927 | 2,920 | 29,952 |

Table 3 shows that correct pairs allowed variations in student utterances, while incorrect pairs included grammatical errors or missing key information. Chats referred to cases where utterances deviated from the expected sentence in the given scenario.

**Table 3.** Comparison of Student Utterances in Tutoring Turns to the Golden Standard

| Label | Student utterance | Golden standard |
|---|---|---|
| Correct | 관람 시간이 언제까지입니까?<br>Until when is the viewing time? | 몇 시까지 관람할 수 있습니까?<br>Until what time can I view it? |
| Incorrect | 네, 펜은 어디든 있나요?<br>Yes, is the pen anywhere? | 네, 펜은 어디에 있나요?<br>Yes, where is the pen? |
| Chat | 펜이 나오지 않아요.<br>The pen isn't coming out. | 이렇게 쓰는 것이 맞습니까?<br>Is this the correct way to write? |

### 3.3 Dataset for Generation

Below is an illustration of the statistics of dialogue datasets for the generative model. The statistics for the dialogue dataset for generation is summarized in Table 4. To utilize high-quality training data, we filtered out data with a length of less than 18 characters, which accounts for about 30% of the total dataset. The statistics of the refined dataset for tutor utterance generation through these processes are as follows:

**Table 4.** Statistics of dialogue dataset for generation

| Train | Valid | Test | Total |
|---|---|---|---|
| 25,274 | 3,200 | 4,393 | 32,867 |

## 4 Development

### 4.1 System Design

The system comprises two key components, featuring a straightforward dialogue manager: a classifier for assessing the learner's utterance and a generator for responding to the learner's chats.

The system flow is relatively simple, especially when compared to previous goal-oriented dialogue systems for language tutoring (refer to Fig. 2). Upon receiving a learner's utterance, it is classified as correct, incorrect, or chat. If the user's utterance is deemed correct, the system outputs the next scenario utterance. In the case of an incorrect utterance, the system provides corrective feedback to guide the learner towards the correct answer. For chat-type utterances, the dialogue generator produces an appropriate response to steer the conversation back to the predefined scenario.

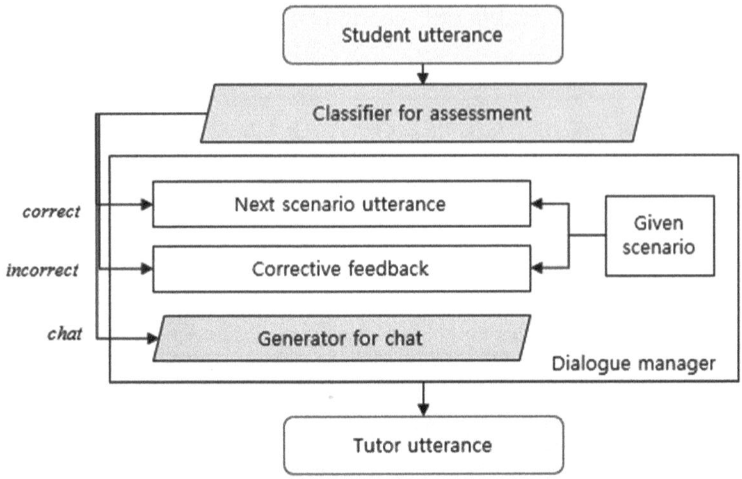


**Fig. 2.** Simplified conceptual schema of the CITS

### 4.2 Implementation

**Classifier and Generator.** Both the classifier for assessing student utterances and the chat response generator (Fig. 2) were implemented using the fine-tuning language model approach. We trained the classifier and generator using pretrained language models of various sizes:

**Mini LM: About 0.2B.** We utilized the compact dialog model eT5-chat [41] as our mini-sized base model. The eT5[1] model, trained on an extensive 136GB corpus comprising Korean Wikipedia articles, newspaper texts, broadcast transcripts, and scripts from movies and dramas, is adept at understanding and generating text. The eT5-chat model was fine-tuned from the eT5-base model using approximately 2 million chat turns (equivalent to around 5.4 million utterances) of conversational data.

**Small LM: Up to 13B.** Small language models (SLMs) have gained attention alongside ChatGPT due to their efficiency and effectiveness in various tasks. While ChatGPT excels in generating rich text, SLMs, with their smaller size, offer a resource-efficient alternative for applications with limited computational resources.

After conducting several preliminary experiments and examining recent trends in Korean language LLMs on the open-ko-llm-leaderboard[2], we have chosen the following models for our study: polyglot_ko-5.8B[3], polyglot_ko-12.8B[4], Kullm-12.8B[5], Llama-2-ko-DPO-13B[6]. The Llama-2-ko-DPO model is a version in which Korean

[1] https://aiopen.etri.re.kr/et5Model.
[2] https://huggingface.co/spaces/upstage/open-ko-llm-leaderboard.
[3] https://huggingface.co/EleutherAI/polyglot-ko-5.8b.
[4] https://huggingface.co/EleutherAI/polyglot-ko-12.8b.
[5] https://huggingface.co/nlpai-lab/kullm-polyglot-12.8b-v2.
[6] https://huggingface.co/daekeun-ml/Llama-2-ko-DPO-13B.

text is instruction-tuned on the Llama-2-13B model utilizing the Direct Preference Optimization (DPO) method [42].

**Advanced GPT Models: GPT-3.5 and GPT-4.** While ChatGPT excels in numerous tasks, its larger parameter counts poses challenges for fine-tuning on specific tasks. In our study, we employed ChatGPT as a benchmark for comparative analysis. Experiments were conducted using OpenAI's APIs, with the utilized models being GPT-4 (gpt-4-1106-preview) and GPT-3.5 (gpt-3.5-turbo).

**Simple Dialogue Manager.** The dialogue manager, simpler than traditional systems, selects turn types based on classification results and generates tutor responses using a straightforward policy.

We enforce a policy allowing students a maximum of two incorrect responses in their utterances. Initially, corrective feedback is given after the first incorrect response. If a second incorrect response occurs, the system provides the correct answer and progresses to the next scenario. Alternatively, the system proceeds to the next utterance or engages in a chat.

Let $L_t$ be the student assessment result, $T_t$ denote the tutor turn type at time $t$, and $T_{t-1}$ represent the tutor turn type in the preceding turn, we have,

$$T_t = \begin{cases} Chat, & \forall L_t = Chat \\ Feedback, & \forall L_t = Incorrect,\ and,\ T_{t-1} \neq Feedback \\ Scenario,\ or\ Chat, & otherwise \end{cases} \quad (1)$$

# 5 Experiment

## 5.1 Evaluation Criteria

We performed prediction experiments involving three primary model categories: eT5, SLMs, and ChatGPT. The classification results for student utterance assessment were evaluated based on Accuracy, Precision, Recall, and F1 scores. The generation results for the tutor utterances were assessed using the following metrics:

**SacreBLEU [43].** BLEU score is calculated based on the precision of matching n-grams (contiguous sequences of n items, typically words) between the candidate and reference sentences [44]. SacreBLEU is designed to standardize and facilitate the consistent computation of BLEU scores.

**METEOR [45]** is one of the metrics used to measure the performance of translation and models at the sentence level. METEOR is based on the harmonic mean of unigram precision and recall.

**ROUGE-L [46].** ROUGE is one of the metrics utilized for assessing model performance in automatic summarization, and involves the unigram (1), bigram (2), and longest substring length ratio (L). ROUGE-L is based on the ratio of the length of the longest common subsequence emphasizing semantic matching.

**Semantic Textual Similarity (STS) [47].** STS is one of the semantic similarity measurements, converting each sentence into a fixed-size vectors with a sentence transformer to measure the cosine similarity between sentence vectors.

## 5.2 Evaluation Results

**Classification Results.** We fine-tuned the eT5-chat and the SLMs using the dataset presented in Table 2. For the fine-tuning and prediction phases, SLMs consistently used the "#classification" instruction, which yielded improved performances. Conversely, the GPT models employed a specialized prompt for classification, detailed in the Appendix. As shown in Table 5, the eT5-chat model, after fine-tuning, achieved the highest accuracy, significantly outperforming the GPT models and the fine-tuned SLMs.

Despite conducting a range of experiments to refine prompts, instances of misclassification occurred in both SLMs and the GPT models, yielding responses that deviated from the predefined categories of correct, incorrect, or chat (for instance, receiving compound responses such as "correct, chat"). These inaccuracies led to a decline in overall performance, adversely affecting accuracy and other evaluation metrics.

**Table 5.** Evaluation results of classifiers for assessing student utterances.

| Base model | Accuracy | Precision | Recall | F1 score |
|---|---|---|---|---|
| eT5-chat | **93.14%** | **92.97%** | **93.05%** | **93.01%** |
| Polyglot_ko-5.8B | 85.14% | 63.81% | 64.89% | 64.18% |
| Polyglot_ko-12.8B | 61.58% | 52.26% | 54.07% | 48.05% |
| Kullm-12.8B | 81.16% | 60.38% | 62.02% | 60.73% |
| Llama-2-ko-DPO-13B | 83.94% | 84.29% | 84.34% | 83.36% |
| GPT-4 | 79.83% | 56.92% | 60.79% | 57.88% |
| GPT-3.5 | 60.72% | 39.33% | 44.87% | 39.80% |

**Generation Results.** We fine-tuned the eT5-chat and the SLMs using the dataset presented in Table 4. Table 6 shows that evaluations using the ROUGE-L word pair matching matrix and semantic text similarity measures from Sentence Transformers (STS) demonstrated comparable performance between fine-tuned SLMs and GPT models, with the fine-tuned mini-LM falling short. In contrast, performance assessments with SacreBLEU and METEOR highlighted the dominance of fine-tuned SLMs.

In terms of overall performance in the generated results, the model fined-tuned with base model Llama-2-ko-DPO-13B exhibited the highest performance over all evaluation matrix, indicating the dominance of models fine-tuned based on SLMs.

## 5.3 Human Evaluation

A human evaluation was conducted to validate the interpretation of quantitative evaluation results. Human evaluation was conducted for models that demonstrated excellent

**Table 6.** Evaluation results of generators for tutor utterance generation

| Base Model | SacreBLEU | METEOR | ROUGE-L | STS |
|---|---|---|---|---|
| eT5-chat | 2.1160 | 14.0428 | 0.6926 | 0.3933 |
| Polyglot_ko-5.8B | 3.2437 | 16.8004 | 0.9056 | 0.4272 |
| Polyglot_ko-12.8B | 3.3489 | 16.4451 | 1.0401 | 0.4231 |
| Kullm-12.8B | 3.4600 | 16.6660 | 1.0075 | 0.4272 |
| Llama-2-ko-DPO-13B | **3.5605** | **17.0900** | **1.2085** | **0.4388** |
| GPT-3.5 | 0.7469 | 13.3495 | 1.0488 | 0.4329 |
| GPT-4 | 1.3196 | 14.6357 | 1.1626 | 0.4341 |

performance in each category, specifically fine-tuned eT5-chat, Llama-2-ko-DPO-13B, and GPT-4 To ensure evaluation quality and consistency, two raters assessed system utterances across a randomly selected sample of 100 dialogues, 1106 turns. To prevent bias, we provided the raters with anonymity, randomly labeling the models as A, B and C. In the initial stages, raters engaged in several discussions, developing a detailed manual with examples to clarify criteria. After assessing the examples, an independent evaluation commenced.

The evaluation criteria consist of three aspects: sensibleness, specificity, and difficulty. Sensibleness and specificity are commonly used in human evaluations of open-domain dialogue systems [48]. Sensibleness measures whether the response aligns with the context of the conversation, while the specificity evaluates the specificity of the utterance. We also incorporate difficulty as a primary criterion for conversational tutoring, specifically in relation to the student's level [49]. In our evaluation, we assume that the difficulty level of the scenario presented aligns with the student's level. Therefore, utterances that deviate from 50 to 200% of the average length of the golden standards in the given scenarios were deemed to not meet the appropriate difficulty criteria. Additionally, the choice of lexicons and expressions should also be taken into account for evaluating difficulty.

Evaluators assessed whether the generated sentences were contextually sensible, specific to the given situation rather than general, and had an appropriate length in relation to the overall difficulty of the dialogue. Each aspect was rated on a scale of 0 or 1 based on the evaluators' judgment of the entire context of the preceding conversation. The scores for all three criteria were then summed up for each model, resulting in an overall score ranging from 0 to 3.

Figure 3 represents the distribution of overall scores after evaluation. Reviewing the proportion of overall scores of 3 each model attained, which indicates fulfillment of all three criteria—sensibleness, specificity, and difficulty—the fine-tuned model utilizing Llama-2-ko-DPO-13B achieved a rate of 53.39%, surpassing the GPT-4 model by more than 10%.

Figure 4 illustrates the human evaluation results by criteria. The results are averaged across two raters for each model, and the overall average is denoted as overall. For the

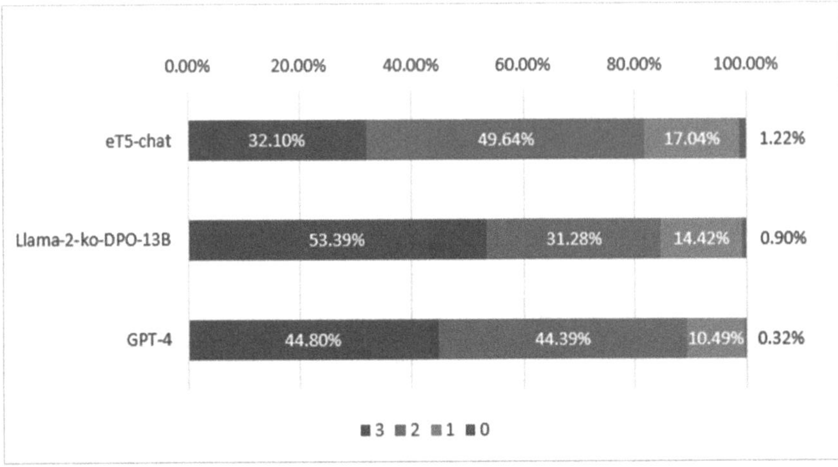


**Fig. 3.** Distribution of overall evaluation scores (0–3) for each model.

sensibleness score, Llama-2-ko-DPO-13B shows a slight advantage, followed by GPT-4, while eT5-chat has a significantly lower performance. This is due to eT5-chat based model responding to the student's utterance by merely echoing a question or repeating the same utterances without considering the preceding conversation context.

In terms of specificity score, GPT-4 surpasses others by more than 10%, followed by eT5-chat and Llama-2-ko-DPO-13B based fine-tuned models. This is because the two fine-tuned models are more inclined to produce generic responses (such as "Yes," "Understood," and "Thank you.") compared to GPT-4, which slightly reduces the specificity score.

Assessing the difficulty of the conversation based on the overall dialogue level, the fine-tuned model based on Llama-2-ko-DPO-13B marginally leads, followed by eT5-chat, and GPT-4 exhibits a performance roughly 20% lower than theirs. The difficulty is evaluated on both ends, encompassing both overly difficult and overly easy responses. The average sentence length for the golden standard was 21.72, whereas eT5-chat had a length of 20.16, Llama-2-ko-DPO-13B had a length of 13.98, and GPT-4 had a length of 34.91. In other words, while eT5-chat generated sentences of similar length to the golden standard, Llama-2-ko-DPO-13B and GPT-4 produced sentences that were relatively shorter or longer, respectively. The reason for the relatively low score of GPT-4 is its tendency to generate sentences that are too long compared to the conversation level, despite including "response briefly" in the prompt.

Cohen's Kappa inter-rater reliability between the two raters score of K = 0.4177. The human evaluation outcomes aligned with the quantitative evaluation results in Table 6.

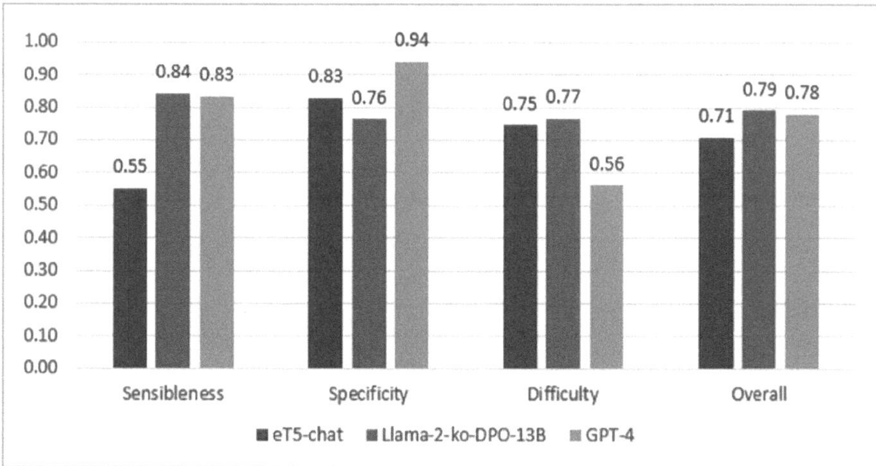


**Fig. 4.** Human Evaluation Results Based on Three Criteria with an Overall Score Scaled to 1

# 6 Conclusion

Our research presents a Conversational Intelligent Tutoring System (CITS) aimed at improving second language learners' speaking skills through immersive experiences. The simplified architecture of CITS, comprising a classifier, dialogue generator, and intuitive dialogue manager, expedites implementation by integrating generative models into the tutoring domain. Addressing the challenge of limited tutoring dialogue resources, we propose a cost-effective approach leveraging existing dialogue datasets, thereby enabling the efficient creation of tutoring dialogue datasets.

Comprehensive experiments, including human evaluation, have been conducted to assess the performance of GPT-4 and fine-tuned models in educational tutoring settings. The evaluation results reveal that although GPT-4 exhibits strong sensibleness and specificity, it faces challenges in aligning difficulty levels with those of individual students, thereby impeding its seamless application in tutoring. In contrast, fine-tuned models based on smaller language models may face difficulties in generating sensible responses or maintaining specificity. Nevertheless, they exhibit effective control over difficulty levels and have demonstrated the potential to either match or surpass GPT-4's performance within specific data domains.

The ongoing need for cost-effective and controllable solutions that can readily adapt user specificity remains critical, particularly within the education sector, given the diverse range of students across various grades and proficiency levels. Our study provides valuable insights and practical guidance for developers grappling with similar challenges in educational systems.

Our experiment focused on a conversational tutoring system for Korean as a Foreign Language (KFL), yet the implementation approach is language-independent. As part of future work, we aim to swiftly extend our research to other language tutoring, facilitated by the multilingual nature of the base dialogue dataset. Additionally, a usability evaluation with a real student group is necessary for further investigation.

**Acknowledgments.** This work was supported by Institute of Information & Communications Technology Planning & Evaluation (IITP) grant funded by the Korea government (MSIT) (2019-0-00004, Development of semi-supervised learning language intelligence technology and Korean tutoring service for foreigners).

**Disclosure of Interests.** The authors have no competing interests to declare that are relevant to the content of this article.

# Appendix

In contrast to the trends in existing language models, the importance of prompt engineering has surged in the LLMs era. This has ushered in an era where even non-developers can easily achieve desired results. However, prompt engineering is still considered a temporary solution applicable only to specific tasks [50]. Although LLMs demonstrate outstanding performance in natural language interactions, crafting appropriate prompts to consistently induce desired results remains a challenging task. Even in the field of

**Table 7.** The refined prompts adopted for the GPT-3.5 and GPT-4 models in our experiments.

| | |
|---|---|
| Classification | `## instruction`<br>`We are in the Korean speaking education.`<br>`Please compare the two given sentences and classify them as correct, incorrect, or chat.`<br>`A is the correct sentence, and B is the sentence for comparison.`<br><br>`## rules`<br>`just select one in correct, incorrect or chat, and print only the results of classification.`<br>`1. correct - if B is semantically and grammatically correct compared to A. they don't have to be exactly same.`<br>`2. incorrect - if B is semantically and grammatically incorrect compared to A but relevant to A.`<br>`3. chat - if two sentences are not relevant.`<br><br>`## two sentences`<br>`A. {}`<br>`B. {}` |
| generation | `## instruction`<br>`You are engaged in role-playing Korean speaking education for second language foreigners.`<br>`Refer to the previous conversation history of <spk1> and <spk2>, and response briefly in Korean to the last utterance.`<br>`Do not output tokens for <spk1> and <spk2>.`<br><br>`## previous conversation`<br>`{}` |

education, various stakeholders, including teachers and students, attempt prompt crafting. However, despite the high performance of LLMs, prompt engineering is not an easy task [51]. Consequently, prompt engineering still has ad hoc and subjective aspects in the current context [52].

Recognizing these limitations, we used prompt engineering to craft prompts and derive optimal results from ChatGPT. The finalized prompts are as follows (Table 7).

## References


1. Alkhatlan, A., Kalita, J.: Intelligent tutoring systems: a comprehensive historical survey with recent developments. arXiv preprint arXiv:1812.09628 (2018)
2. Kwon, O.W., Kim, Y.K., Lee, Y.: Task graph based task-oriented dialogue system using dialogue map for second language learning. In: Taalas, P., Jalkanen, J., Bradley, L., Thouësny, S. (eds.) Future-Proof CALL: Language Learning as Exploration and Encounters – Short Papers from EUROCALL 2018, pp. 153–159 (2018)
3. Sosnowski, T., Abuazizeh, M., Kirste, T., Yordanova, K.: Development of a conversational agent for tutoring nursing students to interact with patients. In: Frasson, C., Mylonas, P., Troussas, C. (eds.) ITS 2023. LNCS, vol. 13891, pp. 171–182. Springer, Cham (2023). https://doi.org/10.1007/978-3-031-32883-1_15
4. Huang, J.X., Lee, K.S., Kwon, O.W., Kim, Y.K.: A chatbot for a dialogue-based second language learning system. In: CALL in a Climate of Change: Adapting to Turbulent Global Conditions–Short Papers from EUROCALL, pp. 151–156 (2017)
5. Aliakbari, M., Jamalvandi, B.: The Impact of 'role play' on fostering EFL learners' speaking ability; a task-based approach. J. Pan-Pac. Assoc. Appl. Linguist. **14**(1), 15–29 (2010)
6. Aljameel, S.S., O'Shea, J.D., Crockett, K.A., Latham, A., Kaleem, M.: Development of an Arabic conversational intelligent tutoring system for education of children with ASD. In: 2017 IEEE International Conference on Computational Intelligence and Virtual Environments for Measurement Systems and Applications (CIVEMSA), pp. 24–29, June 2017. https://doi.org/10.1109/CIVEMSA.2017.7995296
7. Fryer, L.K., Coniam, D., Carpenter, R., Lăpuşneanu, D.: Bots for language learning now: current and future directions. Lang. Learn. Technol. **24**(2), 8–22 (2020). http://hdl.handle.net/10125/44719
8. OpenAI: GPT-3: Generative Pretrained Transformer, vol. 3 (2021). https://beta.openai.com/docs/models/gpt-3
9. Lonsdale, C.: The Third Ear (2006)
10. Mikic, F.A., Burguillo, J.C., Llamas, M., Rodríguez, D.A., Rodríguez, E.: CHARLIE: an AIML-based chatterbot which works as an interface among ines and humans. In: 2009 EAEEIE Annual Conference, pp. 1–6. IEEE, June 2009
11. Crow, T., Luxton-Reilly, A., Wuensche, B.: Intelligent tutoring systems for programming education: a systematic review. In: Proceedings of the 20th Australasian Computing Education Conference, pp. 53–62, January 2018
12. Litovkin, D., Anikin, A., Kulyukin, K., Sychev, O.: Intelligent tutor for designing function interface in a programming language. In: Crossley, S., Popescu, E. (eds.) ITS 2022. LNCS, vol. 13284, pp. 293–302. Springer, Cham (2022). https://doi.org/10.1007/978-3-031-09680-8_27
13. Freedman, R., Edwards, L., Sullivan, I., Brockmann, A., LaBarbera, D., Naples, V.: Teaching cardiovascular physiology with a minigame-based ITS. In: Frasson, C., Mylonas, P., Troussas, C. (eds.) ITS 2023. LNCS, vol. 13891, pp. 137–146. Springer, Cham (2023). https://doi.org/10.1007/978-3-031-32883-1_12

14. Huang, X., Li, S., Lajoie, S.P.: The relative importance of cognitive and behavioral engagement to task performance in self-regulated learning with an intelligent tutoring system. In: Frasson, C., Mylonas, P., Troussas, C. (eds.) ITS 2023. LNCS, vol. 13891, pp. 430–441. Springer, Cham (2023). https://doi.org/10.1007/978-3-031-32883-1_39
15. Salhi, I., El Guemmat, K., Qbadou, M., Mansouri, K.: Towards developing a pocket therapist: an intelligent adaptive psychological support chatbot against mental health disorders in a pandemic situation. Indones. J. Electr. Eng. Comput. Sci. **23**(2), 1200–1211 (2021)
16. Yin, J., Chen, Z., Zhou, K., Yu, C.: A deep learning based chatbot for campus psychological therapy. arXiv preprint arXiv:1910.06707 (2019)
17. Akyuz, Y.: Effects of intelligent tutoring systems (ITS) on personalized learning (PL). Creat. Educ. **11**(6), 953–978 (2020)
18. Tegos, S., Demetriadis, S., Tsiatsos, T.: A configurable conversational agent to trigger students' productive dialogue: a pilot study in the CALL domain. Int. J. Artif. Intell. Educ. **24**, 62–91 (2014)
19. Kaiss, W., Mansouri, K., Poirier, F.: Pre-Evaluation with a personalized feedback conversational agent integrated in Moodle. Int. J. Emerg. Technol. Learn. **18**(6), 177–189 (2023). https://doi.org/10.3991/ijet.v18i06.36783
20. Rus, V., Niraula, N.B., Banjade, R.: DeepTutor: an effective, online intelligent tutoring system that promotes deep learning. In: Proceedings of the Twenty-Ninth AAAI Conference on Artificial Intelligence, AAAI 2015, pp. 4294–4295. AAAI Press (2015)
21. Casas, J., Tricot, M.O., Abou Khaled, O., Mugellini, E., Cudré-Mauroux, P.: Trends & methods in chatbot evaluation. In: Companion Publication of the 2020 International Conference on Multimodal Interaction, pp. 280–286, October 2020
22. Stasaski, K., Ramanarayanan, V.: Automatic feedback generation for dialog-based language tutors using transformer models and active learning. In: 34th Conference on Neural Information Processing Systems, Vancouver, December 2020
23. Budzianowski, P., et al.: MultiWOZ - a largescale multi-domain wizard-of-Oz dataset for taskoriented dialogue modelling. In: Proceedings of the 2018 Conference on Empirical Methods in Natural Language Processing, pp. 5016–5026 (2018)
24. Yu, Z., Black, A.W., Rudnicky, A.I.: Learning conversational systems that interleave task and non-task content. In: Proceedings of the 26th International Joint Conference on Artificial Intelligence, IJCAI 2017, pp. 4214–4220. AAAI Press (2017)
25. Su, H., et al.: MovieChats: chat like humans in a closed domain. In: Proceedings of the 2020 Conference on Empirical Methods in Natural Language Processing, 16–20 November 2020, pp. 6605–6619 (2020)
26. Huang, J.X., Lee, Y., Kwon, O.W.: DIRECT: toward dialogue-based reading comprehension tutoring. IEEE Access **11**, 8978–8987 (2023). https://doi.org/10.1109/ACCESS.2022.3233224
27. Lotze, N.: Goodbye to classroom teaching? Artificial intelligence in language learning. Translation: Chris Cave. Copyright: Goethe-Institut e. V., Redaktion Magazin Sprache (2018). https://www.goethe.de/en/spr/mag/dsk/21290629.html?forceDesktop=1
28. Pardamean, B., et al.: Pengembangan portal pembelajaran online berbasis artificial intelligence dalam kerangka team-based learning, pp. 118–126, December 2020
29. Nugroho, A., Putro, N.H.P.S., Syamsi, K.: The potentials of ChatGPT for language learning: unpacking its benefits and limitations. Regist. J. **16**(2), 224–247 (2023)
30. Baskara, R.: Exploring the implications of ChatGPT for language learning in higher education. Indones. J. Engl. Lang. Teach. Appl. Linguist. **7**(2), 343–358 (2023)
31. Koraishi, O.: Teaching English in the age of AI: embracing ChatGPT to optimize EFL materials and assessment. Lang. Educ. Technol. **3**(1) (2023)

32. Huang, W., Hew, K.F., Fryer, L.K.: Chatbots for language learning—are they really useful? A systematic review of chatbot-supported language learning. J. Comput. Assist. Learn. **38**(1), 237–257 (2022). https://doi.org/10.1111/jcal.12610
33. Lai, T., et al.: Psy-LLM: scaling up global mental health psychological services with ai-based large language models. arXiv preprint arXiv:2307.11991 (2023)
34. Bonner, E., Lege, R., Frazier, E.: Large language model-based artificial intelligence in the language classroom: practical ideas for teaching. Teach. Engl. Technol. **23**(1) (2023)
35. Wang, X., et al.: MINT: evaluating LLMS in multi-turn interaction with tools and language feedback. arXiv preprint arXiv:2309.10691 (2023)
36. Duolingo Team: Introducing Duolingo Max, a Learning Experiment Powered by GPT-4, March 2023. https://blog.duolingo.com/duolingo-max/
37. Xiao, C., Xu, S.X., Zhang, K., Wang, Y., Xia, L.: Evaluating reading comprehension exercises generated by LLMs: a showcase of ChatGPT in education applications. In: Proceedings of the 18th Workshop on Innovative Use of NLP for Building Educational Applications (BEA 2023), pp. 610–625, July 2023
38. Tan, Y., et al.: Can ChatGPT replace traditional KBQA models? An in-depth analysis of the question answering performance of the GPT LLM family. In: Payne, T.R., et al. (eds.) ISWC 2023. LNCS, vol. 14265, pp. 348–367. Springer, Cham (2023). https://doi.org/10.1007/978-3-031-47240-4_19
39. Sun, K., Yu, D., Chen, J., Yu, D., Choi, Y., Cardie, C.: DREAM: a challenge data set and models for dialogue-based reading comprehension. Trans. Assoc. Comput. Linguist. **7**, 217–231 (2019)
40. Reddy, S., Chen, D., Manning, C.D.: CoQA: a conversational question answering challenge. Trans. Assoc. Comput. Linguist. **7**, 249–266 (2019)
41. Lee, J.M., Cho, M.S., Kim, H., Kwon, O.W., Huang, J.X.: Simplified chatbot for Korean language education with learner utterance classification and dialogue generation models. In: Proceedings of the Korean Information Science Society Conference, Jeju, South Korea, pp. 917–919 (2023)
42. Rafailov, R., Sharma, A., Mitchell, E., Ermon, S., Manning, C.D., Finn, C.: Direct preference optimization: your language model is secretly a reward model. arXiv preprint arXiv:2305.18290 (2023)
43. Post, M.: A call for clarity in reporting BLEU scores. In: Proceedings of the Third Conference on Machine Translation: Research Papers, Brussels, Belgium, pp. 186–191. Association for Computational Linguistics (2018)
44. Papineni, K., Roukos, S., Ward, T., Zhu, W.J.: BLEU: a method for automatic evaluation of machine translation. In: Proceedings of the 40th Annual Meeting of the Association for Computational Linguistics, pp. 311–318, July 2002
45. Lavie, A., Denkowski, M.J.: The METEOR metric for automatic evaluation of machine translation. Mach. Transl. **23**, 105–115 (2009). https://doi.org/10.1007/s10590-009-9059-4
46. Lin, C.-Y., Och, F.J.: Automatic evaluation of machine translation quality using longest common subsequence and skip-bigram statistics. In: Proceedings of the 42nd Annual Meeting of the Association for Computational Linguistics (ACL 2004), Barcelona, Spain, 21–26 July 2004 (2004)
47. Reimers, N., Gurevych, I.: Sentence-BERT: sentence embeddings using siamese BERT-networks. arXiv preprint arXiv:1908.10084 (2019)
48. Adiwardana, D., et al.: Towards a human-like open-domain chatbot, arXiv preprint arXiv:2001.09977 (2020)
49. Rus, V., D'Mello, S., Hu, X., Graesser, A.: Recent advances in conversational intelligent tutoring systems. AI Mag. **34**(3), pp. 42–54 (2013)

50. Beurer-Kellner, L., Fischer, M., Vechev, M.: Prompting is programming: a query language for large language models. In: Proceedings of the ACM on Programming Languages, 7(PLDI), pp. 1946–1969 (2023)
51. Zamfirescu-Pereira, J.D., Wong, R.Y., Hartmann, B., Yang, Q.: Why Johnny can't prompt: how non-AI experts try (and fail) to design LLM prompts. In: Proceedings of the 2023 CHI Conference on Human Factors in Computing Systems, pp. 1–21, April 2023
52. Cheng, Y., Chen, J., Huang, Q., Xing, Z., Xu, X., Lu, Q.: Prompt Sapper: a LLM-empowered production tool for building AI chains. arXiv preprint arXiv:2306.12028 (2023)

# SAMI: An AI Actor for Fostering Social Interactions in Online Classrooms

Sandeep Kakar(✉), Rhea Basappa, Ida Camacho, Christopher Griswold, Alex Houk, Christopher Leung, Mustafa Tekman, Patrick Westervelt, Qiaosi Wang, and Ashok K. Goel

Georgia Institute of Technology, Atlanta, GA 30332, USA
{skakar6,rb324,icamacho,cgriswold6,ahouk3,cg2leung,mtekman3, pwestervelt3,qswang,ag25}@gatech.edu

**Abstract.** Learning is a social process. However, online learning is characterized by social isolation. We present an AI social actor, SAMI, for fostering social interactions in online classrooms. SAMI (Social Agent Mediated Interactions) aims to mitigate the potentially adverse impact of social isolation on the learning experience and emotional well-being of geographically dispersed online learners in asynchronous educational settings. SAMI connects learners based on their shared identity considering student location, hobbies, and academic interests. It also aims to enhance the feeling of "belongingness" felt by the students in the community of online students. SAMI has been deployed at Georgia Institute of Technology in several online classes with over 11000 students in the past two years. We describe our findings from student surveys to gauge SAMI's effectiveness.

**Keywords:** Adult Learning · Online Education · Social Presence AI Social Actor · Community Building

## 1 Introduction

Online programs are becoming ubiquitous in higher and continuing education. With their growing popularity, educational institutions must ensure that online learners have a learning experience that is at least as meaningful and effective as that of in-person learners. In this context, an obvious challenge posed by online education is the lack of face-to-face interactions between students who are geographically dispersed and are often receiving asynchronous instruction. This is especially true for adult learners in online education. Adult learners often struggle to accommodate competing commitments to their coursework, full-time jobs, and families, and thus typically have little to no time for building social connections in their online classrooms [1]. The problem is further exacerbated by

This research has been supported by NSF Grants #2112532 and #2247790 to the National AI Institute for Adult Learning and Online Education. We thank members of the Design Intelligence Laboratory for their contributions to this work. This research was conducted in accordance with IRB protocols approved by Georgia Tech.


A. Sifaleras and F. Lin (Eds.): ITS 2024, LNCS 14798, pp. 149–161, 2024.
https://doi.org/10.1007/978-3-031-63028-6_12

the size of online classrooms that have hundreds, if not thousands, of students. Online learners would need to tediously search through faceless posts devoid of social cues on the class discussion forum to identify those with whom they may want to reach out to connect. Even if they did this, they may hesitate to reach out to express their inclination to connect. The resulting lack of social interaction hinders students from projecting themselves as people with emotions and social needs in the class. This social isolation denies online students cognitive learning benefits of collaborative thinking that often leads to shared construction or discovery of knowledge [2–4]. Further, online students may struggle to develop the feeling of "belongingness" in the classroom community, that is, the feeling they identify with other students. This deficit can adversely impact a student's well-being and emotional health, and the desire to stay and complete the program of study [5–7].

Artificially intelligent (AI) social actors offer potential means for fostering social interactions in online classrooms [8]. The current AI techniques seem adept at leveraging natural language generation to bring spontaneity and randomness to online interactions, thus offering the potential for enhanced user (student) engagement. With this perspective, we make the following research contributions. First, we have developed a new version of an social AI actor named SAMI to help online learners make social connections based on their shared identity. Second, critical aspects of SAMI's functionality are enhanced by generative AI sourced from OpenAI's ChatGPT. Third, SAMI uses generative AI in conjunction with a knowledge base of student models represented as knowledge graphs. Fourth, SAMI has been routinely deployed in several online classes with thousands of students. Finally, it requires only modest computational resources to scale SAMI to any number of classes.

## 2 Related Work

The importance of social context in support of learning has been recognized for a long time. Dewey observed in 1897 "that the educational process has two sides - one psychological and one sociological; and that neither can be subordinated to the other or neglected without evil results following" [9]. This viewpoint has gained much urgency with the increasing popularity of online education where social isolation, if left unchallenged, can be more a rule than an exception [10]. More recently, Ashar and Skenes [5] highlighted the role of the social environment in keeping students engaged in learning activities in an online environment.

Garrison et al. [2] put forth the framework of Community of Inquiry that posits social presence - the ability of learners to project their personalities and emotional needs into classrooms - as one of three crucial elements that enable an effective higher education experience, and its implications for building functional online learning communities (cognitive presence and teaching presence are the other two). Sun et al. [11] focus on online learners' community-building practices and find these are motivated either by the discovery of shared identity or the desire to fulfill academic or professional goals. In [12], authors note that discovering students with a common group identity also promotes collective efficacy, the belief in the group's capacity to achieve shared goals.

In earlier work, Brooks et al. [13] note the lack of affordances promoting collaborative learning in traditional learning management systems. To alleviate this shortcoming, the authors present a suite of tools explicitly linking the collaboration of learners to learning artifacts in the learning management system to promote social aspects of learning. More recently, Wang et al. [14] examine the design implications of technology interventions to foster community building in online classes and present an early implementation of a social AI agent. They report results from student surveys that validate the importance of shared identity in creating online communities. They extend this work in [15,16] with co-design workshop studies with online learners to identify learners' design preferences for an AI agent tasked with promoting social connectedness and probe potential ethical concerns. Taking cues from this work, we present here the design and implementation of a new version of SAMI and its deployment in several online classes.

# 3 SAMI System Design

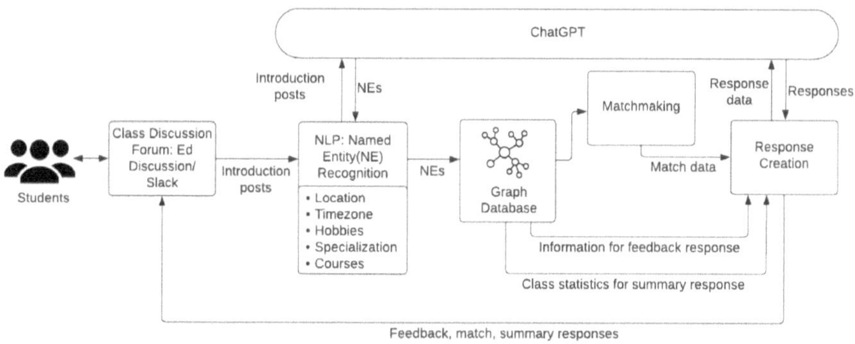


**Fig. 1.** SAMI's architecture

Figure 1 illustrates SAMI's architecture. SAMI has a modular design with five modules: a module that hosts the class discussion forum API; a module for natural language processing (NLP); a knowledge base of graphs representing student models; a module for matchmaking; and a module for response creation. Any module can easily be changed or upgraded independently of other modules. Deployed in an online class, SAMI interacts with students through a dedicated thread on the Ed Discussion forum or a dedicated Slack channel. Students are asked to post their self-introductions at the beginning of the semester and to append hashtag #connectme to consent to SAMI analyzing their posts for matchmaking. Once the number of posts reaches a critical threshold, they are passed to the NLP module in a batch. Figure 2 shows a sample student introduction post.

### 3.1 Natural Language Processing Module

The NLP module is concerned with Named-Entity Recognition (NER). Specifically, it analyzes student posts that contain the #connectme hashtag to extract student location and other places of interest mentioned in the introduction; the time zone; hobbies; the intended specialization; and past and future courses of interest. The NER functionality is sourced from OpenAI's ChatGPT by passing student introduction posts along with an appropriate prompt for each entity type to the OpenAI API. Leveraging ChatGPT for common NLP tasks such as classification and NER obviates the need for gathering training data to build and train task-specific machine learning models, thus greatly simplifying SAMI's architecture and development [17]. It also reduces the task of adding additional named entities for matchmaking to prompt engineering. The extracted named entities are highlighted in the introduction post in Fig. 2.

### 3.2 Knowledge Base Module

The output of the NLP module is a dictionary containing student IDs along with associated named entities, and it is passed to the knowledge base module, which is responsible for constructing a Neo4j graph database using data received from the NLP module. The knowledge graph consists of two types of nodes: student IDs and named entities. A node for a particular student ID is connected to all named entities extracted for that ID; more than one student ID node may be connected to a given named entity node. Figure 3 shows a truncated example of the knowledge graphs for just two students. The knowledge base module exposes its graph data through an API that can be queried using Neo4j's graph query language (Cypher).

### 3.3 Matchmaking Module

The matchmaking module extracts data from the knowledge base to find the best matches for a student based on their shared identity based on student locations and other places of interest; their time zones; hobbies; desired specialization in the program of study; and past and future courses of interest. A student is a match candidate for another student if their respective nodes are connected to one or more of the same named entities, that is they share one or more elements of identity. The matchmaking module computes a pair-wise match score based on the number of shared named identities between students. The higher the number of shared named entity nodes between two students, the higher the match score for the pair. The output of the matchmaking module is sent to the response creation module, and it is a dictionary consisting of student IDs along with five top matches for each student.

Hi everyone,

My name is [student] and I live in Cumming, GA. We moved from CA last and miss the amazing weather all round the year. I am a first year PhD student and have taken CS 7001. I am interested in HCI and have also taken HCC 1 course this semester. I would like my research to focus on humanistic AI and someday hope to become a faculty.

Outside of academics and work, I enjoy hiking, reading classic fiction and spending time with my 3 year old daughter. We moved to GA for my PhD :) and of course the wonderful greenery. #connectme

---

Dear [student] ,

I hope this message finds you well. It's great to learn that you have a passion for reading classic fiction and hiking. As a social agent, I'm excited to help you connect with your classmates who share similar interests and academic pursuits. Your specialization in Human Centered Computing is fascinating, and I'm sure you'll find many like-minded individuals in your upcoming classes. Your primary location in Cumming, Georgia, puts you in a prime position to take advantage of all the opportunities available in the area. We will soon be providing you with a list of matched students once the class registration is completed. Stay tuned for more updates!

Best regards,
SAMI

*If I made a mistake, I would appreciate it if you can correct me. This will help my creators to programmatically correct faults in my brain! To do so, please reply to this post. Your reply should start with* ***#samicorrect.*** *Next depending on what you want me to correct, please add one or more of the following lines to your reply:*

**#primarylocation** [city][state][country]

**#otherlocation** [city][state][country]; [city][state][country]

**#hobbies** [hobby1][hobby2]

**#courses** [course1][course2]

**#specialization** [specialization]

Thank you so much

**Fig. 2.** At the top is an example self-introduction post made by a student in a dedicated thread on the class discussion forum. The named entities in the post are highlighted with a box around them. At the bottom is SAMI's feedback to the student based on this post.

### 3.4 Response Generation Module

The response creation module is responsible for generating SAMI's responses for students. It uses ChatGPT to craft diverse and friendly human-like responses to help increase student engagement. Input data for responses are sent along with an appropriate prompt to the OpenAI API for this purpose. The crafted responses received from ChatGPT are then forwarded to the class discussion forum API for posting as responses to the student introduction posts. The module creates three types of responses: feedback and match responses for each student, and a

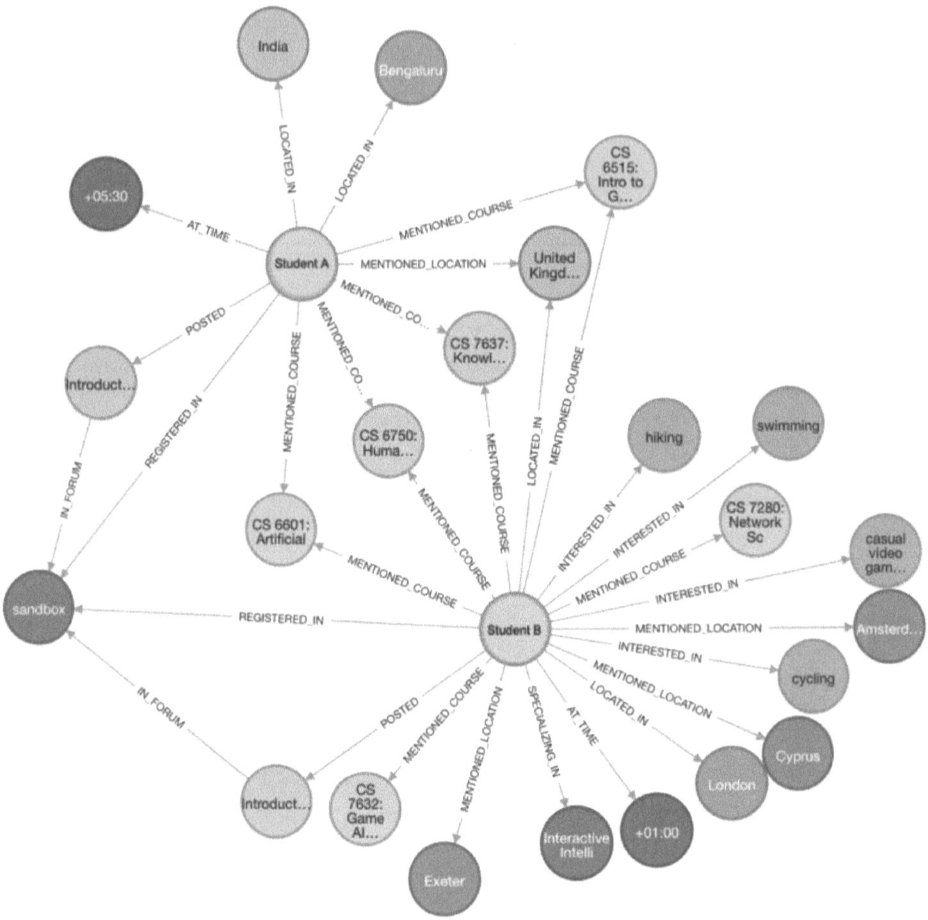


**Fig. 3.** A truncated example of the SAMI's knowledge graphs.

summary response for the class. The type of response created depends on the option selected when SAMI's code is executed.

Figure 2 shows an example of a feedback response. This is the first response a student receives from SAMI, and it uses data queried from the knowledge base. It informs the student what knowledge SAMI has extracted about her from her introduction post. It also asks the student to inform SAMI of any errors in the extracted information.

Figure 4 shows an example of a match response given to a student; the response is constructed using match data output by the matchmaking module. As mentioned above, SAMI suggests the names of five students as potential matches. The name of each suggested match student is an HTML link; clicking on it takes the student to the match student's introduction post. The student can then post a message to the match; or click on a "Click to say Hi" link to show

Hiya [student] . It's good to digitally meet you.

**#CONNECTME** Just take a few minutes to get to know your fellow classmates. You may be interested in connecting with them.

**--SPOTLIGHT BLOCK--**

- ***Spotlight On:*** *[match 1]* ! . Meet [match 1] , a fifth-year PhD candidate in Human-Centered Computing at Georgia Tech. They also lived in Seattle, Washington for their undergrad. Like you, they have taken courses in Cognitive Science and have a passion for Human-Computer Interaction. They enjoy indoor bouldering, working out at Orange Theory, and watching TV shows and movies in their free time. It seems like you both share a love for the outdoors as well, with your interest in hiking and their past experience in Seattle. It's great to see that you both have a lot in common! #ConnectMe

  To say 'Hi!' to [match 1] click here.

- ***Spotlight On:*** *[match 2]* ! . Meet [match 2] , a soon-to-be 3rd year HCC PhD student at GT who does visual analytics and HCI research. They are advised by [advisor] and have a website you can check out. They share your interest in HCI and have taken CS 7001. They also enjoy hiking, just like you, and have a love for American football, baseball, and golf. They live in Atlanta, GA, just like you, and enjoy spending time outdoors. You should definitely connect with them! #connectme

  To say 'Hi!' to [match 2] click here.

- ***Spotlight On:*** *[match 3]* ! . Meet [match 3] a fellow student who recently moved to Atlanta, GA. They share your love for outdoor activities like hiking and enjoy exploring the city. is also enrolled in HCC courses this semester, just like you. Additionally, they are interested in culinary skills and are a movie enthusiast. It seems like you both have a lot in common and could potentially connect over your shared interests. #connectme

  To say 'Hi!' to [match 3] click here.

- ***Spotlight On:*** *[match 4]* ! . Meet [m4] , a fellow OMSCS student from Pittsburgh, PA. They have taken courses in HCI, KBAI, and ICS, and are planning to specialize in II. Like you, they enjoy hiking and spending time with their partner. They also share an interest in video games and have taken a course in video game design. Additionally, they have a background in teaching math and computer science. You both have a shared interest in HCI and could potentially collaborate on research in the future. #connectme

  To say 'Hi!' to [match 4] click here.

- ***Spotlight On:*** *[match 5]* ! . Meet [match 5] , a fellow student who shares your love for hiking and enjoys traveling, photography, and music in their spare time. They live in the San Francisco Bay Area, which is where you moved from last year. They are currently taking DL and SDP, while you have taken CS 7001 and HCC 1 this semester. It's great to connect with someone who shares similar interests and academic pursuits! #connectme

  To say 'Hi!' to [match 5] click here.

**Fig. 4.** An example of SAMI's match response to a student introduction post. SAMI suggests five peers as potential matches based on shared identity. The student can click on a match's name to be taken to her introduction post. They can also click to say "Hi" to a match.

an interest in connecting. We can track student clicks as a measure of SAMI's efficacy in connecting students.

The final response output by SAMI is the summary response. It consists of class statistics derived from student information stored in the knowledge base. Figure 5 shows an example of a summary response. The summary response is motivated by the desire to increase the feeling of belonging among the students, that is, the feeling that they belong to the community (class) and that they identify with other students. This, in turn, can have a salutary effect on their sense of social presence.

**SAMI** has gathered and compiled information from your introduction posts for students who opted in with the **#connectme** hashtag at the end of their posts. This thread gives **summary statistics** for these students, not the entire class. For example, how many students are in certain cities, states and so on. We hope this is helpful to you.

*Please feel free to leave any feedback or comments on this thread about this feature.*

---

**hobbies summary**
-Top Mentions-

- 16.2% of the students are interested in reading.
- 16.2% of the students are interested in hiking.
- 13.1% of the students are interested in running.
- 8.1% of the students are interested in traveling.
- 8.1% of the students are interested in video games.
- 7.1% of the students are interested in soccer.
- 7.1% of the students are interested in watching movies.
- 6.1% of the students are interested in cooking.
- 6.1% of the students are interested in music.
- 5.1% of the students are interested in gardening.

**Fig. 5.** An example of SAMI's summary response. For the sake of brevity, we just show the hobbies summary. Similar statistics are displayed for other named entities, e.g., countries, cities, time zones, hobbies, specializations, courses, etc.

### 3.5 SAMI on Slack

Asynchronous classrooms communicate in different ways, with some utilizing class discussion forums, such as Piazza or Ed Discussion, and others utilizing instant messaging platforms, such as Slack. To make SAMI a truly modular program that can slot into any classroom, it has been our goal to make SAMI work on any online form of communication, and behave consistently across the different platforms. As such, SAMI on Slack behaves the same as previous iterations of SAMI deployed on class discussion forums, including how it communicates with the other modules and the way it directly responds to students who have posted messages addressed to it.

## 4 Results and Discussion

Various versions of SAMI have been deployed in many large online graduate-level classes in the Online Master of Science in Computer Science (OMSCS) program at Georgia Institute of Technology. Versions of SAMI before Summer 2023 used pattern recognition for extracting named entities from introduction posts and provided hard-coded responses to students; these were deployed in classes with about 8000 students enrolled. The current version employing ChatGPT was first deployed in Summer 2023 and it offers a more engaging experience for students with its more varied and human-like responses. Over 3000 students have had an opportunity to interact with this version of SAMI.

### 4.1 Early Results

During the deployment of SAMI in Fall 2019 in two online classes, we conducted three short surveys over the semester to gather student feedback on SAMI [14]. These three surveys served different purposes: Survey 1 (S1, n = 601) to understand online learners' current practices in building social connections, Survey 2 (S2, n = 359) to collect qualitative feedback from students on SAMI, and Survey 3 (S3, n = 431) to quantitatively evaluate the effectiveness of SAMI. Through mixed-methods analysis on these survey results, we found that students were overall positive about SAMI. However, students reported mixed experiences and opinions on the actual usefulness of SAMI in fostering social connections among online learners.

Based on students' responses from S2, we found that students were able to form connections through the shared identity highlighted by SAMI. For example, some students reported that they used SAMI's responses to connect with others who are located in the same area, or even formed local study groups. By highlighting students' shared identity, SAMI also helped online learners foster a sense of "belongingness" in he class. One student said, *"I think the personalized response fosters inclusion and collaboration in the class. It helped me have a sense of belonging."*

However, students also pointed out that while the responses provided by SAMI are interesting, they are not always actionable given that SAMI's response did not trigger an action as much as they had expected. Echoing with this feedback, S3 responses also showed that among all students who opted-in to receive SAMI's recommendations, 53.4% of the students didn't connect with anyone, 19.9% students connected with five or less students, and 7.85% students connected with more than five students.

### 4.2 Intermediate Results

In 2021, we conducted semi-structured interviews with 26 students in the OMSCS program in which SAMI was deployed [16]. We analyzed the interview transcripts using thematic analysis. Through the interviews, we found that

SAMI was able to improve the visibility of social information and increase students' feelings of accountability in remote social interactions. Students reported that SAMI made social signals visible among students by highlighting students' willingness to build social connections. Given that students needed to opt-in by including #connectme in their self-introduction, others also interpreted this as a signal of whether students were willing to build social connections. We also found that SAMI raised awareness of potential social companions for online learners by highlighting online learners' shared identities, such as their similar hobbies and locations.

While SAMI was able to facilitate online learners' social connections by mitigating these challenges, students also voiced their concerns about SAMI. One concern that was frequently brought up by online learners was the lack of transparency of SAMI's working mechanism. We found that students wanted to learn more about how SAMI came up with the recommendation for them to better communicate with SAMI for further improvements. This suggests a need for self-explanation in SAMI [18].

### 4.3 Results from SAMI on Slack

SAMI on Slack was deployed in an in-person course at Georgia Tech in Spring 2023 that utilized Slack as the online communication platform. Using exported data from Slack, it is possible to compare the number of students who were in one channel to another channel. The #general channel, which every student is automatically enrolled in, contained a total of 77 users. Meanwhile, the SAMI channel, which students had to opt in, contained a total of 75 users. This means at maximum, only two students used the Slack server without joining the SAMI channel to interact with SAMI.

In terms of interaction, 81% of students who responded to an in-class survey reported interacting with SAMI. Those students were asked to assess SAMI on a scale of 1 to 5 (with 1 being the worst and 5 being the best). Of the 30 students who responded to this question, 44% responded with a rating of 5, 35% responded with a rating of 4, and 21% responded with a rating of 3.

In terms of efficiency, 76% of students who responded to the survey reached out to other students based on SAMI's suggestions, and of those who were reached out to, 66% responded at least once. Later in the semester, when a project required students to form groups, 80% of students relied on SAMI's suggestions to form their groups. Of that 80%, 25% relied exclusively on SAMI's matches, while 75% relied on a combination of SAMI's suggestions and other previous experience with students.

### 4.4 Recent Deployments

In our more recent deployments, over 3000 students in various classes have been exposed to the ChatGPT-based SAMI. Table 1 lists some of the salient features of these deployments.

**Table 1.** SAMI deployments since Summer 2023 (ChatGPT-based SAMI)

| Semester | Course | Discussion Forum | # Students |
|---|---|---|---|
| Summer 2023 | Human-Computer Interaction | Ed Discussion | 385 |
| Summer 2023 | Knowledge-Based AI | Ed Discussion | 216 |
| Summer 2023 | Introduction to Cognitive Science | Slack | 115 |
| Fall 2023 | Human-Computer Interaction | Ed Discussion | 691 |
| Fall 2023 | Knowledge-Based AI | Slack | 482 |
| Spring 2024 | Knowledge-Based AI | Ed Discussion | 517 |
| Spring 2024 | Machine Learning for Trading | Ed Discussion | 1280 |

**Table 2.** SAMI class usage in Human-Computer Interaction, Fall 2023

| # students | # self-introductions | # opt-ins | # Match name clicks | # click-to-say-hi clicks |
|---|---|---|---|---|
| 691 | 532 (77%) | 249 | 151 | 87 |

Table 2 shows data highlighting the degree of student engagement with SAMI in a class. This class had a student enrollment of 691. 532 (77%) students posted their self-introductions and 249 (47% of those who introduced themselves) opted in to have their posts analyzed by SAMI for match recommendations. We recorded 151 clicks by students on the names of students recommended as potential matches and 81 clicks made by students to say "hi" to these matches.

## 5 Conclusion

We have presented an AI actor, SAMI, for fostering social interactions in online classrooms. SAMI aims to mitigate the potentially adverse impact of social isolation on the learning experience and emotional well-being of online learners by connecting them based on their shared identity derived from their location, time zone, hobbies, and academic interests. It also aims to enhance the feeling of "belongingness" felt by the students in the community of online students. While earlier versions of SAMI used pattern recognition for extracting named entities and methods from knowledge-based AI such as knowledge graph and graph matching, the newer version combines generative AI with knowledge-based methods for better matchmaking and engaging student experience. SAMI has been deployed at Georgia Institute of Technology in several classes with over 11000 students over the past two years and its deployments can be easily scaled to any number of classes. Out initial results from indicate encouraging signs of student engagement with SAMI.

## References


1. Silva, T., Calahan, M., Lacireno-Paquet, N.: Adult education participation: decisions and barriers. Review of Conceptual Frameworks and Empirical Studies. U.S. Department of Education, Washington, DC
2. Garrison, D., Anderson, T., Archer, W.: Critical inquiry in a text-based environment: computer conferencing in higher education. Internet High. Educ. **2**, 87–105 (1999). https://doi.org/10.1016/S1096-7516(00)00016-6
3. Rovai, A.P., Wighting, M.J., Lucking, R.: The classroom and school community inventory: development, refinement, and validation of a self-report measure for educational research. Internet High. Educ. **7**(4), 263–280 (2004). https://doi.org/10.1016/j.iheduc.2004.09.001
4. Stahl, Gerry: Theories of cognition in CSCW. In: Bødker, Susanne, Bouvin, Niels Olof, Wulf, Volker, Ciolfi, Luigina, Lutters, Wayne (eds.) ECSCW 2011, pp. 193–212. Springer, London (2011). https://doi.org/10.1007/978-0-85729-913-0_11
5. Ashar, H, Skenes, R.: Can Tinto's student departure model be applied to nontraditional students? Adult Educ. Q. **43**(2), 90–100 (1993). https://doi.org/10.1177/074171369304300
6. Walton, G.M., Cohen, G.L.: A brief social-belonging intervention improves academic and health outcomes of minority students. Science **331**(6023), 1447–1451 (2011). https://www.science.org/doi/10.1126/science.1198364
7. Yeager, D.S., Walton, G.M.: Social-psychological interventions in education they're not magic. Rev. Educ. Res. **81**(2), 267–301 (2011). https://doi.org/10.3102/0034654311405999
8. Goel, A.: AI-powered learning: making education accessible, affordable, and achievable, arXiv:2006.01908v1 [cs.CY]. https://doi.org/10.48550/arXiv.2006.01908
9. Dewey, J.: My pedagogic creed. Sch. J. **54**(3), 77–80 (1897)
10. Guo, Z., Tan, F.B., Cheung, K.: Students' uses and gratifications for using computer-mediated communication media in learning contexts. Commun. Assoc. Inf. Syst. **27**, 339–378 (2010). https://doi.org/10.17705/1CAIS.02720
11. Sun, N., Wang, X., Rosson, M.B.: How do distance learners connect? In: Proceedings of the 2019 CHI Conference on Human Factors in Computing Systems - CHI 2019, pp. 1–12 (2019). http://dx.doi.org/10.1145/3290605.3300662
12. Sun, N., Rosson, M.B., Carroll, J.M.: Where is community among online learners? Identity, efficacy and personal ties. In: Proceedings of the 2018 CHI Conference on Human Factors in Computing Systems - CHI 2018, Montreal QC Canada, pp. 1–13. ACM (2018). http://dx.doi.org/10.1145/3173574.3173866
13. Brooks, C., Panesar, R., Greer, J.: Awareness and collaboration in the iHelp courses content management system. In: Nejdl, W., Tochtermann, K. (eds.) EC-TEL 2006. LNCS, vol. 4227, pp. 34–44. Springer, Heidelberg (2006). https://doi.org/10.1007/11876663_5
14. Wang, Q., Jing, S., Camacho, I., et al.: Jill Watson SA: design and evaluation of a virtual agent to build communities among online learners. In: Extended Abstracts of the 2020 CHI Conference on Human Factors in Computing Systems - CHI 2020, Honolulu, HI, USA, pp. 1–8. ACM (2020). https://doi.org/10.1145/3334480.3382878
15. Wang, Q., Jing, S., Goel, A.K.: Co-designing AI agents to support social connectedness among online learners: functionalities, social characteristics, and ethical challenges. In: Designing Interactive Systems Conference (DIS 2022), Virtual Event, Australia, pp. 541–556. ACM (2022). https://doi.org/10.1145/3532106.3533534

16. Wang, Q., Camacho. I., Jing, S., Goel, A.K.: Understanding the design space of AI-mediated social interaction in online learning: challenges and opportunities. In: Proceedings of the ACM on Human-Computer Interaction, vol. 6, pp. 1–26 (2022). https://doi.org/10.1145/3512977
17. Qin, C., Zhang, A., Zhang, Z. et al.: Is ChatGPT a general-purpose natural language processing task solver? arXiv:2302.06476 [cs.CL]. https://doi.org/10.48550/arXiv.2302.06476
18. Basappa, R., Tekman, M., Lu, H., Faught, B. Kakar, S., Goel, A.: Social AI agents too need to explain themselves. In: Proceedings of 20th International Conference, ITS 2024, Thessaloniki, Greece. Springer (2024, Accepted for publication)

# Exploring the Methodological Contexts and Constraints of Research in Artificial Intelligence in Education

Irene-Angelica Chounta(✉), Bibeg Limbu, and Lisa van der Heyden

Department of Human-Centered Computing and Cognitive Science, University of Duisburg-Essen, Duisburg, Germany
{irene-angelica.chounta,bibeg.limbu,lisa.van-der-heyden}@uni-due.de

**Abstract.** In this paper, we present a Systematic Literature Review (SLR) on the state-of-the-art in Artificial Intelligence in Education (AIED) focusing on methodological contexts and constraints of the research landscape. To do so, we built on existing works and extended them to cover the latest research advancements in the field over the past five years. We aimed at covering all educational levels and retrieving important data regarding the planning and execution of research studies and the robustness of results. In total, we reviewed 181 papers and answered three research questions, relating to the educational context of AI use, the methodology and study design utilized in AIED research, and the type of AI algorithms and technologies used in education. Our findings suggest that research in AIED primarily focuses on formal, higher education and that there is a demand for robust and rigorous scientific evidence of the effectiveness and impact of AIED. Furthermore, the findings indicate that the most popular AI technologies currently studied are traditional AI algorithms, usually used for prediction, classification, or clustering. Based on our analysis, we discuss practical implications that can serve as inspiration and guidance for future research initiatives.

**Keywords:** artificial intelligence in education · research · methodology · systematic literature review

## 1 Introduction

Research on Artificial Intelligence in Education (AIED) has been a prominent topic for over 30 years. However, recently it gained attention due to technological advances in Artificial Intelligence (AI) and is projected to reach its peak by the year 2025[1]. In the past five (5) years alone, we identified nine (9) systematic literature reviews (SLRs) about AIED that aimed to document the research landscape (see Table 1).

[1] https://www.holoniq.com/notes/2019-artificial-intelligence-global-education-report.


A. Sifaleras and F. Lin (Eds.): ITS 2024, LNCS 14798, pp. 162–173, 2024.
https://doi.org/10.1007/978-3-031-63028-6_13

**Table 1.** Existing Systematic Literature Reviews on AIED

| SLR Title | Years Covered | #Reviewed Publications |
|---|---|---|
| Systematic review of research on artificial intelligence applications in higher education-where are the educators? [20] | 2007–2018 | 146 |
| Application and theory gaps during the rise of artificial intelligence in education [3] | 1999 -2019 | 45 |
| AI in education: A systematic literature review [16] | 2010–2019 | 23 |
| A systematic review of AI role in the educational system based on a proposed conceptual framework [18] | 2005–2021 | 51 |
| Artificial intelligence in online higher education: A systematic review of empirical research from 2011 to 2020 [11] | 2011–2020 | 32 |
| Affordances and challenges of artificial intelligence in K-12 education: A systematic review [6] | 2011–2021 | 169 |
| Artificial intelligence applications in K-12 education: A systematic literature review [19] | 2011–2021 | 210 |
| Systematic literature review on opportunities, challenges, and future research recommendations of artificial intelligence in education [4] | 2012–2021 | 92 |
| Artificial intelligence in higher education: the state of the field [5] | 2016–2022 | 138 |

Most of these reviews explored the integration and use of AI in specific levels of formal education, such as K-12 [6,19] or higher education [5,20], while one review explored the whole range [4]. A common theme addressed in the SLRs was the benefits, opportunities, challenges, and critical implications that follow AIED [4,6,16]. For example, [20] explored – among others – the ethical implications and risks associated with the use of AI in education, while [6] also highlighted several challenges, such as ethical concerns regarding AI use, ensuring fairness and equal opportunities, providing sufficient training and support for teachers, addressing technical infrastructure requirements, and ensuring AI's integration and long-term sustainability in education. [16] pointed out the scarcity of publications presenting the relationship between opportunities, benefits, and challenges. Some reviews focused on the geographical distribution of research, pointing out that certain countries lead the AIED-related publications [3,5]. Finally, other topics discussed in these SLRs were the most prominent AI technologies and algorithms presented in research publications [3,11], the purpose of use, roles, and functions of AI [6,11,18,20].

The above signifies a plethora of research on AIED, especially after the COVID-19 pandemic, strengthened by recent advances in AI technologies, specifically generative AI. It is critical to monitor and document these works and keep an up-to-date state-of-the-art map regarding the AIED research landscape. However, there are evident gaps in the information and level of detail documented. For example, SLRs that examine the use of AI on all levels of education [3,4] focus mostly on the geographical distribution of research, opportunities, and challenges. On the other hand, SLRs that focus on specific education levels (for example, higher education or primary education [19,20]) delve into topics related to the use and purpose of AI in education. Another gap concerns the documentation of data that AI algorithms and AI systems use to achieve their goals. Existing SLRs provide minimal to no information about the data types or data sources, while few point out potential limitations or risks due to data privacy and ownership. We argue that there is a need to systematically document information regarding the AI technologies used for all education levels and their purpose. Most importantly, it is crucial to identify the data sources and types typically employed by AI applications in education. Additionally, there is no systematic evaluation of the research studies under review regarding their scientific rigorousness and robustness of the evidence. We acknowledge the difficulties that the organization and realization of such studies entail. Nonetheless, we argue that it is imperative to document the magnitude of studies in terms of population size, duration, reproducibility, and applicability, along with their methodological designs, to assess the robustness of their findings. This requirement is also imposed by the need to ensure fair, accountable, transparent, and ethical AI [9].

The contribution of this work is to gather insights regarding the methodological contexts and constraints of the AIED research landscape by building on existing works and extending them to cover the latest research advancements in the field over the past five years. In particular, we aimed to retrieve important information regarding the planning and execution of research studies that can potentially provide information about the robustness of results and findings.

For our research purposes, we formulated the following Research Questions (RQs):

**RQ**$_1$. *In which educational contexts is AI used?*

**RQ**$_2$. *What are the methodological and study designs employed in AIED research?*

**RQ**$_3$. *What AI algorithms and technologies are used in education?*

To answer our RQs, we used the SLR of [20] as a blueprint, and we extended it further to: a) cover all research literature from 2019 to 2023 (5 years) appearing in journal publications; b) cover all education levels, including adult and lifelong learning; c) retrieve information regarding the planning and realization of research studies and the robustness of results.

In the following sections, we discuss the methodological setup of this work. Then, we present our findings (Sect. 3), and we answer our research questions along with a contextualized discussion on the need for evidence-based approaches for AIED (Sect. 4). We conclude with a brief summary of our contribution, limitations and future work (Sect. 5).

## 2 Methodology

To carry out the SLR, we followed the PRISMA statement [12,14] that require four phases for selecting articles: a) Identification, b) Screening, 3) Eligibility and 4) Inclusion. For the Identification, we searched the databases Web of Science (WoS)[2], EBSCO[3] and Scopus[4] using the pre-defined search term:

> Search Query = ("artificial intelligence" OR "machine intelligence" OR "intelligent support" OR "intelligent virtual reality" OR "chatbot*" OR "machine learning" OR "automated tutor" OR "personal tutor*" OR "intelligent agent*" OR "expert system" OR "neural network" OR "natural language processing") AND ("higher education" OR college* OR undergrad* OR graduate OR postgrad* OR "K-12" OR kindergarten* OR "corporate training*" OR "professional training*" OR "primary school*" OR "middle school*" OR "high school*" OR "elementary school*" OR "vocational education" OR "adult education") AND (learn* OR student*)

The search string derived from the SLR of [20], and it was used to retrieve relevant journal publications from the pre-selected databases. After retrieving the search results, we concluded the *Indentification* phase by eliminating duplicates. For *Screening*, the publications were reviewed based on their title and abstract by two researchers in parallel who eliminated publications not considered relevant. During the *Eligibility* phase, the remaining records were reviewed based on their full texts: Two reviewers worked in parallel using the exclusion and inclusion criteria (Table 2) adapted from [14]. To support the reviewing process, we compiled a coding scheme with examples for each code. To train the reviewers, we used three papers to demonstrate the coding process. During training, the reviewers could ask for clarifications and take notes. Then, we carried out two reviewing steps. For the first step, we asked the reviewers to code together a set of ten (10), randomly selected papers to establish a common understanding. During this step, we provided additional clarifications and examples for the coding scheme and refined it further when needed. For the second step, we asked the reviewers to code separately a set of 20, randomly selected, papers. Then, we asked the reviewers to compare and discuss their results until they reached a consensus. If consensus was not possible, a third reviewer, an expert on AIED and educational technologies, was involved. This process was repeated until all publications were reviewed.

During the *Inclusion* phase, all remaining publications were included in the corpus for the systematic review. Two of the co-authors split the corpus and

[2] https://www.webofscience.com/wos/woscc/.
[3] https://www.ebsco.com/.
[4] https://www.scopus.com/search/.

**Table 2.** Exclusion and inclusion criteria for formal screening of collected records adapted from [14]. Formal criteria relate to the *formalization* of the publications, such as the working language, the number of pages or the record's availability. Content-related criteria address the topic of the publication and were established in accordance with our RQs.

| Formal Screening | |
|---|---|
| Exclusion Criteria | Inclusion Criteria |
| The full text of the record is not available | The full text can be downloaded |
| The record is not written in English. | The record is written in English |
| The record is not published in a peer-reviewed journal | The record is published in a peer-reviewed journal |
| The record is not substantial (< 7 pages). | The record is substantial (>= 7 pages). |
| Content Screening | |
| Exclusion Criteria | Inclusion Criteria |
| The record does not address the use of AI | The record addresses the use of AI |
| The record does not address education | The record addresses education |
| The record does not involve a research study | The record involves a research study |

reviewed the papers again independently to confirm the original findings. If in doubt, the third co-author was involved. The number of publications over the different phases of the process is shown in Fig. 1. The list of articles that were included in the review and the coding scheme are publicly available at http://tinyurl.com/3rf5jzw6.

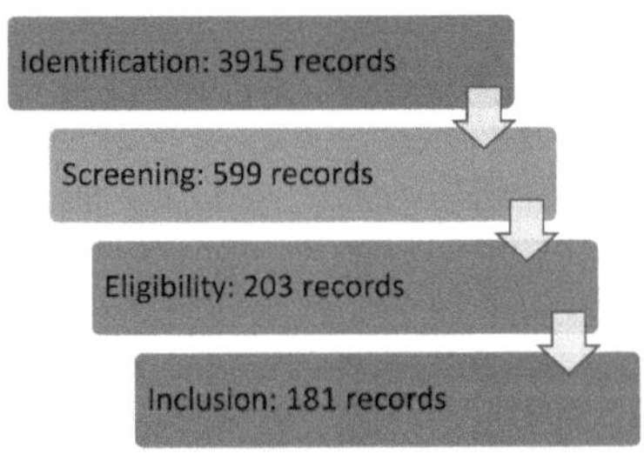


**Fig. 1.** The number of papers for each phase of the reviewing process according to PRISMA.

## 3 Results

In total, we reviewed one hundred and eighty-one (181) articles published in sixty-seven (67) journals from 2019 to 2023. The three (3) leading journals in terms of number of publications were the Education and Information Technologies journal (19 publications, 11%), the British Journal of Educational Technology (11 publications, 6%), and the International Journal of Educational Technology in Higher Education (9 publications, 5%). Figure 2 presents the distribution of publications over the last five (5) years. We note that for 2023, we only considered papers available by April 1st, 2023.

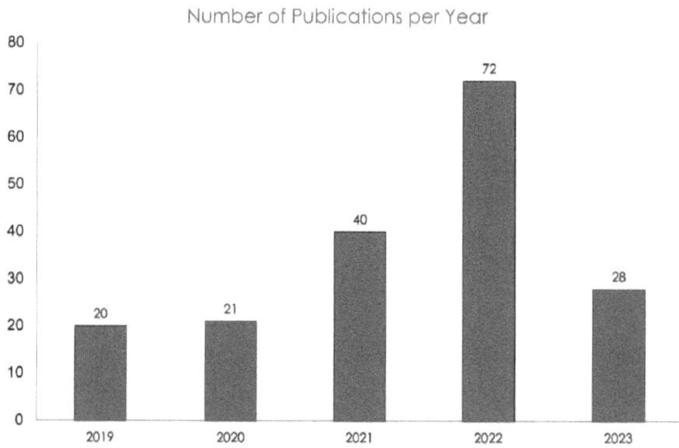


**Fig. 2.** The distribution of published papers over the past 5 years, from January 2019 to April 2023.

To align with existing SLRs, and to gain some understanding regarding potential hubs of AIED research, we will first present some "demographics" of the literature under review. Overall, the first authors of the research publications came from forty-eight (48) countries in terms of affiliation. The most prominent countries in terms of number of publications were the USA (37 publications, 20%), and China (18 publications, 10%). Next, we analyzed the scientific disciplines of the first authors of the publications. To classify various affiliations, we used the taxonomy proposed by the German Research Foundation (DFG)[5]. Our findings showed that most research comes from engineering sciences (88 publications, 49%) followed by humanities and social sciences (62 publications, 34%). Six (6) affiliations could not be retrieved.

### 3.1 Educational Contexts and AI (RQ1)

From our results, we identified four cases regarding the educational contexts that appear in AIED research: a) Higher education (146 publications, 81%); b) K-12 Education (32 publications, 18%); c) Vocational Education (2 publications, 1%); d) Mixed Levels (K-12 and Higher Education) (1 publication, 2%).

Higher education dominates AIED research. This finding was not surprising due to the affordances and potential that higher education offers for conducting

[5] https://www.dfg.de/download/pdf/dfg_im_profil/gremien/fachkollegien/amtsperiode_2020_2024/fachsystematik_2020\discretionary-2024_en_grafik.pdf.

research. One can argue that researchers are inclined to conduct studies within their own institutions since they are already familiar with the context. Other reasons could be stakeholders' familiarity with educational technologies and the level of integration of educational technologies within the curriculum. Also higher education students – as adults – are potentially the most accessible group in terms of ethical requirements that studies must adhere to.

### 3.2 Methodological and Study Designs in AIED (RQ2)

To answer this question, we collected information regarding the methodologies employed (experimental or observational) in state-of-the-art AIED research, the study design regarding population size, and repeatability (that is, whether the study took place only once or repeated times), the analytical methods employed (qualitative, quantitative or mixed-methods) and the data types and sources that researchers collect and/or employ in their approaches. We classified a study as experimental if researchers introduced an intervention, a test under controlled conditions, and studied the effects following the definition[6] provided by the American Psychological Association (APA). Studies that were not classified as experimental were tagged as observational. This scheme did not always align with publications' descriptions that used the term "experiment" in their methodological description but did not meet our criteria for an experiment.

Many studies involved the training of ML models for predictive purposes, such as predicting student dropouts. Although these studies do not qualify as experimental based on our criteria, we acknowledge their importance. Most publications presented studies that followed observational methods (135 publications, 75%) while the rest of the publications (46 publications, 25%) presented experimental studies with two conditions (control, experimental) or more. Among the observational studies, 121 employed quantitative methods (66.85%), 4 employed qualitative methods (2.21%), and 10 conducted mixed methods studies (5.52%). On the other hand, 31 experimental studies used quantitative methods (17.13%)), 1 study used purely qualitative methods (0.55%), and 14 used mixed methods (7.73%). The most common method for data collection was "surveys", used by 76 studies (41.99%) to collect student responses typically via tools such as questionnaires. This was closely followed by the students' "academic data" from platforms such as learning management and student information systems (75 studies, 41.44%). Other data types and sources employed involved assessment data (such as grades and knowledge-tests), student trace data from applications' logfiles, and other learning artifacts (such as essays, and student reports).

Regarding repeatability, most publications (177 publications, 98%) presented one study. Only four (4) publications (2%) reported repeated measures. Finally, in terms of study population size, most publications (53 publications, 29.28%) presented studies with less than 100 participants, followed by 44 publications

[6] https://dictionary.apa.org/experiment.

(24.31%) ranging from 100 to 500 participants. Only 24 studies (13.26%) discussed studies with a population size of more than 10K (Fig. 3). We want to note that, in our case, population size does not always refer to the number of participants. It can instead refer to data entries or data points (such as the matriculation records in a time period). However, we tried to match, based on the information that was available in the reviewed publications, the number of participants to the data records used in the studies.

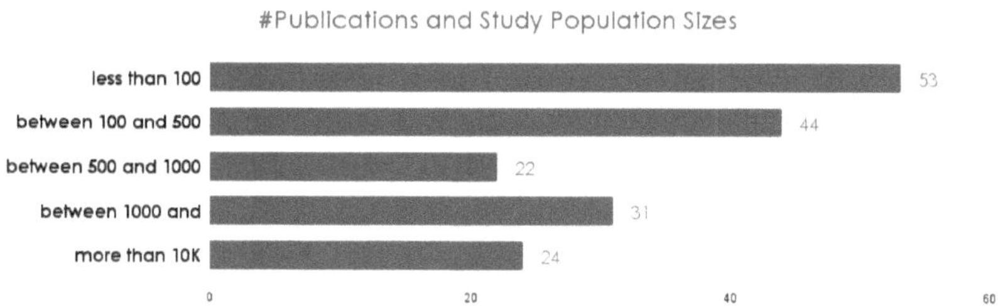


**Fig. 3.** The population sizes of research studies reported in the literature review.

### 3.3 AI Algorithms and AI Technologies Used in Education (RQ3)

We followed a combined bottom-up and top-down approach to retrieve and classify the AI algorithms and technologies used in education as referenced in research publications. First, two reviewers extracted this information from the publications under review, and then we categorized them based on existing literature. Overall, traditional machine learning algorithms were most frequently in the publications, either on their own or in combinations, such as Random Forest (42 references), Regression (36 references), Support Vector Machines (27 references), and Bayesian Networks (20 references). These algorithms were used mainly for prediction, clustering, and classification tasks. NLP methods were referenced 49 times, in relation to conversational agents and chatbots (17 references), and BERT models (11 references). Finally, publications referenced neural networks (12 references), Intelligent Tutoring Systems (5 times), and Recommender Systems (5 times).

Regarding the purpose of using AI, publications focused on predicting the academic performance of students (69 references), and predicting students at-risk of dropping out. Algorithms such as Random Forest, Support Vector Machines and Regression were commonly used for such purposes. Other usages of AI revolved around supporting students in their career choices (23 references), automated evaluation and assessment in academic contexts (12 references).

Our findings confirm prior research [3] suggesting that traditional machine learning algorithms are more popular and heavily used than advanced AI technologies such as deep learning and artificial neural networks. Additionally, we saw a growing interest in NLP and NLP-related technologies, such as chatbots and conversational agents, justified by recent advances in NLP.

# 4 Discussion

## 4.1 In Which Educational Contexts is AI Used? (RQ1)

AIED research focuses, primarily, on higher education (see Sect. 3.1). This may suggest that AI applications are limited to specific settings and not generalized or adapted to serve multiple contexts. Also, the potential and impact of AI on other important sectors, such as workplace and life-long learning, is not sufficiently explored. We perceive this as a unique research opportunity to cross-validate existing AI approaches for learning, such as ITSs, over a wide range of learning contexts. To achieve this, it is necessary to involve stakeholders from diverse settings and explore different aspects of learning.

## 4.2 What are the Methodological and Study Designs Employed in AIED Research? (RQ2)

There is a need for robust and rigorous scientific evidence for the effectiveness and impact of AIED (see Sect. 3.2). Most research studies are observational in nature, with a limited population sample, limited applicability, and transfer in new contexts. For example, studies may focus on AI models' performance but fall short in experimentally testing models in authentic contexts.

It is evident that we need to focus on multilevel, mixed-methods approaches, as recommended by [15,17], and involve triangulation to allow for cross-validation of findings.

Notably, a substantial number of studies have not made their data set open access for various reasons, such as privacy [10] etc. Some authors state willingness to make the data available on request [8,13], however there is a lack of interoperability standards in the community for communication and data exchange. This affects the reproduction and cross-validation of findings necessary for open science. This lack of standardization was also observed in reporting, making it difficult to evaluate scientific rigor. For example, while reporting their choice of AI technology, some authors reported vaguely, simply stating *NLP or chatbots* while some authors were more specific, reporting specific family of NLP algorithms such as *BERT*.

## 4.3 What AI Algorithms and Technologies are Used in Education? (RQ3)

The most popular AI technologies currently explored in the research are traditional AI algorithms, such as random forest and SVMs (see Sect. 3.3), often employed in the context of predicting academic performance and student dropouts. Additionally, the use of NLP is widespread either in combination with chatbots and conversational agents or with regard to text mining and automatic assessment. Although we acknowledge the growing body of literature regarding generative AI for teaching and learning, the research landscape is still dominated by traditional and basic AI approaches rather than performance-demanding AI technologies. This is perhaps due a limitation of our corpus containing studies only up to early 2023.

### 4.4 Theoretical and Practical Implications

The SLR findings entail critical theoretical and practical implications for AIED (in general) and ITS (in particular) research and practice. We envision that these implications can serve as input and guide future research initiatives, ensuring significant impact and innovation. We argue that the findings of this SLR make evident the need for: a) transparent communication of the use of AI in education, its potential benefits and capabilities, and its challenges and opportunities to stakeholders and the general public; b) the need for evidence-based approaches and large-scale, longitudinal studies that will provide sufficient and acceptable indications of the benefits of AI in teaching and learning; c) standardization and open access of data for reproduction and cross-examination of findings experimentally; and, d) the opportunity to revisit traditional AI approaches and cutting-edge technologies from the perspective of feasibility and applicability.

## 5 Conclusion

This paper presented an SLR about the research landscape in AIED that aimed to provide complementary insights to the findings of [20] over the past 5 years, regarding the robustness and rigorousness of methodological approaches applied in the field and in relation to AI technological advancements. To that end, we reviewed 181 research publications published from 2019 to 2023.

In this paper, we retrieved journal publications from three digital libraries (WoS, EBSCO and Scopus). Thus, we acknowledge that we may have failed to include in our review relevant and important publications. To identify AI technologies used in research, we used the descriptions that the authors offered in their publications. Thus, if some AI technology were inadvertently misrepresented, we would not be able to identify it. Similarly, AI technologies that are part of a bigger group or known by different names, might have been not accounted for. For example, BERT models have been categorized as either deep learning or NLP, depending on the authors' descriptions. In the case of reporting population or sample size, we attempted to record the number of participants per study. However, this was not always possible since some papers reported instead population samples in terms of data points or data entries, for example, the number of matriculations per academic year. Although, in some cases, making the connection between data points and participants was straightforward, this was not always the case. We noticed some discrepancies between how authors report their studies' setup and the definitions of these designs, especially regarding experimental studies. We acknowledge that our classification (experimental vs. observational) is restrictive, and one would like to gain further insights regarding diverse study designs employed in AIED research. Therefore, we see a need for future work that will aim to document the methodologies employed in AIED research in relation to the outcomes and robustness of the evidence they produce. At the same time, we acknowledge the complexity, and diversity of study designs in AIED research and the importance of Design-Based Research for the field.

Evidence-based practice indicates the need for building on solid scientific foundations when introducing effective practices into daily life, as a means to eliminate ineffective or plainly wrong approaches that rather rely on tradition, personal beliefs, and assumptions [7]. This is especially important nowadays because rapid technological advances require quick reactions regarding their integration and adoption, as several published calls for evidence regarding the effectiveness and efficacy of AI and education indicate [1,2,9]. Creating opportunities for in-situ research in coordination with practitioners, establishing good practices of rigorous reporting and data sharing, and promoting repeatability and reproducibility efforts can contribute towards bridging the gap between research findings and practical implementation.

We acknowledge the opportunities that AI can introduce for modern education. At the same time, we argue that it is critical to establish solid evidence regarding the impact of such technologies to leverage their potential.

**Acknowledgements.** This research was developed within the augMENTOR ("Augmented Intelligence for Pedagogically Sustained Training and Education") project, co-funded by the European Commission under HORIZON-CL2-2021-TRANSFORMATIONS-01-05, project number: 101061509.

## References

1. Aitken, M., et al.: Generative AI in education: call for evidence. https://www.turing.ac.uk/sites/default/files/2023-08/generative_ai_in_education_-_the_alan_turing_institute_0.pdf. Accessed 01 Mar 2024
2. Cardona, M.A., Rodríguez, R.J., Ishmael, K., et al.: Artificial intelligence and the future of teaching and learning: insights and recommendations (2023)
3. Chen, X., Xie, H., Zou, D., Hwang, G.J.: Application and theory gaps during the rise of artificial intelligence in education. Comput. Educ. Artif. Intell. **1**, 100002 (2020)
4. Chiu, T.K., Xia, Q., Zhou, X., Chai, C.S., Cheng, M.: Systematic literature review on opportunities, challenges, and future research recommendations of artificial intelligence in education. Comput. Educ. Artif. Intell. **4**, 100118 (2023)
5. Crompton, H., Burke, D.: Artificial intelligence in higher education: the state of the field. Int. J. Educ. Technol. High. Educ. **20**(1), 1–22 (2023)
6. Crompton, H., Jones, M.V., Burke, D.: Affordances and challenges of artificial intelligence in k-12 education: a systematic review. J. Res. Technol. Educ. **56**, 1–21 (2022)
7. Dekker, I.: Academic thriving: optimising student development with evidence-based higher education. Erasmus University Rotterdam (2022)
8. Eegdeman, I., Cornelisz, I., Meeter, M., Van Klaveren, C.: Identifying false positives when targeting students at risk of dropping out. Educ. Econ. **31**(3), 313–325 (2023). https://doi.org/10.1080/09645292.2022.2067131, read

9. Holmes, W., Persson, J., Chounta, I.A., Wasson, B., Dimitrova, V.: Artificial intelligence and education: a critical view through the lens of human rights, democracy and the rule of law. Council of Europe (2022)
10. Nagy, M., Molontay, R.: Interpretable dropout prediction: towards XAI-based personalized intervention. Int. J. Artif. Intell. Educ. (2023). https://doi.org/10.1007/s40593-023-00331-8
11. Ouyang, F., Zheng, L., Jiao, P.: Artificial intelligence in online higher education: a systematic review of empirical research from 2011 to 2020. Educ. Inf. Technol. **27**(6), 7893–7925 (2022)
12. Page, M.J., et al.: The PRISMA 2020 statement: an updated guideline for reporting systematic reviews. Int. J. Surg. **88**, 105906 (2021)
13. Phillips, T.M., Saleh, A., Ozogul, G.: An AI toolkit to support teacher reflection. Int. J. Artif. Intell. Educ. **33**(3), 635–658 (2023). https://doi.org/10.1007/s40593-022-00295-1
14. Stracke, C.M., Chounta, I.A., Holmes, W., Tlili, A., Bozkurt, A.: A standardised PRISMA-based protocol for systematic reviews of the scientific literature on artificial intelligence and education (AI&ED). J. Appl. Learn. Teach. **6**(2), 64–70 (2023)
15. Suzuki, H., Hong, M., Ober, T., Cheng, Y.: Prediction of differential performance between advanced placement exam scores and class grades using machine learning. Front. Educ. **7**, 1007779 (2022). https://doi.org/10.3389/feduc.2022.1007779
16. Tahiru, F.: AI in education: a systematic literature review. J. Cases Inf. Technol. (JCIT) **23**(1), 1–20 (2021)
17. Taskiran, A., Goksel, N.: Automated feedback and teacher feedback: writing achievement in learning English as a foreign language at a distance. Turk. Online J. Distance Educ. **23**(2), 120–139 (2022). https://doi.org/10.17718/tojde.1096260
18. Xu, W., Ouyang, F.: A systematic review of AI role in the educational system based on a proposed conceptual framework. Educ. Inf. Technol. **27**, 1–29 (2022)
19. Zafari, M., Bazargani, J.S., Sadeghi-Niaraki, A., Choi, S.M.: Artificial intelligence applications in k-12 education: a systematic literature review. IEEE Access **10**, 61905–61921 (2022)
20. Zawacki-Richter, O., Marín, V.I., Bond, M., Gouverneur, F.: Systematic review of research on artificial intelligence applications in higher education-where are the educators? Int. J. Educ. Technol. High. Educ. **16**(1), 1–27 (2019)

# A Constructivist Framing of Wheel Spinning: Identifying Unproductive Behaviors with Sequence Analysis

John Kos(✉), Dinesh Ayyappan, and Ashok Goel

Georgia Institute of Technology, Atlanta, GA 30332, USA
jkos3@gatech.edu

**Abstract.** Despite the increasing prevalence of inquiry-based learning (IBL) platforms, IBL research still has many open questions in constructivist contexts, such as when to offer help. In this paper, we explore wheel spinning in an open-domain inquiry-based modeling platform. We establish why closed-domain conceptions of wheel spinning do not work well in open domains, and we postulate key features of a working characterization of wheel spinning for an open-domain IBL platform. We also present a comparative quasi-experimental study of two groups of learners: While both groups worked with the same publicly available IBL platform called VERA, one group used VERA in a large graduate class at Georgia Tech and the other group was composed of globally-distributed self-directed learners (SDLs) who accessed VERA through various public websites. We use sequential pattern mining on the results in order to determine what wheel spinning looks like on the VERA platform and how to best identify it. Generalizing, we apply this research to the quitting behaviors of SDLs. Finally, modeling both user groups' action sequences into Markov chains, we identify the stage at which an IBL platform may offer proactive feedback to the learners.

**Keywords:** Inquiry-Based Learning · Wheel Spinning · Self-Directed Learning · Sequential Pattern Mining

## 1 Introduction

As opposed to in-person tutoring, Intelligent Tutoring Systems (ITS) often lack the ability to identify when the user is engaging in unproductive behavior [22]. To alleviate this gap, *wheel spinning* has become a well-researched theme in ITS literature [27]. Research has postulated the value of using wheel spinning as the foundation for ITS [26,27]. Accounting for wheel spinning is critical because it has been correlated with loss of motivation and therefore quitting behaviors [20].

The most frequently used framing for wheel spinning was conceptualized by Beck and Gong [8] and summarized by Zhang et al. (2019) [27] as "failing to get three attempts correct in a row within the first 10 practice opportunities." However, methods to detect wheel spinning in the context of well-defined problems and answers do not transfer well to open-domain educational environments


A. Sifaleras and F. Lin (Eds.): ITS 2024, LNCS 14798, pp. 174–187, 2024.
https://doi.org/10.1007/978-3-031-63028-6_14

because the outputs of the latter are not easily broken down into knowledge components [19].

In inquiry-based learning (IBL) platforms, the process of learning is often more important than the content being taught, and they tend to be grounded in more constructivist theories of education [6,21]. Given that open-domain and IBL platforms vary greatly, it is difficult to develop a framing of wheel spinning that is broadly applicable. Alternative conceptions and framings of wheel spinning used when analyzing these platforms can be read in Sect. 3.2. One difficulty that occurs when defining wheel spinning within these systems is separating it from *productive persistence*, "The ability to steadily maintain an action or complete a task despite failure or adversity." [20] Previous research has demonstrated methods of differentiating between productive persistence and wheel spinning but only in closed-domain problems [17]. Further discussion of the value of productive persistence is discussed in Sect. 3.4.

In summary, it is important to keep students engaging in productive persistence, repeating productive paths of inquiry, while helping them away from wheel spinning, repeating unproductive paths of inquiry. Therefore, we propose the following framing of wheel spinning that applies to constructivist theory: Wheel spinning occurs "when a user is unproductively taking actions that do not correspond to an internal hypothesis or goal state, past the point of productive persistence."

However, since there is no one correct answer in IBL platforms (or open-domain learning systems more generally), how do we know when a users actions do not correspond to their internal hypothesis or goal? In short, one must ask them. There are many ways of doing this including think-alouds, affect recognition, or perhaps deep learning in neural nets using massive data, if available. Given that this research is hoping to serve as the foundation of a proactive IBL platform, we are hoping to determine, in an automated fashion, when would be a good time to offer tutoring in the system. Additionally, because this is prospective research, we are unable to benefit from the large amounts of data produced by an already existing ITS system for data-dependent machine learning methods.

Instead, our research focuses on running a quasi-experiment where we asked 82 students from a graduate class in cognitive science at Georgia Institute of Technology (a R1 university in USA) to click on an in-software coach request button within the inquiry-based ecology modeling tool VERA (Virtual Ecological Research Assistant) [2–4]. We then use sequential pattern mining (SPM) [1] and data mining to develop a generalized conception of when a student might be spinning wheels.

## 2 VERA: A Platform for Inquiry-Based Learning

VERA is made up of two main components: a conceptual modeling tool and a simulation engine. Learners are able to model different ecological systems by creating and modifying the system components and relationships between them. These ecological systems are captured through a Structure-Behavior-Function model [13,23] that allows for agent-based simulations of ecological phenomena [2].

Figure 1 shows the conceptual modeling interface that lets learners imagine and model a diverse set of possible ecologies.

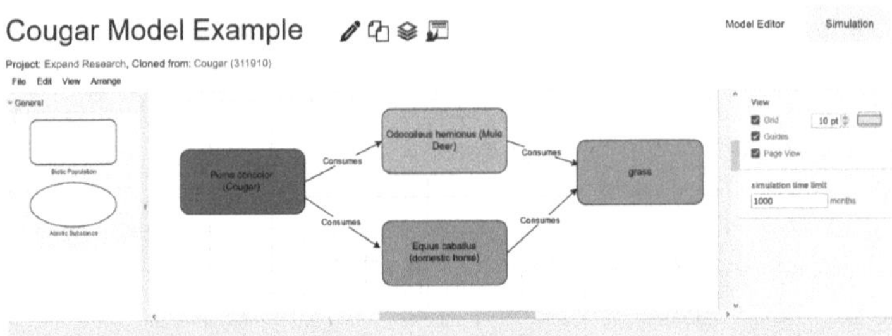


**Fig. 1.** VERA modeling interface. Coach request button looks like teacher in front of chalkboard

Figure 2 shows the interface to the simulation engine, where student can visualize their ecologies interacting as a time series of the population of the species they modeled, where the x-axis tracks time in months and the y-axis is population.

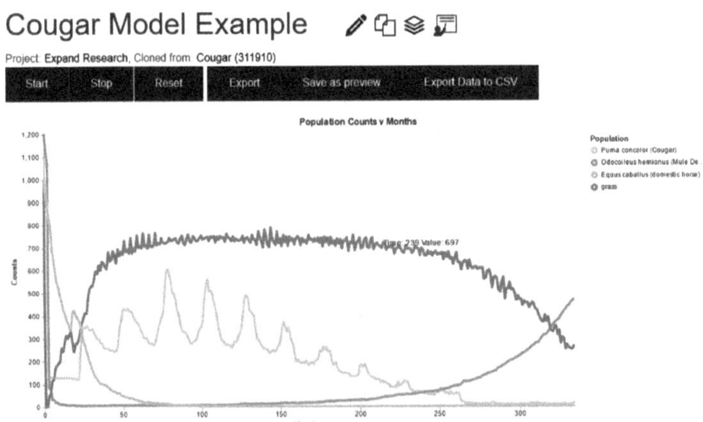


**Fig. 2.** Simulation Environment for VERA

In VERA, the simulation component acts as a feedback or evaluation step where students can check the hypothesis of their conceptual model [2–4]. The core of this process is similar to causal models developed by White et al. which centered around model-simulate-refine loops [25]. VERA also provides access to coaches that provide help on the modeling process to the learners when requested. At present, the coaches in VERA are reactive in that they offer advice only when asked. We seek of develop proactive coaches that would provide guidance to learners when they detect wheel spinning.

This research will demonstrate a methodology for identifying wheel spinning in VERA. First, we will affirm that wheel spinning occurs in VERA. Second, we will use sequential pattern mining to identify common patterns that a user engages in before making a request to a coach for help. Third, we will generalize this identification of wheel spinning to the end-of-session actions of self-directed learners; these are learners that use the VERA platform on their own outside of the classroom, and therefore have modeling behavior that corresponds to internal goal states unknown to us instead of known classroom assignments. Lastly, we will use Markov chains to estimate the best time to offer proactive help as part of VERA.

# 3 Background

## 3.1 Inquiry-Based Learning

Research into IBL in open domains, particularly in the form of interactive learning environments, has seen a massive increase in popularity over the years [11]. IBL gives learners the opportunity to practice meta-cognitive skills, which have been shown to play a significant role in academic achievement and learning outcomes [9,11,12]. Additionally, higher meta-cognitive skills are correlated a higher likelihood to engage in help-seeking behavior [12]. IBL, however, struggles with keeping students on productive learning paths, and the question of how to keep students from engaging in unproductive modes of inquiry is still open [10].

This motivates the need for a proactive coaches in IBL platforms such as VERA that can identify when a student is spinning wheels and offer help. Students who are less likely to ask for help have a direct need for a proactive coaches that can scaffold their experience in an IBL education system, potentially alleviating the lack of meta-cognitive skills that prevented them from seeking help in the first place. This research hopes to answer the question of "when" an IBL would offer feedback by developing a framing for and centering identification of wheel spinning in open domains. The question of what that feedback would look like and how it will be presented is left to future research.

## 3.2 Wheel Spinning

Wheel spinning has been linked to both lower motivation in learners as well as an avoidance in help seeking behaviors [20]. For this reason, it is important to construct and develop a methodology by which wheel spinning can be identified, and with the eventual intervention of ITS, rectified. As mentioned previously the most common conception of wheel spinning involves the failure of answering the same question correctly three times in a row within 10 attempts. This framing is the most popular and works well with the literature on knowledge components [27].

Zhang et al. has research that looked at six different wheel spinning detectors using two different criteria across multiple datasets, but the given detectors or criteria are not generalizable to inquiry-based or open-domain problems [27]. Owen et al. discusses the importance of differentiating wheel spinning in a closed-domain mathematics game [20]. In doing so, they relate wheel spinning to lower gameplay efficiency, effectively tying the conception to a measurable goal state. This manifests as a framing of wheel spinning as "a great deal of effort with very little progress." In this sense, this conception is closer to a constructivist framing, as it does not specify explicit goal states and knowledge components. However, it lacks a differentiation from productive persistence.

Next, this relation of lower gameplay efficiency relates to research from Bauer et al. which uses sequence analysis in a protein folding scientific discovery game *Foldit* [7]. While *Foldit* lacks clear goal states and specification of direct relationships between a student's current state and their final goal state, the game still has a quantitative measure of success based on the energy level of the protein folding. This allows a differentiation of high-performing and lower-performing learners that is not directly applicable to VERA. However comparison with *Foldit* would give us some idea of what wheel spinning would look like in a more open domain.

### 3.3 End-of-Session Activities

End-of-session behavior for educational systems is still a growing field of research [15,26]. There are many reasons to consider end-of-session actions including completion of the goal, frustration, or distraction [15]. Wu et al. researched the quitting behavior of students within a digital game for learning genetics [26]. They found three categories of quitting behavior, one of which is exemplified by students quitting after an extended period of not reaching their goal. This matches our conception of wheel spinning and corroborates previous research on the correlation between wheel spinning behavior and quitting behavior. The authors come to a similar conclusion by suggesting that the research can be used to dynamically change the difficulty of the student problem.

### 3.4 Productive Persistence and Quitting Behavior

Productive persistence, or grit, is highly correlated with achievement and long term outcomes [20]. For this reason, it is important to differentiate between productive persistence and wheel spinning, though it is challenging to do so [17]. Kai et al. (2019) did research on differentiating between wheel spinning students and students engaging in productive persistence within a math game context using a decision tree. This tree included a number of factors such as number of attempts, time between problems, number of hints used, etc. In the context of their closed-domain problem, they were able to identify different categories of students that engage in wheel spinning. A possible indicator that a student is wheel spinning instead of productively persisting is quitting behavior. For this reason, quitting behavior, especially as in seen in self-directed learning, will be our comparison point by which we demonstrate a generalizable framing of wheel spinning in IBL platforms.

### 3.5 Sequential Pattern Mining

SPM has made an impact across many fields in recent decades [24]. It aims to identify patterns of behavior across multiple sequences, though further analysis is required to identify significant or insightful results. Several pattern mining techniques exist [14], and this paper uses a constraint-based SPM library developed by Wang et al. (2022) [24] which allows temporal data to supplement the actions in isolation.

Much work has been done in applying SPM in ITS research where success or performance can be measured objectively and quantitatively. For example, Chen and Wang [9] demonstrated how SPM can be used to understand user actions in a online physics simulation of buoyancy. Hansen et al. used both SPM and Markov Chains to, respectively, quantitatively and qualitatively measure unproductive student behavior in a mathematics educational system [16]. Additionally, Kinnebrew, Loretz, and Biswas used sequence mining in an IBL platform, Betty's Brain, in order to differentiate between high and low performance students and therefore productive and unproductive learning behaviors [18].

There is also recent work with SPM in VERA that grouped users and their behavior into three distinct approaches: observation, construction, and exploration [5]. Our research builds in part on this prior work.

## 4 Methodology

### 4.1 Cohorts

Two groups were compared. The first is a set of independent self-directed learners (SDLs), identified as 19 users who registered on VERA without academic email addresses from 2021 to 2023. It is assumed that these users had less structure and less guided behavior than users for whom working with VERA was part of a directed assignment. While a tutorial is available on the VERA site, there is no guarantee that the users follow the tutorial in order to understand how to use VERA. Additionally, we are unable to know what these users' goal states were and whether they reached them before quitting.

The second group was a set of 82 students who took an online graduate course in cognitive science at Georgia Tech in the summer term of 2023. These users had an assignment that involved performing multiple experiments with VERA. The purpose of the assignment was to give students the experience of cognitive science in action, in the form of tools for conceptual modeling and simulation, based on cognitive theories of scientific reasoning as well as science learning.

Due to the structured nature of the assignment, and the fact that students had to submit their own ecological models, we can assume that the goal state of the users was the final state of their model. Prior to the release of the assignment, students were made aware through a post on the discussion board that there was a mock tutoring feature included in the system. Students were offered extra credit if they filled out a survey and acknowledged the intent to use the mock tutoring feature in the system whenever they needed help while modeling. Other than the note on the discussion forum and an illustration in the survey itself, students were not reminded of the tutoring feature or what it looked like in the VERA interface.

### 4.2 Data Recording and Behavior Classification

The VERA database logs user actions with timestamps, recording a variety of viewing, editing, and simulating behaviors that users attempt. When students clicked on the tutoring feature, an entry was written into the user log of type *coach request.*

Users actions from each cohort were extracted and organized into sessions of work on a model. A user could have multiple concurrent sessions and a model could appear in multiple users' logs. Sessions are defined as consequent action sequences with no more than a five-minute period between two actions or a ten-minute period after a simulation. The following types of actions were recorded: *new model, construct model, revise model, start simulation, stop/reset simulation, edit property, clone model, lookup, view model, coach request. New model* refers to when a student creates a new model in the VERA system. *View model* refers to whenever they open a model from their project page, or refresh the model in the browser. *Construct model* is written to the logs whenever a student adds a new component or relationship. *Revise model* occurs whenever a student either deletes a node or edge or changes relationship type. *Edit property* refers to the students changing the parameters of either the components or relationships. *Lookup* is when a student users the Encyclopedia of Life (EOL) API to fetch real world parameters for a biotic component. *Clone model* is whenever a user copies a model from another source. *Start simulation* occurs when a student runs the simulation for their model and *Stop/Reset Simulation* occurs whenever they click to stop or reset simulation buttons on the simulation page.

In the Markov chain diagram below, construct model, revise model, edit property and lookup are considered "construct model". Clone model, view model and new model are considered "new model". Start simulation and stop/reset Simulation are considered "simulate".

After constructing sessions and action sequences from the logged data, cohorts were further divided into subgroups that focused on coach requests or end-of-session behavior. Within these groups, sequences were analyzed using *Seq2Pat*, a Sequence-to-Pattern Generation Library [24]. This specific library was chosen for its well-documented Python library and ability to incorporate temporal data of the sequence and use this as a constraint. This identified repeated patterns of actions within a given time span across subgroups. For example, the most common sequence among the summer 2023 cohort was *[start simulation, end simulation]* which occurred in about half of nearly 2400 sequences.

Once identified, sequences were compared across different cohorts to identify patterns that could be used to signal a need for coaching with close attention on actions taken before a coach request or the end of a session.

# 5 Results

## 5.1 Actions Before Coach Request

Of the 82 students in the cognitive science class that completed the assignment, 21 users made a coach request with a total of 32 requests. These 32 occurrences of coach requests are our proof of wheel spinning. For three of the coach requests, the previous action before the request was also a coach request. We are omitting these from our Seq2Pat analysis as they do not tell us about user modeling behavior, though we investigate this pattern later in the results. The coach requests occurred across the 2399 total sessions taken by the students in the cognitive science class, meaning that coach requests occurred in 1.21% of all user sessions in the course. *Start simulation* and *stop/reset simulation* are the most common actions immediately before a coach request, and the next most common are viewing and constructing models. Starting and stopping the simulation made up 19 of the total coach requests amounting to 65.52% of the total requests. Four coach requests, additionally, occurred right after viewing a new model.

## 5.2 Sequences of Note

Seq2Pat output the following sequences of note as shown in Table 1. Sequences are ordered on the table based on the prevalence of the coach requests for each sequence divided by the prevalence of the sequence across all modeling sessions. This is the last column Request/Total. This prioritized less common sequences that have a higher number of coach requests. The Cogsci % column refers to the prevalence of coach requests among the sequence in the cognitive science class. The Request number refers to the raw number of coach requests following each sequence. End % refers to the likelihood that end session would follow the sequence for the SDLs. It is also worth noting that very few non-simulation patterns were listed by Seq2Pat. *Start simulation* and *stop/reset simulation* were the most common patterns before quitting actions and coach requests. From this we can also gather that the most common action after a start or stop of the simulation is another start or stop. As we do not want to offer assistance every time a student stops or starts a simulation, it is important that we offer help only after specific patterns of activities. Table 1 shows us which patterns would be useful to offer help after, but more information, which we will examine later, is needed to determine when in the full modeling journey to offer that help.

**Table 1.** Tables showing sequences of note that had a high prevalence of coach request to commonality of action sequence ratio and comparison to end of session ratio

| Pattern | Cogsci % | Request # | End % | Request/Total |
|---|---|---|---|---|
| Stp Sim, Stp Sim, Strt Sim | 71.38 | 6 | 90.90 | 1.922 |
| Stp Sim, Strt Sim, Stp Sim, Strt Sim | 67.03 | 4 | 87.50 | 1.921 |
| Stp Sim, Strt Sim, Stp Sim | 71.19 | 5 | 87.50 | 1.915 |
| Stp Sim, Strt Sim | 83.87 | 9 | 87.50 | 1.899 |
| Stp Sim, Strt Sim, Strt Sim | 76.46 | 6 | 90.00 | 1.897 |
| Stp Sim, Strt Sim, Strt Sim | 76.46 | 6 | 90.00 | 1.897 |

### 5.3 Total User History and Patterns Across Sessions

Table 2 demonstrates where in the modeling process the coach requests occurred. Six of the coach requests took place on the users very first model, with two of those requests occurring before any simulation took place. Similarly another six coach requests occurred on the second model that the user made but only after they had run 10+ simulations in their VERA modeling experience. The vast majority of coach requests occurred deep into the VERA modeling process, after students had run over 100+ simulations, and had created more than four models.

**Table 2.** Coach request by model number and simulation count

| Model # — Sim # | 0 | 1–10 | 11–50 | 50–100 | 101–200 | 201+ |
|---|---|---|---|---|---|---|
| 0 | 2 | 2 | 2 | 0 | 0 | 0 |
| 1 | 0 | 0 | 4 | 1 | 1 | 0 |
| 2–3 | 0 | 1 | 0 | 0 | 1 | 0 |
| 4–5 | 0 | 0 | 0 | 0 | 4 | 3 |
| 6+ | 0 | 0 | 0 | 0 | 3 | 4 |

There were patterns in the coach requests that were not picked up by Seq2Pat because they occurred across sessions. Nine coach requests occurred within three actions of the end of a previous session. For seven of the nine, simulation occurred between the end-of-session and the coach request. This means that the user took a 10+ min break from modeling, but did not close the VERA tab as to prompt the *view model* action. The remaining two of the nine requests followed the pattern of [coach request, end session, coach request]. There were additionally two other patterns of note. First, the open model followed by requesting help, and second, requesting help after interacting with EOL. Students requested help after opening a new model or ending a session in 10 cases. In these cases students did not model or start the simulation. It is important to note, however, in five of these cases, students began their session, clicked *stop/reset simulation* twice when the simulation was not running and then requested help. The last pattern of note is when students lookup on EOL multiple times. This only occurred once, however this pattern is distinct from the modeling and simulating patterns we have already discussed.

## 5.4 Markov Diagram

In Fig. 3, a Markov diagram helps visualize user actions as they move through the modeling process. This allows us to examine when a student would need assistance in their modeling journey. We can see that 15.62% of users that made a coach request then moved directly to the end-session action. Additionally, we see that students requested help 2.27% of the time following the construction of a model and 2.19% of the time following simulation of a model.

Both groups, SDLs and cognitive science students, stayed in the simulation state at similar rates with a simulation action going into another simulation action 86.65% percent of the time with the cognitive science students and 76.24% of the time with the SDLs. Similarly, the movement from simulation to model construction was alike with students moving from simulation to construction 9.18% of the time for cognitive science students and 5.94% of the time for SDLs. The end session statistics were highly different between the two groups with simulation moving to end session only 1.88% of the time in the cognitive science class and 14.85% of the time in the SDLs case. Lastly, cognitive science students moved from new model to end session at a 7.14% rate while SDLs did so at a much higher rate of 18.75%.

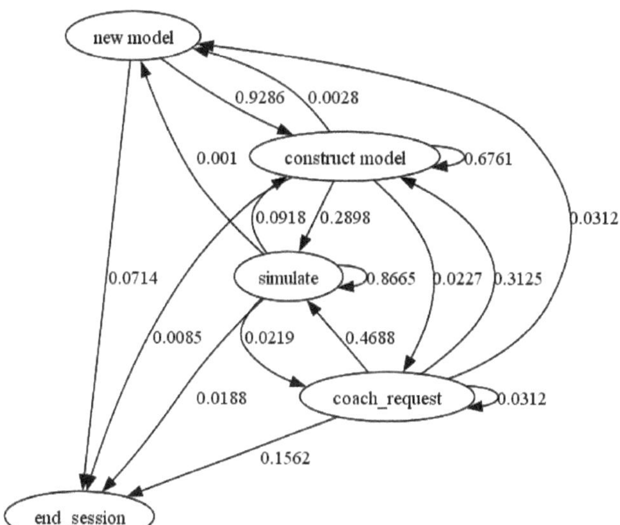


**Fig. 3.** Markov chain for students that requested coaching

# 6 Discussion

## 6.1 When to Offer Proactive Tutoring

There is a tradeoff between the length of a sequence used as a predictor of wheel spinning and the strength of its signal as a unique predictor. Designers of IBL platforms such as VERA with proactive coaching will need to make context-dependent judgments about how much to tolerate coaching that their users might not have needed in order to increase the likelihood of providing coaching to users that actually need it. In this context, the process of IBL in VERA contains simulation as an evaluation step. Running the simulation multiple times presents no cost to the user other than their own time, and this is the only part of the process that provides feedback to the user. We can begin to understand why so much of users' behavior is concentrated in this stage of the process. The feedback from the evaluation, the simulation in this case, is absolutely essential to determining the validity of both the learner's hypothesis and the more elaborate conceptual model.

Looking closely into what happens after the feedback of the simulation is shared with the user, we see some plausible hypotheses emerge about the causes of coach requests. If the feedback is incomprehensible to the user because, for example, the organisms completely fail or behave in a way that the user was not expecting due to lack of ecological knowledge, then the user may struggle to figure out how to revise their model or adjust the simulation parameters based on the feedback. This may be a moment when they feel lost and need coaching. As we can see in Table 2 this can occur even deep into the VERA modeling process.

If a user starts a new model or comes back to a model after a break, which is recorded as the end of a session, they may have some need for coaching. This is especially true if the user stop/resets the simulation without ever starting it. So, a user ending a session and returning may a good way to differentiate productive persistence from wheel spinning. The correlation of wheel spinning behavior with end-of-session behavior goes both ways. Due to the nature of wheel spinning causing users to become help-avoidant and the fact that users often requested help early in their model, it may be useful to offer proactive help once to users at the beginning of their modeling process. This is further reinforced by SDLs quitting early in their modeling process as described in Sect. 5.4.

Future work in this area could investigate different demographics and domains to validate or broaden the current understanding of where in the IBL process learners demonstrate the most wheel spinning. Attempting to measure or deduce more about the users themselves and their learning behaviors and attitudes may help to provide a more differentiated coaching model that is highly responsive to individual users' needs. The identification of patterns from this paper, for example, help seeking during the self evaluation step of instruction or immediately post quitting and restarting a session, might offer insight into important times to offer proactive coaching in an IBL platform. Although this research was designed to bridge a gap in help seeking behavior, it is still prospective. Further research is needed to assess the outcomes of attempting to bridge that gap. Given that learning is so contextual, researchers should be mindful of the balance between striving to find broadly applicable results and being rigorous about precisely naming the domain for which their results are valid.

## 7 Conclusion

In this work we developed a new characterization for wheel spinning that applies to open-domain IBL platforms. Then using data from an experiment where students were asked to flag whenever they were wheel spinning, we explored several methods by which we can find patterns in that data. We found that students most often requested help deep into their modeling journey, specifically during the simulation step of that modeling. We then attempted to generalize using Seq2Pat to determine when to offer help, identifying common patterns and comparing them to end of session behaviors for self-directed learners. We also identified a couple of common patterns in requesting help, for example students beginning a new model, or students stopping a simulation without starting a new one. We believe this research promises to be a useful preliminary step in identifying wheel spinning in open-domain interactive learning environments: it could be a foundation for an inquiry-based learning platforms that is capable of providing proactive assistance to students who may be wheel spinning. This will support more students in finding success in the increasingly complex and open-ended problems they are solving in academic and professional environments.

**Acknowledgements.** This research has been supported by NSF Grants #2112532 and #2247790 to the National AI Institute for Adult Learning and Online Education. We thank members of the VERA project in the Design Intelligence Laboratory for their contributions to this work.

## References

1. Agrawal, R., Srikant, R.: Mining sequential patterns. In: Proceedings of the Eleventh International Conference on Data Engineering, March 1995, pp. 3–14. IEEE (1995)
2. An, S., Bates, R., Hammock, J., Rugaber, S., Goel, A.: VERA: popularizing science through AI. In: Penstein Rosé, C., et al. (eds.) AIED 2018. LNCS (LNAI), vol. 10948, pp. 31–35. Springer, Cham (2018). https://doi.org/10.1007/978-3-319-93846-2_6
3. An, S., Bates, R., Hammock, J., Rugaber, S., Weigel, E., Goel, A.: Scientific modeling using large scale knowledge. In: Bittencourt, I.I., Cukurova, M., Muldner, K., Luckin, R., Millán, E. (eds.) AIED 2020. LNCS (LNAI), vol. 12164, pp. 20–24. Springer, Cham (2020). https://doi.org/10.1007/978-3-030-52240-7_4
4. An, S., Broniec, W., Rugaber, S., Weigel, E., Hammock, J., Goel, A.: Recognizing novice learner's modeling behaviors. In: Cristea, A.I., Troussas, C. (eds.) ITS 2021. LNCS, vol. 12677, pp. 189–200. Springer, Cham (2021). https://doi.org/10.1007/978-3-030-80421-3_21

5. An, S., Rugaber, S., Hammock, J., Goel, A.K.: Understanding self-directed learning with sequential pattern mining. In: International Conference on Artificial Intelligence in Education, pp, 502–505 (2022)
6. Animeh, R.J., Asl, H.D.: Review of constructivism and social constructivism. J. Soc. Sci. Lit. Lang. **1**, 9–16 (2015)
7. Bauer, A., Flatten, J., Popovic, Z.: Analysis of Problem-Solving Behavior in Open-Ended Scientific-Discovery Game Challenges. International Educational Data Mining Society (2017)
8. Beck, J.E., Gong, Y.: Wheel-spinning: students who fail to master a skill. In: Lane, H.C., Yacef, K., Mostow, J., Pavlik, P. (eds.) AIED 2013. LNCS (LNAI), vol. 7926, pp. 431–440. Springer, Heidelberg (2013). https://doi.org/10.1007/978-3-642-39112-5_44
9. Chen, C.M., Wang, W.F.: Mining effective learning behaviors in a web-based inquiry science environment. J. Sci. Educ. Technol. **29**, 519–535 (2020)
10. Cock, J.M., Marras, M., Giang, C., Käser, T.: Generalisable methods for early prediction in interactive simulations for education (2022)
11. Friesen, S., Scott, D.: Inquiry-based learning: a review of the research literature, pp. 1–32. Alberta Ministry Education (2013)
12. Gao, Z., Erickson, B., Xu, Y., Lynch, C., Heckman, S., Barnes, T.: Admitting you have a Problem is the First Step: Modeling When and Why Students Seek Help in Programming Assignments. International Educational Data Mining Society (2022)
13. Goel, A.K., Rugaber, S., Vattam, S.: Structure, behavior, and function of complex systems: the structure, behavior, and function modeling language. AI EDAM **23**(1), 23–35 (2009)
14. Han, J., Kamber, M.: Data Mining. Concepts and Techniques, 2nd edn. Morgan Kaufmann (2006)
15. Hansen, C., Hansen, C., Alstrup, S., Lioma, C.: Modelling end-of-session actions in educational systems. arXiv preprint arXiv:1909.06856 (2019)
16. Hansen, C., Hasen, C., Hjuler, N., Alstrup, S., Lioma, C.: Sequence modelling for analysing student interaction with educational systems. arXiv preprint arXiv:1708.04164 (2017)
17. Kai, S., Almeda, M.V., Baker, R.S., Heffernan, C., Heffernan, N.: Decision tree modeling of wheel-spinning and productive persistence in skill builders. J. Educ. Data Min. **10**, 36–71 (2018)
18. Kinnebrew, J.S., Loretz, K.M., Biswas, G.: A contextualized, differential sequence mining method to derive students' learning behavior patterns. J. Educ. Data Min. **5**, 190–219 (2013)
19. Niazi, M.A., Hussain, A., Kolberg, M.: Verification & validation of agent based simulations using the VOMAS (virtual overlay multi-agent system) approach. arXiv preprint arXiv:1708.02361 (2017)
20. Owen, V., et al.: Detecting wheel-spinning and productive persistence in educational games, June 2019
21. Steffe, L.P., Gale, J.E.: Constructivism in Education. Psychology Press (1995)
22. VanLehn, K.: The relative effectiveness of human tutoring, intelligent tutoring systems, and other tutoring systems. Educ. Psychol. **46**, 197–221 (2011)
23. Vattam, S., et al.: Understanding complex natural systems by articulating structure-behavior-function models. Educ. Technol. Soc. **14**(1), 66–81 (2011)
24. Wang, X., Hosseininasab, A., Colunga, P., Kadıoğlu, S., van Hoeve, W.-J.: Seq2Pat: sequence-to-pattern generation for constraint-based sequential pattern mining. Proc. AAAI Conf. Artif. Intell. **36**(11), 12665–12671 (2022)

25. White, B.Y., Frederiksen, J.R.: Causal model progressions as a foundation for intelligent learning environments. Artif. Intell. **42**(1), 99–157 (1990)
26. Wu, Z., et al.: Predicting challenge outcomes for students in a digital game for learning genetics. In: EDM Workshops, pp. 51–59 (2019)
27. Zhang, C., et al.: Early detection of wheel spinning: comparison across tutors, models, features, and operationalizations. International Educational Data Mining Society (2019)

# Evaluating the Ability of Large Language Models to Generate Motivational Feedback

Angelo Gaeta, Francesco Orciuoli(✉), Antonella Pascuzzo, and Angela Peduto

Dipartimento di Scienze Aziendali - Management and Innovation Systems (DISA-MIS), Università Degli Studi di Salerno, Via Giovanni Paolo II, 132, 84084 Fisciano, SA, Italy
{agaeta,forciuoli,apascuzzo,anpeduto}@unisa.it

**Abstract.** The paper describes and evaluates the use of large language models (LLMs) to provide personalized motivational feedback in the context of Intelligent Tutoring Systems (ITS). Specifically, the main contributions of the present work are the definition of a novel evaluation framework and the early application of such a framework to assess the ability of LLMs to generate textual feedback including motivational features. The experimentation results show that LLMs demonstrate a promising ability to generate motivational feedback and, therefore, a good chance to be integrated as an additional model into the traditional ITS architecture.

**Keywords:** Large Language Model · Intelligent Tutoring Systems · Motivational feedback

## 1 Introduction

Motivating students is essential to their success in academic performance and daily life activities. However, the development of online motivational systems requires knowledge about the strengths and weaknesses of students, including their learning approach, background, and online experience. In [17], motivation is defined as the desire and the willingness of students to engage and persist in learning tasks. Personalizing the learning experiences, identifying areas requiring feedback or scaffolding, and offering individualized support, are some of the external factors [23] that significantly impact students' motivation. On the other hand, also the intrinsic factors such as students' judgments of their ability to complete a task, and their perception of the benefits that task completion will bring, have an influence. Therefore, leveraging extrinsic and intrinsic motivational factors results in enhancement in learning engagement. In this scenario, the introduction of Intelligent Tutoring Systems (ITSs) [5,14] marks a significant turning point in the use of Artificial Intelligence (AI) in the education field.


A. Sifaleras and F. Lin (Eds.): ITS 2024, LNCS 14798, pp. 188–201, 2024.
https://doi.org/10.1007/978-3-031-63028-6_15

In fact, by collecting and storing data on performances and other variables, they can make inferences about students, providing them tailored feedback and hints [18]. These educational systems consist of interconnected components: i) the *Domain (or Expert)* module, which encompasses domain-specific facts and rules, and holds the instructional contents; ii) the *Student (or Learner)* module, in which student profiles including problem-solving states and long-term progress are stored; iii) the *Tutoring (or Instructional)* model, which dictates how the tutor (system) teaches, guides the student, and offers feedback; iv) the *User Interface*, which deals with how learners interact with the ITS [15]. Recent advancements in Generative AI, particularly with the development of large language models (LLMs) leveraging Pre-trained Transformers, have significantly contributed to the field of Natural Language Processing (NLP) [11,21]. Integrating these modules with real-time student-tutor conversations, highly sophisticated texts that closely resemble those authored by humans [20] are provided to students. A list of teaching resources is no longer just presented to students. Instead, ITSs create activities that allow students to analyze a task from various perspectives, aligned with their existing knowledge and learning styles, and to utilize the provided resources effectively [9]. The results presented in this paper aim to evaluate the use of LLMs to generate motivational text in the context of ITSs. The experimentation involved different LLMs such as GPT-3.5-Turbo, Gemini 1.0 Pro (Gemini), Llama 2 70B, and Mixtral $8 \times 7$B, to identify the best-performing model. In the Evaluation Framework, the identification of motivational pillars, the construction of learning situations, prompt engineering, and the setting of qualitative and quantitative analyses are specified. Results from both qualitative and quantitative experiments indicate that the different models can generate motivational texts appropriate for different learning situations. The structure of the remaining part of the paper is as follows: Sect. 2 presents and discusses related works. Section 3 shows, from the conceptual architecture perspective, how an LLM could interact with the main models that are typically included within an ITS. Section 4 describes the novel evaluation framework. Section 5 reports and discusses the experimental results obtained by applying the defined framework. Lastly, Sect. 6 draws conclusions and presents possible future works.

## 2 Related Work

Generative AI represents an innovative and promising approach to meeting the needs of modern education. In fact, by harnessing the power of Generative AI in LLMs such as ChatGPT, it is possible to make them perform extraordinarily complex tasks in the field of education [2]. For instance, promoting teaching and learning, and Virtual Tutoring [6] are complex tasks that can be supported by LLMs. By leveraging interaction and human-like understanding capabilities, these models can assist students efficiently through real-time interactions. Therefore, acting like ITSs, LLMs know perfectly what to teach, who to teach, and how to teach. As a consequence, enhancements in the learning experience [7] are reachable. In [25], students of a foreign language are supported and guided in studying the vocabulary usually housed in foreign language textbooks. Combining the dialogue generation technology with GPT, relevant questions are asked and the answers are evaluated. Moreover, these models help students learn and adopt a growth mindset [13]. Persuasive strategies are used to give students feedback to foster the growth mindset and, at the same time, they are motivated to actively participate in the learning environment. Realizing the potential of acting as tutors, in the present work, the LLMs are integrating into the traditional ITS architecture to evaluate their abilities in generating motivational responses appropriate to specific students' learning situations.

## 3 Overall Picture

This work starts from the hypothesis that a traditional ITS architecture could be enhanced through the integration of an LLM, pre-trained for executing text generation tasks. A traditional ITS architecture should have an interface to communicate with students and three components, domain, tutoring, and student, each having its own category of knowledge. The aforementioned knowledge components respectively deal with: i) what should be learned by the user, ii) the progress of the user, and iii) the behavior of different teaching situations [8].

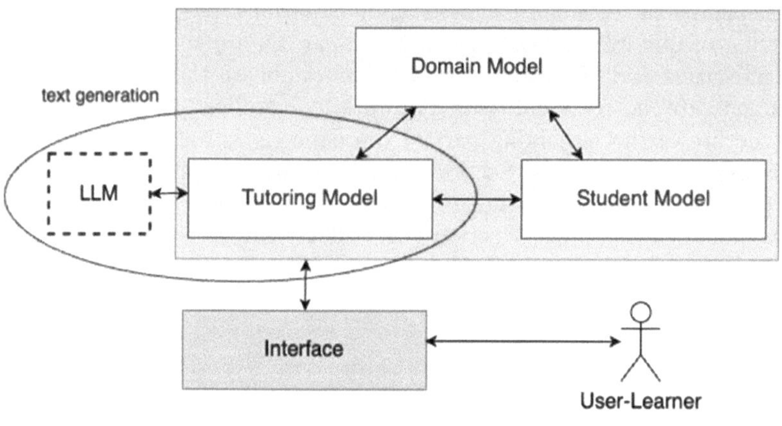


**Fig. 1.** Extended architecture for ITS

Starting from this picture, the main idea is to consider the chance to add a further model (the LLM) to support the generation of textual content aimed at enriching and improving the communication of tutoring actions. One of the main benefits of such an integration could be improving the level of sustainability of intelligent tutoring systems development. In fact, enhancing an ITS with LLMs could lead to decreased efforts related to authoring phases, whose complexity and expensiveness are two of the major barriers to the diffusion of intelligent tutoring systems. Let us see how a LLM could be integrated into a traditional ITS architecture (see Fig. 1). The tutoring component controls the interactions with the LLM, thus it is responsible for invoking the language model, bypassing all necessary input, and pushing its answers into the interface in order to communicate them to the student. Among the other plausible functionalities, the paper assesses how LLMs can help generate appropriate motivational feedback in intelligent tutoring systems, thus providing initial support for the initial hypothesis.

## 4 Evaluation Framework

The main goal of the proposed framework is to assess the ability of LLMs to generate textual content to propose as motivational feedback sent by intelligent tutors to students.

### 4.1 Component View

The proposed framework is structurally defined by seven main components: i) Pillars, ii) Personas and Scenarios Definition, iii) Ground Truth Preparation, iv) Prompt Engineering, v) Human Tutors, vi) Qualitative Evaluation, and vii) Quantitative Evaluation.

- **Pillars** [3] are criteria characterizing the strategies that can be used to create motivational textual content to empower tutors' feedback. In this framework, pillars are used as the main source to generate ground truth and prompts for invoking LLMs. In particular, the identified pillars are six: establishing task value, promoting mastery goals, fostering belongingness, encouraging emotional regulation, promoting expectancy of success, and fostering autonomy (see Table 1).
- **Personas and Scenarios** [1], in the context of this work, are respectively a description of a target student and brief stories describing the interactions of the considered personas with the learning environment. Typically, a persona is combined with one or more scenarios. In this framework, the combination of a persona with a specific scenario is used to instruct prompt engineering to allow LLMs to understand the learning situation and generate suitable motivational texts. It is important to note that in the context of real-world situations, it is possible to extract information related to a pair <persona, scenario> the Student Model and the other main models included in a traditional ITS architecture.
- **Ground Truth Preparation** is the component responsible for generating the dataset that will be used to support the quantitative evaluation of LLM results.
- **Human Tutors** are expert tutors who have two main responsibilities: supervising the ground truth preparation by also considering personas and scenarios, and evaluating LLMs results during qualitative evaluation.

- **Prompt Engineering** is the process of crafting instructions for LLMs to enhance the effectiveness and quality of their outputs [22]. It is the phase in which prompts, i.e. input texts for LLMs, are prepared by using specific approaches and taking into account personas, scenarios, and pillars.
- **Quantitative Evaluation** compares ground truth with motivational texts generated by LLMs. Such comparisons are executed by considering the same learning situations.
- **Qualitative Evaluation** foresees the generation of motivational texts through the invocation of LLMs, which suitable prompts are passed to, and the assessment of their answers by engaging a pool of human tutors.

**Table 1.** The definition of the six motivational pillars

| Pillar | Definition |
|---|---|
| Task value | Students' perceptions of how important, interesting, and useful a particular task is |
| Mastery Goals | Ambition to improve the level of competence, to develop new skills, or to achieve a sense of mastery based on self-referenced (intrapersonal) standards |
| Sense of Belonging | Feeling accepted and liked by the rest of the group. Be connected to others and feeling like a member of a community |
| Manage of emotions | Ability to correctly identify one's own emotions and those of others, and to guide, adjust, and control them purposefully, to achieve healthy development |
| Expectation of success | The degree to which students believe they will accomplish a task or master a skill successfully |
| Autonomy | Take control and responsibility for their learning, both in terms of what they learn and how they learn it. The starting point is that students can self-direction and develop an independent, proactive approach to their studies |

## 4.2 Quantitative Evaluation

The process for applying quantitative evaluation is described in Fig. 2 which shows the creation of a ground truth that is a dataset including actual motivational texts. Each row contains three versions of the same actual motivational text to provide LLMs with more chances to generate a matching response. In particular, three uncontextualized motivational texts are provided for each pillar. Such texts are obtained from specialized literature and supervised by expert human tutors who also contextualize them by using a set of $k$ pairs <persona, scenario>. For the construction of model-generated texts, three main activities are executed. The first one is Prompt Engineering which produces six prompts (one for each pillar) for each one of the $k$ pairs <persona, scenario> that are aligned with the ones used for the ground truth. Prompts are constructed by exploiting the following techniques:

- **Output customization**, to assign the role of a motivating tutor to the model;

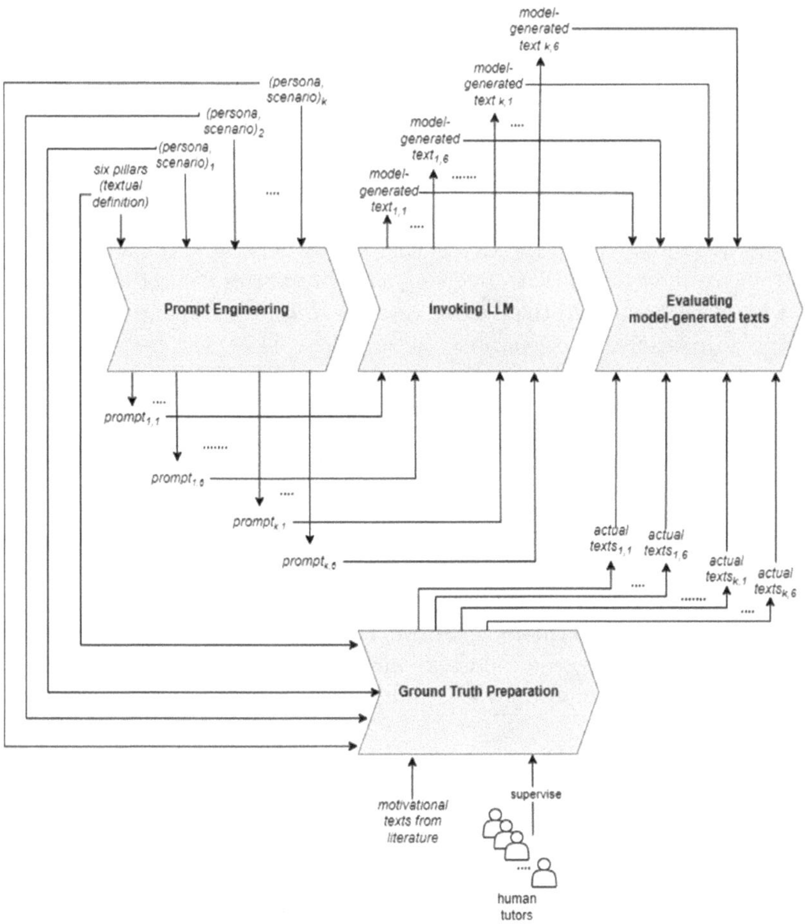


**Fig. 2.** Quantitative evaluation pipeline

- **Context control** [22], to specify the definition of one or more pillars used in order to activate the use of motivational strategies in the model;
- **Personalized prompts** [4] to provide information related to the student's profile and the learning context to the model.

These techniques are employed during the construction process described in Fig. 3. The process, essentially, contextualizes a prompt template by using a specific pair <persona, scenario> and a number of pillars definition. In particular, quantitative evaluation injects only one pillar at a time, while qualitative evaluation puts all six pillars in the same prompt. Subsequently, the prompt is built by composing five fragments. The first one is used to inform the LLM of its role (tutor) and the context (course, class, and faculty name) in which it acts. The second fragment provides the LLM with the information about the student. The third fragment provides the LLM with information about the history of interactions between the student and the learning environment and, in particular, about the last learning activity accomplished by him/her (name, difficulty level, obtained score). The fourth fragment is the task that the LLM must execute. Lastly, the fifth fragment contains additional knowledge transmitted to the LLM and related to the pillars it should consider in its response. The generated prompts are used to invoke a set of different LLMs (Invoking LLM activity). Each LLM answers to these invocations and generates motivational texts that are compared (in the Evaluating model-generated texts activity) with actual texts in the ground truth by using a set of metrics. Note that each model-generated text is compared to all three versions of the corresponding (same pillar and same pair <persona, scenario>) actual text. Thus, the best result among the three is considered. The adopted metrics are BERTScore[1] and ROUGE[2]. BERTScore returns three values, Precision, Recall, and F1-score. Precision indicates the fraction of model-generated text that is correct with respect to the actual text. Recall indicates the fraction of the actual text that is covered by the model-generated text. F1-score is the harmonic mean of Precision and Recall, thus it can be considered as an aggregate result. In this framework, only Precision and F1-score are employed. In particular, the average F1-score is calculated to evaluate how well the model can generate responses closely matching those of a human tutor. Furthermore, ROUGE is used to check whether the vocabulary used in the model-generated text mirrors the one used by human tutors, computing the total number of overlapping units in terms of uni-grams.

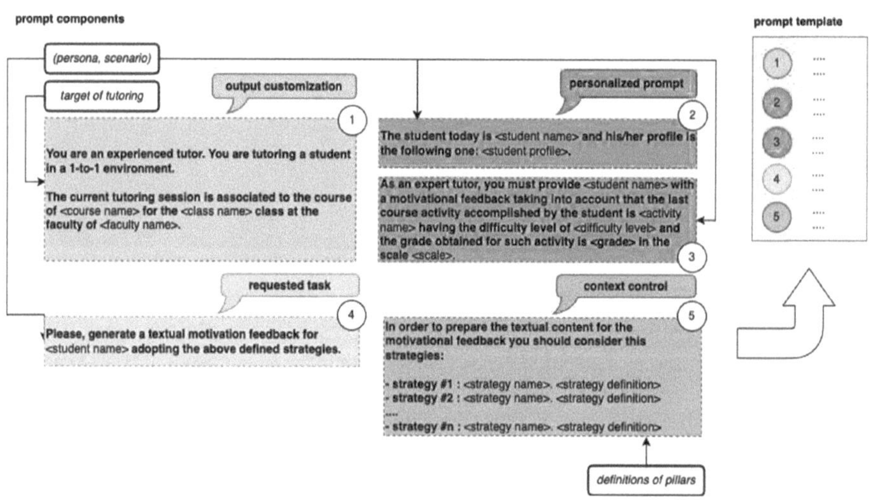


**Fig. 3.** Prompt construction

[1] https://huggingface.co/spaces/evaluate-metric/bertscore.
[2] https://pypi.org/project/rouge-score/.

### 4.3 Qualitative Evaluation

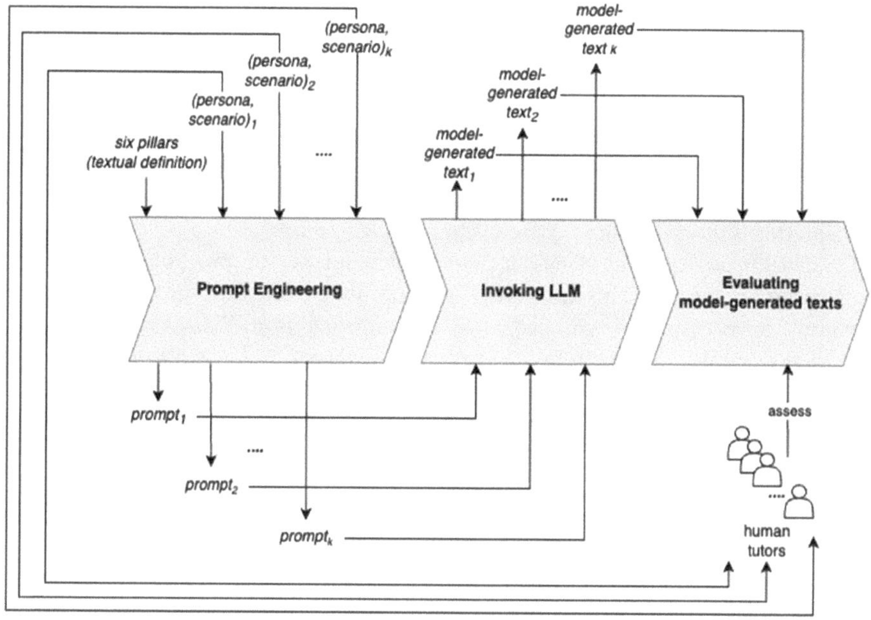


**Fig. 4.** Qualitative evaluation pipeline

The process for applying qualitative evaluation is described in Fig. 4. For the construction of model-generated texts, three main activities are also executed. The first is Prompt Engineering which produces one prompt for each one of the $k$ pairs <persona, scenario>. As well as quantitative evaluation, the same prompt engineering techniques (discussed in Sect. 4.2) and construction process (depicted in Fig. 3) are adopted also in the qualitative evaluation. However, in this case, the fifth fragment of the prompt template (see Fig. 3) simultaneously considers all the six pillar definitions. Then, the generated prompts are used to invoke a set of different LLMs (Invoking LLM activity). LLMs answer to these invocations and generate motivational texts that are provided to human tutors who can evaluate (in the Evaluating model-generated texts activity) them by also considering, from time to time, the pair <persona, scenario> which the LLM response comes from. Human tutors' evaluations are provided by means of a questionnaire adopting the following evaluation criteria:

- **Consistency** to measure how well the responses stay on topic and align with the learning situation [16]. This characteristic allows us to assess the capability of LLMs to provide personalized feedback, similar to a human tutor [12]. For such a criterion, 1 means *completely disconnected* from the provided pair <persona, scenario>, while 5 means *perfectly consistent.*

- **Motivation** to assess whether the six pillars of motivation are clearly and effectively present in the generated text. For this criterion, 1 means *includes no motivational pillar*, while 5 means *includes all six motivational pillars.*
- **Readability** to measure the clarity and fluency of the text to ensure that feedback is easily understood by the students [10,19]. For this criterion, 1 means *the text is difficult to read*, while 5 means *fluent and flowing text.*
- **Correctness** to cover factual accuracy, adherence to common sense, logical flow, and proper grammar. For students to receive valid guidance, tutors must consistently provide appropriate and accurately written responses [24]. For Correctness, 1 means *the text lacks logic and contains errors*, while 5 means *well-organized and logical text with no errors.*
- **Overall quality** that considers every element of the prompt and the general effectiveness of the motivational generated text. For such a criterion, 1 means *confusing, disorganized, and lacking meaningful guidance or encouragement*, while 5 means *highly coherent, engaging, and exceptionally effective in motivating the learner.*

Each criterion is evaluated with a score from 1 to 5.

## 5 Experimentation Activities and Results

### 5.1 Settings and Execution

The selection of the LLMs to be compared was made by considering a mix of open-source and proprietary models, different model sizes in terms of the number of parameters, and different maturity levels. At the end of the selection process, the following models were chosen:

- ChatGPT-3.5-Turbo[3] (OpenAI), 175 billion parameters;
- Gemini 1.0 Pro[4] (Google), 3.25 billion parameters;
- Llama 2 70B[5] (Meta), 70 billion parameters;
- Mixtral-8 × 7B[6] (Salesforce), 46.7 billion parameters.

The experimentation activities were executed by using Python and Jupyter[7]. Moreover, some external libraries were used: BERTScore, ROUGE, and NLTK[8]. The parameter $k$ used in Sects. 4.2 and 4.3 is set to 3, i.e., three specific pairs <persona, scenario> are adopted in the evaluation processes. The role of human tutor for quantitative evaluation and qualitative evaluation was played by six (three for quantitative and three for qualitative) Computer Science teachers from the Dipartimento di Scienze Aziendali - Management & Innovation Systems (DISA-MIS) - Università degli Studi di Salerno.

[3] https://openai.com/.
[4] https://gemini.google.com/app.
[5] https://www.llama2.ai/.
[6] https://mistral-7b.com/mixtral-8x7b-online/.
[7] https://jupyter.org/.
[8] https://pypi.org/project/nltk/.

## 5.2 Results

The analysis of the results obtained revolves around how pillars (activated via prompts) were used by the models. The first interesting result is shown in Fig. 5 where the distribution of F1-scores across the different LLMs shows specific pillars preferred by some models and other pillars preferred by other models.

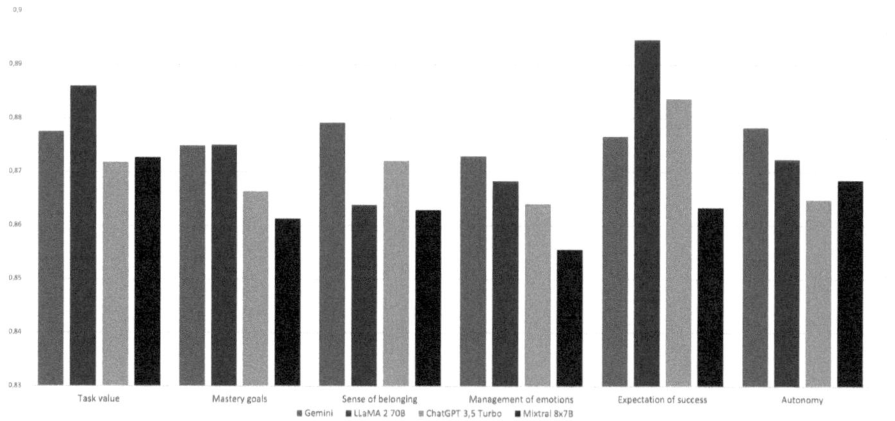


**Fig. 5.** Quantitative BERT results (F1-scores)

In particular, Task Value and Expectation of Success emerge as the most considered pillars by Llama 2 70B and Gemini. While Sense of Belonging and Autonomy pillars are considered especially by Gemini. Moreover, Mixtral-8 $\times$ 7B always offers the lowest values of F1-score, except for Autonomy and Task Value where its performance is slightly better than ChatGPT-3.5-Turbo. Llama 2 70B shows its ability to use all the considered motivational pillars. Gemini prefers to use Sense of Belonging and Autonomy. ChatGPT-3.5-Turbo prefers Expectation of Success. Lastly, Mixtral-8 $\times$ 7B shows evident difficulties in exploiting pillars. This is especially true for the Management of Emotions pillar. In summary, Llama 2 70B is the model that stands out for its superior ability to generate motivational responses by considering all pillars. Furthermore, Fig. 6 shows the degrees of similarity between actual texts and model-generated texts at the vocabulary level, i.e., the number of uni-grams in common between actual and model-generated text was measured. These results are important for assessing the lexical similarity between model-generated texts and motivational texts provided by human tutors, both expressed in the same situation (same person and same scenario). In particular, Llama 2 70B offers the best results with respect to the Expectation of Success pillar, while Gemini is the best model in using Sense of Belonging. Mixtral-8 $\times$ 7B shows always poor results, with respect to other models, except for the pillar Task value in which it reaches the highest value. After considering quantitative evaluation, it is important to enrich the previously reported results also by considering qualitative evaluation.

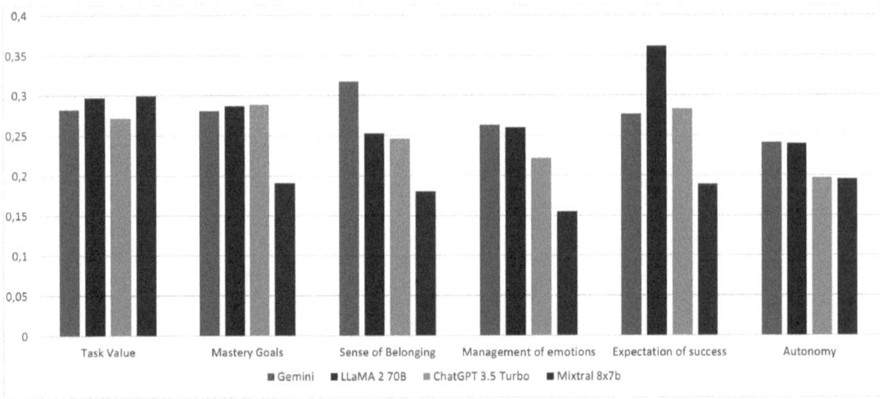


**Fig. 6.** Quantitative ROUGE results

Such a further phase reveals (see Fig. 7) that model-generated texts are lengthy but clear even if readability and fluency could be improved. With respect to these results, it is important to remember that used models are pre-trained without any training for specific domains. Thus, their performance is likely to be enhanced by executing fine-tuning.

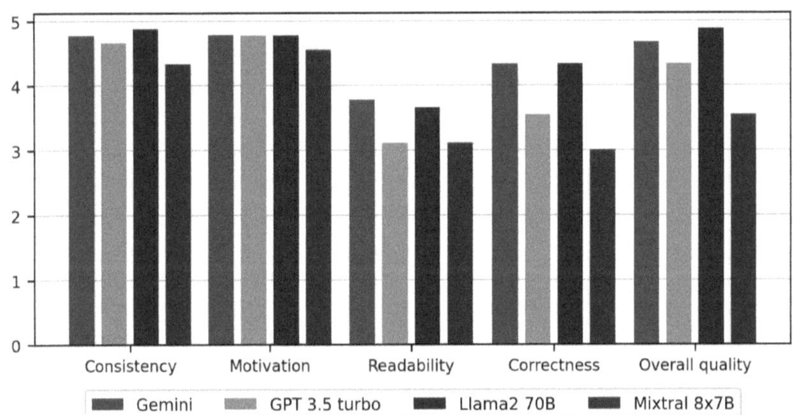


**Fig. 7.** Qualitative results

Human tutors' evaluations (Fig. 8 shows a sample feedback analysis) point out how pillars are used in providing motivational responses. In particular, Management of Emotions is not always included in LLMs' responses.

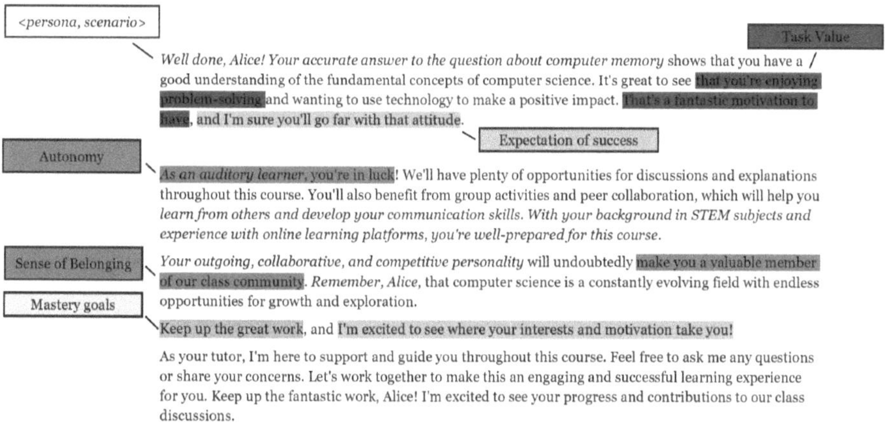


**Fig. 8.** Sample feedback analysis

A very interesting aspect to consider is related to the ability of all LLMs to adapt to different learning situations (determined by the pairs <persona, scenario>. Lastly, if considering both quantitative and qualitative evaluations, it is clear the supremacy of Llama 2 70B. The second best model is Gemini followed by ChatGPT 3.5 Turbo and Mixtral-8 × 7B.

## 6 Conclusions and Future Works

This work aimed at investigating the effectiveness of LLMs when generating personalized motivational feedback in the context of Intelligent Tutoring Systems. A novel evaluation framework is defined and instantiated for accomplishing early experimentation and evaluation activities. The achieved results, in general, show that the considered LLMs are able to create motivational text to be included in tutors' feedback. Such results show also that Llama 2 70B and Gemini are the best-performing models with respect to the evaluated task. In particular, if considering Llama 2 70B, it is confirmed that such a model performs well on text generation and human-like conversation tasks. In contrast, ChatGPT-3.5-Turbo and Mixtral-8 × 7B were found to be less effective overall. With respect to specific pillars, that represent the motivational strategies adopted, both quantitative and qualitative evaluations reveal that the models exploit several pillars when generating motivational textual content, albeit in varying degrees. Notably, some pillars are used in the same way human tutors do. Other pillars, instead, while used correctly are declined differently by LLMs than by human tutors, hence such pillars are not directly recognized by quantitative evaluation but only by qualitative one when the different way to decline them is understood by expert tutors. Among all pillars, Task Value is the most frequently utilized by the models. A very interesting aspect to consider is related to the ability of all LLMs to adapt to different learning situations (determined by the pairs

<persona, scenario>). Encouraged by these promising results, the authors are planning future works to concretely integrate an LLM into an ITS architecture and conduct experimentation activities where students' motivation is measured after the fruition of motivational feedback artificially generated by the LLM.

## References

1. Ali Amer Jid Almahri, F., Bell, D., Arzoky, M.: Personas design for conversational systems in education. In: Informatics. vol. 6, p. 46. MDPI (2019)
2. Baidoo-Anu, D., Ansah, L.O.: Education in the era of generative artificial intelligence (AI): understanding the potential benefits of Chatgpt in promoting teaching and learning. J. AI **7**(1), 52–62 (2023)
3. Belland, B.R., Kim, C., Hannafin, M.J.: A framework for designing scaffolds that improve motivation and cognition. Educ. Psychol. **48**(4), 243–270 (2013)
4. Geng, S., Liu, S., Fu, Z., Ge, Y., Zhang, Y.: Recommendation as language processing (rlp): a unified pretrain, personalized prompt and predict paradigm (p5). In: Proceedings of the 16th ACM Conference on Recommender Systems, pp. 299–315 (2022)
5. Graesser, A.C., Hu, X., Sottilare, R.: Intelligent tutoring systems. In: International Handbook of the Learning Sciences, pp. 246–255. Routledge (2018)
6. Hmoud, M., Swaity, H., Hamad, N., Karram, O., Daher, W.: Higher education students' task motivation in the generative artificial intelligence context: the case of chatgpt. Information **15**(1), 33 (2024)
7. Krahn, T., Kuo, R., Chang, M.: Personalized study guide: a moodle plug-in generating personal learning path for students. In: International Conference on Intelligent Tutoring Systems, pp. 333–341. Springer (2023)
8. Graf von Malotky, N.T., Martens, A.: Analyzing the usage of the classical its software architecture and refining it. In: Intelligent Tutoring Systems: 15th International Conference, ITS 2019, Kingston, Jamaica, June 3–7, 2019, Proceedings 15, pp. 40–46. Springer (2019). https://doi.org/10.1007/978-3-030-22244-4_6
9. Martin, F., Bolliger, D.U.: Engagement matters: student perceptions on the importance of engagement strategies in the online learning environment. Online Learn. **22**(1), 205–222 (2018)
10. McNamara, D.S., Louwerse, M.M., Graesser, A.C.: Coh-metrix: Automated cohesion and coherence scores to predict text readability and facilitate comprehension. Tech. rep., Technical report, Institute for Intelligent Systems, University of Memphis (2002)
11. Moore, S., Nguyen, H.A., Bier, N., Domadia, T., Stamper, J.: Assessing the quality of student-generated short answer questions using gpt-3. In: European Conference on Technology Enhanced Learning, pp. 243–257. Springer (2022). https://doi.org/10.1007/978-3-031-16290-9_18
12. Narciss, S., et al.: Exploring feedback and student characteristics relevant for personalizing feedback strategies. Comput. Educ. **71**, 56–76 (2014)
13. Omar, M.T., Kiron, N., Vassileva, J.: iquiz!: a collaborative online learning system that promotes growth mindset using persuasive feedback. In: International Conference on Intelligent Tutoring Systems, pp. 307–314. Springer (2023). https://doi.org/10.1007/978-3-031-32883-1_27
14. Polson, M.C., Richardson, J.J.: Foundations of intelligent tutoring systems. Psychology Press (2013)

15. Ramesh, V.M., Rao, N.J., Ramanathan, C.: Implementation of an intelligent tutoring system using moodle. In: 2015 IEEE Frontiers in Education Conference (FIE), pp. 1–9 (2015). https://doi.org/10.1109/FIE.2015.7344313
16. Santhanam, S., Shaikh, S.: A survey of natural language generation techniques with a focus on dialogue systems-past, present and future directions. arXiv preprint arXiv:1906.00500 (2019)
17. Schunk, D.H., Pintrich, P.R., Meece, J.L.: Motivation in education: Theory, research, and applications. (No Title) (2014)
18. Shute, V.J., Zapata-Rivera, D.: Adaptive educational systems. Adapt. Technol. Train. Educ. **7**(27), 1–35 (2012)
19. Sommers, N.: Responding to student writing. In: Teaching Secondary English, pp. 148–159. Routledge (2013)
20. Tang, R., Chuang, Y.N., Hu, X.: The science of detecting llm-generated texts. arXiv preprint arXiv:2303.07205 (2023)
21. Wei, J., et al.: Emergent abilities of large language models. arXiv preprint arXiv:2206.07682 (2022)
22. White, J., et al.: A prompt pattern catalog to enhance prompt engineering with chatgpt. arXiv preprint arXiv:2302.11382 (2023)
23. Xiong, Y., Li, H., Kornhaber, M.L., Suen, H.K., Pursel, B., Goins, D.D.: Examining the relations among student motivation, engagement, and retention in a mooc: a structural equation modeling approach. Global Educ. Rev. **2**(3), 23–33 (2015)
24. Zamel, V.: Responding to student writing. TESOL Quart. **19**(1), 79–101 (1985)
25. Zografos, G., Moussiades, L.: A GPT-based vocabulary tutor. In: International Conference on Intelligent Tutoring Systems, pp. 270–280. Springer (2023). https://doi.org/10.1007/978-3-031-32883-1_23

# Towards Cognitive Coaching in Aircraft Piloting Tasks: Building an ACT-R Synthetic Pilot Integrating an Ontological Reference Model to Assist the Pilot and Manage Deviations

Guy Carlos Tamkodjou Tchio[1](✉), Roger Nkambou[1], Ange Adrienne Nyamen Tato[1], and Valéry Psyché[2]

[1] Université du Québec à Montréal, Montréal, Canada
tamkodjou_tchio.guy_carlos@courrier.uqam.ca
[2] Université TÉLUQ, Quebec City, Canada

**Abstract.** Most aviation assistance systems do not take into account the pilot's actual cognitive state when providing assistance. Yet, especially in critical situations such as aircraft takeoff, it is important to determine whether the information presented has been correctly processed and understood by the pilot, or whether some has been omitted or misinterpreted. This paper presents a cognitive synthetic pilot based on the ACT-R cognitive architecture and integrating a reference ontology of standard piloting procedures as a knowledge base. The main purpose is to serve as a coaching system for training pilots in simulation environments to perform critical piloting tasks such as takeoff, by exploiting the advantages of a rich semantic representation of the aeronautical context. In this way, the ontology formally models the expert piloting procedures that will be used by the synthetic pilot to advise an trainee pilots during training sessions. For this, we use two types of ontologies to model the pilot's work: a task ontology describing all the actions the pilot must perform, and a domain ontology containing knowledge about the execution environment. The synthetic pilot uses semantic rules and a reasoner for task automation. The rules define when a task can be executed. The reasoner analyzes these rules and the context to decide which actions to execute. Over time, the actions to be executed are presented in the form of a complex dynamic 3D graph, thus allowing better visualization of the tasks to be performed and intelligent automation of the flight procedures described in the ontological reference model to assist the pilot. This work is an intermediate step towards the implementation of a complete cognitive assistance for novice pilots in a simulation environment. The ultimate goal is to extend the capabilities of the synthetic pilot through machine learning, by analyzing real flight data to extract typical pilot behavioral profiles.

**Keywords:** ACT-R Cognitive Architecture · Ontology · Graph Theory · Cognitive Agent · Synthetic Pilot · SWRL Rules · OWL · Pyactr


A. Sifaleras and F. Lin (Eds.): ITS 2024, LNCS 14798, pp. 202–216, 2024.
https://doi.org/10.1007/978-3-031-63028-6_16

## 1 Introduction

In daily life, the suggestions of our peers significantly influence many of our decisions, whether it's choosing a scientific journal, a candidate for recruitment or a movie [11,12]. Moreover, with the rise of online platforms and their recommendation algorithms, the impact of peer reviews now extends beyond one's close social circle. Technologies enable us to receive personalized proposals based on the analysis of our past preferences and those of a large panel of users with similar tastes. Thus, the tendency to rely on the advice and recommendations from others, whether from those around us or from automated systems, is increasingly shaping our choices in various domains. This tendency to rely on recommendations and feedback is also present in more technical fields like flight training, where new pilots rely on the advice and debriefings of their instructors, who act as guides and experienced peers [4]. Additionally, to enhance the relevance of suggestions to users, recommendation algorithms increasingly incorporate contextual information about the user's situation. These contextual data, aiding in refining recommendations, can either be provided directly by the user or collected automatically by sensors and other devices capable of determining the user's current situation [1]. Despite the availability of automated systems dedicated to pilot training, pilots often face issues of inattention, leading to decreased performance during flights. The causes of this inattention can be diverse, depending on factors such as perception, attention and emotion problems [8]. Due to this decreased attention in the cockpit, it becomes crucial to provide cognitive assistance to pilots [23]. This paper presents a proposal for a cognitive synthetic pilot acting as a coach. It is based on the ACT-R (Adaptive Control of Thought-Rational) cognitive architecture and integrates an ontology defining standard piloting procedures as a knowledge base. The aim is to provide recommendations to novice pilots during simulator training.

The ontological reference model used is described in [6]. It consists of production rules closely linked to the execution context, providing a framework for automatic problem solving. This means that normal and abnormal procedures are decomposed into production rules to identify the actions expected of the pilot in each situation. This automatic resolution is achieved by integrating environmental parameters into the reference framework. The reference model is structured into domain and task ontologies. The domain ontology groups the terminology related to the execution environment, mainly aiming to facilitate execution in a complex context. The task ontology provides a taxonomy of aeronautical procedures specific to the aircraft piloting domain.

Based on Newell's criteria [14] and Sun's desiderata [19], we have opted for the ACT-R cognitive architecture. The principles described by these criteria and desiderata provide guidelines for evaluating and designing relevant, credible and robust cognitive models. ACT-R is used to develop cognitive models that simulate the functioning of the human brain in various tasks, from problem-solving to learning and decision-making [2]. These models help better understand the underlying mechanisms of cognitive processes and predict human behavior in specific contexts such as aircraft piloting [9]. ACT-R is a production system composed of a declarative memory as well as a procedural memory. The former contains knowledge, while the latter contains production rules. The declarative module deals with recognizing what is presented to the model and calculating rule activation, while the procedural part deals with calculating the utility of each activated rule and triggering the most appropriate one. Cognition emerges from the interaction between procedural and declarative structures [3].

Finally, the paper outlines the methodology used to build the synthetic pilot, highlighting the integration of the ontological reference model and the production rules. Thus, in order to ensure the proper functioning of our synthetic pilot, we decided to store the domain ontology and task ontology in its declarative memory. As for the rules used to make inferences about knowledge, such as production rules and SWRL (Semantic Web Rule Language) rules, we have stored them in the procedural memory of our ACT-R cognitive agent. This structuring allows him to have the information he needs to reason and make decisions autonomously in his environment. The decisions made by the cognitive agent are modeled by a 3D directed graph. This graph is dynamically generated over time and displayed in the visual terminal, allowing the synthetic pilot to identify the next task to be performed and provide a visual explanation of the proposed recommendation in the form of a path through the directed graph. To build this directed graph dynamically, the cognitive agent must always know the final goal to be achieved and the current task. The built cognitive pilot is able to detect deviations from standard procedures and provide contextual assistance to the novice pilots in the form of alerts, comments and recommendations.

The results obtained show that cognitive coaching based on the ontological reference model can improve the learning of procedures and accelerate the acquisition of automatisms in novice pilots, compared with unassisted training.

This research opens up new perspectives in designing expert training systems in virtual environments where, in addition to the expert knowledge provided by the ontology, machine learning can be used to increase the cognitive agent's knowledge by learning pilots' behavioral profiles from real flight data.

## 2 Related Work

Several works, such as the ontological representation of knowledge in the aircraft field, the automatic execution of ontological piloting procedures, the automatic flight deviation detection, as well as the execution of a piloting task by an ACT-R agent, have laid the foundations for the development of our cognitive synthetic pilot.

### 2.1 The Reference Model

In order to formally represent the knowledge related to the task, the task environment, and pilot cognitive processes, ontologies can be used. Mizoguchi and Bourdeau [13] have shown the benefits of using an ontological structure to represent rules in order to formally model the knowledge of a domain. In the aeronautical field, ontologies have been developed to formalize knowledge representation. Among these, notable research has been conducted by Aghdam and his team [22], Stefanidis and colleagues [18], as well as Sheng and collaborators [17]. Although these works have contributed to formalizing knowledge, none of them has actively exploited expert domain knowledge, formalized through an ontology, with the aim of directly assisting pilots and providing them with immediate feedback on task execution. The ontological reference model proposed in [6], addresses the challenge of integrating pilots' expertise into an ontology to actively support the execution of flight tasks.

The ontological reference model formalizes expert knowledge of piloting procedures using two linked ontologies developed in OWL (Web Ontology Language): a task ontology that captures in a structured way the sequential, temporal and contextual representation of procedures acquired from expert pilots, and a domain ontology that describes the cockpit environment. This two-step process based on standard formalisms allows for the formal and detailed modeling of these complex procedural knowledge for automated exploitation by a cognitive agent (Fig. 1).

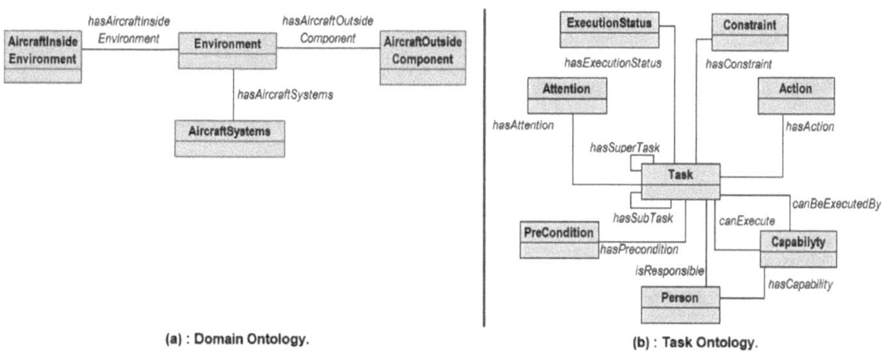


**Fig. 1.** Ontological reference Model.

## 2.2 Automatic Execution of Reference Model

Except for the approach proposed in [7], there is no documented solution in the literature for automating the execution of the ontological reference model. The authors of this paper have proposed a framework for the automatic interpretation and execution of the production rules contained in the reference model. This execution framework uses the procedural and declarative knowledge available in the model. The interpreter uses semantic rules to evaluate environmental constraints, task preconditions and task execution, enabling automatic execution. The simulator used includes a reasoner that manipulates knowledge, evaluates the task and aircraft environment, and autonomously executes required tasks. To support the execution model, the reasoner uses the Semantic Web Rule Language. The set of rules thereby makes the reference model automatically executable.

## 2.3 Automatic Flight Deviation Detection

Pietracupa and colleagues focused on the automatic detection of flight deviations using the ontological reference model for piloting procedures [15].

This paper presents an innovative system, aimed at detecting in real time deviations in the actions performed in the cockpit from the reference procedures established in the reference ontology for pilot procedures. The aim is to anticipate and prevent potential errors that may occur when processing complex data in very short periods, typical of aircraft piloting. To assess these deviations, the authors have developed a model that uses the Needleman-Wunsch global alignment algorithm to compare pilots' actions with reference sequences defined in the ontology. They also integrated a Siamese LSTM network, a type of recurrent neural network, to understand the relationships between different action sequences. This approach facilitated the detection of errors such as added, omitted, or incorrectly ordered actions. This system is limited to detecting deviations from aviation experts' prescriptions, without cognitive modeling or recommendation formulation.

## 2.4 Execution of a Piloting Task by an ACT-R Agent

Other than the research published in [20], we have not found any documentation in the literature dealing with the integration of the ontological reference model of piloting procedures with an ACT-R cognitive agent.

The paper presents a cognitive agent based on the ACT-R cognitive architecture, which integrates an ontological reference model of the aircraft domain to simulate complex piloting tasks. This reference model is part of the ACT-R agent's declarative memory, while the production rules used to extract knowledge are stored in its procedural memory.

The study also introduces an algorithm detailing how the cognitive agent executes a task. Finally, the paper describes the methodology used for implementation, using the pyactr library for the ACT-R model and owlready2 for ontology-oriented programming.

Experimental results demonstrate the successful execution of a piloting task by the cognitive agent, similar to the cognitive cycle observed in human pilots.

## 3 The Cognitive Synthetic Pilot

The cognitive synthetic pilot presented here is based on the ACT-R cognitive architecture and integrates the ontological reference model into its declarative memory. The choice of ACT-R was guided by Newell's criteria and Sun's desiderata, which establish various capabilities, properties and evaluation criteria for cognitive architectures [9]. Cognitive architectures are a significant research topic in cognitive psychology, philosophy of mind, artificial intelligence, and cognitive sciences. The ACT family of architectures was developed by John Robert Anderson in 1973 with the aim of providing a comprehensive theory of human cognition [2]. Kotseruba and Tsotsos [9] define a cognitive architecture as the composition of computer tools aimed at generating perception, reflection, and decision-making capacities similar to those of a human being. The ultimate goal of cognitive architectures is to revive the dream of strong artificial intelligence [10,16]. ACT-R (Adaptive Control of Thought - Rational) [2] is a cognitive architecture that aims to simulate and understand human cognition through a set of modules representing different cognitive processes. ACT-R's main modules are :

- Perceptual modules, receiving sensory information;
- Motor module, controlling motor actions;
- Declarative module, storing factual knowledge in long-term memory;
- Procedural module, containing production rules for action selection;
- Coordination module, selecting production rules and modules to be activated.

Cognitive functioning in ACT-R is based on chunks of information that circulate between modules according to a cognitive cycle: perception, memory retrieval, motor action. Our synthetic pilot, based on the ACT-R model, operate as follows:

- The declarative module contains knowledge provided by the reference model. It includes the domain ontology and task ontology (Retrieval Buffer). It also stores information about the current task state (Imaginal Buffer) and the goal to be achieved (Goal Buffer) ;

- The procedural memory models productions (condition-action-states) based on the current state of the piloting task or the aircraft environment. It also contains SWRL rules to automate task execution and determine their execution status;
- Perceptual modules (Visual Buffer) and motor modules (Manual Buffer) model basic sensory processes and interact with the environment.

Based on information captured in the environment, the coordination module or pattern matcher queries the reference model to deduce whether there is a deviation or not. In the case of a deviation, it proposes actions to manage it.

To successfully complete its mission, the synthetic pilot remains flexible and adaptive during task execution. It also knows the operational context of the ongoing task and related tasks. It also understands what constitutes normative performance for a task and the means to achieve the desired goal. The operating architecture of our synthetic pilot is shown in Fig. 2.

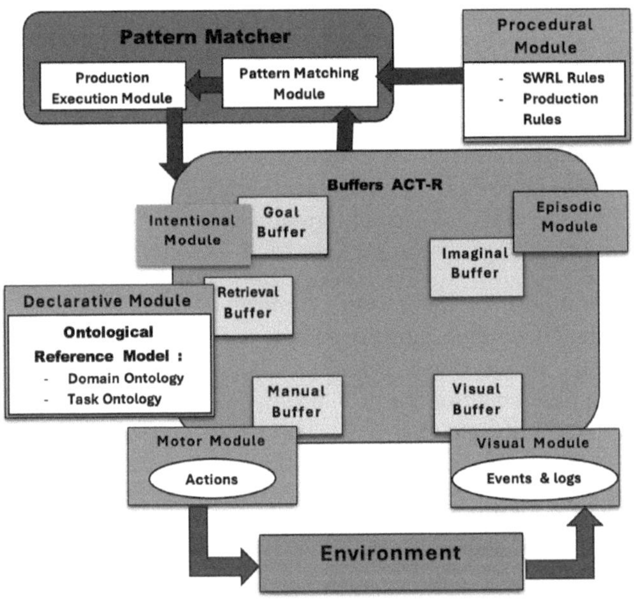


**Fig. 2.** Synthetic pilot internal architecture.

# 4 Methodology and Results

## 4.1 Methodology

To build the synthetic cognitive pilot, we relied on the following tools:

- The Pyactr Python library, which allowed us to create our cognitive agent based on the ACT-R cognitive architecture. Pyactr provides tools to define cognitive models, specify production rules, and simulate cognitive processes such as perception, memory and action;
- The owlready2 Python library, which enabled us to manipulate the ontological reference model (domain and task ontologies). Owlready2 allows representing an ontology, accessing and modifying its classes and properties;
- The Pellet reasoning engine, which facilitated logical deductions on the domain and task ontologies;
- The Semantic Web Rule Language (SWRL), which enabled us to write logical rules to infer task execution status from information extracted from the ontological reference model;
- The NetworkX library enabled representing the network of tasks as a graph with nodes and edges. We could then use NetworkX functions to generate and update the cognitive agent's path through this task network graph over time. The library provided the necessary capabilities to construct, navigate, and analyze the agent's trajectory in the complex, evolving task network. Overall, NetworkX facilitated modeling and tracking the cognitive agent's dynamic pathway within the complex network of tasks. The Pyvis library enabled interactive and dynamic network visualization of the complex graphs created with NetworkX. We could leverage Pyvis to generate web-based visualizations of the node-edge graphs and interact with the network by zooming, dragging, and hovering over elements. This interactivity facilitated analysis and interpretation of the complex networks. Subsequently, Matplotlib empowered 3D visualization of the network graphs, enhancing our ability to understand and present the high-dimensional graph structures. The 3D plots provided more visually intuitive representations of the networks compared to 2D plots. Overall, Pyvis and Matplotlib complemented NetworkX to enable both interactive exploration and 3D visualization of the complex task networks;
- The Protégé Ontology Editor, with its user-friendly graphical interface for manipulating reference model elements (classes, properties, individuals, etc.);
- The Unified Modeling Language (UML), used to visually represent the concepts and relationships in the reference model.

The sequence diagram in Fig. 3 models, in a temporal order, the interactions within the cognitive agent during the execution of a task.

Algorithm 1 shows how the synthetic pilot performs the takeoff procedure described in the ontological reference model.

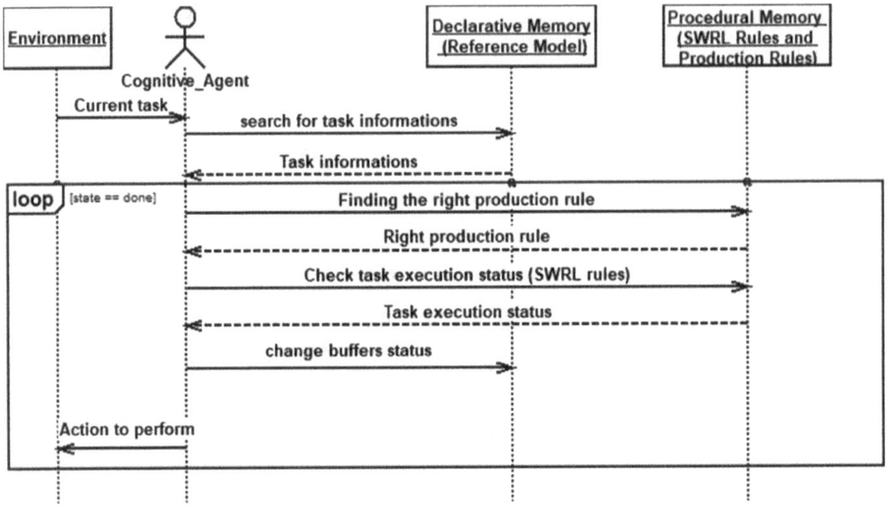


**Fig. 3.** Sequence diagram of the execution of a task by the synthetic cognitive pilot.

**Algorithm 1** : Algorithm of takeoff procedure

**Input**: Ontological Reference Model $O_M$
**Parameter**: Takeoff $T_O$, Current Task $C_T$, Objective $O_B$
**Output**: Execution Time $E_T$, Directed Graph $D_G$, Task T

1: Set takeoff as the goal.
$O_B \leftarrow goal(T_O)$
2: The current task is set as the initial task (1000).
$C_T \leftarrow 1000$
3: The current task status is set to Executed.
status $\leftarrow$ Executed
Repeat the actions below until the current task is task 1035 (last task of Takeoff)
4: **repeat**
5: Generate the directed graph with the current task ($C_T$) as the starting node and task 1035 as the ending node.
$D_G \leftarrow$ generated_path($D_G$,$O_B$)
6: Display the directed graph in the visual interface.
print($D_G$)
7: Select the new current task in the directed graph $D_G$.
T $\leftarrow$ next_task($D_G$)
8: The status will be set to Executed if $C_T$ was executed successfully, NotExecuted otherwise.
status $\leftarrow$ swrl($C_T$)
9: **if** status $==$ Executed **then**
10: The current task $C_T$ is set to the next task T.
$C_T \leftarrow$ T
11: The cognitive agent uses its complex pattern matching mechanism to execute task $C_T$ and make recommendations.
$E_T \leftarrow$ pattern_matcher($C_T$,$O_M$)
12: Display execution time $E_T$.
print($E_T$)
13: **end if**
14: **until** T $==$ $T_O$
15: **return** Buffers

To make the reference model directly executable, we have defined several SWRL rules. Two examples of which are presented in Fig. 4. The first rule (Fig. 4. a) is designed to validate tasks with an action and a precondition (for example: task 1001). The second rule (Fig. 4. b) is intended to validate tasks with a constraint of type 1 and another of type 5 (for example: task 1019).

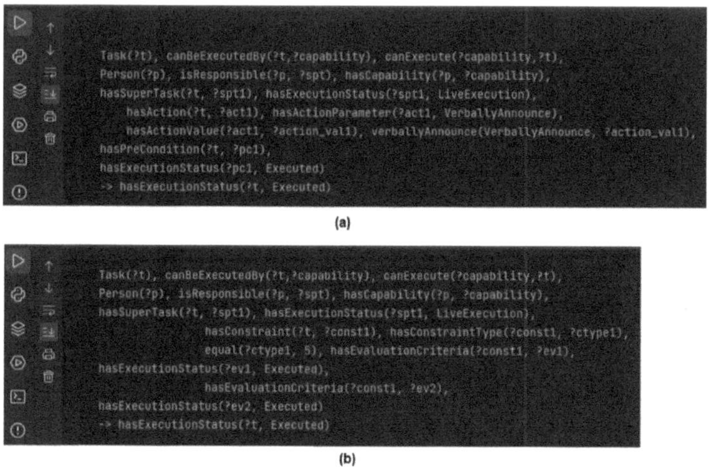


**Fig. 4.** Example of two SWRL constraint evaluation rules.

## 4.2 Results

To assess our model, we conducted several simulations. Initially, we performed complete takeoff procedures. Subsequently, we tested the synthetic pilot by having it perform takeoff recoveries at randomly chosen moments in the takeoff procedure. In each case, we dynamically generated the directed task graph and compared it to the execution expected by the ontological reference model.

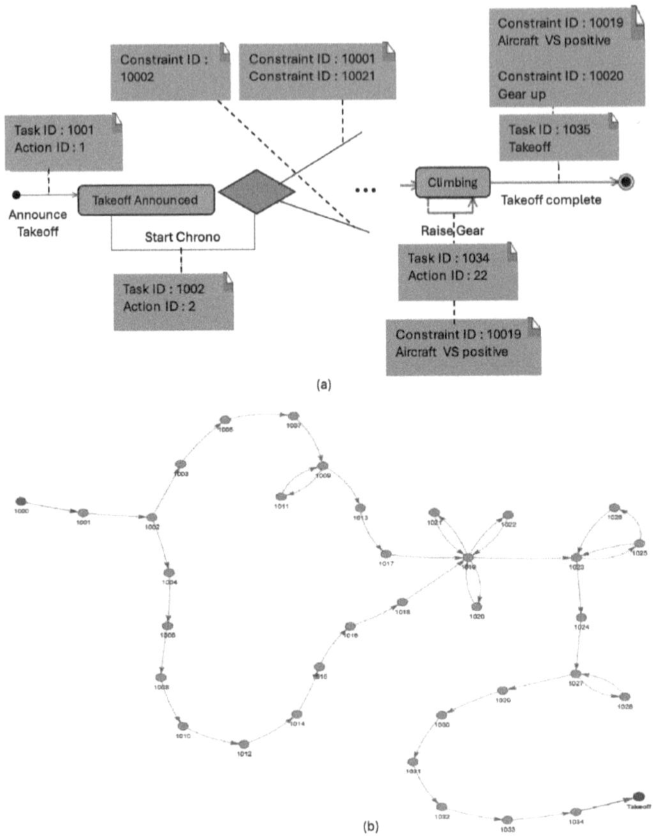


**Fig. 5.** Reference state-transition diagram and directed task graph for the takeoff procedure.

During the complete procedure, the graph (Fig. 5. b) generates tasks identical to those planned by the experts (Fig. 5. a). Based on this graph, the cognitive agent executes the tasks appropriately.

Regarding takeoff recovery procedure, two cases can occur:

- In the first situation, the generated directed task graph (see from task 1024 in the Fig. 6. d) is easy to navigate, and the results provided by the cognitive agent conform to the reference (Fig. 6. a, Fig. 6. b, Fig. 6.c);
- In the second situation, the cognitive agent may find itself in a deadlock (tasks 1025 and 1026), meaning a situation where the ontology has not provided any solution (Fig. 6. a, Fig. 6. b, and Fig. 6. c). To exit this deadlock, we search the ontology for a neighboring task leading to a solution and generate a link to that task (Fig. 6. d). If this is not possible, we end up with a crash. Adding new links allows the agent to complete its task.

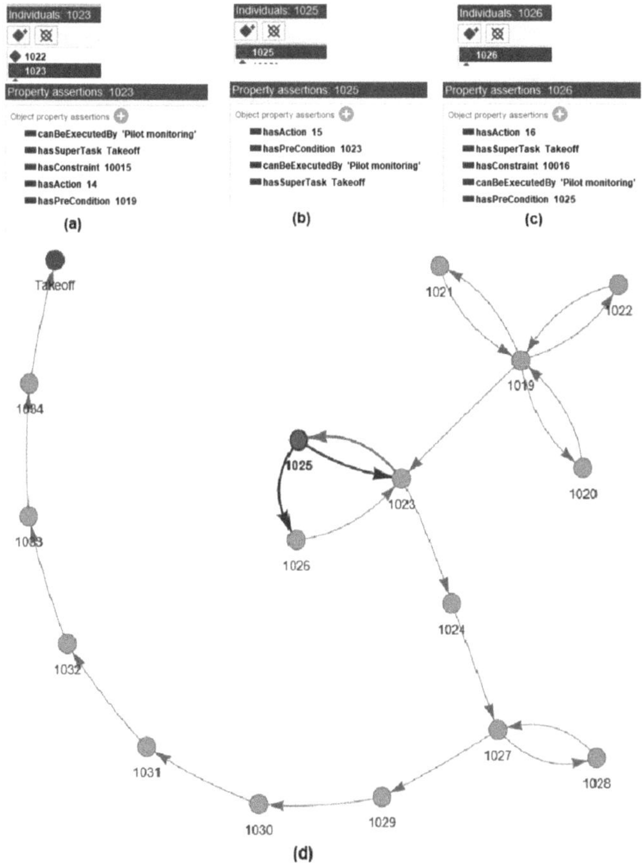


**Fig. 6.** Takeoff recovery : tasks involved from the reference model and directed task graph with added new links.

The agent can function in two modes (Fig. 7): an autonomous mode and an interactive mode. In autonomous mode, it performs the procedure alone, presenting its results on the terminal (Fig. 7. b). In interactive mode, it operates interactively, makes recommendations to avoid deviations (Fig. 7.a), acting as a coach assisting the pilot in his task.

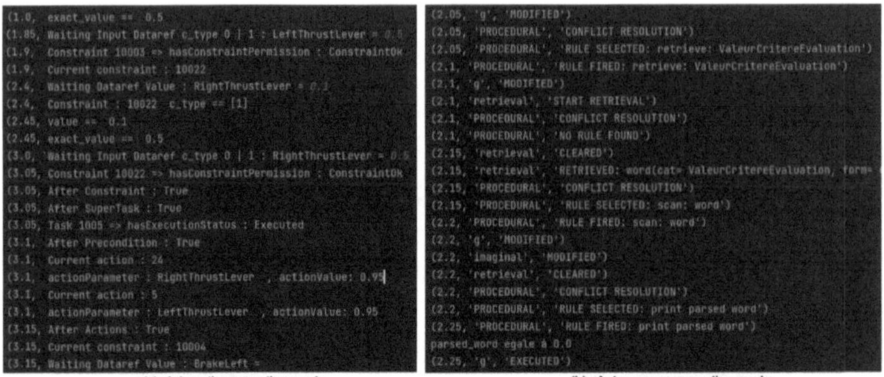


(a) : Interactive execution mode (b) : Autonomous execution mode

**Fig. 7.** Execution modes of the synthetic pilot.

## 5 Conclusion and Future Works

In this paper, we proposed a synthetic pilot based on the ACT-R cognitive architecture and using an ontological reference model as a knowledge base. This reference model includes a domain ontology that captures and formalizes the internal, external environments and navigation systems of aircraft, and a task ontology that captures and formalizes piloting procedures. To carry out its mission, the synthetic pilot uses an interpreter made up of SWRL rules, allowing automatic manipulation of the knowledge provided by the ontological reference model. In its quest for a solution, it dynamically generates and displays a 3D directed graph, which it navigates to determine the tasks to be executed.

Experiments have demonstrated the agent's ability to perform a complete takeoff procedure, similar to a human expert pilot. Furthermore, the agent can execute a takeoff recovery and reconfigure, in certain cases, a path in the form of a directed graph not foreseen in the reference model to achieve the set objective. Finally, the cognitive agent can be used in two modes: an autonomous mode in which it carries out the procedure from A to Z, presenting the different steps, and an interactive mode where it provides recommendations to the human pilot. In this way, the pilot can perform the actions recommended by the system to avoid deviations.

The next stage of this study will be to validate our proposal by testing the synthetic pilot in real-life situations, for example on the X-Plane flight simulator. Another focus will be to develop a synthetic pilot able to perform procedures related to abnormal tasks that occur during takeoff, such as "Dual engine failure with fuel remaining", "Engine failure after V1", "Reactive Windshear", "Rejected Takeoff", "TCAS event" and "Stall recovery'. Finally, a future perspective will focus on enhancing the understanding of our synthetic pilot by integrating knowledge from learning pilot behavioral profiles from real flight data [21].

**Acknowledgement.** We acknowledge the support of Bombardier and all the members of the Pilot-AI project.

## References

1. Adomavicius, G., Tuzhilin, A. : Context-Aware Recommender Systems. In Recommender Systems Handbook, Francesco Ricci, Lior Rokach and Bracha Shapira (eds.). Springer US, pp. 191–226. https://doi.org/10.1007/978-1-4899-7637-6_6, (2015)
2. Anderson, J.R., Bothell, D., Byrne, M.D., Douglass, S., Lebiere, C., Qin, Y.: An integrated theory of the mind. Psychol. Rev. **(111)**(4), 1036–1060 (2004)
3. Anderson, J.R. : How Can the Human Mind Occur in the Physical Universe ? Oxford University Press (2007)
4. Bouzekri, E., et al.: Engineering issues related to the development of a recommender system in a critical context: application to interactive cockpits. Int. J. Hum Comput Stud. **121**, 122–141 (2019)
5. Brasoveanu, A., Dotlačil, J.: Computational cognitive modeling and linguistic theory, berlin: Springer Nature, https://doi.org/10.1007/978-3-030-31846-8, pp. 7–38, (2020)
6. Courtemanche, M.A., Tato, A., Nkambou, R.: Ontological reference model for piloting procedures. In: Crossley, S., Popescu, E. (eds.) Intelligent Tutoring Systems, ITS 2022. LNCS, vol. 13284, pp. 95–104. Springer, Cham (2022). https://doi.org/10.1007/978-3-031-09680-8_9
7. Courtemanche, M.A., Tato, A., Nkambou, R.: Automatic execution of the ontological piloting procedures. In: Frasson, C., Mylonas, P., Troussas, C. (eds.) Augmented Intelligence and Intelligent Tutoring Systems, ITS 2023. LNCS, vol. 13891, pp. 29–41. Springer, Cham (2023). https://doi.org/10.1007/978-3-031-32883-1_3
8. Dehais, F., Roy, R.N., Scannella, S.: Inattentional deafness to auditory alarms : Inter-individual differences, electrophysiological signature and single trial classification. Behav. Brain Res. **360**, 51–59 (2019). https://doi.org/10.1016/j.bbr.2018.11.045
9. Kotseruba, I. , Tsotsos, J.: 40 years of cognitive architectures : core cognitive abilities and practical applications, Artif. Intell. Rev. 17–94 (2020). https://doi.org/10.1007/s10462-018-9646-y
10. Lieto, A., Bhatt, M., Oltramari, A. Vernon, D. : The role of cognitive architectures in general artificial intelligence. Cognitive Systems Research. 48, 1–3, (2018)
11. Mahmood, T., Ricci, F. : Improving recommender systems with adaptive conversational strategies. In: Cattuto, C., Ruffo, G., Menczer, F., (eds.) Hypertext, pp. 73–82 (2009)
12. McSherry, F., Mironov, I. : Differentially private recommender systems: building privacy into the net. In: KDD '09 Proceedings of the 15th ACM SIGKDD International Conference on Knowledge Discovery and Data Mining, ACM, New York, NY, USA, pp. 627–636 (2009)
13. Mizoguchi, R., Bourdeau, J.: Using ontological engineering to overcome common AI-ed problems. J. Artif. Intell. Educ. **11**, 107–121 (2000)
14. Newell, A.: Unified theories of cognition, Coll. " William James lectures 1987", Cambridge, Mass., Harvard University Press, pp. 17–18 (1990)
15. Pietracupa, M., Ben Abdessalem, H., Frasson, C. : An approach to automatic flight deviation detection. In: Frasson, C., Mylonas, P., Troussas, C. (eds) Augmented

Intelligence and Intelligent Tutoring Systems. ITS 2023. LNCS, vol 13891. Springer, Cham (2023). https://doi.org/10.1007/978-3-031-32883-1_47
16. Russell, S.J., Norvig, P.: Artificial intelligence: A modern approach, $4^{th}$ edition. Pearson, Boston (2021)
17. Sheng, Y., Chen, X., Mo, H., Chen, X., Zhang, Y.: An ontology for decision-making support in air traffic management. In: Liang, Q., Wang, W., Mu, J., Liu, X., Na, Z., Chen, B. (eds.) Artificial Intelligence in China. LNEE, vol. 572, pp. 458–466. Springer, Singapore (2020). https://doi.org/10.1007/978-981-15-0187-6_55
18. Stefanidis, D., et al.: The icarus ontology: a general aviation ontology developed using a multi-layer approach. In: Proceedings of the 10th International Conference on Web Intelligence, Mining and Semantics, pp. 21–32 (2020)
19. Sun, R.: Desiderata for cognitive architectures. Philos. Psych. **(17)**(3), 341–373, (2004)
20. Tamkodjou Tchio, G.C., Courtemanche, M.A., Tato, A., Nkambou, R. et Psyché, V.: Integrating an ontological reference model of piloting procedures in ACT-R cognitive architecture to simulate piloting tasks. In: Frasson, C., Mylonas, P., Troussas, C. (eds) Augmented Intelligence and Intelligent Tutoring Systems. ITS 2023. LNCS, vol. 13891, pp. 183–194. Springer, Cham (2023). https://doi.org/10.1007/978-3-031-32883-1_16
21. Tato, A., Nkambou, R., Tato, G.: Automatic learning of piloting behavior from flight data. In: Frasson, C., Mylonas, P., Troussas, C. (eds.) Augmented Intelligence and Intelligent Tutoring Systems, ITS 2023. LNCS, vol. 13891, pp. 541–552. Springer, Cham (2023). https://doi.org/10.1007/978-3-031-32883-1_48
22. Yousefzadeh Aghdam, M., Kamel Tabbakh, S.R., Mahdavi Chabok, S.J., kheyrabadi, M.: Ontology generation for flight safety messages in air traffic management. J. Big Data **8**(1), 1–21 (2021). https://doi.org/10.1186/s40537-021-00449-3
23. Zhang, Z., Russwinkel, N., Prezenski, S.: Modeling individual strategies in dynamic decision-making with ACT-R: a task toward decision-making assistance in HCI. Proc. Comput. Sci. **145**, 68–674 (2018). https://doi.org/10.1016/j.procs.2018.11.064

# Impact of Conversational Agent Language and Text Structure on Student Language

Haiying Li[1(✉)], Fanshuo Cheng[2], Grace Wang[3], Zhiqiang Cai[4], and Art Graesser[5]

[1] University of Pennsylvania, Philadelphia, PA 19014, USA
haiyli@upenn.edu
[2] University of Iowa, Iowa City, IA 52242, USA
fanshuo-cheng@uiowa.edu
[3] University of Southern California, Los Angeles, CA 90007, USA
graceywa@usc.edu
[4] University of Wisconsin, Madison, WI 53706, USA
zhiqiang.cai@wisc.edu
[5] University of Memphis, Memphis, TN 38152, USA
art.graesser@gmail.com

**Abstract.** This study examines how conversational agents' language (formal vs. informal) and text structures (comparison vs. causation) impact student language in written summaries using an intelligent tutoring system (ITS). We used the Coh-Metrix-ENA approach, which integrated Coh-Metrix and epistemic network analysis (ENA), to examine the structure of language connections in students' written summaries. Results revealed both agent language and text structures impacted student language. Specifically, informal agent language elicited a stronger language connection between nonnarrativity and word abstractness in both causation and comparison texts in the posttest network. However, in causation texts, both informal and formal agent language induced a weaker language connection between syntactic complexity and deep cohesion, which improved students' tendency to overuse causal connectives. Moreover, in comparison texts, informal agent language elicited a weaker language association between syntactic complexity and referential cohesion. Implications are discussed regarding the design of conversational agent language and text characteristics for interventions to improve summarization strategies and academic language skills.

**Keywords:** AutoTutor ARC · Coh-Metrix · Conversational agent · Epistemic Network Analysis · Formality · Intelligent tutoring system · Summary writing

## 1 Introduction

It is crucial for K-12 students to master academic language skills and embrace an academic writing style to demonstrate their knowledge and enhance their comprehension [1, 8]. Nevertheless, it is challenging for students to achieve this standard [23]. Increased exposure to academic language, such as teachers' use of academic language, explicit instruction in academic language, and utilizing reading materials in academic contexts,


A. Sifaleras and F. Lin (Eds.): ITS 2024, LNCS 14798, pp. 217–231, 2024.
https://doi.org/10.1007/978-3-031-63028-6_17

is likely to enhance students' academic language skills. Summary writing, particularly in such tasks as reading-to-write or source-based writing [10], is used to assess students' deep reading comprehension and also promotes the development of academic language skills. A recent study found that students improved language use in their written summaries following summarization interventions guided by conversational agents within an Intelligent Tutoring System (ITS) [14]. Informal and formal conversational agents induced distinct changes in language use. However, the study did not delve into how text structures of source texts contribute to student language use beyond the effect of agent language, which is within the scope of the present study.

This study adopts the methodologies and analyses outlined in the previous study [14] to investigate how conversational agent language (formal vs. informal) and text structures (comparison vs. causation) impact student language through a summarization intervention in an ITS, AutoTutor ARC (Adult Reading Comprehension). The research makes two significant contributions to understanding student language use. Firstly, through fine-grained analyses, this study aims to illuminate the interactive effects of agent language and text structures of source texts on student language use. These findings will inform the design of agent language within the ITS and highlight the importance of text characteristics, such as text structures during summarization interventions. Secondly, this study intends to provide additional empirical evidence regarding the efficacy of the Coh-Metrix-ENA approach that integrates Coh-Metrix language features and Epistemic Network Analysis (ENA) to reveal subtle differences in language associations across multiple language and discourse levels. Such a methodology has the potential to advance language research.

### 1.1 Theoretical Framework and Coh-Metrix

The pragmatics-based framework offers a holistic viewpoint on teacher language from diverse language aspects such as linguistic and cognitive attributes [26]. These attributes encompass interpersonal stance, information load, organization of information, lexical choices, representational congruence, genre mastery, command of reasoning or argumentative strategies, and disciplinary knowledge. However, researchers studied teacher language at the lexical, syntactic, and text-based levels. For example, Gámez and Lesaux [3] discovered a positive association between students' vocabulary skills and teachers' use of sophisticated academic vocabulary and complex syntax. More studies have revealed a substantial correlation between teacher language and student language development [17] in English [4], Chinese [27], French [24], Spanish [20], etc.

The multilevel theoretical framework involves six theoretical levels for deeper text comprehension [6]: word, syntax, textbase (e.g., explicit ideas), situation model (e.g., subject matter content), genre and rhetorical structure (e.g., cause-effect), and pragmatic communication (e.g., theme). Coh-Metrix, an automated text analysis tool, operates within the multilevel framework and provides most language features listed in the pragmatics-based framework [26]. Five major Coh-Metrix components align with the first five levels of the multilevel framework, and each represents ease of comprehension or inversely, text difficulty as described below:

(1) **word concreteness** (inverse of word abstractness) gauges the meaningfulness of concrete words that evoke mental images over abstract ones,

(2) **syntactic simplicity** (inverse of syntactic complexity) measures the ease of processing and understanding sentences, represented by fewer words and simple and familiar syntactic structures,
(3) **referential cohesion** evaluates the overlap of words and ideas across sentences, contributing to threads that connect to the explicit textbase,
(4) **deep cohesion** involves the use of causal, intentional, or other connectives or conceptual ideas to facilitate a more coherent and deeper comprehension at the level of the situation model, and
(5) **narrativity** (inverse of nonnarrativity) assesses the extent to which a text tells a story, linking closely to a familiar narrative style, such as everyday conversations.

These components (reversed 1, 2, 5) are aggregated to form a composite formality score, scaling text difficulty [7]. Formal discourse is defined as using language in printed materials or meticulously prepared speeches, requiring precision, coherence, articulation, and persuasion tailored for an educated audience. Informal discourse is at the opposite end of the spectrum, rooted in spontaneous oral communication, narrative elements, and abundant use of pronouns, verbs, and adverbs, relying on shared background knowledge. Therefore, the formality score increases with more abstract words, complex syntax, referential cohesion, deep cohesion, and informational text.

### 1.2 Summarization and Text Structures

Compared to multiple-choice (MC) tests, summarization allows for evaluating deep reading comprehension skills by requiring students to identify and articulate the main ideas of a text and integrate them into a cohesive whole [2, 9]. Established on the Construction-Integration (CI) model of text comprehension [13] and the developmental model of writing, summary writing [12] entails both understanding the source text and accurately conveying its ideas using academic language [2, 24]. Text structures delineate the logical connections and hierarchical relationships among ideas within a text [22]. These connections aid in constructing mental representations in learners, similar to an organizational structure crafted by authors [21]. Previous studies demonstrated the positive impact of instruction on the text structures on learners' comprehension and retention of information across various age groups [11]. However, the impact of language characteristics in source texts on student language remains unexplored, a gap addressed in the present study.

Creating a summary of an expository science text demands written language skills. Summary writing requires articulating abstract concepts in academic settings, and academic language plays a significant role in summarizing scientific expository texts [2]. For instance, proficient writers, whether in their first language (L1) or second language (L2), demonstrated higher levels of syntactic complexity and used more adversative connectors in their written summaries than less proficient writers. Only the L1 writers tended to employ more sophisticated vocabulary and diverse phrases [24]. Furthermore, there was an intrinsic link between syntactic complexity and connectors.

Recent studies manipulated conversational agent language within an ITS, AutoTutor ARC, to investigate the impact of agent language on student language [14–16]. In the formal condition, both teacher and student agents spoke the formal language, whereas in the informal condition, both agents spoke the informal language. No significant difference was detected when student language was measured by the five Coh-Metrix components [14–16]. Interestingly, a significant impact of agent language on student language was identified when the Coh-Metrix-ENA methodology was used to explore the structure of language connections in students' written summaries. These findings highlight the effectiveness of the Coh-Metrix-ENA approach in detecting nuanced variations in student language, outperforming the method of isolated language features.

Specifically, conversational agents using informal language prompted students to employ more abstract vocabulary in their nonnarrative summaries [14]. Conversely, those exposed to formal agent language demonstrated increased usage of referential cohesion in their nonnarrative summaries. Additionally, students in the formal language group exhibited a stronger language connection between deep cohesion and syntactic complexity on the pretest than on the posttest, due to the overuse of causal connectives on the pretest. Nonetheless, the study did not reveal how the text structures of source texts contribute to variations in language use beyond the effect of agent language. To address this gap, the present study utilizes the ENA-Coh-Metrix approach to explore the following research questions:

*Q1. Does conversational agent language impact student language in written summaries when the source texts are comparison texts?*
*Q2. Does conversational agent language impact student language in written summaries when the source texts are causation texts?*

## 2 Method

### 2.1 Participants and Procedures

Individuals who wanted to improve their English summary writing skills were recruited from Amazon Mechanical Turk (AMT) with a compensation of $30 for a three-hour intervention. Participants were screened and then randomly assigned to one of two groups, informal or formal. 118 participants completed the experiment, 56 in the formal group and 62 in the informal group respectively ($M_{Age} = 33.25$, $SD_{Age} = 8.43$; females, 41.8%). Participants had diverse nationalities: 10.7% from the U.S., 61.5% from India, 13.1% from China, and the rest from other Asian, European, and African countries. The country did not show a significant difference. The language learners accounted for 86.9% of participants, studied English for an average of 17.62 years ($SD = 8.02$), and spent 3.95 years ($SD = 7.36$) in a foreign country. Most participants held a bachelor's degree (43.4%) or above (39.3% with a master's degree or higher).

Participants read eight texts and wrote eight corresponding summaries: four comparison and four causation texts. The source text had an average of 260.13 words ($SD = 63.47$) with text difficulty in grades 8–11. Two comparison texts (*Walking and Running*, *Kobe and Jordan*) and two causation texts (*Effects of Exercising*, *Diabetes*) were randomly selected for the intervention. The other two comparison texts (*Butterfly & Moth*, *Hurricane*) and two causation texts (*Floods*, *Job Market*) were used for pretest and posttest, with one comparison text and one causation text on each test. A balanced $4 \times 4$ Latin-square design controlled for the order effect.

Participants' summary writing proficiency was assessed before and after using a summarization intervention delivered by trialogue-based conversational agents in AutoTutor ARC. Two computer agents (see Fig. 1), a tutor agent and a peer agent, led participants interactively to learn summarization strategies. The intervention included a brief lecture introducing text structures and corresponding signal words, such as "*unlike*" for differences in comparison texts and "*therefore*" for effects in causation texts. Then, participants read four expository texts, completed five MC questions for each text, received personalized feedback and scaffolding, and practiced identifying topic sentences, main ideas, text structure, and important information from source texts. They then wrote and evaluated a summary for each text without receiving any feedback or scaffolding. Finally, they evaluated three pre-designed summaries and received personalized feedback. They received no feedback or scaffolding for any task on the pretest and posttest.

Participants were directed to utilize signal words and topic sentences and include main ideas and important information in their summaries. Coh-Metrix 3.0 was employed to compute five Coh-Metrix components (percentile scores), including word abstractness, syntactic complexity, referential cohesion, deep cohesion, and nonnarrativity from their written summaries (see 1.1 for details). These component scores were standardized for the final analysis.

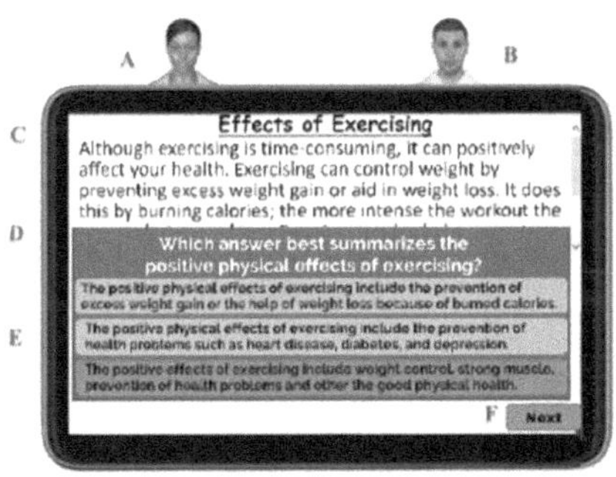


*Note.*

A. Teacher agent, Cristina

B. Student agent, Jordan

C. Text

D. Question

E. Answer choices

F. Submit button

**Fig. 1.** A screenshot of the interface during the training session.

## 2.2 Manipulation for Agents Language

The Expectation and Misconception-Tailored (EMT) dialogue mechanism was employed to design agent conversations [5]. The agent initiated dialogue by posing a challenging question to the learner, anticipating a correct response, and then employed a five-step tutoring frame to guide the learner towards the correct answer (see Fig. 2): (1) the agent presented the question, (2) the learner gave an initial response, (3) the agent gave brief feedback on the response, (4) hint-assertion dialogue moves were used to steer the learner towards the expected answer, and (5) the conversation concluded.

An expert in discourse processes created agent conversations in formal and informal languages, considering five discourse levels: word, syntax, referential cohesion, deep cohesion, and genre. Formal conversations contained more sophisticated words (e.g., statement vs. answer), more complex sentence structures (e.g., complex vs. simple sentences), more content word overlap (e.g., repeating content words), more connective (e.g., so), and a nonnarrative style (e.g., impersonal articles vs. 1st- and 2nd-person pronouns). Another expert validated the naturalness and appropriateness of the generated conversations. Below are two examples of agent language in formal and informal styles, where the tutor agent explained the incorrect choice the student made:

**Formal language:** *The second statement only discusses the positive effect of preventing health problems. Therefore, it fails to summarize all the positive physical effects.*
**Informal language:** *We find this answer shows a specific effect, not general effects. This one is not correct.*

In the formal condition, both the tutor agent, Cristina, and the peer agent, Jordan, utilized formal language, whereas in the informal condition, both agents utilized informal language. The agent language formality in each condition was assessed by Coh-Metrix formality scores: the mean score for conversations in the formal group was 4.70 ($SD = 1.89$), and the mean score for conversations in the informal group was −2.00 ($SD = 0.82$). Both scores aligned with the experts' perceptions of formality.

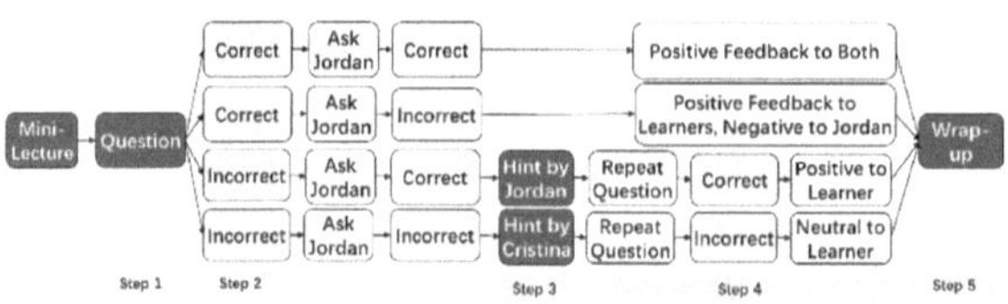


*Note.* Red boxes indicate manipulated agent language. Yellow boxes indicate learners' responses. Gray boxes indicate conversations between two agents.

**Fig. 2.** Dialogue moves during the intervention.

## 3 Analyses, Findings, and Discussions

This study employed the methodology used in prior research [14], visualizing the ENA networks and conducting one-way ANOVA analyses on 10 language connections. The only difference between this study and the prior study lies in dividing the dataset into two subsets: a comparison dataset and a causation dataset. We used the *rENA* package in *R* [18] to generate superimposed and subtracted ENA networks for language connections on the pretest and posttest [25] within a one-moving summary window. The units and conversations were the test (pretest and posttest), condition (formal and informal), and students. In the ENA plot, each node represents an individual learner: red denotes the pretest results, whereas blue signifies the posttest outcomes. The larger and darker nodes indicate stronger connections, and the darker and thicker lines represent the co-occurrence of two Coh-Metrix components. The red lines depict language connections on the pretest, while the blue lines denote those on the posttest.

### 3.1 The Impact of Agent Language Within Comparison Texts

To answer the first question, "*Does conversational agent language impact student language in written summaries when the source texts are comparison texts?*" we first visualized the superimposed and subtracted networks for the comparison texts in the informal condition. Figure 3a and 3b illustrate these networks, displaying a thicker blue line connecting word abstractness and nonnarrativity. This stronger connection shows a pattern of a stronger association between word abstractness and nonnarrativity in students' summaries for the informal condition on the posttest compared to those on the pretest. Moreover, the light red line that connects syntactic complexity and referential cohesion indicates a weaker language connection on the pretest. Figure 3c and 3d illustrate very weak connections between referential cohesion and nonnarrativity, as well as between syntactic complexity and referential cohesion on the posttest. Similarly, weak connections were observed between deep cohesion and nonnarrativity, and between syntactic complexity and deep cohesion on the pretest. While the visualization in the formal condition demonstrates the trend of changes in language connections from the pretest to the posttest, further analyses are necessary to determine the significance of these observed changes.

The results of a one-way ANOVA on the mean of the pretest and posttest indicated a marginally significant effect of agent language on student language, with a small effect size, $F(1, 124) = 3.69, p = 0.057, \eta^2 = 0.03$. Specifically, the mean rotation was marginally higher on the posttest ($M = 0.06, SD = 0.29$) than on the pretest ($M = -0.03$, $SD = 0.25$). The results of one-way ANOVA analyses for 10 language associations (see Table 1) indicated a significant, stronger connection between nonnarrativity and word abstractness on the posttest ($M = 0.23$, $SD = 0.21$) than on the pretest ($M = 0.15$, $SD = 0.19$), with a small effect size, $F(1, 124) = 5.01$, $p = 0.027$, $\eta^2 = 0.04$. However, this trend was not identified in the formal group. These findings were consistent with prior research [14], suggesting that conversational agents' informal language, rather than formal language, promoted students to use more abstract words in nonnarrative summaries with comparison texts as source texts. Thus, these findings are likely to support the personalization principle for the multimedia instruction design [19], indicating that conversational language motivates learners to use more abstract words and write more informational summaries.

Results also indicated a marginally significant, weaker connection between syntactic complexity and referential cohesion on the posttest ($M = 0.30$, $SD = 0.18$) than on the pretest ($M = 0.36$, $SD = 0.19$), with a small effect size, $F(1, 124) = 3.72$, $p = 0.056$, $\eta^2 = 0.03$. Similarly, this pattern was not identified in the formal group. This finding was not detected in prior research [14] when analyzing comparison and causation texts together, suggesting its uniqueness to comparison texts. This trend likely resulted from the characteristics of comparison texts. Specifically, summaries compare the similarities and differences between two objects, which involves repeating the keywords within the adjacent sentences (see underlined words in Example 1). These overlapped words resulted in high referential cohesion. This phenomenon was not seen in the second example, which led to low referential cohesion. Learners are also likely impacted by the informal language agents use, mimicking their conversational style to construct simpler sentences, as illustrated in Example 3.

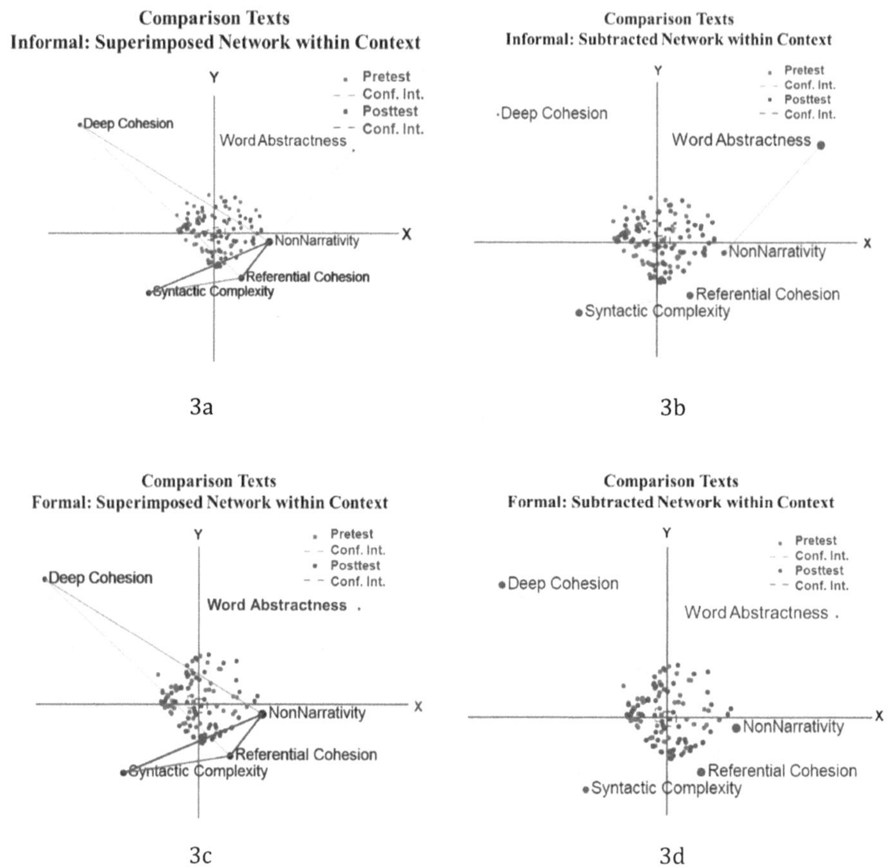


**Fig. 3.** ENA networks for comparison texts.

**Example 1** (Pretest): High Syntactic Complexity = 1.00, High Referential Cohesion = 1.00.

*Hurricane Andrew and Katrina were the most destructive hurricanes to hit the US in 1992 and 2005 respectively. Hurricane Andrew in Homestead Florida was category five with winds measuring 175 miles per hour, seven inches of rain and storm surges of 17 feet resulting in 26 deaths and 25 billion in damages. Hurricane Katrina was a category 3 with 120 miles per hour winds and on the path of the city of New Orleans, flooding 80 of the city leaving 1800 dead and 81 billion in damages.*

**Example 2** (Posttest): High Syntactic Complexity = 0.88, Low Referential Cohesion = 0.17.

**Table 1.** Descriptives and ANOVA results of 10 line weights for comparison texts

| Language | Test | Formal ($F(1, 111)$) | | | | Informal ($F(1, 124)$) | | | |
|---|---|---|---|---|---|---|---|---|---|
| | | Mean | *SD* | *F* | $\eta 2$ | Mean | *SD* | *F* | $\eta^2$ |
| **Nonnarrativity* Word Abstractness** | **Post** | .20 | .21 | .63 | .01 | **.23** | **.21** | **5.01*** | **.04** |
| | **Pre** | .17 | .18 | | | **.15** | **.19** | | |
| Nonnarrativity* Syntactic Complexity | Post | .40 | .20 | .18 | .002 | .39 | .19 | .04 | .0003 |
| | Pre | .42 | .24 | | | .39 | .19 | | |
| Nonnarrativity* Referential Cohesion | Post | .42 | .19 | 2.17 | .02 | .44 | .20 | .09 | .001 |
| | Pre | .37 | .20 | | | .43 | .19 | | |
| Nonnarrativity* Deep Cohesion | Post | .25 | .23 | 1.86 | .02 | .27 | .21 | .00 | .00001 |
| | Pre | .31 | .22 | | | .27 | .21 | | |
| Word Abstractness* Syntactic Complexity | Post | .12 | .12 | .12 | .001 | .14 | .14 | 2.34 | .02 |
| | Pre | .11 | .14 | | | .11 | .12 | | |
| Word Abstractness* Referential Cohesion | Post | .12 | .10 | 1.36 | .01 | .14 | .13 | .94 | .01 |
| | Pre | .09 | .12 | | | .12 | .14 | | |
| Word Abstractness* Deep Cohesion | Post | .11 | .15 | .00 | .00001 | .10 | .12 | .03 | .0003 |
| | Pre | .11 | .14 | | | .09 | .13 | | |
| Syntactic Complexity* Referential Cohesion | **Post** | .35 | .20 | 1.69 | .01 | **.30** | **.18** | **3.72†** | **.03** |
| | **Pre** | .30 | .20 | | | **.36** | **.19** | | |
| Syntactic Complexity* Deep Cohesion | Post | .17 | .16 | 2.54 | .02 | .18 | .16 | .52 | .004 |
| | Pre | .22 | .17 | | | .20 | .16 | | |
| Referential Cohesion* Deep Cohesion | Post | .22 | .21 | .45 | .004 | .22 | .19 | .55 | .004 |
| | Pre | .24 | .21 | | | .24 | .20 | | |

*Note.* **, $p < .01$; *, $p < .05$; †, $p < .10$, which apply to all the tables.

*Hurricanes Andrew and Katrina were some of the most horrendous natural disasters to hit the USA. These were massive catastrophes that are still felt to this day in the south east of the country. Katrina was a category 3 hurricane while Andrew was a category 5. Both of these natural disasters had powerful winds that destroyed significant portions of man made constructions in their respective areas.*

**Example 3** (Posttest): Low Syntactic Complexity = 0.10, High Referential Cohesion = 0.89.

*The two most destructive hurricanes in the United States were Hurricane Andrew and Hurricane Katrina. Both inflicted major damage. 26 people died in Andrew and 1800 died in Katrina. Both caused devastation. Hurricane Andrew caused 25 billion in damage while Katrina caused about 81 billion. Yet when measuring hurricane strength Andrew was the stronger of the two.*

To sum up, the answer to the first question is yes: informal agent language likely facilitates students to write more informational summaries with more abstract words. Moreover, agents' informal language is likely to prompt students to mimic agents' language style, resulting in using fewer complex sentences or fewer content words.

## 3.2 The Impact of Agent Language Within Causation Texts

To answer the second question, "*Does conversational agent language impact student language in written summaries when the source texts are causation texts?*" we also first visualize the superimposed and subtracted networks for the causation texts in the informal condition. Figure 4a and 4b also display a thicker blue line connecting word abstractness and nonnarrativity, indicating a stronger association between word abstractness and nonnarrativity in students' summaries on the posttest compared to those on the pretest in the informal condition. Moreover, the light red lines that connect syntactic complexity and deep cohesion, as well as referential cohesion and deep cohesion, indicate these language connections were stronger on the pretest rather than on the posttest. This pattern was also found in the formal condition (see Fig. 4c and 4d). However, a weak connection between nonnarrativity and deep cohesion was observed in the posttest.

The results of a one-way ANOVA on the mean of the pretest and posttest revealed a significant effect of agent language on student language with a small effect size in both informal group, $F(1, 124) = 5.00, p = 0.027, \eta^2 = 0.04$, and formal group, $F(1, 111) = 5.47, p = 0.021, \eta^2 = 0.05$. In the informal group, the mean rotation was also significantly higher on the posttest ($M = 0.08$, $SD = 0.28$) than on the pretest ($M = -0.03$, $SD = 0.26$). Further analyses of language associations (see Table 2) demonstrated a significant, stronger connection between word abstractness and nonnarrativity on the posttest ($M = 0.26$, $SD = 0.17$) than on the pretest ($M = 0.19$, $SD = 0.17$) with a small effect size, $F(1, 124) = 5.01, p = 0.021, \eta^2 = 0.04$. However, this pattern was not identified in the formal group. These findings were consistent with those identified in comparison texts, implying that agents' informal language is likely to facilitate students in composing more informational summaries with greater use of abstract words, regardless of text structure type (comparison or causation).

Results also revealed a marginally significant, weaker connection between syntactic complexity and deep cohesion on the posttest ($M = 0.25$, $SD = 0.17$) than on the pretest ($M = 0.31$, $SD = 0.17$), with a small effect size, $F(1, 124) = 3.47, p = 0.065, \eta^2 = 0.03$. Interestingly, in the formal group, this connection significantly weakened on the posttest ($M = 0.26$, $SD = 0.18$) in comparison to the pretest ($M = 0.33$, $SD = 0.18$), with a small effect size, $F(1, 111) = 4.39, p = 0.038, \eta^2 = 0.04$. These findings align with previous research [14] (see examples in [14]), confirming that after interventions, students demonstrated increased awareness of the correct use of causal connectives on the posttest more than the pretest, regardless of agent language style (formal or informal) in causation texts.

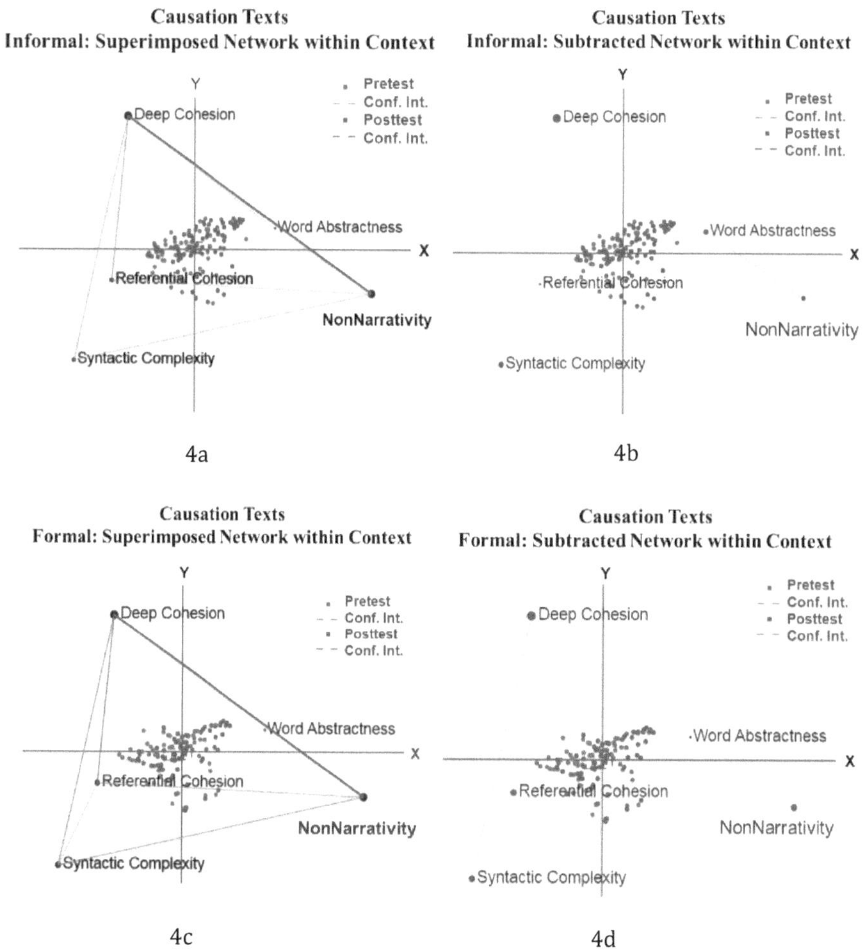


**Fig. 4.** ENA networks for causation texts.

To sum up, the answer to the second question is yes: informal agent language likely facilitates students to write more informational summaries with high use of abstract words. Furthermore, regardless of the language style employed by agents, either formal or informal, conversational agents assisted students in reducing the excessive use of causal connectives in causation texts when students used more complex sentences in summaries.

**Table 2.** Descriptives and ANOVA results of 10 line weights for causation texts

| Language | Test | Formal ($F(1, 111)$) | | | | Informal ($F(1, 124)$) | | | |
|---|---|---|---|---|---|---|---|---|---|
| | | Mean | *SD* | *F* | $\eta 2$ | Mean | *SD* | *F* | $\eta^2$ |
| **Nonnarrativity* Word Abstractness** | Post | .18 | .16 | 1.11 | .01 | **.26** | **.17** | **5.48*** | **.04** |
| | Pre | .15 | .15 | | | **.19** | **.17** | | |
| Nonnarrativity* Syntactic Complexity | Post | .30 | .20 | .02 | .0002 | .27 | .20 | .13 | .001 |
| | Pre | .30 | .21 | | | .26 | .18 | | |
| Nonnarrativity* Referential Cohesion | Post | .29 | .18 | 2.13 | .02 | .26 | .14 | .0000 | .00001 |
| | Pre | .25 | .14 | | | .26 | .15 | | |
| Nonnarrativity* Deep Cohesion | Post | .45 | .24 | 1.71 | .02 | .46 | .22 | .32 | .003 |
| | Pre | .39 | .23 | | | .43 | .20 | | |
| Word Abstractness* Syntactic Complexity | Post | .12 | .12 | .19 | .002 | .14 | .13 | 1.00 | .01 |
| | Pre | .13 | .12 | | | .12 | .12 | | |
| Word Abstractness* Referential Cohesion | Post | .11 | .12 | .05 | .0004 | .13 | .11 | .02 | .0001 |
| | Pre | .11 | .12 | | | .13 | .13 | | |
| Word Abstractness* Deep Cohesion | Post | .18 | .18 | .01 | .0001 | .25 | .18 | .19 | .002 |
| | Pre | .19 | .17 | | | .24 | .20 | | |
| Syntactic Complexity* Referential Cohesion | Post | .23 | .20 | 1.11 | .01 | .19 | .18 | .66 | .01 |
| | Pre | .27 | .19 | | | .22 | .19 | | |
| **Syntactic Complexity* Deep Cohesion** | **Post** | **.26** | **.18** | **4.39*** | **.04** | **.25** | **.17** | **3.47†** | **.03** |
| | **Pre** | **.33** | **.18** | | | **.31** | **.17** | | |
| Referential Cohesion* Deep Cohesion | Post | .29 | .20 | 1.54 | .01 | .28 | .21 | 2.21 | .02 |
| | Pre | .34 | .21 | | | .34 | .20 | | |

## 4 Conclusions, Future Directions, and Implications

The study investigated how conversational agent language (formal vs. informal) and text structures (comparison vs. causation) impact student language in written summaries using the Coh-Metrix-ENA approach. The results revealed that both agent language and text structures impacted students' language use in their written summaries to some extent. Specifically, when conversational agents spoke informal language, students tended to employ more abstract words when writing nonnarrative summaries for comparison or causation texts. Moreover, students tended to reduce the excessive use of causal connectives irrespective of agent language style when they composed summaries containing more complex sentences. Furthermore, students tended to use low referential cohesion when their summaries contained more complex sentences only when they learned with agents who spoke informally, and when the source texts were comparison texts.

This study provides insights into the design of conversational agent language and the consideration of text characteristics for reading-to-write tasks, especially when the objective is to improve students' academic language skills in writing. Our findings revealed three distinct patterns of student language use impacted by: (1) informal agent language regardless of text structures, such as nonnarrativity and word abstractness, (2) causation texts regardless of agent language styles, such as syntactic complexity and deep cohesion, and (3) informal agent language and comparison texts, such as syntactic complexity and referential cohesion. These patterns imply that the design of agent language and curriculum for summarization interventions should consider both the characteristics of text structures and their effect on student language use when the objective is to improve academic language skills. Given that the participants are recruited from AMT and have diverse nationalities, further empirical evidence is essential to generalize the findings to other learners.

Another significant contribution of this study is its validation of the consistent efficacy of the Coh-Metrix-ENA approach in discerning nuanced differences in the structure of language associations compared to individual language features in isolation. Moreover, the ENA network visualizations explicitly illustrate these differences in the structure of language connections, aiding in interpreting results. Furthermore, the ENA networks provide clear visual representations of the discernible patterns of variance in language structures on the pretest and posttests in terms of text structures and agent language styles. Specifically, the visualization suggests that agent language has a greater influence on student language in summaries of comparison texts compared to those of causation texts. However, discerning the significance of these differences remains challenging and statistical analyses are necessary for validating their significance.

In addition, each dataset comprises 10 language connection comparisons within each condition, and applying the Bonferroni correction requires smaller $p$-values than .05, potentially rendering the results marginally significant or non-significant. Thus, additional empirical evidence is needed to examine whether the same patterns of variation in language connections consistently exist and whether the patterns align with linguistic, pragmatic, and communication theories. Further studies could compare language connection patterns between good and poor summaries to discern underlying variations. These insights will guide researchers and educators in designing conversational agent language with the consideration of text structures and agent language to enhance both deep comprehension and academic language skills.

**Acknowledgments.** This work was funded by the Institute of Education Sciences (Grant No. R305C120001).

## References

1. Common Core State Standards Initiative: Common Core State Standards for English language arts and literacy in history/social studies, science, and technical subjects (2010). http://www.corestandards.org/ELA-Literacy/. https://doi.org/10.2139/ssrn.1965026
2. Phillips Galloway, E., Uccelli, P.: Beyond reading comprehension: exploring the additional contribution of Core Academic Language Skills to early adolescents' written summaries. Read. Writ. **32**(3), 729–759 (2018). https://doi.org/10.1007/s11145-018-9880-3

3. Gámez, P.B., Lesaux, N.K.: Early-adolescents' reading comprehension and the stability of the middle school classroom-language environment. Dev. Psychol. **51**(4), 447–458 (2015)
4. Gámez, P.B., Lesaux, N.K.: The relation between exposure to sophisticated and complex language and early-adolescent English-only and language minority learners' vocabulary. Child Dev. **83**(4), 1316–1331 (2012). https://doi.org/10.1111/j.1467-8624.2012.01776.x
5. Graesser, A.C., Li, H., Forsyth, C.: Learning by communicating in natural language with conversational agents. Curr. Dir. Psychol. Sci. **23**(5), 374–380 (2014)
6. Graesser, A.C., McNamara, D.S.: Computational analyses of multilevel discourse comprehension. Top. Cogn. Sci. **3**, 371 (2011)
7. Graesser, A.C., McNamara, D.S., Cai, Z., Conley, M., Li, H., Pennebaker, J.: Coh-metrix measures text characteristics at multiple levels of language and discourse. ESJ **115**(2), 210–229 (2014). https://doi.org/10.1086/678293
8. Graham, S.: Strategy instruction and the teaching of writing: a meta-analysis. In: MacArthur, C.A., Graham, S., Fitzgerald, J. (eds.) Handbook of Writing Research, pp. 187–207. Guilford, New York (2006). https://doi.org/10.1111/j.1467-873x.2008.00423.x
9. Graham, S., Harris, K.R.: Common core state standards and writing: introduction to the special issue. Elem. Sch. J. **115**(4), 457–463 (2015). https://doi.org/10.1086/681963
10. Graham, S., Harris, K.R.: Reading and writing connections: how writing can build better readers (and vice versa). In: Ng, C., Bartlett, B. (eds.) Improving Reading and Reading Engagement in the 21st Century, pp. 333–350. Springer, Singapore (2017). https://doi.org/10.1007/978-981-10-4331-4_15
11. Hebert, M., Bohaty, J.J., Nelson, J.R., Brown, J.: The effects of text structure instruction on expository reading comprehension: a meta-analysis. J. Educ. Psychol. **108**(5), 609–629 (2016)
12. Kim, Y.S.G., Schatschneider, C.: Expanding the developmental models of writing: a direct and indirect effects model of developmental writing (DIEW). J. Educ. Psychol. **109**(1), 35–50 (2017). https://doi.org/10.1037/edu0000129
13. Kintsch, W.: Text comprehension, memory, and learning. Am. Psychol. **49**(4), 294–303 (1994). https://doi.org/10.1037/0003-066x.49.4.294
14. Li, H., Cai, Z., Wang, G., Cheng, F., Marquart, C.: Impact of agent language on student language in the structures of language connections. In: Arastoopour Irgens, G., Knight, S. (eds.) ICQE 2023. CCIS, vol. 1895, pp. 49–65. Springer, Cham (2023). https://doi.org/10.1007/978-3-031-47014-1_4
15. Li, H., Graesser, A.C.: Impact of conversational formality on the quality and formality of written summaries. In: Bittencourt, I., Cukurova, M., Muldner, K., Luckin, R., Millán, E. (eds.) AIED 2020. LNCS, vol. 12163, pp. 321–332. Springer, Cham (2020). https://doi.org/10.1007/978-3-030-52237-7_26
16. Li, H., Graesser, A.C.: The impact of conversational agents' language on summary writing. J. Res. Technol. Educ. **53**(1), 44–66 (2021)
17. Lucero, A.: Teachers' use of linguistic scaffolding to support the academic language development of firstgrade emergent bilingual students. J. Early Child. Lit. **14**(4), 534–561 (2014). https://doi.org/10.1177/1468798413512848
18. Marquart, C.L., Zachar, S., Collier, W., Eagan, B., Woodward, R., Shaffer, D.W.: rENA: Epistemic Network Analysis (2018). https://cran.rproject.org/web/packages/rENA/index.html
19. Mayer, R.E.: Designing multimedia instruction in anatomy: an evidence-based approach. Clin. Anat. **33**(1), 2–11 (2020)
20. Meneses, A., Uccelli, P., Valeri, L.: Teacher talk and literacy gains in chilean elementary students: teacher participation, lexical diversity, and instructional non-present talk. Linguist. Educ. **73**, 101145 (2023). https://doi.org/10.1016/j.linged.2022.101145

21. Meyer, B.J.F.: The Organization of Prose and Its Effects on Memory. North-Holland, Amsterdam (1975)
22. Meyer, B.J.F., Brandt, D.M., Bluth, G.J.: Use of top-level structure in text: key for reading comprehension of ninth-grade students. Read. Res. Q. **16**, 72–103 (1980)
23. NAEP: 2015 Reading Assessment [Data file] (2015). http://nces.ed.gov/nationsreportcard/subject/publications/stt2015/pdf/2016008AZ4.pdf
24. Rivard, L.P., Gueye, N.R.: Syntactic complexity and connector use in the summary writing of L1 and L2 Canadian students. J. Fr. Lang. Stud., 1–30 (2023)
25. Shaffer, D.W., Collier, W., Ruis, A.R.: A tutorial on epistemic network analysis: analyzing the structure of connections in cognitive, social, and interaction data. J. Learn. Anal. **3**(3), 9–45 (2016). https://doi.org/10.18608/jla.2016.33.3
26. Snow, C.E., Uccelli, P.: The challenge of academic language. In: Olson, D.R., Torrance, N. (eds.) The Cambridge Handbook of Literacy vol. 121, pp. 112–133. Cambridge University Press, Cambridge (2009). https://doi.org/10.1017/cbo9780511609664.008
27. Sun, H., Verspoor, M.: Mandarin vocabulary growth, teacher qualifications and teacher talk in child heritage language learners. Int. J. Biling. Educ. Biling. **25**(6), 1976–1991 (2022)

# Analyzing the Role of Generative AI in Fostering Self-directed Learning Through Structured Prompt Engineering

Ashish Garg(✉) and Ramkumar Rajendran(✉)

IDP in Educational Technology, Indian Institute of Technology Bombay, Mumbai, India
{22m1021,ramkumar.rajendran}@iitb.ac.in

**Abstract.** This study explores the use of Generative AI, particularly large language models such as ChatGPT, in promoting self-directed learning among beginners in programming and data analysis, in the study structured prompts were employed as a key tool to enhance educational engagement and skill acquisition. To study the impact, Engineering students participated in a controlled environment where they utilized these prompts in conjunction with Generative AI to tackle programming-based data analysis tasks independently. We measured the impact of this method by comparing pre-test and post-test scores, which showed a significant improvement, indicating its effectiveness. Moreover, 45% of novice participants completed all assigned tasks. We also conducted semi-structured interviews and analyzed participant responses to understand the role of prompt engineering in self-directed learning. The analysis revealed that structured prompts and Generative AI motivate students and empower them to learn independently.

**Keywords:** Chatgpt · Prompt engineering · Self-directed learning · Data analysis

## 1 Introduction

The primary challenge in self-directed computer-based learning is often the absence of robust support systems [1], which can hinder students from effectively engaging with and mastering new technologies and concepts on their own. Traditional Intelligent Tutoring Systems (ITS) and web-based learning environments frequently lack the necessary guidance, especially for complex subjects such as programming and data analysis [2]. In response to these challenges, Generative AI, particularly advanced language models like OpenAI's ChatGPT, offers a promising solution. These AI systems are capable of generating human-like text responses and can be seamlessly integrated into educational environments to facilitate personalized learning experiences [3].

Existing research shows that systems integrating Generative AI with learning environments, such as classrooms, web-based platforms, and mobile learning applications, for example, "Duolingo, EduMentor, and Khanmigo by Khan Academy, etc." utilize these AI capabilities to foster a more engaging learning experience [4–6]. However, it is frequently reported that responses provided by Generative AI may seem irrelevant or


A. Sifaleras and F. Lin (Eds.): ITS 2024, LNCS 14798, pp. 232–243, 2024.
https://doi.org/10.1007/978-3-031-63028-6_18

misleading, which complicates the learning process. One of the possible root causes of these challenges may be identified as inadequate prompting skills, where students do not know how to formulate queries and prompts to extract useful information and guidance from AI systems [7, 8].

To address this gap, this study focuses on integrating structured prompt engineering with Generative AI to enhance its utility for beginners in programming and data analysis. Prior research has predominantly targeted AI code-generators for experienced programmers, leaving novices behind [9]. This research seeks to fill this void by investigating how effective prompt engineering can be implemented to improve learning outcomes and enable students to conduct data analysis independently. The study involved a structured prompt training session in which participants were taught how to use prompting skills effectively with Generative AI. Following this training, students undertook data analysis tasks independently.

Hence, the research focus of our study is:

**RQ1**: How does structured prompt engineering with Generative AI, influence the mastery of programming and data analysis concepts among learners with no prior programming experience?
**RQ2**: What is the role of Generative AI and structured prompt training in fostering self-directed learning and task completion efficiency in data analysis education?

In response to the research questions, this study involved 20 participants aged 24 to 29, all beginners in text-based programming and data analysis. These individuals, from various engineering disciplines, participated in a one-hour training session on prompt engineering and applied this skill in a following 3-h session where they used Generative AI to address data analysis challenges. The effectiveness of this approach was confirmed as 45% of the participants completed all three data analysis tasks. Moreover, the results demonstrated significant learning improvements in programming knowledge with paired sample t-test statistics indicating a substantial effect size of 0.89 and a p-value $<0.05$. Additionally, qualitative data from semi-structured interviews were analyzed using existing themes from the literature: "Empowerment, Joy of Learning, and Task-oriented" [10, 11] These results highlight the effectiveness of using prompt engineering and Generative AI to promote self-directed learning, as participants not only improved their technical skills but also gained the ability to independently navigate and overcome complex challenges, thereby enriching their overall educational experience and autonomy.

The next sections of the paper are discussed as follows: Sect. 2 reviews current research on Generative AI in the programming domain, prompting techniques, and identifies research gaps. Section 3 details the instruments used in this study, including prompt training, and describes the user study and participants. Section 4 presents results and discussions related to the research questions. Finally, Sect. 5 concludes the paper and outlines future work.

## 2 Backgrounds and Literature Review

The literature review explores Generative AI's applications in education, focusing on ChatGPT's role in various learning contexts, structured prompt engineering frameworks, and identifying gaps in research in programming and data analysis.

### 2.1 Generative AI in Education

Generative AI tools, such as ChatGPT, have gained traction for their capacity to generate responses and content that mimic human interaction, using advanced deep learning algorithms and vast amounts of text data [12]. A systematic literature review explores the applications of AI tools in education, highlighting advancements in personalized tutoring, interactive learning, adaptive learning, automated essay grading, language translation, and content creation, contributing to the evolving landscape of Generative AI-enhanced education [13–16].

Transitioning from the vast applications of generative AI to its specific role in programming, recent studies have explored the impactful role of generative AI. An experimental study showcased how the programming tool Codex, powered by generative AI, outperformed learners in a CS1 class on a rainfall problem, ranking in the top quartile [17], Another investigation used the flake8 tool to assess code generated by AI against the PEP8 coding style, revealing a minimal syntax error rate of 2.88 [18]. A notable study involved Github's generative AI platform, which initially failed to solve 87 Python problems; however, applying prompt engineering techniques enabled it to resolve approximately 60.9% of them successfully [19].

These research highlights the efficacy of generative AI in code generation, emphasizing the significance of prompt engineering in maximizing its potential in educational settings.

### 2.2 Prompt Engineering

Mastering prompt engineering is crucial for unlocking Generative AI's potential in education, as it significantly impacts the quality of interactions with AI language models. This skill requires understanding principles influencing AI processing, providing clear prompts for tokenization, embedding, and response accuracy, and providing rich contextual information for relevant connections. It also involves specifying response formats and controlling verbosity to meet user expectations and optimize AI-assisted learning experiences.

However, understanding these principles is just the beginning. Practical application demands a structured approach, embodied in the CLEAR framework. The Framework emphasizes the importance of crafting **Concise** prompts, ensuring brevity and focus; **Logical**, to aid AI in grasping context and concept relationships for coherent outputs; **Explicit**, specifying desired output characteristics to prevent off-target responses; **Adaptive**, encouraging flexible prompt experimentation to find the right mix of creativity and precision; and **Reflective**, advocating for ongoing prompt refinement based on past interactions to enhance future AI engagements [20]. Additionally, to enhance interaction with AI models, openAI suggested tactics including clear instructions, personas, delimiters, task steps, examples, output length, reference texts, breaking down complex tasks, intent classification, dialogue summarization, and piecewise document summarization, allowing GPT models time to think and using external tools like embedding-based search can also enhance knowledge retrieval efficiency [21].

### 2.3 Identification of Gaps in Existing Literature

The literature on Generative AI's technical capabilities in code generation and problem-solving is limited, focusing on its broader educational impact and learner interaction. The underexplored area is the impact of using tools like ChatGPT with prompt engineering on self-directed learning and its effects on learning outcomes.

## 3 Study Design

The study uses a task-based approach to gather detailed data for data analysis, focusing on active participation and exploring learning methodologies to demonstrate how Generative AI and prompt engineering can improve educational outcomes.

### 3.1 Selection of Concept of Data Analysis for the Task

This study emphasizes two key data analysis skills: data aggregation and data merging. Data aggregation is crucial for summarizing and revealing trends in raw data, while data merging integrates different data sets for a unified analysis perspective [22]. These skills are essential for beginners and laying the groundwork for advancing into more complex analytics tasks. The goal is to equip learners with confidence and skills for a seamless transition into the wider realm of data analysis.

### 3.2 Dataset for the Task and Problem Statement for the Task

The dataset, spanning September to January, includes over 10,000 observations of student video usage, student ID, school ID, view count, and last access date and time. It provides a comprehensive view of student engagement with video content, inspired by a school education program where tablets are provided to enhance learning.

Based on the given dataset, the task is designed that way so that it can not be completed with no programming software like Excel and Tableau, etc., The following are the problem statements of the task:

T1: Calculate the total daily video usage for each student throughout the program.
T2: Given the unique data capture cycle of student video usage (the 26th of one month to the 25th of the next), compute the monthly total video usage for each student,
T3: Calculate the monthly video usage for each school over all the months.

To perform the task Python language is selected, the rationale behind Python is chosen for data analytics education due to its simplicity, robust functionality, versatility with big data and machine learning frameworks, strong community support, and practicality for real-world applications [23].

### 3.3 Instrument Designed: Pre-post Test and Sus Survey

In this study, A set of 15 MCQs was created to assess participants' understanding of aggression and merging concepts in Python programming. The test, designed across three levels of Bloom's taxonomy, included five questions each: Understanding (L1), Applying (L2), and Analyzing (L3). Emphasizing practical application, the questions were derived from official pandas documentation and underwent multiple validations by industry experts to ensure their effectiveness.

The System Usability Scale (SUS) was adapted to methodically capture feedback on the Generative AI tool used in data analysis [24].

### 3.4 Design of Structured Prompt Training

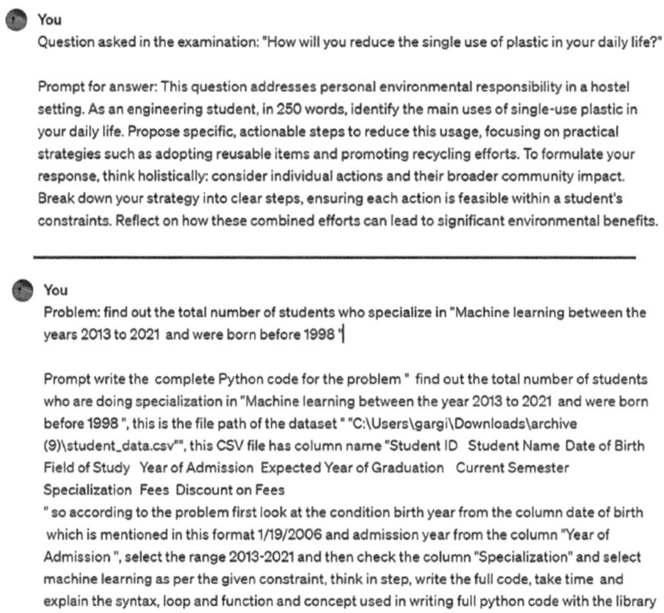


**Fig. 1.** Example used in prompt training: Top image: structured Prompt example-1 regarding the reducing the single-use of plastic from daily life and bottom image structured prompt example-2 regarding the filtering and aggregating of the dataset

A one-hour training session has been designed to introduce participants to prompt engineering, employing an example-based approach. Initially, the CLEAR framework and strategies from OpenAI's documentation are explained to lay the foundation. Subsequently, two examples of structured prompts are presented to illustrate the concepts in practice.

The first example is non-contextual, featuring a question about "reducing the use of single-use plastic from daily life" as shown in Fig. 1 (top-side). This example is chosen for its general nature, ensuring that even students with limited programming or data analysis experience can grasp the concept of structured prompts. The structured prompt for this question is crafted to build trust and provide an easy introduction to the topic.

The second example is contextual and directly related to the field of study. It involves showing students a CSV with a dataset different from the one used in the tasks. For this dataset, a structured prompt is written based on a specific problem statement as shown in Fig. 1 (bottom side). This approach not only demonstrates the application of structured prompts in a relevant context but also prepares students for the types of tasks they will encounter. This careful, step-by-step approach ensures that all participants, regardless of their background, can effectively engage with and understand the principles of prompt engineering, setting a solid foundation for their subsequent tasks in data analysis.

### 3.5 Participant

This study involved 20 graduate-level participants, all familiar with ChatGPT or similar AI tools but without formal training in programming or data analytics. This selection ensured a uniform baseline of understanding across the 12 male and 8 female participants, aged 24 to 29. Each participant had access to ChatGPT 3.5 and shared English as their formal education language, minimizing language barriers. Their lack of prior prompt engineering experience set a consistent starting point for all, crucial for examining the impact of structured prompt training on their data analysis skills using Generative AI. This strategic participant selection was vital for maintaining a controlled study environment and focusing on the specific research objectives.

### 3.6 Study Procedure

In this study, as shown in Fig. 2 participants were initially briefed on the impact of Generative AI in data analysis and consented to ethical data collection and privacy practices. A pre-test then assessed their existing knowledge, establishing a baseline for subsequent phases. During the training phase, they engaged in a one-hour session on structured prompt writing, essential for effective interaction with Generative AI tools like OpenAI's ChatGPT, and practiced crafting prompts through contextual and non-contextual examples. In the task phase, they applied these skills over three hours, tackling various data analysis tasks and refining their proficiency. Post-intervention, their skills were reassessed to quantify the training's effectiveness. Comprehensive data collection included output file assessments of tasks, SUS survey, and semi-structured interviews, providing a multidimensional understanding of the participants' learning experience and the influence of Generative AI tools on enhancing data analysis learning.

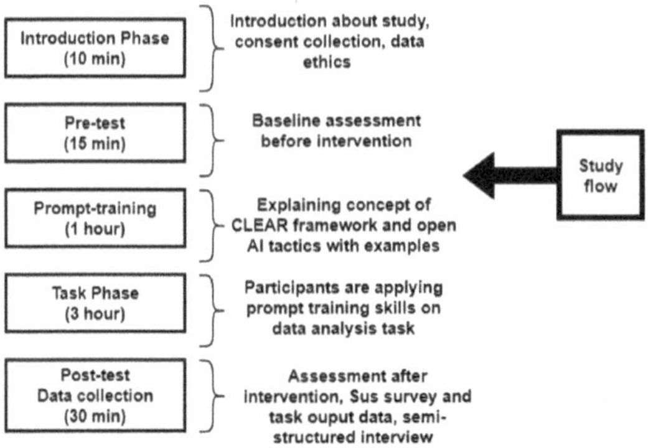


**Fig. 2.** Study Flowchart: Explaining the Elements of Different Phases in the Study

# 4 Results and Discussion

## 4.1 Data Analysis

In response to RQ1, That is to measure the impact of prompt training on data analysis skills. Initially, the homogeneity of variances among participants was verified using the Levene Test applied to pre-test scores across the three cognitive levels of Bloom's taxonomy—understanding, applying, and analyzing—as well as the total score. The Levene Test results indicated no significant difference in variances, with P values greater than 0.05 across all categories, confirming homogeneity within the participant group (Levene's Test values for Total Score Pre-Test = 0.15, P = 0.70). Following this assumption check, a paired sample t-test was conducted to compare pre-and post-intervention test scores. This test revealed a significant improvement in participants' performance, particularly notable in the total score, where the test statistic was $t(19) = 8.66$, $p < .00001$, effect size = 0.89, indicating substantial educational gains attributed to the structured prompt training and Generative AI intervention. The detailed analysis of this result is discussed in [25].

In **response to RQ2**, Which examines the role of Generative AI and structured prompt training in promoting self-directed learning in data analysis education. The following sources of data are analyzed to answer the RQ.

**The System Usability Scale (SUS) Survey.** It resulted in a mean score of 72.38 with a standard deviation of 8.45, reflecting a generally positive reception towards the usability of the Generative AI tool in data analysis learning. This positive perception underscores the tool's effectiveness and user-friendliness, contributing to a satisfactory learning experience.

**Task Completion Rate.** An assessment of task output files further demonstrated that students could perform tasks independently, a capability enhanced by structured prompt training and the use of Generative AI. While 70% of students completed the initial task (T1), the completion rates for more complex tasks (T2 at 55% and T3 at 45%) indicate that although students could handle basic data analysis tasks independently, the increasing complexity of subsequent tasks posed greater challenges. This trend highlights the critical role of foundational data analysis skills, acquired through prompt training, in preparing students to tackle more advanced data analysis tasks using Generative AI, thereby facilitating their independent learning progression.

**Semi-structured Interview.** Interviews were conducted with questions about their interaction with AI tools and structured prompts such as "How do you feel writing prompts affect the learning of programming? Can you share an experience where you faced a challenge during the task, and how you handled it? and What's different about learning with the AI than other ways you've tried to learn?, etc." data from these interviews was analyzed through a deductive coding approach, where three themes and sub-themes were borrowed and adapted from the literature to code the data [10, 11]. These themes were identified as significant patterns in the participants' responses and were

**Table 1.** Decoded themes and participant responses from semi-structured interviews

| Theme | Sub-Theme | Participant Statement |
|---|---|---|
| Empowerment | Self-efficacy<br>Greater Confidence<br>Enhanced decision-making | P3: *"After the AI prompting session, I've realized that programming is within my grasp, and I'm enthusiastic to tackle more coding challenges"*<br>P7: *"Syntax explanation clarified programming concepts for me and demonstrated the practicality of the code, boosted my confidence in my coding"*<br>P9: *"I used to feel lost in programming, but now I feel confident in solving such tasks"*<br>P14: *"Writing structured prompts forced me to think in order and step-by-step, which helped me to instruct ChatGPT effectively and make more informed decisions through clear explanations*<br>*P6: It became easy to understand the reasons behind errors and resolve them through ChatGPT"* |
| Task-oriented | Skill Improvement<br>Problem-Solving<br>Extrinsic motivation | P4: *"Writing code to solve tasks helped me learn programming concepts and how they are used in real life, improved my coding skills"*<br>P20: *"Learning to write prompts correctly helped me break down problems and piece together solutions more effectively."*<br>P12: *"Writing my first prompt was challenging, but seeing the code work successfully boosted my confidence to do more tasks"* |
| Joy of Learning | I want to learn<br>I want to Grow | P5: *"Now, whenever I face a problem, I try tackling it by writing different prompts. It feels like I'm playing a game, exploring various strategies to find the best solution"*<br>P8: *"Chatting with the AI is exciting because I learn something new every time. Unlike textbooks, the AI responds in seconds, making learning fast and fun"* |

subsequently reviewed by experts who have programming experience, expertise in analyzing content generation through Generative AI, and are experts in self-directed learning research. Table 1 details these themes, reflecting the varied experiences and insights of the participants, though this table is limited to participant's responses.

Concluding the data analysis, we observed significant advancements in self-directed learning outcomes through structured prompt engineering and Generative AI. Moving into the discussion section, we explored the deeper implications of these findings.

## 4.2 Discussion

In response to RQ1, we observed significant quantitative improvements in how structured prompt engineering with Generative AI enhances novice learners' understanding of programming and data analysis. First, the Levene Test confirmed a consistent baseline, allowing for valid comparisons. At the same time, paired sample t-tests showed marked advancements in understanding and applying programming concepts, as indicated by significant effect sizes across Bloom's taxonomy levels. Moreover, the positive System Usability Scale (SUS) survey results underscore the tool's user-friendliness, emphasizing its role in reducing cognitive load and enhancing focus on concept application, thereby supporting the study's findings from a usability perspective.

From the analysis of the second research question (RQ2), the results show how structured prompt engineering, coupled with Generative AI, impacts self-directed learning and task completion efficiency within data analysis education. The findings highlight that structured prompts, particularly those crafted using the CLEAR framework and Generative AI, significantly enhance task completion rates, especially as task complexity increases. This is consistent with the self-determination theory (SDT), which suggests that autonomy is the essential component of self-directed learning [26].

High System Usability Scale (SUS) scores confirm the user-friendliness of these tools, promoting sustained engagement and facilitating the transition from dependent to independent learners. A positive perception of the usability of Generative AI with structured prompts can motivate learners to engage in the material and enhance their learning effectiveness, which is crucial for self-directed learning.

Qualitative data from interviews highlight the transformative impact of these tools on learning dynamics. Learners reported feeling confident and believing that they can handle programming and data analysis tasks effectively with the help of generative AI and structured prompts. This reflects their ability to initiate and manage learning processes independently, a sign of empowerment. Additionally, the clarity provided by structured prompts aids learners in decomposing complex tasks into manageable parts, an essential skill in self-directed learning that fosters autonomy and enhances cognitive engagement in the process of solving tasks. Also, the joy of learning and motivation derived from such an interactive and responsive learning tool underscore its effectiveness in fostering an environment where learners are encouraged to explore, experiment, and learn at their own pace, thus enhancing both self-directed learning and task completion efficiency in data analysis education.

## 5 Conclusion and Future Work

This paper presents the role of structured prompts conceptualized based on the CLEAR framework and OpenAI strategies. The quantitative and qualitative findings together demonstrate the effectiveness of Generative AI in enhancing understanding of programming and data analysis concepts. Specifically, structured prompts have been instrumental in guiding learners through complex problem-solving processes. This approach not only improves task completion efficiency but also fosters a self-directed learning environment where students are empowered to explore, experiment, and discover independently, leading to significant learning gains. However, the study acknowledges its limitations, including the absence of log data analysis, which could provide deeper insights into the behavioral patterns of high and low performers, and the relatively small sample size, which limits the generalizability of the findings.

Future research could explore the long-term impacts of Generative AI and structured prompts through a longitudinal study, enhancing our understanding of self-directed learning over time. Additionally, comparative studies could assess the effectiveness of these tools across different groups with varying levels of access to technologies like ChatGPT and structured prompt training. This would help to deepen our insight into the role of Generative AI in learning, which will contribute to refining training methods and improving learning theories to create learning experiences that are more engaging, effective, and tailored to individual needs.

## References

1. Buch, A.C., Rathod, H., Naik, M.D.: Scope and challenges of self-directed learning in undergraduate medical education: a systematic review. J. Med. Educ. **20**(1), Article no. e114077 (2021). https://doi.org/10.5812/jme.114077
2. Crow, T., Luxton-Reilly, A., Wuensche, B.: Intelligent tutoring systems for programming education: a systematic review. In: Proceedings of the 20th Australasian Computing Education Conference (ACE 2018), pp. 1–10. ACM (2018). https://doi.org/10.1145/3160489.3160492
3. Ruiz-Rojas, L.I., Acosta-Vargas, P., De-Moreta-Llovet, J., Gonzalez-Rodriguez, M.: Empowering education with generative artificial intelligence tools: approach with an instructional design matrix. Sustainability **15**(15), 11524 (2023)
4. Chen, O., Zhu, X., Díaz del Castillo, H.F.: Integrating generative AI in knowledge building. Comput. Educ. Artif. Intell. **5**, Article no. 100184 (2023). https://doi.org/10.1016/j.caeai.2023.100184
5. Godwin-Jones, R.: Distributed agency in second language learning and teaching through generative AI. Lang. Learn. Technol. **28**(2). arXiv:2403.20216v1 [cs.CY]. https://doi.org/10.48550/arXiv.2403.20216
6. Dong, C.: How to build an AI tutor that can adapt to any course and provide accurate answers using large language model and retrieval-augmented generation. Preprint submitted to arXiv. arXiv:2311.17696v2 [cs.CL]. https://doi.org/10.48550/arXiv.2311.17696
7. Siontis, K.C., Attia, Z.I., Asirvatham, S.J., Friedman, P.A.: ChatGPT hallucinating: can it get any more humanlike? Eur. Heart J. **45**(5), 321–323 (2024). https://doi.org/10.1093/eurheartj/ehad766
8. Korzynski, P., Mazurek, G., Krzypkowska, P., Kurasinski, A.: Artificial intelligence prompt engineering as a new digital competence: analysis of generative AI technologies such as

ChatGPT. Entrep. Bus. Econ. Rev. **11**, 25–37 (2023). https://doi.org/10.15678/EBER.2023.110302
9. Dhoni, P.: Exploring the synergy between generative AI, data, and analytics in the modern age, 29 August 2023 TechRxiv. https://doi.org/10.36227/techrxiv.24045792.v1
10. McCartney, R., Boustedt, J., Eckerdal, A., Sanders, K., Thomas, L., Zander, C.: Why computing students learn on their own: motivation for self-directed learning of computing. ACM Trans. Comput. Educ. **16**(1), Article no. 2 (2016). https://doi.org/10.1145/274700
11. Rager, K.B.: A thematic analysis of the self-directed learning experiences of 13 breast cancer patients. Int. J. Lifelong Educ. **23**(1), 95–109 (2004). https://doi.org/10.1080/0260137032000172088
12. Dai, Y., et al.: Reconceptualizing ChatGPT and generative AI as a student-driven innovation in higher education. Procedia CIRP **119**, 84–90 (2023)
13. Bahrini, A., et al.: ChatGPT: applications, opportunities, and threats. In: 2023 Systems and Information Engineering Design Symposium (SIEDS), Charlottesville, VA, USA, pp. 274–279 (2023). https://doi.org/10.1109/SIEDS58326.2023.10137850
14. De Silva, D., Mills, N., El-Ayoubi, M., Manic, M., Alahakoon, D.: ChatGPT and generative AI guidelines for addressing academic integrity and augmenting pre-existing chatbots. In: Proceedings of the IEEE International Conference on Industrial Technology, April 2023 (2023). https://doi.org/10.1109/ICIT58465.2023.1014312
15. Kohnke, L., Moorhouse, B.L., Zou, D.: ChatGPT for language teaching and learning. RELC J. **54**(2), 537–550 (2023). https://doi.org/10.1177/00336882231162868
16. Rajabi, P., Taghipour, P., Cukierman, D., Doleck, T.: Exploring ChatGPT's impact on post-secondary education: a qualitative study. In: ACM International Conference Proceeding Series, Article no. 9 (2023). https://doi.org/10.1145/3593342.3593360
17. Denny, P., Kumar, V., Giacaman, N.: Conversing with Copilot: Exploring prompt engineering for solving CS1 problems using natural language. In: Proceedings of the 54th ACM Technical Symposium on Computer Science Education (SIGCSE 2023), pp. 1–7. ACM (2023). https://doi.org/10.1145/3545945.356982
18. Feng, Y., Vanam, S., Cherukupally, M., Zheng, W., Qiu, M., Chen, H.: Investigating code generation performance of ChatGPT with crowdsourcing social data. In: 2023 IEEE 47th Annual Computers, Software, and Applications Conference (COMPSAC), TBD. IEEE (2023)
19. Finnie-Ansley, J., Denny, P., Becker, B.A., Luxton-Reilly, A., Prather, J.: The robots are coming: exploring the implications of OpenAI Codex on introductory programming. In: Proceedings of the 24th Australasian Computing Education Conference, TBD (2022)
20. Lo, L.S.: The art and science of prompt engineering: a new literacy in the information age. Internet Ref. Serv. Q. (2023). https://doi.org/10.1080/10875301.2023.222762
21. OpenAI: Best practices for using GPT (n.d.). https://platform.openai.com/docs/guides/gpt-best-practices. Accessed 20 Oct 2023
22. McKinney, W.: Python for Data Analysis: Data Wrangling with panDas, NumPy, and Jupyter, 3rd edn. (2022)
23. Zheng, Y.: A comparison of tools for teaching and learning data analytics. In: Conference on Information Technology Education, 26 September 2019, p. 160 (2019)
24. Brooke, J.: SUS: a quick and dirty usability scale. In: Usability Evaluation in Industry, vol. 189, 30 November 1995

25. Garg, A., Rajendran, R.: The impact of structured prompt-driven generative AI on learning data analysis in engineering students. In: Proceedings of the 16th International Conference on Computer Supported Education, vol. 2, pp. 270–277 (2024). ISBN 978-989-758-697-2, ISSN 2184-5026
26. Ryan, R., Deci, E.: Self-determination theory and the facilitation of intrinsic motivation, social development, and well-being. Am. Psychol. **55**(1), 68–78 (2000). https://doi.org/10.1037/0003-066X.55.1.68

# Detecting Function Inputs and Outputs for Learning-Problem Generation in Intelligent Tutoring Systems

Kirill Kulyukin, Grigoriy Yakimov, and Oleg Sychev(✉)

Volgograd State Technical University, Volgograd, Russia
o_sychev@vstu.ru
https://vstu.ru

**Abstract.** Designing of the function interface is one of the key skills in programming. That requires feedback, which can be generated in the necessary quantity only by an intelligent tutoring system. In this paper, we propose a method of extracting function descriptions from inline comments in open-source code and find noun phrases that describe the data items passed to and returned from the function. We compare two popular NLP tools for parsing sentences and two different similarity measures to find the best-performing combination and develop sophisticated methods of filtering functions to increase the percentage of correctly marked functions. We achieved correctly marking more than 80% of the automatically selected functions, which significantly speeds up creating banks of learning problems for intelligent tutoring systems in programming learning.

**Keywords:** Natural language processing · Learning problem generation · Feedback generation · Introductory programming learning

## 1 Introduction

Demands for IT professionals and programmers have been growing in the last few years because of the increasing usage of digital technologies in modern society [17]. Learning programming is very difficult because programming requires various knowledge and many different cognitive activities [39].

Modern programs can contain many thousands of lines of code. They are difficult to develop, read, understand, and maintain. They also require the cooperation of teams of software developers to develop and maintain them. The chief method of dealing with the complexity of modern software is decomposing it [20] into smaller modules, which can be developed separately and then linked together into a single system. The object-oriented paradigm [41] is the most popular approach to program decomposition, which can be hard for novice programming students because of the large number of new concepts [15] that should be learned before writing the first program. The procedure-oriented approach is


A. Sifaleras and F. Lin (Eds.): ITS 2024, LNCS 14798, pp. 244–257, 2024.
https://doi.org/10.1007/978-3-031-63028-6_19

easier for beginners; it considers the program a set of procedures interacting with each other in order to perform the program's function. Both approaches require defining interfaces of procedures, which can be called either functions or class methods.

A procedure is a named part of the code that has a well-defined interface consisting of input and output arguments and the return value, so it can be accessed by other parts of the program. One of the central skills when learning to design and implement complex programs is designing function interfaces so that the data are passed to and from the function correctly and conveniently. It often requires repeated exercise to master. One of the common exercises in introductory programming courses is designing the interface of the procedure to perform the required task. The first step in that exercise is extracting the descriptions of data passed to and returned from the procedure from the natural-language formulation of the procedure's goal [24].

Such exercises can be used either for assessing the learners' skills (summative exercises) or for developing those skills, including self-study (formative exercises). Formative assessment [28] is very important for the learning process if it is supplied with appropriate feedback [23]. Face-to-face interaction between student and teacher is an effective way to study, but it is limited because of teachers' time necessary to verify the students' solutions and provide feedback. Many introductory programming courses suffer from a high teacher workload, which leaves little time for teachers to provide individual feedback to their students [10]. Intelligent tutoring systems (ITS) [2,19] can increase the performance of teachers by providing automatic explanatory feedback when students make errors. ITS is a program that simulates student-teacher interaction [9] providing immediate feedback [26] and guidance on incorrect steps [2] while selecting the next learning problem according to the learner's progress. The two key problems when developing ITS are detecting semantic errors to provide meaningful explanatory feedback and creating enough different exercises to maintain effective learning for every kind of student.

In this paper, we propose a method for the automatic extraction of descriptions of data items from a procedures' descriptions that can be automatically extracted from the program code because they are provided in a special format for the purposes of generating program documentation. This method allows increasing the quantity (and so, precision) of explanatory error messages provided to the students and paves the way for automatic generation of procedure-designing learning problems from existing source code.

## 2 Related Works

Many solutions were developed to check the correctness of program code. Static code analyzers [18] are used to check the program code using special templates and report typical errors and deficiencies. Formal verification methods [11] allow to check the algorithm's correctness based on its requirements. However, they work well for experienced programmers; they are not designed to support novice programmers who are still struggling with learning the basic concepts.

Effective feedback belongs to the essential factors of student success in programming courses [34]. However, feedback provided by human teachers and tutors is limited by the specified class time and office time, while poorly-performing students may need more feedback to succeed in the course. Additional feedback can be provided automatically by intelligent tutoring systems.

Many different ITS were developed for programming learning. In [29], the authors discussed a tutor for learning Scratch using automated feedback in the form of hints. In the tutor "AlgoTouch" [1], students create program codes by dragging blocks with algorithmic primitives. "Dodona" [40] is a virtual co-teacher for learning different areas of programming, including data science. It is designed as a set of online courses with practical exercises. Contractor and Rivero described a program that generates feedback using approximate graph matching of abstract syntax trees of the correct (expected) program code and the student's program code [7].

"Ask-Elle" [13] is a tutor teaching writing functions in the Haskel language based on the natural-language text describing the function goal. To create an exercise in that tutor, the teacher should enter the description text and model solutions for the task [12]. But the description's text is not connected with other task's components. The function interface is predefined by the teacher. "CodeQ" [21] is an online tutor for different areas of programming in Python and Prolog. One of the topics in "CodeQ" is writing a code of function with the given goal. The function description is not related to the task solution process. The student has the possibility of getting a hint that was predefined by the teacher. But hints related to the function interface do not provide students with opportunities to understand the errors made and avoid them in the future.

Problets [4,14] and Solvelets [3] are a group of intelligent tutors for different kinds of learning problems used in introductory programming courses. They provide step-by-step feedback if the student takes a wrong action. The steps of Problets and Solvelets correspond to different sub-tasks used in programming practice. Those tutors allow reliable measurements of the students' learning outcomes [25].

Solvelets [3] introduced a task-solving step when the student should select inputs and outputs of the algorithm in the natural-language algorithm description. The tutor gives hints to the student if they select a text fragment that doesn't describe the algorithm's inputs or outputs. That feature relies on the manually entered data in the problem formulation, which makes creating new learning problems more labor-intensive. Also, the tutor provides only basic feedback on errors: it only discerns selecting too little (less than a word), too much (more than necessary), and selecting a wrong phrase. In the last case, the tutor always recommends the student "pick a noun", even if the student selects a noun that is not related to the algorithm's input and output data, which can be misleading. Also, Solvelets only support selecting one noun per data item, which can be confusing if the algorithm interface contains two data items with the same base noun (e.g., calculating a person's age from the birthday date and the current date).

The same step of selecting function inputs and outputs is used in the intelligent tutor for designing a function interface [24]. That tutor has a slightly better system of feedback because it allows noun phrases (not just single nouns) as descriptions of data items, and its basic feedback says, "The selected phrase does not describe any data item", which avoids misleading the student when a noun that does not describe a data item is selected. However, that tutor also requires manual labeling of parts of the function description, and it does not provide detailed feedback to the student on errors.

In order to facilitate automatic learning-problem generation, it is necessary to develop methods of labeling data items corresponding to the input and output data in the function description. Various methods of Natural Language Processing (NLP) [32] can be used to perform the task. The closest to the goals of our study NLP problem is Named Entity Recognition (NER), which concerns extracting named entities mentioned in a natural-language text [6]. NER is often used to extract person names, places, and specific terms [5,16]. However, our problems are more complex than the problems solved by classical NER approaches because data items are represented by common nouns (while most of the named entities are proper nouns), and they belong to different application fields depending on the features of the program from which the pool of function-describing comments is drawn, so domain-specific techniques and ontologies cannot be used.

## 3 Method of Identifying Data Items in Function Description

```
/**
* Find the comparable distance between two points
* @param p1 First point
* @param p2 Second point
* @return The comparable distance between the two
points
*/
```

**Fig. 1.** Function-documenting comment example

Many computer programs have inline comments documenting functions, classes, and other program elements (see Fig. 1). Those comments are used to automatically generate code documentation, which helps keep it updated when the code changes. Comments documenting functions and class methods often contain sections devoted to generally describing the function (which can be used to generate a learning problem in function interface design) and separate descriptions of function parameters and return values, which can be used to facilitate identifying the parts of function descriptions naming data items. Using real-world open-source code allows for the generation of realistic learning problems that do not look artificial [38], unlike the methods based on random generation. Using real program code also allows generating more diverse learning problems than template-based problem generation [36].

We propose a method of finding the phrases mentioning function parameters in its description with the following steps:

1. Extraction of the function data (function description and parameter descriptions) from an inline documentation comment;
2. Pre-filtering of extracted function descriptions;
3. Extraction of noun phrases from descriptions;
4. Matching parameters' noun phrase to description noun phrases;
5. Post-filtering of marked function descriptions.

In the following text, we will use the term "parameter" for any unit of data passed to or returned from the function, including function arguments and returned value.

**Extraction of Function Description and Parameter Descriptions.** Inline documentation comments have fixed patterns, which are necessary to generate structured documents from them. Definitions of parameters and return values are marked with special commands; the paragraph without commands is considered the function description.

**Pre-filtering of Extracted Function Descriptions.** At this stage, incorrect function descriptions are filtered out. Pre-filtering is performed based on the following criteria:

- there are no non-punctuation symbols (e.g., %, $, *, etc.) in the comment (those characters make parsers perform poorly);
- comment contains at least one parameter or return value.

Function descriptions often begin with noun phrases like "This function", "Helper method" and so on. Those noun phrases do not belong to the data elements. If the first word in the function description is not a verb, we exclude the first noun phrase before the verb from the function description. For example, the function description "Helper method to add a setting item to a preset" will be truncated to "add a setting item to a preset".

**Extraction of Noun Phrases from the Descriptions.** A noun phrase [8] is a phrase that has the grammatical function of a noun. Usually, noun phrases describe objects, so data items that are passed to and returned from the function are typically described using noun phrases. Our goal at that stage is to collect all the noun phrases in the descriptions: given a function description and function data descriptions, select all the noun phrases from the function description and parameter descriptions.

In this step, we build a syntax tree of the function description. Then we select all nouns that are not compounds of other nouns. Then we select all direct and indirect dependents of those nouns through relations: "nmod", "amod", "det", "compound", and "case". If a word is linked by the "case" relation directly to the root noun, it is excluded to make the resulting sub-tree a noun phrase (e.g., the word "of" in the example shown in Fig. 2 which is directly related to the root noun "user"). The resulting sub-trees are called "full noun phrases".

Figure 2 shows an example of a sentence's syntax tree. Full noun phrases for that example are "the person's unique identifier of the last registered user", "the last registered user", and "the person". As you can see, full noun phrases can be nested.

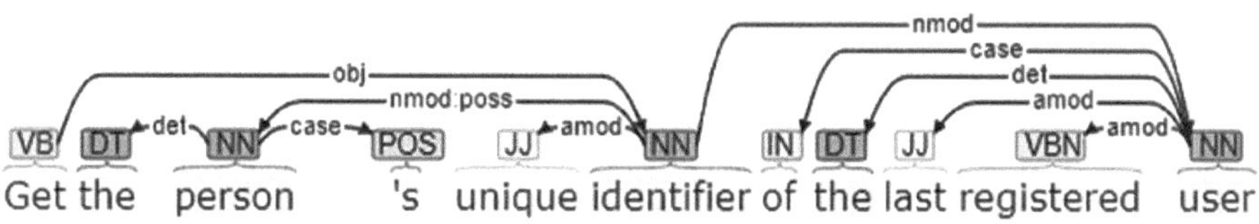


**Fig. 2.** Syntax tree of a sentence

**Matching Parameters' Noun Phrases with Phrases of the Function Description Based on Their Similarities.** To match the parameters with noun phrases in the function description, we propose selecting full noun phrases in the function description with the highest similarity value for each parameter. One noun phrase in the function description can describe more than one parameter as is shown in Fig. 3 (where the box A shows noun phrases extracted from the function description, and the box B shows noun phrases extracted from function parameters), so we can "reuse" the noun phrases for different parameters: the phrase "two points" describes two parameters, "first point" and "second point".

Let's call "main noun phrase" a part of the full noun phrase, which is a noun phrase that is not related through the "nmod" link to other noun phrases. Examples of main noun phrases are shown in Table 1.

A full noun phrase is considered a candidate for a parameter if the similarity between the parameter and the main noun phrase of the full noun phrase is more or equal than 0.5. To choose the best candidate, the similarity of the parameter and the full noun phrase of each candidate are calculated. The candidate with the maximal similarity becomes the parameter's match if its similarity is more or equal than 0.5.

The algorithm is shown in Algorithm 1. Full noun phrases from the function description are denoted *FGNP*; descriptions of parameters are denoted *DE*.

**Table 1.** Examples of main nouns phrases

| Full noun phrase | Corresponding main noun phrase |
|---|---|
| the person's unique identifier of the last registered user | unique identifier |
| the last registered user | the last registered user |
| the person | the person |

**Algorithm 1.** Match similar phrases

$matches = []$ ▷ For each parameter
**for each:** $de \in DE$ **do**
  $candidates \leftarrow []$ ▷ Construct the list of candidate phrases for the parameter
  **for each:** $fdnp \in FDNP$ **do**
    $main\_np\_fdnp \leftarrow get\_main\_np(fdnp)$
    $sim \leftarrow get\_similarity(de, main\_np\_fdnp)$
    **if** $sim \geq 0.5$ **then**
      $candidates.append(fdnp)$
    **end if**
  **end for**

  **if** $length(candidates) > 0$ **then** ▷ Find the most similar function description noun phrase for each parameter
    $curr\_candidate \leftarrow candidates(0)$
    $max\_score \leftarrow -1$
    **for each:** $c \in candidates$ **do**
      $curr\_score \leftarrow get\_similarity(de, c)$
      **if** $curr\_score > max\_score$ and $curr\_score \geq 0.5$ **then**
        $curr\_candidate \leftarrow c$
        $max\_score \leftarrow curr\_score$
      **end if**
    **end for**
   ▷ Connect matched function description noun phrase to parameter description
    **if** $max\_score \neq -1$ **then**
      $matches.append(de, curr\_candidate)$
    **end if**
  **end if**
**end for**

**Post-filtering of Function Descriptions.** At this stage, we aim to increase the percentage of functions with correctly matched parameters by weeding out dubious functions whose descriptions are likely to be matched incorrectly. We keep the functions meeting the following criteria:

- at least one argument of the function and its return value are matched with noun phrases in the function description;

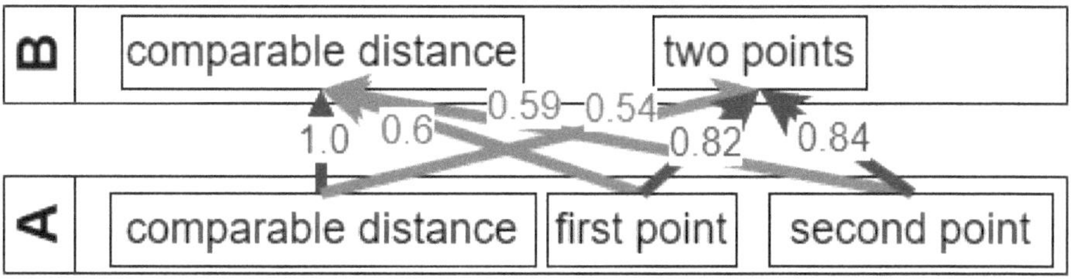


**Fig. 3.** Example of matching noun phrases from function description (A) to its parameters (B).

- if several parameters are matched to the same phrase in the function goal description, they must be similar (similarity no less than 0.5) to each other.

# 4 Results

## 4.1 Test Sample

To test the developed method, we selected inline documentation comments from well-known open-source projects: Moodle, GCC, Linux Kernel, and Doxygen. We used the comments to free functions and static class methods because they have much fewer "hidden parameters" passed through the class fields. We extracted comments from 9 608 functions, which were used to select the best NLP tool for sentence parsing and similarity metrics for matching descriptions.

## 4.2 Evaluation

**NLP Tools Evaluation.** We tried extracting full noun phrases from the function descriptions using two open-source NLP toolkits: "Stanza" and "spaCy". "Stanza" implements a Python interface to use Java Stanford CoreNLP software [31], which uses a neural-network-based method called graph-based parsing. "spaCy" is a Python package using a statistical model based on transition-based parsing algorithms [27].

We considered true positives the full noun phrases that were found manually and by the NLP tool, false positives the phrases that were found by the NLP tool but were not confirmed manually, and false negatives the phrases that were found manually but omitted by the NLP tool.

The metrics for each parser are shown in Table 2.

**Similarity Calculation Methods Evaluation.** We considered two methods of calculating similarity between phrases: editing distance in the form of Levenshtein distance (implemented in the Python package "thefuzz") and semantic similarity in the form of Vector Space Model "GloVe" [35] (implemented in the Python package "Gensim" [33]). The Levenshtein distance between sequences of

**Table 2.** Efficiency of the NLP tools

| NLP tool | Precision | Recall | F1-score |
|---|---|---|---|
| Stanza | 0.941 | 0.961 | 0.951 |
| spaCy | 0.912 | 0.854 | 0.882 |

$A$ and $B$ is the minimum number of changes (inserts, deletes, or substitutions) of one sequence element (usually, a character) in $A$ to transform it into $B$ [22]. The "Glove" Vector Space Model [30] combining features of global matrix factorization and local context window methods and was trained on the data from Wikipedia and Gigaword dataset. Similar words (for example, synonyms) have a small distance from each other.

We measured the percentage of the functions for which all the parameters were matched correctly because only those functions can be used to generate learning problems without a teacher's intervention. The results are shown in Table 3. It can be seen that both filtering stages are crucial to improving the method's performance.

**Table 3.** Evaluation of similarity calculation methods. $N_{func}$ - number of selected functions, $P_{corr}$ - percentage of functions with correctly matched parameters.

| Similarity measure | Full filtration | | No pre-filtration | | No post-filtration | |
|---|---|---|---|---|---|---|
| | $N_{func}$ | $P_{corr}$ | $N_{func}$ | $P_{corr}$ | $N_{func}$ | $P_{corr}$ |
| Levenshtein distance | 127 | 87.62% | 935 | 24.07% | 5839 | 7.1% |
| "GloVe" Vector Space Model | 122 | 63.42% | 1061 | 19.4% | 5839 | 4.9% |

## 5 Discussion

When comparing the NLP tools, the most important metric for us was recall because a wrongly selected phrase is not likely to be matched to any parameter; omitting a valid phrase is a worse error. According to Table 2, "Stanza" performed the best for all metrics, so we consider it more suitable for extracting noun phrases from sentences that are typical in function description comments.

Out of similarity metrics, the Levenshtein distance gave significantly better results than the Vector Space Model "Glove". This can be caused by the semantic similarity metrics using the vector space being too broad, considering different terms used in the same function definition are very close because they belong to the same task performed by the function. For example, the similarity of the phrases $a$ = "an image with new color" and $b$ = "old color of an image" describing two different parameters is $sim(a, b) = 0.96$ when the Vector Space Model is used and $sim(a, b) = 0.62$ when the Levenshtein distance is used. The Levenshtein distance performed better in spite of its obvious disadvantages. The percentage of correctly identified functions (87.62%) is good for giving a teacher prepared problem formulations they can verify and fix if necessary, but it is too low for fully automatic generation [37]. More work on defining a better similarity measure is needed to fully automate learning problem generation in that field.

Our method chose as suitable for learning-problem generations 127 comments out of 9 608. While the rate is only about 1.32%, it is more than enough for large-scale problem generation because of the vast amount of raw data: there are more than 300 million repositories on GitHub alone, and their number is growing. Using the available open-source code, it is possible to generate any practically desired number of learning problems.

Still, the low number of generated learning problems is the biggest limitation of the proposed method. Our aim was to maximize precision so that we can lower the amount of manual work involved in verifying and fixing generated learning problems. Increasing recall will be a challenge for further development of the proposed method. One of the challenges we face in developing that method is using generative artificial intelligence tools to preprocess function comments to increase their quality and so suitability both for machine processing and usage in generating learning problems.

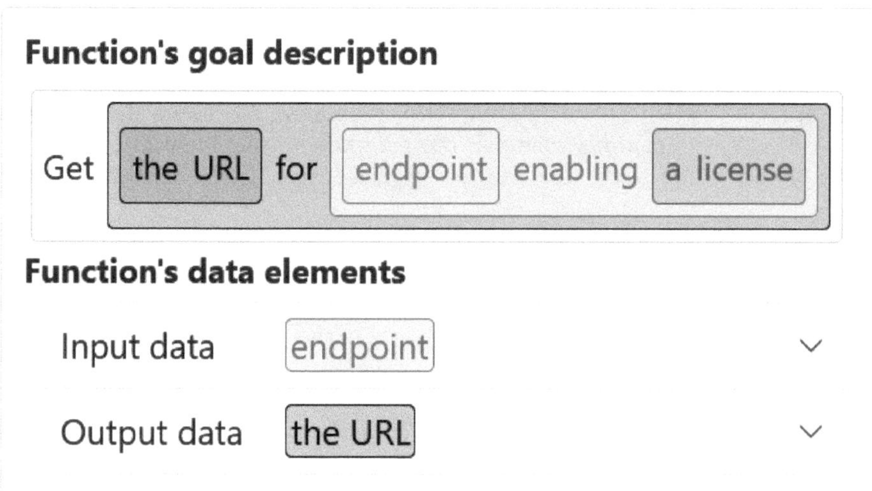


**Fig. 4.** Interface for verifying and correcting mark up of data elements. The noun phrases for the found data elements are shown in the red and blue rectangles; the noun phrase that is not matched to a data element is shown in the gray rectangle. (Color figure online)

To facilitate generating learning problems, we developed a user interface that allows quick verification and correction of the marked function descriptions. Figure 4 shows an example of marked function descriptions with noun phrases highlighted by color rectangles (each element is given its own color); function data elements are shown below. Each data element has two rectangles: the bigger one shows the full noun phrase (i.e., the maximal phrase that can be selected by students to give a correct answer); the smaller rectangle shows the main noun phrase (the minimal phrase that should be selected by students to give a correct answer). Rectangle borders can be adjusted to correct the automatic markup. Noun phrases that were not connected to a data element are shown in a gray rectangle. The interface allows teachers to verify and correct a function description in less than 20 s, which is very fast compared to manual marking. It is then saved in the RDF format to be included in the formal problem definition for the intelligent tutor in developing function interfaces [24].

## 6 Conclusion

Designing function interfaces is an important skill in programming learning. It requires repeated exercise to master. Learning that skill starts with identifying data items passed to and from the function in the natural-language text describing what the function should do.

The current solutions [3, 24] require manual marking of the function description and can give confusing feedback. In this paper, we propose a method of automatic marking of function descriptions extracted from inline documenting comments in the program code to identify the noun phrases describing function parameters. We measured the performance of two NLP tools for parsing sentences and two methods of calculating string similarity and found that the best results (87.62% of functions where all the parameters were identified correctly) can be achieved by using the "Stanza" package and the Levenshtein editing distance.

Those results allow building a tool to support learning-problem generation, which extracts function descriptions from open-source code and gives the teacher pre-marked descriptions they can correct and use in their learning problems. They also help avoid confusing feedback when the tutor tells the learner to select a noun when a non-relevant noun is selected.

Full automation of learning-problem generation requires better precision. We plan to develop a special semantic similarity measure better suited to discern parameters of the same function, which can be based on vector embeddings and/or neural networks.

## References


1. Adam, M., Daoud, M., Frison, P.: Direct manipulation versus text-based programming: an experiment report. In: Proceedings of the 2019 ACM Conference on Innovation and Technology in Computer Science Education, ITiCSE 2019, pp. 353–359. Association for Computing Machinery, New York (2019). https://doi.org/10.1145/3304221.3319738
2. Anderson, J.R., Boyle, C.F., Reiser, B.J.: Intelligent tutoring systems. Science **228**(4698), 456–462 (1985). https://doi.org/10.1126/science.228.4698.456
3. Kumar, A.N.: Solvelets: tutors to practice the process of programming. In: Proceedings of the 27th ACM Conference on Innovation and Technology in Computer Science Education, ITiCSE 2022, Dublin, Ireland, vol. 1, pp. 151–157. Association for Computing Machinery, New York (2022). https://doi.org/10.1145/3502718.3524811. ISBN: 9781450392013
4. Kumar, A.N.: Allowing revisions while providing error-flagging support: is more better? In: Bittencourt, I., Cukurova, M., Muldner, K., Luckin, R., Millán, E. (eds.) AIED 2020. LNCS (LNAI), vol. 12164, pp. 147–151. Springer, Cham (2020). https://doi.org/10.1007/978-3-030-52240-7_27
5. Chantrapornchai, C., Choksuchat, C.: Ontology construction and application in practice case study of health tourism in Thailand. Springerplus **5**, 1–31 (2016). https://doi.org/10.1186/s40064-016-3747-3
6. Chantrapornchai, C., Tunsakul, A.: Information extraction tasks based on BERT and SpaCy on tourism domain. ECTI Transactions on Computer and Information Technology (ECTI-CIT) **15**(1), 108–122 (2021). https://doi.org/10.37936/ecti-cit.2021151.228621
7. Contractor, M.R., Rivero, C.R.: Improving program matching to automatically repair introductory programs. In: Crossley, S., Popescu, E. (eds.) Intelligent Tutoring Systems, pp. 323–335. Springer, Cham (2022). https://doi.org/10.1007/978-3-031-09680-8_30
8. Crystal, D.: A Dictionary of Linguistics and Phonetics. Blackwell Textbooks in Linguistics, Blackwell (1997). https://books.google.ru/books?id=ZfHtAAAAMAAJ
9. Fayaz Ahmad, S., Rahmat, M., Mubarik, M., Alam, M., Hyder, S.: Artificial intelligence and its role in education. Sustainability **13**(22), 12902 (2021). https://doi.org/10.3390/su132212902
10. Figueiredo, J., García-Peñalvo, F.J.: Intelligent tutoring systems approach to introductory programming courses. In: Eighth International Conference on Technological Ecosystems for Enhancing Multiculturality, TEEM 2020, pp. 34–39. Association for Computing Machinery, New York (2021). https://doi.org/10.1145/3434780.3436614
11. Figueroa, I., García, B., Leger, P.: Towards progressive program verification in Dafny. In: Proceedings of the XXII Brazilian Symposium on Programming Languages, SBLP 2018, pp. 90–97. Association for Computing Machinery, New York (2018). https://doi.org/10.1145/3264637.3264649
12. Gerdes, A., Heeren, B., Jeuring, J., van Binsbergen, L.T.: Ask-Elle: an adaptable programming tutor for haskell giving automated feedback. Int. J. Artif. Intell. Educ. **27**(1), 65–100 (2016). https://doi.org/10.1007/s40593-015-0080-x
13. Gerdes, A., Heeren, B., Jeuring, J., van Binsbergen, L.T.: Ask-Elle: an adaptable programming tutor for haskell giving automated feedback. Int. J. Artif. Intell. Educ. **27**(1), 65–100 (2017). https://doi.org/10.1007/s40593-015-0080-x

14. Getseva, V., Kumar, A.N.: An empirical analysis of code-tracing concepts. In: Proceedings of the 27th ACM Conference on on Innovation and Technology in Computer Science Education, ITiCSE 2022, vol. 1, pp. 262–268. Association for Computing Machinery, New York (2022). https://doi.org/10.1145/3502718.3524794
15. Hofuku, Y., Cho, S., Nishida, T., Kanemune, S.: Why is programming difficult?, January 2013
16. Hoppe, T., Qundus, J.A., Peikert, S.: Ontology-based entity recognition and annotation. In: Proceedings of the Conference on Digital Curation Technologies, Qurator 2020, Berlin, Germany, 20th–21st January 2020 (2020). https://ceur-ws.org/Vol-2535/paper_4.pdf
17. Islam, N., Sheikh, G., Fatima, R., Alvi, F.: A study of difficulties of students in learning programming. J. Educ. Soc. Sci. **7**, 38–46 (2019). https://doi.org/10.20547/jess0721907203
18. Knaster, S., Malik, W., Dalrymple, M.: Using the Static Analyzer, pp. 319–328. Apress, Berkeley (2012). https://doi.org/10.1007/978-1-4302-4189-8_19
19. Kurni, M., Mohammed, M.S., Srinivasa, K.G.: Intelligent Tutoring Systems, pp. 29–44. Springer, Cham (2023). https://doi.org/10.1007/978-3-031-32653-0_2
20. Kwon, K., Cheon, J.: Exploring problem decomposition and program development through block-based programs. Int. J. Comput. Sci. Educ. Sch. 3(1), 3–16 (2019)
21. Lazar, T., Sadikov, A., Bratko, I.: Rewrite rules for debugging student programs in programming tutors. IEEE Trans. Lear. Technol. **11**(4), 429–440 (2017)
22. Levenshtein, V.I.: Binary Codes Capable of Correcting Deletions, Insertions and Reversals. Soviet Physics Doklady **10**, 707 (1966)
23. Lin, F., De Silva, S.: An approach to generating adaptive feedback for online formative assessment. In: Frasson, C., Mylonas, P., Troussas, C. (eds.) Augmented Intelligence and Intelligent Tutoring Systems, vol. 13891, pp. 88–99. Springer, Cham (2023). https://doi.org/10.1007/978-3-031-32883-1_8
24. Litovkin, D., Anikin, A., Kulyukin, K., Sychev, O.: Intelligent tutor for designing function interface in a programming language. In: Crossley, S., Popescu, E. (eds.) Intelligent Tutoring Systems, vol. 13284, pp. 293–302. Springer, Cham (2022). https://doi.org/10.1007/978-3-031-09680-8_27
25. Längrich, M., Schulze, J., Kumar, A.: Expression tasks for novice programmers, turning the attention to objectivity, reliability and validity. In: Proceedings of the 2015 IEEE Frontiers in Education Conference (2015). https://doi.org/10.1109/FIE.2015.7344070
26. Marwan, S., Gao, G., Fisk, S., Price, T.W., Barnes, T.: Adaptive immediate feedback can improve novice programming engagement and intention to persist in computer science. In: Proceedings of the 2020 ACM Conference on International Computing Education Research, ICER 2020, pp. 194–203. Association for Computing Machinery, New York (2020). https://doi.org/10.1145/3372782.3406264
27. Montani, I., et al.: explosion/spaCy: v3.1.6: workaround for click/typer issues (2022). https://doi.org/10.5281/ZENODO.1212303
28. Neumann, K.: Formative assessment. In: Gunstone, R. (ed.) Encyclopedia of Science Education. Springer, Dordrecht (2014). https://doi.org/10.1007/978-94-007-6165-0_49-3
29. Obermüller, F., Greifenstein, L., Fraser, G.: Effects of automated feedback in scratch programming tutorials. In: Proceedings of the 2023 Conference on Innovation and Technology in Computer Science Education, ITiCSE 2023, vol. 1, pp. 396-402. Association for Computing Machinery, New York (2023). https://doi.org/10.1145/3587102.3588803

30. Pennington, J., Socher, R., Manning, C.: GloVe: global vectors for word representation. In: Moschitti, A., Pang, B., Daelemans, W. (eds.) Proceedings of the 2014 Conference on Empirical Methods in Natural Language Processing (EMNLP), Doha, Qatar, pp. 1532–1543. Association for Computational Linguistics (2014). https://doi.org/10.3115/v1/D14-1162
31. Qi, P., Zhang, Y., Zhang, Y., Bolton, J., Manning, C.D.: Stanza: a Python natural language processing toolkit for many human languages. In: Proceedings of the 58th Annual Meeting of the Association for Computational Linguistics: System Demonstrations (2020). https://nlp.stanford.edu/pubs/qi2020stanza.pdf
32. Rayhan, A., Kinzler, R., Rayhan, R.: Natural language processing: transforming how machines understand human language (2023). https://doi.org/10.13140/RG.2.2.34900.99200
33. Řehůřek, R., Sojka, P.: Software framework for topic modelling with large corpora. In: Proceedings of the LREC 2010 Workshop on New Challenges for NLP Frameworks, Valletta, Malta, pp. 45–50. ELRA (2010)
34. Rocha, H., Tedesco, P., Costa, E.: On the use of feedback in learning computer programming by novices: a systematic literature mapping. Inf. Educ. **22** (2022). https://doi.org/10.15388/infedu.2023.09
35. Singh, R., Singh, S.: Text similarity measures in news articles by vector space model using NLP. J. Inst. Eng. (India) Ser. B **102** (2020). https://doi.org/10.1007/s40031-020-00501-5
36. Sychev, O.: From question generation to problem mining and classification. In: International Conference on Advanced Learning Technologies, ICALT 2022, Bucharest, Romania, 1–4 July 2022, pp. 304–305 (2022). https://doi.org/10.1109/ICALT55010.2022.00097
37. Sychev, O., Penskoy, N., Prokudin, A.: Generating expression evaluation learning problems from existing program code. In: 2022 International Conference on Advanced Learning Technologies (ICALT), pp. 183–187 (2022). https://doi.org/10.1109/ICALT55010.2022.00061
38. Sychev, O., Prokudin, A., Denisov, M.: Generation of code tracing problems from open-source code. In: Proceedings of the 54th ACM Technical Symposium on Computer Science Education, SIGCSE 2023, vol. 1, pp. 875–881. Association for Computing Machinery, New York (2023). https://doi.org/10.1145/3545945.3569774
39. Turkmen, G., Caner-Yıldırım, S.: The investigation of novice programmers' debugging behaviors to inform intelligent e-learning environments: a case study. Turk. Online J. Distance Educ. **21**, 142–155 (2020). https://doi.org/10.17718/tojde.762039
40. Van Petegem, C., Dawyndt, P., Mesuere, B.: Dodona: learn to code with a virtual co-teacher that supports active learning. In: Proceedings of the 2023 Conference on Innovation and Technology in Computer Science Education, ITiCSE 2023, vol. 2, p. 633. Association for Computing Machinery, New York (2023). https://doi.org/10.1145/3587103.3594165
41. White, G., Sivitanides, M.: Cognitive differences between procedural programming and object oriented programming. Inf. Technol. Manage. 6, 333–350 (2005). doi:10.1007/s10799-005-3899-2

# Automated Analysis of Algorithm Descriptions Quality, Through Large Language Models

Andrea Sterbini[1](✉) and Marco Temperini[2]

[1] Computer Science Department, Sapienza University of Rome, Rome, Italy
sterbini@di.uniroma1.it

[2] Department of Computer, Control and Management Engineering, Sapienza University of Rome, Rome, Italy
marte@diag.uniroma1.it

**Abstract.** In this paper we propose a method to classify the students' textual descriptions of algorithms. This work is based on a wealth of data (programming tasks, related algorithm descriptions, and Peer Assessment data), coming from 6 years of use of the system Q2A, in a "Fundamentals of Computer Programming" course, given at first year in our university's Computer Science curriculum. The descriptions are submitted, as part of the answer to a computer programming task, through Q2A, and are subject to (formative) Peer Assessment. The proposed classification method aims to support the teacher on the analysis of the quite numerous students' descriptions, in ours as well as in other similar systems. We 1) process the students' submissions, by topic automated extraction (BERTopic) and by separate Large Language Models, 2) compute their degree of suitability as "algorithm description", in a scale from BAD to GOOD, and 3) compare the obtained classification with those coming from the teacher's direct assessment (expert: one of the authors), and from the Peer Assessment. The automated classification does correlate with both the expert classification and the grades given by the peers to the "clarity" of the descriptions. This result is encouraging in view of the production of a Q2A subsystem allowing the teacher to analyse the students' submissions guided by an automated classification, and ultimately support fully automated grading.

**Keywords:** Large Language Models · LLM-based Text Similarity · Peer Assessment · Automated Assessment

## 1 Introduction

Computer Programming, as a study discipline in Education, has been growing in the last decade, well beyond its obvious need and placement into Computer Science and Engineering courses [20,21]. Acquiring programming skills, at any level and in any educational context, can be a hard task, as it implies, in the first place, extensive practice and training, by the development of numerous programming exercises [4]. Such practical training is a very useful learning activity, supporting the development and sharpening of programming skills, and often a good part of it is accomplished under the form of homework [17].


A. Sifaleras and F. Lin (Eds.): ITS 2024, LNCS 14798, pp. 258–271, 2024.
https://doi.org/10.1007/978-3-031-63028-6_20

While the assessment of homework can provide a wealth of data about the learner's proficiency, and/or her/his misconceptions, it can be challenging for the teacher, in particular in a large class, for sheer homework numbers, and/or for time constraints. Automated Assessment [16] can then be a great asset in a homework management system: it can provide the student with timely feedback and useful information about the submitted task, also entailing suggestions on how to make it better [5,6,18]. In our Q2A-II system the homework are tested, with a black-box strategy, and grades are given to the submissions according to the number of tests passed. The system also enriches the automated assessment with feedback related to the structure, style, and complexity of the code: feedback that can help the learners to improve and re-submit their solutions.

On the other hand, prior to start coding, the student should make her/his mind about the *Algorithm* to implement. The ability to define an algorithm is very important in computer science and engineering courses, and it's a very important learning objective in several other fields (e.g. medicine, natural sciences, social sciences, music, architecture, and more) [11,12,14].

In our Python programming course, first year in the Computer Science Bachelor, we use the Q2A-II system [15] (Q2A henceforth). Q2A is our question/answer forum, allowing students to help each other while working on the 4 homework tasks to be submitted before of the final exam.

The forum has been extended with some plugins to handle submission, automated testing of the submitted programs, gamification features (badges, points for participation, leader-board), and a *formative peer-assessment* (PA) phase. In it, a student submits the description of the algorithm that is implemented by her/his program. This helps focus on the algorithmic analysis of the student's task. In the PA phase, then, the students are to grade 3 peers' algorithm descriptions and provide three grades: *Clarity* of exposition, *Correctness*, and *Efficiency* of the algorithm. They are also requested to give suggestions on how to improve the algorithm. Unclear algorithm descriptions would make suggestions harder, or even impossible, to give, so the clarity of the algorithm exposition is important. Eventually, the peer receiving a suggestion can grade its perceived usefulness, and is given some more days to submit an improved version of the program.

In this paper, our main goal is to help assess the quality of the algorithm descriptions and to evaluate how the peers' grades relate with such quality. We have first addressed this problem in a very recent conference paper [19], using a modest two-values scale (BAD/GOOD). BAD meant basically "no algorithmic description" (whatever text was in it), so we obtained a partition of the submissions in two classes, where the second class was the one with descriptions bearing at least minimal traces of algorithmic contents.

Here we extend the work using a more powerful Large Language Model (LLM), and a more finely grained classification scale. We also produce a preliminary validation of the classification method, based on the teacher labeling of one year worth of data (about 1600 submissions). (The teacher is one of the authors). The whole dataset we used comprises the submissions from the last six years of Q2A usage, i.e. 10K submissions and 36K grades and suggestions.

The automated classification is produced by first extracting Topic clusters, through BERTopic: each cluster contains a subset of the submissions, and the clusterization is based on the common presence, in such submissions, of the topic keywords. Then the clusters are assigned a label, using the grading scale that was used in the manual classification of 2019/20 dataset. To do this, we have devised a measure of clarity of the algorithm description, based on a comparison with the text of the task description. So the labelling performed by the system is based on the distance between the descriptions of task and single algorithm. We think that cheating, in this setting, can be easily contrasted, while such a measure could provide an assessment of how the algorithm description can be available to be evaluated by the peers (and by the teacher). Eventually, we compare the automated labelling (classification) with the teacher's labelling (limited to year 2019/20) and with the clarity assessment given in the PA.

In both cases, the automated classification correlate with the other classifications.

The rationale of this research is both based on our interest in discovering hidden structure in the students' behaviour, and in our desire to improve our teaching (and the Q2A system) by leveraging the vast amount of data collected. The final goal being to build a good model of the student and of her behaviour when cooperating with her peers, and from that, to be able to help students that find difficulties in their study activity.

### 1.1 Research Questions

Large Language Models (LLM) recently have been able to do sophisticated comparisons between texts "meanings", and to produce texts imitating the human language with a very high level of detail and complexity. This implies that the internal representation used by such models must be precise enough to represent (in some hidden way) the nuances of human languages. This gave us the intuition that LLMs could be used to understand if an algorithm description is actually explaining an algorithm, suitable for the task at hand, and to what degree.

**RQ1:** *Can a LLM be used to classify the algorithm descriptions part of the homework dataset, and so predict the teacher's labelling of the algorithm?*
We'll see that this is possible, through automated topic extraction, and the use of a measure expressing how similar is the algorithm description to the related homework task, as provided by the teacher.
The conjecture is in that the more the algorithm is properly described, the better any kind of assessment will have a chance to be. Notice that here we are not dealing with the *correctness* of the described algorithm, rather with the possibility to say something about it, based on the description, which would be potentially useful to the student author, whether it came from the teacher or from the peers. To validate this, we compared the automated labelling with the teacher's one (2019/20 dataset) and with the clarity assessments given by the peers.
About the last assessment (clarity) naturally a further RQ arose:

**RQ2:** Is there a correlation between the similarity to the task and the peers' grades (clarity)?
In fact, it is interesting to see how the grades given by the peers (about how clearly the algorithm is described) align with the automated evaluation of the algorithm description's quality. This can also shed some light about the student's ability to assess, which can be useful, in turn, for student modelling.

## 2 Related Work

Automated grading of programming tasks in education has been studied for a long time [9], to provide the teacher with needed help, as well to assist learners with prompt feedback during their learning activities. Teachers need support especially when handling high number of students, or just when there are many programming tasks during the course. Prompt feedback, on the other hand, can be crucial in all the activities developing programming capabilities and computational skills, of which "algorithmic skills" are an important part, as mentioned in the introduction [10,16].

Automated analysis of programming tasks is performed to determine the correctness of the submitted solution, and its efficiency. Sometimes also the propriety of the implemented algorithm is considered. In some systems, *Static Analysis* is applied to provide feedback on the syntactic and static-semantic aspects of the program, without actually running the program [2,13,23]. In other systems *Dynamic Analysis* of the program is performed, aiming to measure the success based on tests, carefully defined to allow catching significant behaviors expected, and significant logical errors in the program [5,6,18]. A less frequent approach combines the two above mentioned types of analysis, such as in [22]

Lots of work has been done about the use of PA in courses of Basics of Programming (in Higher education and in other educational settings). However, less literature is available about how PA is connected to the evaluation and development of Higher Order Thinking in general, or Critical Thinking, or Computational capabilities, or algorithmic skills. An experiment analysed the use of PA in the framework of a First Year University course, where the peers were requested to assess a submission according to three criteria, with quality of description and correctness of the algorithm among them [1]. In [3] PA is studied as a fruitful method to "help students and teachers evaluate algorithm problem-solving skills in mathematics" (arithmetic, algebra, statistics, and geometry). Other works are not directly focused on algorithmic skills, while they propose the application of PA to the wider range of Higher Order Skills. In [8] higher order skills range from transfer of knowledge and skills, to critical thinking and problem solving, and it is discussed how "Peer Assessment is a method that is extremely appropriate ... [to] ... help develop the students' abilities" mentioned above. In [24] a critical synthesis of the research on online PA for Higher Order Thinking skills is presented. According to these authors, online PA seems to have better effects on "convergent thinking" learners (guided by logic and respectful of given criteria) than on "divergent thinking" ones (more creative and possibly needing own-developed assessing criteria). In Q2A-II we are not explicitly working on this side of the PA usefulness, while, on the other hand, we leave a very free hand to the peers in their assessment of the algorithms and related suggestions.

## 3 Methods

As we already showed in [19], hierarchical clustering of topics extracted from documents allows us to automatically distinguish between non-algorithms and algorithms.

To summarize, we first did topic extraction by using the BERTopic library [7] on the documents and their embeddings retrieved with the OpenAI API. In particular, BERTopic does the following steps:

- embeddings extraction from text with the selected LLM model
- dimensionality reduction with the UMAP algorithm
- clustering of the embeddings with the HDBSCAN algorithm
- building a topic representation with the most important words representing the topic with the CountVectorizer and the c-TF-IDF (cluster based TF IDF)
- the topic representation is refined by selecting the most important keywords with a KeyBERT inspired algorithm
- the topics found are automatically reduced by joining similar topics

Notice that in the following we call OUTLIERS the (reasonably small) subset of documents that are not placed by BERTopic in any topic.

Once the topics/clusters have been produced, we obtained the hierarchy of topics in Fig. 1, by repeatedly merging pairs of most similar topics/clusters. This automatically produces the hierarchy, with the two topmost categories that distinguish the two most dissimilar groups of documents (in our case, algorithms vs. non-algorithms).

To obtain more precise text similarity results than in the earlier paper, where we were using the **text-embedding-ada-002** model from OpenAI (named ADA from now on), we have processed our texts through the newer OpenAI LLM model **text-embedding-3-large** (named LARGE in the following). This model accepts documents with a context of 8191 tokens as in the ADA model, which is sufficient for the submitted algorithms and suggestions. The LARGE model produces embeddings with 3072 dimensions (twice as much as the ADA model), which should produce better precision in computing text similarity and clustering the topics.

Using the newest model has been especially easy, as one had just to select a different model while using the OpenAI API to retrieve the embeddings of a document.

## 4 Results

We started with the initial automatic classification of algorithms into BAD/GOOD/OUTLIER as explained above. Then we asked ourselves if the

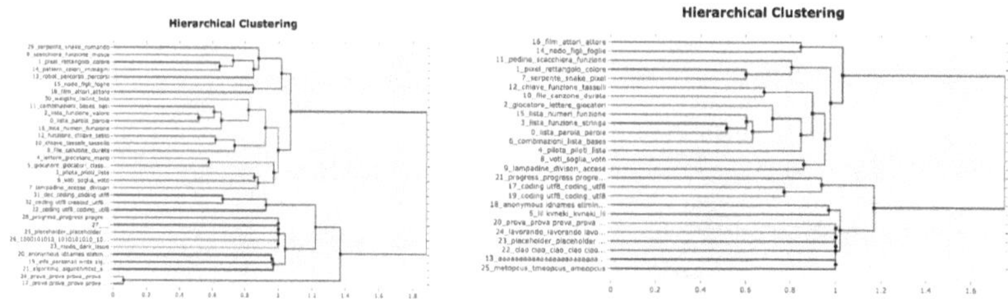


**Fig. 1.** Hierarchical clustering of topics automatically distinguishes non-algorithms (bottom group) from algorithms (top group). ADA (left) and LARGE (right) models.

task description given by the teacher could be used as a reference document to be compared with the algorithms, given the fact that it contained the terminology and the description of the specific homework task.

When we analyse the similarity of algorithms to the task description given by the teachers, we find that non-algorithms (BAD) and algorithms (GOOD) show a distribution with two well separated peaks (see Fig. 2). Similarly, the OUTLIERS show a two-peaks distribution.

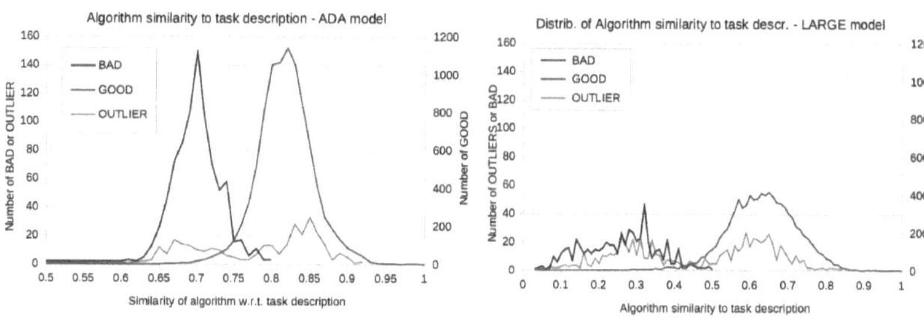


**Fig. 2.** Distribution of documents w.r.t. their similarity to the task description. ADA and LARGE models.

This suggests that the similarity of the algorithm to the task could be used to automatically classify the submitted algorithms.

To understand if the similarity is really connected to the grade a teacher could give to the algorithms, we have manually classified one year of submissions (a.y. 2019–2020, circa 1600 over a total of 10K) with a finer set of labels than the previous BAD/GOOD. The labels are ordered from the lowest grade to the highest: BAD (non-algorithms), LIMBAD, LIMITED, LIMPASS, PASSLIM, PASS, PASSGOOD, GOOD. In the following figures, the columns "GRADES" will refer to such teacher's assigned labels/grades.

When we compute the average similarity of each same-labelled group, and we compare it with the topics extracted and the earlier automatic BAD/GOOD classification, we obtain for the ADA model the distribution shown in Fig. 3

| | | BAD | | | | | | | | | | GOOD | | | | OUTLIER |
|---|---|---|---|---|---|---|---|---|---|---|---|---|---|---|---|---|
| | Topic ID | 17 | 21 | 22 | 23 | 24 | 26 | 27 | 28 | 31 | 32 | 0 | 1 | 2 | 3 | -1 |
| | GRADES | | | | | | | | | | | | | | | |
| Count | BAD | 19 | 2 | 1 | 1 | 2 | 1 | 2 | 4 | 3 | 1 | 2 | 39 | | | 12 |
| | LIMBAD | 1 | | | | | | | | 2 | | 10 | 8 | 1 | 18 | |
| | LIMITED | | | | | | | | | | | 72 | 65 | | 136 | |
| | LIMPASS | | | | | | | | | | | 100 | 74 | | 107 | 1 |
| | PASSLIM | | | | | | | | | | | 93 | 48 | | 55 | |
| | PASS | | | | | | | | | | | 212 | 102 | | 76 | |
| | PASSGOOD | | | | | | | | | | | 143 | 50 | | 33 | |
| | GOOD | | | | | | | | | | | 65 | 23 | | 18 | |
| Avg. Similarity of Algorithm to Task Description | BAD | 0.69 | 0.71 | 0.73 | 0.65 | 0.68 | 0.69 | 0.68 | 0.66 | 0.78 | 0.71 | 0.79 | 0.71 | | | 0.71 |
| | LIMBAD | 0.72 | | | | | | | | 0.76 | | 0.77 | 0.76 | 0.73 | 0.80 | |
| | LIMITED | | | | | | | | | | | 0.80 | 0.78 | | 0.82 | |
| | LIMPASS | | | | | | | | | | | 0.80 | 0.80 | | 0.83 | 0.77 |
| | PASSLIM | | | | | | | | | | | 0.80 | 0.79 | | 0.84 | |
| | PASS | | | | | | | | | | | 0.80 | 0.80 | | 0.84 | |
| | PASSGOOD | | | | | | | | | | | 0.81 | 0.81 | | 0.84 | |
| | GOOD | | | | | | | | | | | 0.81 | 0.81 | | 0.84 | |
| Stdev. Similarity of Algorithm to Task Description | BAD | 0.03 | 0.01 | | | 0.01 | | 0.01 | 0.01 | 0.02 | | 0.03 | 0.02 | | | 0.03 |
| | LIMBAD | | | | | | | | | 0.02 | | 0.04 | 0.02 | | 0.04 | |
| | LIMITED | | | | | | | | | | | 0.02 | 0.03 | | 0.03 | |
| | LIMPASS | | | | | | | | | | | 0.02 | 0.03 | | 0.03 | |
| | PASSLIM | | | | | | | | | | | 0.02 | 0.02 | | 0.03 | |
| | PASS | | | | | | | | | | | 0.06 | 0.02 | | 0.03 | |
| | PASSGOOD | | | | | | | | | | | 0.02 | 0.03 | | 0.03 | |
| | GOOD | | | | | | | | | | | 0.02 | 0.02 | | 0.03 | |

**Fig. 3.** Average similarity for each topic and label. ADA model. Here and in the following figures, we use a red-yellow-green colour scale to highlight the worst-best values.

From the figure, it is clear that automatically classified BAD topics correspond to BAD and LIMBAD, the lowest teacher grades. A small subset of the automatically classified GOOD topics falls also in these lowest grades, possibly corresponding to a few algorithms misclassified by the clusterization step. Almost all outliers fall in the BAD grade (in fact, we manually placed all the outliers in the BAD group in our earlier work).

We compute precision, recall and F1 values for the automatic classification w.r.t. a binary classification obtained by partitioning the 8 teacher labels either in a 2–6 split or in a 3–5 split. We compare these with the same results obtained when using the LARGE model.

**Table 1.** Precision, recall and F1 of the automatic classification w.r.t. the teacher labels over the 2019–20 academic year data.

| Split | ADA model | | LARGE model | |
|---|---|---|---|---|
| | 2–6 | 3–5 | 2–6 | 3–5 |
| Precision | 95.0% | 77.4% | **96.8%** | 77.7% |
| Recall | 100.0% | 100.0% | 100.0% | 100.0% |
| F1 | 97.4% | 87.2% | **98.4%** | 87.5% |
| Accuracy | 95.1% | 77.9% | **97.0%** | 78.9% |
| Specificity | 33.3% | 10.0% | **63.9%** | 20.3% |
| Sensitivity | 100.0% | 100.0% | 100.0% | 100.0% |
| Outliers | **0.81%** | | 11.48% | |

In table 1 we show that a 2–6 split of the 8 labels, when used with the LARGE model, produces the best values, but the number of outliers is 14 times higher than with the ADA model. Therefore, to use the LARGE model, we must find a way to assign the outliers into topics.

From Fig. 4, which shows the similarities for the LARGE model, we see, in fact, that the OUTLIERS are distributed over the whole set of teacher labels. We notice also that the average similarity to task description of each label group increases together with the label grades.

This suggests that using a threshold-based classification strategy to partition outliers w.r.t. their similarity to the task, we could improve the automatic topic-based classification for the LARGE model.

| | | Automatic classification and topic id | | | | | | | | | | | | |
|---|---|---|---|---|---|---|---|---|---|---|---|---|---|---|
| | | BAD | | | | | | | GOOD | | | | | OUTLIER |
| | GRADE | 5 | 13 | 17 | 19 | 20 | 21 | 25 | 0 | 1 | 2 | 4 | 8 | -1 |
| Count | BAD | 38 | 23 | 2 | 3 | 1 | 5 | 2 | 5 | 2 | 1 | | | 8 |
| | LIMBAD | | | | 2 | | | | 7 | 8 | | 19 | 1 | 3 |
| | LIMITED | | | | | | | | 55 | 65 | | 136 | | 17 |
| | LIMPASS | | | | | | | | 82 | 75 | | 107 | | 18 |
| | PASSLIM | | | | | | | | 76 | 48 | | 55 | | 17 |
| | PASS | | | | | | | | 154 | 102 | | 76 | | 58 |
| | PASSGOOD | | | | | | | | 101 | 50 | | 33 | | 42 |
| | GOOD | | | | | | | | 44 | 23 | | 18 | | 21 |
| Avg. Similarity to Task Description | BAD | 0.29 | 0.14 | 0.23 | 0.46 | 0.22 | 0.14 | 0.17 | 0.35 | 0.45 | 0.30 | | | 0.30 |
| | LIMBAD | | | | 0.43 | | | | 0.45 | 0.48 | | 0.55 | 0.35 | 0.46 |
| | LIMITED | | | | | | | | 0.51 | 0.52 | | 0.60 | | 0.51 |
| | LIMPASS | | | | | | | | 0.54 | 0.56 | | 0.63 | | 0.52 |
| | PASSLIM | | | | | | | | 0.55 | 0.57 | | 0.66 | | 0.60 |
| | PASS | | | | | | | | 0.56 | 0.58 | | 0.65 | | 0.59 |
| | PASSGOOD | | | | | | | | 0.58 | 0.60 | | 0.66 | | 0.60 |
| | GOOD | | | | | | | | 0.58 | 0.60 | | 0.68 | | 0.62 |
| StDev. Similarity To Task Description | BAD | 0.04 | 0.03 | 0.04 | 0.01 | | 0.05 | 0.01 | 0.08 | 0.11 | | | | 0.12 |
| | LIMBAD | | | | 0.02 | | | | 0.07 | 0.06 | | 0.09 | | 0.02 |
| | LIMITED | | | | | | | | 0.05 | 0.07 | | 0.07 | | 0.04 |
| | LIMPASS | | | | | | | | 0.05 | 0.07 | | 0.06 | | 0.06 |
| | PASSLIM | | | | | | | | 0.04 | 0.06 | | 0.07 | | 0.07 |
| | PASS | | | | | | | | 0.05 | 0.06 | | 0.07 | | 0.08 |
| | PASSGOOD | | | | | | | | 0.04 | 0.06 | | 0.05 | | 0.06 |
| | GOOD | | | | | | | | 0.04 | 0.08 | | 0.07 | | 0.07 |

**Fig. 4.** Average similarity for each topic and label. LARGE model.

We also wanted to understand if different homework had radically different similarity behaviour. In Fig. 5 we show the average similarity between each labelled group of documents and the homework text, for both ADA and LARGE models. The tables show that, with both models, the lowest grades have lower similarity than the remaining higher labels. This could be used to build an automatic threshold-based classifier. If we look more in detail to the different behaviour of the ADA and LARGE model we notice that the former reaches a plateau, and thus can at most be used for a two-label classification, and cannot be used neither to build a multi-threshold classification strategy, nor to find a linear correlation useful for automatic assessment. The LARGE model instead shows a steady increase in average similarity in concert with the teacher labels. This could be used either to define a multi-threshold assessment strategy (reducing the 8 labels to 3 or 4 levels) or to find a formula interpolating the similarity w.r.t. the labels.

With respect to the homework, we notice that in both models the first, easier, homework shows higher similarity to the task description than the others. This is expected, as the exercise text is shorter and simpler than the other ones. This means also that an automatic assessment model should consider other factors beside the similarity (e.g. the length of the task description or the homework ID).

Algorithms have also been graded by peer students during the peer-assessment phase.

| | | Homeworks | | | | | | | |
|---|---|---|---|---|---|---|---|---|---|
| | | ADA model | | | | LARGE model | | | |
| | Grade | 1 | 2 | 3 | 4 | 1 | 2 | 3 | 4 |
| Count | BAD | 10 | 18 | 26 | 37 | 10 | 18 | 26 | 37 |
| | LIMBAD | 19 | 5 | 9 | 7 | 19 | 5 | 9 | 7 |
| | LIMITED | 135 | 28 | 64 | 46 | 135 | 28 | 64 | 46 |
| | LIMPASS | 106 | 49 | 75 | 52 | 106 | 49 | 75 | 52 |
| | PASSLIM | 55 | 59 | 49 | 33 | 55 | 59 | 49 | 33 |
| | PASS | 75 | 149 | 103 | 63 | 75 | 149 | 103 | 63 |
| | PASSGOOD | 33 | 78 | 50 | 65 | 33 | 78 | 50 | 65 |
| | GOOD | 18 | 45 | 21 | 22 | 18 | 45 | 21 | 22 |
| Avg. Similarity of Algorithm to Task Description | BAD | 0.68 | 0.69 | 0.70 | 0.72 | 0.20 | 0.23 | 0.25 | 0.27 |
| | LIMBAD | 0.80 | 0.74 | 0.76 | 0.78 | 0.55 | 0.42 | 0.47 | 0.45 |
| | LIMITED | 0.82 | 0.78 | 0.78 | 0.80 | 0.60 | 0.51 | 0.52 | 0.51 |
| | LIMPASS | 0.83 | 0.79 | 0.79 | 0.81 | 0.63 | 0.55 | 0.56 | 0.53 |
| | PASSLIM | 0.84 | 0.79 | 0.79 | 0.82 | 0.66 | 0.57 | 0.57 | 0.55 |
| | PASS | 0.84 | 0.79 | 0.80 | 0.82 | 0.65 | 0.58 | 0.58 | 0.55 |
| | PASSGOOD | 0.84 | 0.80 | 0.81 | 0.83 | 0.66 | 0.59 | 0.60 | 0.57 |
| | GOOD | 0.84 | 0.80 | 0.81 | 0.83 | 0.68 | 0.60 | 0.62 | 0.58 |
| Stdev. Similarity of Algorithm to Task Description | BAD | 0.02 | 0.04 | 0.03 | 0.03 | 0.08 | 0.12 | 0.11 | 0.09 |
| | LIMBAD | 0.04 | 0.03 | 0.02 | 0.03 | 0.09 | 0.07 | 0.06 | 0.05 |
| | LIMITED | 0.03 | 0.02 | 0.03 | 0.02 | 0.07 | 0.06 | 0.06 | 0.06 |
| | LIMPASS | 0.03 | 0.02 | 0.03 | 0.02 | 0.06 | 0.04 | 0.07 | 0.07 |
| | PASSLIM | 0.03 | 0.02 | 0.02 | 0.02 | 0.07 | 0.05 | 0.06 | 0.04 |
| | PASS | 0.03 | 0.07 | 0.02 | 0.02 | 0.06 | 0.05 | 0.06 | 0.06 |
| | PASSGOOD | 0.03 | 0.02 | 0.03 | 0.01 | 0.05 | 0.05 | 0.06 | 0.04 |
| | GOOD | 0.03 | 0.02 | 0.02 | 0.02 | 0.07 | 0.05 | 0.06 | 0.07 |

**Fig. 5.** Topic similarity to task description vs the 4 homeworks. ADA and LARGE models.

When we look for correlation between grades and similarity, we find no correlation, because of the variability of grades given by peers to algorithms.

This variability could be related to the fact that peer-assessment is optional, it's not graded, and we suppose the students participate both to get suggestions from others and to have more time to work on their programs. Then they possibly care more about the algorithms and the suggestions than the grades they give/receive to peer's algorithms and suggestions.

If we first extract from the set of submissions the most common topics by using the BERTopic library [7], we find that topics containing similar documents show average similarity and average peers' grade which increase monotonically.

Figure 6 shows how, for each topic extracted and depending on the model, the Clarity grade from peers is related to the average similarity of the topic documents. The size of the dots represents the number of documents belonging to the topic, while the colour shows the automatic classification and the outliers.

If we compute the correlation and plot the interpolating line, we get the following Fig. 7.

As we can see, with both models, there is a high correlation between average topic clarity and average topic similarity ($R^2$ is 0.81 for ADA and 0.79 for LARGE topics).

If we group documents w.r.t. similarity (with 0.01 granularity) the Clarity grades behave like in Fig. 8.

As we can see, the document grades (averaged over each 0.01 similarity bin) and the similarities correlate better by using the LARGE model ($Pearson = 0.57$, $R^2 = 0.32$) than by using the ADA model ($Pearson = 0.22$, $R^2 = 0.05$). The outliers are spread over the whole range and behave like the other automatically classified documents. This could help us to classify them properly.

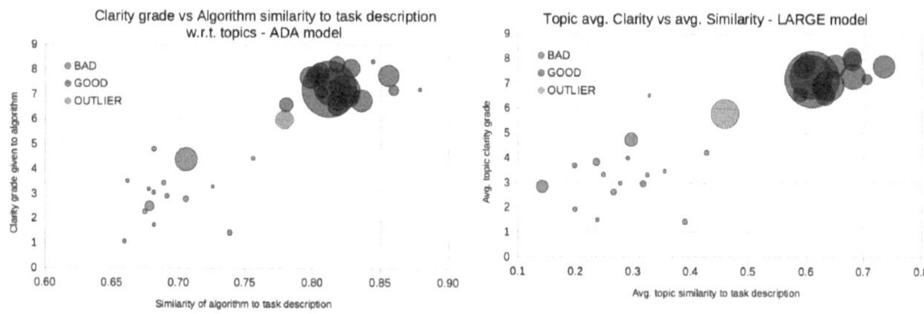


**Fig. 6.** Topic average similarity to the task description vs topic average grade. Colours show the automatic classification (GOOD/BAD/OUTLIERS). Dot size shows the topic's number of documents.

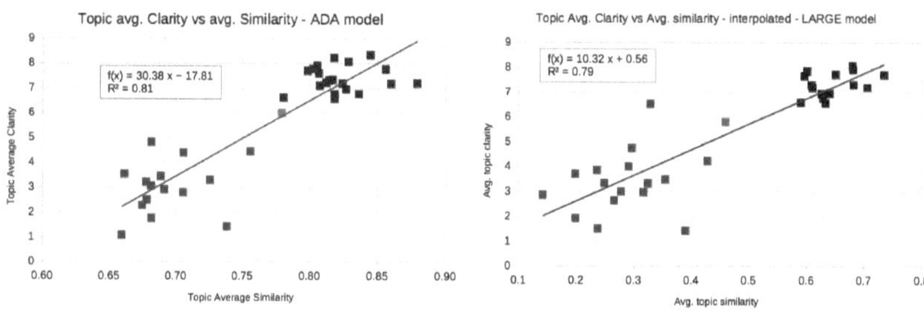


**Fig. 7.** Correlation between topic average similarity to the task description vs topic average clarity grade. Colours show the automatic classification.

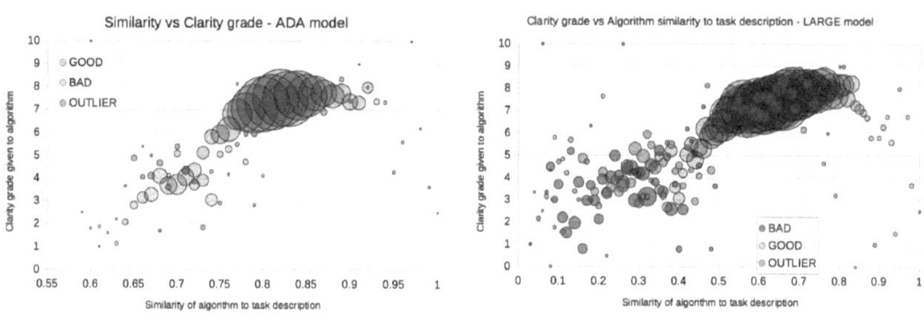


**Fig. 8.** Average grade vs average similarity, for each 0.01 similarity. Colours show the automatic classification. Dot size shows the number of documents with same similarity.

We notice that there are a few documents with very high similarity but with very low Clarity grade. These are wrongly submitted algorithms where the student selected the wrong file. Notice that an automatic assessment based on text similarity to the task description is prone to cheating, when the student just uploads the task description. This type of cheating can be easily detected by considering all documents with similarity above a certain threshold to be a wrong file. If we remove the few documents with very low and very high similarity (above 0.95 and below 0.50 for ADA, and above 0.85 and below 0.1 for LARGE) we get better correlations ($Pearson = 0.78$, $R^2 = 0.60$ for ADA and $Pearson = 0.70$, $R^2 = 0.48$ for LARGE). This suggests adopting a 3-phases assessment strategy:

- first, we compute the similarity of the algorithm to the task description
- then we classify those having similarity below a certain threshold as BAD (non-algorithms) and the ones above a certain threshold as WRONG (wrong file submitted, e.g. the program text, which contains the task description)
- finally, we compute the Clarity grade from the similarity, using the interpolated formula obtained from the data above.

In the next peer-assessment step, after the student has graded her peers' algorithms, we can use the above interpolation to understand if the grades given are coherent with the algorithm quality and give immediate feedback to the student on the grades.

We conclude, to answer RQ2, that just by computing the average topic similarity and by classifying a new document into the corresponding topic, we can predict the Clarity grade of the document and give immediate feedback to the student even before the next phase of the peer-assessment (grading) takes place.

Moreover, by using the similarity, the outliers could be assigned to the correct grade.

When we compute the correlation between teacher grades and average similarity, we get $Pearson = 0.62$ for the ADA model and $Pearson = 0.83$ for the LARGE model. This shows that the LARGE model produces similarities that correlate very well to the teacher grades, better than to the peers' grades (which is expected). This answers RQ1 positively.

## 5 Conclusions and Future Work

We have shown that Large Language Models can be used to analyse algorithm descriptions and compare them to the task description given. Such text similarity correlates well both with the grades given by the teacher (RQ1) and with the grades given by the students (RQ2) (but in this case, first the texts must be clustered into similar topics to reduce grading errors).

The approach, similarly to other distant reading techniques, will be applied to obtain a multi-class classification of the algorithms to be used for automatic assessment. Automatic assessment will be helpful:

- to give immediate feedback to the students submitting the algorithms, and motivate them to work better
- to check if the grades given by peers to algorithms are correct, and give feedback to the peer if needed
- to build a teacher-oriented dashboard showing the state of the class w.r.t. the peer assessment phases
- to automatically suggest remedial activities with tutors for students struggling with the homework assigned

Notice that the topic extraction phase could be enhanced by starting with an initial set of example documents for each desired topic classification grade (BAD/INSUFFICIENT/SUFFICIENT/GOOD), and then use BERTopic to clusterize, when possible, the documents nearest to the examples. The example "seed topics" documents could either be extracted from the available dataset, or be written by the teacher as examples of how s/he would like an algorithm to be described, with different levels of detail.

Notice that the described approach to algorithm classification based on document similarity and topic extraction could be fooled by producing algorithm descriptions through ChatGPT or similar AI systems, or by submitting documents obtained from the task description and some rephrasing. Some of these tricks could be detected by considering as suspect all documents above a given similarity threshold or by preparing a seed topic containing several transformed versions of the task description (e.g. by sorting or scrambling the task description words or by asking ChatGPT to rephrase it) and use it for the topic extraction. This calls for some more research on the mitigation approaches.

Now we have the bases to analyse the remaining steps of our formative peer assessment, i.e. the suggestions given to peers and the final feedback given to the suggestions. Our future goals are: a) understanding what types of suggestions are given, and b) what kind of feedback grades are assigned to the suggestions, depending on the type of algorithm submitted and the initial steps of the peer assessment.

## References

1. Badea, G., Popescu, E., Sterbini, A., Temperini, M.: Integrating enhanced peer assessment features in Moodle learning management system. In: Foundations and Trends in Smart Learning. LNET, pp. 135–144. Springer, Singapore (2019). https://doi.org/10.1007/978-981-13-6908-7_19
2. Bhatia, S., Kohli, P., Singh, R.: Neuro-symbolic program corrector for introductory programming assignments. In: Proceedings of the ICSE'18 (2018)
3. Dahal, N., Luitel, B.C., Pant, B.P., Shrestha, I.M., Manandhar, N.K., Luitel, L.: Procedures for online peer assessment: assessing algorithm problems in school mathematics for future teachers. Adv. Mobile Learn. Educ. Res. **3**(1), 739–747 (2023)
4. Du, J., Wimmer, H., Rada, R.: "Hour of code": can it change students' attitudes toward programming? J. Inf. Technol. Educ. Innov. Pract. **15**, 52–73 (2016)

5. Edwards, S., Perez-Quinones, M.: Web-CAT: automatically grading programming assignments. In: Proceedings of the ITiCSE 2008, pp. 328—328 (2008)
6. Enstrom, E., Kreitz, G., Niemela, F., Soderman, P., Kann, V.: Five years with Kattis - using an automated assessment system in teaching. In: Proceedings of the FIE 2011 (2011)
7. Grootendorst, M.: BERTopic: neural topic modeling with a class-based TF-IDF procedure. arXiv preprint arXiv:2203.05794 (2022)
8. Hadzhikoleva, S., Hadzhikolev, E., Kasakliev, N.: Using peer assessment to enhance higher order thinking skills. TEM J. **8**(1), 242–247 (2019)
9. Hollingsworth, J.: Automatic graders for programming classes. Commun. ACM **3**(10), 528–529 (1960)
10. Hristova, M., Misra, A., Rutter, M., Mercuri, R.: Identifying and correcting Java programming errors for introductory computer science students. In: Proceedings of the SIGCSE 2003 (2003)
11. Hsu, T.C., Chang, S.C., Hung, Y.T.: How to learn and how to teach computational thinking: suggestions based on a review of the literature. Comput. Educ. **126**, 296–310 (2018)
12. Lu, C., Macdonald, R., Odell, B., Kokhan, V., Demmans Epp, C., Cutumisu, M.: A scoping review of computational thinking assessments in higher education. J. Comput. High. Educ. **34**(2), 416–461 (2022)
13. Naudé, K., Greyling, J., Vogts, D.: Marking student programs using graph similarity. Comput. Educ. **54**(2), 545–561 (2010)
14. Ostrowska-Wawryniuk, K., Strzała, M., Słyk, J.: Form follows parameter: algorithmic-thinking-oriented course for early-stage architectural education. Nexus Netw. J. **24**(2), 503–522 (2022)
15. Papandrea, S., Sterbini, A., Temperini, M., Popescu, E.: Q2A-I: a support platform for computer programming education, based on automated assessment and peer learning. In: Hancke, G., Spaniol, M., Osathanunkul, K., Unankard, S., Klamma, R. (eds.) ICWL 2018. LNCS, vol. 11007, pp. 3–13. Springer, Cham (2018). https://doi.org/10.1007/978-3-319-96565-9_1
16. Pieterse, V.: Automated assessment of programming assignments. In: Proceedings of the CSERC 2013, pp. 45–56 (2013)
17. Pozenel, M., Furst, L., Mahnic, V.: Introduction of the automated assessment of homework assignments in a university-level programming course. In: Proceedings of the MIPRO'15, pp. 761–766 (2015)
18. de Souza, D., Maldonado, J., Barbosa, E.: ProgTest: an environment for the sub-mission and evaluation of programming assignments. In: Proceedings of the CSEE&T 2011, pp. 328—328 (2011)
19. Sterbini, A., Temperini, M.: Q2A-II, a system to support peer assessment on homework: a study on four years of use. In: International Symposium on Emerging Technologies for Education, SETE 2023, Sydney, Australia, 26–28 November 2023, pp. 589–602. Springer, Heidelberg (in press)
20. The ACM/IEEE CC2020 Task Force: Computing curricula 2020, paradigms for global computing education. Computing Curricula Series Report, ACM/IEEE-Computer Society (2021). https://www.acm.org/binaries/content/assets/education/curricula-recommendations/cc2020.pdf. Accessed 30 Aug 2023
21. The Joint Task Force on Computing Curricula: Computer science curricula 2023, version beta. ACM, IEEE-CS, AAAI, March 2023 (2023). https://csed.acm.org/wp-content/uploads/2023/03/FPL-Version-Beta.pdf. Accessed 01 Sep 2023

22. Wang, T., Su, X., Ma, P., Wang, Y., Wang, K.: Ability-training-oriented automated assessment in introductory programming course. Comput. Educ. **56**(1), 220–226 (2011)
23. Watson, C., Li, F.W.B., Godwin, J.L.: BlueFix: using crowd-sourced feedback to support programming students in error diagnosis and repair. In: Popescu, E., Li, Q., Klamma, R., Leung, H., Specht, M. (eds.) ICWL 2012. LNCS, vol. 7558, pp. 228–239. Springer, Heidelberg (2012). https://doi.org/10.1007/978-3-642-33642-3_25
24. Zhan, Y., et al.: Effects of online peer assessment on higher-order thinking: a meta-analysis. Brit. J. Educ. Technol. **54**(4), 817–835 (2023). Open Access

# An AI-Learner Shared Control Model Design for Adaptive Practicing

Hongxin Yan[1](✉), Fuhua Lin[2], and Kinshuk[3]

[1] University of Eastern Finland, 80130 Joensuu, Kuopio, Finland
hongya@student.uef.fi
[2] Athabasca University, Athabasca, AB T9S 3A3, Canada
oscarl@athabascau.ca
[3] University of North Texas, Denton, TX 76203, USA
Kinshuk@unt.edu

**Abstract.** Online higher education offers great learning flexibility but demands learners' high self-regulated learning (SRL) skills, especially in self-paced and asynchronous online learning. The lack of SRL skills in many learners often leads to poor academic outcomes, underscoring the need for SRL support. Our study introduces CAP (Confidence-based Adaptive Practicing), a model of adaptive practicing designed to enhance SRL in STEM disciplines. CAP incorporates knowledge tracing and question sequencing as two core functions. Unlike traditional adaptive learning systems that rely solely on machine control, CAP integrates learner confidence feedback and learner control in its rule-based intuitive algorithms. To avert the subjectivities of human judgement on learner confidence, CAP employs Thompson Sampling machine learning to refine the algorithms for adaptive accuracy and efficiency. This innovative AI-learner shared control approach has garnered positive feedback from field experts, highlighting its potential effectiveness in facilitating SRL.

**Keywords:** Self-regulated Learning · Adaptive Practicing · Confidence-based Adaptive Practicing · Knowledge Tracing · Question Sequencing · Wheel-spinning

## 1 Introduction

Online education has become an important educational paradigm in higher education. Self-paced online learning (SPOL) provides even more flexibility because learners can study anywhere and anytime and follow their own study paces. Yet, SPOL faces some inherent challenges due to reduced synchronous interaction when learners study independently and asynchronously [1]. One challenge is that it demands high self-regulated learning (SRL) skills in learners to self-monitor their learning progress, evaluate their knowledge proficiency, identify learning weaknesses, and regulate learning efforts for remediation. [2–4]. Previous research has identified a significant positive relationship between SRL strategies and online academic success [3, 5, 6]. However, not every


A. Sifaleras and F. Lin (Eds.): ITS 2024, LNCS 14798, pp. 272–280, 2024.
https://doi.org/10.1007/978-3-031-63028-6_21

learner has adequate SRL skills. Learners are generally inaccurate when monitoring their learning without additional instruction [7]. Also, in the context of higher education, researchers found that instructors tend to focus on course contents, providing limited opportunities for scaffolding SRL [8, 9]. Hence, it is imperative to provide learners with a means to facilitate their SRL in self-paced online higher education. Also, learners need to consolidate the interrelated concepts and skills covered across units or a whole course to prepare effectively for exams. In some cases, learners may need to detect the root cause of the academic difficulties they experience, such as struggling with an assignment. [1] argue that adaptive practicing could be an effective tool to meet such needs.

Adaptive practicing provides learners with exercises for consolidating knowledge during the post-learning stage. It not only assesses a learner's knowledge level but also includes scaffolding opportunities through hints, instructive feedback, and remediation materials. Adaptive practicing can be accomplished with computed algorithms [10] for two core functions: knowledge tracing and question sequencing. Knowledge tracing estimates and tracks learners' knowledge proficiency based on their responses to questions. Question sequencing determines an optimal order of the exercise questions based on the knowledge tracing results for maximum learning gain each time.

One issue with previous knowledge tracing models is that they mainly rely on the answer correctness of assessment questions [11, 12]. As [12] pointed out, answer correctness alone may not tell whether an exercise is effective, but with certain side information, it could. [13] suggested that humans may have relevant information to which adaptive learning systems are likely blind. [3] included judgments of learning and feelings of knowing in his SRL model. When taking a multiple-choice question, learners can mark which answers they believe are correct while also indicating how confident or certain they feel about their responses [14]. This approach is called confidence-based assessment.

Another limitation of previous research on adaptive learning systems is that instructional sequencing usually assumes exclusive machine control and seldom considers learner control. According to self-determination theory [15], learner control can enhance learning motivation by strengthening the human need for autonomy.

Thus, considering learner confidence feedback and learner control in the adaptive practicing model could promote learning engagement and reflection and potentially increase the model's efficiency. However, to our knowledge, studies have not sufficiently investigated how learners' confidence feedback and learner control are factored into an adaptive practicing model design. As [16] pointed out in a review paper, AI agents could take learner decisions and judgements as inputs to consider during decision-making, but such a form of shared control has not been considered in the context of instructional sequencing.

Therefore, to fill this research gap, our study explores how learner confidence feedback and learner control can be considered in adaptive practicing for knowledge tracing and question sequencing. Given the potential of such an AI-learner shared control model, we will answer the following research question in this paper: *How can learner confidence feedback and learner control improve the efficiency of the AI-based adaptive practicing model?*

## 2 Related Work

Currently, studies have explored some human-AI collaboration approaches in adaptive learning. The term "human-AI collaboration" stresses that humans and AI are partners in achieving the overall goal, and each party contributes according to its strengths and weaknesses [17]. The general ideas of learner control have been extensively explored in the field of education and have formed one of the foundations of self-regulated learning [18]. In the context of online learning system design, learner control refers to certain learning process features, such as control over the path, sequence, flow, etc. [19]. A literature analysis by [19] shows that learner control over time, pace, navigation and design tends to increase learning outcomes.

Some studies have considered how to keep humans in the loop of control in the field of AI for education. [17] summarized four approaches of AI-learner shared control for adaptive content selection. One approach is through the editable learner model [20]. In Weber and Brusilovsky's ELM-ART system, the AI determines the state of learner knowledge and displays it to the learner, while the learner has a chance to correct obvious errors. Another approach is called ranking-based human-AI collaboration [21]. In this case, AI does the work of careful selection and ranking, but the user has the final say in selecting the most relevant content item. A third approach is adaptive navigation support [22]. In this case, AI still works in the background to decide the best links to appropriate content, but AI advice is provided less directly and the final control is left in learners' hands. Those approaches show some possibilities of how AI-learner shared control can be realized in adaptive learning. However, as [17] pointed out, content selection in most cases is done by AI agents alone. At the same time, learners are only involved at the beginning for learner model adjustment or at the end for selecting content from what AI agents recommend.

A couple of approaches are adopted to enable learner control during the decision-making process. For example, the system can allow the user to choose one of the available content selection algorithms [23] or let the learner control some parameters of the recommendation process [24]. However, those approaches require extensive knowledge of learners in computing algorithms and add extraneous cognitive load for learning.

## 3 Our Approach to an AI-Learner Shared Control Model Design

To answer the research questions, we first determine what learner confidence feedback and learner control actions should be considered in the adaptive practicing model. Then, we describe the theories that support our model design.

### 3.1 Confidence-Based Assessment

Traditional knowledge assessments that use multiple-choice questions only report right or wrong answers. [25] found evidence of the obvious, that when learners are given a selection of answers for a problem, they still have a chance to select the correct answer even if they don't know how to solve it. Confidence-based assessment techniques integrate the selection of multiple-choice answers with the learner's self-perceived level of certainty to eliminate guesswork and offer greater efficiency in managing the remediation process [14, 25]. A scale with three confidence levels (low, medium and high) has been used [26] for self-perceived certainty. Inspired by this confidence-based assessment technique, we propose to collect learners' feedback on confidence in answering exercise questions in the adaptive practicing model. We argue that this can improve the model efficiency by eliminating the guesswork or slipping noise in the data.

### 3.2 Learner Confidence Feedback and Learner Control Considered

The idea of increasing interaction between human and machine learning algorithms is to make machine learning more accurate or to obtain the desired accuracy faster through learning with humans [27]. Inspired by the confidence-based assessment, we argue that answer responses combined with learners' feelings about their mastery levels (e.g., confidence or difficulty rating) could make knowledge tracing more efficient. For example, if learners skip a question and indicate it is too easy, or answer it correctly and indicates high confidence, they likely have mastered the knowledge. This could be an algorithmic advantage compared to the traditional knowledge tracing models, such as the Bayesian Knowledge Tracing model, which needs a large number of questions to fit the guessing and slipping parameters. Therefore, the following learner feedback and learner control actions are considered in our model.

a. For learner feedback, our model considers learners' confidence or certainty about their knowledge. A Likert question with three options is asked when a learner answers a question. So, if learners answer a question, they will indicate their confidence level, either "not confident", "somehow confident", or "very confident".
b. For learner control actions, our model allows learners to skip a question if they feel it is too easy or too hard. By this, the learner's choice can override the system's decision on exercise question selection to avoid boredom or frustration. Also, time can be saved by skipping ineffective exercises.

### 3.3 Dynamic Difficulty Adjustment

Dynamic Difficulty Adjustment (DDA) is a technique used in video games to automatically adjust the game's difficulty level in real time based on the player's ability [28]. For education, this technique can be borrowed to adjust the difficulty of learning materials based on learners' skill levels and keep them engaged throughout the learning process. This technique can be instrumental in online learning environments where it can be difficult to provide personalized feedback and support to individual learners. Inspired by DDA, adaptive practicing can be realized through different mechanisms, such as modifying the difficulty level of the exercises, adjusting the pace of the practice or providing additional resources to help the user overcome difficult challenges. For example, suppose a learner is struggling with a particular concept. In that case, adaptive practicing can provide additional resources such as videos, interactive simulations, or practice problems to help the user better understand the concept.

### 3.4 Zone of Proximal Development

The concept of Zone of Proximal Development (ZPD) by Lev Vygotsky refers to a zone where a learner can complete tasks with assistance but cannot independently [29]. According to Vygotsky, concrete growth can only occur in the ZPD, and learning is most effective when timely support is provided in this zone. As a well-known and vastly researched concept in educational psychology, ZPD laid the foundations for personalized learning, and some learning tools have been developed to sequence content [30].

Traditional self-assessment usually contains a set of exercises without any adaptive mechanism. Following such a one-size-fits-all approach, some learners may feel under-challenged and bored, while some may feel over-challenged and frustrated. By Vygotsky's theory, this problem stems from the fact that each learner has a different ZPD at a given time [30]. The adaptive practicing model proposed in our study tries to mitigate this problem by creating an adaptive engine to keep learners exercising in their ZPD.

## 4 The CAP Model and Its Core Modules

Because our adaptive practicing model is built on learners' confidence in their knowledge mastery, we name our model CAP (Confidence-based Adaptive Practicing). Three core modules of CAP are knowledge tracing, question sequencing and system self-learning.

### 4.1 Knowledge Tracing Module

The knowledge tracing module detects a learner's knowledge state and tracks its change during practicing. Relative to the Zone of Proximal Development (ZPD), three cognitive states on a KC are defined in our study:

- Mastered: a KC has been learned, Below-ZPD.
- In-learning: a KC is being learned, In-ZPD
- Unlearnable: beyond a learner's ability to learn, Beyond-ZPD

Additionally, we consider the fourth cognitive state on a KC, Wheel-spinning: unproductive struggling with a KC, a learning phenomenon analogic to a car stuck in snow or mud -- the wheels will spin without getting anywhere despite devoting effort to moving [31].

A learner's ZPD usually keeps moving to higher levels as learners invest time in learning or practicing. Therefore, the knowledge tracing module needs to determine a learner's cognitive state of a KC at any given time based on the answer response and learner feedback. We propose a rule-based knowledge tracing algorithm, as in Table 1.

As illustrated in Table 1, five cognitive zones are identified: Beyond-ZPD, In-Upper-ZPD, In-Mid-ZPD, In-Lower-ZPD, and Below-ZPD. Each zone corresponds to a cognitive state: Unlearnable, In-Learning or Mastered. It is worth pointing out that the cognitive zone and state identified are just a likelihood because of the subjectivity of learners' confidence about their mastery of knowledge.

**Table 1.** Knowledge Tracing Rules

| Answer Response | Learner feedback | Cognitive Zone (likely) | Cognitive State (likely) |
|---|---|---|---|
| **Question Skip** | Too hard | Beyond-ZPD | Unlearnable |
| **Incorrect Answer** | Too difficult | | |
| | Somehow difficult | In-Upper-ZPD | In-learning |
| | Not difficult | In-Mid-ZPD | |
| **Correct Answer** | Not confident | | |
| | Somehow confident | In-Lower-ZPD | |
| | Very confident | Below-ZPD | Mastered |
| **Question Skip** | Too easy | | |

We argue that this rule-based algorithm should be more transparent and interpretable to educators than a machine learning and data-driven algorithm for knowledge tracing. Therefore, it increases the possibility of being adopted in real-world courses by educators.

## 4.2 Question Sequencing Module

The question sequencing module provides individual learners with the optimal question sequences so that the system can keep learners practicing in their ZPD. The exercise question presented to a learner should be based on a learner's current knowledge state. To make the model more transparent and interpretable to educators, a rule-based question sequencing algorithm is decided as in Table 2. Corresponding to the four cognitive states estimated by the knowledge tracing module, four sequencing actions are taken respectively: Move-forward, Move-backward, Jump and Stay. The instructions in the

**Table 2.** Question Sequencing Rules

| Cognitive state (Likely) | Sequencing action (with a certain probability) | Instructions |
|---|---|---|
| **Mastered** | Move-forward | If a KC is detected as mastered, practicing likely needs move forward to the next dependent KC |
| **Unlearnable** | Move-backward | If a KC is detected as unlearnable, practicing likely needs move backward to its prerequisite KC |
| **Wheel-spinning** | Jump | If a KC is detected as wheel-spinning, practicing likely needs jump to a sibling or neighbour KC |
| **In-Learning** | Stay | If a KC is detected as In-learning, practicing likely needs stay with the current KC |

third column explain how each sequencing action works. For example, if a KC is detected as mastered, learners need to move forward to practice with the next dependent KC.

### 4.3 System Self-learning Module

Learning is a complex process. In the environment of adaptive practicing, there are many uncertainties. First, learner confidence feedback is somehow subjective. For example, learners may be overconfident or underconfident in their knowledge mastery, or they may be overestimate or underestimate the task difficulty. Secondly, the prerequisite relationships among KCs could be hard or soft and difficult to quantify in domain modelling. Therefore, the cognitive state deduced by the learner responses is only a likelihood.

To avert the subjectivity of learner confidence feedback and make the CAP model more effective, a system self-learning module is designed. This module aims to fine-tune those likelihoods by analyzing learning data continuously collected from learners' interaction with the system. We propose to utilize a reinforcement learning technique, Thompson Sampling, for system self-learning. Thompson sampling was first proposed by [32] as a reinforcement learning-based algorithm. It is a heuristic strategy for choosing actions among multiple options to address the exploration-exploitation dilemma. [33] proposed to use Thomspon sampling algorithm to generate adaptive quizzes.

In the CAP model, we set the initial likelihood of mastery or the unlearnable in each zone. In the zone Below-ZPD, the initial likelihood of mastery is set 80%. Thus, the initial beta distribution is beta (2, 8) for the Stay action while beta (8, 2) for the Move-forward action. After CAP chooses an action among the two choices based on their beta distributions, a reward is obtained. If the newly selected exercise is detected falling In-ZPD, it means the chosen action is successful. Thus, the reward will be 1. Otherwise, the reward will be 0. This reward is used to update the posterior probability of each action. In the meantime, CAP adjusts the belief in the likelihood of the cognitive state in the mastered and unlearnable zones.

## 5 Model Evaluation

It is crucial to evaluate the design of the CAP model before it is implemented in adaptive practicing. The main evaluation question is: how effectively can CAP trace learners' knowledge and select effective exercises? To answer this question, we planned two phases of evaluation: a) interview experts to gain insights into the strengths and weaknesses of the model design, and b) simulate the model to quantify its effectiveness.

At this stage, we have gathered feedback by interviewing three experts in the field of computing for education and one professor in Physics. All the interviewees had already realized that the SRL-related challenge exists in SPOL and is imperative to be addressed. They all agree that: a) embedding adaptive practicing activities in courses could be an effective solution to address this challenge for STEM disciplines; b) the rule-based algorithms for knowledge tracing and question sequencing are easy to understand and make sense; c) considering learner control would help increase learner engagement.

As a future step, we would like to conduct a simulation of CAP to evaluate its efficiency of the adaptive mechanism. Running a simulation allows for thorough testing of its functionality before implementation, and it becomes possible to optimize the algorithms to make the CAP model more effective, accurate, and robust.

## 6 Conclusion

Our study examines the advantages of considering learner confidence feedback and learner control in adaptive practicing. We have designed an innovative confidence-based adaptive practicing model (CAP) where knowledge tracing and question sequencing rules are created based on learner confidence and the Zone of Proximal Development. To avert the subjectivity of learner confidence feedback, we have creatively employed the Thompson Sampling algorithm for the system to self-learn.

Our CAP model provides a simple yet effective means for knowledge tracing and question sequencing. We believe that this model design can shed some light on researching a new way of keeping human learners in the loop of AI for shared control. Although the CAP model is designed to facilitate SRL for self-paced online higher STEM disciplines, we argue that CAP could apply to many other online learning contexts. However, further research and experiments are needed to validate such hypotheses.

## References


1. Yan, H., Ives, C., Lin, F.: Adaptive practicing design for self-paced online learning. In: Proceedings of the International Conference on Computers in Education (2021)
2. Zimmerman, B.J.: Becoming a self-regulated learner: an overview. Theory Into Pract. **41**(2), 64–70 (2002)
3. Pintrich, P.R.: The role of goal orientation in self-regulated learning. In: Handbook of Self-Regulation, Academic Press, pp. 452–502 (2000)
4. Yan, H., Lin, F., Kinshuk: Including learning analytics in the loop of self-paced online course learning design. Int. J. Artif. Intell. Educ. **31**, 878–895 (2021)
5. Broadbent, J., Poon, W.L.: Self-regulated learning strategies & academic achievement in online higher education learning environments: a systematic review. Internet High. Educ. **27**, 1–13 (2015)
6. Wong, J., Baars, M., Davis, D., Van Der Zee, T., Houben, G.J., Paas, F.: Supporting self-regulated learning in online learning environments and MOOCs: a systematic review. Int. J. Hum.–Comput. Interact. **5**(4–5), 356–373 (2019)
7. Viberg, O., Khalil, M., Baars, M.: Self-regulated learning and learning analytics in online learning environments: a review of empirical research. In: Proceedings of the Tenth International Conference on Learning Analytics & Knowledge (2020)
8. Dignath, C., Büttner, G.: Teachers' direct and indirect promotion of self-regulated learning in primary and secondary school mathematics classes–insights from video-based classroom observations and teacher interviews. Metacogn. Learn. **13**, 127–157 (2018)
9. Moos, D.C., Ringdal, A.: Self-regulated learning in the classroom: A literature review on the teacher's role. Educ. Res. Int. **2012** (2012)
10. Manouselis, N., Drachsler, H., Vuorikari, R., Hummel, H., Koper, R.: Recommender systems in technology enhanced learning. In: Ricci, F., Rokach, L., Shapira, B., Kantor, P.B. (eds.) Recommender Systems Handbook, pp. 387–415. Springer US, Boston, MA (2011). https://doi.org/10.1007/978-0-387-85820-3_12

11. Pelánek, R.: Bayesian knowledge tracing, logistic models, and beyond: an overview of learner modeling techniques. User Model. User-Adap. Inter. **27**(3), 313–350 (2017)
12. B. Clement, D. Roy, P. Oudeyer and M. Lopes, Multi-Armed Bandits for Intelligent Tutoring Systems, 2015
13. Holstein, K., Aleven, V., Rummel, N.: A conceptual framework for human–AI hybrid adaptivity in education. In: Artificial Intelligence in Education: 21st International Conference, AIED 2020, Proceedings, Ifrane, Morocco (2020). https://doi.org/10.1007/978-3-030-52240-7
14. Novacek, P.: Confidence-based assessments within an adult learning environment. Int. Assoc. Dev. Inform. Soc. (2013)
15. Deci, E.L., Vallerand, R.J., Pelletier, L.G., Ryan, R.M.: Motivation and education: the self-determination perspective. Educ. Psychol. **26**(3–4), 325–346 (1991)
16. Doroudi, S., Aleven, V., Brunskill, E.: Where's the reward? Int. J. Artif. Intell. Educ. **29**(4), 568–620 (2019)
17. Brusilovsky, P.: AI in education, learner control, and human-AI Collaboration. Int. J. Artif. Intell. Educ. **34**(1), 122–135 (2023). https://doi.org/10.1007/s40593-023-00356-z
18. Bjork, R.A., Dunlosky, J., Kornell, N.: Self-regulated learning: beliefs, techniques, and illusions. Annu. Rev. Psychol. **64**, 417–444 (2013)
19. Sorgenfrei, C., Smolnik, S.: The effectiveness of e-learning systems: a review of the empirical literature on learner control. Decis. Sci. J. Innov. Educ. **14**(2), 154–184 (2016)
20. Weber, G., Brusilovsky, P.: ELM-ART: an adaptive versatile system for web-based instruction. Int. J. Artif. Intell. Educ. (IJAIED) **12**, 351–384 (2001)
21. Rahdari, B., Brusilovsky, P., He, D., Thaker, K.M., and Lee, Y.J.: Helper: an interactive recommender system for ovarian cancer patients and caregivers. In: Proceedings of the 16th ACM Conference on Recommender Systems (2022)
22. Brusilovsky, P.: Adaptive navigation support. In: Brusilovsky, P., Kobsa, A., Nejdl, W. (eds.) The Adaptive Web, pp. 263–290. Springer, Heidelberg (2007). https://doi.org/10.1007/978-3-540-72079-9_8
23. Ekstrand, B.: What it takes to keep children in school: a research review. Educ. Rev. **67**(4), 459–482 (2015)
24. Papoušek, J., Pelánek, R.: Should we give learners control over item difficulty? In: Adjunct Publication of the 25th Conference on User Modeling, Adaptation and Personalization (2017)
25. Hunt, D.: The concept of knowledge and how to measure it. J. Intellect. Cap. **4**(1), 100–113 (2003)
26. Gardner-Medwin, T., Curtin, N.: Certainty-based marking (CBM) for reflective learning and proper knowledge assessment. In: REAP International Online Conference on Assessment Design for Learner Responsibility (2007)
27. Mosqueira-Rey, E., Hernández-Pereira, E., Alonso-Ríos, D., Bobes-Bascarán, J., Fernández-Leal, A.: Human-in-the-loop machine learning: a state of the art. Artif. Intell. Rev. **56**(4), 3005–3054 (2023)
28. Zohaib, M.: Dynamic difficulty adjustment (DDA) in computer games: a review. Adv. Hum.-Comput. Interact. **2018**, 1–12 (2018)
29. Hedegaard, M.: The zone of proximal development as a basis for instruction. In: An Introduction to Vygotsky, Routledge, pp. 234–258 (2012)
30. Vainas, O., et al.: E-Gotsky: sequencing content using the zone of proximal development. ArXiv 2019
31. Beck, J., Gong, Y.: Wheel-spinning: students who fail to master a skill. In: Artificial Intelligence in Education: 16th International Conference, AIED 2013, Memphis (2013)
32. Thompson, W.: On the likelihood that one unknown probability exceeds another in view of the evidence of two samples. Biometrika **25**(3/4), 285–294 (1993)
33. Lin, F.: Adaptive quiz generation using Thompson sampling. In: Third Workshop Eliciting Adaptive Sequences for Learning (WASL 2020), co-located with AIED 2020 (2020)

# Early Math Skill as a Predictor for Foundational Literacy

Haya Shamir(✉), Mikayla Tom, David Pocklington, Erik Yoder, and Alexander Houchins

Waterford Institute, Taylorsville, U.S.A.
{hayashamir,mikaylatom,davidpocklington,erikyoder, alexanderhouchins}@waterford.org

**Abstract.** This study examined the validity of early math skills as predictors of literacy skills. Data was collected from students using a home-based kindergarten readiness program. Performance on math domain metrics within a kindergarten readiness program was used to generate models predicting scores and grade equivalence on an end of year literacy assessment. Scores on math strands were highly correlated with later reading performance. Performance on math and science metrics were also valid predictors for students reaching literacy benchmarks. This study highlights the interdependence of learning domains while noting areas, such as language concepts, where math performance is a comparatively poor predictor.

**Keywords:** Math · Reading · Predictive Modeling · Young Learners

## 1 Introduction and Literature Review

Research has revealed a strong relationship between literacy and math skills in young learners [1]. Executive functioning skills, including response inhibition, working memory, and cognitive flexibility, are essential for both math and literacy [2]. Many learning factors have been found to be valid predictors for both subjects, and key skills within one domain can identify students at risk in both [3]. Despite this, math and literacy tend to be taught as separate domains.

Literacy and math skills become interwoven with each other very early on in a student's academic development [4, 5]. As a result, it becomes difficult to parse which subject, or subskill, is influencing the development of the other. Early literacy skills have been found to predict the development of later math skills. Longitudinal research has shown that early reading skills lay the foundations for math skills [6], with as much as 56% of the variance in math achievement explained by reading ability [7]. While mathematical language by itself is a strong indicator of later success in the subject [8], general literacy skills are needed to understand the written symbolism and the story-spoken problems in early mathematics [9]. Switching perspectives, early math skills have been shown to be more strongly associated with later literacy skills than even early literacy skills in most cases [10]. Braak et al. [11] investigated the potential mediating


A. Sifaleras and F. Lin (Eds.): ITS 2024, LNCS 14798, pp. 281–290, 2024.
https://doi.org/10.1007/978-3-031-63028-6_22

role of executive functioning in the relationship between early math scores and later literacy scores and found that high early math performance can help with executive functioning development and thus improve literacy skills. Integrating mathematics and reading curricula could support the development of both skill sets [12].

Advances in technology offer potential solutions for both integrating and better understanding each domain. Machine learning describes the use of automated or directed systems that measure performance on a specified task and attempt to improve with experience [13]. Machine learning techniques can be utilized to streamline the prediction-making process for student outcomes. A recent international study examining literacy ability in fourth-grade students used this approach to identify key factors predictive of literacy skills [14]. Using data to make increasingly better decisions in machine learning provides unique benefits to educational settings, such as training an AI tutor to recognize when students are having difficulty understanding concepts, provide intelligent moderation, and decide what learning content to provide students [15]. Multiple machine learning algorithms, such as decision trees, linear support vector machines, and logistic regression, were used in a quantitative study to predict literacy and math performance from students' demographics with up to 90% accuracy [16].

The use of machine learning in academic contexts expanded noticeably during the COVID-19 pandemic [17]. Given this increased prominence, it should be noted that not all research into machine learning in the classroom has yielded positive results. A large-scale study of primary and middle school children conducted prior to the pandemic found that machine-learning approaches were not able to better predict if students would fall below a literacy benchmark than extant regression models [18]. Not all modeling techniques are appropriate for every audience, and when used with young learners, some approaches may under or overestimate student ability [19].

While machine learning in the classroom is not always fruitful, it has been found to be useful in predicting which students may be at risk of falling behind [20]. Identifying at-risk students early on is essential, as later learning success in math and literacy has been shown to be strongly predicted by scores in these subjects from preschool and even prior to preschool [21–23]. A meta-analysis covering 120 studies on early education found significant average effect sizes in the cognitive and social-emotional domains, as well as in academic progress, for children who attended a preschool program when compared to children who received no early educational interventions [24]. In addition to improvement in math and literacy skills, other positive long-term outcomes, such as decreases in grade retention and significant increases in high school graduation rates, are seen when early childhood education programs are implemented [25]. The benefits of early education and interventions have long-term effects that have been found to be predictive of later skills.

## 2 Research Goal

The current study contributes to existing research by seeking to clarify how the development of math skills influences the development of early literacy skills. This study utilizes machine learning algorithms to predict early reading scores from early math scores. It is hypothesized that math scores will be predictive of literacy scores due to the strong relationships between the subjects and based on prior research findings.

## 3 Research Methodology

### 3.1 Participants

This study consisted of pre-kindergarten ($N = 22{,}509$) students who participated in Waterford Upstart during the 2021–2022 program year.

### 3.2 Materials

**Waterford Upstart.** Waterford Upstart is a home-based, technologically enabled kindergarten readiness program that gives students access to an adaptive early literacy, math, and science curriculum. The nationally-implemented program provides families who do not have access to computers or reliable internet equipment. Regular contact with coaches is used to promote student and family engagement.

**Waterford Early Learning (WEL).** WEL is a personalized, computer-adaptive instruction that guides students through an individualized learning path. The software consists of an Early Reading Program (ERP) and an Early Math and Science (EMS) curriculum. The pre-kindergarten ERP curriculum uses the following instructional strands: phonological awareness, phonics, comprehension and vocabulary, and language concepts.

The EMS curriculum uses the following instructional strands: number and cardinality, operations and algebraic thinking, measurement and data, geometry, and science.

**Waterford Assessments of Core Skills (WACS).** WACS is an adaptive assessment that tests key pre-literacy and reading skills. To establish concurrent validity and predictive validity, student performance on WACS was compared to performance on five commonly used standardized tests also measuring early reading skills; all correlations between tests are significant, ranging from $r = .41$ to $r = .78$ (median $r = .63$). Additional analyses indicate that WACS is internally consistent and has strong test-retest reliability ($r = .90$).

### 3.3 Procedure

WACS was administered at the beginning and end of the program. Between testing periods, students who participated in Waterford Upstart were expected to use WEL for 15 min a day, five days per week. Scores were recorded within WEL for each strand. From this data, 11 input variables were collected for each student, including performance on all EMS strands, overall performance within EMS, the total number of objectives encountered, the total number of scored objectives encountered, the number of objectives encountered successfully completed, the percentage of scored objectives successfully completed, and usage of the EMS program. Reading performance metrics within WEL and performance on the WACS assessment at the end of the program were chosen as the target variables. Cut-off thresholds were calculated for each ERP strand within WEL with a criterion of 80 or above. For end-of-year scores for WACS, the criterion was set at a score of 2001, the equivalent of kindergarten beginning.

Data collected from WEL and WACS was partitioned, with 70% of the data used for training the model and the other 30% used for testing.

SPSS modeler used this data to create categorical and regression models that predict students' ERP performance and WACS scores at the end of the program year based on their EMS performance halfway through the program year in December 2021.

# 4 Research Outcomes

## 4.1 Categorical Models

SPSS modeler was used to create categorical models to predict whether a student met the threshold score of 80% on their ERP activities at the end of the program year based on their EMS scores halfway through the program (see Table 1). Analysis of scores was broken down by overall ERP, phonics, phonological awareness, comprehension and vocabulary, and language concepts.

**Overall ERP.** When predicting if a student's overall ERP score passed the 80% threshold, the modeler found the aggregate, Chi-square automatic interaction detector (CHAID) decision tree, exhaustive CHAID, least-squares support vector machine (LSVM), and discriminant models to make the best predictions. The aggregate model predicted overall ERP scores from EMS scores with the highest accuracy rate of 76.71%. The discriminant model had the highest precision at 80.93%. LSVM had the highest recall and F1 percentages at 92.17% and 83.69%, respectively. The greatest difference between the model's metrics was in recall, with a 9.22% difference between the highest recall of 92.17% (LSVM) and the lowest recall of 82.95% (discriminant). Accuracy, precision, and F1 scores all had a difference of 4.30% or less between the models, which resulted in the highest and lowest scores.

The LSVM model had the highest number of true positives and the lowest number of false negatives. This accounts for the model's high recall and F1 score. While the LSVM model had high recall and F1 scores, it resulted in the lowest precision, which is explained by its high count of false positives. The distributions of the aggregate, CHAID, exhaustive CHAID, and discriminant model's false negatives, false positives, true negatives, and true positives were similar.

**Literacy Strands.** When predicting categorical performance on the four constituent literacy strands, CHAID decision tree, exhaustive CHAID, and LSVM models were common to three of the four strands, phonological awareness, phonics, and comprehension and vocabulary. For these three strands, the highest accuracy and F1 values found for these models were associated with either CHAID (comprehension and vocabulary, accuracy 79.92%, F1 88.31%) or exhaustive CHAID (phonics, accuracy 74.28%, F1 83.41%; phonological awareness, accuracy 71.26%, F1 66.83%). Models predicting phonological awareness also included classification and regression (C&R) and C5.0 decision tree models. Models predicting language concepts notably did not include CHAID decision trees. Precision was highest in the aggregated models for phonics and comprehension and vocabulary. For phonological awareness, the greatest precision was identified as LSVM. Performance metrics within each strand were broadly consistent across the range of models considered, with differences between the highest and lowest

**Table 1.** Accuracy, precision, recall, and F1 percentages by reading subject

| Subject | Model | Accuracy | Precision | Recall | F1 |
|---|---|---|---|---|---|
| Overall | Aggregate | 76.71%* | 79.83% | 87.30% | 83.40% |
| | CHAID | 76.59% | 79.43% | 87.80% | 83.41% |
| | Exhaustive CHAID | 76.66% | 79.50% | 87.83% | 83.45% |
| | LSVM | 75.92% | 76.64% | 92.17%* | 83.69%* |
| | Discriminant | 75.48% | 80.93%* | 82.95% | 81.93% |
| Phonological Awareness | Aggregate | 71.26%* | 70.10% | 63.84% | 66.83% |
| | C&R Tree | 70.60% | 68.50% | 65.12% | 66.77% |
| | C5.0 | 70.81% | 68.80% | 65.19%* | 66.95%* |
| | CHAID | 70.34% | 70.18% | 60.13% | 64.77% |
| | LSVM | 69.87% | 71.35%* | 56.09% | 62.81% |
| | Exhaustive CHAID | 71.26%* | 70.10% | 63.84% | 66.83% |
| Phonics | Aggregate | 73.62% | 76.93%* | 88.68% | 82.39% |
| | CHAID | 73.61% | 76.42% | 89.75% | 82.55% |
| | LSVM | 73.92% | 75.01% | 93.73%* | 83.33% |
| | Exhaustive CHAID | 74.28%* | 75.63% | 92.98% | 83.41%* |
| Comprehension and Vocabulary | Aggregate | 79.69% | 82.79%* | 93.34% | 87.75% |
| | CHAID | 79.92%* | 80.79% | 97.39%* | 88.31%* |
| | LSVM | 78.69% | 79.78% | 97.33% | 87.68% |
| | Exhaustive CHAID | 79.70% | 81.60% | 95.49% | 88.00% |
| Language Concepts | Aggregate | 70.18%* | 70.84% | 97.25% | 81.97% |
| | C5.0 | 69.81% | 70.59% | 97.18% | 81.78% |
| | Discriminant | 66.24% | 73.45%* | 80.73% | 76.92% |
| | LSVM | 70.15% | 70.43% | 98.54% | 82.15%* |
| | Exhaustive CHAID | 69.81% | 70.10% | 98.86%* | 82.03% |
| End of Year WACS | LSVM | 85.75% | 86.42% | 98.93% | 92.25% |

metrics of accuracy, precision, and F1 ranging from less than 2% (phonics) to 5.23% (language concepts).

**End-of-Year WACS.** When predicting if students passed a minimum score threshold of 2001 on end-of-year WACS, the equivalent of kindergarten beginning, from EMS scores, the modeler found the LSVM model to be the best predictor. Of the models considered, LSVM was the only approach that resulted in a reasonable recall.

## 4.2 Regression Models

**Table 2.** Correlation and relative error by subject

| Subject | Model | Correlation | Relative Error |
|---|---|---|---|
| Overall | Neural Net | 0.745 | 0.448 |
| | Linear AS | 0.734 | 0.462 |
| | Regression | 0.734 | 0.464 |
| | Generalized Linear | 0.734 | 0.464 |
| | Linear | 0.671 | 0.550 |
| Phonics | Neural Net | 0.671 | 0.550 |
| | Linear AS | 0.674 | 0.546 |
| | Regression | 0.670 | 0.552 |
| | Generalized Linear | 0.670 | 0.552 |
| | Linear | 0.544 | 0.704 |
| Phonological Awareness | Neural Net | 0.643 | 0.587 |
| | Linear AS | 0.635 | 0.597 |
| | Regression | 0.635 | 0.597 |
| | Generalized Linear | 0.635 | 0.597 |
| | Linear | 0.604 | 0.636 |
| Comprehension and Vocabulary | Linear AS | 0.856 | 0.267 |
| | Exhaustive CHAID | 0.853 | 0.273 |
| | XGBoost | 0.852 | 0.345 |
| | C&R | 0.846 | 0.284 |
| | CHAID | 0.847 | 0.283 |
| Language Concepts | Neural Net | 0.212 | 0.956 |
| | Linear AS | 0.223 | 0.951 |
| | Generalized Linear | 0.207 | 0.958 |
| | Regression | 0.207 | 0.958 |
| | CHAID | 0.196 | 0.962 |
| End of Year WACS | Linear AS | 0.496 | 0.757 |
| | Linear | 0.500 | 0.751 |
| | Exhaustive CHAID | 0.481 | 0.772 |
| | XGBoost | 0.493 | 0.790 |
| | Regression | 0.475 | 0.777 |

SPSS modeler was used to build regression models to predict students' ERP and WACS scores at the end of the program year based on EMS scores halfway through the program (see Table 2). The modeler chose the regression models based on the best fit and calculated the Pearson correlation coefficient between the actual and predicted scores and the normalized sum of squares. Correlation strength was defined by absolute value and labeled weak, medium, or strong based on the modeler guide. Analysis of scores was broken down by overall ERP, phonics, phonological awareness, comprehension and vocabulary, language concepts, and WACS.

**Overall ERP.** EMS scores predicted overall ERP scores with strong correlation coefficients, ranging from 0.671 to 0.745. Relative error ranged from 0.448 to 0.550.

**Phonics.** EMS scores predicted ERP scores with medium to strong correlation coefficients, ranging from 0.544 to 0.674. Relative error ranged from 0.546 to 0.704.

**Phonological Awareness.** EMS scores predicted phonological awareness scores with medium correlation coefficients, ranging from 0.604 to 0.643. Relative error ranged from 0.587 to 0.636.

**Comprehension and Vocabulary.** EMS scores predicted comprehension and vocabulary scores with strong correlation coefficients, ranging from 0.846 to 0.856. Relative error ranged from 0.267 to 0.345.

**Language Concepts.** EMS scores predicted language and comprehension scores with weak correlation coefficients, ranging from 0.196 to 0.223. Relative error ranged from 0.951 to 0.962.

**WACS.** EMS scores predicted WACS scores with medium correlation coefficients, ranging from 0.475 to 0.500. Relative error ranged from 0.751 to 0.790.

## 5 Discussion

This study used machine learning models to predict early reading scores from early math scores. Whether students' overall reading scores passed the 80% threshold was predicted with an accuracy ranging from 75.48% to 76.71%. The comprehension and vocabulary strand was predicted with the highest accuracy of 79.92%. The high predictability of mathematics skills on the comprehension and vocabulary strand, in conjunction with the findings of Purpura et al. [9] that vocabulary is predictive of mathematics skills, suggests an interconnectivity between vocabulary and mathematics skills. Whether a student achieved the phonics and phonological awareness literacy threshold was predicted from EMS scores with an accuracy of up to 74.28% and 71.26%, respectively. Passing the 80% threshold in the language concepts literacy strand was predicted by EMS scores with an accuracy of up to 70.18%. These results are consistent with the hypothesis that math scores would be predictive of literacy scores. The ability to predict whether a student passes the 80% threshold in preschool reading skills from preschool math skills with an accuracy of 70% and higher demonstrates the close relationship between the two subjects at an early age, as is consistent with previous findings [4, 5]. These findings suggest that math scores can be a valid measure for predicting whether a student reaches a benchmark in literacy skills, which can be useful for identifying children whose reading skills are at risk and could benefit from interventions.

Furthermore, math skills predicted overall literacy scores using regression models with a strong correlation. These findings reveal a strong linear relationship between students' math and reading scores, further highlighting the interconnectivity of the two domains. When breaking down the predictive analysis by literacy strand, comprehension and vocabulary were predicted by math skills with the highest correlation coefficients ranging from 0.846 to 0.856 and low relative error ranging from 0.267 to 0.345. Comprehension and vocabulary was also the substrand that the categorical model predicted with the highest accuracy, inferring the high predictive power of math skills on this literacy substrand. Math skills predicted phonics and phonological awareness skills with similar medium correlation coefficients. Language concepts had weak correlation coefficients when predicted by math skills. These findings are consistent with previous studies that have found math scores to be predictive of reading scores [10].

Early math performance was also predictive of end-of-year performance on the literacy strands assessed by WACS. This was shown both when looking at whether students would achieve end-of-year Kindergarten readiness, scoring at least 2001, and when assessing the linear relationship between performance in each domain.

## 6 Conclusions

This study demonstrates how two foundational skill sets can grow in tandem, and how growth in one, math and science skills, can predict growth in another, early literacy skills. As students learn the fundamentals of arithmetic and number concepts, they learn and practice skills that will be transferable when learning letters and grammar. By way of acknowledgment, it is possible that practice and repetition in the skills of early knowledge acquisition improve with use, regardless of the subject they are used on. Students learn how to learn, and the skills that facilitate this broadly in math domains are, to a degree, applicable in reading domains.

This study highlights the interdependence of these two learning domains, even at an early age. It is possible to identify students who are at risk of falling behind in one area based on their performance in another. Future research should further define relationships between risk factors, allowing educators to efficiently target interventions that can have the greatest impact during the critical period of early instruction when students are mastering these fundamental concepts. Speculatively, it should also be possible for further research to tailor specific interventions with the goal of promoting cross-domain learning.

Given the relative difficulty in predicting the language concepts, it is also interesting to note that, despite this interconnectedness, there are clearly areas unique to each domain. Language concepts, more so than the other areas of foundational literacy explored in this study, capture something specific to literacy development beyond the foundational learning skills discussed above.

Limitations of the current study should be noted. This study had a specific predictive window, assessing the predictive ability of math scores on reading scores for young students with a six-month delay. Future research should explore the validity of this relationship over more extended periods of time while also using a more diverse range of ages.

## References


1. Koponen, T., Eklund, K., Heikkilä, R., Salminen, J., Fuchs, L., Fuchs, D., et al.: Cognitive correlates of the covariance in reading and arithmetic fluency: importance of serial retrieval fluency. Child Dev. **91**(4), 1063–1080 (2020). https://doi.org/10.1111/cdev.13287
2. Purpura, D.J., Schmitt, S.A., Ganley, C.M.: Foundations of mathematics and literacy: the role of executive functioning components. J. Exp. Child Psychol. **153**, 15–34 (2017). https://doi.org/10.1016/j.jecp.2016.08.010
3. Cirino, P.T., Child, A.E., Macdonald, K.T.: Longitudinal predictors of the overlap between reading and math skills. Contemp. Educ. Psychol. **54**, 99–111 (2018). https://doi.org/10.1016/j.cedpsych.2018.06.002
4. Collins, M.A., Laski, E.V.: Digging deeper: Shared deep structures of early literacy and mathematics involve symbolic mapping and relational reasoning. Early Childhood Res. Q. **46**, 201–212 (2019). https://doi.org/10.1016/j.ecresq.2018.02.008
5. Mulder, H., Verhagen, J., Van der Ven, S.H.G., Slot, P.L., Leseman, P.P.M.: Early executive function at age two predicts emergent mathematics and literacy at age five. Front. Psychol. **8** (2017). https://doi.org/10.3389/fpsyg.2017.01706
6. Erbeli, F., Shi, Q., Campbell, A.R., Hart, S.A., Woltering, S.: Developmental dynamics between reading and math in elementary school. Dev. Sci. **24**(1) (2021). https://doi.org/10.1111/desc.13004
7. Larwin, K.H.: Reading is fundamental in predicting math achievement in 10th graders? Int. Electron. J. Math. Educ. **5**(3), 131–145 (2010). https://doi.org/10.29333/iejme/254
8. Purpura, D.J., Reid, E.E.: Mathematics and language: Individual and group differences in mathematical language skills in young children. Early Childhood Res. Q. **36**, 259–268 (2016). https://doi.org/10.1016/j.ecresq.2015.12.020
9. Purpura, D.J., Hume, L.E., Sims, D.M., Lonigan, C.J.: Early literacy and early numeracy: the value of including early literacy skills in the prediction of numeracy development. J. Exp. Child Psychol. **110**(4), 647–658 (2011). https://doi.org/10.1016/j.jecp.2011.07.004
10. Claessens, A., Engel, M.: How important is where you start? Early mathematics knowledge and later school success. Teach. Coll. Rec. **115**(6), 1–29 (2013). https://doi.org/10.1177/016146811311500603
11. ten Braak, D., Lenes, R., Purpura, D.J., Schmitt, S.A., Størksen, I.: Why do early mathematics skills predict later mathematics and reading achievement? The role of executive function. J. Exp. Child Psychol. **214**, 105306 (2022). https://doi.org/10.1016/j.jecp.2021.105306
12. Purpura, D.J., Litkowski, E.C., Knopik, V.: Mathematics and reading develop together in young children: practical and policy considerations. Policy Insights Behav. Brain Sci. **6**(1), 12–20 (2019). https://doi.org/10.1177/2372732218815923
13. Mitchell, T.M.: Machine Learning, vol. 1. McGraw-Hill, New York (2007)
14. Chen, F., Sakyi, A., Cui, Y.: Identifying key contextual factors of digital reading literacy through a machine learning approach. J. Educ. Comput. Res. **60**(7), 1763–1795 (2022). https://doi.org/10.1177/07356331221083215
15. Rosé, C.P., Ferschke, O.: Technology support for discussion based learning: from computer supported collaborative learning to the future of massive open online courses. Int. J. Artif. Intell. Educ. **26**(2), 660–678 (2016). https://doi.org/10.1007/s40593-016-0107-y
16. Naicker, N., Adeliyi, T., Wing, J.: Linear support vector machines for prediction of student performance in school-based education. Math. Probl. Eng. **2020**, 1–7 (2020). https://doi.org/10.1155/2020/4761468
17. Shaikh, A.A., Kumar, A., Jani, K., Mitra, S., García-Tadeo, D.A., Devarajan, A.: The role of machine learning and artificial intelligence for making a digital classroom and its sustainable impact on education during COVID-19. Mater. Today Proc. **56**, 3211–3215 (2022). https://doi.org/10.1016/j.matpr.2021.09.368

18. Cornell-Farrow, S., Garrard, R.: Machine learning classifiers do not improve the prediction of academic risk: Evidence from Australia. Commun. Stat. Case Stud. Data Anal. Appl. **6**(2), 228–246 (2020). https://doi.org/10.1080/23737484.2020.1752849
19. Montshiwa, T.V., Botlhoko, T.: Stepwise logistic regression, hierarchical logistic regression, CART and Naïve Bayes for predicting learners' numeracy test results. Res. Square (2022). https://doi.org/10.21203/rs.3.rs-1595992/v1
20. Asthana, P., Hazela, B.: Applications of machine learning in improving learning environment. In: Tanwar, S., Tyagi, S., Kumar, N. (eds.) Multimedia Big Data Computing for IoT Applications. ISRL, vol. 163, pp. 417–433. Springer, Singapore (2020). https://doi.org/10.1007/978-981-13-8759-3_16
21. Suggate, S., Schaughency, E., McAnally, H., Reese, E.: From infancy to adolescence: the longitudinal links between vocabulary, early literacy skills, oral narrative, and reading comprehension. Cogn. Dev. **47**, 82–95 (2018). https://doi.org/10.1016/j.cogdev.2018.04.005
22. Pinto, G., Bigozzi, L., Tarchi, C., Vezzani, C., Accorti Gamannossi, B.: Predicting reading, spelling, and mathematical skills: a longitudinal study from kindergarten through first grade. Psychol. Rep. **118**(2), 413–440 (2016). https://doi.org/10.1177/0033294116633357
23. Watts, T.W., Duncan, G.J., Siegler, R.S., Davis-Kean, P.E.: What's What's past is prologue. Educ. Res. **43**(7), 352–360 (2014). https://doi.org/10.3102/0013189x14553660
24. Camilli, G., Vargas, S., Ryan, S., Barnett, W.S.: Meta-analysis of the effects of early education interventions on cognitive and social development. Teach. Coll. Rec. **112**(3), 579–620 (2010). https://doi.org/10.1177/016146811011200303
25. McCoy, D.C., Yoshikawa, H., Ziol-Guest, K.M., Duncan, G.J., Schindler, H.S., Magnuson, K., et al.: Impacts of early childhood education on medium- and long-term educational outcomes. Educ. Res. **46**(8), 474–487 (2017). https://doi.org/10.3102/0013189X17737739

# Explaining Problem Recommendations in an Intelligent Tutoring System

April Clarke(✉) and Antonija Mitrović(✉)

Department of Computer Science and Software Engineering, University of Canterbury, Christchurch, New Zealand
{april.clarke,tanja.mitrovic}@canterbury.ac.nz

**Abstract.** Students learning with intelligent tutoring systems (ITS) do not always trust system recommendations. One solution for this is explainable AI (XAI), which is shown to increase trust in AI. Our research focuses on how students' personality traits affect their interactions with XAI, and how XAI affects students' trust and actions in an ITS. We evaluated this by adding XAI to SQL-Tutor and conducting a pilot study with 15 participants from an introductory database course. We found that personality traits affect students' interactions with XAI, and that students engaging with XAI trust the system more.

**Keywords:** Intelligent tutoring system · SQL-Tutor · explainable artificial intelligence · problem selection

## 1 Introduction

Intelligent tutoring systems (ITSs) improve students' learning outcomes by providing adaptive support based on the student's knowledge and progress [1,17]. SQL-Tutor is a mature constraint-based ITS that teaches students to write SQL queries [13,14]. Previous studies with SQL-Tutor have shown that students who work on problems recommended by the system tend to learn more [12]. However, students accept these recommendations variably, which may be because they do not understand or trust the reasoning behind the recommendations.

A potential solution to increase students' trust in the system, and hopefully their willingness to select recommended problems, is explainable AI (XAI), which has been shown to increase users' trust in decisions made by AI [4]. So far, there has not been extensive research on the factors that affect how students interpret and interact with explanations in an ITS. This paper presents our work on adding explanations to SQL-Tutor and the results of a pilot study we used to investigate the following questions:

- RQ1: How does students' engagement with XAI affect their interactions with the ITS?
- RQ2: How do students' personality traits affect their interactions with explanations?
- RQ3: What explanations do students want?


A. Sifaleras and F. Lin (Eds.): ITS 2024, LNCS 14798, pp. 291–299, 2024.
https://doi.org/10.1007/978-3-031-63028-6_23

Our key findings were: (1) students engaging with explanations accept recommendations more; (2) students want clear steps to apply explanations; and (3) students' personality traits affect their use and understanding of explanations, so personalisation is needed to maximise the benefit of explanations in an ITS.

The paper's structure is as follows: Sect. 2 reviews prior research, while Sect. 3 presents our solution. Section 4 details the experiment design, then results in Sect. 5, and implications in Sect. 6. Finally, Sect. 7 concludes.

## 2 Related Work

XAI exposes decision-making logic to a system's users, allowing them to make informed decisions to trust or distrust the system. However, many factors also influence how students engage with explanations. To implement effective explanations, we need to understand what factors affect students' interactions with explanations, and how to adapt explanations for these factors.

A widely recognised quality attribute for XAI is *completeness* [5,15]. Achieving this requires us to predict what gaps exist in users' knowledge, but these gaps vary between users and over time, which alters what is relevant and useful [10,11]. Also, there is a trade-off with interpretability [5,6,15], so we must limit the depth of explanations. Excessively simple explanations can bore users, making them unwilling to read other explanations, while complex explanations can overwhelm. One option to make explanations more digestible is to split them into smaller parts. This lessens the need to predict users' wants, as they can select relevant explanations. Labelling each part as response to a question, such as *which problems can I solve to improve my ranking in X area?* [2], also promotes reflection [9]. In an ITS for constraint satisfaction problems, the ACSP applet, Conati et al. [4] use explanations that gradually deepen students' knowledge. However, students must review early explanations each time, reducing their freedom. Students who are unwilling to read all explanations miss information from the later explanations. Allowing students to access explanations in any order would give them more freedom, although it risks students skipping important knowledge.

We can help users apply what they learn from explanations by adding actionable steps. Singh et al. [16] found most users preferred explanations with steps when communicating a system's outputs to a third party. However, some users preferred explanations without steps because they were shorter, which confirms the importance of providing explanations in small chunks.

Users' interactions with explanations are affected by factors like personality traits, knowledge, and the task's complexity and risk [2–4]. In the context of the ACSP applet, Conati et al. [4] found the benefits of explanations were affected by students' conscientiousness, need for cognition, and reading comprehension, which indicates a need for personalisation based on user characteristics.

While there is a clear need for adaptive explanations, it is not well established how we can personalise explanations in ITSs.

## 3 Explanations in SQL-Tutor

We added explanations for problem recommendations in SQL-Tutor. When a student requests a new problem, relevant problems are listed by difficulty. The recommended problem is highlighted first, but students can choose any problem.

**Why is this problem being recommended?** Explanation 1 (E1) uses a unique template for each problem recommendation case. For example, if many problems are the right level for the student, unsolved, and not being worked on, then the template will be *There are multiple unsolved problems for the X clause in this database. The recommended problem is the next unsolved problem which is at/above your student level and that you are not already working on, problem Y*, where X is the SQL clause, and Y is the problem's ID.

**Why does problem selection matter?** Explanation 2 (E2) is always *The right problem for you is one that extends your knowledge and helps you improve your skills. A problem that's too easy won't help you learn. A problem that's too challenging will be so difficult that you don't have enough existing knowledge to understand the problem or solution.*

**How is my student level calculated?** The student's level and whether it has changed in the current session affect Explanation 3 (E3). The first half of the explanation is always *Your student level is calculated based on how many problems you have solved or failed recently, their problem levels, and your problem level. You are currently at level X*, where X is the student's level. The second half of the explanation is initially *Your student level hasn't changed this session, yet*, and updates when the student's level increases or decreases.

Each explanation is initially hidden, with the title questions shown. They are toggled by clicking the related question, and have a 5-point Likert scale to gather ongoing feedback on changes in participants' perceptions of the explanations.

## 4 Experiment Design

We recruited 15 volunteers from students enrolled in an introductory database course at the University of Canterbury. The students had been taught to write SQL select queries in lectures, but most had never used SQL-Tutor before. Three participants used SQL-Tutor in lab sessions before participating in this study.

Each participant attended an individual session structured as follows: (1) We asked participants to complete the ten-item personality inventory (TIPI) [7], to determine a score for each of the Big-Five personality traits. (2) We demonstrated the explanations in SQL-Tutor and asked them to view the explanations at least once during their session. (3) They used SQL-Tutor with a Tobii Pro Lab eye tracker capturing their gaze movements. (4) They responded to a questionnaire. (5) We provided them with a $20 voucher and debriefed them.

The questionnaire in part 4 included the System Causability Scale (SCS) [8], and open questions. We modified the SCS to make all statements relevant to this study, and aligned the Likert scale with the 1-to-7 scale used for the TIPI.

## 5 Results

The participants spent on average 33.7 min, with a standard deviation (sd) of 3.5 min, solving problems in SQL-Tutor. They attempted on average 9.5 problems (sd = 3.4), and solved 8.7 problems (sd = 4.3), making 40.3 submissions (sd = 21.0). They visited the problem selection page on average 9.9 times (sd = 3.2) and viewed at least one explanation on 4.1 visits (sd = 3.2). The most explanation views by a participant was 33. Three participants did not view all types of explanations, and we excluded their data from relevant analyses.

Table 1 shows the scores on five SCS questions. The two statements with the lowest mean ratings are *I understood the explanations within the context of my work* and *I was able to use the explanations with my knowledge.* These statements indicate how well the participants felt they could use the explanations. The other three statements with higher mean ratings indicate how well the participants understood the explanations. Therefore, participants rated the consistency and clarity of the explanations more highly than their ability to apply them.

**Table 1.** SCS ratings 1 (Disagree strongly) to 7 (Agree strongly)

| Question (n=12) | M (sd) | Mdn |
|---|---|---|
| I understood the explanations within the context of my work. | 5.75 (1.49) | 6 |
| I did not need support to understand the explanations. | 6.00 (1.41) | 6 |
| I was able to use the explanations with my knowledge. | 5.17 (1.47) | 5.5 |
| I did not find inconsistencies between explanations. | 5.83 (1.64) | 6.5 |
| I think that most people would learn to understand the explanations very quickly. | 5.83 (1.19) | 6 |

### 5.1 RQ1: How Does Students' Engagement with Explanations Affect Their Interactions with the ITS?

To evaluate RQ1, we filtered participants' problem selections to include only the 45 instances where they opened E1, and found they then selected the recommended problem 37 times. The strong Spearman's correlation coefficient ($r_s$ = .90, $p < .001$) indicates that there is a high likelihood that students will select the recommended problem after reading E1.

When asked how explanations affected their problem selection, 8 of the 15 participants agreed the explanations made them more willing to accept recommendations. Those who did not agree either trusted the ITS or their own problem selection already, could not apply the explanations, or viewed no explanations.

### 5.2 RQ2: How Do Students' Personality Traits Affect Their Interactions with Explanations?

To evaluate RQ2, we used a non-parametric Mann-Whitney U test due to the small sample size and non-normal distribution. We combined the personality test data, explanation ratings, gaze data, and system logs, and split participants into low and high-scoring groups around the median score for each personality trait.

Tables 2 and 3 show the results for the Big Five personality traits with multiple significant differences between the high and low groups. More agreeable participants (Table 2) spent less time viewing each explanation without fixating elsewhere on the screen. This may indicate that more agreeable participants are satisfied with less explanation, or are more interested in comparing the explanations with other information on the page. Less agreeable participants also typically used the system for longer before viewing explanations for the first time, which may show a preference for more independent learning.

**Table 2.** Mann-Whitney U Test for Agreeableness

| | Group | M (sd) | Mdn | U | p | r |
|---|---|---|---|---|---|---|
| Average duration of visits to E1 (s) | low (n = 7)<br>high (n = 5) | 4.16 (2.54)<br>1.72 (0.98) | 3.91<br>1.46 | 30.0 | $<.05$ | .59 |
| Average duration of visits to E3 (s) | low (n = 7)<br>high (n = 5) | 4.23 (2.05)<br>2.25 (0.69) | 3.54<br>2.31 | 30.0 | $<.05$ | .68 |
| Average duration of all visits to explanations (s) | low (n = 7)<br>high (n = 5) | 4.21 (2.83)<br>1.75 (0.90) | 2.32<br>1.39 | 31.0 | $<.05$ | .65 |
| Time until first visit to E3 (s) | low (n = 7)<br>high (n = 5) | 327.76<br>(110.07)<br>180.68 (47.87) | 376.47<br>162.09 | 32.0 | $<.05$ | .63 |

Less emotionally stable participants took longer to open E1 for the first time and rated E3 as less useful than their more stable counterparts (Table 3). These differences demonstrate an effect on how participants approach using explanations, and what they want from explanations in an ITS.

**Table 3.** Mann-Whitney U Test for Emotional Stability

| | Group | M (sd) | Mdn | U | p | r |
|---|---|---|---|---|---|---|
| I found the explanation for "How is my student level calculated?" useful | low (n = 6)<br>high (n = 6) | 4.5 (1.64)<br>6.5 (0.55) | 4.5<br>6.5 | 4.5 | $<.05$ | .64 |
| Time to first mouse click on E1 (s) | low (n = 6)<br>high (n = 6) | 331.33<br>(116.89)<br>166.16 (58.63) | 373.41<br>140.93 | 32 | $<.05$ | .65 |

Less conscientious participants spent longer viewing E2 for the first time, (Mann-Whitney U test: $U = 31$, $p < .05$, $r = .60$). The low ($n = 6$) and high ($n = 6$) conscientiousness groups had mean visit lengths of 3.48 s (sd = 5.01) and 0.34 s (sd = 0.23), respectively, and medians of 0.93 s and 0.3 s.

### 5.3 RQ3: What Explanations Do Students Want?

We evaluated RQ3 using questionnaire responses and gaze/click data for each explanation. Participants read E1 for the most time and E3 for the least, but rated E3 more highly than E1 (Table 4). This is consistent with the SCS ratings (Table 5): E3 has the highest mean and median ratings, and the smallest sd, indicating that participants generally found E3 more useful than E1 and E2.

**Table 4.** Explanation ratings 1 (Not useful) to 5 (Very useful)

| Explanation (n = 12) | Total time (s) | Mean time per visit (s) | Times opened | Rating |
|---|---|---|---|---|
| E1 | 42.7 (33.6) | 3.14 (2.32) | 4.66 (2.56) | 3.74 (1.28) |
| E2 | 24.6 (19.1) | 3.16 (3.21) | 3.83 (2.58) | 3.96 (1.08) |
| E3 | 21.9 (14.8) | 3.40 (1.79) | 4.75 (2.83) | 4.08 (0.84) |

**Table 5.** Three SCS questions 1 (Disagree strongly) to 7 (Agree strongly)

| Question (n = 12) | M (sd) | Mdn |
|---|---|---|
| I found the explanation for "How was this problem selected?" useful. | 5.00 (1.95) | 5.5 |
| I found the explanation for "Why does choosing the right problem matter?" useful. | 4.50 (2.15) | 4 |
| I found the explanation for "How is my level calculated?" useful | 5.50 (1.57) | 6 |

Participants sometimes opened E3 to view their student level, and did not read further. Comparing participants' focus in the first and second half of their sessions (Table 6) shows that interest in E3 decreased less over time than for E1 and E2. Figure 1 shows participants focused on their student level in E3, in the second half of the session. This suggests that participants were most interested in their student level, which changed often and informed their choices.

**Table 6.** Time (s) students spent viewing explanations in each half of the session

| Explanation (n = 12) | Time in 1st half | Time in 2nd half | Change |
|---|---|---|---|
| E1 | 437.20 | 75.58 | −82.71% |
| E2 | 258.20 | 36.70 | −85.79% |
| E3 | 228.97 | 56.26 | −75.43% |

In response to the open questions, participants reported increased confidence in the system's problem recommendations, as they were reassured that selecting the recommended problem would aid their learning. They also suggested improvements, including merging explanations, making them visible all the time, adding data to back up recommendations, and adding steps for independent problem selection or changing their student level. Each participant's suggestion was different, so it is unclear which would be the most useful.

The need for clear steps aligns with our earlier observation that participants rated their ability to apply the explanations lower than their understanding of the explanations (Table 1). Clear steps may help students apply what they learn from explanations more easily, as recommended by Arnold et al. [2].

## 6 Discussion

The high correlation between participants viewing E1 and then selecting the recommended problem indicates that engaging with explanations affects trust in the system's recommendations. This shows that XAI can promote behaviours that improve students' learning in ITSs. Participant feedback also reinforces the idea that explanations can increase acceptance of the system's recommendations.

Differences in the way participants' personality factors interacted with the explanations indicate a need for explanations to adapt to students' personality factors. More work is needed to determine what makes explanations more useful for students in different personality groups, alongside other factors that may affect students' use of explanations, such as reading comprehension [4]. While adapting explanations may be costly, our results show that participants who engaged with the explanations more were more likely to select the recommended problem, which is desirable in SQL-Tutor.

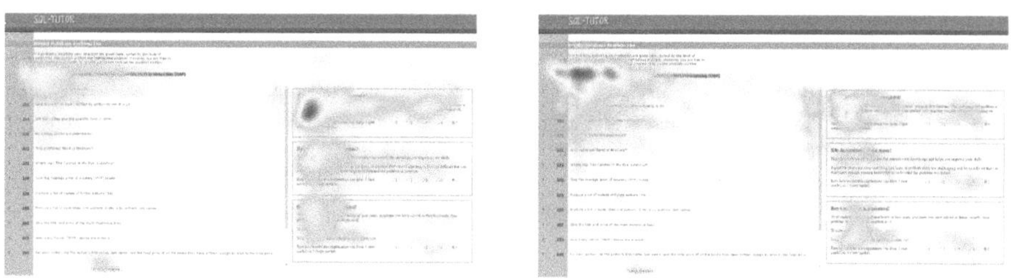

**Fig. 1.** Heat map of the first half (left) and the second half (right) of views of the problem selection page

Participants showed more interest in explanations that showed their progress and change frequently (E1 and E3) than E2, which is static. They also wanted clear steps to help them apply what they learnt from explanations, which may be particularly valuable for students who find explanations less useful.

There are several limitations to this research. Our small sample size makes it difficult to generalise about the wider population of students. We also requested volunteers, creating a selection bias for students more familiar with the course content. The order of the explanations likely influenced participants' interactions with them, as they often read the top explanation first. This explanation order was also different from the order we asked students to rate the explanations in the SCS. Participants who did not read the questionnaire carefully may have assumed the order of the questions. Also for the questionnaires, some participants interpreted 'explanations' as feedback on their problem solving attempts, instead of the explanations we implemented. As a result, we disregarded some responses to the open questions. Finally, measuring factors like reading comprehension would give more insight into students' interactions with explanations.

## 7 Conclusions

This study contributes to our understanding of how students interact with XAI in an intelligent tutoring system and the factors that can affect these interactions. Our results confirm that explanations improve students' trust in the system, and lead to students being more willing to accept recommendations. We also found that students' personality traits can influence their interactions with explanations and perceived benefits, so there is a need for personalisation based on these traits. Finally, we conclude that students are particularly interested in information that helps them apply what they learn from explanations.

In future work we will conduct a larger study for more insight into students' experiences with XAI in ITSs, and evaluate adaptive explanations.

## References

1. Anderson, J., Corbett, A., Koedinger, K., Pelletier, R.: Cognitive tutors: lessons learned. J. Learn. Sci. **4**, 167–207 (1995)
2. Arnold, V., Clark, N., Collier, P.A., Leech, S.A., Sutton, S.G.: The differential use and effect of knowledge-based system explanations in novice and expert judgment decisions. MIS Q. **30**(1), 79–97 (2006)
3. Arnold, V., Sutton, S.: The theory of technology dominance: understanding the impact of intelligent decision aids on decision makers judgments. Adv. Acc. Behav. Res. **1**, 175–194 (1998)
4. Conati, C., Barral, O., Putnam, V., Rieger, L.: Toward personalized XAI: a case study in intelligent tutoring systems. Artif. Intell. **298**, 103503 (2021)
5. Ehsan, U., Tambwekar, P., Chan, L., Harrison, B., Riedl, M.O.: Automated rationale generation: a technique for explainable AI and its effects on human perceptions. In: Proceedings 24th International Conference Intelligent User Interfaces, pp. 263–274. ACM (2019)
6. Gilpin, L.H., Bau, D., Yuan, B.Z., Bajwa, A., Specter, M., Kagal, L.: Explaining explanations: an overview of interpretability of machine learning. In: 2018 IEEE 5th International Conference Data Science and Advanced Analytics, pp. 80–89 (2018)

7. Gosling, S.D., Rentfrow, P.J., Swann, W.B.: A very brief measure of the big-five personality domains. J. Res. Pers. **37**(6), 504–528 (2003)
8. Holzinger, A., Carrington, A., Müller, H.: Measuring the quality of explanations: the system causability scale (SCS). Künstl. Intell. **34**(2), 193–198 (2020)
9. Kay, J., Kummerfeld, B.: From data to personal user models for life-long, life-wide learners. Br. J. Edu. Technol. **50**(6), 2871–2884 (2019)
10. Kveraga, K., Ghuman, A.S., Bar, M.: Top-down predictions in the cognitive brain. Brain Cogn. **65**(2), 145–168 (2007)
11. Miller, T.: Explanation in artificial intelligence: insights from the social sciences. Artif. Intell. **267**, 1–38 (2019)
12. Mitrović, A., Martin, B.: Scaffolding and fading problem selection in SQL-tutor. In: Hoppe, U., Verdejo, F., Kay, J. (eds.) Proceedings 11th International Conference Artificial Intelligence in Education, pp. 479–481 (2003)
13. Mitrovic, A., Martin, B.: Evaluating adaptive problem selection. In: De Bra, P.M.E., Nejdl, W. (eds.) AH 2004. LNCS, vol. 3137, pp. 185–194. Springer, Heidelberg (2004). https://doi.org/10.1007/978-3-540-27780-4_22
14. Mitrović, A., Ohlsson, S.: Implementing CBM: SQL-tutor after fifteen years. Artif. Intel. Educ. **26**, 150–159 (2016)
15. Mueller, S.T., Hoffman, R.R., Clancey, W.J., Emrey, A., Klein, G.: Explanation in human-AI systems: a literature meta-review, synopsis of key ideas and publications, and bibliography for explainable AI. CoRR abs/1902.01876 (2019)
16. Singh, R., et al.: Directive explanations for actionable explainability in machine learning applications. ACM Trans. Interact. Intell. Syst. **13**(4), 23:1–23:26 (2023)
17. Wertheimer, R.: The geometry proof tutor: an intelligent computer-based tutor in the classroom. Math. Teach. **83**(4), 308–317 (1990)

# Implementing Distributed Feedback in a Tool that Supports Peer-to-Peer Simulation in Healthcare

Sandra Katz(✉), Patricia Albacete, Pamela Jordan, Scott Silliman, and Matthew Wrzesniewski

University of Pittsburgh, Pittsburgh, PA 15260, USA
katz@pitt.edu

**Abstract.** MedDbriefer is a web based ITS designed to enable healthcare students to do clinical scenarios anytime, anywhere. While one student "voice treats" a scenario's patient(s) as the leader of a mock Emergency Medical Services (EMS) team, a peer records the team's actions by using the system's checklists, on a tablet. When the scenario ends, MedDbriefer analyzes the event log and generates a debriefing. MedDbriefer also provides a platform for research on simulation-based training. This paper describes how the system's debriefing engine could be extended to deliver feedback *during* a scenario, as well as afterwards. MedDbriefer could then be used to compare the effectiveness of different ways of timing feedback delivery in computer-based simulation systems.

**Keywords:** Automated debriefing · Computer-based simulation systems · EMS training · Feedback · MedDbriefer · Microdebriefing · Peer-to-peer simulation

## 1 Introduction

Computer-based simulation systems allow students to gain supplemental practice outside of their courses' regular simulation-based training (SBT) labs and receive personalized feedback from the automated tutor. Although extensive research has shown that feedback is one of the most critical components of SBT, little is known about how to deliver effective feedback during live or automated simulation exercises [1–4].

In automated simulation systems designed for healthcare provider training, feedback is typically deferred until a debriefing, after a clinical scenario ends. Post-scenario debriefings typically present a step-by-step replay of students' actions, as illustrated in tutoring systems such as the American Heart Association's *Heartcode BLS* and *Heartcode ALS*, and Wolters Kluwer's *VSim for Nursing* [5, 6]. Some human SBT instructors also avoid giving feedback during a scenario, except when students stray far off the path to a successful solution [e.g., 7]. This approach to timing feedback delivery prevents the cognitive overload that can result from students having to shift attention between a scenario (or other simulation exercise) and the instructor's feedback, preserves scenario realism, and provides opportunities for students to experience "productive struggle" and


A. Sifaleras and F. Lin (Eds.): ITS 2024, LNCS 14798, pp. 300–311, 2024.
https://doi.org/10.1007/978-3-031-63028-6_24

self-regulate [e.g., 3, 8] However, several simulation scholars have advocated replacing post-scenario debriefings with within-scenario debriefings—that is, brief pauses to a scenario to address errors or prompt students to reflect on their performance so far.[1] Compared with post-scenario debriefings, within-scenario debriefings position feedback closer to the context in which errors occurred, prevent the frustration that can stem from realizing that the scenario's patient is not improving, and reduce the chance that persistent errors become cognitively ingrained [e.g., 7, 8, 9].

Our observations of human instructor guided scenarios for training emergency medical services (EMS) providers revealed that instructors typically take a hybrid approach, parceling feedback between brief within-scenario debriefings and a post-scenario debriefing. In future work, we plan to compare alternative ways of timing the delivery of feedback, to determine which approach, if any, predicts better learning outcomes in a computer-based simulation system. MedDbriefer, a web based ITS that supports peer-to-peer simulation, will serve as the research platform for these studies [10–12].

After presenting an overview of MedDbriefer, this paper illustrates distributed feedback during human facilitated simulation. It then describes how MedDbriefer analyzes simulation logs to generate post-scenario debriefings, and how this approach could be leveraged to provide within-scenario and distributed debriefings.

## 2 MedDbriefer

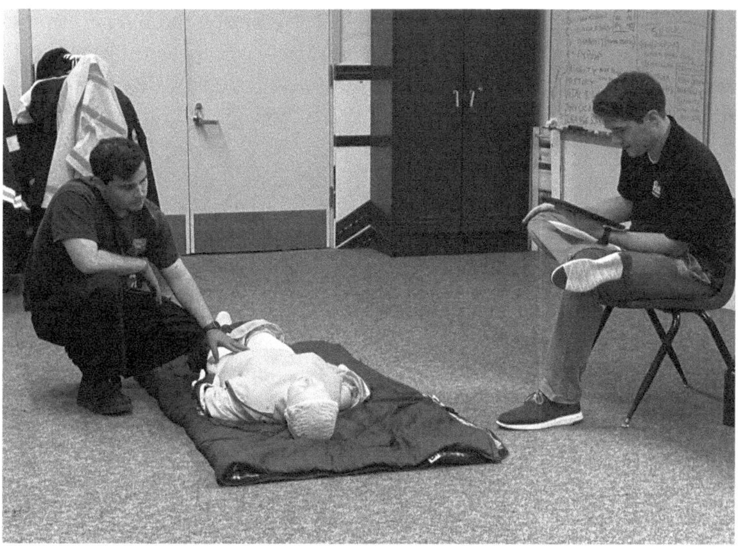

**Fig. 1.** MedDbriefer in use. Paramedic student (at left) treats a simulated patient while peer (at right) uses MedDbriefer's checklists to log actions.

[1] Within-scenario debriefings are alternatively called "microdebriefings," "reflective pauses," "stop-and-go debriefings," among other terms.

Students who struggle to acquire clinical skills often benefit from supplemental simulation practice, outside of their regular SBT labs. Unfortunately, programs across healthcare specialties face a shortage of simulation instructors [e.g., 13]. To address this problem, many instructors encourage students to get together with peers and practice scenarios. However, left unguided, peer-to-peer simulation often deteriorates, emblemizing "the blind leading the blind" [14].

When fully developed MedDbriefer will enable pairs or small groups of paramedic trainees to engage in clinical scenarios on their own—anytime, anywhere. While one student "voice treats" a virtual patient as the leader of a mock EMS team, a peer uses the system on a tablet to log the team leader's verbalized actions, by selecting these actions from the interface's checklists. (See Figs. 1–2.) After the scenario ends, the system analyzes the event log and generates a debriefing. In a randomized trial that is nearing completion, we used MedDbriefer to compare two ways to structure post-scenario debriefings [10, 12]. Table 1 illustrates the traditional approach: a chronological replay of students' scenario actions, with feedback.

MedDbriefer implements several affordances to foster beneficial interaction between the student who voice treats the simulated patient (the "EMS team leader") and a peer who uses the tablet to log the team's actions (the "observer"). As shown in Fig. 2, MedDbriefer's observer interface (OI) provides two main checklists: an assessment checklist (Fig. 2, left) and an intervention checklist (Fig. 2, right). When the observer checks an assessment action, the system displays a finding to call out. The observer does not need to invent a finding that is realistic and accurate. For example, if the team leader states that he is checking breathing quality, the observer may be cued to call out "gurgling," as highlighted in yellow in Fig. 2. Similarly, the intervention checklist includes routine actions that EMS providers perform, such as ventilating a patient and securing a patient onto a spinal board. Interspersed throughout this menu are prompts for the observer to issue if the team leader fails to provide sufficient detail about how he would perform an intervention. For example, Fig. 2 (right) displays a respiratory intervention, bag-valve mask ventilation, with questions the observer should ask if the team leader doesn't specify the ventilation rate, oxygen flow rate, etc.

Providing feedback during a post-scenario debriefing is MedDbriefer's most important affordance. Immediately after the observer clicks on the Done button, the system analyzes the event log to generate a debriefing (e.g., Table 1), as described presently (Sect. 4.1). Ultimately, MedDbriefer could be scaled to support peer-to-peer simulation in other areas of healthcare education, such as physician and nurse training.

## 3 An Example of Distributed Feedback

Table 2 shows excerpts of distributed feedback that took place during a live, human instructor guided paramedic training scenario. At the start of the scenario, the instructor (simulation facilitator, abbreviated "Fac" in Table 2) stated the dispatch information:

*You are dispatched to a 26-year-old female having trouble breathing. She's at a bus terminal, sitting on the curb.*

The facilitator paused the scenario several times to achieve an overarching goal: to get the team leader (abbreviated "TL" in Table 2) to do a more thorough patient

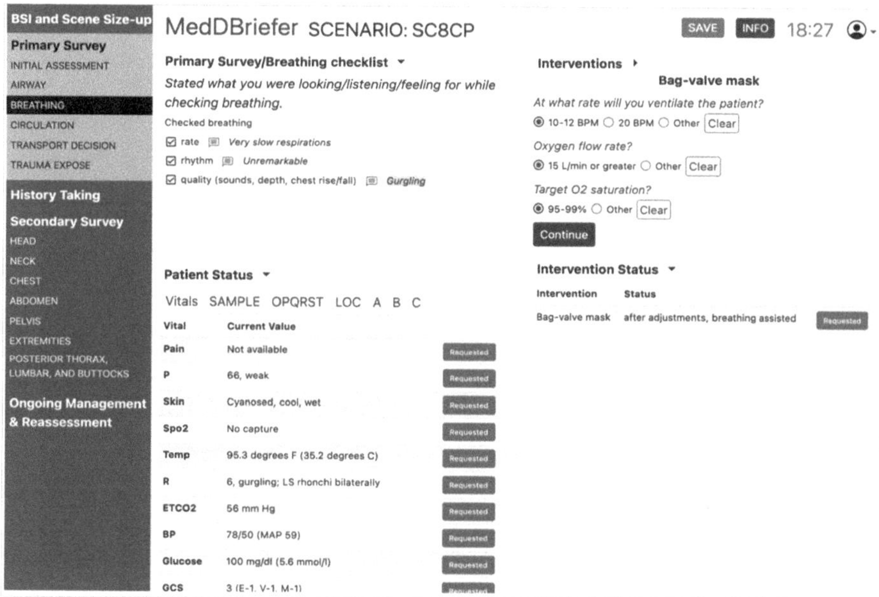


**Fig. 2.** MedDbriefer's observer interface.

assessment before settling on a diagnosis—specifically, to understand *why* the patient is in respiratory distress. Through within-scenario debriefings, often extended during the post-scenario debriefing, the instructor addressed a common problem in healthcare education: premature closure, aka "jumping to conclusions" [e.g., 15]. Especially when patients present with medical conditions, as opposed to physical injury, paramedics must gather enough evidence to determine which of several possible conditions is the most likely cause of ambiguous symptoms like "difficulty breathing," so that they can manage the patient appropriately until they arrive at a definitive care facility.

During the scenario excerpted in Table 2, the team leader suspected early on that the patient was suffering from a pulmonary embolism (PE) (e.g., Pause 2, turn 7), which is a clot that blocks blood flow to an artery in a lung. Although the student happened to be correct in this case, the facilitator was not happy with the *process* by which the student reached this diagnosis. The student had gathered other findings besides difficulty breathing that could indicate a PE such as chest pain, low blood pressure, and poor oxygen saturation (not shown in Table 2). However, a similar cluster of findings could indicate a cardiac issue, including a heart attack. At each pause in the scenario, the instructor prodded students to gather more evidence, to rule out other possible conditions and strengthen the team leader's proposed diagnosis (i.e., a PE).

Errors trigger within-scenario pauses. For example, Pause 1 in Table 2 is triggered by the team leader's failure to take a patient history after administering oxygen and realizing that the patient still had difficulty breathing (i.e., SAMPLE and OPQRST

**Table 1.** Excerpt from a MedDbriefer post-scenario debriefing on a child near-drowning

| ID | Action description | Feedback |
|---|---|---|
| 15 | Performed bag-valve mask ventilation. **Purpose:** Oxygenation **Oxygen flow rate:** 15 liters/min or greater **Target O2 saturation rate:** 95-99% **Ventilation rate:** 10-12 BPM | *Incorrectly administered intervention.* You were incorrect about ventilation rate. This patient should have been ventilated at a rate of 20 breaths per minute, which is the recommended rate for a child aged 2-12. When performing BVM ventilation, you use 15LPM O2 to both oxygenate and ventilate the patient to a target SpO2 >90%. |
| 16 | Checked skin condition (moisture). **Found:** *Wet* | |
| 17 | Performed a gross blood sweep. **Found:** *No major external bleeding* | *Missing assessment step.* A gross blood sweep (negative in this patient) will help you identify any life-threatening bleeding you may have missed earlier when forming your general impression. |
| 18 | Checked skin color. **Found:** *Cyanosed* | |
| 19 | Which pulse? **Pulse to check:** carotid and radial | |
| 20 | Checked pulse rate. **Found:** *Slow* | *Mistimed assessment step.* All unconscious patients should have a pulse check before starting the ABCs. However, paramedics often check breathing while doing a pulse check. If the patient is pulseless, you will start high-quality CPR immediately... |

history, referred to in turn 5).[2] Findings gathered from history taking would strengthen or weaken the likelihood of a PE. Continuing in the same vein, Pause 2 is triggered by TL's failure to ask focused questions that would reveal more about the possible causes of the patient's "breathing problem" (turn 8). Similarly, Pause 3 (turns 9–17) is triggered by the student's failure to inquire about other telltale factors that could lead to a PE, such as being a smoker and/or sedentary for considerable time.

During the post-scenario debriefing, the facilitator clarified why he prodded the team leader to "ask all those questions" (turn 19): because the patient could be experiencing a "STEMI" (i.e., an "**ST**-Elevation **M**yocardial **I**nfarction," aka a "heart attack"), not a

[2] SAMPLE and OPQRST are acronyms for history-taking questions; for example, S = Signs/Symptoms; A = known Allergies; M = Medications; O = Onset of pain; P = Palliation/Provocation (i.e., what makes the pain better/worse?).

**Table 2.** Example of distributed debriefing during a human facilitated scenario

| Pause# (elapsed time in minutes) | Within-scenario Debriefings | Excerpts from the post-scenario debriefing that extend within-scenario debriefings |
|---|---|---|
| 1 (~12:00) | 1. Fac: OK; let's stop. What else do you know about her?<br>2. TL: She's a 26-year-old female<br>3. Fac: OK. What else do you know?<br>4. TL: Nothing<br>5. Fac: What about SAMPLE, OPQRST? | 18. TL: I didn't think it was a cardiac problem once I put her on the monitor…<br>19. Fac: Don't females have them…especially if they're pregnant, diabetic, blah blah blah, right?…That's why you need to ask all those questions. She could be having a STEMI |
| 2 (~15:00) | 6. Fac: So, let's pause again. What's the problem? Why are we here?<br>7. TL: Shortness of breath. I think she might have a PE<br>8. Fac: But is it a breathing problem? Does she have a cough? Cold? Is the cold productive? Does she smoke? You know…think of all the breathing questions. When you have belly pain it's all the belly questions… | |
| 3 (~19:00) | 9. Fac: What's going on?<br>10. TL: I think she has a PE<br>11. Fac: Why?<br>12. TL: Pleuritic chest pain on one side. She's on birth control<br>13. Fac: There's many people that have pleuritic chest pain. Maybe she lifted an air conditioner yesterday…What else do you know about her?<br>14. TL: Shortness of breath. Are you a smoker?<br>15. Patient: yes…<br>16. Fac: Where is she?<br>17. TL: Bus terminal…She's been sitting for a long time. That's a contributing factor for an expected PE | 20. Fac: Ok…She's 26, she's on birth control, she's been sedentary for a couple of days. She smokes. She does have the pleuritic chest pain. She's a little bit tachycardic, her oxygen saturations are low. Is that a much better story for a PE?… Like you hit PE super early on, but you didn't know why PE. You had like, it was a little piece of the puzzle it was a good guess…I think you did a really good job. You got to the point where you went from a guess to an educated informed, medical—I think they call it a "differential diagnosis" or something; a field impression |

PE. As stated in turn 20, the facilitator tried to steer students from taking a "shot in the dark" (guess) towards deriving an "informed, medical…differential diagnosis."

## 4 Towards Automated Distributed Feedback in MedDbriefer

MedDbriefer analyzes the entire event log after a scenario ends in three phases to generate a debriefing (e.g., Table 1). This section summarizes the log analysis process (Sect. 4.1; see [11] for more detail) and how it could be leveraged to implement within-scenario and distributed feedback (Sect. 4.2). In essence, instead of analyzing the entire log at the end of a scenario, the system would analyze the log dynamically, at selected "checkpoints," pausing to provide feedback on students' performance between checkpoints. Examples in this section refer to the near-drowning scenario associated with the interface screenshot shown in Fig. 2 and the debriefing excerpt shown in Table 1. The scenario starts when the observer reads the dispatch information:

*You and your partner are working in a suburban EMS service. You are dispatched to a single-family home for a child drowning. It is 19:30 h and the air temperature is 87 °F. From the scene you are 11 min to a level 2 trauma center and 16 min by air to a level 1 pediatric trauma center.*

### 4.1 How MedDbriefer Generates Post-scenario Debriefings

In addition to the scenario event log (EL), each analysis phase uses two other types of data: the assessment hierarchy (AH) and the management hierarchy (MH). The AH is a downward branching tree whose parent node is the goal of completing a full patient assessment and branches are assessment phases and subphases. Figure 2 (left) shows the top two levels of the assessment hierarchy. Lower levels are displayed when the observer selects a menu item. For example, Fig. 2 shows the checklist that would appear when the observer selects *Breathing* in the *Primary Survey* menu.

Like the assessment hierarchy, the management hierarchy is a downward branching tree whose parent node is the goal of managing the clinical problems identified during patient assessment, children are separate problems (e.g., severe bleeding, hypovolemic shock), and grandchildren are interventions necessary to address these problems, including appropriate alternatives. For example, in the near-drowning scenario, the main management goals are to control the patient's obstructed airway and compromised breathing. Managing the child's airway requires suctioning and, eventually, intubation.

***Analysis Phase 1: Interpreting the Event Log.*** During the first phase of analysis, observed events in the EL are interpreted by comparing them to two models: the expected patient assessment actions specified in the AH and solutions to clinical problems specified by domain experts, represented in the MH. In addition, the system scores any responses to the observer's requests for additional details (e.g., Table 1, ID 15). Interventions (the leaf nodes) in the MH, are designated as either "required" or "optional" and there may be more than one acceptable alternative for required interventions. Interventions that are not part of any solution are designated as "not indicated."

There is usually a simple one-to-one mapping between assessment actions in the EL and the AH, and between interventions in the EL and the lowest levels and leaf nodes in the MH. The analysis system picks the solution path that best fits the EL. By associating events in the EL with items in the AH and the MH, the system gains knowledge about the possible role of each event, such as what to expect some time before or after a particular event and the purpose of that event. This information facilitates recognition of assessment sections and management goals that may not have been completed during one contiguous time frame—for example, the student interrupted an assessment section to start a different one and returned to the interrupted section later. It is also used as part of checking temporal constraints in the second analysis phase and organizing the final debriefing presentation in the third phase, as described presently.

The AI in Analysis Phase 1 is this matching process—a search to find the solution path that best explains the events logged. Similar approaches have been used in other intelligent tutoring systems [16, 17]—that is, generate solutions and do plan recognition by matching observations of what the student did to possible solutions [18].

***Analysis Phase 2: Applying temporal constraints.*** Some interventions must be performed in an expected order to be effective, whereas timing is less critical for other interventions. For example, in the near-drowning scenario, it is important to suction the child's airway to clear it before oxygenating and ventilating him. We represent temporal constraints as decision rules and use these rules to assess the ordering of actions recorded in the EL. For example, Table 1 (ID 20) illustrates a temporal constraint violation. The student checked the unconscious patient's pulse late. Temporal representations and constraints, and constraints in general, are part of problem solving and plan recognition and thus are important in reasoning [e.g., 19, 20].

***Analysis Phase 3: Identifying and Marking Missing Actions.*** In the final phase of analysis, missing actions are identified and inserted in the section of the annotated EL in which they best fit and are assigned a status of "missing." The suggested orderings implied by the AH and MH are utilized so that missing actions are inserted in the annotated log where they are inferred to be most appropriate. The insertion heuristic first tries to locate other events related to the same assessment phase or management goal and inserts the missing one relative to the ordering specified in the AH or MH. If a management goal is missing entirely from the student's solution, the missing intervention is inserted at the end of the assessment section in which the MH indicated it should appear. For example, if the student doesn't check the patient's pulse at all, as opposed to checking it late, "checks pulse" would be inserted in the *Primary Survey/Circulation* section of the debriefing narrative and tagged as a "missing assessment step," with a red X (e.g., Table 1, line 17). Missing interventions are likewise identified and inserted into the annotated debriefing based on the solutions specified for their management goal in the MH and relative to where they best fit in the student's solution (the EL).

## 4.2 Adapting the Log Analysis System to Vary the Timing of Feedback

Most complex tasks can be divided into subtasks, each with a goal, possible subgoals, and actions to achieve these (sub)goals. For example, the assessment hierarchy shown in Fig. 2 (left) represents the goal structure for managing a trauma patient during prehospital emergency care. Its subtasks include performing a *Primary Survey*, *History Taking*, *Secondary Survey*, etc., referred to herein as "assessment phases." Phases can be subdivided into subphases and their associated actions—for example, *Check Breathing* is a subphase of the *Primary Survey*, whose leaf node actions include checking the patient's breathing rate, rhythm, and quality (Fig. 2, center).

This hierarchical goal structure can be used to specify when an automated simulation system should initiate within-scenario debriefings. Transitions between scenario phases offer natural assessment "checkpoints"—for example, when the student shifts focus away from the *Primary Survey.* As illustrated in the examples discussed previously (Tables 1–2), students often leave a phase prematurely, before conducting all necessary assessment actions and interventions. MedDbriefer's log analysis system can detect phase transitions because each assessment action is associated with only one phase or subphase. For example, if the student had been performing actions that belong to the *Primary Survey's* branch of the AH and then performs actions that belong to the *Secondary Survey's* branch (e.g., checking the patient's abdomen for distension), the system can infer that the student considers the *Primary Survey* completed (although it may not be), analyze the event log segment that includes *Primary Survey* actions, and initiate a within-scenario debriefing if it detects errors.

MedDbriefer's log analysis system could be modified to enable it to dynamically apply similar rules and procedures to the log segment that corresponds to a phase that the student has shifted focus away from (perhaps prematurely) as the system currently uses to retrospectively analyze the entire log, as described in Sect. 4.1. Specifically, the system would compare the student's plan for the corresponding (sub)phase with an expert plan for that (sub)phase, searching for missing actions, temporal constraint violations, and incorrectly performed interventions (e.g., see Table 1). User testing will enable us to determine what adjustments to the current log analysis procedure, additional decision rules, etc. are needed to generate within-scenario debriefings.

In future randomized trials, we plan to compare different ways of timing feedback delivery in MedDbriefer, keeping feedback content constant across conditions. At this writing, we are examining our corpus of human facilitated EMS scenarios to gain insight into the types of errors that trigger within-scenario debriefings and how experienced simulation facilitators parcel feedback between these discussions and post-scenario debriefings. To our knowledge, these questions have not yet been investigated. Initial corpus analysis suggests that facilitators tend to keep within-scenario pauses brief, focused on keeping students on track towards a successful solution (e.g., Table 2). For example, instead of addressing every assessment action that a team leader skipped, human facilitators tend to focus on those that would have yielded significant findings in the current scenario (e.g., checking the patient's pulse would have indicated an abnormal heart rate). Similarly, facilitators focus feedback on missing critical, life-saving interventions, not less critical interventions (e.g., dressing minor wounds). We plan to emulate this "focused feedback" behavior in MedDbriefer. Ultimately, a more adaptive system will assess students' performance and gradually address less critical errors after the student consistently and correctly performs critical interventions.

To keep within-scenario debriefings as brief as possible and encourage student self-regulation, we plan to have the system issue feedback in increasingly directive doses. For example, if the log analysis system detects that a student left the *Primary Survey* prematurely—such as advancing to the *Secondary Survey* without first managing the patient's difficulty breathing—the observer would be cued to click on the Feedback button. This would invoke audio-recorded feedback, to preserve the peer observer's role as a simulation assistant, not an instructor. Initial feedback would offer a high-level reminder of what the *Primary Survey* entails, for example: "Make sure that you have fully assessed the patient's airway, breathing, and circulation and managed any problems before you move onto the focused, Secondary Survey." If the student then checks breathing but does not oxygenate and ventilate the patient, the next level of feedback would prompt the student to interpret his findings, as the facilitator does in the example shown in Table 2 (lines 1 and 3), for example: "What do you know about this patient?" If the student still does not manage the patient's breathing, the system would interpret significant findings and tell the student what to do but not how to do it, for example: "You checked the patient's breathing and found it to be slow, with gurgling. You should manage his breathing." Finally, if the student still does not ventilate and oxygenate the patient, feedback would specify what the student should do, for example: "The patient's bradypnea [slow breath rate] and gurgling should have prompted you to administer oxygen and perform bag-valve mask ventilation, or another type of ventilatory support. Perform BVM ventilation with high flow oxygen at this time."

In a randomized trial to compare the effectiveness of within-scenario debriefing, post-scenario debriefing, and distributed debriefing, the within-scenario condition would present increasingly directive feedback, as illustrated in the previous paragraph. Some within-scenario debriefings might elaborate on this basic feedback. Referring to the previous example, a possible elaboration would be: "Always check BVM compliance. If relevant vital signs do not improve or ventilations do not seem to be working, reassess the patient's head position (nose tilted upright), body position (thorax elevated) and ensure a proper BVM seal." The distributed debriefing condition would provide the same increasingly directive feedback as within-scenario debriefings but defer any elaboration until the post-scenario debriefing. The post-scenario debriefing condition would summarize the information that unfolds through the within-scenario sequence and include any elaborated feedback, entirely after the scenario ends.

## 5 Conclusion

The debate concerning the timing of feedback delivery during simulation-based training echoes the well-documented, unresolved problem in instructional science known as the assistance dilemma: "...how, when, and if support should be given to learners during training" [8, p. 442]. Most research on feedback timing during simulation focuses on technical skills training (i.e., procedural, motor, and psychomotor skills) [e.g., 3, 4, 8, 21]. Studies typically compare the effectiveness of *concurrent feedback* versus *terminal feedback* for initial skill acquisition and retention. Concurrent feedback takes place while a task or action is in progress, while terminal feedback takes place after a task/action, with variable delay. Due to mixed results, these studies have yielded few guidelines on timing feedback delivery for technical skills training [4]. Nonetheless, they are important for having uncovered factors that can moderate the effectiveness of feedback delivery, such as skill level, type of feedback (e.g., outcome vs. process), training context, and outcome measures (e.g., user acceptance vs. performance gains).

In contrast to the abundant research on feedback for technical skills training, few studies have investigated feedback timing in scenario-based training [9]. Scenarios challenge students to apply technical and non-technical skills (e.g., clinical decision making and team coordination). Echoing the distinction between concurrent and terminal feedback, two studies compared within-scenario with post-scenario debriefings during human guided clinical simulations [7, 9]. Their primary aim was to test the common belief that students would find within-scenario feedback disruptive. Both studies found no between-condition differences for user satisfaction, as measured by survey. Unfortunately, due to methodological limitations that the study authors acknowledge (e.g., lack of an objective measure of learning in [7]; lack of a baseline measure of performance in

[9]), these studies do not indicate whether within-scenario or post-scenario debriefings are more effective for improving students' clinical knowledge and scenario performance, regarding technical and non-technical skills.

To our knowledge, no research to date has examined the effectiveness of distributing feedback across within-scenario and post-scenario debriefings, which we observed to be the norm for human facilitated EMS training scenarios (e.g., Table 2). Future research is needed to compare alternative ways of timing feedback delivery during scenario-based training in various domains—that is, within-scenario, post-scenario, and/or distributed debriefings. These studies should investigate gains in students' knowledge, technical and non-technical skills, as well as user satisfaction. We expect that findings will be moderated by the same factors that moderate the effectiveness of feedback timing for technical skills training. This paper and our prior work [e.g., 10] illustrate how computer-based simulation systems like MedDbriefer can serve as a research platform to investigate feedback delivery and other aspects of simulation-based training.

**Acknowledgements.** This research is supported by grant 2016018 from the National Science Foundation. The ideas and opinions expressed are those of the authors and do not necessarily represent the views of the NSF. We thank Audrey Aronis, John Gallagher, Priya Gupta, Karen Kornblum, Emily Miller, Lily Nong, Collin O'Connor, Erin O'Meara, Thomas Platt, Stuart Prunty, Samuel Seitz, Emma Sennott, Keith Singleton, Zachary Smith, Marideth Tokarsky, Jingyi Xiong, and Tiffany Yang for their contributions.

## References

1. Cook, D.A., et al.: Technology-enhanced simulation for health professions education: a systematic review and meta-analysis. JAMA **306**(9), 978–988 (2011). https://doi.org/10.1001/jama.2011.1234
2. Cheng, A., et al.: Debriefing: the state of the art and science in healthcare simulation. In: Healthcare Simulation Education: Evidence, Theory and Practice, pp. 158–164 (2017). https://doi.org/10.1002/9781119061656.ch21
3. Hatala, R., et al.: Feedback for simulation-based procedural skills training: a meta-analysis and critical narrative synthesis. Adv. Health Sci. Educ. **19**(2), 251–272 (2014). https://doi.org/10.1007/s10459-013-9462-8
4. Wijewickrema, S., et al.: Feedback techniques in computer-based simulation training: a survey. arXiv preprint arXiv:1705.04683 (2017). https://doi.org/10.48550/arXiv.1705.04683
5. Oermann, M.H., et al.: Advantages and barriers to use of HeartCode BLS with voice advisory manikins for teaching nursing students. Int. J. Nurs. Educ. Sch. **7**(1) (2010). https://doi.org/10.2202/1548-923X.1949
6. Oermann, M.H., et al.: HeartCode BLS with voice assisted manikin for teaching nursing students: preliminary results. Nurs. Educ. Perspect. **31**(5), 303–308 (2010). https://pubmed.ncbi.nlm.nih.gov/21086869/. PMID: 21086869
7. Van Heukelom, J.N., Begaz, T., Treat, R.: Comparison of post simulation debriefing versus in-simulation debriefing in medical simulation. Simul. Healthcare **5**(2), 91–97 (2010). https://doi.org/10.1097/SIH.0b013e3181be0d17
8. Tullis, J.G., Goldstone, R.L., Hanson, A.J.: Scheduling scaffolding: the extent and arrangement of assistance during training impacts test performance. J. Mot. Behav. **47**(5), 442–452 (2015). https://doi.org/10.1080/00222895.2015.1008686

9. Schober, P., et al.: Effects of post-scenario debriefing versus stop-and-go debriefing in medical simulation training on skill acquisition and learning experience: a randomized controlled trial. BMC Med. Educ. **19**(1), 1–7 (2019). https://doi.org/10.1186/s12909-019-1772-y
10. Katz, S., et al.: MedDbriefer: a debriefing research platform and tool to support peer-led simulation-based training in healthcare. In: Proceedings of the 17th International Conference of the Learning Sciences—ICLS (2023). https://par.nsf.gov/biblio/10443688
11. Katz, S., et al.: Debriefings on prehospital care scenarios in MedDbriefer—a tool to support peer learning. In: Kabassi, K., Mylonas, P., Caro, J. (eds) NiDS 2023. LNNS, vol. 783, pp. 102–113. Springer, Cham (2023). https://doi.org/10.1007/978-3-031-44097-7_10
12. Katz, S., et al.: Comparing alternative approaches to debriefing in a tool to support peer-led simulation-based training. In: Crossley, S., Popescu, E. (eds.) ITS 2022. LNCS, vol. 13284, pp. 88–94. Springer, Cham (2022). https://doi.org/10.1007/978-3-031-09680-8_8
13. McKenna, K.D., et al.: Simulation use in paramedic education research (SUPER): a descriptive study. Prehosp. Emerg. Care **19**(3), 432–440 (2015). https://doi.org/10.3109/10903127.2014.995845
14. Haraldseid, C., Aase, K.: Variability among groups of nursing students' utilization of a technological learning tool for clinical skills training: an observational study. J. Nurs. Educ. Pract. **7**(7), 66–76 (2017). https://doi.org/10.5430/jnep.v7n7p66
15. Rencic, J., Trowbridge Jr., R.L., Fagan, M., Szauter, K., Durning, S.: Clinical reasoning education at US medical schools: results from a national survey of internal medicine clerkship directors. J. Gen. Intern. Med. **32**(11), 1242–1246 (2017). https://doi.org/10.1007/s11606-017-4159-y. Epub 2017 Aug 24. PMID: 28840454; PMCID: PMC5653563
16. Koedinger, K.R., Corbett, A.: Cognitive tutors: technology bringing learning sciences to the classroom. In: Sawyer, R.K. (ed.) The Cambridge Handbook of: The Learning Sciences, pp. 61–77. Cambridge University Press (2006). https://www.researchgate.net/publication/255519934_Cognitive_Tutors_Technology_Bringing_Learning_Science_to_the_Classroom
17. Chu, Y.-S., et al.: Implementation of a model-tracing-based learning diagnosis system to promote elementary students' learning in mathematics. J. Educ. Technol. Soc. **17**(2), 347–357 (2014). https://www.jstor.org/stable/jeductechsoci.17.2.347
18. Carberry, S.: Techniques for plan recognition. User Model. User-Adap. Inter. **11**, 31–48 (2001). https://doi.org/10.1023/A:1011118925938
19. Allen, J.F.: Towards a general theory of action and time. Artif. Intell. **23**(2), 123–154 (1984). https://doi.org/10.1016/0004-3702(84)90008-0
20. Köckemann, U., Karlsson, L.: Configuration planning with temporal constraints. In: Proceedings of the AAAI Conference on Artificial Intelligence (2017). https://doi.org/10.1609/aaai.v31i1.11186
21. Cheng, A., et al.: Debriefing for technology-enhanced simulation: a systematic review and meta-analysis. Med. Educ. **48**(7), 657–666 (2014). https://doi.org/10.1111/medu.12432

# Keeping Humans in the Loop: LLM Supported Oral Examinations

Ansgar Fehnker(✉) and Luke Glover

Macquarie University, Sydney, Australia
ansgar.fehnker@mq.edu.au

**Abstract.** This paper investigates the use of generative AI to prepare oral examinations. The aim is to support oral exams regardless of whether the student uses generative AI. Oral exams have long been viewed as inefficient, subjective, or unfair. Generative AI has the potential to mitigate some of these concerns. This paper reports on a prototype developed to prepare vivas for essays in software engineering. This position paper discusses underlying principles, a proposed design and workflow, as well as limitations on both the technology and its use.

**Keywords:** Large-Language-Models · examinations · oral · essays

## 1 Introduction

Oral examinations, often called viva or viva voce, are widely used for assessment in various educational settings such as lab sessions, tutorials, doctoral defences, and certification or bar exams. This paper examines vivas as supplements to writing assessments, especially in technical degrees like software engineering.

Written assignments are significant in engineering education. Bushwell et al. [2] found that 86% of engineering instructors incorporate writing assignments to prepare students for writing in a professional context. The Seoul Accord [14] emphasises graduates' need to "communicate effectively with the computing community and with society at large about complex computing activities". Similarly, the SWEBOK v3.0 [1] underscores the importance of the ability to generate written artefacts, including reports, documentation, and justifications.

Large language models (LLMs) can author human-like text on a wide range of topics, including written assessments. In a 2023 survey, 30% of US college students reported using essay-generating software [3]. Educational institutions responded, from outright banning their use to accepting or even promoting the responsible use of generative AI. The Australian government agency TESQA, tasked with quality assurance in higher education, advises that trustworthy assessment will require assessments of different types [9]. Pearce and Chiavaroli [13] suggest"rehabilitating" oral exams and vivas for this purpose.

This paper addresses the research question: How to build a system using generative AI to generate questions for vivas that supplement written assessments. The paper will first discuss vivas as an assessment type, and large language models in Sect. 2, the design and implementation in Sect. 3, and observations from experiments in Sect. 4.


A. Sifaleras and F. Lin (Eds.): ITS 2024, LNCS 14798, pp. 312–319, 2024.
https://doi.org/10.1007/978-3-031-63028-6_25

## 2 Preliminaries

*Generative artificial intelligence* is an umbrella term for AI systems capable of creating content based on user prompts, such as images, audio, and text. *Large language model* (LLM) is a similarly broad term for the application of large-scale neural networks to natural language processing problems, encompassing tasks from spelling and grammar correction to automatic sentiment analysis and machine translation [11].

The release of OpenAI's chatbot, powered by GPT-3.5 and GPT-4, showcased their ability to perform on academic and professional exams, demonstrating high accuracy and human-like responses. It was reported that GPT-4 was able to perform within the 90th percentile of human test takers for several academic and professional level exams including the Uniform Bar Exam, the Law School Admission Test (LSAT), several Scholastic Aptitude Test (SAT) exams, and several Advanced Placement (AP) exams [12]. The most commonly mentioned risks include the production of offensive content, the reproduction of copyrighted content, and the spread of false information [4]. OpenAI recommends avoiding "high-stakes uses" of GPT4 altogether because of hallucinations [12,15].

Besides risks, the use of LLMs in education also offers opportunities. They have been used, for example, to explain code snippets in detail [10], or to generate quizzes and example problems based on existing educational material [8].

*Oral examinations and vivas* serve various purposes across different contexts. Joughin outlined six key dimensions [6,7], which we'll use to frame the intended use of our prototype tool and inform its workflow.

**Objective** Within our setting, vivas aim to test *knowledge of concepts, theories, and procedures. Integrated practice* plays some role, as practising engineers must regularly orally explain written reports. *Applied problem-solving* plays less of a role, as the problems were solved to write the essay. The viva will not introduce new problems. The vivas will not explicitly assess *interpersonal competence*, such as audience interaction, or *intrapersonal competence*, such as resilience to stress.

**Interaction** While the vivas include an aspect of *presentation* – the student has to present a response to the given questions – the intent is that the examiner will use the answer for a *dialogue*.

**Authenticity** This dimension refers to whether the assessment emulates "real life". While practising graduates will have to explain their written work, as mentioned before, it does usually not appear in a confined exam setting.

**Structure** The *structure* of the vivas that our prototype tool supports, is by construction *semi-structured*. The tool will produce a set of pre-determined and personalised questions. However, the examiner has the opportunity (and the task) to follow up on the answer if necessary.

**Examiners** The *examiners* in the viva will be tutors, lecturers, or other authorised assessors. While conceivable, the prototype is not targeted at self-assessment or peer assessment.

**Orality** The last dimension is *orality*. As mentioned, the prototype suggests viva questions based on a written essay. This means that *orality is secondary*, while the written document is the primary artefact of assessment.

The discussion so far does not address why vivas are increasingly used alongside written assessments, especially in the context of generative AI. Pearce and Chiavaroli, recommend viva to ensure the trustworthiness of written assessments [13]. They differentiate between *unassisted* and *assisted assessments*. The former prohibits explicitly the use of (certain) external tools, while the second will (explicitly) permit their use. For our prototype, we assume that an assignment may be assisted (even if not explicitly stated) and that the focus is to assess the student's *intellectual ownership* of the written report.

Our goal is not to assess the complete depth of a student's knowledge or definitively prove the absence of external tools. Instead, we focus on evaluating *intellectual ownership* – which should not be confused with intellectual property – using three key criteria: (1) *Familiarity*: Is the student prepared and familiar with the text as written? (2) *Discussion Proficiency*: Can the student engage in a meaningful conversation about the concepts as presented in the essay? (3) *Critical Expansion*: Can the student expand upon the essay's content by exploring related ideas and concepts? These criteria could be used as the rubric for the viva, independent of the rubric used for grading the essay, which remains the primary artefact of assessment.

## 3 Design and Implementation

The assumed workflow for the prototype is that all essays are first submitted and downloaded by an assessor, who then uses the tool to generate viva questions ahead of time in a printable format. We assume that the input files are either in PDF or Microsoft Word format.

The application is designed to be modular and model-agnostic, providing wrappers to handle different LLMs. We used GPT-3.5 from OpenAI, GPT-4 from OpenAI, and PaLM 2 from Alphabet (Google) in our application, but others could be used as well. The prototype is a desktop application that uses a bundled web browser for user interfacing, communicating with a back-end component via HTTP. This means the application could potentially be adapted to be a public web app given more development time and if such adaptation is necessary.

All models distinguish between two types of input prompts. PaLM 2's *context* input and the GPT family's *system* input perform the same function and are intended to provide instructions that cannot be overridden by further instructions in the *user* or *test* input. While separating *system* from *user* input is considered best practice, there are reported instances where this protection fails. We furthermore noticed that GPT-3.5 tends to ignore the system prompt in favour of the user prompt. This led to the decision to use the GPT-3.5 user prompt for both the instruction and the essay text itself.

## 4 Experiments and Observations

The aim is to assess an essay with respect to generic criteria for *intellectual ownership*, as described in Sect. 2. We developed a prompt that creates five questions for a viva, independently from the rubric used for the essay, which will be marked separately. This section illustrates the process using a student essay, written by a student applying to enrol in a software engineering program.

The first prompt we tried was simply "`Generate 5 questions about the essay text.`" which resulted for GPT3.5 in the suggested following questions:

> 1. What is the role of software engineering in the development of software?
> 2. Why is software engineering needed?
> 3. What is the author's reason for applying to Georgia Tech's Computer Science program?
> 4. What is the field of study that the author finds most interesting within engineering?
> 5. What are some of the skills and interests of the author in the field of Computer Engineering?

The initial prompt was iteratively refined, based on the following observations: The question should address the author of the essay. Short and general questions should be avoided, and the questions should refer to the text of the essay. The question may use quotes to refer to the text, however, quoting phrases with poor word choice or poor grammar should be avoided. The questions should be pitched at different levels, from recall to further exploring ideas present in the essay. This led to the prompt depicted in Table 1. Interestingly, the prompt resembles instructions that could be given to a human examiner before a viva.

Table 2 depicts the questions generated for the sample essay. PaLM 2's questions are simpler compared to those from the GPT models. Even the probing question (Question 5) is superficial and ambiguous, referring to "your discipline" without specifying old or new. Both GPT models outperform PaLM 2, with GPT-4 producing more specific and tailored questions, even quoting from the source text, unlike GPT-3.5, which struggles with accurate quoting.

While the ability to quote is useful to make questions more specific, we noticed for one of the intermediate prompts, that GPT-4 selected the unusual phrase "the body of the computer" several times. We are concerned that repeating a poorly worded phrase, especially in a quote-unquote style, may be interpreted as an attempt to hone in on a language error. It has been reported that foreign language learners [5] show higher anxiety in an oral exam, and tools that hone in on a mistake, may add to that anxiety.

The quality of the question seems to come with costs, as running all three models will incur costs. Generating questions for a 2500-word essay, as for our example, costs approximately USD 0.25 with GPT-4, but only USD 0.002 with GPT-3.5. Google's PaLM2, which charges per character instead of per token, would charge approximately USD 0.04 per 2500-word essay. Pricing may vary with new models and providers, but it's crucial to consider the significant cost differences between models.

**Table 1.** Chosen System Prompt

```
Context: You are a tutor or teaching assistant for an
undergraduate software engineering course. Students are
required to submit written essays and then participate in a
face-to-face viva where their tutor discusses the essay.

Instruction: For the essay text, generate five (5) questions
that are 2 or 3 sentences in length for the author's viva.

Use phrases such as ``you mentioned'', ``where you said'', or
``in the section'' to refer back to the essay text when
appropriate.

For some of the questions, when referring to a specific
statement in the essay text, directly quote it with quote
marks. Avoid quoting poorly worded phrases unless you are
specifically asking for clarification on the meaning of the
phrase. If you are not directly quoting the text, you can
reword ambiguous or poorly worded statements to make them
clearer.

Questions should gradually progress in difficulty from the
first to the last question. The first two questions (1 and 2)
should be easily answered by all students at a pass level and
require students to recall or clarify the content of the essay.
The third question (3) should be answerable for students at a
credit level and require students to explain in more detail a
point from the essay. The fourth question (4) should be
answerable by students at a distinction level and require the
student to significantly elaborate on a point made in the
essay. The final question (5) should be answerable by students
at a high distinction level, and require the student to explore
new ideas based on but not directly addressed in the essay.
```

## 5 Discussion

The previous sections described the nature of the viva and the technology used to generate questions for three different LLMs. This section reflects on the effect the prototype may have on the disadvantages and risks of vivas. It should be noted that these are early observations, which should be further investigated before such a tool is used at scale.

Wang discusses several shortcomings of vivas, among lack of reliability, standardisation and objectivity [16]. Using LLMs to generate questions mitigates these concerns, as it will standardise how questions are generated. They will be independent from one assessor to the next, or from how tired an assessor is. However, LLMs will not address all concerns, as verbal cues, gender, intonation, or gestures can still influence both the student and the assessor.

Using LLMs to prepare viva questions introduces also risks. The first is that the tool may misunderstand parts of the essay, or create ambiguous questions.

**Table 2.** Model responses for the sample software engineering essay

**GPT-3.5**

1. In the essay, you mentioned that software engineering provides a possibility to develop software with less cost and more reliability. Can you explain how software engineering principles contribute to achieving these goals?

2. You stated that you chose Computer Science as a major because you wanted to learn machine learning and algorithms. Can you elaborate on how these areas are relevant to Computer Engineering and how they can be applied in practice?

3. In the essay, you mentioned the importance of learning how to design memory chips and hardware in Computer Engineering. Could you provide some examples of how this knowledge can be applied in real-world scenarios and the impact it can have on the development of computer systems?

4. You quoted a statistic from bls.gov about the growth rate of careers in Computer Engineering. How do you interpret this statistic in terms of job prospects and the future of the field? What factors do you think contribute to this growth?

5. Towards the end of your essay, you discussed the importance of Cybersecurity and advanced communications. Given the increasing prevalence of cyber threats, how do you envision the role of a Computer Engineer evolving in the context of Cybersecurity? How can software engineering principles be utilized to enhance Cybersecurity measures?

**GPT-4**

1. In the introduction, you mentioned that software engineering provides a possibility to develop software with less cost and more reliability. Can you elaborate on how software engineering principles contribute to this cost-effectiveness and reliability?

2. You mentioned that you chose Computer Science as a major because you wanted to learn machine learning and algorithms. Can you explain how these two areas are integral to your studies and future career in Computer Engineering?

3. In the section where you said, "I find it important to learn how to design memory chips and hardware in Computer Engineering", could you explain why you believe this knowledge is crucial and how it might be applied in real-world scenarios?

4. You quoted from bls.gov stating that the growth rate of careers in the field of Computer Engineering is 6% from 2018 to 2028. How do you interpret this statistic in terms of job opportunities and the future of the field? What factors do you think might be driving this growth?

5. Towards the end of your essay, you touched on the importance of Cybersecurity and advanced communications. Given the increasing prevalence of cyber threats, how do you see the role of a Computer Engineer evolving in the context of Cybersecurity? How might the principles of software engineering be applied to enhance Cybersecurity measures?

**PaLM 2**

1. You mentioned that software engineering is needed to provide a possibility to develop the same software with less cost and more reliability. Can you give an example of a software engineering principle that can be used to achieve this?

2. Why do you want to apply to Georgia Tech's Computer Science program?

3. What are the goals of computer engineering?

4. What are some of the skills that you have that are matched with computer engineering?

5. What are some of the advances in technology in the last 5 years that have altered your discipline?

Although an LLM was used to create the question, the assessor still retains the responsibility to check their validity.

Wang identified as a risk that assessors may focus on their preferred content [16]. While the use of an LLM mitigates this risk, we now rely on the assessor being able to assess any topic the LLM suggests. Assessors may be less accurate when the LLM selects a topic that is not in their focus area.

Another risk is that LLMs may be unaware of social norms. We encountered an example where the LLMs repeatedly quoted a language error, with the request for clarification. This can be a legitimate question, but it can also be easily misunderstood as unnecessarily confronting. A related risk, that needs to be further evaluated, is that we have to ensure that the level of the questions is not dependent on the quality of the writing, and whether grammar or word choice influences the viva questions.

The prototype, coupled with human assessors, mitigates some risks by limiting individual assessor influence while allowing assessors to counter LLM-related risks. To do this effectively, assessors should be trained in the use of the tools, and be made aware of their limitations and risks.

## 6 Conclusion

This paper presents a prototype tool that uses LLMs to prepare viva questions. This tool is not just a response to the increased use of generative AI. The aim is to mitigate risks of vivas, reducing the workload, while making the assessment more personal and tailored to the student. This paper focuses on vivas that supplement written essays and defines criteria that the viva aims to assess. It is not a replacement for marking the essay itself, but a tool to assess *intellectual ownership* as a supplementary viva.

The prototype currently exists as a desktop application but should be turned into a web application for use in a variety of units. At present, the tool employs a single generic prompt. Exploration of user-configurable prompts is planned, with LLMs potentially generating prompts from assessment details, learning outcomes, or model answers.

The current tool was developed for essays in the field of software engineering and IT. An obvious future extension would be support for coding assessments. Other uses may include combining it with invigilated written exams that ask students to reflect on their essays given generated questions. The prototype could also be used to prep students for vivas, to reduce exam anxiety, and as another way to engage with the material.

It should also be noted that LLMs are a very dynamic field. The field of prompt engineering is developing quickly, and the models used in this paper have been superseded in the meantime. The preview of GPT4-turbo, for example, has a larger token limit, allows fine-tuning, runs faster, and is cheaper than GPT-4. It can return a seed, which makes it possible to run repeat experiments. The upcoming developments and improvements, however, will not undermine the use of LLMs in teaching; they will likely make the approach presented in this paper more efficient and effective.

**Acknowledgements.** We like to thank Cameron Edmond, Malcolm Ryan, Michael Johnson and Kate Stefanov for helpful feedback on our prototype.

## References

1. Bourque, P., Fairley, R.E.: Guide to the software engineering body of knowledge, version 3.0. IEEE Computer Society (2014). https://www.swebok.org
2. Buswell, N.T., Jesiek, B.K., Troy, C.D., Essig, R.R., Boyd, J.: Engineering instructors on writing: perceptions, practices, and needs. IEEE Trans. Prof. Commun. **62**(1), 55–74 (2019). https://doi.org/10.1109/TPC.2019.2893392
3. Chan, C.K.Y.: A comprehensive AI policy education framework for university teaching and learning. Int. J. Educ. Technol. High. Educ. **20**(1), 38 (2023). https://doi.org/10.1186/s41239-023-00408-3
4. Dwivedi, Y.K., Kshetri, N., et al.: So what if ChatGPT wrote it? Int. J. Inf. Manage. **71**, 102642 (2023). https://doi.org/10.1016/j.ijinfomgt.2023.102642
5. Hewitt, E., Stephenson, J.: Foreign language anxiety and oral exam performance: a replication of Phillips's MLJ study. Mod. Lang. J. **96**(2), 170–189 (2012)
6. Joughin, G.: Dimensions of oral assessment. Assess. Eval. High. Educ. **23**(4), 367–378 (1998). https://doi.org/10.1080/0260293980230404
7. Joughin, G.: A Short Guide to Oral Assessment. Leeds Met Press in Association with University of Wollongong (2010)
8. Kohnke, L., Moorhouse, B.L., Zou, D.: ChatGPT for language teaching and learning. RELC J. **54**(2), 537–550 (2023). https://doi.org/10.1177/00336882231162868
9. Lodge, J.M., Howard, S., Bearman, M., et al.: Assessment reform for the age of artificial intelligence. TEQSA (2023)
10. MacNeil, S., Tran, A., Mogil, D., Bernstein, S., Ross, E., Huang, Z.: Generating diverse code explanations using the GPT-3 large language model. In: Proceedings of the 2022 ACM Conference on International Computing Education Research-Volume 2, ICER 2022, August 2022, pp. 37–39. ACM, New York (2022). https://doi.org/10.1145/3501709.3544280
11. Nadkarni, P.M., Ohno-Machado, L., Chapman, W.W.: Natural language processing: an introduction. J. Am. Med. Inform. Assoc. **18**(5), 544–551 (2011). https://doi.org/10.1136/amiajnl-2011-000464
12. OpenAI: GPT-4 Technical Report. Technical report, OpenAI, March 2023. https://doi.org/10.48550/arXiv.2303.08774
13. Pearce, J., Chiavaroli, N.: Rethinking assessment in response to generative artificial intelligence. Med. Educ. **57**(10), 889–891 (2023). https://doi.org/10.1111/medu.15092
14. Seoul Accord Secretariat: The Seoul Accord (2022). https://www.seoulaccord.org/
15. Shen, Y., et al.: ChatGPT and other large language models are double-edged swords. Radiology **307**(2), e230163 (2023). https://doi.org/10.1148/radiol.230163
16. Wang, L., et al.: Structured oral examination as an effective assessment tool in lab-based physiology learning sessions. Adv. Physiol. Educ. **44**(3), 453–458 (2020). https://doi.org/10.1152/advan.00059.2020

# Generating Learning Sequences Using Contextual Bandit Algorithms

Le Minh Duc Nguyen, Fuhua Lin(✉), and Maiga Chang

Athabasca University, 1 University Dr, Athabasca T9S 3A3, Canada
lnguyen12@learn.athabascau.ca, {oscarl,magaic}@athabascau.ca

**Abstract.** Personalized learning paths have become a promising instructional strategy in online learning, as they can cater to individual learners' needs and preferences. However, creating effective personalized learning paths is a complex task due to the high degree of variability in learners' characteristics, behaviors, and learning contexts. Existing recommendation methods do not adequately address this challenge, as they do not work effectively in dynamic environments. This paper tries to address this gap by proposing a personalized learning path recommendation system using a contextual multi-armed bandit approach to offer a student an optimal learning sequence and provide the student with a modified sequence when re-planning is required.

**Keywords:** Multi-Armed bandit (MAB) algorithms · knowledge components (KC) · adaptive learning · exploration and exploitation · personalized learning

## 1 Introduction

The effectiveness of traditional one-size-fits-all approaches to course designing has been a subject of debate due to their limited ability to address the diverse needs and interests of learners. However, the advent of personalized learning has introduced a transformative paradigm that can tailors instruction to match the unique characteristics of each learner. This approach acknowledges the inherent differences among learners, including their backgrounds, learning strategies, and preferences, emphasizing the importance of providing personalized learning paths to help them achieve their learning goals more efficiently. Personalized learning involves the customization of learning trajectories, which consist of carefully selected sequences of learning activities and resources, designed to facilitate learners in attaining their specific educational goals [1].These tailored trajectories act as individualized roadmaps, guiding learners through a set of activities that have been specifically adapted to address their distinct needs and aspirations. Achieving this level of customization in learning trajectories requires an in-depth understanding of learners' characteristics, encompassing their prior knowledge, areas of interest, and preferred modalities of learning, in order to effectively improve the learning experience and optimize learning outcomes[2].

Our research proposes a contextual multi-armed bandit (MAB) approach for personalized learning path recommendation in the domain of online education. The contextual


A. Sifaleras and F. Lin (Eds.): ITS 2024, LNCS 14798, pp. 320–329, 2024.
https://doi.org/10.1007/978-3-031-63028-6_26

bandits approach, also referred to as associative Reinforcement Learning[3], is an iterative process. An agent at every time step receives a context vector generated by the environment and selects an option from the set of choices (which are referred to as "arm"). Each selected arm is associated with a stochastic reward that the environment reveals to the agent. The primary objective is for the agent to optimize its acquired rewards over the long term by leveraging the historical data of its previous actions.

We structure our paper into the following sections: Related Work (Sect. 2 to discuss recent related research of personalized learning), Research Problem (Sect. 3 to define a formalized research problem), Methodology (Sect. 4 to describe the methods in our research), Proposed Algorithm (Sect. 5 to propose algorithms), Experiment &Simulation (Sect. 6), and Conclusion (Sect. 7).

## 2 Related Work

The field of personalized learning paths has been extensively researched in recent years. Various approaches have been proposed to personalize learning paths based on individual learners' characteristics, behaviors, and learning contexts. According to [4], those approaches can be categorized into two main types: Course Generation and Course Sequence. Course Generation (CG) approaches involve generating and recommending the entire learning path to a user in a single recommendation. In this approach, the user is presented with a complete set of learning content and activities to follow to learn a course. The evaluation of the learning path effectiveness occurs only after the completion of the entire path, rather than at each step along the way. In CG approaches, Shi et al.[5] proposed a graph traversal algorithm in their paper to generate all paths considering the students' learning objectives and learning need and recommending the one with the highest score. Niknam et al. [6] proposed Ant Colony Optimization algorithm, combined with Fuzzy C-Mean Cluster algorithm to select a path for a cluster of learners based on their prior knowledge. While Course Generation methods are commonly used by researchers to generate personalized learning paths, they are associated with several limitations. One of the major drawbacks of this approach is that it often fails to account for changes that may occur during the learning process, such as a user's evolving skills, interests, or preferences. Consequently, learners may be at risk of receiving an inappropriate or unmanageable learning path, leading to inefficiencies or disengagement. Another challenge is the potential for CG methods to become slow when presented with a large amount of data, such as a high volume of learning objects or user profiles. This sluggishness can negatively impact the user experience, as it may take too long to generate a personalized learning path or respond to the learner's needs in a timely manner. In contrast to the CG approach, Course Sequence (CS) methods suggest personalized learning paths to users one step at a time, considering their current progress and performance. This method allows for ongoing evaluation and adaptation of the learning path, ensuring that users are not overwhelmed by information and can focus on mastering one concept at a time. By dynamically adjusting the learning path as a user progresses, CS methods are better able to accommodate changes in users' performance and adapt to their unique learning needs. Xu et al. [7] proposed Naïve Bayes algorithm, combined with KNN to recommend an optimized learning objective to a student. Cai et al. [8]

proposed a Reinforcement Learning based method, combined with Neural Network and Knowledge Tracing Model (KTM) to recommend the most suitable learning path based on the specific knowledge points and the individual learner's needs throughout the entire learning journey. The study of Cai et al. (2019), however, posts some limitations [8]. It does not address dependencies and constraints among learning modules. In addition, the proposed method is not efficient in online learning, as the reinforcement-learning model can only be trained after the training of the knowledge tracing model is completed. Lastly, there is no handling of altering or adjusting the recommended learning path once required.

Although the field of learning path personalization has seen significant attention from researchers, a number of challenges and limitations still persist. First and foremost, it is essential to consider the learners' time constraints when designing personalized learning paths. Time is a valuable resource for learners, and an effective learning path personalization method should consider learners' schedules to optimize their learning outcomes. Another challenge in learning path personalization is scalability. Designing methods that can handle large-scale datasets is a complex problem that has only been addressed by a few studies in the literature. Scalability is critical to the success of personalized learning, as the method must be able to efficiently process and respond to large amounts of data to maintain learners' engagement. In addition, learners' profiles should be regularly updated to reflect changes in their responses and learning progress. This requires the learning path personalization method to adapt to the learners' changing needs and provide them with the most appropriate learning content. Evaluation is also a significant challenge in learning path personalization methods. The lack of a general evaluation framework makes it difficult to compare different methods, and a reliable evaluation framework should include guidelines for data sources and principles to ensure a consistent and accurate evaluation. The ability to update the learning sequence actively and dynamically, when one or more student's surrounding factors alter is another challenge. Finally, recommender systems play a crucial role in adaptive learning by predicting student preferences. However, they face the exploration-exploitation dilemma when making recommendations. They must balance exploiting their knowledge about the content chosen by previous students with exploring new materials that may be better suited to the current student's needs.

Reinforcement learning (RL) has been utilized to create effective and adaptable pedagogical policies. Recently, there has been a growing interest in the use of MAB algorithms for adaptive learning. MAB algorithms fall under the broader category of RL and are named after the problem faced by a gambler who must decide which arm of a K-slot machine to pull in order to maximize their total reward in a series of trials. These algorithms can navigate exploration-exploitation trade-offs and make sequential decisions under uncertain conditions. They have been employed in real-world applications to solve optimization problems, such as experimental design and website optimization. As MAB algorithms actively select which data to receive and analyze in real-time, they lend themselves naturally to the problem of eliciting adaptive sequences of content and assessment in adaptive learning environments [9]. The multi-armed bandit framework has the potential to address the challenge faced by many applications when no prior information is available, especially for large-scale recommender systems. Their continuous exploration approach can also help address the cold start problem in recommender systems.

Although some initial, isolated, or purely theoretical research has been conducted on using MAB to elicit sequences for adaptive learning, there are still many questions that need to be answered. For example, due to the complexity of adaptive learning, standard MAB models cannot be directly applied. When an MAB-based adaptive engine makes sequential decisions to optimize learning, how does it define rewards? Which metrics should be optimized? Which algorithm of the MAB family in what parameter settings, would be best for a particular sequencing problem in adaptive online learning?

To our knowledge, none of the proposed algorithms have adequately addressed the challenges associated with the learning sequence recommendation problem. Another consideration is the contextual bandit algorithm, which is an extension of the MAB approach used to discover which actions are effective in specific contexts. Xu et al. [10] used a contextual bandit approach to recommend entire sequences of courses within a program, rather than sequencing knowledge components in an online course. In their work, courses were planning elements with fixed completion times. The work did not address knowledge component sequencing within individual courses. Additionally, after recommending a whole sequence to complete a degree, the sequence could not be altered. We recognize that one of the drawbacks of recommending an entire KC learning path to a learner is that it ignores the learner's actualized learning performance and the context changes that occur during the learning process. As a result, the learner may waste time by receiving a path that may not be optimal.

In the next section, we will formally define the research problem, followed by our proposed methodology and algorithm.

## 3 Research Problems

MAB algorithm is a subset of RL algorithm, and contextual MAB (CMAB) is an extension of the MAB approach where environment contexts are factored in. MAB (or CMAB) approach is different from the general RL approach in that MAB is for solving a stateless Markov Decision Process (MDP) problem, where all the states (observations) are independent, and the agent gets a reward immediately after choosing an action. In order to fit the adaptive sequence learning problem into CMAB approach, we have the option to follow the CG approach (i.e... Generate entire learning path). However, due to the disadvantage of CG approach, we give favors to the CS approach. It is a challenge to creatively model our problem to fit CMAB in the CS approach. Another challenge is that even when our problem is well modelled, the standard CMAB approach does not well support re-planning (i.e., the current recommended learning module failed to fit a student's current competency, and a new different learning module should be recommended). For this challenge, Wacharanwan et al. in their research [11] proposed applying correlation analysis in CMAB approach. It recommends the closest learning path having the highest rank of correlation measurement. However, the approach is not effective as the learning problem is non-stationary [11]. Before we discuss further, we first consider how we are going to model our learning problem.

There are many ways to model a modular content hierarchy. Duval and Hodgins [12] introduced the content hierarchy consisting of 5 levels: Course, Lesson, Learning Object, Raw Content, and Information Object. Nabizadeh et al. in their research paper [4] suggested another level named Topic. Referencing these articles, we modeled our knowledge domain into two levels: Course and Knowledge Component (KC). A course is composed of a few learning units, each learning unit covers a concept. A KC is a learning unit, and a Course is composed by few KCs. Some KCs are the prerequisites in order to learn other KCs. Some KCs can be exchangeable or other KCs.

## 4 Methodologies

We can model a course domain as a KC AND-OR graph where each node in the graph presents a knowledge component. A KC AND-OR graph represents the search space for solving the problem in "Goal". We can define the root node "Goal" as the initial problem and every other node is a sub-problem.

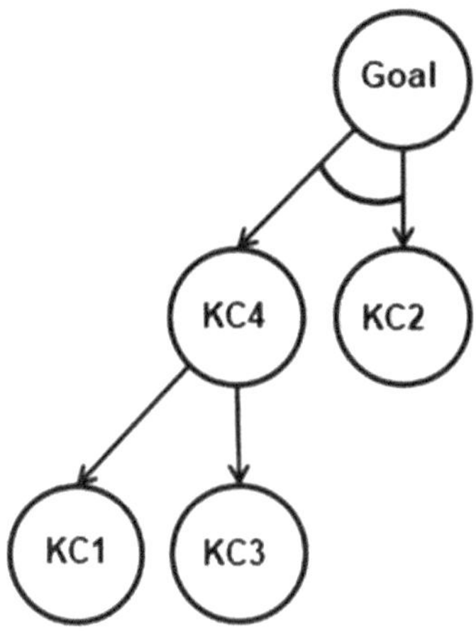


**Fig. 1.** A KC AND-OR graph sample.

In Fig. 1, we use goal-reduction methods to break down the graph:

$$\boldsymbol{GOAL} if \boldsymbol{KC}4 and \boldsymbol{KC}2$$

$$\boldsymbol{KC}4 if \boldsymbol{KC}1 or \boldsymbol{KC}3$$

The KCs are modeled as a knowledge structure in Knowledge Space Theory (KST) [13]. To this end, the domain experts first identify the set of KCs for a course. After that, the domain experts specify the prerequisite relations among the KCs.

A learning path is also called a policy or a learning sequence. Formally, the set of KCs in a course is denoted as $list(KC) = \{KC_1, KC_2, \ldots, KC_n\}$, where $n$ is the total number of the KCs of the course. For example in Fig. 1, the possible learning sequences are

$\{\{KC_1 \rightarrow KC_4 \rightarrow KC_2\}, \{KC_2 \rightarrow KC_1 \rightarrow KC_4\}, \{KC_3 \rightarrow KC_4 \rightarrow KC_2\}, \{KC_2 \rightarrow KC_3 \rightarrow KC_4\}\}$. The contextual multi-armed bandit algorithm is an extension of the classical multi-armed bandit algorithm [14] that considers the context in which the decisions are made. In the CMAB problem, besides the observed rewards, the agent also considers the additional information received about the context to make the decision. The context can be thought of as a set of features that describe the state of the system, and the objective is to learn a policy that maps the context to the best action to take.

## 5 The Proposed Algorithms

We propose a contextual multi-armed bandit algorithm for recommending the next KC for learners to learn based on two types of context information as follows.

- The similar profile, characteristics, and backgrounds of past learners
- The current situation of learners in the course. Current situation of learners can be seen as the current completion status of the KCs

Let's denote $f_g^k$ to be $k$ global features that are included in the first type of context. $f_g^k \in [0, 1]^k$ is a binary feature matrix of fixed dimensionality $k$.

Let's denote $f_a^l$ to be $l$ per-arm (per selection) features that are included in the second type of context. $f_a^l \in [0, 1]^l$ is a binary feature matrix of fixed dimensionality $l$, where $l = 2n$.

Each KC is presented by two binary features: 1- If KC is taken and 2- If KC is completed (i.e., passed/failed).

$1 \leq i \leq n|KC_i = \left[f_{gi}^k; f_{ai}^l\right]$ - KC feature matrix presenting both global features and per-arm features for each of KC (a horizontal concatenating matrix).

There are a fixed number of arms $n$ in CMAB which are equal to the number of KCs (each KC presents an arm). At each time step$t$, there are a number of $n_t \leq n$ possible arms to select. The $n_t$ possible arms are dependent on two factors: 1- the remaining KCs to complete and 2 – possible KCs from the AND-OR graph to take. If the selected arm is completed (i.e., the student passes the selected KC), the agent receives a binary reward of 1; otherwise, 0. Let's denote $r_i^t \in \{0, 1\}$ as the binary reward at time step $t$ for selecting arm i. The KC feature matrix is then updated before the next time step.

The framework that we propose consists of offline and online learning, where offline learning stores the structure of domain model, student database and policy base [2]. On the other hand, online learning is the agent using CMAB algorithm to select the next KC for a learner. Every time a learner puts his/her attempt on a recommended KC, either he/she can complete or cannot complete the KC, the binary reward and the KC features are recorded into the student database. We use the binary classification algorithm proposed by David Cortes [15] as black-box oracles for finding the best policy on observed context and rewards. The contextual Multi-Armed Bandit algorithms have the dilemma of balancing exploration and exploitation. Some methods have been proposed such as Epsilon-Greedy, UCB, or Thompson Sampling. In this research, we compare three methods by simulating CMAB using logistic regression as black-box oracles. However, we need to establish baselines for each method first.

**Algorithm 1**: Epsilon-Greedy

Input probability $p \in (0,1]$, decay rate $d \in (0,1]$, oracle $\hat{f}_{1:n}$

For each successive round t with context $x^t$ do<br>
  With probability (1 – p):<br>
    Select action a = $argmax_n \hat{f}_{1:n}(x^t)$<br>
  Otherwise:<br>
    Select action a uniformly at random from 1 to k<br>
  Update $p := pxd$<br>
  Obtain reward$r_a^t$, Add observation $\{x^t, r_a^t\}$ to history for arm a<br>
  Update oracle $\hat{f}_a$ with its news history

**Algorithm 2**: Bootstrapped-UCB

Input number of re-samples$m$, percentile$p$, oracle $\hat{f}_{1:n,1:m}$

For each successive round t with context $x^t$ do<br>
  For arm $q$ in 1 $ton$ do<br>
    Set $\hat{r}_q^{ucb} = Percentile_q\{\hat{f}_{q,1}(x^t), \ldots, \hat{f}_{q,m}(x^t)\}$<br>
  Select action a = $argmax_q \hat{r}_q^{ucb}$<br>
  Obtain reward$r_a^t$, Add observation $\{x^t, r_a^t\}$ to history for arm a<br>
  For re-sample $s$ in 1 $tom$ do<br>
  Take bootstrapped re-sample $X_s, r_s$ from $X_\alpha, r_\alpha$<br>
  Refit $\hat{f}_{a,s}$ to this re-sample

**Algorithm 3:** Bootstrapped-TS

Input number of re-samples$m$, percentile$p$, oracle $\hat{f}_{1:n,1:m}$

For each successive round t with context $x^t$ do<br>
  For arm $q$ in 1 $ton$ do<br>
    Select re-sample s uniformly at random from 1 $tom$<br>
    Set $\hat{r}_q^{ts} = \hat{f}_{q,s}(x^t)$<br>
  Select action a = $argmax_q \hat{r}_q^{ts}$<br>
  Obtain reward$r_a^t$, Add observation $\{x^t, r_a^t\}$ to history for arm a<br>
  For re-sample $s$ in 1 $tom$ do<br>
    Take bootstrapped re-sample $X_s, r_s$ from $X_\alpha, r_\alpha$<br>
    Refit $\hat{f}_{a,s}$ to this re-sample

**Re-planning in the CMAB:** Given the systematic capture of the learner's performance within the framework of per-arm features, the management of failures assumes significance, particularly in the context of re-planning. In scenarios necessitating re-evaluation and adjustment, the agent's role extends to the discerning recommendation of the next Knowledge Component, incorporating a nuanced consideration of the failures attributed to the previously suggested KC. This approach not only ensures a meticulous handling of learning dynamics but also underscores the agent's capacity for informed decision-making and adaptive planning within the broader educational framework. The integration of failure-aware considerations into the re-planning process emerges as a pivotal aspect, contributing to the resilience and effectiveness of the learning algorithm.

## 6 Experiments and Simulations

In our research, we plan to conduct the incorporation of experiments and simulations. in assessing the efficacy and performance of the proposed Contextual Multi-Armed Bandit approach. The experimental design encompasses the deployment of the CMAB algorithm in diverse educational contexts, involving real-time interactions with learners. Both experiments and simulations are carried out in the environment context of course COMP 272 (Data Structures and Algorithms) from Athabasca University. We especially chose Unit 7 (sorting algorithm) of the course to model the KC spaces.

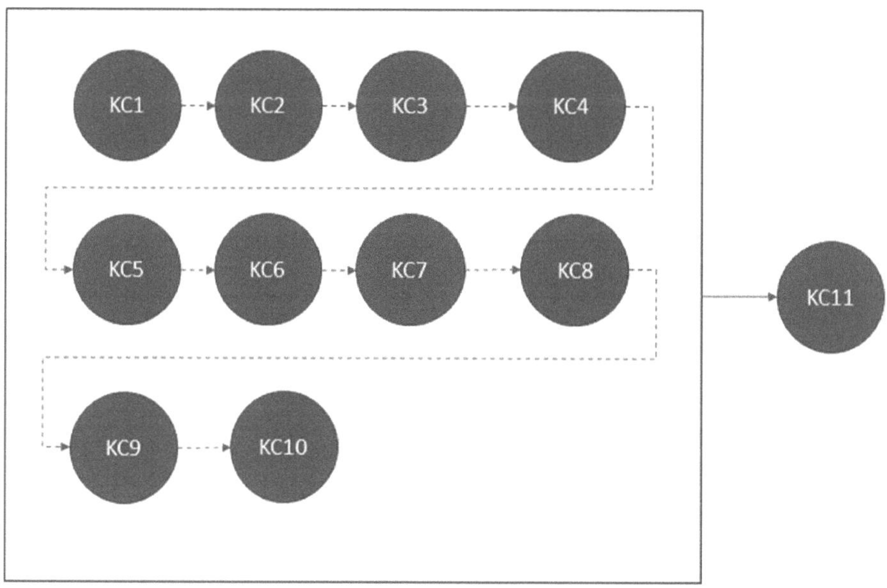


**Fig. 2.** KC graph of sorting algorithm Unit.

Figure 2 shows the KC graph of 11 sorting algorithms in the unit of the course.

In the experiment, participants will engage with a learning system designed to recommend a KC for their learning at each step, based on their individual background and performance, and the system will adapt to their progress. On the other hand, the simulation will produce student data and emulate their learning progression within the learning system. Our primary objective is to assess and compare the performance of the adaptive learning system across various learning curves using four foundational algorithms: Bootstrapped UCB, Epsilon-Greedy, Bootstrapped TS, and Random Action Selection.

## 7 Conclusion

In conclusion, this research highlights the potential of personalized learning paths as a promising instructional strategy in the realm of online learning. By catering to the unique needs and preferences of individual learners, personalized learning paths have the potential to enhance the learning experience and outcomes. However, the complexity of creating effective personalized learning paths arises from the significant variability in learners' characteristics, behaviors, and learning context. As is known, existing recommendation methods have limitations in dealing with the dynamic nature of learning environments, leading to suboptimal recommendations. To address this gap, our study proposes a novel approach: a personalized learning path recommendation system based on a contextual multi-armed bandit framework. This approach aims to overcome the challenges posed by dynamic learning contexts and adaptively offer students optimal learning sequences. By utilizing the contextual multi-armed bandit approach, the system can dynamically adjust learning paths based on real-time feedback, ensuring that students receive the most relevant and suitable content as they progress. This adaptability allows the system to respond to changes in learners' preferences and needs, providing them with a modified sequence when re-planning is required. Through this research, we hope to contribute to the advancement of personalized learning in online education and provide educators and learners with a more effective, and responsive learning path recommendation system. The findings and insights from this study have the potential to inform the design of future personalized learning platforms, enhancing the overall learning experience and promoting better learning outcomes for diverse learners in various educational settings.

**Acknowledgements.** We acknowledge the support of the Natural Sciences and Engineering Research Council of Canada (NSERC) and Alberta Innovates.

## References

1. Graf, S., Lin, F., Kinshuk, McGreal, R.: Intelligent and adaptive learning systems: technology enhanced support for learners and teachers. Inf. Sci. Ref. (2011)
2. Lin, F., Howard, L., Yan, H.: Learning optimal and personalized knowledge component sequencing policies. AIED **2**, 338–342 (2022)
3. Auer, P.: Using confidence bounds for exploitation-exploration trade-offs. J. Mach. Learn. Res. **3**(Nov), 397–422 (2002)

4. Nabizadeh, A.H., Leal, J.P., Rafsanjani, H.N.: Learning path personalization and recommendation methods: a survey of the state-of-the- art. Expert Syst. Appl. **159**, 113596 (2020). https://doi.org/10.1016/j.eswa.2020.113596
5. Shi, D., Wang, T., Xing, H., Xu, H.: A learning path recommendation model based on a multidimensional knowledge graph framework for e- learning. Knowl.-Based Syst., 105618 (2020)
6. Niknam, M., Thulasiraman, P.: A bio-inspired intelligent learning path recommendation system based on meaningful learning theory Educ. Inf. Technol., 1–23 (2020)
7. Xu, D., Wang, Z., Chen, K., Huang, W.: Personalized learning path recommender based on user profile using social tags. In: 2012 Fifth International Symposium on Computational Intelligence and Design (ISCID), vol.1, pp. 511–514 (2012)
8. Cai, D., Zhang, Y., Dai, B.: Learning path recommendation based on knowledge tracing model and reinforcement learning. In: IEEE 5th International Conference on Computer and Communications (ICCC), pp. 1881–1885 (2019)
9. Mui, J., Lin, F., Dewan, M.A.A.: Multi-armed bandit algorithms for adaptive learning: a survey. AIED **2**, 273–278 (2021)
10. Xu, J., Xing, T., Schaar, M.V.D.: Personalized course sequence recommendations. Pers. IEEE Trans. Signal Process. **64**(20), 5340–5352 (2016)
11. Wachanrawan, I., Chayapol, K., Punnarumol, T.: Reinforcement learning based on contextual bandits for personalized online learning recommendation systems. Springer Nature (2020). https://doi.org/10.1007/s11277-020-07199-0
12. Duval, E., Hodgins, W.: A LOM research agenda. In: Twelfth International Word Wide Web Conference (WWW2003), Budapest, Hungary (2003)
13. Falmagne, J.-C., gnon, J.-P.: Learning Spaces: interdisciplinary applied mathematics. Springer-Verlag (2011). https://doi.org/10.1007/978-3-642-01039-2
14. Giuseppe, B., Jason, L., Ramon, L.: A survey of online experiment design with the stochastic multi-armed bandit (2015). arXiv preprint arXiv:1510.00757
15. David, C.: Adapting multi-armed bandits policies to contextual bandits scenarios (2019). arXiv:1811.04383v2 [cs.LG]

# A Generative Artificial Intelligence Empowered Chatbot: System Usability and Student Teachers' Experience

Stavros A. Nikou[1(✉)], Arjun Guliya[2], Suraj Van Verma[3], and Maiga Chang[2]

[1] Strathclyde Institute of Education, University of Strathclyde, Glasgow, Scotland, UK
stavros.nikou@strath.ac.uk
[2] School of Computing and Information Systems, Athabasca University, Edmonton, Canada
arjunguliya19@gmail.com, maiga.chang@gmail.com
[3] McGill University, Montreal, Canada
suraj.verma@mail.mcgill.ca

**Abstract.** Generative Artificial Intelligence empowered conversational agents (chatbots) seem to be increasingly used in various settings including education. While student teachers are key stakeholders in supporting and improving education, not many studies exist in student teachers' views on the educational use of chatbots. The current study performs a usability evaluation and explores student teachers' views on the academic use of the VIP-Bot, an advanced academic Discord chatbot, which leverages the OpenAI's gpt-3.5-turbo-instruct model. Student teachers, within the context of the formative task of writing a literature review, interacted with the chatbot and self-reported their experiences through an online survey. The usability evaluation returned a relatively high SUS score (76.36) for the chatbot. Moreover, student teachers' view on the chatbot acceptance, effectiveness and motivation were positive. The chatbot can be helpful in developing ideas and initiating further engagement with the literature. Academic misconduct concerns have been expressed if the chatbot is not used properly. The study, as a usability evaluation, is an essential step in further chatbot development and, as an investigation of student teachers' views, it is an essential step on the chatbot employment in teaching and learning.

**Keywords:** chatbot · Discord bot · Generative Pre-trained Transformer (GPT) · gpt-3.5-turbo-instruct · system usability · acceptance · effectiveness · motivation

## 1 Introduction

Chatbots, also known as Conversational User Interfaces (CUI), are software applications with the capacity to conduct online conversations with users via text or speech, acting as virtual assistants [1]. Conversational user interfaces can be based on various underlying technologies such as rule-based systems, Natural Language Processing (NLP), Machine Learning models include Generative Pre-trained Transformer (GPTs) in Generative AI.

Generative AI is a type of artificial intelligence that trains models with large amount of data in order to generate new digital content (text, images, video, or audio clips) [2].


A. Sifaleras and F. Lin (Eds.): ITS 2024, LNCS 14798, pp. 330–340, 2024.
https://doi.org/10.1007/978-3-031-63028-6_27

One example of Generative AI is the GPT (Generative Pre-trained Transformer) models and the first GPT was introduced by OpenAI [3]. GPT models are based on Large Language Models (LLMs) that autonomously learn from text data and can generate human-like text responding to a human-provided prompt. These models can be embedded in a variety of applications. In particular, they can offer dynamic and accessible forms of online interactions with chatbots providing human-like conversational experiences to users [4].

Generative AI empowered conversational agents seem to be increasingly used in various settings including education [5, 6]. However, related research is still at an early stage [2]. Moreover, with few exceptions (e.g., [7]) not many empirical studies examining the use of chatbots in student teachers' education exist [8]. Student teachers can be the ambassadors of any educational change such as the use of Generative AI in the educational context, transferring their skills and knowledge into their teaching. To the best of our knowledge, not many studies have explored the use of Generative AI empowered chatbots to assist student teachers in their formative essay-type assessments. The current study performs a usability evaluation and explores student teachers' views on the academic use of the VIP-Bot, an advanced academic Discord chatbot, which leverages the OpenAI's gpt-3.5-turbo-instruct model. The current study is aiming to answer the following research questions:

1) What is the perceived System Usability toward the Discord academic chatbot, VIP-Bot?
2) What is student teachers' experience with using the VIP-Bot in terms of its acceptance, perceived effectiveness, and motivation?

## 2 VIP-Bot, Generative AI Empowered Discord Chatbot

The VIP-Bot is an advanced academic chatbot on Discord, which leverages the OpenAI API to access gpt-3.5-turbo-instruct model (See Fig. 1) to provide assistances ranging from general conversational advice. It makes use of /chat command and public thread to achieve this, giving its users control over their conversation and focus on the chatbot interactions and given responses.

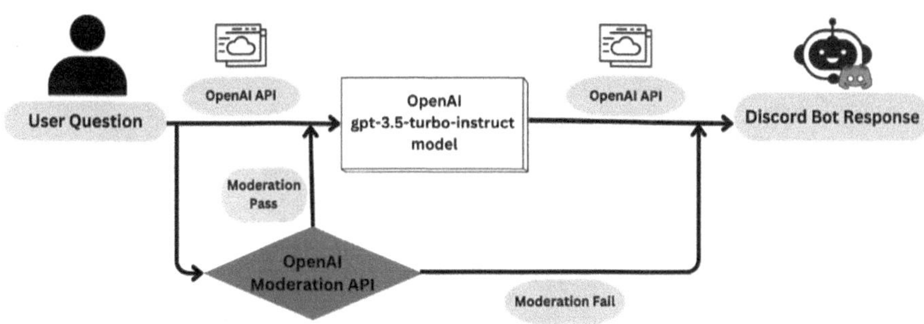


**Fig. 1.** Flowchart showing the system Workflow of the /chat command.

The /chat command creates a public thread, where each message is used as a prompt to get a response from the OpenAI gpt-3.5-turbo-instruct model, utilizing the message history to create context for the model. Along with the message and context, personality and behaviour instructions are also passed into the model, which are completely customizable using a separate config file. The default personality is set to imitate a typical discord user, complete with regular slang and internet shorthand usage.

The GPT model's response is returned through the API, and captured by the bot, which is then written out directly in the created thread. When the context limit or the maximum message count for the model is reached, VIP-Bot automatically closes the thread. Additionally, Since /chat communicates directly with OpenAI's model, each message is first moderated using the OpenAI Moderation API to assess the content of each message. If a message triggers any moderation flags, then it is either directly blocked or flagged, and not passed onto the OpenAI API.

When a user initiates interactions with the bot via the primary command: /chat (See Fig. 2), VIP-Bot sees the command, it creates a new public thread to allow the user and itself to have a conversation without interfering with the original channel's activity. It also allows multiple users to have simultaneous conversations with the bot and allows the bot to differentiate between each conversation. During the initial thread creation process the user also passes in a 'message' argument which serves as the initiating text with the chatbot.

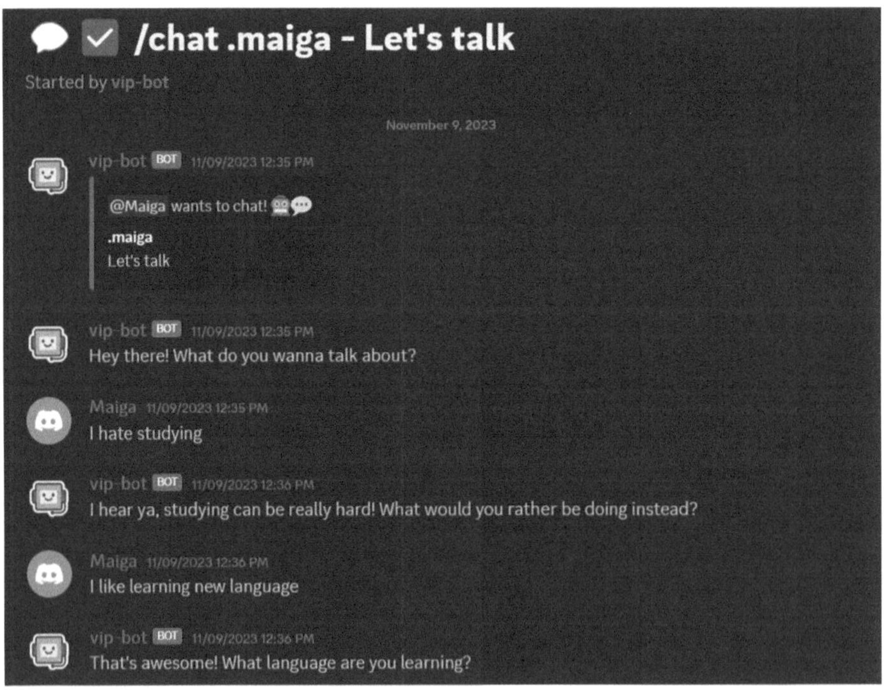


**Fig. 2.** Screenshot showing an example use case of the /chat command. The chatbot can hold a conversation with the user even when prompted with questions not related to coursework.

# 3 Methodology

## 3.1 Participants and Procedures

Data collected based on a convenience sampling. The participants were 10 student teachers, 4 males (40%) and 6 females (60%), enrolled in a post-graduate course in Technology Enhanced learning at the Department of Education of a UK University. Student teachers were five primary school teachers, four secondary school teachers and one higher education lecturer. Participants had not had any previous experience in using chatbots for learning. The study has been granted Ethics approval by the Ethics Committee of the University and has been conducted during the fall semester 2023.

Student teachers have been asked to write a brief literature review type essay on the challenges and benefits of using a specific educational technology of their choice in their own educational context. In alignment with one of the course learning objectives, e.g., students to explore new technologies and adapt as necessary, all students had access to the VIP-Bot on Discord. Therefore, student teachers have been encouraged to interact with the VIP-Bot to help them to prepare for and complete their formative type of assignment.

It has been also communicated to student teachers that, while this could be seen as an opportunity to re-think assessment in ways that could be transformative, under no circumstances the use of AI-generated content be permitted verbatim without clear indication and acknowledgement. Indicatively, among other topics, students have chosen to write about augmented, virtual reality, learning analytics, etc. After engaging with the VIP-Bot, student teachers were asked to complete an online survey with closed and open-ended questions self-reporting their experience in using the VIP-Bot.

## 3.2 Instruments

The survey consisted of two parts. The first part intended to evaluate the system usability and the second part to explore student teachers' acceptance levels, perceived effectiveness, motivation, and concerns. Usability is a pragmatic attribute that refers to the fulfilment of users' functional goals and therefore it is important to be measured [9]. Usability, as defined in ISO 9241–11:2018 (Sect. 3.1.1) [10] as 'the extent to which a system, product or service can be used by specified users to achieve specified goals with effectiveness, efficiency, and satisfaction in a specified context of use.'

For the system usability of the VIP-Bot we have used the System Usability Scale (SUS) [11] because of its validity and reliability [12] and its wide acceptance and easy administration. The questionnaire consists of 10 items that are answered using a 5-point Likert scale ranging from "strongly disagree" to "strongly agree", resulting in a single score between 0 and 100 (in 2.5 points increments) where higher scores indicate better usability.

To explore chatbot's acceptance, effectiveness, and student teachers' motivation we have used a 10-item questionnaire. For the acceptance we adopted 3 items from [13], for perceived effectiveness we used a 4-items self-developed scale and for motivation we adopted 3 items from the intrinsic motivation inventory [14]. Sample items for acceptance are "I indent to use the Discord chatbot in the future" and "I find the Discord bot chatbot easy to use", for perceived effectiveness "The Discord bot chatbot provides me with helpful responses relevant to my queries", "The Discord bot chatbot engaged me in meaningful conversations" or "The Discord bot chatbot can have an impact on student learning outcomes and educational practices" and for motivation "I enjoy using the Discord bot chatbot" and "I would describe interacting with Discord bot chatbot as very interesting".

Cronbach's alpha tests were applied to examine the reliability of the instrument with the results to show acceptable (>0.70) levels of internal consistency. Cronbach's value for acceptance was 0.95, for perceived effectiveness was 0.77 and for motivation 0.81. For an external validation of the scale properties, we compared the findings with measurements from similar studies [15, 16]. To further capture student teachers' experience, we have used open-ended questions focusing on the acceptance and the effectiveness of the VIP-Bot and participants' motivation. Moreover, student teachers' concerns on the use of the chatbot have been explored.

# 4 Data Analysis and Results

## 4.1 System Usability

To answer the first research question regarding system's usability, we have used the overall System Usability Score (SUS) questionnaire. A total of ten responses were collected. The number of participants is within the usability study's general rule $10 \pm 2$ for optimal sample size [25]. The overall SUS of the VIP-Bot, representing the composite measure of the overall usability of the system [11], was found 76.36. Based on [17, 18] the result found is above average and it is considered as **Good**. This indicates that the VIP-Bot and its functionality is good for using it. SUS is a unidimensional instrument with its questionnaire items better not considered individually [11], however we report in Table 1 the responses on the individual questionnaire items along with the median, the mean and standard deviation to highlight each one questionnaire item.

## 4.2 Student Teachers' Experience

To answer the second research question regarding student teachers' experience in using the VIP-Bot, we have used an online survey with a) quantitative data collected from a survey on chatbot's acceptance, effectiveness and participants' motivation and b) qualitative data from open-ended questions on the above constructs.

For the quantitative data, participants responded online to Likert-type questions related to their acceptance level toward the chatbot, perceived effectiveness and their motivation. Table 2 presents the descriptive statistics for student teachers' experience in terms of their acceptance and their perceived effectiveness of the chatbot and their motivation in using it. Students self-reported a high-level of acceptance for the VIP-Bot (3.81, SD = 1.16) in the 5-point Likert scale. Student teachers also reported that they perceived the effectiveness of the chatbot as high (3.19, SD = 0.81). Moreover, student teachers self-reported their level of motivation while interacting with the chatbot as high (3.85, SD = 0.97).

A visual representation of the above sub-scales is depicted in the following Fig. 3 with box plots with the overall patterns of student teachers' responses. Acceptance and

**Table 1.** SUS questionnaire and statistics for each item.

| | Strongly Disagree | | | | Strongly Agree | Median | Mean | SD |
|---|---|---|---|---|---|---|---|---|
| | 1 | 2 | 3 | 4 | 5 | | | |
| 1. I think that I would like to use this system frequently | 0 | 0 | 3 | 6 | 2 | 4 | 3.91 | 0.67 |
| 2. I found the system unnecessarily complex | 1 | 10 | 0 | 0 | 0 | 2 | 1.91 | 0.29 |
| 3. I thought the system was easy to use | 0 | 0 | 1 | 7 | 3 | 4 | 4.18 | 0.57 |
| 4. I think that I would need the support of a technical person to be able to use this system | 0 | 6 | 5 | 0 | 0 | 2 | 2.45 | 0.49 |
| 5. I found the various functions in this system were well integrated | 0 | 0 | 5 | 6 | 0 | 4 | 3.55 | 0.49 |
| 6. I thought there was too much inconsistency in this system | 7 | 4 | 0 | 0 | 0 | 1 | 1.36 | 0.48 |
| 7. I would imagine that most people would learn to use this system very quickly | 0 | 0 | 2 | 8 | 1 | 4 | 3.91 | 0.51 |
| 8. I found the system very cumbersome to use | 4 | 6 | 1 | 0 | 0 | 2 | 1.73 | 0.61 |

*(continued)*

**Table 1.** (*continued*)

| | Strongly Disagree | | | | Strongly Agree | Median | Mean | SD |
|---|---|---|---|---|---|---|---|---|
| | 1 | 2 | 3 | 4 | 5 | | | |
| 9. I felt very confident using the system | 0 | 0 | 2 | 6 | 3 | 4 | 4.09 | 0.66 |
| 10. I needed to learn a lot of things before I could get going with this system | 4 | 7 | 0 | 0 | 0 | 2 | 1.64 | 0.48 |

**Table 2.** Student teachers' acceptance, perceived effectiveness, & motivation toward VIP-Bot.

| | N | Minimum | Maximum | Mean | Std. Deviation |
|---|---|---|---|---|---|
| Acceptance | 10 | 1.33 | 5.00 | 3.81 | 1.16 |
| Effectiveness | 10 | 2.00 | 4.25 | 3.19 | 0.81 |
| Motivation | 10 | 1.67 | 5.00 | 3.85 | 0.97 |

motivation have high medians (around 4) while the median for the perceive effectiveness of the chat is lower (approximately 3). Comparing the interquartile ranges, we identified a rather similar dispersion.

For the qualitative data, participants responded online to open-ended questions providing a few interesting insights. Qualitative data were analysed using thematic analysis [19] following a deductive approach using a pre-determined coding scheme based on the constructs of acceptance, effectiveness, and motivation, rather allowing the themes to be determined by the data [20].

In terms of the chatbot acceptance, student teachers found the chatbot to be useful and easy to use and they "would like to use it in the future". Participants expressed their willingness to embrace and integrate the chatbot as a valuable resource for learning and skill development, e.g., "I will use it to clarify terms and concepts as I am engaging with the literature" and "I would encourage my students to use it during their preparation of class" or "to improve their writing skills" since it "can provide useful language structures". Moreover, "it is good tool for reflecting critically on its output." The above statements imply student teachers' acceptance of the VIP-Bot and their willingness to incorporate it into the educational process.

In terms of the chatbot's effectiveness, it is prominent in terms of the evaluation of response quality, consideration of prompting techniques, and emphasis on clarity in questioning to achieve optimal outcomes. A participants mentioned "I received clear and

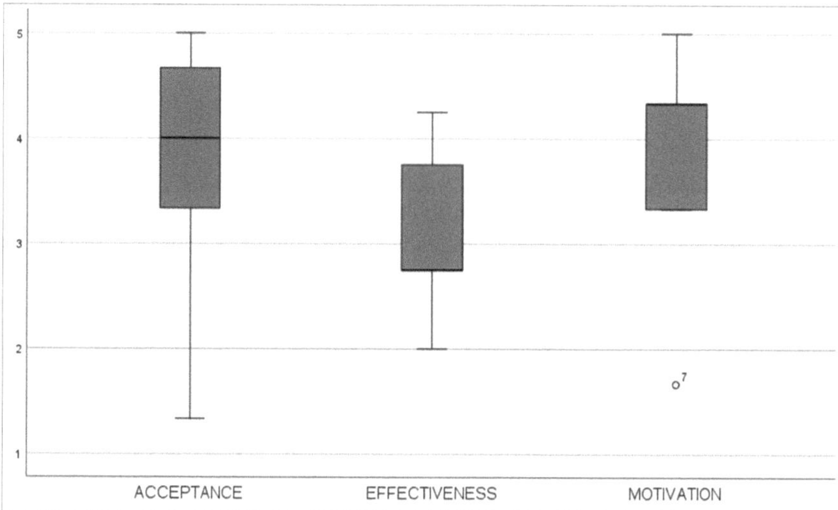


**Fig. 3.** Visual box-plot representation of the descriptive findings.

conscience answers" however, another said, "some of the responses were not comprehensive", while most participants reported that "clear and specific prompting obviously results in better results". The influence of clear and specific prompting on the quality of responses has been acknowledged as "using straightforward words such as (simplify) to indicate the purpose of the prompt can have better results to my questions" and "following up questions to clarify and breaking down questions into smaller sub questions" is important.

In terms of motivation, student teachers enjoyed the interaction with the VIP-Bot (e.g., "I enjoyed using the chatbot a lot"), and they would like to use it because it can be helpful in supporting them in their study. A participant said that the VIP-Bot can help to "discover the key thinkers/writers and their works in relation to a field of study" implying a motivation to deepen one's understanding and knowledge base. Additionally, participants mentioned that the VIP-Bot "is good additional for initial research, ideas, or guidance", by providing "initial explanations of concepts, before exploring these in greater depth in the literature" and "it is good additional for initial research, ideas, or guidance." The above statements imply an underlying motivation to further explore and engage with scholarly literature to inform and enhance one's own work.

However, student teachers reported a few concerns on the use of the VIP-Bot. Concerns have been expressed about students simply copying the answers without verifying their accuracy or engaging in critical thinking, e.g., "taking the answers as 'fact' and using these as the basis for assignments, which could be limiting and sometimes incorrect." Also, few concerns that students might view the VIP-Bot as a complete alternative to doing their own work, potentially undermining academic integrity, e.g., "my only concern would be that students use it as a complete alternative to do all the work for them."

## 5 Discussion and Conclusion

Interest in Generative AI empowered chatbots development is growing. Moreover, its employment in education is promising [2, 21]. The current study is a usability evaluation and an investigation of student teachers' views on the academic use of the VIP-Bot, an advanced academic Discord chatbot, which leverages the OpenAI's gpt-3.5-turbo-instruct model. The study examines usability, acceptance, effectiveness, and motivation as main indicators of how well users can learn and use chatbots and how satisfied and motivated users are during the interaction. Similar metrics have been identified by a recent systematic overview of various chatbots usability studies [15]. Student teachers used the VIP-Bot to assist them in completing their formative assessment and self-reported their views on the potential use of the VIP-Bot in education for similar purposes.

Study findings found for the SUS of the VIP-Bot to be 76.36 which is considered as Good (B+) based on [11]. Considering the structure of the SUS questionnaire of having two factors i.e., usability (items #1, #2, #3, #5, #6, #7, #8 and #9) and learnability (items #4 and #10) [22], student teachers' responses indicated that the system was easy to learn (the median values for items 4 and 10 were quite low) and highly usable.

Since student teachers found the chatbot useful and easy to use they indent to use it in the future. The effectiveness of the chatbot attributed mainly to its ability to provide responses relevant to user queries offering opportunities for meaningful conversations. Students self-reported also that they enjoyed using the chatbot which is in agreement with similar studies exploring students' intrinsic motivation while interacting with chatbots [21, 23]. Student teachers also acknowledged the educational value of the VIP-Bot if used appropriately. They agreed that generative AI supported chatbots pose both opportunities and challenges to education.

While they can be helpful in supporting essay writing and assignments completions, several challenges have been identified as well. "Students use it as a complete alternative to do all the work for them" has been identified as the main concern of the participants. However, student teachers agreed that if "a discussion would have taken place either prior to use, or after use to reflect/discuss critically on the use of VIP-Bot, how it works, what it can do, it's limitations" would be useful. Participants seem to agree that it is not always the case that using Generative AI in educational settings is considered academic misconduct if this resource is used critically. The chatbot can be a "positive tool to generate and develop ideas and for developing critical thinking" as long as "both students and teachers depend in original sources".

Research provides evidence that Generative AI empowered chatbots can introduce new ways of teaching and learning transforming such education [2, 24]. Our study is significant because it provides an evaluation of a generative AI empowered chatbot with potential in education and in particular to assist students with their formative assessments. As a usability evaluation, the study is an essential step in further chatbot development. As an investigation of student teachers' views, the study is an essential step on the chatbot employment in teaching and learning. Our study has limitations. One limitation is the small sample size and especially for eliciting quantitative data. Future research will use larger cohorts and moreover it will develop a more structured instructional design based on the use of the VIP-bot, the Generative AI empowered Discord chatbot.

## References


1. Luo, X., Tong, S., Fang, Z., Qu, Z.: Frontiers: machines Vs. humans: the impact of artificial intelligence chatbot disclosure on customer purchases. Market. Sci. **38**(6), 913–1084. (2019). https://doi.org/10.1287/mksc.2019.1192
2. Chiu, T.K.F.: Future research recommendations for transforming higher education with generative AI. Comput. Educ. Artif. Intell. **6** (2024) https://doi.org/10.1016/j.caeai.2023.100197
3. Radford, A., Narasimhan, K., Salimans, T., Sutskever, I. : Improving language understanding by generative pre-training (2018). https://cdn.openai.com/research-covers/language-unsupervised/language_understanding_paper.pdf
4. Skjuve, M., Følstad, A., Brandtzaeg, P.B.: The user experience of ChatGPT: findings from a questionnaire study of early users. In: Proceedings of the 5th International Conference on Conversational User Interfaces (CUI 2023), pp. 1–10. Association for Computing Machinery, New York, NY, USA, Article 2 (2023). https://doi.org/10.1145/3571884.3597144
5. Adeshola, I., Adepoju, A.P.: The opportunities and challenges of ChatGPT in education. Interact. Learn. Environ. (2023). https://doi.org/10.1080/10494820.2023.225385
6. Mariani, M.M., Hashemi, N., Wirtz, J.: Artificial intelligence empowered conversational agents: a systematic literature review and research agenda. J. Bus. Res. **161**, 113838 (2023). https://doi.org/10.1016/j.jbusres.2023.113838
7. Nikou, S.A., Chang, M.: Learning by building chatbot: a system usability study and teachers' views about the educational uses of chatbots. In: Frasson, C., Mylonas, P., Troussas, C. (eds.) ITS 2023. LNCS, vol. 13891, pp. 342–351. Springer, Cham (2023). https://doi.org/10.1007/978-3-031-32883-1_31
8. Hwang, G.J., Chang, C.Y.: A review of opportunities and challenges of chatbots in education. Interact. Learn. Environ. **31**(7), 4099–4112 (2023). https://doi.org/10.1080/10494820.2021.1952615
9. Hassenzahl, M.: User experience and experience design. The Encyclopedia of Human-Computer Interaction. Interaction Design Foundation (2013) Accessed. https://www.interaction-design.org/literature/book/the-encyclopedia-of-human-computer-interaction-2nd-ed/user-experience-and-experience-design
10. ISO.2018. 9241-11:2018: Ergonomics of Human-System Interaction–Part11: Usability: Definitions and concepts. International Standardization Organization (ISO) (2018)
11. Brooke, J.: SUS: a 'quick and dirty' usability scale. In: Jordan, P.W., Thomas, B., Weerdmeester, B.A., McClelland, A.L. (eds.) Usability Evaluation in Industry, pp. 189–194. Taylor and Francis, London/UK (1996)
12. Bangor, A., Kortum, P., Miller, J.: An empirical evaluation of the system usability scale. Int. J. Hum.-Comput. Interact. **24**(6), 574–594 (2008). https://doi.org/10.1080/10447310802205776
13. Davis, F.D.: Perceived usefulness, perceived ease of use, and user acceptance of information technology. MIS Quart. **13**(3), 319–340 (1989). Accessed. http://www.jstor.org/stable/249008
14. McAuley, E., Duncan, T., Tammen, V.V.: Psychometric properties of the intrinsic motivation inventory in a competitive sport setting: a confirmatory factor analysis. Res. Q. Exerc. Sport **60**, 48–58 (1987)
15. Ren, R., Zapata, M., Castro, J.W., Dieste, O., Acuña, S.T.: Experimentation for chatbot usability evaluation: a secondary study. IEEE Access **10**, 12430–12464 (2022). https://doi.org/10.1109/ACCESS.2022.3145323
16. Casas, J., Tricot, M.-O., Khaled, O.A., Mugellini, E., Cudré-Mauroux, P.: Trends & methods in chatbot evaluation. In: Companion Publication of the 2020 International Conference on Multimodal Interaction (ICMI 2020 Companion), pp. 280–286. Association for Computing Machinery, New York, NY, USA (2021). https://doi.org/10.1145/3395035.3425319

17. Sauro, J.: 5 Ways to Interpret a SUS Score. Measuring U (2018). Accessed. https://measuringu.com/interpret-sus-score/
18. Sauro, J., Lewis, J.: Quantifying the User Experience: Practical Statistics for User Research. Elsevier/Morgan Kaufmann, Amsterdam, Waltham, MA (2016)
19. Braun, V., Clarke, V.: Using thematic analysis in psychology. Qual. Res. Psychol. **3**(2), 77–101 (2006). https://doi.org/10.1191/1478088706qp063oa
20. Saldana, J.: The Coding Manual for Qualitative Researchers, 3rd edn. Sage Publications Ltd. (2015)
21. Lai, C.Y., Cheung, K.Y., Chan, C.S.: Exploring the role of intrinsic motivation in ChatGPT adoption to support active learning: an extension of the technology acceptance model. Comput. Educ. Artif. Intell. **5**, 100178 (2023). https://doi.org/10.1016/j.caeai.2023.100178
22. Lewis, J.R., Sauro, J.: The factor structure of the system usability scale. In: Kurosu, M. (ed.) Human Centered Design. LNCS, vol. 5619, pp. 94–103. Springer, Heidelberg (2009). https://doi.org/10.1007/978-3-642-02806-9_12
23. Chiu, T.K., Moorhouse, B.L., Chai, C.S., Ismailov, M.: Teacher support and student motivation to learn with Artificial Intelligence (AI) based chatbot. Interact. Learn. Environ. (2023). https://doi.org/10.1080/10494820.2023.2172044
24. Wollny, S., Schneider, J., Di Mitri, D., Weidlich, J., Rittberger, M., Drachsler, H.: Are we there yet? - A systematic literature review on chatbots in education. Front. Artif. Intell. **4**, 654924 (2021). https://doi.org/10.3389/frai.2021.654924
25. Hwang, W., Salvendy, G.: Number of people required for usability evaluation: the 10±2 rule. Commun. ACM **53**(5), 130–133 (2010). https://doi.org/10.1145/1735223.1735255

# Predicting Rough Error Causes in Novice Programmers Using Cognitive Level

Deok Yeop Kim and Woo Jin Lee(✉)

School of Computer Science and Engineering, Kyungpook National University, Daegu, Republic of Korea
woojin@knu.ac.kr

**Abstract.** Novice programmers face various errors during the learning of a programming language. Most of them need help from instructors since they lack error resolution skills. On the other side, instructors spend a lot of time figuring out students' error causes. Long error detection times result in delayed and failed feedback, leading to a loss of student motivation. To support instructor's fast feedback, a detection method of error cause is needed. Existing detection methods, which are code-based, detect common and specific errors that can be identified by analyzing source code. These methods do not cover the diverse error patterns of novice programmers sufficiently, such as logical defects. To resolve this issue, it may be beneficial to detect rough and correct error causes of diverse error patterns. In this paper, a prediction method of rough error cause is proposed by considering not only source code, but also problem information, execution results, and the cognitive level indicating programming skills. We assume that different programming skills lead to different error patterns, which can help roughly but precisely predict error causes of runtime and logic errors in novice programmers. For performance evaluation, data from two introductory programming courses are used to validate the effectiveness of the cognitive level. Additionally, the usability for fast feedback is validated by comparing the error causes detection times of the instructors in each case.

**Keywords:** Error Detection · Cognitive Level · Programming Error · Introductory Programming Course · Learning Taxonomy

## 1 Introduction

An introductory programming course (IPC) involves not only learning coding concepts but also programming exercises. Novice programmers are challenged by various programming errors [1]. They need help from the instructor because they lack the ability not only to correct errors but also to identify their causes [2]. To provide feedback to the student, the instructor looks at the source code, execution result, and problem information to detect the error cause. Since it takes a lot of time to detect the error cause, the more students there are, the more delays and failures in instructor's feedback [3]. This late feedback demotivates students, making it difficult for them to achieve their learning goals [4]. Fast feedback requires instructors to quickly identify the error cause.


A. Sifaleras and F. Lin (Eds.): ITS 2024, LNCS 14798, pp. 341–350, 2024.
https://doi.org/10.1007/978-3-031-63028-6_28

Recently, various methods have been proposed to detect errors through source code analysis. Programming error types are categorized into compilation error, runtime error and logic error. Compilation errors are caused by incorrect syntax usage, which are perfectly detectable because the error message and location are precise [5]. Runtime errors occur during code execution due to poor software design or mechanical defects. They can be detected by debugging since it is possible to know where the error occurred. However, this method is applicable only to memory-related errors detectable through source code analysis [6]. In the case of a logic error, since the program does not produce the expected results without any information, logic errors are hard to detect by analyzing the source code [7]. Since existing methods focus on common and specific error causes through source code analysis, they do not sufficiently cover the diverse error patterns of novice programmers. For instructors who want to provide fast feedback, correct detection of rough error causes may be more beneficial than incorrect detection of specific error causes. To correctly detect the rough causes of novice programmers' diverse errors, it is necessary to use additional data beyond the source code.

In this paper, a method is proposed to predict the rough causes of runtime and logic errors by considering the programming skills of novice programmers. The proposed method is based on the research question that different programming skills lead to different error patterns and that programming skill data may be helpful in predicting error causes. To support fast instructor feedback, a machine learning classification model classifies data such as source code, problem information, execution results, and programming skills into rough error causes. For data collection, errors from the programming exercises of the introductory programming courses are analyzed. Programming skill data are obtained through cognitive level assessments. Cognitive level refers to student's programming skills as measured by learning results. The cognitive level is assessed by learning topic using the learning taxonomy as a framework. To evaluate the prediction performance of rough error causes, classification models are compared on two introductory programming courses data. The effectiveness of the cognitive level is validated by comparing the prediction performance with and without cognitive level. Additionally, instructors' error cause detection times are compared to validate whether the proposed method helps instructors to provide fast feedback.

## 2 Related Work

### 2.1 Programming Error Detection

Compilation errors are easy to detect because the error message at compile time indicates the error's location. Li [8] classifies compilation errors based on program tokens, the smallest unit of a program. He divides 16,926 error codes into 13 category labels and trains the model. The model shows a high classification accuracy of about 98%. Ahmed [5] uses the classification model trained on over 15,000 error repair codes to provide alternative feedback on errors. The model finds existing code that matches compilation errors in new code and provides feedback on corrections made by other students. The model demonstrates 97.7% classification accuracy for 212 error category labels. The results show that compilation errors can be perfectly classified and detected.

Runtime errors can be detected by debugging with a debugger. However, novice programmers are not familiar with debuggers, so debugging is often not done well. For this reason, Egan [6] built a debugging tool that enables runtime error detection for novice programmers. The study targets runtime errors that are memory-related, such as invalid memory accesses, uninitialized memory reads, and overflows. Delev [9] reports the results of static analysis of solutions submitted by students in an exam at IPC. The study detects and analyzes runtime errors. However, the errors that can be detected are limited since they are only detected by analyzing the code without executing it. For example, it only detects errors that can be detected by code alone, such as unused variables, unexecuted code, variable initialization, and out-of-bound access.

Logic errors are difficult to detect because there is no information available to specify the error cause. Nakayama [3] estimates logic error causes based on pattern matching analysis between strings. However, only a few logic errors are applicable to this approach, specifically those focusing on source code statements. In addition, for estimation, an existing case base of identical error causes must exist. Yoshizawa [7] proposes a logic error detection algorithm based on structural pattern and error degree. The proposed method detects logic errors by comparing the source code containing the error with the correct source code. Therefore, it is applicable only to some problems where students' solutions may be similar. In other study [10], the detection is done through comparison with the correct source code. Therefore, this approach has limitations, as it requires extensive source code or is applicable only to some common errors.

### 2.2 Cognitive Level Assessment Based on Learning Taxonomy

A learning taxonomy describes and categorizes the cognitive levels that a student may experience in the learning process. The most representative is the revised Bloom's Taxonomy [11], which is based on Bloom's taxonomy [12]. It has a hierarchy of six cognitive levels that build on each other. In programming education, learning taxonomy is a framework for assessing student learning results by classifying them into cognitive levels. Therefore, learning data such as problems or learning outcomes must first be classified into cognitive levels. Students are mapped to the corresponding cognitive level based on the learning data collected at the end of learning.

Fuller [13] modified the Revised Bloom's Taxonomy to reflect the various learning paths and the semi-independence of program understanding skills and creation skills. Fuller's Taxonomy provides a more practical framework for assessing students by designing a two-dimensional assessment grid that separates two skills. Also, the programming activities mapped to cells in the grid strengthen the discriminatory power, making it easier to assess a student's skills. Separating program understanding skills and creation skills can help classify error causes according to students' programming skills. Therefore, in this study, Fuller's taxonomy is used as a cognitive level assessment.

## 3 Analysis of Programming Errors by Novice Programmers

The target IPC was a compulsory course in the first semester of the bachelor's degree curriculum determined by the Computer Science faculty at the School of Computer Science and Engineering. Table 1 details the programming language and curriculum.

Theoretical tests and programming exercises must be completed within a time limit and are graded using an intelligent tutoring system (ITS). Theoretical tests are graded by comparing answers to problems such as short-answer. Programming exercises are graded on student-submitted code against test cases prepared by the instructor.

**Table 1.** Introductory Programming Course Details.

| Type | Description | |
|---|---|---|
| Programming Language | C | |
| Learning Topics | 1. Variable, Conditional | 2. Loop |
| | 3. Array, String | 4. Function |
| | 5. Variable scope | 6. Recursive function |
| | 7. Pointer | 8. Structure |
| Course Structure (each topic) | Learning, Theoretical test, Programming exercise | |

The analysis of students' error data are performed on two IPCs in 2021: 1,841 errors from 37 students in IPC-A and 2,098 errors from 34 students in IPC-B. Data are analyzed in the following format: student, learning topic, problem number, code features, execution result, exit value, and error causes. For error causes classification, the IEEE Software Anomalies Standard's Type criteria were referenced [14]. Among the types, Data, Interface, Logic, and Syntax were used to classify the error causes, and 10 rough error causes were defined for these types, except for Syntax. Table 2 displays the error types and rough error causes, and Table 3 displays the classification results.

**Table 2.** Error types and rough error causes.

| Type | Definition | Rough error causes |
|---|---|---|
| Data | Defect in data definition, initialization, mapping, access, or use, as found in a model, specification, or implementation | 1. Wrong memory access |
| | | 2. Wrong parameter |
| | | 3. Overflow |
| | | 4. Floating point error |
| Interface | Defect in specification or implementation of an interface | 5. Wrong input interface |
| | | 6. Wrong output interface |
| Logic | Defect in decision logic, branching, sequencing, or computational algorithm, as found in natural language specifications or in implementation language | 7. Wrong solution |
| | | 8. Wrong expression-statements |
| | | 9. Wrong loop condition |
| | | 10. Wrong loop termination control |
| Syntax | Nonconformity with the defined rules of a language | (Exclude from error prediction) |

**Table 3.** Result of the classification of the analyzed error causes.

| Type | Data | | | | Interface | | Logic | | | | Syntax |
|---|---|---|---|---|---|---|---|---|---|---|---|
| | 1 | 2 | 3 | 4 | 5 | 6 | 7 | 8 | 9 | 10 | |
| IPC-A (1,841) | 39 | 72 | 11 | 6 | 13 | 194 | 878 | 186 | 97 | 57 | 288 |
| | 2% | 4% | 1% | 0.3% | 1% | 10% | 48% | 10% | 5% | 3% | 16% |
| IPC-B (2,098) | 75 | 30 | 14 | 7 | 52 | 337 | 974 | 119 | 125 | 66 | 299 |
| | 4% | 1% | 1% | 0.3% | 3% | 16% | 46% | 6% | 6% | 3% | 14% |

# 4 Cognitive Level Assessment

## 4.1 Classification of Learning Data by Cognitive Level

To assess cognitive level, theoretical test problems and programming exercise problems are classified into appropriate cognitive levels. Problems are classified using the Fuller's Taxonomy and criteria defined in [15]. Among the cognitive levels, the Evaluate level requires programming activities such as peer review and refactoring for assessment. These activities are not usually part of the IPC curriculum, so the Evaluate level is excluded from this study.

The theoretical tests consisted of five problems, each with one or more sub-questions. The programming exercises consisted of five problems that required students to write complete program code. Simple problems provided solutions or conditions to write code, whereas Advanced problems only provided a program's requirements. Table 4 displays the problem classification results for the eight learning topics. Since problems alone cannot assess all cognitive levels, learning outcomes are used for assessment. Table 5 details the learning outcomes used for assessment.

**Table 4.** Cognitive level classification results of the problems.

| Category | Problem type | Level | Classification result | | | | | | | | |
|---|---|---|---|---|---|---|---|---|---|---|---|
| | Fill-in-the-blank | Rem. | | T1 | T2 | T3 | T4 | T5 | T6 | T7 | T8 |
| | Short-answer | Rem. | Rem. | 1 | 2 | 1 | 2 | 2 | 2 | 2 | 2 |
| Theoretical test | True/False | Rem. | Und. | 3 | 2 | 2 | 0 | 2 | 0 | 1 | 1 |
| | Write output value | Und. | Ana. | 0 | 0 | 1 | 1 | 1 | 1 | 1 | 1 |
| | Write code | Apply | None | 0 | 0 | 0 | 0 | 0 | 0 | 0 | 0 |
| | Correct code error | Ana. | Apply | 3 | 3 | 4 | 5 | 3 | 5 | 4 | 3 |
| Programming exercise | Simple | Apply | Create | 3 | 3 | 2 | 2 | 2 | 2 | 2 | 3 |
| | Advanced | Create | Total | 10 | 10 | 10 | 10 | 10 | 10 | 10 | 10 |

Rem.: Remember; Und.: Understand; Ana.: Analyze; T: Topic

**Table 5.** Learning outcomes to cognitive level assessment.

| Learning outcome | Description | Level |
|---|---|---|
| Executable code submission | Student's minimal program creation skills | None |
| Number of solved problems | Solution creation skills and testing skills | Understand, Analyze |
| Number of occurred error types | Incomplete understanding of syntax and semantic rules, problem comprehension, solution structure, and testing | Analyze |
| Number of occurred errors | Lack of awareness of program errors or solution flaws | Analyze |
| Consecutive errors of same type | Lack of error correction skills | Analyze |

### 4.2 Cognitive Level Assessment Process

The cognitive level is quantified into program understanding skills and creation skills. Program understanding skills are assessed through the levels Remember, Understand, Analyze, and program creation skills are assessed through the levels None, Apply, and Create. Assessment process required five steps.

First, categorical data are preprocessed to be closer to 1 if it reflects a cognitive level and closer to 0 otherwise. Second, the data are scaled to have a minimum value of 0 and a maximum value of 1. However, the scaling result of error data in learning outcomes is closer to 1 the more errors there are, so 1 minus the scaling value is used. Third, sum the scaled data by cognitive level. Fourth, the summed data are scaled once again. Fifth, apply different weights to the data for each cognitive level. The weighting was 1x for Remember and None, 2x for Understand and Apply, and 3x for Analyze and Create. Since cognitive levels are a strict hierarchy, the better the metrics associated with the higher levels, the better the assessment should be. Table 6 presents an assessment example of a student in learning topic 4.

**Table 6.** Example of assessing a student's cognitive level.

| Step | Theoretical test | | | | | Programming exercise | | | | | Learning outcomes | | | | |
|---|---|---|---|---|---|---|---|---|---|---|---|---|---|---|---|
| 1 | 5 | 2 | 1 | 2 | 1 | 1 | 0 | 1 | 1 | 0 | 1 | 3 | 2 | 5 | 1 |
| 2 | 1 | 1 | 0.5 | 1 | 0.5 | 1 | 0 | 1 | 1 | 0 | 1 | 0.6 | 0.5 | 0.7 | 0.9 |
| Step | Remember | Understand | Analyze | None | Apply | Create | | | | | | | | | |
| 3 | 2 | 0.6 | 3.2 | 1 | 3.5 | 1 | | | | | | | | | |
| 4 | 1 | 0.6 | 0.6 | 1 | 0.7 | 0.5 | | | | | | | | | |
| 5 | 1 | 1.2 | 1.8 | 1 | 1.4 | 1.5 | | | | | | | | | |
| Understanding skills | 4 | Creation skills | 3.9 | | | | | | | | | | | | |

# 5 Prediction of Rough Error Causes

## 5.1 Model Training

The training dataset for the prediction model includes data on cognitive levels, topic numbers, exercise problem numbers, execution results, program exit values, and counts of code features such as identifiers, keywords, and operators. Cognitive level data are used in the form of the understanding skills and creation skills of the previous learning topic and the average of the accumulated understanding skills and creation skills. Students solve problems based on their accumulated knowledge and newly learned knowledge. Therefore, the cognitive level of the previous study topic is closest to the cognitive level of the current. Also, the average of the cognitive level is used as the generalized cognitive level of the student accumulated from past learning topics.

Since the error causes have different ratios, the data for training and validation are sampled using a stratified method to maintain these ratios. Table 7 displays the training information for the models and the performance comparison according to the cognitive level data. Without cognitive level data, the Extreme Gradient Boosting model achieves the best performance, with 66% accuracy. With cognitive level data, the Light Gradient Boosting Machine model outperforms others, reaching 85% accuracy.

**Table 7.** Model training and validation information and performance comparison results.

| Model training dataset | IPC-A dataset | | IPC-B dataset | Total dataset |
|---|---|---|---|---|
| | 1,553 set | | 1,799 set | 3,352 set |
| Model performance (without cognitive level data) | Model | Accuracy | Precision | F1 score |
| | Xgboost | 0.662 | 0.615 | 0.618 |
| | Gradient boosting | 0.636 | 0.608 | 0.610 |
| Model performance (with cognitive level data) | Model | Accuracy | Precision | F1 score |
| | Lightgbm | 0.851 | 0.844 | 0.843 |
| | Xgboost | 0.847 | 0.840 | 0.839 |

Xgboost: Extreme gradient boosting; Lightgbm: Light gradient boosting machine.

## 5.2 Cognitive Level Effectiveness Testing and Validation

For cognitive level effectiveness validation, Split the data from the IPC-B by student to test per student. Use the students' data except the test student data and the IPC-A data for training. Repeat this for all IPC-B students data. Table 8 displays the test results of rough error causes for validation of cognitive level effectiveness.

**Table 8.** Test results of rough error causes for validation of cognitive level effectiveness.

| Type | | Without cognitive level data | | | | With cognitive level data | | | |
|---|---|---|---|---|---|---|---|---|---|
| Test Performance | | Accuracy | | Precision | F1 score | Accuracy | | Precision | F1 score |
| | | 0.629 | | 0.636 | 0.623 | 0.852 | | 0.845 | 0.845 |
| Details | | True | Ratio | False | Ratio | True | Ratio | False | Ratio |
| Data | 1 | 46 | 61% | 29 | 39% | 74 | 99% | 1 | 1% |
| | 2 | 14 | 47% | 16 | 53% | 29 | 97% | 1 | 3% |
| | 3 | 9 | 64% | 5 | 36% | 12 | 86% | 2 | 14% |
| | 4 | 7 | 100% | 0 | 0% | 7 | 100% | 0 | 0% |
| Total&Average | | 76 | 60% | 50 | 40% | 122 | 97% | 4 | 3% |
| Interface | 5 | 10 | 19% | 42 | 81% | 31 | 60% | 21 | 40% |
| | 6 | 128 | 38% | 209 | 62% | 249 | 74% | 88 | 26% |
| Total&Average | | 138 | 35% | 251 | 65% | 280 | 72% | 109 | 28% |
| Logic | 7 | 777 | 80% | 197 | 20% | 901 | 93% | 73 | 7% |
| | 8 | 20 | 17% | 99 | 83% | 63 | 53% | 56 | 47% |
| | 9 | 79 | 63% | 46 | 37% | 119 | 95% | 6 | 5% |
| | 10 | 42 | 64% | 24 | 36% | 47 | 71% | 19 | 29% |
| Total&Average | | 918 | 71% | 366 | 29% | 1,130 | 88% | 154 | 12% |

Without the cognitive level, the accuracy is 63%. The accuracy is 60% for data, 35% for interface, and 71% for logic. In the case of logic, considering the performance of predicting wrong solution causes, error causes are not predicted well. On the other side, the accuracy is 85% when cognitive levels are included. Prediction performance is 97% for data, 72% for interface, and 88% for logic. The test results show that the cognitive level is effective at predicting roughly but precisely the error causes.

To validate the usability for fast feedback by instructors, compare the time spent detecting and providing feedback on detailed error causes for each case. The experiment uses one error data per error cause. Instructors are given common problem information, test case, execution result, and source code. The experiment was conducted using tutors from IPCs to minimize differences in instructors' abilities. Table 9 displays the time spent by instructors to provide feedback. Compared to the manual case, the average feedback time is 23% faster without cognitive level and 34% faster with cognitive level.

**Table 9.** Comparison of time to feedback from instructors by case.

| Type | | | Instructor 1 (manually) | | Instructor 2 (without cognitive level) | | Instructor 3 (with cognitive level) | |
|---|---|---|---|---|---|---|---|---|
| Information | | | Seconds | | Seconds (Prediction) | | Seconds (Prediction) | |
| Data | 1 | 2 | 487 | 511 | 448 (False) | 577 (False) | 192 | 191 |
| | 3 | 4 | 365 | 163 | 285 | 76 | 310 | 125 |
| Interface | 5 | 6 | 190 | 288 | 210 (False) | 92 | 358 (False) | 98 |
| Logic | 7 | 8 | 320 | 417 | 128 | 510 (False) | 160 | 550 (False) |
| | 9 | 10 | 320 | 354 | 191 | 104 | 188 | 79 |
| Average | | | 342 | | 262 | | 225 | |

# 6 Conclusion

The proposed method to support fast feedback from instructors predict the rough but precise causes of runtime and logic errors of novice programmers in an introductory programming course. This method covers diverse error causes such as logical defects, unlike existing approaches that focus on common and specific error causes. Existing error detection methods are source code-based and do not use students' programming skills, such as cognitive level. Our approach uses not only source code, but also problem information, execution results, and cognitive level.

The effectiveness of cognitive level in error cause prediction was validated for students in two introductory programming courses. The prediction accuracy was 63% without cognitive level and 85% with cognitive level, and cognitive level enhanced the prediction of most error causes. This indicates that different programming skills of students lead to different error causes, and thus cognitive level may be useful in the programming error causes detection. Additionally, the proposed method helped instructors detect error causes and compared to manual, the instructor's feedback was 23% faster without cognitive level and 34% faster with cognitive level.

**Acknowledgments.** This study was supported by the BK21 FOUR project (AI driven Convergence Software Education Research Program) funded by the Ministry of Education, School of Computer Science and Engineering, Kyungpook National University, Korea (4199990214394) and the Basic Science Research Program through the National Research Foundation of Korea funded by the Ministry of Education (NRF-2018R1A6A1A03025109).

## References


1. Mendonça, A., de Oliveira, C., Guerrero, D., Costa, E.: Difficulties in solving ill-defined problems: a case study with introductory computer programming students. In: 39th IEEE Frontiers in Education Conference, pp. 1–6. San Antonio, TX, USA (2009)
2. Yalagi, P.S. Indi, T.S., Nirgude, M.A.: Enhancing the cognitive level of novice learners using effective program writing skills. In: International Conference on Learning and Teaching in Computing and Engineering (LaTICE), pp. 167–171. Mumbai, India (2016)
3. Nakayama, H., Yamamoto, K., Ogane, K., Kaminaga, H., Nakamura, S., Miyadera, Y.: Estimation of the error factors in programming exercises based on dynamic revisions of case-bases. In: IEEE Conferences on Ubiquitous Intelligence & Computing, Advanced and Trusted Computing, Scalable Computing and Communications, Cloud and Big Data Computing, Internet of People, and Smart World Congress, pp. 475–481. Toulouse, France (2016)
4. Karam, M., Awa, M., Carbone, A., Dargham, J.: Assisting students with typical programming errors during a coding session. In: 7th International Conference on Information Technology: New Generations, pp. 42–47. Las Vegas, NV, USA (2010)
5. Ahmed, U.Z., Sindhgatta, R., Srivastava, N., Karkare, A.: Targeted example generation for compilation errors. In: 34th IEEE/ACM International Conference on Automated Software Engineering (ASE), pp. 327–338. San Diego, CA, USA (2019)
6. Egan, M.H., Mcdonald, C.: Runtime error checking for novice C programmers. In: 4th Annual International Conference on Computer Science Education: Innovation and Technology (CSEIT), Bangkok, Thailand (2013)
7. Yoshizawa, Y., Watanobe, Y.: Logic error detection algorithm for novice programmers based on structure pattern and error degree. In: 9th International Conference on Awareness Science and Technology (iCAST), pp. 297–301. Fukuoka, Japan (2018)
8. Li, Z., Sun, F., Wang, H., Ding, Y., Liu, Y., Chen, X.: CLACER: a deep learning-based compilation error classification method for novice students' programs. In: 45th Annual Computers, Software, and Applications Conference, pp. 74–83. Madrid, Spain (2021)
9. Delev, T., Gjorgjevikj, D.: Static analysis of source code written by novice programmers. In: IEEE Global Engineering Education Conference (EDUCON), pp. 825–830. Athens, Greece (2017)
10. Gulwani, S., Radiček, I., Zuleger, F.: Automated clustering and program repair for introductory programming assignments. ACM SIGPLAN Not. **53**(4), 465–480 (2018)
11. Anderson, L.W., Krathwohl, D.R., et al.: A taxonomy for learning, teaching, and assessing: a revision of bloom's taxonomy of educational objectives. Addison Wesley Longman Inc. (2001)
12. Bloom, B.S., Englehard, M.D., Furst, E.J., Hill, W.H., Krathwohl, D.R.: Taxonomy of educational objectives: the classification of educational goals. Handbook I Cognitive Domain. Harlow, U.K.: Longmans (1956)
13. Fuller, U., et al.: Developing a computer science-specific learning taxonomy. ACM SIGCSE Bull. **39**(4), 152–170 (2007)
14. IEEE Standard Classification for Software Anomalies. IEEE Std. 1044–2009, 1–23 (2010)
15. Dorodchi, M., Dehbozorgi, N., Frevert, T.K.: I wish I could rank my exam's challenge level!: an algorithm of Bloom's taxonomy in teaching CS1. In: IEEE Frontiers in Education Conference (FIE), pp. 1–5. Indianapolis, IN, USA (2017)

# Social AI Agents Too Need to Explain Themselves

Rhea Basappa(✉), Mustafa Tekman, Hong Lu, Benjamin Faught, Sandeep Kakar, and Ashok K. Goel

Georgia Institute of Technology, Atlanta, GA 30332, USA
{rb324,mtekman3,bfaught3,skakar6,ag25}@gatech.edu, hlu07@tufts.edu

**Abstract.** Social AI agents interact with members of a community, thereby changing the behavior of the community. For example, in online learning, an AI social assistant may connect learners and thereby enhance social interaction. These social AI assistants too need to explain themselves in order to enhance transparency and trust with the learners. We present a method of self-explanation that uses introspection over a self-model of an AI social assistant. The self-model is captured as a functional model that specifies how the methods of the agent use knowledge to achieve its tasks. The process of generating self-explanations uses Chain of Thought to reflect on the self-model and ChatGPT to provide explanations about its functioning. We evaluate the self-explanation of the AI social assistant for completeness and correctness.

**Keywords:** Social AI · XAI · Self-Explanation · Self-Models · Generative AI · Combining Knowledge-Based and Generative AI

## 1 Introduction

Learning at scale, and particularly online learning at scale, offers many well-established benefits such as geographically distributed and self-paced asynchronous learning that meets the reskilling and upskilling needs of working learners and learning workers. However, learning at scale, and again particularly online learning at scale, also have several well-known drawbacks such as lack of social presence, i.e., the ability of learners to establish and maintain a sense of connectedness both with one another and with the instructor [1].

SAMI (Social Agent Mediated Interaction) is an AI social assistant that helps students in large online classes form social connections by introducing them to one another based on shared characteristics and interests [2–4]. This is posited to increase social presence in an online class environment [3]. However, students interacting with SAMI often have questions regarding its inner workings [4]. Knowing how SAMI works internally may help students build trust in its recommendations. Thus, the specific research question for us in this paper becomes: How might an AI social assistant, such as SAMI, provide an explanation of its inner workings to online students?


A. Sifaleras and F. Lin (Eds.): ITS 2024, LNCS 14798, pp. 351–360, 2024.
https://doi.org/10.1007/978-3-031-63028-6_29

We present a computational technique for self-explanation in SAMI. Our self-explanation technique consists of several parts. First, we view self-explanation as a process of question answering in which a user provides the AI agent input in natural language (English), the agent then introspects on its knowledge of its own reasoning and then produces an answer back to this question also in natural language (English). Second, this introspection requires the AI agent to have a self-model of its goals, knowledge, and methods. We use the Task, Method and Knowledge (TMK) framework [5–7] for representing this self-model. Third, we replace logical propositions in the traditional TMK models with short descriptions in English while still retaining their task-method-knowledge decomposition. Fourth, we conduct a similarity search on the input question and the English descriptions in TMK model to find the relevant snippets for answering the question. Fifth, we use Chain of Thought [8] to walk step-by-step over the TMK model to generate prompts into ChatGPT to produce an answer from the identified snippets. Thus, the self-explanation technique of SAMI combines the strengths of generative AI (training over a very large corpus and the ability to address a large variety of natural language tasks) with that of knowledge-based AI (knowledge representation and organization at multiple levels of abstraction).

## 2 Related Work

Self-explanation has re-emerged as an important topic in AI. Muller et al. (2019) [9] provide a fairly comprehensive and a very useful summary of the history of AI research on self-explanation. Confalonieri et al. (2021) [10] present another and more recent take on the history. The need for interpretability of the representations and processing in modern neural networks is one of the main reasons for the resurgence of interest in self-explanation in AI agents [11]. Rudin [12] advocates the construction and use only of AI agents capable of self-interpretation and self-explanation.

It is useful here to distinguish between two kinds of AI assistants: AI assistants that interact with individual humans and AI assistants that enable interaction among humans. In the context of AI in learning and teaching, teaching assistants such as Jill Watson [13,14] that answer a student's questions are an example of the former; AI social assistants such as SAMI [2–4] that help foster interactions among students are an example of the latter. The latter class of assistants exemplify the paradigm of "computers are social actors" [15]. It is important to note that self-explanation in social assistants is as important as it is in personal teaching and learning assistants.

One of the key ideas to emerge out of this early research on explanation was the importance of explicit representation of knowledge of the design of an AI assistant [16,17]. An explicit representation of the design knowledge of an AI assistant enables the generation of explanations of the tasks it accomplishes, the domain knowledge it uses, as well as the method that use the knowledge to achieve the tasks. This raised the question of how this design knowledge can be identified, acquired, represented, stored, accessed, and used for generating explanations [7]. One possible answer was to endow the AI agent with meta-knowledge of its own design [18] and enable the agent to generate explanations through introspection on its meta-knowledge.

# 3 Computational Architecture and Process for Self-explanation

## 3.1 SAMI, the Social AI Agent

SAMI accesses the self-introduction posts of students in an online discussion forum and extracts information such as their location, hobbies and academic interests. Using this, SAMI builds a knowledge graph for each student. It then uses this knowledge graph to 'match' students who share one or more similarities. SAMI communicates its recommendations of matches to the online students who elect to contact the recommended matches [2–4].

## 3.2 Semantic Representation of SAMI

From its code base, we manually create a symbolic representation of SAMI in the Task-Method-Knowledge (TMK) framework [5–7]. Briefly, the TMK model specifies SAMI's tasks (or goals), methods (or mechanisms for achieving the goals) and the domain knowledge of the environment. The TMK is organized hierarchically. The top-level task specifies SAMI's method for accomplishing it; the method specifies the finite state machine for accomplishing the task in terms of a sequence of information states and state transitions. The state transitions are annotated by either subtasks or domain knowledge. This decomposition continues until all leaf nodes in the TMK model are primitive tasks that can be directly accomplished by the available domain knowledge. Figure 1 illustrates the hierarchical organization of the TMK model of SAMI. Figure 2 illustrates the state-transition specification of a method in the TMK model in detail.

Having built the TMK model of SAMI, we manually translate the logical propositions in the TMK model into brief natural language descriptions to obtain a semantic representation of SAMI. This semantic representation becomes the self-model of SAMI that empowers our self-explanation technique.

## 3.3 Self-explanation Technique

The self-explanation technique utilizes the information from SAMI's TMK self-model to provide explanations about its inner workings. As Fig. 3 illustrates, the technique has three main stages: Classification, Localization and Reasoning. When a question is asked, the Classifier first analyses the question to determine which of the pre-defined classes the question belongs to. These classes are 'mmodel', 'kmodel', 'multimodel' (along with 'can't answer') and are used to determine which part(s) of the self-model of SAMI are later used in the self-explanation pipeline. A 'kmodel' classification would lead to using information

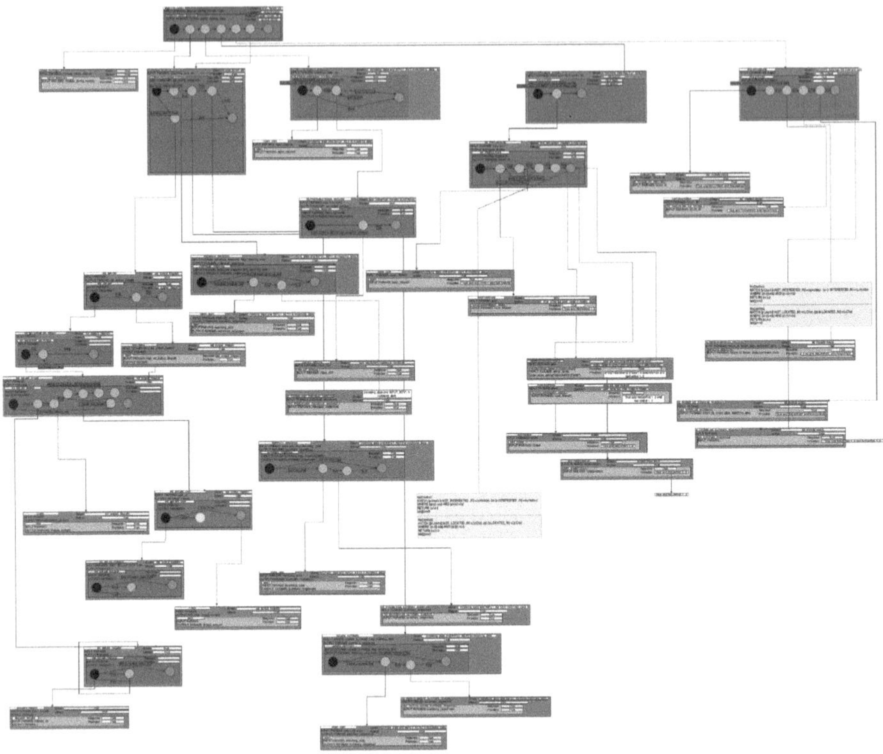

**Fig. 1.** The organization of the TMK model of SAMI. Outer rectangles represent high-level goals. Inner rectangles represent methods, with the circles within them representing sub-tasks and the arrows between them representing transitions. (We know that the text in this figure is not readable). Our goal here is to convey the hierarchical decomposition of the TMK model of SAMI, along with its size and complexity.

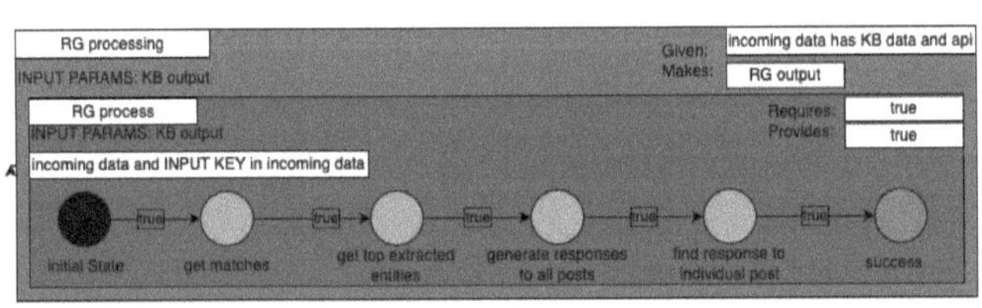


**Fig. 2.** This figure illustrates the state-transition specification of one method ('RG process') in the TMK model of SAMI. The circles within the method represent the individual tasks. The arrows connecting the tasks represent the state by state transitions within this particular method.

only from the domain knowledge part of the self-model. An 'mmodel' classification would lead to localizing the relevant task and method information within the self-model. With a 'multimodel' classification, a similarity search would be conducted to find the relevant pieces of information from all knowledge, method, and task parts of the self-model. Lastly, any question deemed as not being relevant to SAMI would be classified as 'can't answer'. The Classifier employs LangChain[1] to create a prompt that uses pre-written templates describing each of these classifications, along with the question to be answered. This prompt is then sent to ChatGPT[2], which returns a value for the classification, along with a complexity 'k' value which is used to control the verbosity of the final answer in later stages.

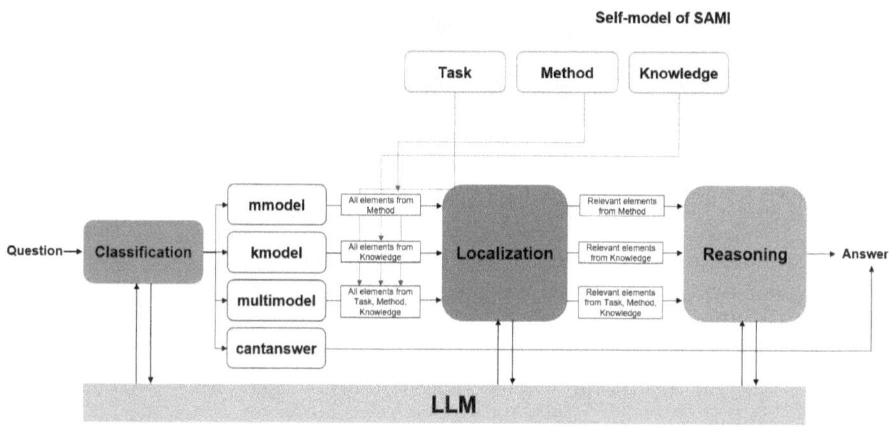


**Fig. 3.** The computational architecture and process flow of the self-explanation technique.

Next, the Localizer conducts the similarity search to find the most relevant k pieces of information within the sub-model(s) identified as relevant by the classifier. The Localizer uses the FAISS library[3] to do a similarity search on the input question and the natural language descriptions in the relevant sub-model(s). The hierarchical organization of the TMK model (see Fig. 1) helps in this localization. Like the Classifier, the Localizer employs LangChain and prompts ChatGPT to determine the names of the relevant items from the sub-model(s). These are then passed to the reasoning stage.

In the final stage, if the relevant items identified by the Localizer include a method, the Reasoner uses Chain of Thought to walk step-by-step over the specification of the identified method including the subtasks in the method

[1] LangChain documentation.
[2] OpenAI's gpt3.5-turbo-instruct model has been used.
[3] Meta's FAISS documentation.

(see Fig. 2). This enables the answer to include descriptions of task annotations on the state transitions within a method that might have led to a particular outcome of SAMI. Like the Classifier and the Localizer before it, the Reasonser once again uses LangChain to construct prompts to ChatGPT to compose the final answer. Thus, the self-model technique makes multiple calls to ChatGPT for different purposes in different stages.

## 4 Evaluation

**Correctness and Completeness Study Design:** To evaluate the self-explanation technique, we used high-level, non context-dependent questions taken directly from XAI question banks [19,20] such as *"What is the source of the data?"* [19], *'How often does the system make mistakes?"* [19] and *"What is the scope of the output data?"* [20]. Additionally, we modified some questions so that they become more relevant to SAMI. For example, *"What are the results of other people using the system?"* [20] was adapted as *"What is the result of other students opting-in to use SAMI?"*.

In total, 57 questions were borrowed and adapted from the question banks. Additionally, 9 questions specific to SAMI were created. These include questions such as *"What is a match?"* and *"How do you find matches for students?"*. The self-explanation technique of SAMI was prompted with each of these 66 questions and SAMI developers assessed each explanation for correctness and completeness. We considered the definition of correctness as "nothing but the truth" [21] and completeness as "the whole truth" [21]. For correctness, three categories - yes, partial and no - were noted, and for completeness, two categories - complete and incomplete - were used.

**Result of the Correctness and Completeness Study:** Table 1 summarizes the completeness and correctness scores for each question category. The self-explanation technique provided correct answers to 49 out of 66 questions; 37 of these 49 correct answers were also complete. For example, for the question, *"What is a match?"*, the self-explanation method provided the answer *"A match is a student recommended by SAMI to the user who shares one or several similarities with the user. This information is based on the task, method and goals of the Social AI agent provided, which contains information about objects and their properties that SAMI tracks in its system. The task, method and goals of the Social AI agent states that a match is a student recommended by SAMI, and this recommendation is based on shared similarities between the user and the recommended student. These similarities could include location, hobbies, specialization, classes taken, and timezone"*. Since this explanation did not contain any incorrect information nor did it miss any other relevant correct information, it was assessed to be both correct and complete.

The question *"What are the different types of responses you are capable of giving?"* was answered with *"I am capable of giving Individual Responses, which are recommendations for matches based on the information provided by the user.*

**Table 1.** Results of categorising all 66 questions that were used to evaluate the self-explanation technique, a representative question for each category along with their adaptation and corresponding completeness and correctness results

| Category | # of Questions | Example Question(s) | Completeness Scores | Correctness Scores |
|---|---|---|---|---|
| Input | 4 | What kind of data does SAMI learn from?<br>What is the source of the data? | Complete: 2/4<br>Incomplete: 2/4 | Correct: 3/4<br>Partially Correct: 1/4<br>Incorrect:0/4 |
| Output | 22 | How can I best utilise SAMI's output?<br>What kind of output does SAMI give? | Complete: 16/22<br>Incomplete: 6/22 | Correct: 14/22<br>Partially Correct: 2/22<br>Incorrect:6/22 |
| How (global) | 17 | Is location used or not used in matchmaking?<br>Are hobbies used or not used in matchmaking? | Complete: 12/17<br>Incomplete: 5/17 | Correct: 14/17<br>Partially Correct: 2/17<br>Incorrect: 1/17 |
| Why not | 1 | Why would two students not be matches? | Complete: 1/1<br>Incomplete: 0/1 | Correct: 1/1<br>Partially Correct: 0/1<br>Incorrect: 0/1 |
| Others | 10 | What are the result of other students opting-in to SAMI?<br>How will I be affected if other students use or not use SAMI? | Complete: 10/10<br>Incomplete: 0/10 | Correct: 9/10<br>Partially Correct: 1/10<br>Incorrect: 0/10 |
| Others (context) | 3 | Who is responsible for this system?<br>Who are the authors? | Complete: 2/3<br>Incomplete: 1/3 | Correct: 0/3<br>Partially Correct: 2/3<br>Incorrect: 1/3 |
| SAMI Specific Questions | 9 | Why am I matched with a particular student?<br>What entities do you use in matchmaking? | Complete: 6/9<br>Incomplete: 3/9 | Correct: 8/9<br>Partially Correct: 0/9<br>Incorrect: 1/9 |

*These responses are based on the entities I extract from the user's introduction post, such as location, hobbies, specialization, classes taken, and timezone.".* Whilst this is correct, it is incomplete because SAMI is capable of providing individual, summary and feedback responses. Saying it only provides individual response makes the answer incomplete. 12 of the correct answers were incomplete. Some answers given by the self-explanation method were partially correct. Such partially correct answers were given to 8 of the 66 questions. The question, *"What are your limitations?"* received an answer as, *"I am a software system called SAMI, and my main limitation is that I can only mediate social interactions among students who have opted in to use me. I do this by extracting entities such as location, hobbies, specialization, classes taken, and timezone from their introduction post and connecting them to others based on similar entities. However, I am limited to only students who have opted in and have included the #connectme optin tag in their introduction post in the ED online discussion forum. Additionally, I am limited to only students who are enrolled in one of the five specializations offered by Georgia Institute of Technology for its Computer Science Masters students."*. This answer is evaluated to be partially correct because even though the first part around the opt-in limitation is correct, the second part around being only limited to students in one of the five specializations is incorrect. On the other hand, the answer is complete as it's not missing any other relevant information.

Incorrect answers were given to only 9 out of the 66 questions. 6 of these 9 incorrect answers were to questions belonging to the 'Output' category - this could be attributed to the fact that there's no output specified in SAMI's self-model, since it does not have a static output. For example, *"What does the output of SAMI mean?"* received an answer as, *"The output of SAMI refers to the result or outcome of the system's task, which is to mediate social interactions among students who have opted in to use SAMI. However, according to the given task, method and goals of the Social AI agent, the output for this specific task is not specified, so it is not possible to provide a specific answer. It is recommended to ask other questions that may be answered with the information provided in the task, method and goals of the Social AI agent"*. This answer was evaluated to be incorrect (and incomplete) as it doesn't correctly explain what the output of SAMI means.

In total, 48 out of 66 answers were complete (with 18 being incomplete). Questions like *"What does a match mean?"*, *"What type of matches does SAMI give?"* and *"What kind of output does SAMI give?"* received complete answers, whilst questions such as *"What data is the system not using?"* [19] and *"What is the system's overall logic?"* [19] received incomplete explanations. We expect the completeness of SAMI's self-explanations to improve with the completeness of its TMK self-model.

# 5 Conclusions

Our computational technique for self-explanation in AI social assistants combines classical knowledge-based methods with modern generative AI methods. The technique for self-explanation leverages ChatGPT to introspect over a TMK self-model of the AI social assistant to generate explanations about its functioning. Our preliminary analysis of the self-explanation technique showed that it is capable of providing complete and correct explanations about the inner workings of SAMI provided that the question asked was relevant to the TMK self-model of SAMI and the self-model itself was complete and correct. We tentatively conclude that introspection by generative AI on a self-model of the AI social assistant is a promising way of generating self-explanations and thus merits further investigation.

**Acknowledgements.** This research has been supported by NSF Grants #2112532 and #2247790 to the National AI Institute for Adult Learning and Online Education. We thank members of the Design & Intelligence Laboratory for their contributions to this work.

## References


1. Garrison, D., Anderson, T., Archer, W.: Critical inquiry in a text-based environment: computer conferencing in higher education. Internet High. Educ. **2**, 87–105 (1999)
2. Wang, Q., Jing, S., Camacho, I., Joyner, D., Goel, A., Jill Watson, S.A.: Design and evaluation of a virtual agent to build communities among online learners. In: Extended Abstracts of the 2020 CHI Conference on Human Factors in Computing Systems, pp. 1–8 (2020)
3. Goel, A.: AI-powered learning: making education accessible, affordable, and achievable. arXiv preprint arXiv:2006.01908 (2020)
4. Kakar, S., et al.: SAMI: an AI actor for fostering social interactions in online classrooms. In: Proceedings of 20th International Conference (ITS 2024). Springer, Thessaloniki (2024)
5. Murdock, J., Goel, A.: Meta-case-based reasoning: self-improvement through self-understanding. J. Exp. Theor. Artif. Intell. **20**, 1–36 (2008)
6. Goel, A., Rugaber, S.: GAIA: a CAD-like environment for designing game-playing agents. IEEE Intell. Syst. **32**, 60–67 (2017)
7. Goel, A., Sikka, H., Nandan, V., Lee, J., Lisle, M., Rugaber, S.: Explanation as Question Answering based on a Task Model of the Agent's Design. arXiv preprint arXiv:2206.05030 (2022)
8. Wei, J., et al.: Chain-of-thought prompting elicits reasoning in large language models. Adv. Neural Inf. Process. Syst. **35**, 24824–24837 (2022)
9. Mueller, S., Hoffman, R., Clancey, W., Emrey, A., Klein, G.: Explanation in human-AI systems: a literature meta-review, synopsis of key ideas and publications, and bibliography for explainable AI. arXiv preprint arXiv:1902.01876 (2019)
10. Confalonieri, R., Coba, L., Wagner, B., Besold, T.: A historical perspective of explainable Artificial Intelligence. Wiley Interdiscip. Rev. Data Mining Knowl. Discov. **11**, e1391 (2021)
11. Gilpin, L., Bau, D., Yuan, B., Bajwa, A., Specter, M., Kagal, L.: Explaining explanations: an overview of interpretability of machine learning. In: 2018 IEEE 5th International Conference on Data Science and Advanced Analytics (DSAA), pp. 80–89 (2018)
12. Rudin, C.: Stop explaining black box machine learning models for high stakes decisions and use interpretable models instead. Nat. Mach. Intell. **1**, 206–215 (2019)
13. Goel, A., Polepeddi, L.: Jill Watson: A Virtual Teaching Assistant. Theoretical Contexts And Design-based Examples. Routledge, Learning Engineering For Online Education (2018)
14. Eicher, B., Polepeddi, L., Goel, A., Watson, J.: doesn't care if you're pregnant: grounding AI ethics in empirical studies. In: Proceedings of the 2018 AAAI/ACM Conference on AI, Ethics, and Society, pp. 88–94 (2018)
15. Lee, J., Nass, C.: Trust in computers: the computers-are-social-actors (CASA) paradigm and trustworthiness perception in human-computer communication. In: Trust and Technology in a Ubiquitous Modern Environment: Theoretical and Methodological Perspectives, pp. 1–15 (2010)
16. Chandrasekaran, B., Tanner, M., Josephson, J.: Explaining control strategies in problem solving. IEEE Intell. Syst. **4**, 9–15 (1989)
17. Chandrasekaran, B., Swartout, W.: Explanations in knowledge systems: the role of explicit representation of design knowledge. IEEE Expert **6**, 47–49 (1991)

18. Goel, A., Silver Garza, A., Grué, N., Murdock, J., Recker, M., Govindaraj, T.: Explanatory interface in interactive design environments. In: Artificial Intelligence in Design 1996, pp. 387–405 (1996)
19. Liao, Q., Gruen, D., Miller, S.: Questioning the AI: informing design practices for explainable AI user experiences. In: Proceedings of the 2020 CHI Conference on Human Factors in Computing Systems, pp. 1–15 (2020)
20. Sipos, L., Schäfer, U., Glinka, K., Müller-Birn, C.: Identifying explanation needs of end-users: applying and extending the XAI question bank. Proc. Mensch Comput. **2023**, 492–497 (2023)
21. Nauta, M., et al.: From anecdotal evidence to quantitative evaluation methods: a systematic review on evaluating explainable AI. ACM Comput. Surv. **55**, 1–42 (2023)

# Students' Perceptions of Adopting Learning Analytics

Dimitrios Tzimas(✉) and Stavros Demetriadis

Aristotle University of Thessaloniki, Thessaloniki, Greece
{detzimas,sdemetri}@csd.auth.gr

**Abstract.** Learning analytics (LA) refers to the collection, analysis, and presentation of big data to assist teachers in optimising learning conditions. Although LA has made contributions, it still has not met students' needs because it does not provide sufficient actionable insights that prioritise learning over analytics. Moreover, the degree of LA adoption is still limited, and students and teachers who do adopt LA do not engage with it consistently. Our research aims to examine students' perspectives of adopting LA. The research question is as follows: "What are students' learning perceptions and satisfaction under learning analytics-based guidance?" A qualitative study that included interviews and a perception survey was conducted at a university in Greece. The factors that affected the adoption of LA were performance expectancy, feelings, and guidance, according to the findings. Student satisfaction was also high with LA-based guidance. We discuss the implications and future research for students adopting LA.

**Keywords:** Learning analytics adoption · Higher education · Co-design · Students' perceptions · Qualitative study

## 1 Introduction and Related Work

Learning analytics (LA) is a growing community that has emerged for identifying students' behaviour and performance. Learning analytics is a type of intelligent data use transforming data into valuable knowledge, offering students and educators learning insights and evidence-based interventions (Guzmán-Valenzuela et al., 2021). However, there exist issues, particularly with student learning and its implications (Banihashem et al., 2022). According to Viberg et al. (2018), LA appears to place greater emphasis on analytics than on learning (Gašević et al., 2015). Furthermore, a transition from a technological to an educational perspective is required (Tzimas & Demetriadis, 2024). Learning analytics has not yet been used to its potential because LA recommendations do not provide enough actionable information to instructors and students (Tzimas & Demetriadis, 2023). Furthermore, Tzimas and Demetriadis (2021b) reported a slight increase in student learning performance through LA. While a substantial corpus of literature about technology adoption in the context of higher education exists, there is limited research on LA about factors that might promote the decision to adopt and implement LA in HEIs (Hilliger et al., 2024). Our focus is on how students perceive


A. Sifaleras and F. Lin (Eds.): ITS 2024, LNCS 14798, pp. 361–368, 2024.
https://doi.org/10.1007/978-3-031-63028-6_30

the adoption of LA and, thus, how they describe their motivation for LA adoption. In particular, we enacted an intervention that involved displaying a traffic signal indicator message to convey the performance of each student and an online interview with the instructor for self-assessment. The objective of the research was to investigate students' learning perceptions with LA-based guidance.

There are specific studies on students' perceptions and emotions around LA (Kitto et al., 2017). In Ifenthaler's (2017) study, network graph analysis demonstrated the ability of LA design to improve learner satisfaction. Because there is limited research on LA-based feedback satisfaction (Demmans Epp et al., 2020), we investigated whether our results align with the existing findings. Nonetheless, after guidance from LA support, students' opinions require further research in order to extract insights regarding feedback satisfaction and thus students' motivation to adopt LA. Qualitative techniques may be valuable for investigating students' perceptions of LA and how they can become more actively involved (Guzmán-Valenzuela et al., 2021). Finally, we investigate the following research question:

"What are students' learning perceptions and satisfaction under learning analytics-based guidance?".

In the following sections, we illustrate the research design and study results, followed by a discussion and conclusions.

## 2 Proposed Methodology

### 2.1 Learning Design

Our instructional design adheres to the flipped classroom, motivational interviewing, and ethical pedagogical concepts. The flipped classroom instructional strategy is commonly used in blended and online learning environments. It allows students to manage time specifically for completing tasks that need higher-order knowledge (Jovanovic et al., 2017). Moreover, motivational interviewing teacher guidance for effective classroom management is a collaborative conversation approach that strengthens students' incentives to modify their behaviours (Zuckoff, 2012). Finally, we use ethics to foster trust among educational stakeholders by addressing the following guidelines (Tzimas & Demetriadis, 2021a): providing informed consent, promoting student autonomy, and ensuring that instructor feedback motivates students.

During the third week, we sent messages to all the students about LA-supported actions. The instructor initiated the messages. Similar interventions were conducted weekly, as follows; "We are providing you feedback after reviewing your participation and performance. I am attaching for self-reflection your grades in the exercises and the grades of your fellow students. I encourage you to study the learning management system options for your participation concerning your peers." Finally, we modified motivational interviewing into an intervention that addressed student behaviour through Zoom discussions. The time was selected during the fifth week in order to ensure sufficient data for discussion following the monitoring of student performance and participation. Every interview lasted approximately 20 min. The students participated in a reflective process, explaining how the interventions made sense.

### 2.2 Research Design

This research was conducted in a thirteen-week undergraduate course during the COVID-19 pandemic. An informatics department of a Greek HEI provided this course online. A total of one hundred and ten students took the course. Finally, twelve students dropped out, and fifty-eight passed the course. The course covered how to conduct scientific research and write a thesis. The instruments used to collect student opinion data (regarding perceptions and satisfaction) included an opinion-mining survey after the course, interviews, and a poll. The researchers designed a survey consisting of three open-ended questions and twenty-two Likert scale items.

**Table 1.** Guide for interviewing with the students

| Questions |
|---|
| How would you describe your learning analytics-based learning experience? |
| What changes should you use to enhance your performance? |
| How would you evaluate your current progress? |
| To what extent do your test scores align with those of your peers? |
| What emotions are evoked in you by learning analytics? |
| Do you have any further observations that haven't yet been discussed? |

Qualitative data were gathered: perception survey data were used to measure student satisfaction, and semi-structured interviews were used to extract student perspectives regarding the adoption of LA. We employed content analysis to interpret patterns in the survey data. In parallel, we used thematic analysis to gather motivational interview data and extract common themes. Consequently, we posed questions in order to obtain viewpoints (Table 1). We used open responses from students and frequency analysis to develop a taxonomy for categorising comments. This inductive reasoning approach indicates that the detected themes are closely linked to the data, but they do not align with a pre-established coding scheme.

## 3 Results

Thirty-four students participated in the survey (Table 2), with questions emphasising student satisfaction and LA-based guidance usefulness. The findings from the content analysis indicate that students expressed satisfaction with the quality of the interventions. Most participants reported that the interventions were beneficial, comprehensible, and actionable. The question "What emotions does the use of learning analytics evoke?", primarily elicits feelings of encouragement ($n = 14$), self-confidence (9), and worry (8).

Following the response to the open-ended question, "Please share your thoughts on the experience of using learning analytics," the students' perspectives were gathered as follows: "I desire to have this guidance available in other courses"; "Learning analytics

**Table 2.** Overview of the descriptive statistics from the student survey.

| Survey Statements | Mean (Standard Deviation) |
|---|---|
| LA quality | |
| Learning analytics helped increase participation | 4.9 (1.6) |
| The guidance on how to utilise learning analytics was sufficient | 5.0 (1.6) |
| Efficacy of LA on self-regulated learning skills | |
| I prefer using learning analytics in the educational process over traditional ways | 4.7 (1.6) |
| Learning analytics led to putting more effort into the course | 4.4 (1.7) |
| Student satisfaction with LA | |
| Learning analytics provided an enjoyable educational experience | 4.9 (1.5) |
| Learning analytics increased my motivation to actively engage in the course | 4.8 (1.5) |
| Motivation to use LA | |
| A discussion was held to elucidate the learning analytics findings | 5.0 (1.6) |
| Learning analytics facilitated my course awareness | 5.2 (1.3) |

assisted me in understanding my performance compared to other students"; and "I prefer to configure learning analytics to suit my needs". Responses to the question "How did learning analytics facilitate the learning process?" centred on the themes of motivation, awareness, and persistence.

In parallel, we extracted the subsequent findings from a poll of seventy-five students completed in the seventh week. In the question "Do you monitor analytics for your academic performance?", forty-eight students answered affirmatively, whereas ten answered negatively. In response to the question "Do you find reflection needful?", thirty-six students answered "Yes, I am more aware", eleven answered "Yes, I am becoming competitive", and nine answered, "No, it makes me anxious". Finally, when asked "What positive emotions do learning analytics evoke in you?", thirty-five students answered that they considered it interesting, twenty-five were motivated, and twenty were satisfied. On the contrary, for the question "What negative emotions do learning analytics evoke in you?", twenty-seven students answered curiosity, eighteen answered anxiety, and 10 answered irritability.

Additionally, a thematic analysis was used during the interviews. The analysis of the discussions revealed eleven common themes. Combining the themes and refining their semantics yielded the eight critical themes listed in Table 3. For instance, a number of students indicated modifying their behaviour throughout the semester. This pattern indicated that students at risk of withdrawing may change their behaviour following the intervention, and the use of motivational interviewing may intensify this risk. Five students stated that they considered dropping out when they finally passed the course. Finally, some students reported that they were not involved in the design process.

**Table 3.** Interview results.

| Concept | Evidence Quotations | Frequency % |
| --- | --- | --- |
| Behaviour change | The learning analytics-based alert woke me up, and I made the decision to begin exercising | 52 |
| Guidance | My grades were lower than the class average, so this comparison prompted me to change my study habits | 45 |
| Support seeking | Learning analytics services encouraged me to seek help | 39 |
| Motivation | Learning analytics motivated me to persist in my efforts | 34 |

## 4 Research Outcomes

Table 2 demonstrates a high level of student satisfaction, aligning with the results reported by Nguyen et al. (2017). The positive attitudes of the students on the efficacy of LA services were in line with existing literature (Smith, 2019; Tzimas & Demetriadis, 2024) and our poll findings (where most students acknowledged the utility of LA). As stated by Viberg et al. (2018), the findings mentioned above enhance our comprehension of LA in a qualitative manner, rather than relying on technical approaches. Moreover, the students' responses revealed emerging themes related to the quality of LA, the efficacy of LA, and the incentive to utilise it. Specifically, the requirement for timely feedback to facilitate self-reflection (Bodily & Verbert, 2017) is derived from the following quotations: "It is inadequate to obtain good grades without receiving feedback"; and "Few teachers are concerned about whether students are progressing at a similar rate."

According to the interviews, our conclusion is that students held a favourable perception of LA-based guidance. The main subjects we identified were behavioural change, motivation, seeking support, and time allocation. We observed students' satisfaction with LA to support awareness and self-reflection, aligning with the conclusions stated by Arnold and Pistilli (2012). According to a student's description, "The guidance I received for utilising LA was helpful". However, students were initially unfamiliar with working with LA-based feedback.

To investigate the differences between datasets, some students expressed dissatisfaction and anxiety; thus, HEIs cannot overlook this crucial perspective. This unexpected insight generates an unforeseen interpretation because previously identified themes highlight that LA-based feedback may improve learning outcomes. A plausible hypothesis is that peer comparisons have a demotivating effect. Roberts et al. (2016) found that certain students were not interested in utilising services that facilitated comparisons with their peers. When questioned about their views on progress, the students expressed anxiety. Barreiros et al. (2023) proposed the inclusion of student opinions in LA-based decision-making, namely through participatory and co-design approaches. However, these opinions are often not considered (Buckingham Shum et al., 2019). Thus, while a university may see feedback and teacher effort as beneficial, they may not always consider what students want (Dwivedi et al., 2019).

In contrast, most students acknowledged the value of LA-based guidance. Many quotations exemplified this mindset: "Learning analytics provides motivation and reflection, fostering students to be more productive"; and "Using learning analytics enabled me to achieve high rankings and boost my self-confidence". We conclude that LA-based guidance can have a significant impact on improving self-regulation and performance expectancy. Additionally, peer comparisons have the potential to motivate students to enhance their skills (Tzimas & Demetriadis, 2024).

A scenario in student-facing LA involves students being presented with a dashboard but failing to comprehend its significance to them (Bodily & Verbert, 2017) due to the lack of explanatory feedback. This statement contradicts the students' extracts throughout the study interviews: "It is advantageous. I wish we had this specific guidance in every class" (obligation to take action) and "The use of learning analytics helped me gain insight into my level compared to other students" (reflection).

Regarding self-regulated learning skills, LA-based guidance facilitates students practising them methodically. By adhering to the motivational interviewing rules and expressing their thoughts regarding their study behaviour, the students were more likely to practise these skills. Ultimately, by reflecting on the students' subjective perceptions, we noted that the students reported adequate assimilation of self-regulated learning abilities as the interventions progressed. This finding provides evidence in favour of Kitto et al.'s (2017) claim that students should evaluate their behaviour by employing self-regulation techniques.

Engaging students in the LA design process can be complicated and time-consuming. Nevertheless, involving them in participatory and codesign approaches can transform a failing prototype into a successful system. As a result, shifting LA to something done with students is a human-centred learning analytics strategy (Campos et al., 2024). Understanding students' values and needs through inter-stakeholder communication leads to learners' agentic positioning (Dimitriadis et al., 2021). Students' statements, "Learning analytics tools should be tailored to my requirements" and "It would be advantageous if I could adjust LA according to my personal preferences," provide the above insights.

The poll results indicate that most students recognised the usefulness of LA feedback, with a percentage of 83%. The predominant positive emotions encompass motivation, satisfaction, and encouragement, whereas the negative emotions consist of anxiety, irritability, and confusion. An analysis of the survey, poll, and motivational interviewing data sources revealed similarities among the datasets. The consistent themes observed were encouragement, self-confidence, persistence, and stress.

## 5 Conclusions

This paper addresses the critical issue of students' perceptions of LA adoption in educational environments. Through a qualitative study conducted at a Greek university, the research investigates factors influencing the adoption of LA and examines student satisfaction with LA-based guidance. The findings reveal positive attitudes towards the usefulness of LA services and highlight the significance of high-quality feedback and timely guidance in supporting students' self-reflection and motivation.

Finally, we acknowledge the constraints in interpreting the results. The sample size was small, and the data only covered one semester of a specific course. Our intention is to replicate this study in nonformal education settings, with new groups of teachers and students from varied backgrounds, who represent large populations. This way, we could observe the applicability of our findings to various contexts. Future studies could investigate the confirmation stage in order to have a thorough understanding of the adoption process.

## References


Arnold, K.E., Pistilli, M.D.: Course signals at Purdue: using learning analytics to increase student success. ACM Int. Conf. Proc. Ser. **2012**, 267–270 (2012). https://doi.org/10.1145/2330601.2330666

Banihashem, S.K., Noroozi, O., van Ginkel, S., Macfadyen, L.P., Biemans, H.J.A.: A systematic review of the role of learning analytics in enhancing feedback practices in higher education. Educ. Res. Rev. **37**, 100489 (2022). https://doi.org/10.1016/j.edurev.2022.100489

Barreiros, C., Leitner, P., Ebner, M., Veas, E., Lindstaedt, S.: Students in focus – moving towards human-centred learning analytics. In: Viberg, O., Grönlund, Å. (eds.) Practicable Learning Analytics. Advances in Analytics for Learning and Teaching, pp. 77–94. Springer, Cham (2023). https://doi.org/10.1007/978-3-031-27646-0_5

Bodily, R., Verbert, K.: Trends and issues in student-facing learning analytics reporting systems research. ACM Int. Conf. Proc. Ser., 309–318 (2017). https://doi.org/10.1145/3027385.3027403

Buckingham Shum, S., Ferguson, R., Martinez-Maldonado, R.: Human-centred learning analytics. J. Learn. Anal. **6**, 1–9 (2019). https://doi.org/10.18608/jla.2019.62.1

Campos, F., Nguyen, H., Ahn, J., Jackson, K.: Leveraging cultural forms in human-centred learning analytics design. Br. J. Edu. Technol. **55**, 769–784 (2024). https://doi.org/10.1111/bjet.13384

Demmans Epp, C., Phirangee, K., Hewitt, J., Perfetti, C.A.: Learning management system and course influences on student actions and learning experiences. Educ. Technol. Res. Dev. **68** (2020). https://doi.org/10.1007/s11423-020-09821-1

Dimitriadis, Y., Martínez-Maldonado, R., Wiley, K.: Human-centered design principles for actionable learning analytics. In: Tsiatsos, T., Demetriadis, S., Mikropoulos, A., Dagdilelis, V. (eds.) Research on E-Learning and ICT in Education, pp. 277–296. Springer, Cham (2021). https://doi.org/10.1007/978-3-030-64363-8_15

Dwivedi, Y.K., Rana, N.P., Jeyaraj, A.: Re-examining the Unified Theory of Acceptance and Use of Technology (UTAUT): towards a revised theoretical model. Inf. Syst. Front. **21**, 719–734 (2019). https://doi.org/10.1007/s10796-017-9774-y

Gašević, D., Dawson, S., Siemens, G., Gašević, B.D., Dawson, S.: Let's not forget: learning analytics are about learning. TechTrends **59**, 64–71 (2015)

Guzmán-Valenzuela, C., Gómez-González, C., Rojas-Murphy Tagle, A.: Learning analytics in higher education: a preponderance of analytics but very little learning? Int. J. Educ. Technol. High. Educ. **18**, 23 (2021). https://doi.org/10.1186/s41239-021-00258-x

Hilliger, I., Miranda, C., Celis, S., Pérez-Sanagustín, M.: Curriculum analytics adoption in higher education: a multiple case study engaging stakeholders in different phases of design. Br. J. Edu. Technol. **55**, 785–801 (2024). https://doi.org/10.1111/bjet.13374

Ifenthaler, D.: Are higher education institutions prepared for learning analytics? TechTrends **61**, 366–371 (2017). https://doi.org/10.1007/s11528-016-0154-0

Jovanovic, J., Gašević, D., Dawson, S., Pardo, A., Mirriahi, N.: Learning analytics to unveil learning strategies in a flipped classroom. Internet High. Educ. **33**, 74–85 (2017). https://doi.org/10.1016/j.iheduc.2017.02.001

Kitto, K., Lupton, M., Davis, K., Waters, Z.: Designing for student-facing learning analytics. Australas. J. Educ. Technol. **33**, 152–168 (2017). https://doi.org/10.14742/ajet.3607

Nguyen, Q., Rienties, B., Toetenel, L., Ferguson, R., Whitelock, D.: Examining the designs of computer-based assessment and its impact on student engagement, satisfaction, and pass rates. Comput. Hum. Behav. **76**, 703–714 (2017). https://doi.org/10.1016/j.chb.2017.03.028

Roberts, L.D., Howell, J.A., Seaman, K., Gibson, D.C.: Student attitudes toward learning analytics in higher education: "The Fitbit version of the learning world." Front. Psychol. **7**, 1959 (2016). https://doi.org/10.3389/fpsyg.2016.01959

Smith, P.: Engaging online students through peer-comparison progress dashboards. J. Appl. Res. High. Educ. **12**, 38–56 (2019). https://doi.org/10.1108/JARHE-11-2018-0249

Tzimas, D., Demetriadis, S.: Ethical issues in learning analytics: a review of the field. Educ. Technol. Res. Dev. **69**, 1101–1133 (2021). https://doi.org/10.1007/s11423-021-09977-4

Tzimas, D., Demetriadis, S.: The impact of learning analytics on student performance and satisfaction in a higher education course. In: Proceedings of the 14th International Conference on Educational Data Mining (EDM21), Paris, France, 29 June–2 July, pp. 654–660 (2021)

Tzimas, D., Demetriadis, S.: Culture of ethics in adopting learning analytics. In: Frasson, C., Mylonas, P., Troussas, C., (eds.) ITS 2023. LNCS, vol. 13891, pp. 591–603. Springer, Cham (2023). https://doi.org/10.1007/978-3-031-32883-1_52

Tzimas, D.E., Demetriadis, S.N.: Impact of learning analytics guidance on student self-regulated learning skills, performance, and satisfaction: a mixed methods study. Educ. Sci. **14**, 92 (2024). https://doi.org/10.3390/educsci14010092

Viberg, O., Hatakka, M., Bälter, O., Mavroudi, A.: The current landscape of learning analytics in higher education. Comput. Hum. Behav. **89**, 98–110 (2018). https://doi.org/10.1016/j.chb.2018.07.027

Zuckoff, A.: Welcome to MITRIP. Motiv. Interviewing Train. Res. Implement. Pract. **1**, 1 (2012). https://doi.org/10.5195/mitrip.2012.5

# *AI4LA*: An Intelligent Chatbot for Supporting Students with Dyslexia, Based on Generative AI

Stefano D'Urso and Filippo Sciarrone(✉)

Faculty of Technological and Innovation Sciences, Universitas Mercatorum, P.zza Mattei, 10, Rome, Italy
stefano.durso@studenti.unimercatorum.it,
filippo.sciarrone@unimercatorum.it

**Abstract.** In the last two years, thanks to the advent of generative AI, new avenues are opening up in its use in the educational field, e.g. through the use of ChatGPT. But, while generative AI is opening up new avenues for both teaching and learning, there are no proposals for its use in the context of students with Dyslexia and in general for students with Specific Learning Disorders (SLD), that afflict between 10 and 15 percent of people worldwide. In this paper we present AI4LA, a web intelligent chatbot based on generative AI, with the aim to help dyslexic students during their learning process. This system is capable of analyzing conversational data to model students' understandings and misconceptions, thereby offering personalized educational support. Significantly, we highlight the chatbot's ability to create Concept Maps from conversations, visually representing the student's knowledge structure and progression. An evaluation of the effectiveness of the system is presented, in a real-world educational settings, based on feedback from a sample of dyslexic students. The findings suggest that our system holds great promise in revolutionizing the way dyslexic students engage with educational content, making learning more accessible, interactive, and effective.

**Keywords:** Dyslexia · Intelligent Chatbot · LLM

## 1 Introduction

The shift towards distance learning has gained momentum in recent years, especially due to the COVID-19 pandemic, leading to an increase in the adoption of Massive Open Online Courses (MOOCs) across all educational levels [7]. This transition has posed significant challenges in providing personalized support to students, particularly those with Specific Learning Disorders (SLDs) like *Dyslexia*, *Dysorthographia*, and *Dyscalculia*, who face substantial hurdles in environments lacking direct teacher engagement [12,14]. Dyslexia, the most prevalent SLD, affects between 5% and 15% of the global population, impacting reading, writing, and occasionally spoken language comprehension [1,2]. The development


A. Sifaleras and F. Lin (Eds.): ITS 2024, LNCS 14798, pp. 369–377, 2024.
https://doi.org/10.1007/978-3-031-63028-6_31

of assistive technologies such as speech recognition, text-to-speech, and smart pens has been crucial in supporting dyslexic learners [3,6,11,16]. Furthermore, advances in Deep Learning and Large Language Models (LLMs) like ChatGPT have facilitated the creation of tools like the system we present here: *AI4LA-Artificial Intelligence for Learning Assistant*, which supports dyslexic students by adapting dialogues and generating personalized Concept Maps (CM)s based on their specific needs[1]. Our initial trials of *AI4LA* in a high school setting have shown promising results, enhancing engagement and learning outcomes for students with dyslexia. This paper details these findings, discusses the integration of generative AI in educational settings, and outlines future research directions

## 2 Related Work

This section examines support systems for individuals with dyslexia, particularly highlighting the *AI4LA* system's use of CMs, which visually represent a knowledge domain as a direct graph, formed by nodes (the concepts) and the connections among them (the semantic relationships). These CMs, dynamically generated from chatbot-learner dialogues, help minimize the reliance on textual explanations, addressing the challenges dyslexic learners face in creating such maps due to difficulties with reading and key relationship identification [8].

Beyond CMs, *AI4LA* leverages advanced generative AI technologies like *Retrieval Augmented Generation* (RAG) to enhance learning by generating topic summaries, distinguishing it from other tools that lack dynamic CM customization capabilities. Comparative analysis shows that other applications also support dyslexic learners. The ALEXZA application [13] offers features like text-to-speech and adjustable reading speeds, using machine learning to classify text difficulty. The GARY system enhances reading through eye-tracking and auditory narration, significantly improving comprehension [15]. Additionally, the RALF framework uses Cellular Learning Automata (CLA) to tailor educational content for Persian students with dyslexia, enhancing learning effectiveness by 27% during COVID-19 lockdowns [10]. In [5], the TutorChat system is presented. This system is a chatbot based on ChatGPT, able to automatically build multimedia CMs: each node is connected to images and video concerning the knowledge domain under study. Our system, however, offers different types of CMs whereas Tutorchat only builds them based on the answer to a specific question using Google for images and youtube for videos.

Overall, the *AI4LA* system's integration of generative AI and CMs uniquely positions it in the educational support landscape for dyslexic learners, setting new standards for personalized educational tools.

## 3 The System

In the rapidly evolving landscape of Natural Language Processing (NLP), two powerful techniques have emerged as game-changers, reshaping the way we harness the potential of language models: *Fine-Tuning* [4] and *Retrieval Augmented*

[1] https://dyslexia2024.replit.app.

*Generation* (RAG) [9]. These methodologies have revolutionized the capabilities of language models, addressing critical limitations and unlocking new possibilities in various NLP applications. Since our system uses both of the above technologies, it is worth briefly summarising their key features and how were used for a full understanding of the system.

Fine Tuning is essentially a re-training of a Deep Learning model. In the context of refining LLMs, Adaptive Fine-Tuning (AFT) and Behavioral Fine-Tuning (BFT) refer to specific methodologies used to adjust and improve the model based on additional data or feedback. AFT involves further training a pre-trained model on a specific, often smaller, dataset that is tailored to the needs of a particular application or domain, adapting the model to be more proficient in areas that might not have been adequately covered during the initial broad training phase. BFT, on the other hand, focuses on adjusting the model's outputs to match desired behaviors more closely, often in response to specific user feedback or desired interaction styles. This method is less about domain knowledge and more about how the model interacts-its style, tone, response formulation and so on. In our case, the fine-tuning process we employed is an example of BFT. The dataset we used was specialized on a set of simulated conversations between the chatbot and dyslexic students, with the aim to train the chatbot to interact properly with students with dyslexia. This work was supported by a cognitive psychologist. The dataset is composed of 80 conversations, in the form: $C_i \equiv \{s_i, (u_{ij}, a_{ij})\}$, where $s_i$ (i=1,...,80) is that part of the conversation used to train the role of the system and $(u_{ij}, a_{ij})$ are a set of interactions in the form: <*question posted by the user,answer prompted by the chatbot*>. So, while each record $C_i$ has only one $s_i$, it can have a variable number of couples $(u_{ij}, a_{ij})$, depending on the knowledge domain concerning the interaction. Figure 1 shows an example of such kind of record with $j = 2$.

| | |
|---|---|
| system | Your role is to be a helpful assistant with a friendly, understanding, patient, and user-affirming tone. You should: explain topics in short, simple sentences; keep explanations to 2 or 3 sentences at most. If the user provides affirmative or brief responses, take the initiative to continue with relevant information. Check for user understanding after each brief explanation using varied and friendly-toned questions. Use ordered or unordered lists (if longer than 2 items, introduce them one by one and check for understanding before proceeding), or simple text in replies. Provide examples or metaphors if the user doesn't understand. |
| user | Tell me something about Planet Earth |
| assistant | Planet Earth is the third planet from the Sun in our Solar System. It's the only known planet to support life. Are you following? |
| user | Yes, please continue. |
| assistant | It has diverse climates and terrains, from icy polar regions to vast deserts. About 71% of its surface is covered by water, mainly oceans. Clear so far? |
| user | Absolutely clear. |

**Fig. 1.** A complete record of the fine-tuning dataset. In this example, first we train the chatbot to have the role of an assistant to answer to dyslexic people. Second, we have two simulated interactions chatbot-user. In this case, $j = 2$.

In this way, we obtained a neural model customized to properly interact with dyslexic people.

RAG provides a way to optimise the production of an LLM with targeted information without changing the model behind it; that targeted information can be more up-to-date than the LLM, but also more precise in the case of specific organisations and sectors. This means that the generative AI can provide more appropriate responses to prompts, and base those responses on highly current data [9]. A RAG model acts in a pipeline configuration, following these steps: Retrieve, Augment and Generate.

The system RAG pipeline uses *Chroma DB*[2]. Chroma DB is an open-source vector store designed for storing and retrieving vector embeddings. Its primary function is to save embeddings along with metadata for use later by large LLMs. It supports the creation, storage, and querying of embeddings, making it a valuable tool for developers building AI applications that require efficient handling of vector embeddings, as in the case of our system. Figure 2 shows the functional architecture of the system.

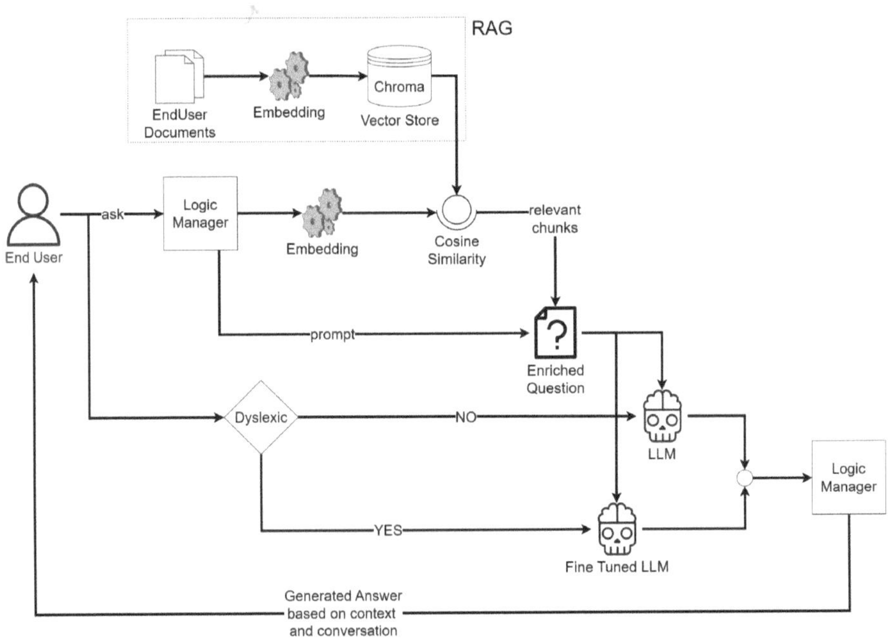


**Fig. 2.** The Fine-Tuned RAG Pipeline embedded in the AI4LA system. For dyslexic people the system makes use of the fine-tuned model.

In particular, our system empowers users to gather data from various sources such as PDFs, text documents, and YouTube videos. Subsequently, this collected

[2] https://www.trychroma.com/.

data are utilized to generate a Chroma DB collection, which serves as valuable context for enhancing the capabilities of the RAG model. When a user submits a query, the RAG system uses the indexed data and vectors to perform efficient searches. The system identifies relevant information by comparing the query vector with those stored in Chroma DB. In our implementation we used the cosine similarity measure to find the most relevant chunks inside the vector DB. The LLMs then use the retrieved data to craft appropriate responses. Finally, we have enriched the RAG Pipeline with those finely-tuned models specifically designed to meet the unique requirements of dyslexic users and discussed in the previous paragraph.

The system offers a range of features which ensure that every interaction is tailored to the student's unique preferences and needs: (i) a typeface designed by Google, against some common symptoms of dyslexia; (ii) Context Summarization: When the learner uploads her own context, the system enables her to request a summary. This summary provides an overview of the context's key points, ensuring the learner has a clear understanding of the topic at hand during conversations; (iii) Contextual Concept Maps: When the chatbot provides an answer, the user can generate a CM for that response; (iv) Speech-to-Text: The student can post the question using voice instead of writing and the system will transcribe it into text, streamlining communication; (v) Export of Full Conversation: The system allows users to conveniently export the entire conversation, preserving it for reference or future analysis. In addition, we placed a significant emphasis on user customization. In fact, users have the power to adjust the level of contextual CM generation and conversation memory. This allows the chatbot to fully adapt to their needs and preferences, making the interaction even more personal and tailored to the user.

Here we show a brief case study of the chatbot at work. After entering the system using his credentials, the (dyslexic) student entered a PDF document into the system, concerning operations between binary numbers. He then asked the following question: *Please show me an example of addition of two binary numbers*. Consequently, the chatbot prompts the example. After that, the student asks for the CM that is immediately drawn in the space below the answer, as shown in Fig. 3. Finally, the student can download the CM in order to better fix the concepts to be studied.

## 4 Methods

This section details the initial experimentation with the system, which involved a sequence of steps: selecting a sample, administering a text comprehension test, and distributing a happiness questionnaire. The study included 23 dyslexic students, aged 14 to 18, from a technical high school in Italy. The test chosen was based on a newspaper article titled *His Majesty the Owl Blinded by Lights*, selected due to its relevance to text comprehension-a critical skill for dyslexic students-and because it mimics the standardized *Invalsi Test* used in Italian education. Students used the intelligent chatbot pre-loaded with the text to

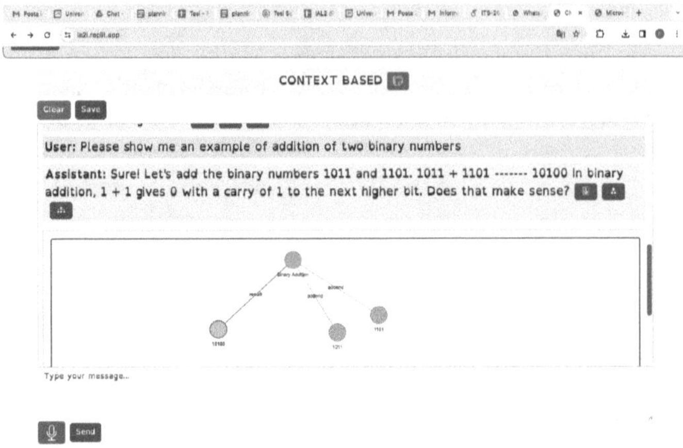


**Fig. 3.** The brief case study concerning the learning of binary numbers.

assist them in understanding and answering questions about the article. They had 45 min to complete the test in a fully anonymized setting to protect their privacy, using unique credentials and pseudonyms. Prior to the test, students were briefed on how to use the chatbot, despite their previous general experience with ChatGPT. This was their first opportunity to query about self-provided texts, a feature enabled by this system. Both paper and digital versions of the test were available, and each student worked at a dedicated PC station. After the test, they completed a feedback questionnaire. Data analysis was performed on both the chatbot interactions and questionnaire responses.

In the analysis of the data generated by the experiment, we distinguished two keys of study the first concerns an analysis of student-system interactions and utilization, as retrieved from the log file. The second concerns the questionnaire taken by the sample after the session.

**Student-System Interactions.** Our analysis identified four key variables in student interactions with the system: Question Precision, Seeking Clarifications, Use of CMs, and Low Usage. From the data (see Table 1), we observed that slightly more than 50% of students asked *Precise Questions*, indicating that the chatbot is a valuable resource for direct answers, aiding in test preparation. Approximately 20% sought clarifications or engaged more deeply with the chatbot's responses, demonstrating its role in fostering an interactive learning environment. Notably, 65% of students utilized the CMs generated by the system, showing the effectiveness of this feature in helping students visualize and organize information. However, a small segment, about 5%, showed *Low Usage* of the system, either by not using it or interacting minimally. Investigating the reasons behind this could provide insights into potential improvements in system design and functionality. Overall, the chatbot appears to effectively meet the needs of most students by providing direct answers, enabling deeper understanding, and supplying helpful visual aids, though further research could enhance its appeal to all users.

**Table 1.** The four variables on which the system utilisation analysis was based.

| Chat Activities | % |
|---|---|
| Question Precision | 50% |
| Seeking Clarifications | 20% |
| Use of CMs | 65% |
| Low Usage | 5% |

**The Questionnaire.** After the work session, all students completed a questionnaire designed to assess their enjoyment, engagement, and the usability of the system. The questionnaire was distributed using the Google Form module[3] and consisted of sixteen closed-ended questions and one open-ended question. The questionnaire is depicted in Fig. 4. Crafted with the assistance of a psychologist specializing in dyslexia, the questions primarily focused on usability, engagement, and the potential effectiveness of *AI4LA* as a supportive tool for dyslexic learners.

| ID | Question | ID | Question |
|---|---|---|---|
| $Q_1$ | What is your age? | $Q_9$ | Are the text characters with which AI4LA communicates clear and understandable to you? |
| $Q_2$ | What kind of school you attend | $Q_{10}$ | Do you think AI4LA can help you in your studies? |
| $Q_3$ | Would you like to use IA4LA often to learn? | $Q_{11}$ | Do you like that AI4LA can read your answer? |
| $Q_4$ | Did you find IA4LA easy to use? | $Q_{12}$ | Do you like that you can communicate with your voice without writing? |
| $Q_5$ | Did you need technical help to use AI4LA? | $Q_{13}$ | Did AI4LA's explanations help you? |
| $Q_6$ | Did you feel confident using AI4LA? | $Q_{14}$ | Did you find the concept map AI4LA proposed easy to read? |
| $Q_7$ | Did you have to learn many technical things before you could start communicating with AI4LA? | $Q_{15}$ | Did the concept map help you? |
| $Q_8$ | Did you feel encouraged by AI4LA? | $Q_16$ | Did you enjoy using AI4IA? |

**Fig. 4.** The questions composing the questionnaire submitted to the sample after the use of the system.

The closed-ended questions were grouped according to three research themes:

- Group $G_1 = \{Q_4, Q_5, Q_6, Q_7, Q_8, Q_9, Q_{12}\}$ focused on assessing the system's ease of use.

[3] https://forms.gle/RNKCxDjuEyu1RjdU9.

- Group $G_2$={$Q_3$, $Q_8$, $Q_{10}$, $Q_{11}$, $Q_{12}$, $Q_{13}$, $Q_{14}$, $Q_{16}$, $Q_{15}$} aimed to evaluate the acceptance and appreciation of IA4LA as a study support tool.
- Group $G_3$={$Q_3$, $Q_6$, $Q_8$, $Q_9$, $Q_{10}$, $Q_{11}$, $Q_{14}$} intended to measure the perceived effectiveness of the system.

Responses were gathered using a 5-point Likert scale, with specific questions designed inversely to ensure analytical consistency. Normalization was applied to invert responses for $Q_5$ and $Q_7$ during analysis, aligning them with the standard scale direction used in other questions. Data analysis involved calculating the average number of occurrences for each scale value across the groups, facilitating a detailed evaluation of user feedback.

**Table 2.** Occurrences of the 5-scale values in the answers to the questionnaires, aggregated according to the three groups/RQs.

| | Avg. 1 | Avg. 2 | Avg. 3 | Avg. 4 | Avg. 5 |
|---|---|---|---|---|---|
| Group 1 | 0 | 0.78 | 1.8 | 4.23 | 8.98 |
| Group 2 | 0 | 0.41 | 2.21 | 4.31 | 8.76 |
| Group 3 | 0 | 0.22 | 1.9 | 4.78 | 8.89 |

Initial findings from this analysis indicate a lack of low-value responses, with the higher values on the scale dominating, suggesting a positive reception towards the *AI4LA* system. The detailed results from each group are summarized in Table 2, providing a clear indication of high user engagement and the perceived effectiveness of the system.

## 5 Conclusions

In this article, we presented *AI4LA*, an intelligent web chatbot based on generative AI to support the learning of dyslexic students. The system has the characteristic of exploiting all the potential offered by generative AI, through the use of two procedures: Fine-Tuning and Retrieval-Augmented Generation, which allow the system to offer good student support, such as the possibility of constructing concept maps and contextual summaries. We presented an initial experiment with a sample of 23 dyslexic students, coming from an Italian technical high school, obtaining positive feedback, along three lines: usability, engagement and perceived effectiveness. As future developments, we plan to carry out a more wide-ranging experiment to validate the system.

**Acknowledgement.** We would like to express our sincere gratitude to Universitas Mercatorum for its financial support in the development of this project (Grant No. 16-FIN/RIC 2023).

## References


1. American, Psychiatric, Association, DSM-5, Task, Force. Diagnostic and Statistical Manual of Mental Disorders: DSM-4$^{\text{TM}}$, 4th edn. American Psychiatric Publishing Inc. (2000)
2. American, Psychiatric, Association, DSM-5, Task, Force. Diagnostic and Statistical Manual of Mental Disorders: DSM-5$^{\text{TM}}$, 5th edn. American Psychiatric Publishing Inc. (2013)
3. Athanaselis, T., Bakamidis, S., Dologlou, I., Argyriou, E., Symvonis, A.: Making assistive reading tools user friendly: a new platform for greek dyslexic students empowered by automatic speech recognition. Multim. Tools Appl. **68**, 681–699 (2014)
4. Church, K.W., Chen, Z., Ma, Y.: Emerging trends: a gentle introduction to fine-tuning. Nat. Lang. Eng. **27**(6), 763–778 (2021)
5. De Marco, V., Sciarrone, F., Temperini, M.: Tutorchat: a chatbot for the support to dyslexic learner's activity through generative AI. In: The 24th IEEE International Conference on Advanced Learning Technologies (in Press) (2024)
6. Gotesman, E., Goldfus, C.: The impact of assistive technologies on the reading outcomes of college students with disabilities. In: Proceedings of the Chais Conference on Instructional Technologies Research (2009)
7. Kara, A.: Covid-19 pandemic and possible trends into the future of higher education: a review. J. Educ. Educ. Develop. **8**(1) (2021)
8. Lami, G., Locatelli, M.: Dyslexia and concept maps: an indispensable tool for learning. In: 3rd International Conference on Concept Mapping "Concept Mapping–Connecting Educators", pp. 152–154. Citeseer (2008)
9. Lewis, P., et al.: Retrieval-augmented generation for knowledge-intensive NLP tasks. Adv. Neural. Inf. Process. Syst. **33**, 9459–9474 (2020)
10. Minoofam, S.A.H., Bastanfard, A., Keyvanpour, M.R.: Ralf: an adaptive reinforcement learning framework for teaching dyslexic students. Multim. Tools Appl. **81**(5), 6389–6412 (2022)
11. Olabisi, S.B.: Digital smart pen: a portable media with endless benefits. Int. J. Comput. Appl. **74**(14), 28–30 (2013)
12. Peng, H., Ma, S., Spector, J.: Personalized adaptive learning: an emerging pedagogical approach enabled by a smart learning environment. Smart Learn. Environ. **6**(9) (2019)
13. Rajapakse, S., Polwattage, D., Guruge, U., Jayathilaka, I., Edirisinghe, T., Thelijjagoda, S.: Alexza: a mobile application for dyslexics utilizing artificial intelligence and machine learning concepts. In: Proceedings of the 3rd International Conference on Information Technology Research (ICITR 2018) (2018)
14. Richardson, G.: Dyslexia in higher education. Educ. Res. Rev. **16**(4), 125–135 (2021)
15. Schiavo, G., Mana, N., Mich, O., Zancanaro, M., Job, R.: Attention-driven read-aloud technology increases reading comprehension in children with reading disabilities. J. Comput. Assist. Learn. **37**(3), 875–886 (2021)
16. Taylor, P.: Text-to-Speech Synthesis. Cambridge University Press (2009)

# EvaAI: A Multi-agent Framework Leveraging Large Language Models for Enhanced Automated Grading

Paraskevas Lagakis(✉) and Stavros Demetriadis

Software and Interactive Technologies (SWITCH) Lab, Computer Science Department, Aristotle University of Thessaloniki, Thessaloniki, Greece
{plagakis,sdemetri}@csd.auth.gr

**Abstract.** In recent times, Massive Open Online Courses (MOOCs) have become increasingly popular for offering accessible and versatile learning opportunities to a broad audience. However, specific tasks that are necessary in such systems and usually require human involvement, like grading assignments, can be difficult to automate and scale. Furthermore, recent studies have highlighted the capabilities of Large Language Models (LLMs) in a variety of natural language processing tasks, yet the effectiveness of these models in evaluating assignments in educational settings like MOOCs is still an under-researched field. In this paper, we introduce a novel multi-agent architecture, powered by LLMs and the AutoGen framework, that aims in automating the grading of subject-agnostic student assignments. Additionally, we present interaction examples between the agents during grading coding assignments, shedding light on the system's potential to mimic human-like grading nuances and incorporate the tutor's feedback. This research aims to demonstrate the advancements in automated grading, emphasizing the role of multi-agent systems in educational technology.

**Keywords:** Automated Grading · Large Language Models · Multi-Agent Systems · MOOCs

## 1 Introduction

Massive Open Online Courses (MOOCs) have made quality education more accessible, but the scalability of personalized assessment remains a challenge as automated grading systems often lack the nuance of human graders. Recent advancements in AI and Machine Learning, especially Large Language Models (LLMs) like GPT-3.5 and GPT-4, have transformed the field of Natural Language Processing (NLP) [1] and show potential in implementing classic NLP tasks without the need for explicit supervision [2], thus showcasing their potential as valuable tools in the educational sector, especially for tasks like the automation of grading processes in MOOCs [3].

This paper proposes EvaAI, a novel multi-agent framework powered by AutoGen [4], designed to automate the grading of student assignments using LLM-powered agents, building on the foundation laid by previous research, which explored their efficacy


A. Sifaleras and F. Lin (Eds.): ITS 2024, LNCS 14798, pp. 378–385, 2024.
https://doi.org/10.1007/978-3-031-63028-6_32

in such a task [5]. EvaAI employs a two-step process: a Reverse Proxy Agent routes the grading task to the appropriate Expert grader, which can have its own multi-agent architecture and specialized LLMs.

The study focuses on EvaAI's ability to provide accurate grades using minimal initial information compared to a single-agent system, the potential for customizing the grading process through educator input, and the system's capacity to offer meaningful feedback to students. EvaAI aims to streamline grading in MOOCs and enrich the feedback process, contributing to the ongoing dialogue on AI's role in providing quality, accessible, and personalized education globally.

## 2 Related Work

The exploration of automated systems for grading and providing feedback on programming assignments has a long history. Tools like Web-CAT [6], BOSS [7], and CourseMaker [8] represent significant advancements in this area. Web-CAT offers automated feedback and grading for programming tasks with a suite of analysis tools. BOSS delivers an automated platform for grading and managing submissions, whereas CourseMaker supports educators with tools for test case creation and automated grading.

In 2013, a study [9] introduced a tool for generating feedback on Python assignments in an MIT MOOC, notably using an error model to offer personalized advice beyond identifying failing tests. Another system [10] for grading JAVA assignments employed regular expressions for comparing student submissions against instructor solutions, though this method has limitations due to the complexity of crafting regex patterns and format constraints.

A semi-automated system for JAVA, ASys [11], evaluates submissions through Compilation, Analysis, and Testing phases, using a domain-specific language (DSL) for code analysis via an assessment template, facilitating programmable evaluation of Java assignments for correctness.

Research in [12] investigated the application of Machine Learning to assess correctness in code submissions, testing various models including Naïve Bayes, SVM, Logistic Regression, and NLP techniques such as RNNs, CNNs, and LSTMs, with CNNs emerging as particularly effective for analyzing student code.

With the advent of Large Language Models (LLMs) like GPT from OpenAI, recent studies [13] have examined their use in creating programming exercises, solutions, and code explanations. Despite their benefits, these studies underscore the necessity for human review to maintain the quality of AI-generated educational content.

## 3 System Architecture

EvaAI introduces a novel, two-tiered architecture aimed at automating the grading of student assignments across various subjects. This system is designed to be both subject- and rubric-agnostic, capitalizing on the flexibility and efficacy of Large Language Models (LLMs) in NLP tasks, to adapt to diverse educational needs. The architecture is primarily divided into two critical steps: the initial routing of assignments and the specialized grading process.

**Assignment Routing**

The first step in EvaAI's grading process involves the Reverse Proxy Agent. This agent acts as the central coordinator within the EvaAI framework, responsible for the initial assessment of incoming assignments. Upon receiving a task, the Reverse Proxy Agent evaluates the nature and requirements of the assignment to determine the most appropriate Expert grader to handle it. This determination is based on the assignment's subject matter, complexity, and specific grading rubrics provided. The Reverse Proxy Agent's role is pivotal in ensuring that assignments are directed to Expert graders with the optimal expertise and resources for accurate and efficient grading.

**Specialized Grading**

Once an assignment has been routed to the appropriate Expert grader, the second step of the process begins. Each Expert grader within the EvaAI framework is a multi-agent system itself, comprising several specialized agents that collaborate to grade assignments. These Expert graders are subject-specific, such as coding exercises handled by a coding expert, mathematics problems by a mathematics expert, and essays by an essay expert. Two exemplary architectures of Expert graders are discussed to illustrate the grading process:

- *Grader-Reviewer Approach*: The First Expert Architecture includes a Teacher agent, a Grader agent, and a Reviewer agent. This configuration simulates a comprehensive human educator's grading process. The Teacher agent provides initial evaluations and feedback, the Grader agent assesses the assignments against specific criteria, and the Reviewer agent performs a final review to ensure accuracy and fairness in grading.
- *Multiple Graders Approach*: The Second Expert Architecture comprises a Teacher agent and two or more independent Grader agents. This setup allows for multiple independent evaluations of an assignment, enhancing the reliability and objectivity of the grading process. The independent Grader agents assess the assignment and provide their grades, which are then consolidated and reviewed under the supervision of the Teacher agent.

In both configurations, a Group Chat Manager orchestrates collaborative dialogue among agents in EvaAI, enabling them to assess, review, and finalize grades for assignments, mimicking the nuanced decision-making processes of human grading committees. EvaAI's dynamic group chat feature, supported by AutoGen, facilitates seamless communication among specialized agents during the grading process. Agents share a common context and engage in conversations without adhering to a predefined order, simulating a natural, human-like discussion akin to a team of educators collaboratively grading assignments. The dynamic group chat, guided by role-play style prompts, ensures that conversation flow remains relevant and aligned with the task, leading to more effective problem-solving and decision-making among the agents.

## 4 Methodology and Preliminary Results

For the purposes of this study, a number of characteristic examples from using EvaAI in the automated grading of coding assignments were used, with the purpose of showcasing the potential of using such a multi-agent architecture in this specific context. The dataset used, as mentioned before, refers to the grading of code submissions in a Greek MOOC setting, focusing on an introductory Python course, where EvaAI was asked to grade such submissions. The specific Expert implementation used, named "Coder", follows the Grader-Reviewer approach, meaning that the Teacher agent asks the Grader agent to initially grade the exercise, and the Group Chat Manager then asks for the Reviewer agent to review the grade.

In terms of technical specifications for this specific experiment, the LLM that was used to power all agents was GPT-4, more specifically the "gpt-4–0125-preview" version of the model, through OpenAI's API. As described before, all agents were created by utilizing the AutoGen framework, and the agents' name, description and system message for the specific examples which used the Grader-Reviewer approach, were the following:

**Grader.**

```
name="grader",
description="A grader that grades the student's solution to a coding
exercise based on a grading rubric. After initial grading, the grader
receives a one-time feedback from the reviewer and revises the grade.
Finally the grader return the final, reviewed grade to the teacher.",
system_message="You are a grader. You break down the grading rubric
into bullet points. You apply the rubric to the student's solution
and provide a grade (0-10). If needed, revise the grade based on
feedback from the reviewer.
```

**Reviewer.**

```
name="reviewer",
description="A reviewer of the grader, that provides a one-time feed-
back to the grader's initial grade.",
system_message="You are a reviewer of the grader. Your job is to
check the grade's validity, based on the grading rubric. Provide a
one-time feedback to the grader. If you find any mistakes and the
grade has to be corrected, let them know. Do not disagree with the
grader if the grading rubric has been applied correctly. You are a
reviewer, not a critic."
```

Finally, we utilized the Group Chat and Group Chat Manager functionalities of AutoGen for implementing the conversation between agents, with the max rounds of messages being set to 12.

The assignment that the system was tasked with grading, asked the students to create a Python program that evaluates whether a given year is a leap year. The program was required to correctly apply the rule that a year is leap if it's exactly divisible by 4, except for century years, which are leap only if they're exactly divisible by 400.

The sample rubric that was provided to the system for grading the student's code, had two main guidelines:

- Execution error: If the student's code caused an error during execution, two points were to be deducted for each occurrence of such an error.
- Wrong result: Four different sample inputs were provided as test values. Those were "2004", "1800", "1600" and "1999", with the purpose of testing if the student implemented the correct logic in their code, to calculate the appropriate response for each of these cases in regards to the year being leap or not. Two points were to be deducted for each wrong result.

While the aggregated, quantitative results of the study, that includes this as well as different experiments with different assignments, are still in the process of being calculated and will be published in the future, in this section two characteristic examples of such grading runs of EvaAI are being presented together with the appropriate context for each run, that provide qualitative and promising insights regarding the ways that such an architecture can be an improvement over single-agent approaches in automated grading, how it can incorporate the tutor's feedback in grading and how it can provide useful feedback to the student, that is based on the specific scoring rubric. Since generated text data from the agents was too lengthy to be presented here as a whole, excerpts are being provided, and "..." represents extra generated text that has been omitted.

The first example refers to a case where the student's code response to the assignment was correct, however the Grader agent hallucinated by considering there was a typo in the variable used for the results:

```
grader (to chat_manager):
Grading the student's code based on the provided rubric:
...
**Execution error**: The student's code will execute without errors
but there's a typo in the variable name ("disekto" is used instead of
"disekto" after the condition) which would lead the program to always
print `False`.
...
For the first, third, and fourth test cases, the output will be af-
fected by the typo, making the code return incorrect results for 2
out of 4 tests due to the logical mistake rather than execution er-
ror. That would lead to a deduction of 4 points (2 points deducted
for each incorrect result).
...
Final grade: **6/10**
```

In this case, the Reviewer agent corrected the Grader and explained that there was no typo in the variable name, resulting in the grader revising the grade, showcasing how such multi-agent approaches with dynamic conversation between agents have the potential to avoid similar errors due to a single agent hallucinating.

```
reviewer (to chat_manager):
Upon reviewing the grading done for the student's code against the
provided rubric, there appears to be a misunderstanding regarding the
issue with the variable name. The feedback mentioned a typo in the
variable name ("disekto" is used instead of "disekto"), which seems
to be a mention of an error that doesn't exist in the provided code
snippet. The variable "disekto" is consistently named throughout the
code, so there's no actual typo affecting the logical functionality.
Thus, any deductions made due to this perceived typo are incorrect.
...
**Final grade should be: 10/10**

grader (to chat_manager):
Upon receiving the reviewer's feedback, I realize my mistake regard-
ing the variable name "disekto" in the student's code. My initial as-
sessment incorrectly identified a non-existent typo which influenced
the grading outcome improperly.
...
**Revised final grade: 10/10**
```

The second example, refers to a case where we used a sample tutor's feedback for the Reviewer agent to be more lenient, meaning that they should not get stuck up to the letter of the grading rubric but grade more holistically. In the example, the student' code printed out the result instead of storing it to a boolean variable and returning that, which was the instruction in the prompt. Here, the Grader agent originally tried to deduct eight points (since all four test values would result in a string result instead of a boolean), but the Reviewer agent corrected them, and suggested that the error should be considered as one instance rather than four, but relevant feedback should be provided to the student.

We should also note that when as a tutor we used the opposite instruction to the Reviewer, that is to stick to the grading rubric to the letter, there were multiple instances where when the Grader agent wanted to deduct less points for such an error, the Reviewer actually advised for the full eight points to be deducted, suggesting that customizing the system's behaviour according to the tutor's feedback is feasible to an extent.

```
grader (to chat_manager):
The provided student's code does not follow the exact instructions
from the exercise prompt, specifically with the required output for-
mat and variable usage. Here's a breakdown based on the provided ru-
bric:
...
Initial grade: 10
Deductions: 8 (for the variable name 'disekto' not being used and the
lack of a return statement)
Final grade: 2

reviewer (to chat_manager):
...
Wrong result: The program provides the correct True or False output
for the tested years; however, according to the exercise prompt, the
code should assign the result to a variable named 'disekto' and not
print it. Since the end result should be stored in 'disekto' and not
printed, points should be deducted. There is no instruction in the
rubric for this particular issue, but it would be reasonable to count
it as one mistake despite occurring in four tests because it's a sys-
tematic error rather than separate occurrences.
... from a holistic pedagogical perspective, and per the exercise
prompt, the student should be instructed to correct the code to align
with the required structure of output and use of variables.
...
Recommended actions:
- Provide feedback to the student to adjust their code according to
the exercise instructions.
```

## 5 Conclusions and Discussion

In this paper, we introduced EvaAI, a novel framework leveraging Large Language Models (LLMs) and a multi-agent architecture for automated grading. EvaAI has the potential to offer improvements over single-agent systems. The collaborative nature of the multi-agent model can add depth to the grading process, potentially reflecting a more human-like assessment. Preliminary observations suggest that the multi-agent approach contributes to grading precision and dependability. Leveraging a network of specialized agents could streamline the grading process and provide feedback similar to human educators, reducing educators' grading workload.

Further research is needed to explore the full potential of multi-agent frameworks for automated grading across a broader range of subjects and assignment types. Limitations include the dependency on LLM availability and quality, as well as the increased cost associated with multi-agent approaches. Ethical considerations surrounding AI in education also warrant careful consideration.

EvaAI represents a promising approach to automate and enhance the grading process in educational settings. This study contributes to the academic discourse on Generative AI in education and paves the way for more innovative, efficient, and nuanced educational technologies.

## References


1. Wei, J., et al.: Emergent abilities of large language models. arXiv preprint arXiv:2206.07682 (2022)
2. Radford, A., et al.: Language models are unsupervised multitask learners. OpenAI blog 1.8, 9 (2019)
3. Kasneci, E., et al.: ChatGPT for good? On opportunities and challenges of large language models for education. Learn. Individ. Diff. **103**, 102274 (2023)
4. Wu, Q., et al.: AutoGen: enabling Next-Gen LLM applications via multi-agent conversation, pp. 1–43 (2023). http://arxiv.org/abs/2308.08155
5. Lagakis, P., et al.: Automated grading in coding exercises using large language models. In: IMCL (2023)
6. Edwards, S.H., Perez-Quinones, M.A.: Web-CAT: automatically grading programming assignments. ACM SIGCSE Bull. **40**(3), 328–328 (2008)
7. Joy, M., Griffiths, N., Boyatt, R.: The BOSS online submission and assessment system. J. Educ. Resour. Comput. **5**(3), 2 (2005). https://doi.org/10.1145/1163405.1163407
8. Higgins, C.A., Gray, G., Symeonidis, P., Tsintsifas, A.: Automated assessment and experiences of teaching programming. J. Educ. Resour. Comput. **5**(3), 5 (2005). https://doi.org/10.1145/1163405.1163410
9. Singh, R., Gulwani, S., Solar-Lezama, A.: Automated feedback generation for introductory programming assignments. ACM SIGPLAN Notices **48**(6), 15 (2013). https://doi.org/10.1145/2499370.2462195
10. Akahane, Y., Kitaya, H., Inoue, U.: Design and evaluation of automated scoring: java programming assignments. Int. J. Softw. Innov. **3**(4), 18–32 (2015)
11. Insa, D., Silva, J.: Semi-automatic assessment of unrestrained java code: a library, a DSL, and a workbench to assess exams and exercises, pp. 39–44 (2015)
12. Tarcsay, B., Vasić, J., Perez-Tellez, F.: Use of machine learning methods in the assessment of programming assignments. In: Sojka, P., Horák, A., Kopeček, I., Pala, K. (eds.) Text, Speech, and Dialogue: 25th International Conference, TSD 2022, Brno, Czech Republic, September 6–9, 2022, Proceedings, pp. 151–159. Springer International Publishing, Cham (2022). https://doi.org/10.1007/978-3-031-16270-1_13
13. Sarsa, S., Denny, P., Hellas, A., Leinonen, J.: Automatic generation of programming exercises and code explanations using large language models. In: Proceedings of the 2022 ACM Conference on International Computing Education Research V.1 (ICER 2022), August 7–11, 2022, Lugano and Virtual Event, Switzerland. ACM, New York, NY, USA, p. 17 (2022). https://doi.org/10.1145/3501385.3543957

# Optimising a Peer Based Learning Environment

Aidan Murphy[1,2(✉)], Mahsa Mahdinejad[1], Syed Saeed Ahmad[3], Joe Kenny[3], and Anthony Ventresque[1,4]

[1] Lero - the Science Foundation Ireland Research Centre for Software, Limerick, Ireland
[2] University College Dublin, Dublin, Ireland
aidan.murphy@ucd.ie
[3] Zeeko, NovaUCD, Dublin, Ireland
[4] Trinity College Dublin, Dublin, Ireland

**Abstract.** Primary School education in Ireland is in the process of updating its pedagogical approaches, embracing new teaching methods and desiring new learning outcomes. In particular, the new curriculum emphasizes developing skills necessary for modern-day life. Peer-led interactive group learning is an effective method of teaching those desired skills. One such technology embracing these methods of learning is the "Magical Leaders" programme. However, creating an environment that allows for optimum delivery of the content is difficult as the teacher needs to deal with the new method of content delivery as well as any behavioral or social issues that exist in the classroom. We investigate three factors that affect the successful delivery of the "Magical Leaders" programme: group composition; peer leader selection; and preparation time. We find that classes in which the teacher selects the groups complete the challenges more than 10 min quicker than those classes in which the peers select the groups or they are randomly assigned. The mean time to complete each challenge was approximately the same for groups in which the peer leaders were selected by the teacher and those groups were volunteers. However, the number of volunteer-led groups that finished on or before schedule was higher. Groups with peer leaders who completed less than 30 min of preparation time finished on average 9 min quicker than groups with peer leaders who did more than 30 min of preparation time. However, while the mean time is much less the number of classes finishing on time is higher for those with more preparation time, 60%, than those will 30 min of less preparation time, 52%.

**Keywords:** Peer Led Learning · Education Technology · Optimisation

## 1 Introduction

Maximising the learning and development of all school students is an important goal for all countries, with education earmarked by the United Nations as a pillar for a sustainable future [4]. However, creating and fostering learning environments that allow each student to fulfill their potential is a key challenge.


A. Sifaleras and F. Lin (Eds.): ITS 2024, LNCS 14798, pp. 386–394, 2024.
https://doi.org/10.1007/978-3-031-63028-6_33

Primary education in Ireland is undergoing a dramatic transformation, with new updated pedagogical approaches being implemented. The National Council for Curriculum and Assessment (NCCA) want to move primary education in Ireland away from traditional rote learning to problem-based learning [9]. In their draft primary curriculum framework, the NCAA identifies seven key competencies (being creative, a digital learner, mathematical, an active citizen, communicating and using language, fostering well-being and learning how to learn) and stress experiential learning. In particular they want to "support children to become curious, creative, confident and critical users of digital technology".

Implementing this new curriculum, while at the same time creating new, efficient learning environments is a formidable challenge. This transformation also comes at a time when teachers in Ireland are reporting record levels of burnout [5].

To achieve these ambitious goals, the education sector must embrace technology. Zeeko Education[2], a Dublin based education technology company, are creating this technology. Among their products is "Magical Leaders", a peer led immersive digital learning programme. This innovative programme allows students to practice and develop the core competencies desired by the NCAA. However, no research to date has been conducted on how to best deploy "Magical Leaders" (or any peer-to-peer course) in schools in Ireland. This paper is the first study examining this topic. These results will help guide teachers on how to create an environment to efficiently complete the tasks, thereby giving the largest amount of time for important self-reflection to the students [7].

We study three components and examine how they impact the time taken to complete the various challenges within "Magical Leaders". They are: how the peer-led groups were composed; how the various peer leaders were selected; and how much preparation time was done before the challenge.

Section 2 reviews the main background concepts and discusses the NCCA and peer-to-peer learning in more detail and introduces the "Magical Leaders" programme. Section 3 discusses each component of our data capture and describes our experimental setup in detail. Section 4 presents the main results of the experiments described in 3 and discusses their findings. Finally, Sect. 5 summarises the research and discusses future work suitable for investigation.

## 2 Background and Related Work

### 2.1 Irish Primary School Curriculum

The NCAA wants to drastically reform the Irish primary school curriculum and the current pedagogical approaches in schools. The unprecedented rate of change in modern society brought about by technological innovation has resulted in mass disruption to a variety of industries and disciplines. The Primary Curriculum Framework, launched in 2023, aims to transform education in Ireland around key competencies that ensure children practice and learn transferable skills, such

[2] https://zeeko.ie/

as creatively and problem-solving, to deal with an unknowable future. They wish to place students at the core of this new learning process. This must be done efficiently to maximise students' potential while ensuring teacher burnout is mitigated. This second goal is of particular importance as primary school teachers in Ireland have reported record levels of stress and feel overworked [3].

A teacher is well placed to design individualised learning environments for their students, but a teacher's knowledge of their students' learning needs, speed and capacity cannot be easily scaled. Augmenting teachers with technology to deliver their lessons is scalable, however. A key component of this new technology is that it must efficiently deliver these lessons to all the students. This will allow teachers to focus better on educating and not on administration, behavior correction and would ensure students' potential has the best chance of being achieved. However, to date there has been no work examining how to make the deployment of any technology more efficient in primary education schools.

## 2.2 Peer Based Learning

Peer based learning is a collaborative form of education in which one or more peers (e.g. students) lead the learning of the group (or class). Peer-to-peer learning has been shown to improve learning outcomes and provides an opportunity for students to practise skills essential for later stages of life, such as team work and communication [6]. There is much overlap between these skills and those the NCAA aim to instill in students in their updated curriculum. Therefore, peer based learning offers itself as an attractive method of content delivery. A flexible paradigm with many ways to be implemented, peer interaction has shown positive effects in enhancing learning in both children and adolescents [8]. It has been shown that peer led learning can be improved upon by adding additional incentives and changing to the needs of the particular group [2].

Indeed, peer-based approaches have been shown to have a large, positive impact on learning, with a potential effect equivalent to approximately 5 additional months' progress for both peer educators and peer-educated pupils according to the Education Endowment Foundation [1].

Some challenges must be overcome to successfully implement such peer based learning systems, however. It can be difficult for peer leaders to maintain discipline within the group and ensure the correct lesson plan is followed. There may also be complicated social dynamics within the class that need to be navigated to ensure tension or other problems in any group are mitigated. Supervision and optimum arrangement of the classroom for the lesson therefore becomes a key concern in many peer learning settings.

## 2.3 Magical Leaders Programme

The "Magical Leaders" Programme is a peer led education programme for 10–13 year old primary education students developed by Zeeko Education, a Dublin based Eduction Technology company. It focuses on developing transferable,

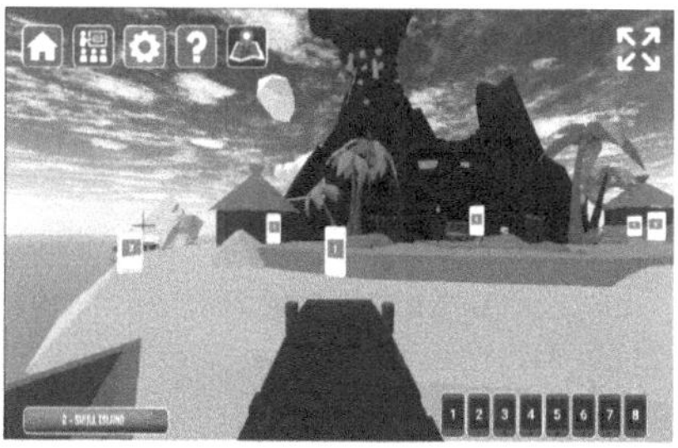

Fig. 1. Challenge map which is navigated by the Driver. The Driver will move the avatar in the virtual world and enter each phone and uncover the activity to be performed.

Fig. 2. Screen seen entering a phone. The screen describes a challenge or concept that must be performed by the group. Upon successful completion, the driver will exit the phone.

higher order skills and knowledge. Zeeko have shown this knowledge acquisition, complemented by skills practice, progresses young people's skills and fosters positive attributes.

The program aims to complement the new curriculum envisioned by the NCAA, teaching skills such as communication, collaboration, critical thinking, and creativity through the lens of entrepreneurship.

This study examines the introductory programme of "Magical Leaders", consisting of 6 lessons - or 'Challenges'. Each challenge focuses on a particular concept and contains unique learning outcomes, key messages, presentations and discussion activities. Specifically, pupils are presented with details based on real-life situations and are tasked with making decisions based on the evidence given. The challenges are designed to raise questions and to present just enough data to stimulate/engage pupils to find their own answers. Each challenge is navigated virtually through online software and also led locally by peer leaders reading from instructional material. An example of the online software is seen in Figs. 1 and 2. Each challenge ends with a period of self-reflection for the pupils.

The "Magical Leaders" programme has received very positive feedback and has been created to ensure all the knowledge outcomes are met, however, there has been no research done on the optimum environment and classroom setup to achieve these goals.

### 2.4 Peer Leader Roles Within Magical Leaders

The "Magical Leaders" Programme requires multiple students to perform various roles during each challenge. These roles include:

**Presenters** are peer educators who facilitate the lesson's key messages to the Pupils via the online software. They are required to stand at the front of the class and deliver the content of the lessons provided to them, aided by the online software that is shown to the pupils on the screen.

**Drivers** are peer educators who control the online software. They are required to sit at the computer, select the correct lesson, navigate the online software, find the various phones contained in the challenge and navigate and show the slides that the presenters are explaining.

**Group Leaders** are peer educators who sit at the table with the pupils in their groups and facilitate and lead the discussion about the lesson. They facilitate group discussions when asked to do so by the presenters and ensure discussions remain constructive and on schedule.

## 3 Experimental Setup

Each "Magical Leaders" challenge is designed to take up 45 min of activity. Before beginning the lesson, the class must be divided into groups of 6 or 7 and the peer leaders chosen. Each peer leader must undertake preparation to ensure they are fully able to fulfil their role. The composition of the groups, the selection of the peer leaders and the amount of preparation done is at the discretion of the teacher. While the "Magical Leaders" instructional manual gives suggestions to teachers of what is best, there has been no research to date investigating how a teacher can most optimally create an environment to efficiently complete each lesson.

This paper analyses the performance of classes undertaking "Magical Leaders" challenges and investigates the effect of three criteria on their outcome. The criteria examined are: Group composition; Peer Leader Selection; and Preparation Time.

Group composition investigates how the groups were chosen. There are three possible approaches to create groups for the challenge: the teacher can select the groups, the peers form the groups themselves or the groups are created randomly. Zeeko does not recommend that the groups be created randomly as students with animosity or some other form of incompatibility may be inadvertently placed into the same group, unsettling the social dynamic and creating a tense atmosphere in which other members may be unwilling to participate fully.

Peer Leader Selection examines how the student presenters, leaders and drivers were selected. Pupils will have different levels of self-confidence, which will be affected differently by the environment and size of the group. Some will naturally want to be a presenter, others may prefer to be a group leader or computer driver. There are three methods to chose the peer leaders: The teacher will select them; the students will volunteer themselves for the various roles; or some other method which could be random or a mixture of the previous two approaches. While the teacher may be best suited to choose which students are best suited to the roles and are primed to develop their presentation, assertiveness, and interpersonal skills it may be that a child's self confidence, illustrated by them volunteering for the roles, is a key factor. Pupils will have different levels of self-confidence and this may be an important factor in fostering efficient peer learning.

Lastly, Preparation Time considers the preparation time undertaken by the peer leaders before commencing the lesson. Zeeko recommends at least 30 min of preparation time before each challenge for each peer leader to familiarise themselves with the content, their role in the challenge and to answer any questions they may have. This is a binary category: less than 30 min of preparation or 30 min or more of preparation time.

Each of the challenge follows a similar format. The lesson is broken down into sub-parts/ points. Each sub-part/ point corresponds to a phone location in the online programme. Our data capture found the time to compete each phone and aggregated them to find the total time to complete the challenge. This allowed for classes which did not complete the challenge in one block (interrupted by lunch, etc.) to still be included in the final dataset.

## 4 Results

42 different classes, taking part in 116 challenges were recorded with each class taking part in between 1 and 5 challenges. After data cleaning and removing challenges which had errors or were not fully completed, the final dataset contained 26 classes taking part in 67 challenges.

The summary of the results collected is shown in Table 1. Challenges 1 and 2 are the largest in the dataset, with 15 and 17 classes undertaking them. 5 and 3 have roughly half as many, 7 and 8 respectively. 10 classes completed challenges 4 and 6.

**Table 1.** Summary of data used in results after cleaning.

| Challenge Num | Number | Mean | Median | SD |
|---|---|---|---|---|
| 1 | 15 | 57.49 | 55.5 | 19.17 |
| 2 | 17 | 56.67 | 55.08 | 17.39 |
| 3 | 8 | 50.29 | 48.89 | 8.79 |
| 4 | 10 | 58.89 | 55.53 | 14.19 |
| 5 | 7 | 49.74 | 46.88 | 15.59 |
| 6 | 10 | 46.14 | 47.72 | 9.81 |

Challenges 1, 2 and 4 take an average of over 55 min to complete. This is perhaps not too surprising as the first time classes attempt challenges they make take longer. Challenges 3 and 5 take around 50 min to complete while challenge 6 was the quickest, taking just over 46 min. Challenges 1, 2, 4 and 5 show a large distribution of times taken, while challenges 3 and 6 show that most classes took a similar amount of time.

Each challenge is designed to take approximately the same time complete. As our results reflect this design, we combine all challenges for our next stage of analysis. We next investigate the various factors affecting the length of time taken to complete each challenge, as described in Sect. 3.

Some teachers reported that group composition was a mixture of one of the options (i.e. some groups were selected by the teachers, others randomly). These challenges were excluded from analysis, leading to less that 67 challenges included in the analysis.

The overwhelming majority, 43, of groups were composed by the teacher. 4 were composed by the group leader and 8 were randomly put together. Teacher selected groups were much quicker finishing the challenges than both other group selection types. Teacher selected finished in an average of 51.59 min, while Group Leader selected and Randomly selected took 63.41 and 63.93 min to complete challenges, respectively. Wilcoxan signed rank tests were performed to assess the significance of the difference between Teacher selected and the other methods. The results of these tests, as well as other results, are shown in Table 2

**Table 2.** Experimental Results. Results which are bolded indicate significance according to our Wilcoxon tests.

| Type | Selection | Number | Mean Time | Median Time | p-value |
|---|---|---|---|---|---|
| Group Composition | Teacher Selected | 43 | 51.59 | 49.73 | – |
| | Group Leader | 4 | 63.41 | 59.98 | 0.2908 |
| | Random | 8 | 63.93 | 59.53 | **0.0882** |
| Presenter, Leader and Driver Selection | Teacher Selected | 23 | 58.03 | 55.50 | – |
| | Volunteered | 29 | 54.31 | 53.63 | 0.4355 |
| | Other | 3 | 48.57 | 45.75 | **0.0786** |
| Preparation Time | $< 30mins$ | 23 | 48.98 | 50.05 | |
| | $> 30mins$ | 30 | 57.73 | 55.38 | **0.0220** |

The number of challenges that finished on time and those that did not, split by each factor, is shown in Table 3. The results further reinforce the conclusion that challenges are completed more efficiently when the teacher selects the groups. 53% of teacher-selected groups finish the challenge on time, while other methods only finish on schedule 17% of the time.

Volunteered leaders and drivers are seen to finish challenges on time 44% of the time, while teacher selected only finish on schedule 30% of the time.

Finally, when the preparation time exceeds 30 min 60% of the time the challenge finished on schedule, compared to only 52% when the preparation time is less than 30 min. This is despite the average time taken for groups with more than 30 min preparation time being far larger (and statistically significantly longer) than those with 30 min or less preparation time.

**Table 3.** Experimental Results on Time Keeping.

| Type | Selection | Times Over Schedule | Times On Schedule |
|---|---|---|---|
| Group Composition | Teacher Selected | 20 | 23 |
| | Group Leaders | 3 | 1 |
| | Random | 7 | 1 |
| Presenter, Leader and Driver Selection | Teacher Selected | 16 | 7 |
| | Volunteered | 16 | 13 |
| | Other | 1 | 2 |
| Preparation Time | $< 30mins$ | 11 | 12 |
| | $> 30mins$ | 12 | 18 |

## 5 Conclusion and Future Work

We analysed the performance of various primary school classes in Ireland completing the "Magical Leaders" programme, a peer led interactive learning course. Specifically, we considered three factors (group composition, peer leader selection and preparation time) and investigated their influence on the successful and efficient completion of challenges within the programme. Keeping to the prescribed schedule and completing the challenges in an efficient way results in each child maximising their personal reflection time.

We found that teachers overwhelmingly chose the members of groups and those groups were seen to more efficiently complete the program, taking on average 10 min less to complete each challenge than peer-selected or randomly assigned groups.

There was no difference in mean time to complete a challenge found between peer leaders that were selected by the teacher and those who volunteered for the position. However, when analysing the number of challenges that remained on schedule, we see that teacher-selected leaders remained on schedule 30% of the time while leaders that volunteered stayed on schedule 45% of the time.

Leaders who undertook less than 30 min of preparation time were seen to complete challenges faster than leaders who undertook more than 30 min of preparation. The reasons for this are an open question and an avenue for future work. Interestingly, despite having a lower mean and median time to complete each challenge, the number of challenges completed on time when having less than 30 min of preparation was 52%. The number of challenges completed on time when leaders had more than 30 min preparation time was 60%. The amount of preparation time needed is an open question and may be influenced by other factors not examined in this study.

The next step of this work is to investigate the effectiveness of the peer learning environments, which can only be measured using student post-challenge surveys and feedback. These surveys will measure how much a student's skills have improved after completion of each challenge and will allow more context to be placed on the information captured.

**Acknowledgement.** This work was supported, in part, by Science Foundation Ireland grants 20/FFP-P/8818 and 13/RC/2094_P2.

## References

1. Peer Tutoring Evidence Education Endowment Foundation. https://educationendowmentfoundation.org.uk/education-evidence/teaching-learning-toolkit/peer-tutoring. Accessed 30 Feb 2024
2. Chen, C.M., Wang, J.Y., Zhao, R.H.: An effective method for incentivizing groups implemented in a collaborative problem-based learning system to enhance positive peer interaction and learning performance. Interact. Learn. Environ. **30**(3), 435–454 (2022)
3. Minihan, E., Adamis, D., Dunleavy, M., Martin, A., Gavin, B., McNicholas, F.: COVID-19 related occupational stress in teachers in Ireland. Int. J. Educ. Res. Open **3**, 100114 (2022)
4. Nations, U.: Transforming our world: the 2030 agenda for sustainable development. United Nations, Department of Economic and Social Affairs, New York (2015)
5. Nohilly, M., O'Toole, V., Collins, B.: The impact of primary school closures in Ireland resulting from the coronavirus pandemic on principal and teacher wellbeing. Ir. J. Sociol. **31**(3), 324–353 (2023)
6. Preszler, R.W.: Replacing lecture with peer-led workshops improves student learning. CBE-Life Sci. Educ. **8**(3), 182–192 (2009)
7. Rienties, B., Willis, A., Alcott, P., Medland, E.: Student experiences of self-reflection and peer assessment in providing authentic project-based learning to large class sizes. Facilitating learning in the 21st century: leading through technology, diversity and authenticity, pp. 117–136 (2013)
8. Tenenbaum, H.R., Winstone, N.E., Leman, P.J., Avery, R.E.: How effective is peer interaction in facilitating learning? A meta-analysis. J. Educ. Psychol. **112**(7), 1303 (2020)
9. Walsh, T.: Redeveloping the primary school curriculum in Ireland. Center for Universal Education at The Brookings Institution, Case Study (2023)

# Difficulty Estimation and Simplification of French Text Using LLMs

Henri Jamet(✉), Yash Raj Shrestha, and Michalis Vlachos

Department of Information Systems, Faculty of Business and Economics (HEC), University of Lausanne, Lausanne, Switzerland
henri.jamet@unil.ch

**Abstract.** We leverage generative large language models for language learning applications, focusing on estimating the difficulty of foreign language texts and simplifying them to lower difficulty levels. We frame both tasks as prediction problems and develop a difficulty classification model using labeled examples, transfer learning, and large language models, demonstrating superior accuracy compared to previous approaches. For simplification, we evaluate the trade-off between simplification quality and meaning preservation, comparing zero-shot and fine-tuned performances of large language models. We show that meaningful text simplifications can be obtained with limited fine-tuning. Our experiments are conducted on French texts, but our methods are language-agnostic and directly applicable to other foreign languages.

**Keywords:** Digital Education · Machine Learning · Large Language Models

## 1 Introduction

Today, there exist many online foreign-language learning tools, including Duolingo, Frantastique, and ReadLang which incorporate gamification elements to increase appeal and retention [25]. However, they do not offer personalization based on learners' interests nor do they provide relevant, contemporary content. Oftentimes, the educational content fails to be matched to the learners knowledge level. Content that is too easy bores learners; too difficult discourages them.

In this work, we use large language models (LLMs) to estimate and potentially reduce the difficulty of foreign content. Such an approach, can be used to identify appropriate contemporary content in the target learning language, thus increasing learners' motivation. Moreover, such an approach could be used in conjunction with a recommendation system to discover content appropriate for the learner's knowledge level. The **contributions** of this work include:

- A machine learning solution to estimate foreign text difficulty, more accurate than traditional *readability* metrics.
- Use of fine-tuned LLMs to simplify the difficulty/level of a foreign French text while preserving its meaning as well as possible. We propose a technique for automatically assessing simplification quality and report performance benchmarks.


A. Sifaleras and F. Lin (Eds.): ITS 2024, LNCS 14798, pp. 395–404, 2024.
https://doi.org/10.1007/978-3-031-63028-6_34

## 2 Difficulty Estimation

### 2.1 Related Work

From a pedagogical perspective, our solution builds upon already established theory of *extensive reading* [7,15], which constitutes a crucial means of reinforcing one's language skills. However, it is important to find content that is appropriate for the learner's knowledge level of the foreign language. One approach to estimating the difficulty of a foreign language text is to use "readability" formulas[1]. They are regression approaches that calculate the complexity of a text based on various text features, including sentence length and word frequency. Some commonly used readability formulas for foreign language texts include the **Flesch-Kincaid Grade Level**, the **Simple Measure of Gobbledygook** (SMOG), and the **Gunning Fog Index**.

Another approach to tackle difficulty estimation is to use machine learning techniques to predict the difficulty level based on various linguistic features [5,10]. A particularly notable advancement in this field in recent years is the integration of pre-trained word- and sentence- embeddings into text readability architectures [11,12,16,27]. However, our review indicates that prior research has not yet investigated the predictive accuracy of difficulty estimation using LLMs.

### 2.2 Our Approach

We model the estimation of difficulty as a classification problem. Let $\mathcal{D}$ be the set of documents, $Y$ the random variable representing the linguistic difficulty class. For the linguistic difficulty, we wish predict the Common European Framework of Reference for Languages, or CEFR difficulty level of a text $\{A1, A2, B1, B2, C1, C2\}$), where A1,A2 signify easy text, B1,B2 intermediate level and C1,C2 advanced level. $f : \mathcal{D} \rightarrow Y$ is a classifier mapping a document $d \in \mathcal{D}$ to a difficulty class $y \in Y$. The classifier $f$ is built using text-label pairs, where the label corresponds to the linguistic difficulty. We use LLMs like **BERT** [8], **GPT** [20], **GPT-3** [2], **LLaMa** [24], and **Palm** [6], which convert text tokens into embeddings capturing the meaning of each token. The models vary in data volume, training methodology, size, and language capabilities, resulting in embeddings of different lengths (e.g., 768 for **BERT**, 1,536 for OpenAI's "ada-002").

**GPT-3+ Models:** Advanced models like **GPT-3** and **GPT-4** [20] have been trained on massive multilingual datasets and post-trained using reinforcement learning from human feedback. They achieve state-of-the-art performance across tasks like summarization, translation, and question-answering [3]. These models excel at generating human-like text and can be fine-tuned for classification tasks. We use **GPT** models for their good performance-versus-cost ratio.

[1] Note, that these readability formulas are primarily targeted to estimate the difficulty of a text for native speakers rather than for second language learners [28]. These methods were initially developed for the English language, and progressively have been extended for other languages such as French, Chinese and Italian [5,19].

## 3 Text Simplification

In the context of a foreign language learning app, we now explore the scenario assuming we have discovered content that matches the user's interests (such as, sports or politics), but it is more advanced than their current language proficiency level.

Evaluating text simplification systems is a non-trivial task that requires metrics robust enough to account for both readability and semantic preservation. Traditional n-gram based metrics such as **BLEU** or **ROUGE**, though popular in translation tasks, have limitations when applied to text simplification due to the fundamental requirement of simplification to alter the text structure while maintaining the same meaning [1] [22]. The **SARI** metric, designed specifically for simplification tasks, measures the goodness of words added, deleted, and kept by the system. Current research, such as [22], is exploring new methods like **QUESTEVAL**, which uses semantic questioning of texts to assess simplifications. This approach aims to overcome the limitations of earlier metrics and may result in improved alignment with human evaluations.

While text summarization and text simplification may appear similar as both involve altering the original text, their objectives are distinct. Summarization aims to condense a text by trimming down its length and retaining only the main points. Simplification seeks to lower the linguistic complexity, making content more accessible [22]. Simplification may or may not alter the length of text. Unlike summarization, simplification is deals with adjusting the text to a particular knowledge or comprehension level.

The hybrid task of combining both text summarization and simplification has been investigated in the context of generating summaries for lay audiences. This task known as "lay summarization" aims to render complex scientific content accessible to a general audience, requiring the extraction of key points and simultaneously a reduction in linguistic complexity [4,26]. Transformer models based on **BERT** [8] and **PEGASUS** [29] have been used in this context.

Recent advancements in LLMs, have greatly contributed to the field of text simplification [21]. However, the efficacy of these models varies, and not all are equally suited for the task, calling for evaluation and fine-tuning on specialized datasets [23]. A recent analysis by [9] highlights that when evaluated on public datasets, contemporary LLMs like **GPT-3** can match or even outperform systems explicitly designed for text simplification.

### 3.1 Our Approach

We model simplification in a similar way as for content difficulty estimation. However, instead of predicting the level of difficulty, we predict the simplified sentence token by token. We provide labelled examples of original and simplified sentences and train a machine learning model. Because we only fine-tune LLMs, we need to provide very few pairs of examples, since the LLMs have already encapsulated in them large amounts of textual knowledge. In our experiments, we only post-train the LLMs using 125 pair sentences, and show large improvements compared to the zero-shot LLM counterpart. Because our goal is to assist learners in improving their language skills by reading content close to their knowledge/experience level, simplification of a given text is approached as a sentence-by-sentence simplification, and not as a complete synthesis of new text.

A key challenge in text simplification involves evaluating and balancing the trade-off between preserving the meaning and semantics of the original text and achieving effective simplification. The more we simplify, the more we may lose the original meaning, depending on the complexity of the original text. To evaluate these conflicting aspects, we introduce two metrics: simplification accuracy, and semantic similarity. Therefore, given a set of original sentences $\mathcal{O}$, their simplified versions $\mathcal{T}$ by a model $m$ that we seek to evaluate $\mathcal{O} \xrightarrow{m} \mathcal{T}$, and $\epsilon(\cdot)$ is the embedding representation of a text, we define: **A. Simplification Accuracy** $A \in \{0, 1\}$ is a binary output indicating if a text $t \in \mathcal{T}$ is exactly one CEFR level of difficulty lower than their associated original text $o \in \mathcal{O}$. As an example, if a text of level `C2` is simplified to `C1` with a given model then $A = 1$, but if the resulting simplification leads to `B2` level text, then $A = 0$. For a set of texts, we average $A$. **B. Semantic Similarity** $S \in [0 \ldots 1]$ is a real number between zero and one, and captures the preservation of semantic meaning of simplified text with respect to original text, which can be measured as the cosine similarity between the embedding representation $\epsilon(\cdot)$ of the original text and the embedding representation of the simplified text. The choice of model used to calculate embbedings is described below. For a set of texts, we average $S$. Note, that this measure of similarity allows texts to have completely different words, but still have high similarity if their vectors are close in the (semantic) embedding space. We integrate both aspects, simplification and semantic similarity, into a single weighted-score by drawing inspiration from the *F1-score*:

$$\text{w-Score} = 2 \times \frac{w_1 \times A \times w_2 \times S}{w_1 \times A + w_2 \times S}$$

where $w_2 = (1 - w_1)$. The coefficients $w_1$ and $w_2$ are chosen in such a way to balance the importance of the two aspects (equal in our experiments). This metric allows us to compare the performance of each of the models evaluated. Note that the $A$ and $S$ components would benefit from being kept separate to easily distinguish the strengths and weaknesses of each model.

There is one fine aspect still to be discussed. While $S$ can be easily computed, evaluating the simplification accuracy $A$ is more challenging. Even though we have the difficulty of the original text, when a text is simplified by a model $m$, then we do not have at our disposal the difficulty level of the simplified text (`A1`-`C2`). In our experiments, we address this by using the fine-tuned **CamemBERT** model as the *proxy* evaluator of the simplification accuracy. We compute the difficulty of the original text and the simplified text, and if the difficulty is reduced by one level, we consider the transformation as valid. For example, if the original label was `C2`, and **CamemBERT** classified it as `C1`, but then it classified the simplified text as `B2`, then we assign $A = 1$ since the difficulty reduction was one level. Notice, that this approach should cater for constant biases or potential errors that the model might introduce.

## 4 Experiments

The goal of the following experiments is to demonstrate that (a) fine-tuned LLMs can significantly improve the difficulty estimation offered by traditional readability metrics. (b) simplification methodology driven by fine-tuned LLM models outperforms zero-shot approaches. The code for the experiments can be retrieved here.

### 4.1 Difficulty Estimation

We evaluated the difficulty estimation on three labeled **datasets**: **1)** Littérature de jeunesse libre (`LjL`) which we obtained from [11]. Each content item here contains several sentences and a label (labels: level1, level2, level3, level4). **2)** A collection of sentences collected from the Internet (`sentencesInternet`). Each of these sentences was then annotated by at least three annotators (students recruited in our university) in difficulty levels. Only sentences in which all participants agreed on the difficulty annotation were retained (labels: A1,A2,B1,B2,C1,C2). Here, the labels correspond to the levels designed by the Common European Framework of Reference for Languages (CEFR). **3)** A collection of sentences from literature books (`sentencesBooks`). Each book was annotated with a difficulty level by a Professor of French. All sentences in that book were then given that label. This process involved an OCR pipeline which could lead to faulty detection of characters, so only the sentences without any errors were retained. (labels: A1,A2,B1,B2,C1,C2). The characteristics of these datasets are provided in Table 1. To train and evaluate our model, we used an 80/20 train-test split, and the results that we present are for examples which the model saw for the first time.

**Table 1.** Characteristics of datasets for difficulty estimation experiments

| Dataset | Sentences | Words | Chars | Labels |
|---|---|---|---|---|
| `LjL` [11] | 2,060 | 334,026 | 1,532,442 | level1–4 |
| `sentencesInternet` | 4,800 | 85,941 | 421,045 | A1–C2 |
| `sentencesBooks` | 2,400 | 56,557 | 281,463 | A1–C2 |

**Evaluation.** As a simple benchmarking, we compare the accuracy of our difficulty estimation approach to traditional readability-based metrics, such as the **GFI** (Gunning Fog Index), **FKGL** (Flesch Kincaid grade level), **ARI** (Automated Readability Index) in Table 2. Initially, all of these metrics have been developed for English content, but language specific models, such as for French text, as used in our application, have also been developed [10].

These techniques are inherently regression techniques and output a floating point value of the text difficulty. As a result, we cannot make a direct comparison, because our difficulty estimator predicts discrete labels. To address this challenge, we trained a logistic regression model $\mathbb{R} \rightarrow \mathcal{L}$ with $\mathcal{L}$ being the space of our labels equal to $\{\text{level1}, \text{level2}, \text{level3}, \text{level4}\}$ for the `LjL` dataset and $\{A1, A2, B1, B2, C1, C2\}$ for the `sentencesBooks` and `sentencesInternet` datasets. In this way, we transformed our regression into a classification, which we can evaluate with the usual metrics and compare with the other classification methods. For LLM-based difficulty estimation, we train the following classifiers using the examples from the training set and test how they behave on the unseen test set: **1. GPT**-based models: We use the **GPT-3.50-turbo-1106** and **Davinci-002**. Both these models have been fine-tuned for the task at hand using the examples with the labelled difficulties of the text. **2. CamemBERT**: This is essentially the well-known **BERT** model trained on French data [18]. **CamemBERT** is based on the **RoBERTa** architecture [17]. While **BERT** was initially trained on a diverse range of texts in multiple languages, **CamemBERT** is specifically fine-tuned for the French language. This fine-tuning process involves training the model on a massive amount of French text data, which enables it to capture the nuances, idioms, and syntactic structures unique to the French language. Because **CamemBERT** is tailored to French, it excels in various language-related tasks such as text classification, sentiment analysis, and named entity recognition within the context of French text. **3. Mistral-7B**: This is an open-source LLM [13] with a modest size that we fine-tuned in the same manner as GPT-based models.

To take advantage of the inherent knowledge in LLMs, we tested different contexts and selected the one which offered the best performance. We then evaluated which models could potentially benefit with and without this context.[2] Table 2 shows the F1-score across the three datasets. The column *context* indicates whether the model has been trained with or without a task-related context. The various models were sorted by average ranking of their F1-score on each dataset. Our results suggest that the **GPT-3.5** is the best performing model. The second place is shared by the **Mistral-7B** and the **CamemBERT**, but we draw the attention of the reader to the much smaller size of these models: 7 Billion parameters for **Mistral-7B**, 110 Million for **CamemBERT**, compared to 175 B parameters of **GPT-3.5**.

### 4.2 Text Simplification

For the training and the evaluation of the LLM models, we have constructed two different datasets: **1) Training-set.** To fine-tune our models for the task of

[2] The context used consists of a French text whose translation is given by: *You are a language assessor using the Common European Framework of Reference for Languages (CEFR). Your task is to assign a language proficiency score to this text, using the CEFR levels from A1 (beginner) to C2 (advanced/native). Evaluate this text and assign it the corresponding CEFR score.*

**Table 2.** Difficulty estimation metrics for all datasets

| model | context | LjL | SentencesInternet | SentencesBooks |
|---|---|---|---|---|
| **GPT-3.5-turbo-1106** | ✓ | 0.72 | 0.90 | 0.50 |
| | - | 0.73 | 0.87 | 0.49 |
| **CamemBERT** | - | 0.62 | 0.82 | 0.52 |
| **Mistral-7B** | ✓ | 0.64 | 0.75 | 0.51 |
| **Davinci-002** | - | 0.59 | 0.82 | 0.47 |
| | ✓ | 0.61 | 0.81 | 0.47 |
| **Mistral-7B** | - | 0.47 | 0.63 | 0.35 |
| **FKGL** | - | 0.42 | 0.34 | 0.35 |
| **GFI** | - | 0.45 | 0.32 | 0.34 |
| **ARI** | - | 0.40 | 0.34 | 0.34 |

simplification, we need a dataset of French sentences with their simplifications at an associated lower CEFR level. We used **GPT4** to generate 125 sentences (*25 from each level* `A2, B1, B2, C1, C2`) and their simplified versions. This dataset was further reviewed by a native French speaker. **2) Test-set.** We take, per difficulty level `A2, B1, B2, C1, C2` (*Level A1 cannot be simplified*), 100 random sentences from the `sentencesBooks` and `sentencesInternet` dataset. The test-set consists of $5 \times 100 \times 2 = 1000$ sentences.

**Model Evaluation.** We examine the performance of **GPT-4**, **Davinci** and **GPT-3.5-turbo-1106** from OpenAI, and the **Mistral-7B** model. We provide the results of our evaluation in Table 3. Among the different models evaluated, GPT-4 Zero-shot has the highest w-Score. The 0.5 in the simplification accuracy of GPT-4 shows that in 50% of the cases, the text was simplified to one-level

**Table 3.** Performance of LLMs for the text simplification task.

| Model | Simplification Accuracy | Semantic Similarity | w-Score |
|---|---|---|---|
| **GPT-4 Zero-shot** | *0.50* | *0.89* | *0.64* |
| **Mistral-7B Fine-Tuned** | 0.35 | 0.91 | 0.51 |
| **GPT 3.5 Fine-Tuned** | 0.34 | 0.91 | 0.50 |
| **GPT 3.5 Zero-Shot** | 0.31 | 0.93 | 0.47 |
| **Mistral-7B Zero-Shot** | 0.28 | 0.93 | 0.43 |
| **Davinci Fine-Tuned** | 0.24 | 0.83 | 0.38 |

lower of difficulty. At the same time the meaning is highly preserved with the cosine similarity between the original and simplified embeddings of the text being 0.89 on average.

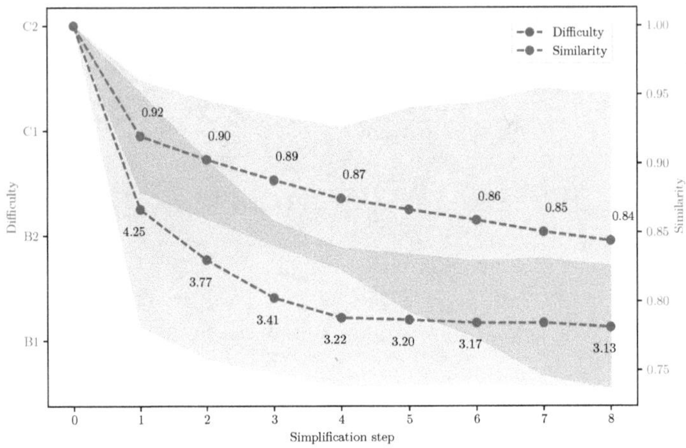


**Fig. 1.** Iterative simplification of sentence difficulty of CEFR level C2 with Mistral-7B model where CamemBERT was used to estimate difficulty and cosine similarity to evaluate text similarity. We report average value over 100 experiments.

**Iterative Simplification.** Finally, we illustrate how a simplification model, the Mistral in this case, behaves for the task of an iterative simplification of French sentences. We randomly selected 100 level `C2` sentences from the `training-set` correctly classified by **CamemBERT** as being of level `C2`. We then iteratively applied the simplification steps to the sentence using the fine-tuned version of **Mistral-7B** before evaluating the difficulty of the resulting sentence and the cosine similarity with the original sentence (from iteration 0). For a performance model, that always reduces the difficulty one-difficulty level at a time, we could only do this operation 5 times (`C2` $\longrightarrow$ `A1`). Since, we don't have a perfect model, we perform this 8 times to observe the trend. We see that the model successfully reduces both the difficulty and the semantic similarity is also reduced as a consequence of the simplification, as shown in Fig. 1.

## 5 Conclusion

This study demonstrates the potential of LLMs to enhance the estimation of foreign text difficulty and simplification. These advancements open new perspectives for personalizing language learning. By integrating these models into educational platforms, it becomes possible to adapt content to each learner's interests and level, making the experience more engaging and effective. Moreover, these models could help bridge gaps in existing pedagogical resources by generating simplified content on-demand. Future work should explore the possibility of working with entire paragraphs rather than isolated sentences for difficulty estimation and simplification. It would also be interesting to include state-of-the-art models like **GPT-4**, **Claude 3 Opus**, **Gemini 1.0 Ultra**, and larger open-source models such as **Mistral 8x22b** in the comparisons [14].

## References


1. Al-Thanyyan, S., Azmi, A.M.: Automated text simplification. ACM Comput. Surv. (2021)
2. Brown, T., Mann, B., et al.: Language models are few-shot learners. NeuRIPS **33**, 1877–1901 (2020)
3. Bubeck, S., et al.: Sparks of artificial general intelligence: early experiments with GPT-4. arXiv:2303.12712 [cs] (2023)
4. Chaturvedi, R., et al.: Divide and conquer: From complexity to simplicity for lay summarization. SDP (2020)
5. Chen, X., Meurers, D.: Ctap: a web-based tool supporting automatic complexity analysis. In: Proceedings of the Workshop on Computational Linguistics for Linguistic Complexity (CL4LC), pp. 113–119 (2016)
6. Chowdhery, A., et al.: Palm: scaling language modeling with pathways. arXiv preprint arXiv:2204.02311 (2022)
7. Day, R., Bamford, J.: Top ten principles for teaching extensive reading (2002)
8. Devlin, J., Chang, M., Lee, K., Toutanova, K.: BERT: pre-training of deep bidirectional transformers for language understanding. In: Burstein, J., Doran, C., Solorio, T. (eds.) NAACL-HLT, pp. 4171–4186 (2019)
9. Feng, Y., Qiang, J., Li, Y., Yuan, Y., Zhu, Y.: Sentence simplification via large language models. arXiv (2023)
10. François, T., Fairon, C.: An "AI readability" formula for French as a foreign language. In: Empirical Methods in Natural Language Processing and Computational Natural Language Learning, pp. 466–477 (2012)
11. Hernandez, N., Oulbaz, N., Faine, T.: Open corpora and toolkit for assessing text readability in French. In: Workshop on Tools and Resources to Empower People with REAding DIfficulties (READI), pp. 54–61 (2022)
12. Imperial, J.M.: Bert embeddings for automatic readability assessment. arXiv preprint arXiv:2106.07935 (2021)
13. Jiang, A.Q., Sablayrolles, A., et al.: Mistral 7b (2023)
14. Kevian, D., et al.: Capabilities of large language models in control engineering: a benchmark study on gpt-4, claude 3 opus, and gemini 1.0 ultra (2024)
15. Krashen, S.D.: The power of reading: Insights from the research: insights from the research. ABC-CLIO (2004)
16. Lee, J.S.: An editable learner model for text recommendation for language learning. ReCALL **34**(1), 51–65 (2022)
17. Liu, Y., et al.: Roberta: a robustly optimized bert pretraining approach (2019)
18. Martin, L., et al.: CamemBERT: a tasty French language model. In: Annual Meeting of the ACL, pp. 7203–7219 (2020)
19. Okinina, N., Frey, J.C., Weiss, Z.: Ctap for Italian: integrating components for the analysis of Italian into a multilingual linguistic complexity analysis tool. In: LREC, pp. 7123–7131 (2020)

20. Radford, A., Narasimhan, K., Salimans, T., Sutskever, I., et al.: Improving language understanding by generative pre-training (2018)
21. Radford, A., Wu, J., Child, R., Luan, D., Amodei, D., Sutskever, I.: Language models are unsupervised multitask learners (2019)
22. Scialom, T., Martin, L., Staiano, J., Clergerie, E.V.D.l., Sagot, B.: Rethinking automatic evaluation in sentence simplification. arXiv (2021)
23. Shatilov, A., Rey, A.: Sentence simplification with ruGPT3 (2021)
24. Touvron, H., Lavril, T., et al.: Llama: open and efficient foundation language models. arXiv preprint arXiv:2302.13971 (2023)
25. Tuncay, H.O.: App Attrition in Computer-Assisted Language Learning: Focus on Duolingo. Ph.D. thesis, McGill University (Canada) (2020)
26. Vinzelberg, O., Jenkins, M., Morison, G., McMinn, D., Tieges, Z.: Lay text summarisation using natural language processing: a narrative literature review. arXiv.org (2023)
27. Wilkens, R., et al.: Fabra: French aggregator-based readability assessment toolkit. In: Language Resources and Evaluation Conference, pp. 1217–1233 (2022)
28. Xia, M., Kochmar, E., Briscoe, T.: Text readability assessment for second language learners. arXiv preprint arXiv:1906.07580 (2019)
29. Zhang, J., Zhao, Y., Saleh, M., Liu, P.J.: Pegasus: pre-training with extracted gap-sentences for abstractive summarization (2020)

# LLM-Based Course Comprehension Evaluator

George Zografos, Vasileios Kefalidis(✉), and Lefteris Moussiades

Democritus University of Thrace, 65404 Kavala, Greece
{gezozra,vskefal,lmous}@cs.ihu.gr

**Abstract.** Large language models (LLMs) like GPT-4 reshape intelligent tutoring systems by enabling nuanced natural language interactions. Leveraging LLMs' capabilities, this study introduces an innovative Lesson Comprehension Evaluator, utilizing advanced Natural Language Processing (NLP) methods and Augmented Retrieval Generation (RAG) to assess course material comprehension. Through a web interface, students engage with tailored questions and receive feedback, fostering immersive learning experiences. Each response undergoes rigorous evaluation against a ground truth LLM-generated knowledge base, encompassing semantic comprehension, specificity, and correctness metrics. These evaluations provide insights into students' course understanding, informing future pedagogical strategies. By incorporating auditory options for accessibility and gamification elements for enhanced engagement, this approach facilitates self-paced, deeper learning, fostering dynamic and enriching learning environments.

**Keywords:** Intelligent Tutoring Systems · GPT-4 · Retrieval Augmented Generation (RAG)

## 1 Introduction

In the realm of Intelligent Tutoring Systems (ITS), several significant advancements have been made in recent years, as evidenced by a series of papers published from 2019 to 2024. Explainable Artificial Intelligence was introduced in ITS to foster student engagement and understanding [1]. The integration of ITS with personalized learning (PL) gained traction [2]. Systematic literature reviews underscored the evolution of ITSs with natural language, showcasing various mechanisms for simulating human dialogue and pedagogical strategies [3, 4].

Papers explored the potential of LLMs in generating reading comprehension exercises [5] and developing adaptive practicing systems [6], highlighting their efficiency in question generation and mastery detection algorithms. However, challenges such as bias mitigation and evaluating multi-turn conversations remained focal points for future research [7]. Additionally, studies investigated the mathematical capabilities of LLMs and emphasized the need to address knowledge gaps and misconceptions in educational contexts [8, 9].

Innovative solutions, such as AI Tutors and Virtual Teaching Assistants (TA), showcased the integration of advanced AI technologies, including Large Language Models


A. Sifaleras and F. Lin (Eds.): ITS 2024, LNCS 14798, pp. 405–414, 2024.
https://doi.org/10.1007/978-3-031-63028-6_35

(LLMs), for personalized and adaptive learning experiences [10, 11]. These systems leveraged state-of-the-art LLMs, such as GPT-4, to provide accurate answers, tailored tutoring, and comprehensive feedback [11–13]. However, challenges such as scalability, interpretability, and ethical considerations remained pertinent [10, 11, 14].

In parallel, the research explored the authoring scaling of AutoTutors and the real-life usability of LLMs in science education [15, 16]. Studies on Retrieval Augmented Generation (RAG) systems emphasized the importance of careful design considerations and domain-specific fine-tuning [17, 18].

The transformative breakthroughs in NLP arrived with the ascent of deep learning methodologies and the development of LLMs, such as OpenAI's GPT [20] series and Google's BERT [21]. These LLMs are characterized by their massive scale, parameter counts, and ability to generate coherent and contextually relevant text.

The proliferation of LLMs has catalyzed a revolution in NLP, enabling unprecedented capabilities in tasks ranging from machine translation and question-answering to text summarization and dialogue generation. RAG is a pioneering paradigm within the domain of NLP. It integrates LLMs with external knowledge sources to leverage the retrieved knowledge to augment text generation capabilities.

This study introduces an innovative Course Comprehension Evaluator using LLMs (LLMCCE). The web interface allows students to engage with tailored questions and receive feedback, providing insights into their understanding and facilitating self-paced, deeper learning.

Subsequent sections concisely expose the technical underpinnings pertinent to the terminologies utilized. Finally, an exposition of the evaluation outcomes, which at the same time evaluate GPT-4 effectiveness in creating meaningful and on-target questions from textual content, derived from domain expert assessments and pilot study findings is presented, complemented by examining associated limitations and avenues for future research in this domain.

## 2 LLM-Based Course Comprehension Evaluator (LLMCCE)

The main modules that comprise our proposed approach are the User Interface, Timeline Creation Module, Evaluation Module, and Vector Database. A high-level architecture is shown in Fig. 1.

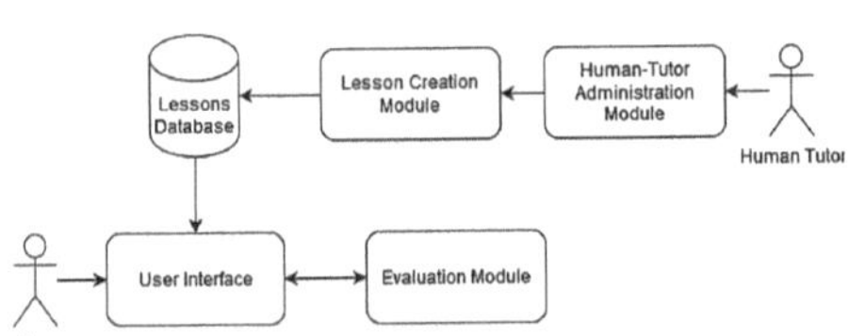


**Fig. 1.** High-level architecture of LLMCCE

## 2.1 User Interface Module

In general, several elements are included in the intelligent tutoring system's user interface to make learning easier and more comfortable. In our approach, one notable feature is the flexibility for students to choose the precise lesson file they want to practice. This feature empowers students to actively engage with the educational information in a way that is in line with their learning preferences and aims while also encouraging autonomy and agency among students and a sense of ownership over the learning process.

After the student chooses the desired lesson, in our case History, the main interaction screen changes and shows the corresponding timeline chosen.

Central to this new screen is the prominent display of the timeline, strategically positioned to facilitate student engagement and navigation through the educational material. The timeline is presented in a vertical orientation, commencing at the topmost portion of the screen and extending downwards, affording students a comprehensive overview of the chronological progression of events or learning milestones, as shown in Fig. 2.

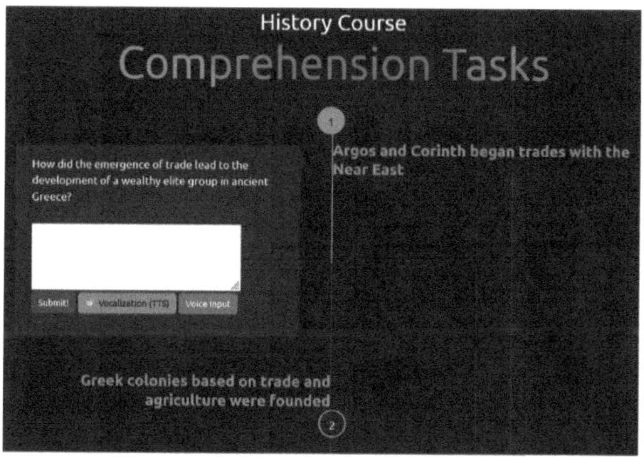


**Fig. 2.** The Timeline student interaction screen

## 2.2 Human Tutor Administration Module

In the administrative interface of the intelligent tutoring system, the human tutor is vested with significant autonomy and flexibility in shaping the pedagogical trajectory of the educational experience. A key feature of this interface empowers the human tutor to define the parameters governing the generation of a specific number of questions by the model or to directly input custom questions onto specific textual content, thereby circumventing the conventional Lesson Creation Module.

By bypassing the Lesson Creation Module, described in later sections, in favor of direct intervention by the human tutor, the system transitions into an evaluative role, wherein the focus shifts towards assessing learner comprehension and mastery of the educational content. The lesson is promptly saved to the database upon completion of the instructional design process, ensuring seamless integration into the overarching educational framework.

This approach not only expedites the content creation process but also affords the human tutor greater freedom and flexibility in tailoring pedagogical pathways to address learners' diverse needs and preferences. By emphasizing human expertise and input, the system fosters a collaborative educational environment wherein the complementary strengths of automated technology and human ingenuity converge to facilitate enriched learning experiences.

### 2.3 Lesson Creation Module

In creating lessons within the intelligent tutoring system, a structured procedure is followed to harness the capabilities of both human input and advanced natural language processing technologies. Initially, a human tutor accesses an administration panel designed for lesson creation, wherein they are prompted to insert textual content that forms the basis for constructing a timeline within the educational material. This textual content (TC) can range from concise excerpts to comprehensive passages, encompassing various educational resources such as book paragraphs, chapters, or entire books. Subsequently, upon submission of the inserted text, it undergoes processing within a Python script specifically engineered for this task.

Within the confines of the Python script, a meticulously crafted prompt is formulated, tailored to elicit pertinent information from the provided text and to guide subsequent question generation. This prompt encompasses instructions for extracting key points from the text, a predefined template for structuring responses, and the number of questions the tutor requested [NQ]. Leveraging the robust capabilities of the GPT-4 language model, this prompt is then deployed to generate responses that align with the specified template. The structure of this prompt is as follows:

*"Create a timeline of [NQ] important events covering all of the given text. The presentation of the timeline will be presented without break lines and three keywords [referring_date, event, question] separated by comma as follows: referring_date: [Date], event: [Event], question: [Question] of understanding about the event. The keywords must be mentioned every time in the response. Text: [TC]".*

The resultant responses generated by GPT-4 are subject to post-processing procedures, wherein the data is organized and stored in individual PHP files. A salient feature involves automatically generating PHP files each time a timeline is created, facilitating the storage and dissemination of educational content. This innovative functionality underscores a commitment to seamless collaboration and knowledge sharing among students and tutors within the educational ecosystem. A detailed low-level architecture of the lesson creation module is presented in Fig. 3.

This structured procedure underscores a symbiotic relationship between human expertise and artificial intelligence, wherein the computational power and natural language processing capabilities of state-of-the-art language models complement human tutors' nuanced understanding and instructional insights. By seamlessly integrating human input with advanced technological solutions, the intelligent tutoring system facilitates the creation of dynamic and engaging educational content tailored to learners'

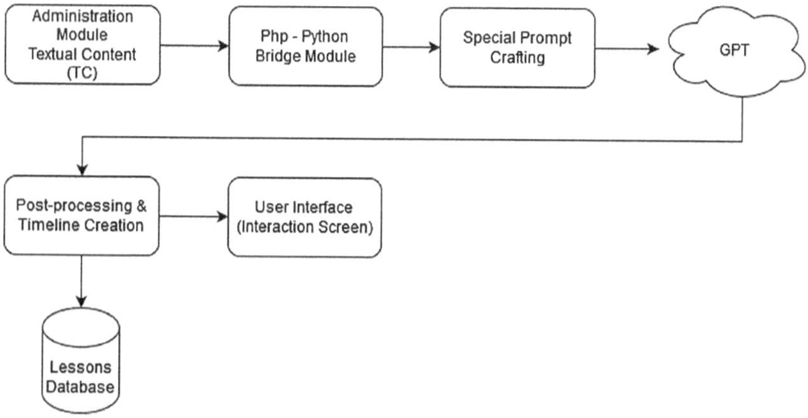


**Fig. 3.** Detailed low-level architecture of Lesson Creation Module.

diverse needs and preferences. Moreover, this procedure exemplifies a synergistic approach toward educational content creation, wherein the fusion of human creativity and machine intelligence culminates in developing pedagogically sound and intellectually stimulating learning experiences.

## 2.4 Evaluation Module

In the context of this step, the utilization of a vector database [22] plays a pivotal role in facilitating the storage and manipulation of textual data within the intelligent tutoring system. A vector database, in essence, is a specialized repository designed to store vectors, which are mathematical representations of data points in a multi-dimensional space. These vectors capture semantic relationships and contextual information inherent within the textual content, thereby enabling efficient retrieval and analysis of information.

Specifically, in our approach, the vector database serves as a repository for storing vectors generated from textual inputs provided by human tutors. Upon submission of a text by the human tutor to create a timeline within the educational material, the system initiates an auxiliary procedure. This procedure involves tokenizing the text and segmenting it into predefined chunk sizes, breaking the textual content into manageable units for processing.

Subsequently, each chunk of text transforms into a vector embedding utilizing an embedding model, with the specific model employed herein denoted as "text-embedding-ada-002" [20]. This embedding model facilitates the conversion of textual information into dense numerical representations, capturing the semantic nuances and contextual intricacies embedded within the text. Through this process, the textual content provided by the human tutor is encoded into vector embeddings, effectively encapsulating the semantic essence of the input within a mathematical framework.

This database is meticulously calibrated to operate using cosine similarity as its primary similarity metric, a mathematical measure widely acknowledged for its efficacy in capturing the degree of similarity between vectors in a multi-dimensional space. Furthermore, the dimensionality of vectors stored within the database is meticulously defined to adhere to the text embedding model's specifications. Specifically, the dimension size is set at 1536, aligning precisely with the dimensional requirements of the employed embedding model.

Completing this encoding process, the vectorized representations of the human tutor's text are inserted into the vector database for storage and subsequent retrieval within the system's operational workflow.

Within the architectural framework of our approach, incorporating a dynamic timeline feature serves as a cornerstone in facilitating interactive learning experiences.

Integral to this timeline are questions generated by the Lessons Creation Module, strategically positioned to prompt learner engagement and comprehension. Each question is complemented by a textarea input field, allowing students to articulate their responses effectively. To enhance accessibility and accommodate diverse learner needs, the system incorporates text-to-speech functionality, enabling auditory presentation of questions and automatic speech recognition (ASR) for seamless input through spoken responses.

Upon submission of a student's response (UR), the system initiates a comprehensive evaluation process orchestrated by a designated Python file. This evaluative procedure commences with a retrieval operation targeting the vector database to source relevant information pertinent to the question. Employing sophisticated retrieval algorithms, the system identifies the top three most relevant records from the vector database, contextualizing the subsequent evaluation process.

With relevant data, the system proceeds to solicit responses from the GPT-4 model, leveraging its advanced natural language processing capabilities. These responses, generated in response to the same question (UQ) presented to the student, serve as the benchmark ground truth (GT) against which student responses are evaluated. RAG's response is considered as the authoritative reference point for subsequent evaluations.

Subsequently, the system engages GPT-4 again, this time tasking it with the role of evaluator. A specialized prompt is crafted to guide the model in assessing the student's response vis-à-vis the generated ground truth, focusing on evaluating detail, semantic comprehension, and correctness. Each aspect is meticulously scrutinized, and a score ranging from 0 to 20 is assigned to quantify the quality and accuracy of the student's response relative to the established ground truth. The prompt follows:

*"Act as a kind assistant, History Teacher Assistant. I want you to evaluate answers [UR] and [GT] against each other for question [UQ]. Taking [GT] as the correct reference, answer for [UR] the following: Detail:[Grade from 1 to 20], Semantic:[Grade from 1 to 20], Correctness: [Grade from 1 to 20]. Then average the three ratings and display Final Score:[Average from 1 to 20]".*

The evaluation results are returned to the user interface. Additionally, a brief explanation of how GPT-4 evaluated the student's response is returned for better interpretability of the procedure.

### 2.5 LLMCCE Evaluation

In evaluating the correctness and effectiveness of the intelligent tutoring system's question generation and response capabilities, a rigorous assessment methodology is employed, leveraging the expertise of domain-specific professionals. This evaluative process involves soliciting feedback from three domain experts who possess specialized knowledge and proficiency in the subject matter under consideration. The experts evaluate questions and corresponding model-generated answers, assessing their relevance, accuracy, and alignment with the provided context.

The domain experts are provided with a standardized questionnaire comprising 15 question-answer pairs, each representing a distinct instance of model-generated content to structure the evaluation process. The experts are instructed to employ a classification method wherein they assign a score based on the question's relevance to the provided context and the adequacy of the model-generated answer in addressing the corresponding question. Specifically, a score of 2 is assigned if both the question and answer are deemed relevant and satisfactory, and a score of 1 is assigned if the question is relevant but the answer falls short of expectations. A score of 0 is reserved for instances where the question is deemed irrelevant to the context. This evaluation approach also evaluates how well an LLM such as GPT-4 can extract specific questions from a text and identify its main points.

Upon completion of the evaluation process, the results from each domain expert are compiled and analyzed to gauge the accuracy and effectiveness of the model's question generation and response capabilities. Notably, the evaluation results indicate a high degree of alignment between the model-generated content and the provided context, with the vast majority of question-answer pairs receiving scores of 2 or 1. Specifically, the first domain expert submits 13 pairs with a score of 2 and 2 pairs with a score of 1, while the second domain expert assesses 12 pairs with a score of 2 and 3 pairs with a score of 1. Remarkably, the third domain expert's evaluations mirror those of the first expert, further validating the consistency and reliability of the assessment process.

Crucially, none of the domain experts identify instances where the model-generated content deviates significantly from the provided context, as evidenced by the absence of scores of 0. This observation underscores the robustness and accuracy of the model in generating contextually relevant questions and responses (Table 1).

**Table 1.** The model generated Q&A pairs evaluation from domain experts.

| Domain Experts | Domain Expert Evaluation | | |
|---|---|---|---|
| | 0 | 1 | 2 |
| $1^{st}$ DE | 0 | 2 | 13 |
| $2^{nd}$ DE | 0 | 3 | 12 |
| $3^{rd}$ DE | 0 | 2 | 13 |

In aggregate, the evaluation results yield an overall accuracy rate of 84.4%, indicating a high level of proficiency and effectiveness in the system's question generation and response capabilities. This percentage is a key metric in assessing the system's performance and guiding decisions regarding its implementation and utilization within educational settings. Ultimately, the favorable evaluation outcomes affirm the system's efficacy in facilitating effective question generation and response, thereby contributing to enhanced user learning experiences and outcomes.

### 2.6 LLMCCE Pilot Study

To gauge the intelligent tutoring system's practical efficacy and user experience, access was extended to a select group comprising 8th-grade students and their dedicated history lesson human tutor. This endeavor aimed to solicit firsthand feedback from end users regarding their engagement with the system and overall satisfaction with its functionality and utility within the educational context.

During the evaluation period, students and their tutor interacted with the system, engaging in various activities designed to assess its effectiveness in facilitating learning and comprehension of historical concepts. Notably, participant feedback indicated a high level of engagement and enthusiasm with the system, with students expressing a keen interest in revisiting the procedures multiple times in pursuit of improved outcomes.

## 3 Limitations

The evaluation procedure for an intelligent tutoring system's question generation and response capabilities has limitations due to subjective evaluations from domain experts. Future research should include a larger pool of experts to improve the robustness and generalize ability of evaluation outcomes.

Moreover, the evaluation process in educational domains is influenced by contextual nuances, with the effectiveness of model question-answer pairs varying based on the context and instructional material complexity. Understanding these factors is crucial for making informed decisions about the model's applicability.

The model's relevance issue highlights the need for ongoing research and refinement of RAG approaches. Strategies like optimizing prompts or exploring alternative methodologies can enhance contextual relevance and accuracy, addressing evolving needs and expectations.

## 4 Conclusion

Our proposed methodology integrates natural language processing and interactive learning methodologies to enhance educational experiences, engaging learners, fostering active participation, and facilitating knowledge acquisition and retention. Simultaneously, an assessment is conducted by specialists in the field of LLM Model efficiency, namely the GPT-4 in our instance, concerning the task of identifying the salient features of the provided text and crafting focused questions around them.

Our system effectively delivers relevant and engaging educational content, with an intuitive interface and interactive features. However, further research is needed to address limitations, improve performance, and enhance user satisfaction. This will help the system evolve to meet diverse user needs and expectations.

**Acknowledgements.** This work was supported by the MPhil program "Advanced Technologies in Informatics and Computers", hosted by the Department of Computer Science, Democritus University of Thrace, Greece.

## References

1. Putnam, V., Conati, C.: Exploring the need for explainable artificial intelligence (XAI) in intelligent tutoring systems (ITS). Los Angel (2019)
2. Akyuz, Y.: Effects of intelligent tutoring systems (ITS) on personalized learning (PL). Creat. Educ. **11**(06), 953–978 (2020). https://doi.org/10.4236/ce.2020.116069
3. Sychev, O., Anikin, A., Penskoy, N., Denisov, M., Prokudin, A.: CompPrehension - model-based intelligent tutoring system on comprehension level. In: Cristea, A.I., Troussas, C. (eds.) Intelligent Tutoring Systems: 17th International Conference, ITS 2021, Virtual Event, June 7–11, 2021, Proceedings, pp. 52–59. Springer International Publishing, Cham (2021). https://doi.org/10.1007/978-3-030-80421-3_6
4. Paladines, J., Ramirez, J.: A systematic literature review of intelligent tutoring systems with dialogue in natural language. IEEE Access **8**, 164246–164267 (2020). https://doi.org/10.1109/ACCESS.2020.3021383
5. Xiao, C., Xu, S.X., Zhang, K., Wang, Y., Xia, L.: "Evaluating reading comprehension exercises generated by LLMs: a showcase of ChatGPT in education applications. In: Proceedings of the 18th Workshop on Innovative Use of NLP for Building Educational Applications (BEA 2023), Toronto, Canada: Association for Computational Linguistics, pp. 610–625 (2023). https://doi.org/10.18653/v1/2023.bea-1.52
6. Kabir, R., Lin, F.: An LLM-powered adaptive practicing system (2023)
7. Pillera, G.C.: In dialogue with ChatGPT on the potential and limitations of AI for evaluation in education. Pedagog. OGGI **21**(1), 301–315 (2023). https://doi.org/10.7346/PO-012023-36
8. Liu, N., Sonkar, S., Wang, Z., Woodhead, S., Baraniuk, R.G.: Novice learner and expert tutor: evaluating math reasoning abilities of large language models with misconceptions. arXiv (2023). Accessed 23 Feb 2024. http://arxiv.org/abs/2310.02439
9. Niño-Rojas, F., Lancheros-Cuesta, D., Jiménez-Valderrama, M.T.P., Mestre, G., Gómez, S.: Systematic review: trends in intelligent tutoring systems in mathematics teaching and learning. Int. J. Educ. Math. Sci. Technol. **12**(1), 203–229 (2023). https://doi.org/10.46328/ijemst.3189
10. Hicke, Y., Agarwal, A., Ma, Q., Denny, P.: AI-TA: towards an intelligent question-answer teaching assistant using open-source LLMs. arXiv (2023). Accessed 23 Feb 2024. http://arxiv.org/abs/2311.02775
11. Sajja, R., Sermet, Y., Cikmaz, M., Cwiertny, D., Demir, I.: Artificial intelligence-enabled intelligent assistant for personalized and adaptive learning in higher education. arXiv (2023). https://doi.org/10.48550/arXiv.2309.10892
12. Chenxi, D.: How to build an AI tutor that can adapt to any course and provide accurate answers using large language model and retrieval-augmented generation (2023)
13. Latif, E., et al.: AGI: artificial general intelligence for education. arXiv (2023). Accessed 23 Feb 2024. http://arxiv.org/abs/2304.12479
14. Owan, V.J., Abang, K.B., Idika, D.O., Etta, E.O., Bassey, B.A.: Exploring the potential of artificial intelligence tools in educational measurement and assessment. Eurasia J. Math. Sci. Technol. Educ. **19**(8), em2307 (2023). https://doi.org/10.29333/ejmste/13428
15. Chowdhury, S.P., Zouhar, V., Sachan, M.: Scaling the authoring of AutoTutors with large language models. arXiv (2024). Accessed 23 Feb 2024. http://arxiv.org/abs/2402.09216
16. Chevalier, A., et al.: Language Models as Science Tutors. arXiv (2024). Accessed 23 Feb 2024. http://arxiv.org/abs/2402.11111

17. Lewis, P., et al.: Retrieval-augmented generation for knowledge-intensive NLP tasks. arXiv (2021). Accessed 22 Nov 2023. http://arxiv.org/abs/2005.11401
18. Castleman, B., Turkcan, M.K.: Examining the influence of varied levels of domain knowledge base inclusion in GPT-based intelligent tutors. arXiv (2023). Accessed 27 Feb 2024. http://arxiv.org/abs/2309.12367
19. Chen, Y., Ding, N., Zheng, H.-T., Liu, Z., Sun, M., Zhou, B.: Empowering private tutoring by chaining large language models. arXiv (2023). Accessed 23 Feb 2024. http://arxiv.org/abs/2309.08112
20. OpenAI Platform. Accessed 24 Jan (2024). https://platform.openai.com
21. Devlin, J., Chang, M.W., Lee, K., Toutanova, K.: BERT: pre-training of deep bidirectional transformers for language understanding. arXiv (2019). https://doi.org/10.48550/arXiv.1810.04805
22. What is a vector database? | IBM. Accessed 29 Feb 2024. https://www.ibm.com/topics/vector-database

# Exploring Item Difficulty Prediction: Data Driven Approach for Item Difficulty Estimation

Mohamed Lamgarraj[1], Céline Joiron[1], Aymeric Parant[2], and Gilles Dequen[1(✉)]

[1] Laboratoire de Modlisation, Information et Systèmes (MIS), Picardie Jules Verne university, Amiens 80000, France
{mohamed.lamgarraj,gilles.dequen}@u-picardie.fr

[2] Centre de Recherche en Psychologie: Cognition, Psychisme et Organisations (CRP-CPO), Picardie Jules Verne university, Amiens 80000, France

**Abstract.** This paper presents a comprehensive study of learning assessment, delving into the concept of item difficulty and learner perception. It addresses two critical dimensions: the methodologies employed, particularly data-driven approaches, and the necessary data for this analysis. Traditional difficulty estimation methods focus on question content or student performance. Recent studies suggest using machine learning and natural language processing to predict question difficulty. These models are subject-specific and often overlook individual student differences, limiting their wider application. The work aims to examine data of real-world testing scenarii, so that assembling and building a rich and diverse dataset. It offers valuable insights into the factors influencing item difficulty by giving the maximum amount of information considering the test and the student. It presents experiments to build and train predictive machine learning models for difficulty prediction. At the end, thanks to experiments, we can show a nuanced understanding of the assessment challenge and lay the groundwork for incorporating psychological factors into difficulty estimation as a subsequent phase.

**Keywords:** Computer Human Learning Environments · Education · Assessments · Item Difficulty · Machine Learning

## 1 Introduction

In higher education, learning assessment plays a determining role in the academic progress of students. In this context, estimating the difficulty of test questions (items) is crucial to guarantee the accuracy, or even fairness, of student evaluations. The complexity of this task arises from the diversity of assessment methods that can be employed, as well as factors affecting the perception of the difficulty of a question or task. The latter include not only the content of the question, its structure (depending on its nature), or its wording, but also the individual characteristics of the students evaluated. Faced with this complexity, the use of


A. Sifaleras and F. Lin (Eds.): ITS 2024, LNCS 14798, pp. 415–424, 2024.
https://doi.org/10.1007/978-3-031-63028-6_36

digital tools for an automatic and more objective assessment of difficulties constitutes a research avenue for our work, which focuses in this article on Multiple Choice Questions (MCQ) type items.

In this context, the characterization of assessment items difficulty raises a complex problem. Our research aimes at this characterization through the construction of a model oriented towards the measure of this difficulty strating from traces, as well as integrating psychometric characteristics into this process. This work aims to examine the approaches and methodologies used in the literature to predict the difficulty of assessment items, as well as the datasets used in these studies. Based on this analysis, our goal is to develop a dataset designed specifically to refine difficulty predictions via machine learning.

In this paper, we focused on two pivotal aspects. First, building an extensive dataset incorporating a range of factors that affect the perception of item difficulty. Second, Machine Learning methods to achieve more precise difficulty estimations. Our goal is to improve the accuracy and efficacy of item difficulty prediction models. It aims to establish the foundations for a more sophisticated and nuanced estimation, integrating more complex psychometric factors.

## 2 Related Works

The concept of difficulty has been the subject of study in psychology, especially within educational and cognitive domains, by exploring the socio-cognitive processes underlying its individuals perceptions. Researchers have examined factors such as working memory capacity, cognitive load, attentional resources, and meta-cognitive strategies employed for challenging tasks. These researches have analyzed factors contributing to difficulty, such as question attributes and examined abilities [4]. Other studies announced that some attributes were relevant to question difficulty, such as question types, question structures and knowledge depth [12]. These studies are based on manual intervention and human expertise [3,13]. Complementarily, Yen (1981) demonstrated how statistical simulations of latent trait models could be employed to rigorously analyze these perceptions of difficulty in educational assessments, providing a quantitative approach to understanding these complex psychological constructs [18].

Data-driven approaches are also used for some MCQ-type item difficulty prediction tasks. The majority of works related to predicting question difficulty, processed the test items based on the text or a history of previous answers. Most of them have been done in the field of Natural Language Processing (NLP). Data-driven approaches, although limited, utilize psychometric models like the Linear Logistic Test Model (LLTM) to predict question difficulty, leveraging a linear relationship between latent traits and response probabilities [10]. These models are based on item response theory (IRT) [16], wich is a statistical framework used to develop, evaluate, and score assessments. Its goal is to predict the probability that a student with a specific ability level, will correctly answer an item. Morever, Classical Test Theory (CTT) provides a foundational framework for understanding test score reliability and validity [1]. It introduces item difficulty and discrimination indices, shedding light on how well test items differentiate between individuals of varying abilities. The reliability coefficient, often measured by Cronbach's alpha [17], assesses score consistency, indicating how accurately observed scores reflect true individual differences. CTT presents limitations in handling tests with differing difficulty levels.

Additionally to these works, some studies have adopted text-based methods to predict question difficulty, employing advanced NLP models. Early works focused on MCQs, and employed deterministic bag-of-words approaches to measure similarity between question elements [2]. Additionally, transformer-based pre-trained architectures, such as BERT (Bidirectional Encoder Representations from Transformers) [8] can be fine-tuned for difficulty prediction by understanding contextual relationships between questions and answers [5]. Furthermore, machine learning algorithms such as Support Vector Machines (SVM) or Random Forests can be trained on features derived from text, like semantic similarity scores between distractors, to predict question difficulty.

According to this state-of-the-art analysis, both in terms of the methodologies used to estimate question difficulty and the data employed for this purpose, our investigations have revealed several notable gaps that present opportunities for significant contributions to the field. Primarily, the data utilized in these works typically comprise only text data from questions and answers or traces from students' interactions during tests. Such datasets tend to include basic information like the content of questions or answers, time elapsed, and expected responses. While these elements are undoubtedly valuable, they fall short of providing a comprehensive understanding of item difficulty. They capture only a limited aspect of the data necessary to discern real patterns in student performance.

This critical review indicates that current models overly depend on surface-level data, which might lead to incomplete or skewed analyses of difficulty. There is a conspicuous absence of deeper, more nuanced data inputs such as students' cognitive processes, affective states, and interaction dynamics during the test-taking process. Incorporating such multidimensional data could unveil richer insights into the complexities of test difficulty and student performance.

In this context, we aim to create and enrich a significant dataset of educational traces, which will serve as a foundation for building machine learning models to predict item difficulty accurately.

## 3 Data

For research purposes in computer-based learning environments, publicly available datasets are released such as the ASSISTments dataset [9], an online tutoring system assessing students while providing pedagogical assistance. Additionally, the Academy dataset[1], offered by an online learning provider, focuses on computer science courses, with all questions being multiple-choice. Those datasets have been evaluated extensively, and they don't meet our needs due

[1] https://cloudacademy.com/.

to inadequate information, high missing data rates, and limited data volume, hindering comprehensive and reliable analysis. Our research focus on the EdNet Dataset [7], a large-scale hierarchical dataset that spans over two years, gathering student interaction logs from Santa[2] a multi-platform self-study solution designed to assist students in preparing for the TOEIC test (Test of English for International Communication).

EdNet considered the largest publicly accessible dataset, with 131,441,538 interactions of 784,309 students and 13,170 questions, with an average of 8,687 observations per question, it comprises four extensions, labeled from KT1 to KT4. After thorough evaluation, we opted to use KT1 due to its completeness and the relatively high level of missing values in the other extensions. KT1 contains 784,309 individual files, each corresponding to a unique user (learner). These files capture the test-taking history of each student, detailing question IDs, solving IDs, timestamps, user answers, and elapsed times. Additionally, EdNet includes a 'contents' file housing a 'questions' file, which provides comprehensive information on each of its 13,170 questions, including question IDs and correct answers. This dataset offers a land to develop a more accurate dataset.

However, characterizing difficulty in educational assessment requires a dataset that includes detailed student interactions, task completion times, and learning resource efficiency. Thus, we organized and aggregated data to create a tailored dataset, enabling accurate difficulty characterization across subjects and levels. The work was executed in several stages:

- **Merging learners traces:** EDNet-KT1 consists of 784,309 CSV files related to each user. All files were merged into a single flat file integrating the user's ID. The result is a file composed of 95,293,926 lines and 6 columns.
- **Combine question information with user information:** in this phase we merge questions information from the 'Contents' file to users traces. This combination not only facilitates correlating user responses with specific question characteristics but also adds information to the dataset, such as the correct answer to the question, topics, or other relevant metadata.
- **Data enhancement:** this step consists on increasing the extracted data with calculated and deduced characteristics. These designed characteristics may include ratios, statistics, or other metrics derived from the initial data that provide a deeper understanding of the underlying patterns in the dataset.

The final dataset takes two forms providing specific analysis perspectives:

- **User-Question oriented dataset:** contains information on each question attempted by every learner. This version enables the inclusion of parameters related to perceived difficulty and human factors in difficulty prediction and characterization work. It comprises 35 columns (Table 1) and a total of 79,929,968 entries.

[2] https://www.aitutorsanta.com/vn/.

- **Question oriented dataset:** focuses on the characteristics and nuances embedded in each evaluation item. It highlights essential question features, facilitating targeted analysis. This file contains data aggregated from each question, resulting in 13,170 entries(the number of questions proposed in all tests), and 27 columns of questions only features, extracted from the (Table 1).

**Table 1.** Column Names for User-Question-Oriented Dataset

| user_id | question_id | correct_answer | user_answer |
|---|---|---|---|
| is_correct | elapsed_time | bundle_id | explanation_id |
| solving_id | part | tags | deployed_at |
| PassCountPerQues | PassCountPerUser | Tot_answers_false | Tot_answers_correct |
| falseCountPerUser | correctCountPerUser | TotalTimeforQues | TotalTimeforQuesperUser |
| TotalTimeforCorrect | TotalTimeforFalse | UserTimeforCorrectr | UserTimeforFalse |
| AverageTimeperQues | AverageTimeperUser | AvergeTimeforCorrect | averageTimeforFalse |
| averageTimeforCorrect | averageTimeforfalse | VarTimeforCorrect | VarTimeforFalse |
| VarTimeforCorrectUser | VarTimeforFalseUser | difficulty (GT) | |

The next section presents some experiments of building predictive models, applied to these datasets and the results obtained.

# 4 Models and Results

Before refining our dataset for enhanced predictive capabilities, we initiated our process by training machine learning models on the intiial (non enhanced) dataset. This preliminary phase aimed to establish a baseline for the performance of various algorithms in predicting question difficulty. By contrasting these first results with those obtained from our final, enriched and treated dataset, we aim to underscore the substantial impact of our data preparation, and the value of the elements we added to difficulty characterization. Our approach involves identifying and integrating significant features that can improve the representation and estimation of difficulty. Through this comparative analysis, we not only evaluate the predictive power of different machine learning models but also assess the quality and relevance of our dataset at various stages of enhancement. This methodology allows us to experimentally demonstrate the added value of our work (Fig. 1) in the context of difficulty prediction tasks.

For establishing ground truth labels in our supervised learning training tasks, we employed a straightforward and fundamental criterion: the rate of correctness among all provided answers for every question. Predicting the exact value is challenging due to the inherent difficulty in identifying patterns that precisely correlate with specific values. As a result, we have opted to define three classes of ground truth difficulty: questions with a difficulty lower than 0.3 are identified as easy (class 0), those whose difficulty is between 0.3 and 0.6 are considered

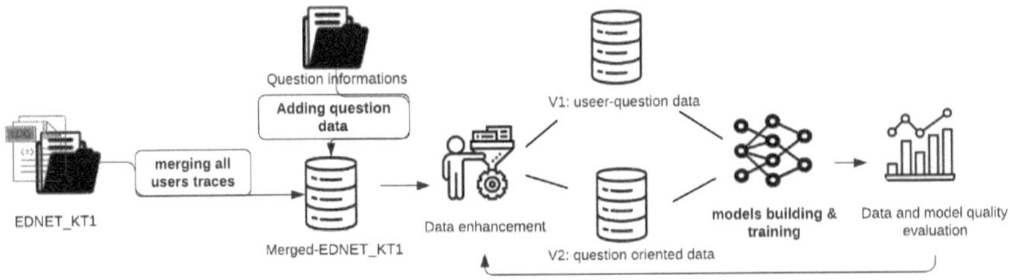


**Fig. 1.** *Workflow of our Data Enhancement and Model Training tasks*

of midium difficulty (class 1), and those with a difficulty greater than 0.6 are considered difficult (class 2).

During our experiment, we systematically trained four distinct machine learning models: Logistic Regression (LR) [15], Decision tree (DT) [11], Random Forests (RF) [14] and XGBoost (XGB) [6] These models were trained on data before and after enhancement, on HPC MatriCS platform[3]. We used a classical training process involving 80% of data, randomly chosen. The validation is simple, using the remaining 20% of the dataset.

Insights from this comparative analysis pave the way for informed decisions regarding the most suitable model for our particular dataset and predictive goals. To assess model performance on our dataset, we used the F1-score as we require both good precision and recall simultaneously, to correctly identify both challenging and non-challenging items (precision) while also capturing as many of the truly challenging items as possible (recall). For the original data, we obtained the results presented in the table (Table 2):

**Table 2.** Models performance on the initial question-user oriented data.

| **Model** | LR | DT | RF | XGB |
|---|---|---|---|---|
| **Accuracy** | 0.64 | 0.72 | 0.72 | 0.69 |
| **F1 score** | 0.59 | 0.70 | 0.70 | 0.65 |

After the data enrichment tasks, the same models were trained on our two final versions of data. For the second version of our dataset, which comprises a set of 79,929,968 rows and 35 columns, 40% of the data were used. The sample of data selected took into consideration factors such as homogeneity and data integrity, insuring that the data samples are representative of the entire dataset and do not disproportionately favor any particular subgroup, and verifying the accuracy, completeness, and consistency of the data. The data selected around the average number of instances per question, which is 8687 user responses per

[3] https://www.matrics.u-picardie.fr.

question, and also in an acceptable range of timing for questions to avoid questions with outlier values. Evaluation of the trained models yielded the following results (Table 3):

**Table 3.** Models performance on enriched data.

| Dataset | Model | LR | DT | RF | XGB |
|---|---|---|---|---|---|
| Question oriented data | Accuracy | 0.54 | 0.91 | 0.91 | 0.93 |
| | F1 score | 0.50 | 0.85 | 0.81 | 0.82 |
| User-question oriented data | Accuracy | – | 0.80 | 0.89 | 0.74 |
| | F1 score | – | 0.65 | 0.70 | 0.71 |

Comparing performances before and after data enrichment reveals the positive impact of adding new features and data processing on the models' ability to predict difficulty. Prior to enrichment, models struggled to achieve acceptable levels of accuracy and F1 scores, as shown in (Table 2). However, following the introduction of additional features and the improvement of data quality, (Table 3 demonstrate a significant increase in the performance of all tested models. This substantial improvement in results justifies the effort spent on data enrichment and processing. The addition of relevant features and information about the item led us to better characterize the difficulty and hence a better prediction of it. The performance variations among the models are notable between the question-oriented dataset and the user-question-oriented dataset, showing the impact of data composition on predictions. Model performance is better on the question-oriented dataset because the data precisely concerns the questions, with only one row per question, making it easier for models to find patterns. However, for the user-question-oriented dataset, question data is also linked to users, and questions appear multiple times in the dataset based on the number of students who attempted the question. Then it makes more challenging for models to find patterns in these data. The examination of the distribution of question density across targeted and predicted difficulty values (Fig. 2) provides clearer vision into the alignment between intended difficulty levels and the model predictions (in the figure the results for XGBoost model) for the questions-oriented data. The distribution of predicted values are more centred than targeted. However models demonstrates commendable accuracy in both instances, and that is the purpose of using classes for labeling the ground truth, the density in each class is the same in factor of the accuracy of the model.

By comparing model performance before and after data enhancement, we can clearly see the impact of our data processing and enhancement efforts, focused on adding the most important details and features about the items to help us better understand and characterize item difficulty. These preliminary results serve as the basis on which we will build a more complete and refined analysis, thus marking the beginning of our exploration. Comparing model performance

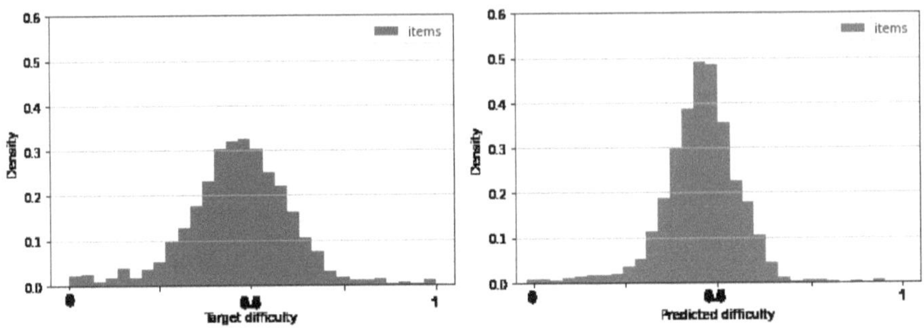


(a) Question density by ground truth difficulty values

(b) Question density by predicted difficulty values for question-oriented data

**Fig. 2.** Distribution of ground truth difficulty vs predicted values.

highlights the importance of the richness of our dataset in characterizing item difficulty and provides direction for future approaches to explore and implement in our quest for the optimal difficulty characterization and estimation.

## 5 Conclusion

In this paper, we focus on characterizing the difficulty of evaluation items. Beginning with a detailed exploration of existing methodologies, we then concentrated on constructing a robust and rich dataset containing maximum information about items, suitable for the complexities of difficulty estimation. The process involved data preparation resulting in a dataset ready for in-depth analysis. After laying the groundwork, we proceeded to test our dataset, using different predictive models to assess their effectiveness in capturing and predicting challenges. The results of these model evaluations not only provide valuable insights but also highlight the importance of our rich dataset for characterizing item difficulty and give us an idea of the next approaches to explore and implement for effective difficulty estimation techniques. Looking ahead, an ongoing experimental study, particularly with students in computer science and psychology, aims to verify several hypotheses about inherent item characteristics influencing perceived difficulty, as well as mechanisms supporting this perception, involving continuous improvement and expansion of the dataset by incorporating psychological dimensions. This work should lead to the definition and implementation of a difficulty "estimator", improving our understanding of the complex interaction between learners and the components of the assessment. In the longer term, it will be a matter of integrating this prediction into the algorithms for the automatic generation of assessment tests with targeted difficulty and of focusing on other types of items.

**Acknowledgments.** This research is funded as part of the Ap.Res project (Apprentissage en Réseaux - in French) resulting from the call for projects Digital Demonstrator in Higher Education of France 2030 (https://www.economie.gouv.fr/france-2030).

## References

1. Alagumalai, S., Curtis, D.: Classical test theory. In: Applied Rasch Measurement: A Book of Exemplars. Education in the Asia-Pacific Region: Issues, Concerns and Prospects, vol. 4. Springer, Dordrecht (2005). https://doi.org/10.1007/1-4020-3076-21
2. Alsubait, T., Parsia, B., Sattler, U.: A similarity-based theory of controlling MCQ difficulty. In: e-Learning and e-Technologies in Education (ICEEE), 2013 Second International Conference on, pp. 282–288 (2013)
3. Attali, Y., Saldivia, L., Jackson, C., Schuppan, F., Wanamaker, W.: Estimating item difficulty with comparative judgments. ETS Res. Rep. Ser. **2014**(2), 1–8 (2014)
4. Beck, J., Stern, M., Woolf, B.P.: Using the student model to control problem difficulty. In: User Modeling: Proceedings of the Sixth International Conference UM97, pp. 277–288. Springer, Vienna (1997)
5. Benedetto, L., Aradelli, G., Cremonesi, P., Cappelli, A., Giussani, A., Turrin, R.: On the application of transformers for estimating the difficulty of multiple-choice questions from text. In: Proceedings of the 16th Workshop on Innovative Use of NLP for Building Educational Applications, pp. 147–158 (2021)
6. Chen, T., et al.: Xgboost: extreme gradient boosting, r package version (2015)
7. Choi, Y., et al.: EdNet: a large-scale hierarchical dataset in education. In: Bittencourt, I.I., Cukurova, M., Muldner, K., Luckin, R., Millán, E. (eds.) Artificial Intelligence in Education: 21st International Conference (AIED 2020), Part II. LNCS, 12164, pp. 69–73. Springer, Cham (2020). https://doi.org/10.1007/978-3-030-52240-7_13
8. Devlin, J., Chang, M.W., Lee, K., Toutanova, K.: Bert: pre-training of deep bidirectional transformers for language understanding. arXiv preprint arXiv:1810.04805 (2018)
9. Feng, M., Heffernan, N., Koedinger, K.: Addressing the assessment challenge with an online system that tutors as it assesses. User Model. User-Adap. Inter. **19**, 243–266 (2009)
10. Fischer, G.H.: The linear logistic test model as an instrument in educational research. Acta Physiol. (Oxford) **37**(6), 359–374 (1973)
11. Kotsiantis, S.B.: Decision trees: a recent overview. Artif. Intell. Rev. **39**, 261–283 (2013)
12. Kubinger, K.D., Gottschall, C.H.: Item difficulty of multiple choice tests dependant on different item response formats-an experiment in fundamental research on psychological assessment. Psychol. Sci. **49**(4), 361 (2007)
13. Lane, S., Raymond, M.R., Haladyna, T.M. (eds.): Handbook of Test Development. Routledge (2015)
14. Liu, Y., Wang, Y., Zhang, J.: New machine learning algorithm: random forest. In: Proceedings of the Information Computing and Applications: Third International Conference (ICICA 2012), Chengde, 14–16 September 2012, vol. 3, pp. 246–252. Springer, Heidelberg (2012)
15. Menard, S.: Applied Logistic Regression Analysis, vol. 106. Sage (2002)

16. Richards, D., Ekers, D., McMillan, D., et al.: Cost and outcome of behavioural activation versus cognitive behavioural therapy for depression (cobra): a randomised, controlled, non-inferiority trial. Lancet **388**(10047), 871–880 (2016). https://doi.org/10.1016/S0140-6736(16)31140-0
17. Taber, K.: The use of cronbach's alpha when developing and reporting research instruments in science education. Res. Sci. Educ. **48**, 1273–1296 (2018)
18. Yen, W.M.: Using simulation results to choose a latent trait model. Appl. Psychol. Meas. **5**(2), 245–262 (1981). https://doi.org/10.1177/014662168100500212

# Author Index





A. Sifaleras and F. Lin (Eds.): ITS 2024, LNCS 14798, pp. 425–427, 2024.
https://doi.org/10.1007/978-3-031-63028-6

SPRINGER NATURE

# GPSR Compliance

*The European Union's (EU) General Product Safety Regulation (GPSR) is a set of rules that requires consumer products to be safe and our obligations to ensure this.*

*If you have any concerns about our products, you can contact us on ProductSafety@springernature.com*

In case Publisher is established outside the EU, the EU authorized representative is:

Springer Nature Customer Service Center GmbH
Europaplatz 3
69115 Heidelberg, Germany

FSC
www.fsc.org
MIX
Papier | Fördert
gute Waldnutzung
FSC® C083411

Kolibri 360 GmbH
Ferdinand-Jühlke-Straße 7
99095 Erfurt, Deutschland
produktsicherheit@kolibri360.de